KIERKEGAARD'S INTERNATIONAL RECEPTION

TOME II: SOUTHERN, CENTRAL AND EASTERN EUROPE

Kierkegaard Research: Sources, Reception and Resources
Volume 8, Tome II

Kierkegaard Research: Sources, Reception and Resources
is a publication of the Søren Kierkegaard Research Centre

General Editor
JON STEWART
*Søren Kierkegaard Research Centre,
University of Copenhagen, Denmark*

Editorial Board
KATALIN NUN
PETER ŠAJDA

Advisory Board
ISTVÁN CZAKÓ
FINN GREDAL JENSEN
DAVID D. POSSEN
JOEL D. S. RASMUSSEN
HEIKO SCHULZ

This volume was published with the generous financial support
of the Danish Agency for Science, Technology and Innovation

Kierkegaard's International Reception
Tome II: Southern, Central and Eastern Europe

Edited by
JON STEWART

ASHGATE

© Jon Stewart 2009

All rights reserved. No part of this publication may be reproduced, stored in a retrieval system or transmitted in any form or by any means, electronic, mechanical, photocopying, recording or otherwise without the prior permission of the publisher.

Jon Stewart has asserted his right under the Copyright, Designs and Patents Act, 1988, to be identified as the editor of this work.

Published by
Ashgate Publishing Limited
Wey Court East
Union Road
Farnham
Surrey GU9 7PT
England

Ashgate Publishing Company
Suite 420
101 Cherry Street
Burlington, VT 05401-4405
USA

www.ashgate.com

British Library Cataloguing in Publication Data
Kierkegaard's international reception
   Tome 2: Southern, Central and Eastern Europe. –
(Kierkegaard research : sources, reception and resources ; v. 8)
   1. Kierkegaard, Soren, 1813–1855
   I. Stewart, Jon (Jon Bartley)
   198.9

Library of Congress Cataloging-in-Publication Data
Kierkegaard's international reception / edited by Jon Stewart.
Tome 2: Southern, Central and Eastern Europe.
      p. cm. (Kierkegaard research ; v. 8)
   Includes bibliographical references and index.
   ISBN 978-0-7546-6350-8 (hardcover : alk. paper)
   1. Kierkegaard, Soren, 1813–1855. I. Stewart, Jon.

198'.9–dc22

ISBN 978-0-7546-6350-8

Cover design by Katalin Nun.

Printed and bound in Great Britain by
TJ International Ltd, Padstow, Cornwall

Contents

List of Contributors   *vii*
List of Abbreviations   *ix*

PART I   SOUTHERN EUROPE

Portugal:
Discontinuity and Repetition
Elisabete M. de Sousa   1

Spain:
The Old and New Kierkegaard Reception in Spain
Dolors Perarnau Vidal and Óscar Parcero Oubiña   17

Italy:
From a Literary Curiosity to a Philosophical Comprehension
Ingrid Basso   81

PART II   CENTRAL EUROPE

Hungary:
The Hungarian Patient
András Nagy   155

Slovakia:
A Joint Project of Two Generations
Roman Králik   189

The Czech Republic:
Kierkegaard as a Model for the Irrationalist Movements
Helena Brezinova   205

Poland:
A Short History of the Reception of Kierkegaard's Thought
Antoni Szwed   213

PART III EASTERN EUROPE

Russia:
Kierkegaard's Reception through Tsarism, Communism, and Liberation
Darya Loungina   247

Bulgaria:
The Long Way from Indirect Acquaintance to Original Translation
Desislava Töpfer-Stoyanova   285

Romania:
A Survey of Kierkegaard's Reception, Translation, and Research
Nicolae Irina   301

Macedonia:
The Sunny Side of Kierkegaard
Ferid Muhic   317

Serbia and Montenegro:
Kierkegaard as a Post-Metaphysical Philosopher
Safet Bektovic   323

Index of Persons   *329*
Index of Subjects   *339*

List of Contributors

Elisabete M. de Sousa, Centro de Filosofia da Universidade de Lisboa, Faculdade de Letras, Alameda da Universidade, 1600-214 Lisbon, Portugal

Dolors Perarnau Vidal, Universitat Autònoma de Barcelona, Departament de Filosofia, Edifici B, Campus de la UAB, 08193 Bellaterra (Cerdanyola del Vallès), Spain

Óscar Parcero Oubiña, Facultade de Filosofía, Universidade de Santiago de Compostela, Praza de Mazarelos, 15782 Santiago de Compostela, Spain

Ingrid Basso, Universita Cattolica del Sacro Cuore, Dipartimento di Filosofia, Largo, A. Gemeli, 1-20123 Milano, Italy

András Nagy, Hungarian Theatre Museum and Institute, Krisztina körút 57, 1013 Budapest, Hungary

Roman Králik, Kierkegaard Collection, Mestská knižnica v Šali, Hlavná 61/15, Šala 927 01, Slovakia

Helena Brezinova, Karlova Univerzita, Ustav germanskych studii, nam. Jana Palacha 2, 118 00 Prague, Czech Republic

Antoni Szwed, Department Dean, B. Janski High School in Cracow, ul. Witosa 9, 30-612 Cracow, Poland

Darya Loungina, Moscow State University, Philosophy Faculty, Department of History and Theory of World Culture, 119899 Moscow Vorob'evy Gory, Russia

Desislava Töpfer-Stoyanova, c/o Søren Kierkegaard Research Centre, Farvergade 27D, 1463 Copnehagen K, Denmark

Nicolae Irina, York University, Department of Philosophy, S428 Ross Building, 4700 Keele St., Toronto, ON, Canada M3J 1P3

Ferid Muhic, Faculty of Philosophy, Katedra za filozofija, Univerzitet SV. Kiril i, Metodij, Krste Misirkov b.b., 1000 Skopje, Macedonia

Safet Bektovic, Center for europæisk islamist tænkning, Det Teologiske Fakultet, Købmagergade 44-46, 1150 Copenhagen K, Denmark

List of Abbreviations

Danish Abbreviations

B&A *Breve og Aktstykker vedrørende Søren Kierkegaard*, ed. by Niels Thulstrup, vols. I–II, Copenhagen: Munksgaard 1953–54.

Bl.art. *S. Kierkegaard's Bladartikler, med Bilag samlede efter Forfatterens Død, udgivne som Supplement til hans øvrige Skrifter*, ed. by Rasmus Nielsen, Copenhagen: C.A. Reitzel 1857.

EP *Af Søren Kierkegaards Efterladte Papirer*, vols. 1–9, ed. by H.P. Barfod and Hermann Gottsched, Copenhagen: C.A. Reitzel 1869–81.

Pap. *Søren Kierkegaards Papirer*, vols. I to XI–3, ed. by Peter Andreas Heiberg, Victor Kuhr and Einer Torsting, Copenhagen: Gyldendalske Boghandel, Nordisk Forlag, 1909-48; second, expanded ed., vols. I to XI–3, by Niels Thulstrup, vols. XII to XIII supplementary volumes, ed. by Niels Thulstrup, vols. XIV to XVI index by Niels Jørgen Cappelørn, Copenhagen: Gyldendal 1968–78.

SKS *Søren Kierkegaards Skrifter*, vols. 1–28, K1–K28, ed. by Niels Jørgen Cappelørn, Joakim Garff, Jette Knudsen, Johnny Kondrup, Alastair McKinnon and Finn Hauberg Mortensen, Copenhagen: Gads Forlag 1997ff.

SV1 *Samlede Værker*, ed. by A.B. Drachmann, Johan Ludvig Heiberg and H.O. Lange, vols. I–XIV, Copenhagen: Gyldendalske Boghandels Forlag 1901–6.

English Abbreviations

AN *Armed Neutrality*, trans. by Howard V. Hong and Edna H. Hong, Princeton: Princeton University Press 1998.

AR *On Authority and Revelation, The Book on Adler*, trans. by Walter Lowrie, Princeton: Princeton University Press 1955.

ASKB *The Auctioneer's Sales Record of the Library of Søren Kierkegaard*, ed. by H.P. Rohde, Copenhagen: The Royal Library 1967.

BA	*The Book on Adler*, trans. by Howard V. Hong and Edna H. Hong, Princeton: Princeton University Press 1998.
C	*The Crisis and a Crisis in the Life of an Actress*, trans. by Howard V. Hong and Edna H. Hong, Princeton: Princeton University Press 1997.
CA	*The Concept of Anxiety*, trans. by Reidar Thomte in collaboration with Albert B. Anderson, Princeton: Princeton University Press 1980.
CD	*Christian Discourses*, trans. by Howard V. Hong and Edna H. Hong, Princeton: Princeton University Press 1997.
CI	*The Concept of Irony*, trans. by Howard V. Hong and Edna H. Hong, Princeton: Princeton University Press 1989.
CIC	*The Concept of Irony*, trans. with an Introduction and Notes by Lee M. Capel, London: Collins 1966.
COR	*The Corsair Affair; Articles Related to the Writings*, trans. by Howard V. Hong and Edna H. Hong, Princeton: Princeton University Press 1982.
CUP1	*Concluding Unscientific Postscript*, vol. 1, trans. by Howard V. Hong and Edna H. Hong, Princeton: Princeton University Press 1982.
CUP2	*Concluding Unscientific Postscript*, vol. 2, trans. by Howard V. Hong and Edna H. Hong, Princeton: Princeton University Press 1982.
EO1	*Either/Or, Part I*, trans. by Howard V. Hong and Edna H. Hong, Princeton: Princeton University Press 1987.
EO2	*Either/Or, Part II*, trans. by Howard V. Hong and Edna H. Hong, Princeton: Princeton University Press 1987.
EOP	*Either/Or*, trans. by Alastair Hannay, Harmondsworth: Penguin Books 1992.
EPW	*Early Polemical Writings, among others: From the Papers of One Still Living; Articles from Student Days; The Battle Between the Old and the New Soap-Cellars*, trans. by Julia Watkin, Princeton: Princeton University Press 1990.
EUD	*Eighteen Upbuilding Discourses*, trans. by Howard V. Hong and Edna H. Hong, Princeton: Princeton University Press 1990.
FSE	*For Self-Examination*, trans. by Howard V. Hong and Edna H. Hong, Princeton: Princeton University Press 1990.

List of Abbreviations

FT   *Fear and Trembling*, trans. by Howard V. Hong and Edna H. Hong, Princeton: Princeton University Press 1983.

FTP   *Fear and Trembling*, trans. by Alastair Hannay, London and New York: Penguin Books 1985.

JC   *Johannes Climacus, or De omnibus dubitandum est*, trans. by Howard V. Hong and Edna H. Hong, Princeton: Princeton University Press 1985.

JFY   *Judge for Yourself!*, trans. by Howard V. Hong and Edna H. Hong, Princeton: Princeton University Press 1990.

JP   *Søren Kierkegaard's Journals and Papers*, ed. and trans. by Howard V. Hong and Edna H. Hong, assisted by Gregor Malantschuk, vols. 1–6, vol. 7 Index and Composite Collation, Bloomington and London: Indiana University Press 1967–78.

KAC   *Kierkegaard's Attack upon "Christendom," 1854–1855*, trans. by Walter Lowrie, Princeton: Princeton University Press 1944.

KJN   *Kierkegaard's Journals and Notebooks*, vols. 1–11, ed. by Niels Jørgen Cappelørn, Alastair Hannay, David Kangas, Bruce H. Kirmmse, George Pattison, Vanessa Rumble and K. Brian Söderquist, Princeton and Oxford: Princeton University Press 2007ff.

LD   *Letters and Documents*, trans. by Henrik Rosenmeier, Princeton: Princeton University Press 1978 (A translation of *B&A*).

M   *The Moment and Late Writings*, trans. by Howard V. Hong and Edna H. Hong, Princeton: Princeton University Press 1998.

P   *Prefaces / Writing Sampler*, trans. by Todd W. Nichol, Princeton: Princeton University Press 1997.

PC   *Practice in Christianity*, trans. by Howard V. Hong and Edna H. Hong, Princeton: Princeton University Press 1991.

PF   *Philosophical Fragments*, trans. by Howard V. Hong and Edna H. Hong, Princeton: Princeton University Press 1985.

PJ   *Papers and Journals: A Selection*, trans. by Alastair Hannay, London and New York: Penguin Books 1996.

PLR   *Prefaces: Light Reading for Certain Classes as the Occasion May Require*, trans. by William McDonald, Tallahassee: Florida State University Press 1989.

PLS	*Concluding Unscientific Postscript*, trans. by David F. Swenson and Walter Lowrie, Princeton: Princeton University Press 1941.
PV	*The Point of View* including *On My Work as an Author*, *The Point of View for My Work as an Author*, and *Armed Neutrality*, trans. by Howard V. Hong and Edna H. Hong, Princeton: Princeton University Press 1998.
PVL	*The Point of View for My Work as an Author* including *On My Work as an Author*, trans. by Walter Lowrie, New York and London: Oxford University Press 1939.
R	*Repetition*, trans. by Howard V. Hong and Edna H. Hong, Princeton: Princeton University Press 1983.
SBL	*Notes of Schelling's Berlin Lectures*, trans. by Howard V. Hong and Edna H. Hong, Princeton: Princeton University Press 1989.
SLW	*Stages on Life's Way*, trans. by Howard V. Hong and Edna H. Hong, Princeton: Princeton University Press 1988.
SUD	*The Sickness unto Death*, trans. by Howard V. Hong and Edna H. Hong, Princeton: Princeton University Press 1980.
SUDP	*The Sickness unto Death*, trans. by Alastair Hannay, London and New York: Penguin Books 1989.
TA	*Two Ages: The Age of Revolution and the Present Age. A Literary Review*, trans. by Howard V. Hong and Edna H. Hong, Princeton: Princeton University Press 1978.
TD	*Three Discourses on Imagined Occasions*, trans. by Howard V. Hong and Edna H. Hong, Princeton: Princeton University Press 1993.
UD	*Upbuilding Discourses in Various Spirits*, trans. by Howard V. Hong and Edna H. Hong, Princeton: Princeton University Press 1993.
WA	*Without Authority* including *The Lily in the Field and the Bird of the Air, Two Ethical-Religious Essays, Three Discourses at the Communion on Fridays, An Upbuilding Discourse, Two Discourses at the Communion on Fridays*, trans. by Howard V. Hong and Edna H. Hong, Princeton: Princeton University Press 1997.
WL	*Works of Love*, trans. by Howard V. Hong and Edna H. Hong, Princeton: Princeton University Press 1995.

PART I

Southern Europe

Portugal:
Discontinuity and Repetition

Elisabete M. de Sousa

The reception of Kierkegaard in Portugal may give the impression of being a succession of discontinued efforts and repeated endeavors; nonetheless, this uneven path has recently smoothed, as we shall conclude from a close analysis of the Portuguese translations and of the studies on Kierkegaard's works. In the first section, the translations of Kierkegaard into Portuguese published in Portugal are discussed. These are referred first by the title in English of the original work, with the title of the Portuguese edition noted in the footnotes; when the Portuguese title shows any significant dissimilarity to the original title, a literal translation in English is also provided. In the second section, the most noteworthy Portuguese Kierkegaard scholars and their contributions are commented on, taking into account their particular academic and scholarly relevance.

I. The History of Kierkegaard Translations in Portugal

Shortly after the 1910 Italian translation of "The Diary of the Seducer," Livraria Clássica, then one of the best-known publishing houses in Lisbon, published the first Portuguese translation of Kierkegaard, using Luigi Redaelli's text as indirect source. Mário Alemquer was a regular translator of esoteric books, and his translation of "The Diary of the Seducer" *The Diary of the Seducer: The Art of Love* came out in 1911.[1] Besides the Ovidian touch in the title, Alemquer also wrote a short introduction, portraying Kierkegaard as a kind of romantic novel hero, who tried helplessly to forget the love of his life by writing. This translation seems to have had some success in Spain, since Valentín de Pedro made a version of *The Diary of the Seducer* using the Portuguese text as source and choosing the same title.[2]

This early start actually set a pattern of discontinuity in Kierkegaard reception in Portugal. Though most of the ten Portuguese translations were edited by well-known publishers in their Philosophy Series, none of the publishers seemed to be concerned

---

[1] *O diário do seductor: a arte de amar*, trans. by Mário Alemquer, Lisbon: Livraria Clássica 1911. (Translated from *Il diario del seduttore*, trans. by Luigi Redaelli, Torino: Fratelli Bocca Editori 1910.)

[2] *Diario de un seductor (arte de amar)*, version by Valentin de Pedro, Madrid: Sucesores de Rivadeneyra 1922 (later published in *Colección Austral*, Madrid: Espasa Calpe SA 1953).

about an accurate or a sequential publication of Kierkegaard's works. All but one used French or Italian translations as source texts, with only four translations of complete volumes, namely, *The Point of View* (published together with *Two Ethical-Religious Essays*), *The Sickness unto Death* and *The Concept of Anxiety*. Somehow obsessively, these translations linger on in a pattern of repetition—there are two translations of "The Diary of the Seducer," two of *The Sickness unto Death* and another two of the first chapter of *Stages in Life's Way*, "In Vino Veritas," scattered between the years 1911 and 2000.

Twenty-five years after the first translation, in 1936, Adolfo Casais Monteiro (1908–72) wrote a concise but quite informative introduction to his translation of *The Sickness unto Death*, presenting it as a "complex, vast and contradictory" text, as the work of a philosopher, practically unknown in Portugal until then, whose writings invariably show some paradoxical non-philosophical characteristics, the result of a unique combination of talents and feelings. Casais Monteiro used the French translation by Knud Ferlov (1881–1977) and Jean J. Gateau,[3] translating its title as well,[4] and, to support his commentaries, he quoted Jean Wahl, among others, focusing mainly on the use of pseudonyms, the biographical nature of Kierkegaard's works (the customary reference to the relevance of his father's curse and the broken engagement), the theory of the three stages, the experimental and exemplary character of his writings, permeated as they are by the notions of repetition and the leap. The translation is dedicated to Leonardo Coimbra (1883–1935), Casais Monteiro's mentor, the Portuguese philosopher and professor at the University of Porto (1919–31), who was responsible for the Philosophy Series of Livraria Tavares Martins, and hence, for the publication of *The Sickness unto Death*. Coimbra had intended to write the introduction to this translation himself; however, his sudden death robbed posterity of the opportunity of evaluating rigorously his role in Kierkegaard's reception. It is also worth mentioning that Casais Monteiro was a poet, a literary critic and a busy translator, a founding member of the most important Portuguese literary movement of the 1930s,[5] who later settled in Brazil where he taught Portuguese Literature at the State University of São Paulo.[6]

---

[3] *Traité du désespoir: la maladie mortelle*, trans. by Knud Ferlov and Jean J. Gateau, Paris: Gallimard 1932. It produced an immediate impact in Catholic circles, claiming Kierkegaard as a religious philosopher; see António Pinto de Carvalho, "A Filosofia Religiosa de Sören Aabye Kierkegaard," *Brotéria*, vol. 22, 1936, pp. 361–9.

[4] *O desespero humano: doença até à morte*, trans. and introduced by Adolfo Casais Monteiro, Oporto: Livraria Tavares Martins 1936. Two subsequent reprints in 1947 and new editions in 1957, 1961, and 1979.

[5] Known as "Presença," it is not related to the publishing house of the same name, which published three Kierkegaard translations in the 1960s. Leonardo Coimbra was a member of the previous influential literary movement "Renascença Portuguesa," thus placing Casais Monteiro in a unique position between these two movements. Casais Monteiro also held links with the modernist movement "Orpheu" and his founding member, Fernando Pessoa (see footnote 13 and works by Eduardo Lourenço in the Bibliography).

[6] Casais Monteiro's publications in Portugal and in Brazil are now published under the title *Obras Completas de Adolfo Casais Monteiro*, Lisbon: Imprensa Nacional Casa da Moeda 2003.

The impact of existentialism during the 1950s and the 1960s fostered a steady interest in the works of Kierkegaard. These years witnessed several reprints of Casais Monteiro's translation of *The Sickness unto Death* as well as new translations from two important Lisbon publishing houses, Presença and Guimarães. The sixth edition of Casais Monteiro's translation came out in 1979, when Presença had already published two editions of *The Concept of Anxiety* translated by João Lopes Alves,[7] using Ferlov's and Gateau's French translation. Presença also published separately two chapters taken from *Either/Or* using the Prior and Guignot French translation[8] as source text: Carlos Grifo translated "The Diary of the Seducer" and Margarida Schiappa translated the first chapter of Part 2 under the title *Aesthetics of Matrimony* in 1965.[9] The Presença editions have no *apparatus criticus* whatsoever.

On the contrary, the Guimarães editions showed some concern in contextualizing Kierkegaard's works, in the line of Casais Monteiro's introduction. The editors and translators belonged to the circle of the former disciples of Coimbra; a significant number of them had been barred from public teaching posts (be it secondary or university education) and dedicated themselves mainly to translating and reviewing, regularly lecturing and publishing articles or books, which were often excluded from the official mainstream. Nevertheless, the prefaces to *Fear and Trembling*[10] and "In Vino Veritas"[11] clearly reveal the state of Kierkegaard's reception at the time. Álvaro Ribeiro (1905–81) used another French translation as source text and chose *O Banquete* as title for "In Vino Veritas," the same title used in the Portuguese translations of Plato's *Symposium*. His preface (1953) dwells extensively on Ribeiro's own views on love and marriage, revealing his readings of Kierkegaard's criticism of romantic literature, particularly in Judge William's "The Esthetic Validity of Marriage" and in *The Concept of Irony*. Ribeiro briefly compares Plato's and Kierkegaard's texts and considers Kierkegaard's view on love and marriage as fundamental to the construction of a new ethical order, capable of contradicting the idea that "moral pessimism coincides with the highest intellectual insight."[12] Moreover, Ribeiro draws attention to a possible link between Kierkegaard and

---

[7]   *O conceito de angústia*, trans. by João Lopes Alves, Lisbon: Presença 1962 (2nd ed., 1972). (Translated from *Traité du désespoir: la maladie mortelle*, trans. by Knud Ferlov and Jean J. Gateau, Paris: Gallimard 1932.)

[8]   *Ou bien...ou bien*, trans. by F. and O. Prior and M.H. Guignot, Paris: Gallimard 1943.

[9]   *Diário de um Sedutor*, trans. by Carlos Grifo, Lisbon: Presença 1971; *Estética do Matrimónio*, trans. by Margarida Schiappa, Lisbon: Presença 1965.

[10]   *Temor e Tremor*, trans. by Maria José Marinho, introduced (13 unnumbered pp.) by Alberto Ferreira, Lisbon: Guimarães Editores 1959. Subsequent editions 1990, 1998. (Translated from *Crainte et Tremblement: Lyrique-dialectique par Johannes de silentio*, trans. by P.-H. Tisseau, introduced by Jean Wahl, Paris: Aubier-Montaigne 1935.)

[11]   *O Banquete*, trans. and introduced by Álvaro Ribeiro, Lisbon: Guimarães Editores 1953. Subsequent editions 1962, 1963, 1985, 1997, 2002. (Probable source text: *In Vino Veritas*, trans. by André Babelon and C. Lund, Abbeville: Éditions du Cavalier 1933.)

[12]   *O Banquete*, pp. 7–12.

Fernando Pessoa (1888–1935),[13] Portugal's most important twentieth-century poet, in the latter's particular use of a multiple authorship, to be further discussed in his relation to Kierkegaard in the next section of this article.

The 1959 preface to *Fear and Trembling*, by Alberto Ferreira (1920–2000), remained the most accessible presentation of Kierkegaard's thought until 1967, the year the philosopher Eduardo Lourenço (b. 1923) published the essay "Sören Kierkegaard, The Spy of God," which will be presented under Lourenço's contribution below. *Fear and Trembling* was translated from Tisseau's *Crainte et Tremblement*[14] by Maria José Marinho (b. 1928), Ferreira's wife and daughter of José Marinho (1904–75), another philosopher and writer belonging to Coimbra's circle, whose work also discloses a serious reading of Kierkegaard, as will be mentioned below. In a three-part introduction, Ferreira quotes numerous works by Kierkegaard and French commentators, namely Wahl and Tisseau. As central ideas, Ferreira emphasized the responsibility of the individual facing the challange of the leap, the unsystematic character of Kierkegaard's writings and the interaction between paradox and doubt, especially in what concerns the roles of Abraham and Job.

In 1986 two new translations came out, both using Tisseau's French translation as indirect source: a new translation of *The Sickness unto Death* by Ana Keil,[15] and the translations by João Gama of *The Point of View* and *Two Ethical-Religious Essays*,[16] corresponding exactly to volume 16 of Editions de l'Orante, Gama's source. None of these editions has critical notes, and some of the statements of both editors are bewildering; in the first case, a small introductory text misleads the reader into thinking that *The Sickness unto Death* and *The Concept of Anxiety* are one and the same book; in the second case, the inattentive reader may read the whole book, only to find out in the last three pages some information about the nature of the works, having thus been denied a proper critical approach to the two texts.

The 150th anniversary of Kierkegaard's death brought the first Portuguese translation using the original source, offering a very good *apparatus criticus* as well. José Miranda Justo (b. 1951, German Department, Humanities Faculty, University of Lisbon) translated "In Vino Veritas," supplying his own notes and further sources of information, such as the Hong edition and *Søren Kierkegaards*

---

[13]   Fernando Pessoa worked for Livraria Clássica, which had published the first Portuguese translation of "The Seducer's Diary" in its *Theosophy and Religion* series. From 1914 onwards, Pessoa translated six titles by exactly the same authors that Alemquer had translated before for the same series (namely Annie Besant and C.W. Leadbeater). During his lifetime, he published poetry under four different authorial personalities, and since his death, many more authors have been discovered in his papers.

[14]   *Crainte et Tremblement*, trans. by Poul-Henri Tisseau, Paris: Éditions de l'Orante 1972.

[15]   *Desespero: a doença mortal*, trans. by Ana Keil, Porto: Rés-Editora 1986 (2nd ed., 2003). (Translated from *La maladie à la mort*, trans. by Poul-Henri Tisseau and Else Marie Jacquet-Tisseau (*Œuvres de Sören Kierkegaard*, vol. 16), Paris : Éditions de l'Orante 1971.)

[16]   *Ponto de vista explicativo da minha obra como escritor*, trans. by João Gama, Lisbon: Edições 70 1986. (Translated from *Point de vue explicatif de mon œuvre d'écrivain, Deux petits traités éthico-religieux*, trans. by P-H Tisseau and Else Marie Jacquet-Tisseau (*Œuvres de Sören Kierkegaard*, vol. 16), Paris: Éditions de l'Orante 1971.)

Skrifter.[17] In his Supplement,[18] he contextualizes "In Vino Veritas" within *Stages on Life's Way*, including a brief commentary of the discourses. He also addresses the issue of the pseudonyms and analyzes Kierkegaard's alterity as a constitutive mode of experimentation and representation, a combination of his continual experimenting with a plural *logos* directly linked to a plurality of *pathos*. Furthermore, Miranda Justo comments on the works of different pseudonyms and, all along, introduces the reader to key concepts, namely the notion of anxiety, which is shown to be a consequence of the repeated experiments with a "positive subjectivity," continually pushing the individual away from his finite condition towards the infinite ideal status. Other concepts discussed are contradiction, melancholy and humor and, naturally, recollection; the use of *Witz* in the case of Johannes Climacus is also discussed. Hopefully, this edition will set the Portuguese translations on a more fortunate path, the one it might well have taken long before, especially after a sequence of articles and essays published between the early 1950s and the late 1960s.

II. The History of Portuguese Secondary Literature

Although Kierkegaard is never directly mentioned in Leonardo Coimbra's works, some aspects may be linked to key concepts in Kierkegaard's writings. Coimbra's theory, known as Creationism, confronts, on the one hand, Positivism and, on the other, Hegelianism; very briefly, it defends, among other things, the freedom of human thought, evolving to a form of Gnosticism where religion, art, and philosophy are equally vital for the emergence of an *ethos*, capable of leading man to cosmological harmony. Nevertheless, there is no consensus about Kierkegaard's influence on Coimbra's philosophical works, since the two scholars who have discussed this issue disagree on this point.[19] It is known that Coimbra had in his library a Spanish translation (1930) of *The Concept of Anxiety*, besides the French translation (1934) of Carl Koch's *Sören Kierkegaard*. Yet, what might be more meaningful is the fact that a great number of his former students came to be actively interested in Kierkegaard. Besides two of the translators, Álvaro Ribeiro and Casais Monteiro, two other philosophers in Coimbra's sphere of

---

[17] *Kierkegaard: In Vino Veritas*, trans. and ed. by José Miranda Justo, Lisbon: Antígona 2005. Miranda Justo has translated quite a large number of works for the same publisher (among other authors, Herder, Voltaire, H.E. Jacob, Kleist, Wagner, and Jacob) and has published on the philosophy of language and esthetics.

[18] "Supplement: Polinomy-Kierkegaard, presentation of a segment of 'experimentation in thinking'" (Posfácio: Polinómio-Kierkegaard, Apresentação de um segmento de 'experimentação em pensamento').

[19] Manuel Cândido Pimentel claims that there is no influence of Kierkegaard on Coimbra's thought, see *A Ontologia Integral de Leonardo Coimbra*, Lisboa: Imprensa Nacional Casa da Moeda 2003, no. 55, pp. 65–6; Ângelo Alves claims exactly the opposite ("Notas e Comentários: As Influências na Elaboração do Criacionismo. A Biblioteca de Leonardo Coimbra," *Humanística e Teologia*, vol. 9, no. 2, 1988, pp. 223–44; pp. 367–80). For a detailed study of Leonardo Coimbra's Creationism, see Manuel Cândido Pimentel, *A Ontologia Integral de Leonardo Coimbra*.

influence deserve a reference—the previously mentioned José Marinho and Delfim Santos (1907–66), who started mentioning Kierkegaard regularly as early as 1933, i.e., before Casais Monteiro's translation of *The Sickness unto Death*.[20] Marinho frequently quotes Kierkegaard, and in his main work, *Theory of the Being and the Truth* (1961), Marinho presents his ontology of the spirit using a three-part schematic division which shows some organic similarities to the three Kierkegaardian stages.[21] Although they actually never held teaching posts, Marinho and Ribeiro were very influential in Lisbon literature and philosophy circles, and they have been the object of recent research, Kierkegaard being a thinker who has been acknowledged as one of their sources.[22]

On the other hand, Delfim Santos' influence was predominantly institutional; a professor at the University of Lisbon, he was, among Coimbra's disciples, the one who left an indelible presence in Philosophy and Pedagogy Studies until his death. Though he did not hold a Philosophy chair, he was the head of the Pedagogical Sciences Department for almost twenty years; this enabled him to influence various generations of graduate students who had to pass difficult entrance examinations to be admitted to teaching posts at public secondary schools.[23] Delfim Santos read Kierkegaard in German, and his main philosophical interest and points of references were Heidegger and Nikolai Hartmann; he contributed regularly to general and philosophical publications and to the daily press, besides publishing four main works. From 1933 until one of his last articles in 1966, he made constant reference to Kierkegaard, though he focused especially on his role in the emergence of the philosophy of Heidegger and on his influence on existentialism. He always underscored the unique nature of Kierkegaard's thought, accurately presenting the philosopher's point of view on irony, subjectivity, anxiety, despair, among other key

---

[20] In an article published in *Seara Nova* (no. 398, 1934), Marinho commented on "Reflection and Spontaneity" in Nietzsche, Kierkegaard, and Amiel ("Reflexão e Espontaneidade," *Obras Completas de José Marinho (1994–2005)*, vol. 2: *Ensaios de Aprofundamento e Outros Textos*, Lisbon: Imprensa Nacional Casa da Moeda 1995, pp. 210–12). In the essay "Dialéctica Totalista" (*Presença*, vol. 2, no. 39, 1933) Delfim Santos reviewed the theory of stages and the concept of liberty as action (see *Obras Completas de Delfim Santos (1971–1977; 1995)*, vol. 1, Lisbon: Fundação Gulbenkian 1971, pp. 31–8).

[21] See José Marinho, *Obras Completas de José Marinho*, vol. 1: *Aforismos sobre o que mais importa*, Lisbon: Imprensa Nacional Casa da Moeda 1994; *Teoria do Ser e da Verdade*, Lisbon: Guimarães Editores 1961. Marinho's stages are labelled "The Being of Truth," "The Truth of Being," and "The Other Truth."

[22] See Maria José Pinto Cantista, "Tendências Dominantes na Filosofia Portuguesa do Século XX: Algumas achegas acerca da Contribuição de José Marinho," *Filosofia, Hoje—Ecos no Pensamento Português*, Porto: Fundação Eng. António de Almeida 1993, pp. 242–65.

[23] In an "In Memoriam" article, his role as professor and his philosophy (including the role of Kierkegaard in his thought) are acknowledged by eight representative personalities of his time (from editors to academy colleagues). See "Delfim Santos: um Destino Português," *O Tempo e o Modo*, nos. 43–4, 1966, pp. 1080–1101.

concepts, not forgetting to signal the first centenary of Kierkegaard's death in the opening speech of the first Philosophy Congress in Portugal in 1955.[24]

However, the most important reference to the centenary came from a group of Jesuit scholars, headed by Júlio Fragata, S.J. (1920–85), an expert on Husserl and phenomenology and a professor of Philosophy at the Catholic University of Braga. Fragata hosted the first Philosophy Congress in 1955 and founded the *Revista Portuguesa de Filosofia* (1945); though he argued for a religious existentialism, he also warns the reader against Kierkegaard's point of view on religious categories, drawing the line between the true theological Christianity and Kierkegaard's anthropological Christianity.[25] Other essays followed this line in *Cadernos de Filosofia*, published by the Scholastics Center of the University of Braga, and the first number of *Filosofia* (1956) of the Lisbon Scholastics Center, celebrated the centenary by claiming Kierkegaard as a religious thinker, not as an existentialist philosopher. Together with a translation of a long article by Cornelio Fabro on Kierkegaard and Catholicism, and an article by Fragata on the theological existentialism of Kierkegaard, this *Filosofia* issue contains a long essay by Maria Manuela Saraiva (better known for her contributions on phenomenology), which gives an appreciation of Kierkegaard as one of the voices capable of bringing new dynamics into Scholastic studies.[26] Fragata is also the author of the entry "Kierkegaard" in the *Verbo Enciclopédia Luso-Brasileira de Cultura* and in *Logos*, the philosophy dictionary published by the same house.[27] Despite giving an honest account of Kierkegaard's thought and work, he introduces him as a thinker and *literatus*, thus bypassing any consideration of Kierkegaard as a religious writer or a philosopher.

Manuel Antunes, S.J. (1918–85), a professor at the University of Lisbon for over twenty-five years, gave courses on ancient and modern culture and ontology which were attended by almost every undergraduate Humanities student at the time.

---

[24] Among other texts by Delfim Santos, see "The Value of Irony" ("O valor da Ironia," 1943, in his *Obras Completas*, vol. 1, pp. 349–53); "The Existential Meaning of Anxiety" ("Sentido Existencial da Angústia," 1952, in his *Obras Completas*, vol. 2, pp. 154–64); "Jaspers in Contemporary Philosophy" ("Jaspers na Filosofia Contemporânea," in his *Obras Completas*, vol. 2, pp. 268–79); "Philosophy as Fundamental Ontology" ("Filosofia como Ontologia Fundamental," in his *Obras Completas*, vol. 2, pp. 213–16).

[25] Júlio Fragata, "Filosofia da Existência," *Revista Portuguesa de Filosofia*, vol. 16, 1960, pp. 336–50 (also published in a collection of essays, *Problemas da Filosofia Contemporânea*, Braga: Publicações da Faculdade de Filosofia da UCP 1989, pp. 99–112). Apart from this essay by Fragata, only Diamantino Martins (1910–79) focused more consistently on Kierkegaard in *Revista Portuguesa de Filosofia*. See Bibliography.

[26] Angelino Barreto, "Kierkegaard e a sua Visão Existencial do Homem," *Cadernos de Filosofia*, vol. 5, 1956, pp. 24–30; E. Luís Jardim, "Kierkegaard e o Catolicismo," *Cadernos de Filosofia*, vol. 6, 1957, pp. 1–9; Eurico da Rua Júnior, "Desespero e Consciência em Kierkegaard," *Cadernos de Filosofia*, vol. 14, 1965, pp. 5–20. See also Júlio Fragata, "O Existencialismo Teológico de Kierkegaard" and Maria Manuela Saraiva, "Kierkegaard e o Problema Filosófico do Homem," *Filosofia*, vol. 2, no. 8, 1956.

[27] Júlio Fragata, "Kierkegaard," in *Enciclopédia Luso-Brasileira de Cultura*, vol. 11, Lisbon: Editorial Verbo 1971, pp. 1124–8; Fragata, "Kierkegaard," *Logos*, vol. 3, Lisbon: Editorial Verbo 1991, pp. 162–7.

He was also a prolific essayist, more focused on anthropological and educational issues than on philosophy or religion. In his many articles for *Brotéria*,[28] which he published over several years, he presents Kierkegaard's thought as the result of his work as "an existential thinker," someone who put his human condition above all, in its relation to transcendence or to the world he lived in. He further underlines his value as a witness, as a testimony of "the eternal youth of Christianity,"[29] going thus beyond the arguments proposed by Fragata.

Eduardo Lourenço (b. 1923), a contemporary thinker who has steadily contributed to making Kierkegaard's thought better known in Portugal, held the chairs of Portuguese Culture in the Universities of Hamburg, Heidelberg (Germany), São Salvador da Baía (Brazil), Montpellier and Nice (France). His forty-page long essay, "Sören Kierkegaard, the Spy of God" dates from 1967 and belongs to the second volume of his essays, *Heterodoxia II*.[30] Lourenço takes Kierkegaard as a "poet of the religious" and a disciple of Socrates, continually and simultaneously living his faith in God and his condition of philosopher by experimenting with different stances in his authorship, which enable the philosopher to develop the fundamental notions of his thought. To explain Kierkegaard's role in the pamphlet nature of *The Moment*, Lourenço takes into consideration the intricate relationship between, on the one hand, faith and truth as subjectivity and paradox, and on the other hand, the individual character of the public, taken as *Enkelte*.

Lourenço has written extensively on Fernando Pessoa and produced two major essays on Kierkegaard and Pessoa, one in the mid 1950s, "Kierkegaard and Pessoa or Indirect Communication" and another one in 1981, "Kierkegaard and Pessoa or the Masks of the Absolute."[31] Lourenço points out some differences and similarities between Kierkegaard's and Fernando Pessoa's authorships; their use of pseudonyms is explained not as lack of sincerity, but as proof of their authenticity as authors and poets living in a hostile environment dominated by non-authenticity. He draws the line between the two by emphasizing the ontological nature of Pessoa's pseudonyms (named by the poet as heteronyms), whereas Kierkegaard's gallery of authors is described as a collection of characters psychologically designed as a requirement for the apologetic demands of Kierkegaard's endeavor. Lourenço also focuses on the literary stance of the pseudonyms in both poets, one mainly in permanent dialogue with the representatives of the religious, philosophical and political sectors of his milieu, and the other with the dominant poets of the different literary spheres he was

---

[28] *Revista Brotéria* (1902ff.) edited by the Portuguese Jesuits publishes mainly on humanities, sciences and arts, on Christianity and for the last twenty years also on bioethics, anthropology, and geopolitics.

[29] Manuel Antunes S.J., "Kierkegaard" (1955), in *Obras Completas*, vol. 3, Tome I, Lisbon: Fundação Calouste Gulbenkian 2005, pp. 347–55.

[30] Eduardo Lourenço, "Sören Kierkegaard, O Espião de Deus," in *Heterodoxia II*, Lisbon: Gradiva 2005, pp. 121–99 (first publication: *Heterodoxia II Ensaios*, Coimbra: Coimbra Editora 1967).

[31] Eduardo Lourenço, "Kierkegaard e Pessoa ou as Máscaras do Absoluto" (1981) and "Kierkegaard e Pessoa ou a Comunicação Indirecta" (1954–6), both included in *Fernando Rei da Nossa Baviera*, Lisbon: Imprensa Nacional Casa da Moeda 1986, pp. 97–109; pp. 121–44.

immersed in (from Walt Whitman and John Milton, to Virgil and Horace, besides Teixeria de Pascoaes (1877–1945) and Camilo Pessanha (1867–1925), two major Portuguese poets). On the other hand, Luís de Oliveira e Silva's (b. 1945) essay on Kierkegaard and Pessoa (1988) explains the relationships between Pessoa's heteronyms by means of Kierkegaardian concepts, taking their position as romantic writers as his starting point.[32]

As mentioned before, the advent of the new millennium finally brought a translation from Danish and research based on direct sources. In a long article, "The Concept of 'Experience' in the work of Kierkegaard" (2000), Nuno Ferro (b. 1961) comments on the *Upbuilding Discourses*, in particular "The Expectancy of Faith" (1843).[33] Among other things, Ferro discusses how the recurrent idea of "obscure discourse" in the *Upbuilding Discourses* conditions both subject and object. Furthermore, he develops a cross-analysis of several upbuilding discourses, focusing mainly on the way experience posits the individual in temporality, thus determining his relation to the past, the present and the future, while setting his imagination in motion at the same time. Ferro argues that the individual gains experience not merely by experimenting but chiefly by recollecting experience, which eventually enables the individual to think prospectively, with the inevitable emergence of doubt and indifference in his horizon.

In "The Hand of Mozart" (2004),[34] Elisabete M. de Sousa (b. 1954) discusses Kierkegaard's reception of Mozart's *Don Giovanni*, based on some chapters of *Either/Or* ("The Immediate Erotic Stages," "Diapsalmata," "The Diary of the Seducer," and Victor Eremita's Preface). Besides contextualizing Kierkegaard's point of view on *Don Giovanni* in the musical criticism of the nineteenth century, Sousa argues that the deliberate absence of any commentaries on Zerlina and on the famous love duet, "Là ci darem la mano," displaces the *locus* of seduction and the presence of *Eros* from the conflicts between the different pairs of seducers and seduced in *Either/Or* to a new standpoint, where the philosopher takes the role of the seducer, and philosophy is taken as the object of love and the reader as the seduced part.

A final word needs to be said about two Portuguese novelists, Vergílio Ferreira (1916–96) and Agustina Bessa-Luís (b. 1922), the former as the most famous representative of existentialist writers, the latter for her particular reception of Kierkegaard. Ferreira published over twenty volumes of novels and short stories, often taking a reflective path on the border between literature and philosophy. Acknowledged as a philosopher,[35] Kierkegaard is constantly referred to in Ferreira's journals and essays, as well as in the introduction to his own translation of Sartre's

---

[32] Luís de Oliveira e Silva is a professor of Literature at Universidade Nova de Lisboa. See "Estética e Ética em Kierkegaard e Pessoa" ("Aesthetics and Ethics in Kierkegaard and Pessoa"), *Revista da Faculdade de Ciências Sociais e Humanas da UNL*, 1988, pp. 261–72.

[33] Nuno da Rosa Ferro, "A Noção de Experiência na Obra de Kierkegaard," *Quid, Revista de filosofia* (1: *Sobre a Experiência*), 2000, pp. 251–317.

[34] Elisabete M. de Sousa, "A mão de Mozart," *Dedalus*, vol. 9, 2004, pp. 147–71.

[35] Vergílio Ferreira deserves a full chapter in the most comprehensive study on Portuguese philosophers; see José Antunes de Sousa, "Vergílio Ferreira," *História do Pensamento Filosófico Português*, vol. V–II, ed. by Pedro Calafate, organized by Centro de Filosofia da Universidade de Lisboa, Lisbon: Caminho 2000, pp. 434–57.

L'Existentialisme est un Humanisme,[36] which probably stands out as the best account of existentialism in Portugal in the early 1960s. Agustina Bessa-Luís, another prolific novelist, produced in 1992 an interesting example of her readings of Kierkegaard in the form of a play, under the title *The Immediate Erotic Stages of Sören Kierkegaard*.[37] Introducing her work as "an arrangement for the theater" based on "The Diary of the Seducer," the essay on the musical-erotic and her own understanding of Kierkegaard's writings and life, Bessa-Luís explicitly announces in a small introductory text that she will present Kierkegaard's dead remains "in the costume of Don Juan." Besides Sören, the other characters include Regine Olsen, Frederik Schlegel, an Aunt (Regine's), Don Juan, Paul (*sic*) Martin Möller, Johanne Louise Heiberg and five young women. Through three acts, Sören is depicted by all the other characters as a demoniac seducer, especially by Don Juan, who fears Sören might rob him of his place in history as the only genuine seducer. Far from assuming a farcical tone, Bessa-Luís reveals her awareness of the misunderstandings of a biographically biased reading of Kierkegaard's writings and emphasizes the role of the woman in the construction of Kierkegaard's view of seduction and love.

Although four of the major Portuguese universities (Lisbon, New University of Lisbon, Coimbra, and Porto) have had well-established philosophy departments since the late 1950s (philosophy and history used to be a single department and area of studies), and the Portuguese Catholic University has Theology and Philosophy degrees at three different campuses, Kierkegaard has practically remained a secondary author and thinker. Only the Library of the Lisbon Catholic University contains a good stock of works, including all the translations in Portuguese and the complete writings in French, German, and English (the Hong edition). Moreover, the debate concerning different churches or creeds, when it occurs at all, traditionally takes place outside the university; in addition to this, the presence of Lutheranism or Presbyterianism is hardly felt in Portugal, in what concerns education, research or religious studies, which might contribute to the deflation of such a debate. As already noted, a significant number of the articles and essays on Kierkegaard came from philosophers and thinkers outside philosophy departments. In Spring 2006, nevertheless, two professors of the same generation, the previously mentioned Nuno Ferro (New University of Lisbon) and Manuel Cândido Pimentel (b. 1961, Lisbon Catholic University) regularly taught doctoral seminars on Kierkegaard.[38] This will hopefully contribute to further research on Kierkegaard, who has remained a point of reference in the areas of esthetics, ethics, with implications in religious studies and theology, but has seldom been the main object of study—there are only five occurrences of his name in titles of dissertations

---

[36] Vergílio Ferreira's journals and essays comprehend about ten volumes, covering fifty years, and are published under the titles *Conta-Corrente* and *Espaço do Invisível*. For his essay on Existentialism, see "Da Fenomelogia a Sartre," in Jean Paul Sartre, *O Existencialismo é um Humanismo*, trans. by Vergílio Ferreira, Lisbon: Livraria Bertrand 2005 [1961], pp. 11–192.

[37] Agustina Bessa-Luís, *Estados eróticos imediatos de Sören Kierkegaard*, Lisboa: Guimarães Editores 1992.

[38] Ferro's seminar is based on "The moods of Kierkegaard" and Cândido Pimentel includes Kierkegaard among the authors discussed in the seminar "Modernity and Post-Modernity: from Lucidity to Labyrinth."

from 1962 until now.[39] However, three of these have been produced in the last seven years, and two of them relied on updated research in American institutions, giving new dimensions to the bibliographies (which previously tended to be based on Éditions de l'Orante and mostly French commentators) and consequently the scope of the research. Besides signalling a renewed interest in the thought and writings of Kierkegaard, these dissertations, together with the last translation of "In Vino Veritas" and the recent inclusion of Kierkegaard in doctoral programs in two different universities, may eventually set a new path and leave behind a time of indomitable trials, unavoidable errors, and customary tribulations for Kierkegaard scholars in Portugal.

[39] See Bibliography, section II.

Bibliography

I. Portuguese Translations of Kierkegaard's Works

O diário do seductor: a arte de amar ["The Seducer's Diary"], trans. by Mário Alemquer, Lisbon: Livraria Clássica 1911.

O desespero humano: doença até à morte [*The Sickness unto Death*], trans. and introduced by Adolfo Casais Monteiro, Oporto: Livraria Tavares Martins 1936 (reprinted twice in 1947, several later editions).

O Banquete ["In Vino Veritas"], trans. and ed. by Álvaro Ribeiro, Lisbon: Guimarães Editores 1953 (several later editions).

Temor e Tremor [*Fear and Trembling*], trans. by Maria José Marinho, introduced by Alberto Ferreira, Lisbon: Guimarães Editores 1959 (republished in 1990 and 1998).

O conceito de angústia [*The Concept of Anxiety*], trans. by João Lopes Alves, Lisbon: Presença 1962 (2nd ed., 1972).

Estética do Matrimónio ["The Esthetic Validity of Marriage"], trans. by Margarida Schiappa, Lisbon: Presença 1965.

Diário de um Sedutor ["The Seducer's Diary"], trans. by Carlos Grifo, Lisbon: Presença 1971.

Desespero: a doença mortal [*The Sickness unto Death*], trans. by Ana Keil, Oporto: Rés Editora 1986 (2nd ed., 2003).

Ponto de vista explicativo da minha obra como escritor [*The Point of View of My Work as an Author; Two Ethical-Religious Essays*], trans. by João Gama, Lisbon: Edições 70 1986.

Kierkegaard: In Vino Veritas, trans. and ed. by José Miranda Justo, Lisbon: Antígona 2005.

II. Secondary Literature on Kierkegaard in Portugal

Aguiar, M., "A guerra Anti-hegeliana" [The Anti-Hegel War], *Brotéria*, vol. 30, 1940, pp. 410–25.

Antunes, S.J., Manuel, "Kierkegaard," in *Obras Completas*, vol. 3, Tome I, Lisbon: Fundação Calouste Gulbenkian 2005, pp. 347–55 (first published in *Brotéria*, vol. 46, 1956; published also in *Do Espírito e do Tempo*, Lisbon: Edições Ática 1960, pp. 79–93).

Araújo, Alberto Fonseca, "Kierkegaard, um meditativo da existência cristã" [Kierkegaard Meditating on Christian Existence], *Chave*, no. 1, 1964, p. 7.

Barreto, Angelino, S.J., "Kierkegaard e a sua visão existencial do Homem" [Kierkegaard and his Existential View of Man"], *Cadernos de Filosofia*, vol. 5, 1956, pp. 24–30.

Bessa-Luís, Agustina, *Estados eróticos imediatos de Sören Kierkegaard* [Søren Kierkegaard's Immediate Erotic Stages], Lisbon: Guimarães Editores 1992.

Carvalho, António Pinto de, "A Filosofia Religiosa de Sören Aabye Kierkegaard" [The Religious Philosophy of Sören Aabye Kierkegaard"], *Brotéria*, vol. 22, 1936, pp. 361–9.

Espinha, Bruno José Neves, *Origem de uma ideia na Obra de Sören Kierkegaard?* [On the Origin of an Idea in the Work of Sören Kierkegaard], Masters' Thesis, Universidade Nova de Lisboa, Lisbon 1998.

Ferro, Nuno da Rosa, "A Noção de Experiência na Obra de Kierkegaard" [The Notion of Experience in Kierkegaard's Work], in *Quid Revista de filosofia* (1: *Sobre a Experiência*), Lisbon: Livros Cotovia 2000, pp. 251–317.

Fragata, Júlio Moreira, S.J., "Kierkegaard," in *Enciclopédia Luso-Brasileira de Cultura*, vol. 11, Lisbon: Editorial Verbo 1971, pp. 1124–8.

— "Kierkegaard," in *Logos*, vol. 3, Lisbon: Editorial Verbo 1991, pp. 162–7.

— "O Existencialismo teológico de Kierkegaard" [The Logical Existentialism of Kierkegaard], *Filosofia*, vol. 8, 1956, pp. 250–5.

— "Filosofia da Existência" [The Philosophy of Existence] (1960), in *Problemas da Filosofia Contemporânea*, Braga: Publicações da Faculdade de Filosofia da UCP 1989, pp. 99–112.

Gomes, F. Soares, "Revoluções do pensamento: Redescoberta da Categoria Afectiva do Outro" [Revolutions in Thought: the Rediscovery of the Affective Category of the Other], *Revista Portuguesa de Filosofia*, vol. 31, 1975, pp. 3–27.

Gonçalves, Daniela Alexandra Ramos, *Ironia e Humor. A perspectiva existencial de Kierkegaard* [Irony and Humor. Kierkegaard's Existencial Perspective], Masters' Thesis, Universidade do Porto, Porto 2002.

Gouveia, Maria Carmelita Homem de, *Meditação sobre* Temor e Tremor *de Kierkegaard* [A Meditation on *Fear and Trembling* by Kierkegaard] Coimbra 1957 (Separata das publicações do Congresso Luso-Espanhol para o Progresso das Ciências).

Guerra, Maria Luísa, "Kierkegaard ou a Paixão do Indivíduo" [Kierkegaard or the Passion of the Individual], *Palestra*, vol. 18, 1963, pp. 45–60.

Jardim E. Luís, S.J., "Kierkegaard e o Catolicismo" [Kierkegaard and Catholicism], *Cadernos de Filosofia*, vol. 6, 1957, pp. 24–30.

Júnior Eurico da Rua, S.J., "Desespero e Consciência em Kierkegaard" [Despair and Consciousness in Kierkegaard], *Cadernos de Filosofia*, vol. 14, 1965, pp. 5–20.

Lima, Salviano Paixão Zagalo de, *O Movimento Kierkegaardiano de Interiorização do Instante* [The Kierkegaardian Movement towards the Interiorization of the Moment], Ph.D. Thesis, Universidade de Lisboa, Lisbon 1962.

Lourenço, Eduardo, "Sören Kierkegaard, O Espião de Deus" [Sören Kierkegaard, God's Spy], *Heterodoxia*, vol. 2, Lisbon: Gradiva (3rd ed.), pp. 121–99.

— "Kierkegaard e Pessoa ou as Máscaras do Absoluto" [Kierkegaard and Pessoa or the Masks of the Absolute] (1981), in *Fernando Rei da Nossa Baviera*, Lisbon: Imprensa Nacional Casa da Moeda 1986, pp. 97–109.

— "Kierkegaard e Pessoa ou a Comunicação Indirecta" [Kierkegaard and Pessoa or the Indirect Communication] (1954–6), in *Fernando Rei da da Nossa Baviera*, Lisbon: Imprensa Nacional Casa da Moeda 1986, pp. 121–44.

Lopes, António Costa, "Kierkegaard e o Catolicismo" [Kierkegaard and Catholicism], *Theologica*, 1957, pp. 221–4.

Malpique, Manuel Cruz, "Kierkegaard: o Misógino e o Obsessivo do Pecado (1813–55) [Kierkegaard: the Misogynist Obsessed by Sin (1813–55)], *Labor*, vol. 29, nos. 236–7, pp. 229–41; pp. 277–97.

Marinho, José, "Reflexão e Espontaneidade" [Reflection and Spontaneity], *Obras Completas de José Marinho*, vol. 2, Lisbon: Imprensa Nacional Casa da Moeda 1995, pp. 210–12.

Martins, Diamantino, "O Problema da Demonstração de Deus em Kierkegaard" [The Question about the Proof of God in Kierkegaard], *Revista Portuguesa de Filosofia*, vol. 24, 1976, pp. 429–39.

Mourujão, Alexandre Fradique, "Em Torno do Existencialismo" [On Existentialism] (1954), *Estudos Filosóficos*, vol. 2, Lisbon: Imprensa Nacional Casa da Moeda 2004, pp. 465–86 [part 2, pp. 468–73].

Murteira, José Maria, "Kierkegaard: Angústia e Fé" [Kierkegaard: Anguish and Faith], *Brotéria*, vol. 126, 1988, pp. 340–5.

Niner, Elaine Cecília, "Sören Kierkegaard e a problemática humana" [Sören Kierkegaard and the Question of Mankind], *Convivium S.P.*, no. 8, 1969, pp. 14–32.

Pinto José Rui Gaia da Costa, S.J., "A Verdade em Kierkegaard" [The Truth in Kierkegaard], *Revista Portuguesa de Filosofia*, vol. 33, 1977, pp. 84–8.

Quadros, António, "Filosofia e Sentimento – Gnoseologia do Amor" [Philosophy and Feeling – Gnoseology of Love], *Tempo Presente*, no. 8, 1959, pp. 28–40 [on Kierkegaard, see pp. 35–7].

Ribeiro, Álvaro, "Balanço e Equilíbrio do Ano Filosófico" [Evaluation and Balance of the Philosophical Year] (1954), *Dispersos e Inéditos II*, ed. by Joaquim Domingues, Lisbon: Imprensa Nacional Casa da Moeda 2004, pp. 89–93.

— "Filosofia Portuguesa Actual" [Current Portugese Philosophy] (1962), *Dispersos e Inéditos III*, ed. by Joaquim Domingues, Lisbon: Imprensa Nacional Casa da Moeda 2005, pp. 51–8.

Santos, Delfim, "Dialéctica Totalista" [Total Dialectics], in *Obras Completas de Delfim Santos*, Lisbon: Fundação Gulbenkian 1971–7, vol. 1, pp. 31–8 (originally published in *Presença*, no. 39, 1933, pp. 8–9; p. 12).

— "O valor da Ironia" [The Value of Irony], in *Obras Completas de Delfim Santos*, vol. 1, pp. 349–53 (originally published in *Variante*, Winter 1943, pp. 74–6).

— "Temática Existencial," in *Obras Completas de Delfim Santos*, vol. 2, pp. 79–85 (originally published in *Atlântico*, vol. 2, 1950).

— "Sentido Existencial da Angústia" [The Existential Meaning of Anxiety], in *Obras Completas de Delfim Santos*, vol. 2, pp. 154–64 (originally published in *Anais Portugueses de Psiquiatria*, vol. 4, 1952).

— "Prefácio à tradução de um livro de Régis Jolivet" [Preface to a Translation of a Book by Régis Jolivet], in *Obras Completas de Delfim Santos*, vol. 2, pp. 168–72

(originally published as preface to Régis Jolivet, *As Doutrinas Existencialistas*, Oporto: Tavares Martins 1953).
— "Humanismo em Pascal" [Humanism in Pascal], in *Obras Completas de Delfim Santos*, vol. 2, pp. 189–202 (originally published in *Revista Brasileira de Filosofia*, vol. 3, no. 2, 1953, pp. 199–212).
— "Filosofia como Ontologia Fundamental" [Philosophy as Fundamental Ontology], in *Obras Completas de Delfim Santos*, vol. 2, pp. 213–16.
— "Jaspers na Filosofia Contemporânea" [Jaspers in Contemporary Philosophy] (1958 conference), in *Obras Completas de Delfim Santos*, vol. 2, pp. 268–79 (originally published in *O Tempo e o Modo*, nos. 43–4, 1966).
Saraiva, Maria Manuela Simões, "Kierkegaard e o Problema Filosófico do Homem" [Kierkegaard and the Philosophical Problem of Man], *Filosofia*, vol. 8, 1956, pp. 256–66.
Silva, José Manuel Bártolo da, *O Labirinto interior: o pensamento de Sören Kierkegaard a partir das suas reacções ao sistema (1843–1846)* [The Inner Labyrinth: Sören Kierkegaard's Thought Seen from his Reactions to the System], Masters' Thesis, Universidade Nova de Lisboa, Lisbon 1999.
Silva, Luís de Oliveira e, "Estética e Ética em Kierkegaard e Pessoa" [Esthetics and Ethics in Kierkegaard and Pessoa], *Revista da Faculdade de Ciências Sociais e Humanas*, 1988, pp. 261–72.
Sousa, Elisabete Marques de, "A mão de Mozart" [The Hand of Mozart], *Dedalus*, vol. 9, 2004, pp. 147–71.
— *Formas de Arte: a Prática Crítica de Berlioz, Kierkegaard, Liszt e Schumann* [Forms of Art: the Practical Criticism of Berlioz, Kierkegaard, Liszt and Schumann], Ph.D. Thesis, Universidade de Lisboa, Lisbon 2006.
Zeferino, Maria de Lourdes, "Dialéctica do Espírito e da Matéria em Alguns Filósofos Contemporâneos" [The Dialectic of Spirit and Matter in Some Contemporary Philosophers], *Brotéria*, no. 100, 1975, pp. 154–64.

III. Secondary Literature on Kierkegaard's Reception in Portugal

Valls, Álvaro L.M., "*The Concept of Anxiety* in Spanish and Portuguese," *Kierkegaard Studies. Yearbook*, 2001, pp. 335–40.

Spain:
The Old and New Kierkegaard Reception in Spain

Dolors Perarnau Vidal and Óscar Parcero Oubiña

As normally happens with other thinkers, the reception of Kierkegaard in Spain has been belated and a bit precarious, especially when one compares it with that of other European countries. In spite of the fact that already in the very first decade of the twentieth century both Miguel de Unamuno and Joan Estelrich i Artigues had discovered the Dane and tried to present him to the Spanish reader,[1] there was not a general interest in Kierkegaard in the following years. For a long time, there were only personal approaches to him in Spain. There were partial and isolated contributions which did not constitute a solid ground for a future reception.

This situation paved the way for a massive influx of foreign literature in Spain which strongly shaped the picture of Kierkegaard for many years. From that moment on, the Spanish readings were tinged by two major perspectives, mainly imported from Italy and France: Catholicism and existentialism. Both of these perspectives and the tragic and romantic view that Unamuno had already presented of Kierkegaard gave rise to the picture of a melancholic, solitary, pessimistic, and tormented Christian. This is the image that would remain until the arrival of a group of scholars who, from the late 1970s and for the very first time, would dedicate their efforts to introducing to the Spanish audience "Kierkegaard's real face" taken directly from his original works.

In the meantime, a very important event was taking place. From 1961, a complete translation of Kierkegaard's works and journals had begun to appear. This project also had the significance of being made directly from the Danish originals, which constituted a novelty in the rather poor tradition of the Spanish translation of Kierkegaard. However, it was never completed. Just a few works, some of them only partially translated, were published; and yet these translations were an important step forward in the Kierkegaard reception, inasmuch as they provided the readers with more accurate and reliable material to work with. In this sense, they

---

[1] In this respect, some Spanish scholars have argued that Kierkegaard's influence on Unamuno was first in relation to countries such as Russia, France or Italy. (Cf. Jorge Uscatescu, "Unamuno y Kierkegaard o la interioridad secreta," *Arbor*, vol. 103, nos. 403–4, 1979, p. 27; Joan Estelrich i Artigues, "Kierkegaard dins del pensament nòrdic," *La revista*, vol. 5, nos. 81–3, 1919, p. 68.)

established a new way of approaching Kierkegaard that would eventually lead to the aforementioned group of scholars.

Finally, out of this group, a whole new generation of specialists appeared in the field of Spanish Kierkegaard studies. They were people whose approaches to Kierkegaard differed greatly from those of the previous interpreters, insofar as their main concern was to develop rigorous studies, rather than to simply reflect upon an already given picture of Kierkegaard. As a consequence, this new generation of scholars gave—and continues to give—to the Spanish research not only a more scholarly view of Kierkegaard but also new perspectives for reading his works. Furthermore, they put the Spanish research directly in contact with the international research and made it possible to begin to compensate for the delay that had been the distinctive mark of the Spanish reception for a very long time. In what follows, we will divide the history of the reception of Kierkegaard in Spain into five periods, corresponding to what can be considered its five main stages.

I. The First Period 1901–1930s:
A. Two Forerunners of Kierkegaard: Miguel de Unamuno and Joan Estelrich

It is a well-known fact that to date the beginning of Kierkegaard's reception in Spain is to date the encounter of the Basque writer Miguel de Unamuno (1864–1936) with his admired Danish thinker. Traditionally, this has been ascribed to 1901, since this was the year in which Unamuno received the first three volumes of the first Danish edition of Kierkegaard's collected works and started to study the author who attracted him so much that he called him a "brother."[2] In the preface to the Danish translation of *The Tragic Sense of Life in Men and Nations*, Unamuno explains:

> I discovered a brother in him, almost another I, and I decided to embrace his soul. Since at that time I could not get any translation of his collected works, I requested the Danish original. With the help of my knowledge of German and English, I began to translate it for myself. In this way, I learned enough Danish to be able to understand Kierkegaard.[3]

---

[2]   It was not until Jesús Antonio Collado's work that the date of 1901 was academically accepted. Previously, the critics had considered 1900 to be the year of the encounter, on the grounds that in a letter to Clarín from that year Unamuno says he is going to "take a dip in the Danish theologian." (Cf. Jesús Antonio Collado, *Kierkegaard y Unamuno. La existencia religiosa*, Madrid: Gredos 1962, p. 388.) After Collado's work, most of the scholars agree with the date of 1901. (Cf. Juan Carlos Lago Bornstein, "Unamuno y Kierkegaard: dos espíritus hermanos," *Anales del Seminario de Metafísica*, vol. 21, 1986, pp. 60–1; Gemma Roberts, *Unamuno: afinidades y coincidencias Kierkegaardianas*, Colorado: Society of Spanish and Spanish-American Studies 1986, p. 21; and Jaime Franco Barrio, "Kierkegaard en español," *Azafea*, no. 2, 1989, p. 212.)

[3]   Miguel de Unamuno, *Den tragiske Livsfølelse hos Mennesker og Folkeslag*, Copenhagen: Haase 1925, p. 5. All translations into English are ours, unless otherwise noted.

Nevertheless, Unamuno's contact with the Danish language dates back to his youth, when he used to teach Spanish to a group of Danish sailors in his hometown, Bilbao.[4] It would not be until later on that this first approach to the language would continue to be developed by an attempt to read the works of Kierkegaard, which he purchased as soon as they were published in Copenhagen.

Unamuno read most of the volumes of Kierkegaard's *Samlede Værker*. As we know from the marginal notes, marks, and underlinings in his own copies, he worked with most of the pseudonymous works, some of the discourses and the late articles; he did not have access to the edition of the *Papirer*. It is difficult to say, however, to what extent Unamuno was familiar with the works of Kierkegaard which he possessed, since he sometimes left books half read, and he hardly alludes to them in his own writings.[5] Only two works could be considered as having been clearly worked on by Unamuno, namely, *Either/Or* and the *Concluding Unscientific Postscript*, which are, in fact, the ones which he quotes in his writings.[6]

Throughout his work, Unamuno mentioned or, better said, praised Kierkegaard in different places. The most important and extensive allusions to the Danish author appear in the essays "Ibsen and Kierkegaard"[7] and "Manuel Machado's 'Soul,'"[8] and in the books *The Tragic Sense of Life in Men and Nations* and *Against This and That*.[9] In these texts, Unamuno refers to Kierkegaard as "the powerful Danish thinker and 'feeler,' the great melancholic, the philosopher of irrationalism, contradiction and leap, of disjunctions and *either all or nothing*, the main model of that great and shadowy *Brand* of Ibsen."[10] As a matter of fact, the expressions Unamuno uses to name Kierkegaard are quite repetitive and said as prayers:

---

[4] Cf. Juan David García Bacca, "Kierkegaard y la filosofía contemporánea española," *Cuadernos Americanos*, vol. 151, no. 2, 1967 (Mexico), p. 95.

[5] In the prologue to *San Manuel Bueno, Mártir, y tres historias más*, Unamuno writes: "Precisely now, when I am writing this prologue, I have just finished the reading of *Either/Or* of my favorite Søren Kierkegaard, whose reading I interrupted years ago—before my exile—, and in the section entitled 'The Balance between the Aesthetic and the Ethical in the Development of the Personality' I have found a fragment which has wounded me deeply, and it comes as rope for the tholepin to hold the oar—here pen—with which I am rowing in this writing" (Miguel de Unamuno, *San Manuel Bueno, Mártir*, Madrid: Espasa-Calpe 1942, p. 90).

[6] Cf. Oscar A. Fasel, "Observations on Unamuno and Kierkegaard," *Hispania*, vol. 38, no. 4, 1955 (Los Angeles), p. 448.

[7] Miguel de Unamuno, "Ibsen y Kierkegaard," in his *Mi religión y otros ensayos breves* [My Religion and Other Short Essays], Madrid: Renacimiento 1910.

[8] Miguel de Unamuno, "El 'alma' de Manuel Machado," *Heraldo de Madrid*, March 19, 1901.

[9] Miguel de Unamuno, *Del sentimiento trágico de la vida en los hombres y en los pueblos*, Madrid: Renacimiento 1912, p. 7; pp. 111–3; pp. 117–8; p. 124; p. 154; pp. 176–7; p. 197; p. 253; p. 280; p. 318; and Miguel de Unamuno, *Contra esto y aquello*, in *Ensayos*, vols. 1–2, Madrid: Aguilar 1945 [Madrid: Renacimiento 1912], vol. 2, p. 1080; p. 1107; p. 1147.

[10] Miguel de Unamuno, *Libros y autores españoles contemporáneos*, in *Obras completas*, vols. 1–16, Madrid: Afrodisio Aguado, 1951–60, vol. 5, 1952, p. 194. With regard to Ibsen, Unamuno writes: "It was the Ibsenian critic, Brandes, who introduced me to Kierkegaard, and if I began to study Danish by translating, before anything, Ibsen's *Brand*, it has been the

"brother," "my favorite," "the great Dane," "that heroic Kierkegaard," "that lonely theologian of Copenhagen," the "man of the secret," "that mysterious Dane who lived in constant inward despair," "the tragic poet of heroic loneliness," "the great Danish theologian and dreamer," the "tormented and heroic soul," "that master of resigned despair." All these are words of admiration, enthusiasm, and compassion for a man who, like him, was "of flesh and blood" and felt "the tragic sense of life." Thus, the affection and respect that Unamuno had for Kierkegaard was for the man, the person, rather than for the thinker, the philosopher, or theologian. In this sense, the allusions we find in his writings are references in passing rather than detailed or elaborated reflections on Kierkegaard and his work.

Nevertheless, there is also a strictly intellectual relationship that can be found in the way in which the Basque author uses Kierkegaard's texts. In some of his references, Unamuno includes quotations that he himself translates into Spanish, becoming the first person in Spain to venture into the difficult task of translating Kierkegaard. These translated fragments allow us not only to observe Unamuno's capability to understand the Danish text (which was more precarious than what sometimes is taken for granted), but also to examine the topics he was most interested in.

One of the main themes of Unamuno's writings is the strong objection to the rational knowledge of life. Like Kierkegaard, Unamuno thinks that rationality is not sufficient to explain existence and its dimension of faith. In this way, most of the fragments he chooses from Kierkegaard stress the contrast between an objective and pure thought and a subjective and passionate existence. It is not surprising, therefore, that Kierkegaard's major philosophical work, the *Concluding Unscientific Postscript*, is almost omnipresent in Unamuno's major philosophical work, *The Tragic Sense of Life in Men and Nations*.

An interesting point of contact between the two authors is Unamuno's notion of the "man of flesh and blood," which finds an echo in Kierkegaard's claim about "*den Enkelte*." Both authors condemn the loss of the individual in the decadence of the times and, particularly, in Christianity, which no longer expresses its true sense and has become a mere cultural habit.

> Let others complain that the times are evil. I complain that they are wretched, for they are without passion....The thoughts of their hearts are too wretched to be sinful. It is perhaps possible to regard it as sin for a worm to nourish such thoughts, but not for a human being, who is created in the image of God. Their desires are staid and dull, their passions drowsy....Fie on them! That is why my soul always turns back to the Old Testament and to Shakespeare. There one stills feels that those who speak are human beings; there they hate, there they love, there they murder the enemy, curse his descendants through all generations—there they sin.[11]

This quotation, used by Unamuno on two occasions in his works, shows the kind of relationship he had with Kierkegaard, a relation of brotherhood that made them join hands in their fight against the mediocrity of the times. But Unamuno had his

---

works of Kierkegaard, his spiritual father, which have especially made me happy with myself for having learned it" ("Ibsen y Kierkegaard," p. 426).

[11] *SKS* 2, 50 / *EO1*, 27–8.

own voice in this brotherhood, and his ideas have origins and aims different from Kierkegaard's, in such a way that at times these conceptions are in conflict with each other. In fact, Unamuno did not really follow Kierkegaard but rather used him occasionally to reaffirm his own ideas. It is in this sense that the question of the relation between the two authors arises. What kind of relation was it? Was there a real influence of Kierkegaard on Unamuno or was it only a coincidence, a spiritual brotherhood? To answer this question, many studies have been written in the context of both Unamuno and Kierkegaard scholarship.

On the one hand, some scholars claim that Unamuno did not follow Kierkegaard's texts, but that he just excerpted fragments from them in order to enrich and illustrate his own ideas. Moreover, he is also accused of having been a capricious reader who manipulated the texts in such a way that his reading loses all objective value.[12] Instead of simply quoting the text, he adapted it for his own benefit and made it say just what he wanted it to say.[13] However, not everybody agrees with this accusation, and we can also find those who defend Unamuno by saying that "his interpretation is penetrating and deep, although his interest was, above all, to develop his own concerns or 'obsessions' and not merely to give an erudite account of someone else's thought."[14] These two positions are, in fact, not as opposed to each other as they initially seem to be. It is true that Unamuno's translations are quite close to the original text and that he does not manipulate the text in his translations. But it is also true that he just selects the passages that best fit with his thought, overlooking others that could be in conflict with his ideas.[15] The controversy that arose in Unamuno's relation to Kierkegaard, however, is not only based on the question of faithfulness or unfaithfulness to the texts, but also on the themes that the Basque author developed himself. Here we find a number of scholars who stress the distance between the two thinkers. The permanent and tragic contradiction between reason and faith, the topic of immortality, the status of art in relation to religiousness, the relation between the individual and society, between man and God, or the importance of sin are themes where one finds profound differences between the two authors. Although it is true that Unamuno took some elements from Kierkegaard, it cannot be said, according to these scholars, that Kierkegaard exercised an influence on Unamuno.[16]

On the other hand, there have also been interpreters who have defended the thesis of an influence. According to them, Unamuno would have developed some of his

---

[12] Cf. Paul L. Landsberg, "Reflexiones sobre Unamuno," *Cruz y Raya*, no. 31, 1935, pp. 7–54; François Meyer, "Kierkegaard et Unamuno," *Revue de Littérature Comparée*, vol. 29, 1955 (Paris), p. 482.

[13] Cf. Bornstein, "Unamuno y Kierkegaard: dos espíritus hermanos," pp. 59–71.

[14] Roberts, *Unamuno: afinidades y coincidencias Kierkegaardianas*, pp. 21–2.

[15] Unamuno's peculiar reading is then a sign of a completely different approach to the work that has little to do with the question of faithfulness or unfaithfulness. We could regard this reading as that of the genius, according to what Kierkegaard writes in his journals in 1837: "A thesis: great geniuses are essentially unable to read a book. While they are reading, their own development will always be greater than their understanding of the author" (*SKS* 17, 136, BB:46 / *JP* 2, 1288).

[16] Cf. Bornstein, "Unamuno y Kierkegaard: dos espíritus hermanos"; Fasel, "Observations on Unamuno and Kierkegaard," pp. 478–91.

themes only after his encounter with Kierkegaard.[17] As a reaction to this reading, many studies came to defend the view that Unamuno's thought was already mature when he first came upon Kierkegaard, and so it is not possible to talk about an influence but just a coincidence.[18] But most of the papers written in this regard were not solely against the thesis of the influence; but they also tried to present a thesis themselves. The well-known interpretation of the "spiritual brotherhood" seems to have been the reading that has most succeeded in both Unamuno and Kierkegaard scholarship. Basically, this thesis consists in defending the view that there is not only a thematic overlap between the two authors but, furthermore, that the core of this intellectual overlap lies in an encounter of two similar souls, a similar existential attitude towards life. Several texts from both Kierkegaard's journals and Unamuno's private diary would support this argument. "Unamuno did not possess the *Papirer*, edited later, among which one can find the decisive notes from the journals. And it is curious to find in Unamuno passages that seem to be inspired precisely by Kierkegaard's journals."[19] Therefore, rather than an influence of Kierkegaard on Unamuno, we should speak of an encounter of two kindred spirits who felt so similarly as to make one of them feel that he was the reincarnation of the other:[20]

> It is nearly three and a half years ago [the summer of 1916], in Mallorca, when Miguel de Unamuno talked, or better said, gave a monologue in front of others and said:
>
> — The last time I died was the year of 1855 in Copenhagen; my name was Søren Kierkegaard.
> — And before?—Some of the people present asked.
> — Pascal.
> — And still before?
> — Before, my name was Íñigo de Loyola.
> — And before?—We insisted.
> — Before—another one interjected—before Paul of Tarsos.
> — No, that would be too much—warned Miguel de Unamuno.[21]

---

[17] Cf. Pierre Mesnard and Robert Ricard, "Aspects nouveaux d'Unamuno," *La vie intellectuelle*, vol. 14, no. 2, 1946 (Paris), pp. 112–39; Alain Guy, "Miguel de Unamuno, pèlerin de l'absolu," *Cuadernos de la cátedra Miguel de Unamuno*, vol. 1, 1948, pp. 75–102; Luis S. Granjel, *Retrato de Unamuno*, Madrid: Guadarrama 1957, p. 169; and Antonio Sánchez Barbudo, *Estudios sobre Unamuno y Machado*, Madrid: Guadarrama 1959, pp. 65ff.

[18] Cf. Andrés M. Tornos, "Sobre Unamuno y Kierkegaard," *Pensamiento*, vol. 18, 1962, pp. 131–46.

[19] Collado, *Kierkegaard y Unamuno. La existencia religiosa*, p. 15.

[20] Cf. Collado, *Kierkegaard y Unamuno. La existencia religiosa*; Bacca, "Kierkegaard y la filosofía contemporánea española," pp. 94–105; José Luis Abellán, "Influencias filosóficas en Unamuno," *Ínsula*, no. 181, 1961, p. 11; Uscatescu, "Unamuno y Kierkegaard o la interioridad secreta"; Bornstein, "Unamuno y Kierkegaard: dos espíritus hermanos." The thesis of the "spiritual brotherhood" is defended by many scholars. Nevertheless, as far as the intellectual relation is concerned, this is not a thesis that necessarily enters into conflict with others, since it basically stresses the fact of a personal relationship.

[21] Joan Estelrich i Artigues, "Kierkegaard i Unamuno," *La Revista*, vol. 5, no. 84, 1919, p. 83.

Spain: The Old and New Kierkegaard Reception in Spain 23

This anecdote is recounted by Joan Estelrich (1896–1958), the versatile Majorcan writer who was, together with Unamuno, the first forerunner of Kierkegaard in Spain and, particularly, in Catalonia.[22] If Unamuno was the first to discover Kierkegaard, then Estelrich was the first to study his work in a more rigorous and scholarly way. Estelrich's studies stand out for their astonishing novelty and familiarity with both the secondary literature and Danish.[23] He explains:

> [The reading of Unamuno] incited me to get a direct approach to the work of the great Danish writer. Despite the difficulties of the war, I got the German edition of Gottsched and Schrempf, plus the studies of Brandes, Høffding and some others; later I acquired the Danish edition of the collected works....In the second semester of 1918, I wrote my essay on Kierkegaard, caught by the fascination of his personality. My first piece was quite long (more than 150 pages) and was published by *La Revista*....In 1926 I reprinted it in the volume *Entre la vida i els llibres*. Here, the book did not have any influence, and one must rather find it used in foreign works such as Daniel-Rops' *Carte d'Europe*. Given that the book was the first extensive study on Kierkegaard in a non-Germanic language, Daniel-Rops and Jean Cassou asked for permission to translate it into French; I refused, because no one better than me knew the deficiencies of my work, without getting my modesty so far as to ignore the happy discoveries and correct intuitions that later studies of more learned authors have confirmed and developed.[24]

---

[22] Estelrich was a politician, journalist, editor, and essayist. As a matter of fact, his interest in Kierkegaard was closely related with his political concerns, which focused, among other things, on the Scandinavian countries. Estelrich drew a certain parallelism between the political situation of Scandinavia and Iberia (cf. "Escandinàvia i Ibèria," *La Revista*, no. 112, 1920, pp. 134–6).

[23] The well-documented bibliographical note he elaborated in 1919 is good evidence of this. It must be said that Estelrich also translated a fragment of Høffding's speech at the University of Copenhagen (1913) in 1918, which could make us think he mastered the Danish language. However, it is difficult to say to what extent Estelrich knew Danish since, on the one hand, an early French translation of Høffding's Speech had already been published (*Revue de Métaphysique et de Morale*, vol. 21, no. 6, 1913 (Paris), pp. 713–32)—as Estelrich himself remarks in his "Bibliography on S. Kierkegaard"; and, on the other hand, the Danish titles, categories and expressions he used from Kierkegaard's work could also have been taken from other studies on Kierkegaard. As a matter of fact, Estelrich's letter from February 1920 seems to verify this hypothesis: "My friend Kjersmeier also sent me a copy of his translation. I do not know anybody who could do a good and exactly literal translation either. The little knowledge I have of Danish, due to the resemblance of German, only helps me to be aware of the content, without being able to give a literal translation" ("Letter to Joan Alcover," in *Joan Alcover i Maspons personal archives*, Obra cultural Balear copyright, Palma: Regne de Mallorca Archives). Likewise, in a *curriculum vitae* written by Estelrich himself at the end of his life, Danish is not given as a language of his knowledge (*Joan Pons i Marquès personal archives*, Palma de Mallorca). Taking these documents into account, we could practically confirm that Estelrich neither translated the fragment of Høffding's speech nor the passages and categories quoted from Kierkegaard's work since, despite that "little knowledge" of Danish, he was only able to "be aware of the content" but not "to give a literal translation." We are indebted to Isabel Graña for these documents.

[24] Joan Estelrich i Artigues, "Kierkegaard en España," *Destino*, August 9, 1947, p. 9.

The chapter on Søren Kierkegaard, which is part of Estelrich's *Between Life and Books*, consists of two essays: "Søren Kierkegaard. 'El més infeliç,'" and "Kierkegaard dins del pensament nòrdic," plus a "Bibliografia de S. Kierkegaard."[25] Having gone through a critical period in which the problem of existence worried him, Estelrich states that he turned to those tormented souls who had most felt it. Hence the title of the first essay: "Søren Kierkegaard, The Unhappiest One," which Estelrich says is "not something absolutely objective," but an "imagined construction, purely poetic" account of the work and life of a man who, in a certain moment, impressed him very deeply.[26] Even though this first essay had already been conceived of as a book,[27] the project was frustrated, and Estelrich ended up publishing the written material in installments in *La Revista* from October to December of 1918.

As far as the content of this essay is concerned, Estelrich starts with a brief portrait of the most characteristic elements of Kierkegaard's biography and goes on with the main topics of Kierkegaard's work. Together with the same melancholic and solitary image of Kierkegaard found in Unamuno, the Majorcan depicts the Dane as a man who knew everybody and enjoyed talking to people in the streets: "He always came up in Østergade—'the Passeig de Gràcia,' so to speak, of the Danish capital—masterly and with downcast eyes, the umbrella under his arm and waving his hat from left to right. He talked to everyone with prodigality. But he locked himself in his home afterwards."[28] A representative feature of Estelrich's approach to Kierkegaard is that of attempting to bring him nearer to the Catalan reader. Here, it is the "Passeig de Gràcia" (a centrally situated avenue in the city of Barcelona), and a few pages later it will be count Arnau (a traditional Catalan myth), which will be put in relation to Don Giovanni. Both references are made in order to set the aspects of Catalan culture in a European context. It is also in this sense that Estelrich praises Kierkegaard's masterly use of Danish, which he relates to his claim for the minority Catalan language.

In contrast to this study, "Kierkegaard dins del pensament nòrdic," the second of these essays published in *La Revista* in 1919, was "only erudite and better documented," written this time "with perfect objectivity."[29] In this text, Estelrich returns to the distinction, already drawn in the last chapters of his previous essay, between northern and southern thought, developing the peculiar features of the northern spirit. Given that Kierkegaard was the center of his reflection, Estelrich analyzes those thinkers and writers who preceded him, who were contemporary with him, and who were influenced by him. Among the followers, he focuses particularly on Unamuno, whom he surprisingly regards as a northern thinker. According to Estelrich, the Basque author lacks the Latin roots and, in this sense, he should be

---

[25] Joan Estelrich i Artigues, *Entre la vida i els llibres*, Barcelona: Llibreria Catalonia 1926, pp. 63–218.
[26] Ibid., p. 66.
[27] "The first of these essays about the fascinating figure of Søren Kierkegaard had to be—its elements being properly coordinated and amplified—a book for *La Revista* publications." (Estelrich, *Entre la vida i els llibres*, p. 65).
[28] Ibid., p. 74.
[29] Ibid., p. 67.

regarded as "a northern consciousness, a heavy spirit, a reconcentrated intelligence."[30] This must be the reason why Kierkegaard is so unknown in the southern countries, remarks Estelrich, and he adds: "Unamuno will die alone, without disciples, in the petrified loneliness that surrounds him. Many people applaud or condemn Unamuno, but his religious ideas—even though, according to him, his tragic sense of life is the tragic sense of Spaniards—have not been of interest to anybody."[31]

Pío Baroja (1872–1956), a Basque writer contemporary with Unamuno, supports Estelrich's thesis. He asserts that Kierkegaard's thought "is a way of thinking that exists among Protestants and that cannot be found among us who have a Catholic and Latin tradition."[32] In the second part of the novel *The Great Whirl of the World*[33] Baroja talks about Kierkegaard, presenting the Spanish reader with an image very similar to Unamuno's, although, this time, Baroja's evaluation of this image is one not of admiration but, on the contrary, of rejection. He starts by making allusion to Kierkegaard's name, which he translates literally into Spanish as "Severo Cementerio" [Severe Churchyard],[34] and with this gloomy mood, he claims Kierkegaard was a man "as sad as his surname; a fellow very difficult to understand for a southerner." He writes:

> It is foolish. He thought he was a Socrates, and he was, at most, a northern Saint Ignacio de Loyola. Maybe the difference lies in the fact that Loyola's disciples tried to make Christianity something easy, available to everyone, and Kierkegaard's system has been to set the Christian model as something so superior that it is impossible to actualize. Here, men like Kierkegaard drive people to insanity with their delirious Christianity and their *Either/Or*. There are men who, having been trained by fellows like this theologian, spend their lives torturing themselves with a religious masochism, thinking about their sins and eternal condemnation, in which, however, they do not believe. With their moral hyperesthesia, they martyr themselves for sins that are not sins, and they think about a condemnation that is not condemnation and about an eternity that is not eternity either.[35]

This one-sided view turned out to be the standard picture of Kierkegaard for many years in Spain. The "dark side" of the works of the Dane became the only one to be taken into consideration in such a way that there was no place for other readings that also stressed its "bright side." Tragedy, pessimism and darkness overwhelmed everything, and Kierkegaard became a masochist who "wishes anxiety and despair

---

[30] Ibid., p. 209.
[31] Ibid., p. 84.
[32] Pío Baroja, *Obras completas*, vols. 1–8, Madrid: Biblioteca Nueva 1946–51, vol. 5, 1948, p. 238 [1918].
[33] Pio Baroja, *El gran torbellino del mundo*, Madrid: Caro Raggio 1926.
[34] Also Estelrich opens his "Søren Kierkegaard, 'el més infeliç'" translating Kierkegaard's surname into Catalan as "jardí d'església, cementiri" [churchyard, cemetery]. In fact, this way of referring to Kierkegaard would become a cliché to introduce him in Spain and would last for many years.
[35] Pio Baroja, *El gran torbellino del mundo*, Madrid: Espasa-Calpe 1964, p. 119.

almost as a rule…a sick man, arbitrary and shadowy, who not only does not want to be healed but recreates himself in his own pains."[36]

To make matters worse, Ortega y Gasset's (1883–1955) revocation of Unamuno's "tragic sense of life" would consolidate later on not only the aforementioned tragic image but also Kierkegaard's bad reputation in Spain. In *The Idea of Principle in Leibnitz and the Evolution of Deductive Theory*, Ortega writes:

> I do not, then, believe in the "tragic sense of life" as the ultimate form of human existence. Life is not, cannot be a tragedy. It is within life that tragedies are produced and are possible.
>
> That idea of the tragic sense of life is the product of a romantic imagination, and as such it is arbitrary and crudely melodramatic. Romanticism poisoned the Christianity of a born actor who lived in Copenhagen: Kierkegaard, and from him the refrain went first to Unamuno and then to Heidegger.[37]

It must be said that the Madrilenian philosopher did not really have a reading of Kierkegaard of his own, but he just borrowed it from Unamuno without any intermediate critical reflection.[38] As a result, his rejection of Kierkegaard became solely an unfair consequence of his opposition to Unamuno's conception of life.[39] Thus, Kierkegaard receives from Ortega a very rude treatment:

> In the narrow environment of Copenhagen, where everything is small, absurdly crowded, where every man automatically becomes a "type," a "bonhomme," a public marionette, and a byword, Kierkegaard, superlative at dramatizing himself, a very frequent occurrence in those last two romantic generations (the other, the later one, is that of Baudelaire)—a marionette of Hegel who wants to "act" the antiHegel—needs to make and be made a spectacle of himself and to be a great "type," an "original," at whom children laugh in the street and point with a finger when he turns the corner, in the little town where all the corners are familiar….Thus Kierkegaard in Copenhagen. The great provincial personality there was the theologian Mynster. So Kierkegaard will make it his business to be "he who attacks and insults the theologian Mynster."[40]

---

[36] Pio Baroja, *Las horas solitarias*, Madrid: R. Caro Raggio 1918, p. 238.

[37] José Ortega y Gasset, *The Idea of Principle in Leibnitz and the Evolution of Deductive Theory*, trans. by Mildred Adams, New York: Norton 1971, p. 313 (in Spanish as *La idea de principio en Leibniz y la evolución de la teoría deductiva*, Buenos Aires: Emecé 1958).

[38] "I have known another man singularly like Kierkegaard in this, and hence I know the latter well." (Ibid., p. 316.) In another work, Ortega openly confirms the fact of having a "borrowed" reading of Kierkegaard: "As far as Kierkegaard is concerned, I have not been able to read him, neither then nor after…I am unable to absorb a book of Kierkegaard" (José Ortega y Gasset, *Prólogo para alemanes*, Madrid: Revista de Occidente 1974, pp. 58–9).

[39] From his very first writings, Ortega opposed to the "tragic sense" of Unamuno a "jovial sense" of life. As a matter of fact, the harsh words Ortega wrote against Kierkegaard were the response to the fact of having been accused of being related to existentialism. With anger, Ortega decided to run down Kierkegaard, whom he regarded as the "father of existentialism," and extended his attack to his so-called followers, such as Unamuno and Heidegger.

[40] Unamuno, *The Idea of Principle in Leibnitz*, pp. 315–8.

Finally, and in contrast with the negative views of both Baroja and, later, Ortega, we must also point out in this first period the modest contribution of Eugeni d'Ors (1881–1954), the Catalan essayist, journalist, philosopher, scientist, and art critic who created the movement of "Noucentism," a personal project of renovation and education of the individual and society. We do not find in d'Ors any personal account of how he knew Kierkegaard's work. Nevertheless, everything seems to point to the fact that the intellectual movements in Europe might have been the meeting point of the Catalan and the Dane. Eugeni d'Ors was very familiar with the European intellectuals, and he knew the work of authors such as the Danish scholar Harald Høffding (1843–1931), from whom it is very likely d'Ors discovered Kierkegaard.

In the *Glosari*, a daily column d'Ors wrote from 1906 in the newspapers, he refers a few times to Kierkegaard, always almost exclusively in relation to two topics. First, he alludes to Kierkegaard's conception of the ethical as a model for the individual. Second and closely related to the ethical, he takes the category of *repetition* and draws a parallel to his own idea of "la Santa Continuació" [the Holy Continuity], the secret of the authentic moral life:

> It is a man who knows how to continue (Søren Kierkegaard, the Scandinavian philosopher). He who loses enthusiasm for continuity is a Philistine. He who lets himself be tempted by new paths is an aesthete. He who with the same initial enthusiasm knows how to continue on the same path, this person is a man (Søren Kierkegaard, again).[41]

As we have seen, the first years of Kierkegaard's reception in Spain have an ambiguous significance. It is true that neither Unamuno nor Estelrich (the two authors who really studied Kierkegaard) had a real impact on the following generations. In the case of the former, it was the personal aspect of his approach which failed to produce any impact on the more objective and academic reception. Besides, his tragic sense of life would not be well regarded for many, particularly in the years after the Spanish Civil War. As far as Estelrich is concerned, it is very likely that his use of Catalan could have worked as an obstacle for his influence. And yet both authors contributed to creating an image of Kierkegaard—the melancholic and solitary one—that would last a long time, later to be consolidated by many others.

---

[41] Eugeni d'Ors, "No un alçament: una ascensió," *La veu de Catalunya*, May 7, 1910.

B. The Early Translations

The first translation of Kierkegaard into Spanish was published in 1918 in Madrid under the title *Prosas de Søren Kierkegaard*.[42] The Uruguayan translator Álvaro Armando Vasseur (1878–1969)[43] opens the book with a "dedication" that echoes Unamuno's reincarnation: "I offer to the reader some pages I wrote, a little more than half a century ago, in a previous existence. Then, I lived in Denmark, and they called me Søren Kierkegaard. [Signed] Álvaro Armando Vasseur."[44]

These words clearly show the spirit in which Vasseur selects and translates the texts of Kierkegaard: he appropriates and recreates the works in such a capricious way that he manipulates them without any consideration. Furthermore, there is no mention whatsoever about where the texts are taken from or how shamelessly they are transformed into isolated paragraphs and aphorisms. As for the translation itself, it is remarkably deficient.[45] Vasseur cuts out parts of individual sentences as carelessly as he does with the entire structure of the text itself. Additionally, his text is rife with misprints and surprisingly outlandish mistakes, such as his use of the name "Parmenides" instead of "Parmeniscus," or his reference to *Either/Or* as "Entaaweder-Oder" and even "Enterríveder-Oder" (*sic*).[46]

The second Spanish translation of Kierkegaard's works, a translation of "The Seducer's Diary," would be the first of many versions of this work, becoming the most popular text of Kierkegaard, with up to eight different translations to date (seven in Spanish and one in Basque).[47] Nonetheless, we should note that the fact of having been translated so many times has not contributed to a better reception of the work, since it has always been published separately and, therefore, has never reflected its real status as a part of *Either/Or*. With regard to Valentín de Pedro's translation, it is

---

[42]   *Prosas de Søren Kierkegaard*, trans. by Álvaro Armando Vasseur, Madrid: América 1918. The book, 259 pages in small format, consisted of excerpts from *Either/Or* and "In vino veritas," plus two studies on Kierkegaard by Harald Høffding (pp. 13–42) and Henri Delacroix (pp. 45–99).

[43]   It is shocking to see that in different pages, different "versions" of the author's name are given. Vasseur shares his authorship together with an imagined Vassend who will accompany him forever, since many scholars and catalogues of libraries continue to refer indistinctively to Vasseur and Vassend. After having researched about this issue, we choose Vasseur as the most likely option.

[44]   *Prosas de Søren Kierkegaard*, p. 9.

[45]   About this translation, Estelrich writes: "Almost everything clearly translated—and with many imperfections, by the way—from the Italian version of Knud Ferlov...This awful translation, deservedly criticized by E. Díez-Canedo in the literary section of *El Sol* newspaper, will contribute, without question, to Kierkegaard's bad reception" (Joan Estelrich i Artigues, "Bibliografia de S. Kierkegaard," *La Revista*, vol. 5, no. 85, 1919, p. 108).

[46]   They obviously correspond to the German translation (*Entweder-Oder*), which constitutes the first step of what would become a quite normal habit for many Kierkegaard scholars in Spain, namely, to refer to Kierkegaard's works as if they were German. This would be, for example, the case of Francisco Jarauta.

[47]   *Diario de un seductor*, trans. by Valentín de Pedro, Madrid: Sucesores de Rivadeneyra 1922. In 1980, this translation was reissued (Barcelona: Fontamara) with the title *Diario del seductor*, which is in fact a more accurate translation of the Danish original title.

rather poor: there is no critical apparatus whatsoever, and it lacks Don Giovanni's quotation at the beginning.

In 1930, José Gaos' translation of *The Concept of Anxiety* was published in Madrid.[48] Despite being made based on the German version, this translation would become the most used text by Kierkegaard scholars in Spain. Its countless reprints, unique in the Spanish Kierkegaard literature, would capture almost all the attention for decades, even though a direct translation of this work would be issued in 1965.

II. The Second Period 1940s–1950s
A. Kierkegaard through Others

Except for the early translation of Harald Høffding's *Søren Kierkegaard som Filosof*,[49] we do not find any work on Kierkegaard in Spain until the period after the Second World War. It is not until 1945 that a number of studies began to appear in the Spanish language. All of them were translations of foreign studies and represented two main perspectives of reading Kierkegaard: a philosophical perspective that regarded Kierkegaard as the "father of existentialism," and a religious one that tried to put him in relation to Catholicism.

The existentialist approach, particularly the French one, was the most predominant in these years. In 1947, the book by the Russian philosopher exiled in France, Lev Shestov (1866–1938), *Kierkegaard and the Existential Philosophy*, was translated in Argentina.[50] This would be the first of a series of French books that would have a significant influence in Spain, such as Emmanuel Mounier's (1905–50) *Introduction aux Existentialismes*,[51] Régis Jolivet's (1891–1966) *Introduction à Kierkegaard* and *Les Doctrines existentialistes de Kierkegaard à J.P. Sartre*,[52] and Jean Wahl's (1888–

---

[48] *El concepto de la angustia. Una sencilla investigación psicológica orientada hacia el problema dogmático del pecado original*, trans. from German by José Gaos, Madrid: Revista de Occidente 1930. A later edition of this translation (Madrid: Espasa-Calpe 1940) was introduced by the the well-known Spanish philosopher José Luis Aranguren (1909–96).

[49] Harald Høffding, *Søren Kierkegaard*, trans. from German by Fernando Vela, Madrid: Revista de Occidente 1930 (originally as *Søren Kierkegaard som Filosof*, Copenhagen: Gyldendalske Boghandel 1892).

[50] Lev Shestov, *Kierkegaard et la philosophie existentielle*, trans. by Josep Ferrater Mora, Buenos Aires: Editorial Sudamericana 1947 (originally in Russian as *Киргегард и экзистенциальная философия (Глас вопиющего в пустыне)*, Paris: Sovremenniye zapiski i Dom Knigi 1939).

[51] Emmanuel Mounier, *Introducción a los existencialismos*, trans. by Daniel D. Montserrat, Madrid: Revista de Occidente 1949 (originally, *Introduction aux Existentialismes*, Paris: Denoël 1947).

[52] Régis Jolivet, *Introducción a Kierkegaard*, trans. by Manuel Rovira, Madrid: Gredos 1950 (originally, *Introduction à Kierkegaard*, Saint-Wandrille: Éd. de Fontenelle 1946); Régis Jolivet, *Las doctrinas existencialistas desde Kierkegaard a J.P. Sartre*, trans. by Arsenio Pacios, Madrid: Gredos 1950 (originally, *Les Doctrines existentialistes de Kierkegaard à J.P. Sartre*, Saint-Wandrille: Éd. de Fontenelle 1948).

1974) *Études Kierkegaardiennes* and *Les philosophies de l'existence*,[53] despite the fact that the latter work was not translated into Spanish. Among them, we should point to Wahl's and Jolivet's as the most influential one, especially Jolivet's, since his works played a role in the Catholic reading of Kierkegaard as well.

Regarding other countries, the presence of foreign studies on existentialism and related to Kierkegaard, though not particularly abundant, was yet of some importance. From Denmark, a brief presentation written by Peter P. Rohde (1902–78) was published by the Danish Ministry of Foreign Affairs under the title *Søren Kierkegaard: Father of Existentialism*.[54] It is an introduction to the life and work of the Danish thinker with many illustrations that reveal its popular character, and in which there is a special emphasis on showing the relations between Kierkegaard and existentialism. From Germany, the contribution of Karl Jaspers (1883–1969) should also be noted; his texts on Kierkegaard began to be translated into Spanish in the 1950s. From America, Marjorie Glicksman Grene's (b. 1910) book on Kierkegaard was translated in 1952 with a Spanish study: "Unamuno, Existential Philosopher" by Amando Lázaro Ros.[55]

As far as the Catholic approaches are concerned, first and foremost the 1948 translation of Theodor Haecker's (1879–1945) *Der Buckel Kierkegaards* must be emphasized.[56] The title of this book became a constant when referring to the psychoanalytic interpretations that regard Kierkegaard's work as a mere consequence of his physical constitution. Yet these references to Haecker's work were unfair, since it was precisely he who opposed this kind of interpretation.[57] Theoderich Kampmann's (1899–1983) *Kierkegaard als religiöser Erzieher* agrees with Haecker in presenting Kierkegaard as a religious author. The translator José Artigas talks about the necessity of having "a clean voice of Kierkegaard in Spain," which is precisely what, according to this author, the works of Haecker, Guardini and Kampmann himself provide.[58] In 1959, the lectures on Kierkegaard and Catholicism

---

[53] Jean Wahl, *Études Kierkegaardiennes*, Paris: Vrin 1949; Jean Wahl, *Las filosofías de la existencia*, trans. by Alejandro Sanvisens, Barcelona: Vergara 1956 (originally as *Les philosophies de l'existence*, Paris: A. Colin 1954).

[54] Peter P. Rohde, *Søren Kierkegaard: Padre del existencialismo*, Copenhagen: Ministry of Foreign Affairs 1963.

[55] Marjorie Glicksman Grene, *El sentimiento trágico de la existencia. Análisis del Existencialismo existencialismo*, trans. by Amando Lázaro Ros, Madrid: Aguilar 1952 (originally as *Dreadful Freedom. A Critique of Existentialism*, Chicago: University of Chicago Press 1948).

[56] Theodor Haecker, *La joroba de Kierkegaard*, trans. by Valentín García Yebra, Madrid: Rialp 1948 (originally as *Der Buckel Kierkegaards*, Zürich: Thomas Verlag 1947). The Spanish edition of Haecker's book is preceded by an introductory study of Ramón Roquer in which he starts by taking Kierkegaard as a possible way out from existentialism to Christianity. However, he criticizes Haecker for making Kierkegaard a Catholic author and later on he confesses his prejudices against the Dane, whose Protestant view he dislikes. He ends wondering: "Why have they not just immediately and straightaway resorted to the full and fertile Christianity of the Catholic church?" (Haecker, *La joroba de Kierkegaard*, Madrid: Rialp 1956, p. 13).

[57] See Rikard Magnussen, *Det særlige Kors*, Copenhagen: Munksgaard 1942.

[58] See Theoderich Kampmann, *Kierkegaard como educador religioso*, trans. by José Artigas, Madrid: CSIC 1953 (originally as *Kierkegaard als religiöser Erzieher*, Paderborn: Schöningh 1949).

given by the Danish Jesuit Heinrich Roos (1904–77) were also translated, and still the works of two more scholars with Catholic readings appeared in Spain during these years, the American James Daniel Collins (1917–85) and the Italian Cornelio Fabro (1911–95). Only a few of Fabro's articles could be read in Spanish (most of them translated in South America), and yet this Italian translator and interpreter had a radical influence in Spain. As a matter of fact, some Spanish scholars became direct disciples of him, and, in general, his Italian translations, particularly those of the journals attracted the attention of many for years. As for Collins, his introductory study *The Mind of Kierkegaard* has always had a good reputation in the Spanish academic world, and it has been used as a reference work, even though it has been criticized precisely on the grounds of its Catholic tendency.[59]

These foreign studies were, to a great extent, responsible for the reception of Kierkegaard in Spain. They not only represented most of the secondary literature of these decades, but also brought about Spanish interpretations intimately connected with their trends. This is the case, for example, of the Thomist philosopher Ángel González Álvarez (1916–91), who wrote a chapter on Kierkegaard in his book *The Idea of God in Existential Philosophy*.[60] He was not the only one who devoted himself to the study of Kierkegaard and existentialism; others, such as José Ignacio Alcorta y Echeverría (b. 1910), and Conde or José Ramón San Miguel (b. 1932), wrote a few articles about the same issue.

As for the Catholic-influenced Spanish studies, we find an interesting case in the brief article of Eugenio Frutos "La enseñanza de la verdad en Kierkegaard." The interest of this study lies in the fact that it combines a strong influence of the French Catholic reading of Paul Petit (1893–1944) with the originality of dealing with a work that had never been and would not be treated for many years in Spain, namely *Philosophical Fragments*.[61]

Along with the narrow framework of the existentialist and Catholic readings, there was also a significant group of Spanish authors who made original contributions, mostly individually. It is actually a pity that a good deal of these autochthonous studies have only played a secondary role in the Spanish Kierkegaard reception, for in some cases they offer readings of Kierkegaard which are much richer and more independent than the ones suggested by the aforementioned two tendencies. This is the case, for example, of José Luis López Aranguren (1909–96), whose scattered contributions to the Kierkegaard research are original and valuable. The central question of his studies on Kierkegaard is the latter's relation to Lutheranism. According to Aranguren, Jolivet's claim that Kierkegaard went in the direction of Catholicism is the "obsession" of many Catholics who, "driven by the pious desire of a 'good end' for the lives of non-Catholics, tend to 'drag them by their

---

[59]   James Daniel Collins, *El pensamiento de Kierkegaard*, trans. by Elena Landázuri, Mexico City: FCE 1958 (originally, *The Mind of Kierkegaard*, Chicago: Henry Regnery 1953).
[60]   Ángel González Álvarez, "Kierkegaard y el existencialismo" [Kierkegaard and Existentialism], in his *El tema de Dios en la filosofía existencial*, Madrid: Instituto Luis Vives de filosofía 1945, pp. 67–102.
[61]   *Miettes philosophiques*, trans. by Paul Petit, Paris: Gallimard 1941 (see Paul Petit's postscript to his translation).

hair' to Catholicism."[62] Thus, the Spanish philosopher sees Kierkegaard clearly as a Protestant, "profoundly Lutheran," writer, and yet as a very influential religious thinker for Catholicism, in the sense that he recovers elements that the Counter Reformation had suppressed.[63]

Another remarkable original contribution to the Kierkegaard research during these years comes from the field of psychiatry. They were a few varied studies that examined particular Kierkegaardian topics such as anxiety or melancholy. Far from reducing Kierkegaard's work by interpreting him as nothing more than a psychiatric case, they aimed to enrich the philosophical discussion with medical-oriented analyses. An example of this is the case of Juan José López Ibor (b. 1906), a psychiatrist who took up Kierkegaard in order to show, for example, anxiety as a privileged access to the intimate structure of the human being. Other examples worth mentioning are Xoan Rof Carballo (1905–94), who focused on the topic of the seducer, and Carlos Castilla del Pino (b. 1922).

B. The Indirect Translations

In the twenty years between 1941 and 1961 a remarkable number of new translations of Kierkegaard into Spanish appeared in Buenos Aires, which obviously had an impact on the reception of Kierkegaard in Spain. These works, mostly translated from French, English or Italian, revealed, in general, very little loyalty to the Danish originals. In some cases, new titles were given; in others, mere excerpts were issued without any indication of their fragmentary character and, in general, an obvious deficiency in the translation itself was common to all them. *Etapas en el camino de la vida* is a good example of all this. The title corresponds literally to *Stages on Life's Way*, but it is a fragmentary translation of this work, since it lacks the "Letter to the Reader from Frater Taciturnus."[64] This was later issued by the same publishing house, entitled *Love and Religion*, which has nothing at all to do with either the original title of the work or the title of the part it contains.[65] Yet nothing is said about it and both texts are published as whole works.

---

[62] José Luis López Aranguren, "Exposición de Kierkegaard," *Cuadernos Hispano-americanos*, no. 22, 1951, p. 440.

[63] Even though his contribution with regard to Protestantism is noteworthy for the Spanish reception of Kierkegaard, Aranguren was not properly a Kierkegaard scholar, which can be seen in the way he follows some stereotypes and makes mistakes in relation to pseudonymity ("Vigilius Haufmizuri," "William Ashan," or "Anticlimax"). As we will see, this lack of care in relation to the names of the pseudonyms will have, unfortunately, its own followers in the future.

[64] *Etapas en el camino de la vida*, trans. from French by Juana Castro, Buenos Aires: Santiago Rueda 1952.

[65] Moreover, the translator of these two books claims to include footnotes "elaborated after the commentaries of professor J. Himucelstrup" (*sic*). We dare to deduce that she is referring to Jens Himmelstrup (cf. Prologue to *Etapas en el camino de la vida*, Santiago Rueda, Buenos Aires 1952).

Another example of this tendency is Maria Angélica Bosco's *Intimate Diary*.[66] The book is a selection and translation of Cornelio Fabro's first Italian translation of texts from Kierkegaard's journals, and it makes use of the French version as well.[67] The dubious nature of this work is clearly evident in the case of the translation of one of the most important Kierkegaardian terms, namely *"den Enkelte,"* which is rendered into Spanish as *"el ente"* ["being," the Latin *ens*]. With this term, the translator destroys all the strength of Kierkegaard's expression, insofar as she identifies it with a central notion of metaphysics. In this way, *"den Enkelte"* passes over into a universal and abstract concept totally opposed to the concreteness and existential meaning of the Kierkegaardian individual. The choice of this term is particularly surprising, for Bosco's translation is made from the Italian *"il Singolo,"* which has nothing to do with *"el ente."* Fortunately, this was well criticized by Aranguren in the introduction which he wrote to the second edition of this book.[68]

Alberto Colao's translation of *Fear and Trembling*, entitled *Eulogy on Abraham*, gathers together all the imagined cases of carelessness towards Kierkegaard's originals.[69] First of all, Colao capriciously recreates the original work, which is only named in a footnote. He does not explain anything about the text he is presenting, and he omits both isolated sentences and entire sections. Additionally, he changes titles and even turns Kierkegaard's prose into verse, for, according to him, this is something the very text demands. As for the translation, it contains numerous mistakes and misunderstandings that make any contact with the real work of Kierkegaard impossible for the reader. Last but not least, Colao's introduction and footnotes distort even more the already negative image of Kierkegaard who is referred to as a "flagellant philosopher and as well as cripple, crippling."[70] Calao confuses the reader with claims, such as "the expression ['go further'] is readily identified: it is Nietzschean."[71] Finally, we have to refer to two other translations from this period: *Philosophical Fragments* and *The Point of View*.[72] The former constituted the first attempt to offer to the Spanish reader a central text of Kierkegaard's philosophy. The

---

[66] *Diario íntimo*, trans. from Italian by María Angélica Bosco, Buenos Aires: Santiago Rueda 1955 (reissued with an introduction by José Luis López Aranguren, Barcelona: Planeta 1993).

[67] See, *Journal*, trans. by Knud Ferlov and Jean-J. Gateau, Paris: Gallimard 1941; and *Diario* [Diary], trans. by Cornelio Fabro, vols. 1–3, Brescia: Morcelliana 1948–51.

[68] *El amor y la religión (Puntos de vista)*, trans. by Juana Castro, Buenos Aires: Santiago Rueda 1960 (published also, Mexico City: Tomo 2002). There is something else interesting to say about this work. The first edition of 1955 seems to have been completely ignored by the Spaniards, since every time they refer to it they give the reissue in Planeta, Barcelona 1993, as the first and only edition of this translation (See, for example, María García Amilburu's introduction to *El Concepto de la angustia. 150 años después*, *Thémata*, vol. 15, 1995, p. 10).

[69] *Elogio de Abraham (páginas líricas)* (excerpts from *Fear and Trembling*), trans. by Alberto Colao, Cartagena: Athenas 1959.

[70] Ibid., p. 13.

[71] Ibid., p. 15.

[72] *Fragmentos filosóficos*, trans. from French and English by Arnoldo Canclini, Buenos Aires: La Aurora 1956; *Mi punto de vista*, trans. by José Miguel Velloso, Buenos Aires: Aguilar 1959 (published also, Madrid: Sarpe 1985).

latter is of importance, inasmuch as many Spanish scholars would regard it as the key to Kierkegaard and his authorship.[73]

III. The Third Period 1961–9: the Direct Translations

In 1961, an important event for Kierkegaard's reception in Spain took place. Demetrio Gutiérrez Rivero, a Spanish scholar educated at the University of Munich who was interested in the work of Kierkegaard, started to publish a series of translations under the generic *Kierkegaard's Works and Papers*.[74] As this shows, the original project of Gutiérrez was very ambitious, but the final result turned out to be much more humble and only nine volumes were ultimately published. These contained just a few of the works and not a word from the journals. However, it is possible that this frustrated project has made a significant contribution to the Spanish reception. Aside from the evident advantage of enabling the reader to hear a more authentic voice of Kierkegaard—as Gutiérrez put it, his translations were "almost literal" and were made directly from the Danish originals[75]—the diversity of the works translated offered new faces of the Dane and, consequently, the possibility of overcoming the traditional clichés.

The first volume appeared in 1961 and was a translation of *Practice in Christianity*. After that date, other texts would be translated: parts of *Stages on Life's Way* and *Either/Or*, various religious discourses, *Works of Love*, *The Concept of Anxiety*, and *The Sickness unto Death*. As already mentioned, this group of writings made possible a new way of approaching Kierkegaard, since the reader could now have access to works that had been ignored for a long time and find in them new voices.[76] Nonetheless, the novelty of Gutiérrez's translations was not unqualified since they repeated the disrespectful treatment that had been common to many previous translations; he manipulated some works by creating new titles and new structures in which different parts of different works were published. This is the case of volume 2, entitled *Two Dialogues on the First Love and Marriage* (which brings together "The

---

[73]   It is very difficult to think about this translation as having been made directly from the Danish text, since it refers to the original work as "Synspunkiel for min foraftterwirksomhed" (*sic*). Although the translator does not mention anything about his source, we suspect it to be Lowrie's translations, for Velloso occasionally inserts some Danish terms, which are exactly the same ones that Lowrie includes in his translation.

[74]   *Obras y Papeles de Kierkegaard*, vols. 1–9, trans. and ed. by Demetrio Gutiérrez Rivero, Madrid: Ediciones Guadarrausa 1961–9. Although some bibliographies persist in including a tenth volume, entitled *Estudios Estéticos III: Diario de un seductor. In vino veritas*, which was, actually, part of the original project but was never issued as such.

[75]   Cf. *Ejercitación del Cristianismo* [*Practice in Christianity*], trans. by Demetrio Gutiérrez Rivero, vol. 1 (1961) of *Obras y Papeles de Kierkegaard*, pp. 28–9.

[76]   In this respect, it is worth noticing that some of the new translated works were of religious nature. As a matter of fact, Gutiérrez Rivero's work, both in the translation and in the critical apparatus, tended to emphasize the religious dimension of Kierkegaard and to criticize those readings, such as the existentialists', which used Kierkegaardian categories without taken the religious context into account (cf. translator's prologue to *El concepto de la angustia* [*The Concept of Anxiety*], vol. 6 (1965) of *Obras y Papeles de Kierkegaard*).

Esthetic Validity of Marriage" from *Either/Or* and "Some Reflections on Marriage in Answer to Objections by Married Man" from *Stages on Life's Way*), volume 3, entitled *The Lilies in the Field and the Birds of the Air* (which is a selection of different discourses on the same motif), and the two last volumes, entitled *Esthetical Studies* (which are collections of texts from the first part of *Either/Or*).

Finally, we have to mention two further translations from this period: *Diapsalmata*, a translation of two parts of *Either/Or*[77] and *The Immediate Erotic Stages or the Musical–Erotic*, a translation of the part of *Either/Or* with the same title.[78] Mariona Serra de Sala also translated into Catalan Jacques Colette's excerpts from Kierkegaard's writings, *The Difficulty of Being Christian*.[79] This work was the first text of Kierkegaard's translated into Catalan, and it would remain the only one for a long time.

In the field of research literature, the 1960s were not so fertile in comparison with the translations, and yet some remarkable works were published. There was a clear predominance of comparative studies between Kierkegaard and his Spanish forerunner, Unamuno. Although the studies of this kind had already arisen years before, it was during this decade that they really burst out. In 1954, Luis Farré (b. 1902) published an article on the relationship between Unamuno, William James, and Kierkegaard.[80] However, it is Antonio Sánchez Barbudo (1910–95) who really stands out: already in 1949 he studied these three authors and would come back to Unamuno and Kierkegaard in 1950 and 1959.[81] The authors who dealt with the relation between Unamuno and Kierkegaard were both Unamuno scholars, who paused briefly to consider the influence of the Dane on the Basque writer, and others whose studies were dedicated to both authors equally. Of these, the work of Jesús Antonio Collado stands out. He was a scholar who, in his dissertation and some articles, studied the possible influence of Kierkegaard's existential-religious conception of the individual on Unamuno's thought.[82] It must be said that Collado's study was particularly important

---

[77]   *Diapsalmata*, trans. by Javier Armada, Buenos Aires: Aguilar 1961.
[78]   *Los estadios eróticos inmediatos o lo erótico musical*, trans. by Javier Armada, Buenos Aires: Aguilar 1967.
[79]   *La dificultat d'ésser cristià*, trans. from French by Mariona Serra de Sala, Barcelona: Ariel 1968 (in French as *La difficulté d'être Chrétien. Présentation et choix de textes*, ed. by Jacques Colette, Paris: Éditions du Cerf 1964).
[80]   Luis Farré, "Unamuno, William James y Kierkegaard," in *Cuadernos Hispanoamericanos*, no. 57, 1954, pp. 279–99 and no. 58, 1954, pp. 64–88.
[81]   Antonio Sánchez Barbudo, "La intimidad de Unamuno: Relaciones con Kierkegaard y W. James" [Unamuno's Intimacy: Relations to Kierkegaard and W. James], *Occidental*, no. 7, 1949 (New York), pp. 10–13; Antonio Sánchez Barbudo, "La formación del pensamiento de Unamuno. Una experiencia decisiva: La crisis de 1897" [The Development of Unamuno's Thought. A Decisive Experience: The Crisis of 1897], *Hispanic Review*, vol. 18, 1950 (Philadelphia), pp. 218–43; and Antonio Sánchez Barbudo, "Unamuno y Kierkegaard" [Unamuno and Kierkegaard] and "Diferencia entre Unamuno y Kierkegaard" [Difference between Unamuno and Kierkegaard], in his *Estudios sobre Unamuno y Machado*, Madrid: Guadarrama 1959, pp. 65–79 and pp. 189–93.
[82]   See, for example, Collado's Ph.D. Thesis entitled *La existencia religiosa en Kierkegaard y su influencia en el pensamiento de Unamuno* [The Religious Existence in

in the context of comparative studies between the two authors, since his work, for the very first time, made a direct reading of both Unamuno's and Kierkegaard's texts. It is in this sense and, especially, because of his rigorous research, that Collado's study became a reference work for all those interested in this topic.

Out of this context of comparative studies, we find another significant work, which is, along with Collado's, the only dissertation on Kierkegaard of this decade. The study of Consuelo Ferrer Bonifaci entitled *Kierkegaard and Love* attracted the attention of many, judging by the numerous reviews written.[83] This work is a psychological study of the life of Kierkegaard, with special attention to the love relations with his father and Regine. Kierkegaard is here seen again as a solitary and tormented author whose personal features resemble those of the genius. In spite of its complete bibliography, Bonifaci's study is too partial in its use of Kierkegaard's works and, in general, reduces him to a few non-critical ideas.

Finally, the translations of works that offered new perspectives for interpreting Kierkegaard, such as that of irrationalism (Lukács),[84] Western intellectual history (Löwith),[85] and aesthetics (Adorno's dissertation),[86] also appeared in these years. Together with these, we must include new studies that continued to read the work of Kierkegaard from an existentialist approach, both originals, such as Juan José Rodríguez Rosado (1933–93) or Jorge Vidiella[87] and translations, such as works by

---

Kierkegaard and its Influence in Unamuno's Thought], Madrid: Facultad de Filosofía y Letras 1961.

[83] Consuelo Ferrer Bonifaci, *Kierkegaard y el amor*, Barcelona: Herder 1963. The author has several times been confused with Conrad Bonifazi, author of *Christendom Attacked, a Comparison of Kierkegaard and Nietzsche*, in such a way that one can see their respective works mixed up in some of the Spanish bibliographies.

[84] Georg Lukács, "Kierkegaard," in *El asalto a la razón: La trayectoria del irracionalismo desde Schelling hasta Hitler*, trans. by Wenceslao Roces, Barcelona: Grijalbo 1967, pp. 202–48 (in German as *Die Zerstörung der Vernunft. Der Weg des Irrationalismus von Schelling zu Hitler*, Berlin: Aufbau Verlag 1954).

[85] Karl Löwith, *De Hegel a Nietzsche. La quiebra revolucionaria del pensamiento en el siglo XIX. Marx y Kierkegaard*, trans. by Emilio Estiú, Buenos Aires: Editorial Sudamericana, 1968 (originally as *Von Hegel zu Nietzsche. Der revolutionäre Bruch im Denken des neunzehnten Jahrhunderts: Marx und Kierkegaard*, Zürich and New York: Europa Verlag 1941).

[86] Theodor W. Adorno, *Kierkegaard: Ensayo*, trans. by Roberto J. Vernengo, Caracas: Monte Ávila 1969 (originally as *Kierkegaard: Konstruktion des Ästhetischen*, Tübingen: Mohr 1933).

[87] See, for example, Juan José Rodríguez Rosado "La angustia existencial: 'Kierkegaard'" [The Existential Anxiety: "Kierkegaard"], in his *La aventura de existir*, Pamplona: EUNSA, 1976, pp. 38–43 and Jorge Vidiella, *De Kierkegaard a Sartre. El existencialismo* [From Kierkegaard to Sartre. Existentialism], Barcelona: Bruguera 1963.

Peter P. Rohde (1902–78),[88] Harold John Blackham,[89] Paul Roubiczek,[90] or Henri de Lubac (1896–1991).[91]

IV. The Fourth Period 1970–85: Awakening Kierkegaard

The Spanish secondary literature on Kierkegaard from the early seventies seemed to experience the same kind of awakening that the translations had experienced before. In comparison with the previous decade, we notice a considerable increase of studies on Kierkegaard, both qualitatively and quantitatively. The works of scholars such as Francisco Jarauta Marión and Rafael Larrañeta Olleta (1945–2002) announce a shift of emphasis in the way of approaching Kierkegaard, since, from now on, we start to find studies that, far from the clichés, go into particular topics in a systematic and academic fashion.

In 1973, Francisco Jarauta began to publish a series of comparative studies on Kierkegaard and other thinkers such as Schleiermacher, Schelling, and Hegel. In this respect, he opened new focuses of study in the Spanish research since the comparative studies on Kierkegaard and nineteenth-century thinkers had been a topic completely neglected until then. Moreover, works of such a decisive importance from a philosophical viewpoint as the *Concluding Unscientific Postscript* or *Philosophical Fragments*, which had been little known hitherto, became important objects of study in the work of Jarauta.

Jarauta's main contribution to the Spanish Kierkegaard research is the book, entitled *Kierkegaard: the Limits of the Individual's Dialectics*.[92] Here, he critically approaches the Kierkegaardian question of subjectivity by presenting its grounds, structure, and dialectic. Taking the analysis of the concept of existence and its contradiction as a point of departure, the Spanish author goes on through the different spheres of existence until he arrives at the problem of subjectivity itself. Once there, Jarauta follows Climacus' approach to subjectivity and carefully analyzes his position.

---

[88]   Peter P. Rohde, *Søren Kierkegaard. El filósofo danés* [Søren Kierkegaard. The Danish Philosopher], Copenhagen: Ministry of Foreign Affairs, 1955 and Rohde, *Søren Kierkegaard: Padre del existencialismo* [Søren Kierkegaard: Father of Existentialism], Copenhagen: Ministry of Foreign Affairs 1963.

[89]   Harold John Blackham, *Seis pensadores Existencialistas. Kierkegaard, Nietzsche, Jaspers, Marcel, Heidegger, Sartre*, trans. by Ricardo Jordana, Barcelona: Ediciones de Occidente 1964 (in English as *Six Existentialist Thinkers. Kierkegaard, Nietzsche, Jaspers, Marcel, Heidegger, Sartre*, London: Routledge & Kegan Paul 1951).

[90]   Paul Roubiczek, "Kierkegaard" and "Kierkegaard y el existencialismo" [Kierkegaard and Existentialism], in *El existencialismo*, trans. by J.M. García de la Mora, Barcelona: Labor 1967, pp. 59–74; pp. 97–111 and passim (in English as *Existentialism for and against*, Cambridge: Cambridge University Press 1964).

[91]   Henri de Lubac, "Nietzsche y Kierkegaard" [Nietzsche and Kierkegaard], in *El drama del humanismo ateo*, trans. by Carlos Castro Cubells, Madrid: Epesa 1967, pp. 79–128 (in French as *Le Drame de l'humanisme athée*, Paris 1944).

[92]   Francisco Jarauta Marión, *Kierkegaard: Los límites de la dialéctica del individuo*, Cali: Universidad del Valle 1975.

The other important scholar of this period is Rafael Larrañeta, who in 1975 and 1976 published the two parts of a long study on Kierkegaard, entitled "Existence as Dialectical Crossroad between Philosophy and Faith. A Study on Søren Kierkegaard."[93] As we will see later, Rafael Larrañeta launched a trajectory that would become a decisive point of reference for the next generation of Spanish Kierkegaard scholars.

In addition to these two principal figures who embodied the new way of studying Kierkegaard in Spain, there were many other valuable contributors who, from various disciplines, helped to make this period a fertile and promising one. This is the case, for example, of the self-taught writer Rosa Chacel (1898–1994), who included Kierkegaard in her book *The Confession*, in which she deals with confessions in literature, analyzing Kierkegaard together with Rousseau and St. Augustine.[94] Already in 1948, she had written an article, entitled "Kierkegaard and Sin."[95] Another example, still further from the traditional approaches to Kierkegaard, was the play of Pedro Antonio Urbina (b. 1936) *Søren Kierkegaard: The Seducer*, based on "The Seducer's Diary."[96] In this play, the author splits the seducer's personality into two characters, showing, in this way, the conflict between the impulse of seduction and the consciousness of the seducer.

In the field of essay, Ignacio Gómez de Liaño (b. 1946) made use of Kierkegaard's categories of the moment and repetition to reflect upon the role of memory, imagination, and time in philosophy.[97] Alfonso López Quintás (b. 1928) made use of Kierkegaard's notions as well, specifically the stages of life, which he understands in a conciliatory way. With regard to new topics on Kierkegaard, Fermín de Urmeneta and Juan Plazaola wrote articles about aesthetics in Kierkegaard's work.[98]

The anthologies, histories, and handbooks of philosophy also composed a new group of works that began to take Kierkegaard into consideration during these years. This is very significant in the sense that it shows how the work of the Dane was opened to a broader field of study and, especially, how Kierkegaard was beginning to be recognized as a major name in the history of philosophy. The anthologies of texts by Clemente Fernández (b. 1942) and Francisco Canals Vidal (b. 1922) and the handbooks of Teófilo Urdanoz (b. 1946), Pedro Fontán Jubero, and Manuel Maceiras Fafián are good evidence of this. In this context, it is important to note that Maceiras'

---

[93] Rafael Larrañeta Olleta, "La existencia como encrucijada dialéctica entre la filosofía y la fe. Un estudio sobre Søren Kierkegaard," *Estudios Filosóficos*, no. 24, 1975, pp. 337–81 and no. 25, 1976, pp. 17–70.

[94] Rosa Chacel, *La confesión*, Barcelona: Edhasa 1971, see pp. 9–44.

[95] Rosa Chacel, "Kierkegaard y el pecado," *Sur*, no. 162 (Buenos Aires), pp. 71–96 (reissued in her *La lectura es secreto*, Madrid: Júcar 1989).

[96] Pedro Antonio Urbina, *Søren Kierkegaard: el seductor*, Seville: Universidad de Sevilla 1975.

[97] See Ignacio Gómez de Liaño, "El instante decisivo" [The Decisive Moment], in *El Idioma de la Imaginación* [The Language of the Imagination], Madrid: Taurus 1982, pp. 413–42.

[98] See Alfonso López Quintás, "Los tres estadios en el camino de la vida, según Søren Kierkegaard" [The Three Stages on Life's Way, according to Søren Kierkegaard], in *Estrategia del lenguaje y manipulación del hombre*, Madrid: Narcea 1979, pp. 48–84.

work *Schopenhauer and Kierkegaard. Feeling and Passion* has played a significant part in the academic reception as one of the texts most consulted in the initial studies on Kierkegaard at the universities.[99] The book, which presents Kierkegaard together with Schopenhauer as the two great opponents of the Hegelian system, is written in a very didactic fashion, containing chronologies, diagrams, texts, and definitions of the main categories—besides an original contribution in the form of portraits of the philosophers drawn by the author. Finally, for his numerous and persistent articles, the North American professor George J. Stack also deserves to be named.[100]

Along with all these new lines of research, we also find in this period those contributions that resume the trajectories plotted in the last two decades, although they have now a secondary prominence. As for the foreign studies on Kierkegaard translated into Spanish, we can mention the works of Georg Lukács (1885–1971), Ágnes Heller (b. 1929), and Nelly Viallaneix.[101] There is also the translation of Frederik Billeskov Jansen's (1907–2002) anthology of Danish literature, which gives the reader the opportunity to approach Kierkegaard in a literary way.[102]

Existentialist interpretations experienced a relative continuation in the studies of the aforementioned Rodríguez Rosado,[103] and the translations of Leo Gabriel (1902–87), Karl Jaspers (1883–1969), and Jean Wahl's history of existentialism.[104]

---

[99] Manuel Maceiras Fafián, *Schopenhauer y Kierkegaard: sentimiento y passion*, Madrid: Cincel 1985.

[100] See, for example, George J. Stack, "Ética de la subjetividad en Kierkegaard" [The Ethics of Subjectivity in Kierkegaard], *Folia Humanística*, vol. 9, no. 99, 1971, pp. 193–220 and Geroge J. Stack, "La verdad como subjetividad. Interpretación (Kierkegaard)" [Truth is Subjectivity: An Interpretation (Kierkegaard)], *Folia Humanística*, vol. 15, no. 177, 1977, pp. 607–18.

[101] The work of Lukács would give cause for Manuel Ballestero's reference to Kierkegaard, in what constituted an attempt to restore the importance of the individual from within a Marxist viewpoint (cf. Manuel Ballestero, "Kierkegaard, sujeto y realidad," in *Crítica y marginales. Compromiso y trascendencia del símbolo literario*, Barcelona: Barral 1974, pp. 33–44); to Ágnes Heller, see her "Fenomenología de la conciencia desdichada: Sobre la función histórica de *La alternativa* de Kierkegaard," in her *Crítica de la Ilustración: las antinomias morales de la razón*, trans. by Gustau Muñoz and José Ignacio López Soria, Barcelona: Península 1984, pp. 135–77 (originally in Hungarian as "A szerencsétlen tudat fenomenológiája," *Magyar Filozófiai Szemle*, nos. 3–4, 1971, pp. 364–94); to Nelly Viallaneix, see her *Kierkegaard, el único ante Dios*, trans. by Joan Llopis, Barcelona: Herder 1977 (originally as *Kierkegaard. L'Unique devant Dieu*, Paris: Éditions du Cerf 1974).

[102] Frederik Billeskov Jansen and Uffe Harder (eds.), *Panorama de la literatura danesa* [Anthologie de la littérature danoise, Paris 1964] (bilingual edition), Madrid: Turner 1984, pp. 222–41.

[103] Rodríguez Rosado, *El tema de la nada en la filosofía existencial* [The Question of Nothingness in Existential Philosophy], Madrid: Escorial 1966, see pp. 19ff.

[104] Leo Gabriel, *Filosofía de la existencia. Kierkegaard, Heidegger, Jaspers, Sartre. Diálogo de posiciones*, trans. by Luis Pelayo Arribas, Madrid: Editorial Católica 1973 (in German as *Existenzphilosophie von Kierkegaard bis Sartre*, Vienna: Herold 1951); to Karl Jaspers, see his "Origen de la situación filosófica actual (El significado histórico de Kierkegaard y Nietzsche)" [Origin of the Contemporary Philosophical Situation (the Historical Meaning of Kierkegaard and Nietzsche], in his *Razón y Existencia. Cinco lecciones*, trans. by Haraldo

As far as comparative studies are concerned, Jorge Uscatescu went on practically alone with the question about the relation between Kierkegaard and Unamuno.[105] Martín Gelabert resumed the study of the relation between Kierkegaard and Luther in a couple of articles written in 1981.[106] With regard to Hegel, the Thomist philosopher Leonardo Polo included a chapter devoted to Kierkegaard in his book *Hegel and Posthegelianism*.[107] There, Polo tackles the thought of Kierkegaard from a Hegelian perspective and regards him as the author who best expresses the psychological dimension of the crisis of Hegelianism. Polo criticizes, however, the form of Kierkegaard's critique of Hegel, which he regards as only a point of view, and suggests the need for a general and rigorous science to correct the excess of Hegelian reflection.

In contrast to the multiplicity of studies produced, we find very few translations of Kierkegaard in the 1970s and none in the 1980s, with the exception of a new version of "The Seducer's Diary."[108] Apart from a few indirect translations published in Argentina and Mexico, among which the Spanish version of the French edition of Kierkegaard's letters to Regine and Emil Boesen stands out, two more volumes of Gutiérrez Rivero appeared in 1975 and 1976, this time outside the aforementioned series, *Søren Kierkegaard's Works and Papers*.[109] But the most remarkable publication in these years is without question Vicente Simón Merchán's translation of *Fear and Trembling*, which includes a valuable preliminary study on Kierkegaard and his intellectual context.[110] This edition would be printed many times by different publishing houses through the years, and it would become an essential book about Kierkegaard in Spain. It is striking that Merchán's work started and ended with this single edition, since both the translation and the preliminary study are significant.

Kahnemann, Buenos Aires: Nova 1959, pp. 9–42 (in German as *Vernunft und Existenz, Fünf Vorlesungen*, Groningen: Wolters 1935); Jean Wahl, *Las filosofías de la existencia*.

[105] See, for example, Jorge Uscatescu, "Unamuno y Kierkegaard" [Unamuno and Kierkegaard], in *ABC*, August 18, 1978 and "Unamuno y Kierkegaard o la interioridad secreta" [Unamuno and Kierkegaard or the Secret Inwardness], *Arbor*, vol. 103, nos. 403–4, 1979, pp. 25–40.

[106] See, for example, Martín Gelabert, "Dimensión hermenéutica de la doctrina luterana de la justificación" [Hermeneutic Dimension of the Lutheran Doctrine of Justification], in *El método en teología* [The Method in Theology], Valencia: Facultad de Teología San Vicente Ferrer 1981, pp. 237–49.

[107] Leonardo Polo, "Kierkegaard, crítico de Hegel: la dialéctica como tedio y desesperación" [Kierkegaard, Critic of Hegel: Dialectic as Boredom and Despair], in *Hegel y el posthegelianismo*, 2nd ed., Pamplona: EUNSA 1999, pp. 101–74 [Peru: Universidad de Piura 1985].

[108] *Diario de un seductor*, trans. from French by Jacinto León Ignacio, Barcelona: Ediciones 29 1971 (published also, Barcelona: Río Nuevo 1997); *Diario de un seductor*, trans. by Ramón Alvarado Cruz, Mexico City: Juan Pablo 1984.

[109] *In vino veritas. La repetición* ["In vino veritas," *Repetition*], trans. by Demetrio Gutiérrez Rivero, Madrid: Guadarrama 1975; *Temor y temblor. Diario de un seductor* [*Fear and Trembling*. "The Seducer's Diary"], trans. by Demetrio Gutiérrez Rivero, Madrid: Guadarrama 1976.

[110] *Temor y temblor*, trans. by Vicente Simón Merchán, Madrid: Editora Nacional 1975.

V. The Fifth Period 1986–Present Time: the Scholarly Kierkegaard

In the second half of the 1980s, Kierkegaard studies in Spain followed the new direction that the work of authors such as Larrañeta or Jarauta had started. There is not a particular date at which we could place the beginning of this new period, but 1986 seems to be the most appropriate one to choose, since, from this year on, an important number of dissertations on Kierkegaard began to be defended at different universities in Spain. This fact, which has no equivalent in the past, can be considered as a positive sign of the maturity of the Spanish reception of Kierkegaard.

One of the first dissertations to appear, in 1986, was Jaime Franco Barrio's study entitled *Kierkegaard against Hegelianism in the Context of Nineteenth Century Philosophy*.[111] This work offers a good historical introduction to Kierkegaard with many references to some of his contemporaries, even though it is basically descriptive and without much criticism. Franco Barrio later published other articles on Kierkegaard, among them "Kierkegaard in Spanish," which is a study on the reception of Kierkegaard in Spain.[112]

Also in 1986, Virginia Careaga Guzmán defended her dissertation entitled *Kierkegaard: Ingenuity and Paradox*.[113] This study considers Kierkegaard from a religious background and a Hegelian context, not trying to present a doctrine, which she says is not there, but "some existential categories on which his [Kierkegaard's] multiple discourses, moods and situations are based."[114] In Careaga's work, one can find a well-documented bibliography of the works of Kierkegaard and, in general, a first approach to the question of pseudonymity. This scholar would continue to publish several articles and to take part in various seminars and congresses.

Two years later, Rafael Larrañeta defended his dissertation on Kierkegaard's categories of truth and love.[115] Even though this is just another doctoral thesis among the many written in these years, this author deserves a more detailed commentary for what he represents in the Spanish Kierkegaard reception. As we have seen before, Larrañeta had already begun his study in 1975. It was, however, the year 1987, when he carried out his research for one year at the Kierkegaard Library in Copenhagen, that constituted a turning point in his work. During this stay, he not only worked directly with the original texts of Kierkegaard, but also established the first contact with the international research. Besides, part of Larrañeta's work was directed at the task of presenting to the Spanish reader a more reliable picture of

---

[111] Jaime Franco Barrio, *Kierkegaard frente al hegelianismo en el contexto de la filosofía decimonónica*, Salamanca: Universidad de Salamanca 1986.
[112] Franco Barrio, "Kierkegaard en español, *Azefa*, no 2, 1989, pp. 211–34. Together with Rafael Larrañeta's article, "Recepción y actualidad de Kierkegaard en España" [Reception and Present of Kierkegaard in Spain], *Estudios Filosóficos*, vol. 37, no. 105, 1988, pp. 317–46, Barrio's study is the only one on the reception of Kierkegaard in Spain.
[113] Virginia Careaga Guzmán, *Kierkegaard: Ingenuidad y paradoja*, San Sebastián: Universidad del País Vasco 1986.
[114] Ibid., pp. 11–12.
[115] Rafael Larrañeta, *La interioridad apasionada. El concepto de verdad y amor en la obra de Søren Kierkegaard* [Passionate Inwardness. The Concept of Truth and Love in the Work of Søren Kierkegaard], Salamanca: Universidad de Salamanca 1988.

Kierkegaard in contrast to the traditional one, namely, the one-sided portrait of the pessimistic, deformed, and solitary thinker. The article "Kierkegaard's Real Face" is a good example of this.[116] As the title shows, Larrañeta here denies the traditionally accepted false image of Kierkegaard and contributes new contrasting information about the writer from Copenhagen:

> We have been noticing quite frequently that, while in the international contexts Kierkegaard enjoys quite a balanced reputation, sometimes constituted by admiration and, in any case, with a halo of respect and affection, in Spain, and from spheres so diverse as religious conservatism or certain pseudo-agnostic progressism, the idea persists, though with nuances, of a pessimistic Kierkegaard, depressed to despair, embittered, psychologically depressed due to his physical ailments, doubtful in his profound convictions, mistrustful of love, in short, a picture wholly distant from actuality.[117]

Larrañeta's task of giving an accurate picture of Kierkegaard would also be performed by means of works of a more popular nature, which would accompany the more learned ones. Among the latter, his doctoral research on truth and love in Kierkegaard is obviously his major contribution.[118] It contains a rich critical apparatus and a complete bibliography of Kierkegaard's works as well as secondary literature. Along with his dissertation, Larrañeta published a number of articles in which he related Kierkegaard to different topics and authors in the field of philosophy and religion. As far as his "popular" work is concerned, we must point out his brief introduction to Kierkegaard written in 1997 for a major series on philosophers.[119] *Kierkegaard's Magnifying Glass* is another introduction to the Dane that became his last work, published shortly before his untimely death.[120] As a matter of fact, this book can be regarded as the result of many years devoted to Kierkegaard. In this work, Larrañeta brings together the different Kierkegaardian topics he had studied throughout his writings and offers an overall view of the life and work of Kierkegaard.

Last but not least, Larrañeta's contribution to the Kierkegaard research would be completed in the form of different activities such as the organization of seminars, doctoral courses, supervision of several dissertations and, above all, his participation in a very ambitious and decisive project, namely, the translation of the complete works of Kierkegaard into Spanish, to which we will later refer.

In 1991, a new dissertation on Kierkegaard appeared. At the University of Navarra, the Mexican Luis Ignacio Guerrero Martínez (b. 1957) defended his doctoral thesis on faith and reason in Kierkegaard's anthropology.[121] He was not the only one

---

[116] Rafael Larrañeta, "El verdadero rostro de Kierkegaard," *Revista de Filosofía*, vol. 10, no. 18, 1997, pp. 83–112.

[117] Ibid., p. 84.

[118] Rafael Larrañeta, *La interioridad apasionada. Verdad y amor en S. Kierkegaard* [Passionate Inwardness. Love and Truth in S. Kierkegaard], Salamanca: San Esteban–Universidad Pontificia 1990.

[119] Rafael Larrañeta, *Kierkegaard*, Madrid: Ediciones del Orto 1997.

[120] Rafael Larrañeta, *La lupa de Kierkegaard*, Salamanca: San Esteban 2002.

[121] Luis Ignacio Guerrero Martínez, *Fe y Razón en la antropología de Kierkegaard* [Faith and Reason in Kierkegaard's Anthropology], Pamplona: Universidad de Navarra 1991. The work of Guerrero would last a little longer in Spain, by means of a few articles published in

who studied Kierkegaard at this university, since, one year later, two more scholars related to the University of Navarra defended their dissertations on Kierkegaard: María García Amilburu and Teresa Aizpún de Bobadilla. The former presented a systematic study on the notion of existence in Kierkegaard following the computer methods of Alastair McKinnon.[122] The work of Amilburu has the originality of being the first one in Spain to use computer analysis of the Kierkegaardian texts. Her study does not seem, however, to offer any new interpretation as far as the question of existence itself is concerned since her results do nothing but confirm the traditional ones. Thus, her dissertation becomes valuable as a demonstration of the legitimacy of using these computer methods rather than as a new reading of Kierkegaard's notion of existence.

Aizpún de Bobadilla started her studies on Kierkegaard at the University of Navarra, under the supervision of Rafael Alvira.[123] Later on, she decided to leave the Catholic ambience of this University and look for a more Kierkegaardian environment in Protestant lands. As a result, she defended her doctoral thesis on Kierkegaard's concept of the exception in Munich in 1992. She actively carried on her studies on Kierkegaard with different articles and collaborations with some of the most representative Spanish Kierkegaard scholars. Apart from her stay in Germany, she also did research in Copenhagen under the supervision of Julia Watkin. Her studies focus on philosophical questions such as Kierkegaard's anthropology and freedom, considering the religious writings as well.

Other works that took Kierkegaard into account in order to approach different philosophical, theological, or even literary questions were written in Spain contemporaneously with these specialized studies. These works, which are important inasmuch as they confirm the new way of studying Kierkegaard, are represented, for instance, by Cèlia Amorós' (b. 1944) study entitled *Søren Kierkegaard or the Gentleman's Subjectivity. A Study in the Light of Patriarchy's Paradoxes*.[124] In this work, Amorós proposes a feminist view of Kierkegaard, not as an analysis of isolated claims on women in his work but as a methodology to interpret some of its central questions. In this sense, the author relates Abraham's religious suspension of the ethical in *Fear and Trembling* to Don Juan's aesthetic one in *Either/Or*. According to Amorós, the latter foreshadows the former, and both are to be understood from within a common conception in which the woman is excluded and the idea of

---

different Spanish periodicals. However, his main contribution to the Kierkegaard research is to be found in his native country, where he has been responsible, among other things, for the foundation of the *Sociedad Iberoamericana de Estudios Kierkegaardianos*.

[122] The supervisor of Amilburu's work was Alastair McKinnon himself, which confirms once again the contact, in these years, of Spanish studies with international Kierkegaard research.

[123] Although not a Kierkegaard scholar himself, Rafael Alvira was supervisor of some other studies on Kierkegaard as, for example, the aforementioned dissertation of Luis Guerrero. It is worth mentioning that the University of Navarra has been an important focus in the Spanish reception of Kierkegaard. The reason of this interest could lie in the religious tendency of this institution that belongs to the Opus Dei.

[124] Cèlia Amorós, *Søren Kierkegaard o la subjetividad del caballero. Un estudio a la luz de las paradojas del patriarcado*, Barcelona: Anthropos 1987.

sacrifice is romantically sublimated. Another example of Kierkegaard's recognition in the field of academic studies can be seen in the different histories of philosophy and other handbooks that included Kierkegaard in their repertoires. Among the various cases, it is worth noting that of José María Valverde (1926–96), an influential Spanish figure who concentrates on the religious as well as the literary dimension of Kierkegaard's thought.[125] His brief introductions to the Dane are always well documented and highlight the general ignorance of the work of Kierkegaard in Spain and the difficulties of making it accessible to the Spanish language. Patricio Peñalver Gómez is also a noteworthy example inasmuch as he symbolizes a new approach to Kierkegaard, namely, that of seeing him as an autonomous thinker in the context of the history of philosophy, without reducing him to the traditional limited readings of the "father of existentialism" or the "antiHegel."[126]

In this context, the recent work of José Luis Cañas, *Søren Kierkegaard. Between Immediacy and Relation*, is representative.[127] Without being a Kierkegaard scholar himself, Cañas turns to the Dane as "a powerful hermeneutical key to understand modern philosophy and the current trends of thought."[128] He interprets the whole work of Kierkegaard in terms of a tension between two forces which correspond to the aesthetic and the religious and which the author conceives as "the force of the immediate" and "the force of the relational." Despite being of importance for its philosophical approach, the work of Cañas forces us to relativize the optimism of these years, since the total ignorance of the complexity of Kierkegaard's pseudonymity and the lack of familiarity with Danish evinced in this study make it clear that there is still a long way to go.[129]

The work of Manuel Suances Marcos, a very prolific professor whose devotion to Kierkegaard has taken various forms, including contributions to radio and television, is worth taking into consideration. Apart from his articles and academic activities related to Kierkegaard's thought, his major work is three monograph volumes on Kierkegaard's life, philosophy, and religious thought, addressed to university students as didactic material. These three volumes have the curious peculiarity of being written in the first person which, according to Suances, is the result of not only a personal identification with Kierkegaard, but also the conviction that this

---

[125] See, for example, José María Valverde, "Kierkegaard: correctivo del Cristianismo, adversario de la Cristiandad" [Kierkegaard: Christianity's Corrective, Christendom's Opponent], in *La entrada en el siglo XX* in *Historia de la literatura universal*, vols. 1–10, ed. by Martín de Riquer and José María Valverde, Barcelona: Planeta 1984–6, vol. 8, 1986, pp. 94–105; pp. 126–33.

[126] See, for example, Patricio Peñalver Gómez, "Kierkegaard," in *La filosofía del siglo XIX*, ed. by José Luis Villacañas, Madrid: Trotta 2001, pp. 113–61.

[127] José Luis Cañas, *Søren Kierkegaard. Entre la inmediatez y la relación*, Madrid: Trotta 2003.

[128] Ibid., p. 11.

[129] Like many other authors, who venture themselves into the risky Danish language, Cañas falls into some spelling mistakes such as "Synspunkiel for min foraftterwirksomhed" (*sic*, p. 12; p. 122; See note 73) or the use of verbs instead of nouns, for instance. This makes one wonder what the use of these authors' references to Danish original titles and categories is.

literary resource can help to better present Kierkegaard's thought.[130] This approach to Kierkegaard, however, has the disadvantage of lacking some critical reflection. Suances claims to introduce Kierkegaard himself directly and to be faithful to his thought, but he ends up being faithful rather to an interpretation of Kierkegaard, namely, the traditional Spanish one. In any case, his study does provide the reader with a lot of information about the Dane, and it is a reliable and valuable introduction for all those to whom it is addressed.

To continue with the dissertations written in these years, we must mention Francesc Torralba, a scholar educated in the field of philosophy and theology who has become an unavoidable point of reference in the Spanish Kierkegaard research for his numerous studies. Apart from many articles and some translations, Torralba has published four books on Kierkegaard's thought, one of them being the result of his doctoral dissertation in Philosophy at the University of Barcelona. *Point of Inflection. A Reading of Kierkegaard* was his first work which appeared in 1992, after a research stay at the Kierkegaard Library in Copenhagen.[131] The book is a longer essay in which Kierkegaard is taken as an encouraging example to follow for the critical situation of religiosity in post-modernity.[132]

Despite being a work written in a free and essayistic fashion, Torralba already here points to the keys of his reading of Kierkegaard. According to him, and owing to the multiplicity of voices, one has to be very cautious when facing Kierkegaard's work and protect oneself from the risk of getting lost in the author's "labyrinth of masks": "In the textual skin, one has the impression that Kierkegaard's work is a brutal cacophony which completely lacks order and unity" and, nevertheless, "there is a thread, an Ariadne's thread that [the interpreter] must discover in the textual subsoil."[133] Throughout his work, Torralba proposes that we use the well-known academic distinction between direct communication (works signed by Kierkegaard himself) and indirect communication (pseudonymous works) as the "Ariadne's thread." In light of this, he considers *The Point of View* and the journals as the main

---

[130] With respect to the former, Suances writes: "I have had a full identification with him; I have lived his experiences as mine" (Manuel Suances Marcos, *Søren Kierkegaard, tomo I: Vida de un filósofo atormentado* [Søren Kierkegaard, vol. I: Life of a Tormented Philosopher], Madrid: UNED 1997, p. 17); about the latter, he says in his second volume: "I decided to do it also in first person because I believe that it makes the comprehension and immediate access to Kierkegaard's thought easier...especially, if one tries to be faithful to his thought and not make use of the opportunity to lumber Kierkegaard with thoughts and positions that are not his" (Suances Marcos, *Søren Kierkegaard, tomo II: Trayectoria de su pensamiento filosófico* [Søren Kierkegaard, tome 2: Trajectory of His Philosophical Thought], Madrid: UNED 1998, p. 26).
[131] Francesc Torralba, *Punt d'inflexió. Lectura de Kierkegaard*, Lleida: Pagès Editors 1992.
[132] In general, Torralba sees Kierkegaard as a religious author who could be a very valuable reference for the crisis of faith as long as theology and philosophy adjust or even correct his lucid intuitions in order to save them from a mere fideism (cf. Francesc Torralba, "Kierkegaard," in *Història del pensament cristià. Quaranta figures* [History of Christian Thought. Forty Figures], ed. by Pere Lluís Font, Barcelona: Proa 2002, p. 774).
[133] Francesc Torralba, *Poética de la libertad. Lectura de Kierkegaard* [Poetics of Freedom. Reading of Kierkegaard], Madrid: Caparrós 1998, p. 27; p. 30.

texts where we can find the true voice of Kierkegaard. He writes: "[the journals] could be defined as Kierkegaard's selfhood textually articulated or, in another sense, the actual self expressed narratively...In the autobiographical texts collected in Group A of the *Papirer*, the literary and the actual self of Kierkegaard constitute a monolithic unity."[134]

In this way, Torralba follows the hierarchical interpretation of *The Point of View*, in accordance with which the whole work and Kierkegaard, as its author, are religious, pseudonymity being an instrument in the service of Christianity.[135] Regarding this, he adds in the introduction to his translation of *Christian Discourses*:

> We think that the pseudonymous works have a referential value. That means that the authentic and true thought of Kierkegaard is expressed in the texts of direct communication, which, on the other hand, are much more extensive; while the pseudonymous works are useful to complement and illuminate some of the author's theses.[136]

Following this reading, Torralba approaches various topics of Kierkegaard's work in his studies, particularly those of a theological nature. Thus, he deals, for example, with the central questions of his thesis, namely, God, individual and freedom; the relation between Kierkegaard and other religious authors such as Urs von Balthasar and Saint Thomas Aquinas; the problem of communication; the biblical roots of Kierkegaard's thought or the religious nature of Kierkegaard as an author.[137] With regard to the latter, it is curious to see that Torralba seems to use a Janus-faced interpretation. On the one hand, he says that the interpreter cannot let himself be deceived by the pseudonymous authors since they are not the true voice of Kierkegaard. Whereas, on the other hand, he repeatedly uses the claim of a "non-reliable author," Johannes de silentio, as an argument to defend one of his main theses, namely, that Kierkegaard is neither a philosopher nor a theologian but a religious poet.[138] Unfortunately, this lack of rigor in adhering to his own methodological distinctions is not the only questionable aspect of Torralba's work. In his studies we surprisingly find fault with the following: a persistent confusion of the pseudonyms, misprints, numerous

---

[134] Ibid., p. 23.

[135] There have been many scholars in Spain who have followed the same interpretation. It is very likely that a strong influence of the aforementioned Cornelio Fabro lies behind it.

[136] *Discursos Cristians*, trans. by Francesc Torralba, Barcelona: Proa-Enciclopèdia Catalana 1994, p. 23.

[137] See, for example, Francesc Torralba, "Santo Tomás y Kierkegaard ante el dilema abrahámico" [Saint Thomas and Kierkegaard before Abraham's Dilemma], *Pensamiento*, vol. 196, no. 50, 1994, pp. 75–94; Francesc Torralba, "Teologia de l'angoixa. Kierkegaard i Urs von Balthasar" [Theology of Anxiety. Kierkegaard and Urs von Balthasar], in *Fe i teologia en la història. Estudis en honor del prof. Dr. Evangelista Vilanova* [Faith and Theology in History. Studies in Honor of Prof. dr. Evangelista Vilanova], ed. by Joan Busquets and Maria Martinell, Barcelona: Abadia de Montserrat 1997, pp. 449–56.

[138] "Kierkegaard explicitly says that he is not a philosopher *sensu stricto*, but a poet" (Introduction to *Discursos Cristians*, p. 8)—says Torralba just before quoting Johannes de silentio, who claims: "The present author is by no means a philosopher. He is *poetice et eleganter* a supplementary clerk who neither writes the system nor give promises of the system" (*SKS* 4, 103 / *FT*, 7).

spelling mistakes (particularly in the Danish references), and a significant lack of familiarity with current international Kierkegaard research—all things that, sadly, diminish the value of his studies.[139]

Like Francesc Torralba, Carlos Goñi Zubieta defended his dissertation at the University of Barcelona. In 1996, he published the resulting book of his doctoral research, *The Eternal Value of Time: Introduction to Kierkegaard*.[140] This work is divided into two parts. In the first part, Goñi tackles the topic of pseudonymity and its role in Kierkegaard's work; he is in line with other scholars in regarding Kierkegaard's guidelines in *The Point of View* as the criterion for an interpretation of the authorship.[141] The second part of Goñi's work concentrates on the relation

---

[139] In his dissertation (*Dios, individuo y libertad. La lírica-dialéctica de Kierkegaard* [God, Individual and Freedom. Kierkegaard's Lyrics-Dialectics], Barcelona: Universidad de Barcelona 1992) and in *Love and Difference. The Mystery of God in Kierkegaard* (*Amor y diferencia. El misterion de Dios en Kierkegaard*, Barcelona: PPU 1993), he refers to "Anticlimacus" as the author of *Works of Love, Judge for Yourself!* and *Two Ethical-Religious Essays* (cf. Torralba, *Dios, individuo y libertad*, p. 36 and Torralba, *Amor y diferencia*, p. 49). As a matter of fact, there is in his dissertation a chapter devoted specifically to the analysis of *Works of Love*, which is made under the assumption that it belongs to Anti-Climacus (cf. Torralba, *Dios, individuo y libertad*, p. 487). He would persist in ascribing to "Anticlimacus"—sometimes "Johannes Anticlimacus" (*sic*)—*Works of Love* in other studies. Moreover, he also claims, for example, Frater Taciturnus to be the author of *Fear and Trembling* (cf. Torralba, *Punt d'inflexió*, p. 21) and *Repetition* (cf. Francesc Torralba, *Kierkegaard en el laberinto de las mascaras* [Kierkegaard in the Labyrinth of Masks], Madrid: Fundación Emmanuel Mounier 2003, p. 20)—even though he writes correctly in other cases the pseudonyms of these two works. As far as the spelling mistakes in his use of Danish are concerned, they not only are abundant but also denote problems of comprehension, as it is in the case of *Tre Taler ved taenker Liligheder* (*sic*) [*Three Discourses on Imagined Occasions*], which Torralba renders into Spanish as "Tres discursos concretamente circunstanciales" [Three Concretely Circumstantial Discourses] or the translation of *Judge for Yourself!*, which he turns upside down as "Juzgaos a vosotros mismos!" [Judge yourselves!] (cf. Torralba, *Dios, individuo y libertad*, p. 1174; p. 36 and Torralba, *Amor y diferencia*, p. 53; p. 49). Finally, the bibliographies he includes in his studies suffer from the same careless treatment too. There are mistakes in the titles, authors, and years of publication; for example—a case that fulfils the three—"Lerrañeta, F, *Kierkegaard o la subjetividad apasionada*, Salamanca," (*sic*) (cf. Torralba, *Amor y diferencia*, p. 373), which might correspond to Rafael Larrañeta, *La interioridad apasionada. Verdad y amor en S. Kierkegaard*, Salamanca: San Estaban-Universidad Pontificia 1990). Major references are also missing. To mention two examples, the Hongs' English translations are not included in the bibliographies given but only Lowrie's and Swenson's (cf. Torralba, *Dios, individuo y libertad*, ; Torralba, *Amor y diferencia*, ; and Torralba, "Kierkegaard,") and, in a study in 2002 meant to introduce Kierkegaard both thematically and methodologically, the new critical edition of Kierkegaard's works, *Søren Kierkegaards Skrifter*, is not listed, but the third edition of Drachmann, Heiberg and Lange—"the latest edition until now"—is the only one he offers to the would-be scholar (cf. Torralba, "Kierkegaard," pp. 775ff.).

[140] Carlos Goñi Zubieta, *El valor eterno del tiempo: Introducción a Kierkegaard*, Barcelona: PPU 1996.

[141] Ibid., pp. 35–53. Goñi's reading of Kierkegaard resembles the theses of Torralba on how to face pseudonymity. On this regard, it is curious to find in Goñi's work some mistakes

between time and eternity in the pseudonymous works, a relation that he regards as the fundamental question of Kierkegaard's thought.

As we can see, pseudonymity began to be taken into consideration in Spanish Kierkegaard studies of this period.[142] However, the first approaches to this issue were still limited, since they took pseudonymity as a preliminary question that soon was overlooked for the sake of an interpretation of the work. It would not be until later that pseudonymity would be regarded as a topic in itself. This is the case of Begonya Sáez Tajafuerce (b. 1967), another scholar from Catalonia, who studies pseudonymity, not as a rhetorical device but as "an *essential* basis in the *production* itself," to put it in Kierkegaard's words.[143] In 1997, at the University Autònoma of Barcelona, she defended her dissertation on *Søren Kierkegaard: the Ethical Seduction*.[144] Seduced by the textual strategy of Kierkegaard's work, Sáez reads the work of the Dane as "a philosophical-literary project which has as a primordial object the ethical, although not as an *object* subjected to considerations of a different kind, but as a *project of existence to which every individual must be led*."[145] In many articles and lectures, Sáez continues to develop this interpretation of Kierkegaard, by means of specific studies on particular topics and works. These studies always offer an internal reading of the works that emphasizes their formal dimension, showing thus the intimate relation between the aesthetic and the ethical in Kierkegaard's writings.

With her contribution, Sáez opens a new perspective of study for the Spanish Kierkegaard research, namely, the aesthetic one, which takes the role of Kierkegaard as an author into account.[146] The most important aspect of Sáez's contribution, however, probably lies in her promotion of Kierkegaard, which she has done by means of different activities. From the very beginning, Sáez has been a scholar with close ties to the international Kierkegaard Research. She made long stays at the Søren Kierkegaard Research Centre in Copenhagen and at the Hong Kierkegaard Library in Northfield, Minnesota, which gave her work not only an outstanding quality but

---

in the pseudonyms that coincide exactly with Torralba's. This is the case, for example, of claiming Anti–Climacus to be the author of *Works of Love, Judge for Yourself!* and *Two Ethical–Religious Essays* (ibid., p. 23).

[142] In this context, the translation of Marion Holmes Hartshorne's *Kierkegaard, The Godly Deceiver: The Nature and Meaning of his Pseudonymous Writings* (New York: Columbia University Press 1990, in Spanish as *Kierkegaard, el divino burlador: Sobre la naturaleza y el significado de sus obras pseudónimas*, trans. by Elisa Lucena Torés, Madrid: Cátedra 1992) stands out as a reference for some Spanish Kierkegaard scholars who began to take pseudonymity into account. Among the few foreign works translated into Spanish in this period, this work can be regarded as the most influential one.

[143] *SKS* 7, 569 / *CUP1*, 625.

[144] Begonya Sáez Tajafuerce, *Søren Kierkegaard: la seducció ètica*, Barcelona: Universitat Autònoma de Barcelona 1997.

[145] Ibid., p. v.

[146] Although the interest in aesthetics had already been dealt with by some individual contributors as, for example, Ricardo Gullón, who already in 1965 had published a brief article in which he compared the multiplicity of voices in the works of Kierkegaard and Dostoevsky to Unamuno's work, it is not until now that this interest really has a place in the Spanish Kierkegaard studies.

also an important international renown. With the former, she has collaborated in different activities, of which the project of translation of Kierkegaard's collected works into Spanish stands out as surely the most significant. As far as the Hong Kierkegaard Library is concerned, Sáez has been the main person responsible for the "Seminario Iberoamericano," an important seminar of Spanish-speaking scholars from Latin America and Spain who meet every second year at the library with the aim of discussing questions related to the recent Spanish translations.[147] Lastly, we must also call attention to Sáez's work as supervisor of—to date—two doctoral dissertations on Kierkegaard.[148]

As a result of the work of all these scholars, many collective activities pertaining to the study of Kierkegaard have been taking place for the first time in Spain. The first one was the congress, *Encuentros de Filosofía en Denia*, which was held from the 6th to the 9th of May 1987. This was a course of meetings held every year and dedicated to different works of various authors. It was in 1987 that the works chosen for the seminars were Kierkegaard's *Fear and Trembling* and "The Seducer's Diary." Different scholars contributed with papers on these texts, and the congress was also the occasion to present a couple of audiovisual documents on Kierkegaard. In 1990, the conference proceedings, edited by Javier Urdanibia (chairman of the meetings), were published together with the ones of another meeting on Schopenhauer. It must be said that the scholars who contributed with papers in these two works were not, strictly speaking, Kierkegaard scholars, in the sense that they did not publish any other study on the Dane apart from these contributions; the lone exception is Cèlia Amorós, who presented a paper from her only book on Kierkegaard, published just one month before the meeting.

Another case of collective work was the monographic issue of the Mexican periodical *Tópicos*, published as the result of a conference entitled "Las publicaciones de Søren Kierkegaard de 1843." The seminar took place in Mexico on September 23 and 24, 1993. In this case, some Spanish Kierkegaard scholars contributed to the conference with papers on *Either/Or* (María García Amilburu), *Fear and Trembling* (Leonardo Polo) and *Three Upbuilding Discourses* (Teresa Aizpún). Whereas Leonardo Polo had only studied Kierkegaard in his book on Hegelianism, both Amilburu and Aizpún were Kierkegaard scholars, properly speaking, who, as we have seen, had already defended their dissertations on Kierkegaard and published some studies as well. In this sense, we can regard their presence in this international conference (in which, apart from the Mexican scholars, important figures of the Kierkegaard research such as Arne Grøn, Alastair McKinnon, and Julia Watkin were present) as a significant step forward for Spanish research.

---

[147] We refer to the new translation project *Escritos de Søren Kierkegaard* [Kierkegaard's Writings], ed. by Rafael Larrañeta, Darío González and Begonya Sáez Tajafuerce, Madrid: Trotta 2000ff.

[148] Along with Sáez, other scholars are currently supervising doctoral dissertations on Kierkegaard. This is the case of Montserrat Negre in Seville or Tomás Melendo in Malaga. Also, the late Rafael Larrañeta, who was the supervisor of three different dissertations when he died.

Shortly after this conference, García Amilburu herself took charge of the edition of a monograph on Kierkegaard edited by the Sevillian periodical *Thémata*.[149] While the Mexican conference had been held to commemorate the 150 years of Kierkegaard's publications of 1843, the Spanish publication celebrated the 150 years of *The Concept of Anxiety*. On this occasion, the study was limited solely to this work and most of the outstanding Spanish scholars contributed with papers. As a matter of fact, according to what Amilburu says in the introduction of this issue, all the contributions requested for the volume were from authors exclusively of Spanish language, with the exception of two cases: Arne Grøn (as head of the Kierkegaard Department at the University of Copenhagen) and Julia Watkin (as editor of the *International Kierkegaard Newsletter*). The aim of making Spanish Kierkegaard studies meet the international standard was the reason for this exclusivity. This volume became one of the most significant events in Spanish reception and contributed to the "Kierkegaard renaissance" that Amilburu wished also for Spain. The monograph includes papers by Rafael Alvira, Begonya Sáez, Teresa Aizpún, Rafael Larrañeta, Virginia Careaga, Montserrat Negre, Carlos Díaz and the Mexican Leticia Valádez; some of these were documented and analytic papers, others, more essayistic approaches.[150]

Three years after Amilburu's, another monograph on Kierkegaard came out in Spain, edited by Begonya Sáez in the periodical *Enrahonar*.[151] In contrast to the volume on *The Concept of Anxiety*, it consists of essays by exclusively foreign contributors. We could consider this monograph as the fulfillment of a long awaited event, namely, to put the Spanish Kierkegaard research in contact with the international one. In this sense, this collection resumes and completes the task initiated by Amilburu's.

The volume is opened by an introduction by the editor in which the main readings of Kierkegaard are presented. Apart from following the ones already mentioned by André Clair (Paris, 1976), Sáez speaks of the "aesthetic reading," a reading that watches over the poetics and rhetoric of Kierkegaard's work. In this respect, she announces that most of the articles of the volume are examples of this kind of reading, which tries to reconcile at the same time the form and the content of Kierkegaard's works. The monograph is divided into four parts: the first one consists of a group of articles on the ethical stage; all of them offer a "problematic" reading that calls into doubt the conventional one of the theory of the stages and the authority of Judge Wilhelm to determinate how to understand the ethical stage in Kierkegaard. The

---

[149] María García Amilburu (ed.), *El Concepto de la Angustia: 150 años después* [*The Concept of Anxiety*: 150 Years After], Seville: Universidad de Sevilla 1995 (*Thémata*, vol. 15).

[150] As for the latter, the article of Rafael Alvira aims to draw a parallel between the phenomenon of anxiety (which he prefers to translate into Spanish as *ansiedad* instead of the academically accepted *angustia*) and the Socratic phenomenon of the longing for knowledge. Although his reading is quite suggestive for Kierkegaard's thought, the parallel is drawn out of the context of *The Concept of Anxiety*. For his part, Carlos Díaz writes a "rhapsodic auto-confession" which is conceived of as a "Non-Edifying and Non-Academic Postscript to the volume."

[151] Begonya Sáez (ed.), *Enrahonar*, no. 29, Barcelona: Universitat Autònoma de Barcelona 1998.

second part gathers together brief articles that show the multiplicity of faces that the work of the Danish author suggests: Kierkegaard as philosopher, teacher, poet, pathologist, lover, etc. The third presents for the first time to the reader a translation into Catalan of "A First and Last Explanation" by Begonya Sáez. And, finally, the monograph ends with some practical information for the Kierkegaard scholar, such as news about the different Kierkegaard research centers and a bibliographical list of the translations of Kierkegaard's works into Spanish.

Along with the publication of these monograph volumes, we should also note several seminars, doctoral courses, and lectures that were given in these years by scholars such as Manuel Suances, Virginia Careaga, María García Amilburu, Begonya Sáez, Montserrat Negre, and Tomás Melendo. The contributions of Montserrat Negre include a couple of articles and papers, besides her work as supervisor of a dissertation. Tomás Melendo is also currently supervising a dissertation that echoes the Fabro influence of his beginning with Kierkegaard in Rome, since it analyzes the topic of "*el singular*" (Fabro's *il singolo*) in Kierkegaard's journals. In 1997, the author of this dissertation, José García, and Tomás Melendo himself held a series of meetings on Kierkegaard, in which the Dane was, so to speak, brought to trial. Melendo and García played the role of counsel for the defence, while the students acted as the jury. Apart from holding these original meetings, they also had the ambition to create a Kierkegaardian society in Málaga.[152] Despite their enthusiasm, the idea never got any further and remained a personal wish, rather than a common Spanish undertaking.

Regarding the translations of this period, we should first point out the absence of works characteristic of the 1980s. In fact, it was not until 1992 that a new resurgence of Kierkegaard translations took place. From this year, a number of translations appeared in Spain in different languages, particularly in Catalan, which constituted a significant novelty.

The first translation to appear in 1992 was Begonya Sáez's *Repetition*, a well-documented work that demonstrates a good knowledge of both Danish and Kierkegaard's thought.[153] Furthermore, Sáez's translation shows a respectful treatment of the original text that stands out as a rarity in the tradition of Spanish translations. In contrast to this rigorous approach, we find another Catalan translation one year later, this time of "In vino veritas," by Anna Pascual.[154] This work contains several mistakes as, for example, the fact of completely ignoring the separation between the preface and the rest of the work, in such a way that we find 142 pages of preface to no work whatsoever.

In 1994, the first and only—as far as we know—Basque translation of Kierkegaard appeared; once again the text was the popular "The Seducer's Diary."[155] Unfortunately, we cannot make any comment about this translation, given the language of it. In the same year another Catalan translation, that of *Christian*

---

[152] Cf. "Søren Kierkegaard i krydsforhør," in the Danish review issued in Málaga *Solkysten* (May 12, 1997).
[153] *La repetició*, trans. by Begonya Sáez Tajafuerce, Barcelona: Edicions 62 1992.
[154] *In vino veritas*, trans. by Anna Pascual, Barcelona: Llibres de l'índex 1993.
[155] *Seduzitzailearen egunkaria*, trans. by J.M. Mendizábal, Bilbao: Klasikoak 1994.

Discourses by Francesc Torralba, was published.[156] This work has the value of presenting to the Catalan reader a non-pseudonymous text, which contributes to the broadening of the very limited field of the so-called religious works in Spain. As for Torralba's translation, it must be said that it is made in a very free way, sacrificing some of the features of Kierkegaard's writing, supposedly for the sake of style. To give an example, he decides to use seven different sentences to translate a single Danish expression that is constantly repeated by Kierkegaard with exactly the same words.[157] In this way, the reader of this translation allegedly reads a richer text but misses a meaningful resource that Kierkegaard uses in his writings: repetition. Apart from this questionable way of translating, we find in Torralba's text some mistakes and oversights that, again, diminish the potential value of his work.[158]

Another translation that has the value of presenting to the Spanish reader the underestimated "spiritual dimension" of Kierkegaard's work is the selection of Kierkegaard's prayers, also by Francesc Torralba, published in 1996. Made on the basis of the second Danish edition of Kierkegaard's collected works and contrasted with the already existing selections of prayers such as Tisseau's, Lefevre's, and Fabro's,[159] this work is not a scholarly book and does not claim to provide a Kierkegaardian theology but a "guide of prayers for completely personal use."[160] Thus, the intention of the book is rather to make the reader a participant in Kierkegaard's spirituality.

In 1997, Rafael Larrañeta offers for the very first time to the Spanish reader a rigorous and reliable translation of one of the most important works of Kierkegaard from a philosophical point of view, namely, *Philosophical Fragments*.[161] As we said earlier, this work had already been translated by Arnoldo Canclini in 1956.[162] Yet

---

[156] *Discursos Cristians*, trans. by Francesc Torralba, Barcelona: Proa-Enciclopèdia Catalana 1994.

[157] "Efter alt saadant søge Hedningene" (ibid., p. 53; p. 62; p. 74; p. 84; p. 95; p. 106; and p. 116).

[158] In 1992, Francesc Torralba had already translated into Spanish *Armed Neutrality*, *The Changelessness of God* and, partially, "The Dialectic of Ethical and Ethical-Religious Comunication. A Little Sketch" (in *Pap.* VIII–2 B 81) as an appendix to his dissertation *Dios, individuo y libertad* (see pp. 1178–88; pp. 1235–43; pp. 1192–1202; and pp. 1211–34). These translations are not very reliable, since, in his version of *The Changelessness of God*, Torralba skips two pages of the original, without any apparent reason and without giving any explicit warning; he also omits lines from *Armed Neutrality* and translates incompletely "The Dialectic of Ethical and Ethical–Religious Comunication," which he inexplicably says is taken from the second edition of Kierkegaard's *Samlede Værker*.

[159] See *Prières et fragments sur la prière* [Prayers and Fragments of the Prayers (excerpts from Kierkegaard's Journals and Papers)], trans. by Paul–Henri Tisseau, Nancy et al.: Berger-Levrault 1937; *The Prayers of Kierkegaard*, trans. and ed. by Perry D. Le Lefevre, Chicago: Chicago University Press 1956 and *Preghiere* [Prayers (selected religious passages from Kierkegaard's writings)], ed. by Cornelio Fabro, Brescia: Morcelliana 1951.

[160] See *Pregàries* [Prayers], trans. by Francesc Torrelba, Barcelona: Publicacions Abadia de Montserrat 1996, p. 26.

[161] *Migajas filosóficas o Un poco de filosofía*, trans. by Rafael Larrañeta, Madrid: Trotta 1997.

[162] *Fragmentos filosóficos*, trans. from French and English by Arnoldo Canclini, Buenos Aires: La Aurora 1956.

that translation was made from the English and French versions, and it was quite deficient and erroneous. In contrast, this new translation is a critical edition that has all the elements necessary for reliability, such as a good knowledge of both Danish and Kierkegaard's work, which is shown in the introduction and footnotes that accompany the body of the text. The style of this translation is very respectful to the Danish original, which, according to Larrañeta, makes the Spanish text "suffer" in some passages, although this is compensated by the rigor and the literality of the translation. The edition includes the pagination of the second Danish edition in the margins, a feature obviously meant for scholars that is quite representative of the intentions of Larrañeta, which are not only to present the work of Kierkegaard to a broad audience, but also to do it in a scholarly way for those who want to go deeper in the study of the Dane.

We must highlight the beginning of a long awaited and important project in 2000: the translation of Kierkegaard's collected works into Spanish. This ambitious undertaking started in 1997 in the context of the aforementioned "Seminario Iberoamericano" (at the Hong Kierkegaard Library). After a period in which different potential translators were taken into consideration, three scholars were assigned for the project: Rafael Larrañeta, Begonya Sáez, and the Argentinian Darío González. The plan of the work consisted of translating all the works written by Kierkegaard, including the posthumous and unfinished ones, which normally were published in the editions of the *Papirer*. In order to carry this out, the new Danish critical edition of the texts (*Søren Kierkegaards Skrifter*) would be used, in such a way that the Spanish translation would be issued so that each volume corresponded to a volume of *Søren Kierkegaards Skrifter*. The criteria for the translation and edition of the Spanish text would also correspond to the Danish one; that is to say, they would present to the reader a very rigorous text, without any personal interpretation. The comprehensive critical apparatus included in the Danish edition would also be the main source for the elaboration of the explanatory notes that, in the case of the Spanish version, would be considerably shorter and adapted to the needs of the Spanish reader. Additionally, the edition would include a glossary with the most significant and problematic Kierkegaardian terms, an index of names and a table of concordances between the first and second Danish editions and the new edition, *Søren Kierkegaards Skrifter*.

The first volume of *Escritos de Søren Kierkegaard*, the generic title of this project, included the works *From the Papers of One Still Living* and *The Concept of Irony*, translated by Begonya Sáez and Darío González, respectively. In both cases, it was the first time that these works were translated into Spanish. This first volume was presented at an international seminar that took place in Madrid in May 2000, held by Rafael Larrañeta and Trotta, the publishing house co-responsible for the project. The seminar included papers of both Sáez and González, who talked about the works they had translated; Niels Jørgen Cappelørn, co-editor of the Spanish edition and editor of *Søren Kierkegaards Skrifter*, who talked about Kierkegaard's writings in Denmark; and Rafael Larrañeta, who read a paper on the "Aventuras y Desventuras de Kierkegaard en España." Two brief speeches by the Danish Ambassador in Spain and the director of Trotta concluded the meeting. The latter presented the schedule of the project, which initially consisted of the optimistic plan of a volume per half year.

According to this plan, the next volume to supposedly appear in 2001 would correspond to *Either/Or*. Afterwards, the translations of *The Concept of Anxiety, Fear and Trembling* and *Repetition* would be published in 2002 and *Concluding Unscientific Postscript* in 2003.[163] Unfortunately, things turned out to be much slower than expected, and the second volume is still to be published, not to mention the other ones.[164] The unfortunate death of Rafael Larrañeta has been the main reason for this extraordinary delay, which makes the Spanish reader wait still longer for such an important and needed translation.

It goes without saying that in the last twenty years, we also find translations of Kierkegaard's works in Spanish America. This is the case of a couple of texts translated in the "Sociedad Iberoamericana de Estudios Kierkegaardianos" in Mexico and the *Biblioteca Kierkegaard* in Buenos Aires, respectively. The translation of "The Present Age," which was issued in Chile in 2003, is also worth mentioning.

A century ago, Kierkegaard entered Spain by the hand of Miguel de Unamuno, not a scholar but a personal thinker who had been seduced by the personality of the Dane. As a matter of fact, this way of receiving Kierkegaard became one of the most significant features in the Spanish reception. From Unamuno's "brotherhood" to Suances' personal identification, which led him to write his studies in the first person, the seduction of Kierkegaard's work and life seems to have been a constant in Spain. This could explain, on the one hand, the prevalence of essayistic approaches to the work of the Dane. It is true that this way of studying has been, in general, customary in Spain, but it is also true that in the case of Kierkegaard this tendency has predominated in most of the cases. On the other hand, this "seduced" approach could also have something to do with another characteristic of the reception: the individual nature of many works, which has delayed the rise of a real tradition of Kierkegaard studies.

It was not until the arrival of foreign studies that we began to find a common reading of Kierkegaard. This is the case for both the existentialist and the Catholic readings. The former became the mainstream interpretation of Kierkegaard for many years, and it would be closely related to the tragic and pessimistic picture of the Dane that Unamuno had already depicted—an image that would take many years to change and that even today has a strong influence. The latter would also become a distinctive mark of Kierkegaard in Spain since after the first foreign studies, a considerable group of scholars emerged who approached and continued to approach Kierkegaard from a Catholic-influenced viewpoint. Whereas, in the beginning, these approaches were rather straightforward and aimed basically to show Kierkegaard as a Catholic, in the most recent years these studies have turned to more specific topics, and yet they have continued to reveal a strong influence of an interpretation *à la* Fabro and the like. This is clearly noticeable, for example, in the work of some Thomist scholars and also others related to the prelature of the Opus Dei.

---

[163] We should include in this list *Philosophical Fragments*, which had already been published in 1997, as we have seen, and was later reissued as part of *Escritos de Søren Kierkegaard*.

[164] In an optimistic haste, Rafael Larrañeta included the second volume of *Escritos de Søren Kierkegaard* in the bibliography of his last book, *La lupa de Kierkegaard*, 2002, with 2002 as date of issue. This reference is obviously not true and one must not let oneself be deceived by it.

Finally, as the third group of common contributions, we should allude to the studies of a scholarly and rigorous kind that have prevailed in the last two decades. Apart from providing the reader with a more accurate picture of Kierkegaard, these studies have made the participation of Spanish Kierkegaard research in the international context possible. In this sense, the new project of translating Kierkegaard's works has to be seen as occurring parallel to other translation projects that are being made in other languages. However, we cannot be very optimistic in relation to this advance since we will still have to wait many years before we enjoy a complete translation of Kierkegaard's works in Spanish—not to mention that we are still lacking the *Papirer*. Until this happens, the reception of Kierkegaard in Spain will continue to be rather precarious.

Bibliography

I. Spanish Translations of Kierkegaard's Works

Prosas de Søren Kierkegaard [Prose of Søren Kierkegaard] (excerpts from "In vino veritas," "Diapsalmata," "The Unhappiest One," "The Esthetic Validity of Marriage"), trans. by Álvaro Armando Vasseur, Madrid: América 1918.

Diario de un seductor: arte de amar ["The Seducer's Diary": The Art of Love], trans. by Valentín de Pedro, Madrid: Sucesores de Rivadeneyra 1922 (republished, Buenos Aires: Espasa-Calpe 1951, and with the title *Diario del seductor*, Barcelona: Fontamara 1980).

El concepto de la angustia. Una sencilla investigación psicológica orientada hacia el problema dogmático del pecado original [*The Concept of Anxiety. A Simple Psychologically Orienting Deliberation on the Dogmatic Issue of Hereditary Sin*], trans. (from German) by José Gaos, Madrid: Revista de Occidente 1930 (republished, Madrid: Espasa-Calpe 1940).

"Fragmentos sobre la angustia" [Fragments on Anxiety] (excerpts from *The Concept of Anxiety*), trans. by José Gaos, *Revista de Occidente*, vol. 30, no. 89, 1930, pp. 204–23.

"Søren Kierkegaard. Fragmento" [Søren Kierkegaard. Fragment] (extracts from "In vino veritas)", trans. by Álvaro Armando Vasseur, 1918, *Revista Rosalía*, vol. 1, no. 4 (Centro Gallego de La Habana, Santiago de Cuba), 1937, pp. 20–2.

Tratado de la desesperación [*The Sickness unto Death*], trans. from French by Carlos Liacho, Buenos Aires: Santiago Rueda 1941 (republished, Buenos Aires: Leviatán 1997).

Antígona [Antigone] (translation of "The Tragic in Ancient Drama Reflected in the Tragic in Modern Drama" from *Either/Or*, Part 1), trans. by Juan Gil Albert, Mexico City: Séneca 1942 (republished, Seville: Renacimiento 2003).

"El Espíritu es el que da vida" ["It Is the Spirit Who Gives Life?"] (translation of Part III of *For Self-Examination*), *El Predicador Evangélico*, vol. 4, no. 16, 1946–7, pp. 356–62.

Temor y temblor [*Fear and Trembling*], trans. by Jaime Grinberg, Buenos Aires: Losada 1947 (republished, Buenos Aires: Hyspamérica 1985, and Barcelona: Orbis 1987).

Diario de un seductor ["The Seducer's Diary"], trans. by Arístides Gregori, Buenos Aires: Santiago Rueda 1951.

Etapas en el camino de la vida [*Stages on Life's Way*] (partial translation), trans. (from French) by Juana Castro, Buenos Aires: Santiago Rueda 1952.

Antígona: El sentido de la tragedia [Antigone: The Meaning of Tragedy] (translation of "The Tragic in Ancient Drama Reflected in the Tragic in Modern Drama"), trans. by Edmundo Fontana, Buenos Aires: Losange 1954.

Diario íntimo [Personal Diary] (excerpts from Kierkegaard's journals), trans. (from Italian) by María Angélica Bosco, Buenos Aires: Santiago Rueda 1955 (reissued with an introduction by José Luis López Aranguren, Barcelona: Planeta 1993).

Estética y ética en la formación de la personalidad ["The Balance between the Esthetic and the Ethical in the Development of the Personality"] (also translated in this volume, "Ultimatum," both from *Either/Or*, Part 2), trans. by Armand Marot, Buenos Aires: Nova 1955.

Fragmentos filosóficos [*Philosophical Fragents*], trans. from French and English by Arnoldo Canclini, Buenos Aires: La Aurora 1956.

Elogio de Abraham (páginas líricas) [Eulogy on Abraham (Lyrical Pages)] (excerpts from *Fear and Trembling*], trans. by Alberto Colao, Cartagena: Athenas 1959.

Mi punto de vista [My Point of View] (translation of *The Point of View for My Work as an Author*; *The Point of View: On My Work as an Author*), trans. by José Miguel Velloso, Buenos Aires: Aguilar 1959 (republished, Madrid: Sarpe 1985).

El amor y la religión (Puntos de vista) [Love and Religion (Points of View)] (translation of "Letter to the Reader from *Frater Taciturnus*" from *Stages on Life's Way*), trans. by Juana Castro, Buenos Aires: Santiago Rueda 1960 (republished, Mexico City: Tomo 2002).

Estética del matrimonio: Carta a un joven esteta [The Esthetic Validity of Marriage: Letter to a Young Esthete], trans. from French by Osiris Troiani, Buenos Aires: Dédalo 1960 (republished, Buenos Aires: Pléyade 1972, and Buenos Aires: Leviatán 1991).

El amor de Cristo [Love of Christ] (translation of "Love Will Hide a Multitude of Sins" from *Two Discourses at the Communion on Fidays*), *El Predicador Evangélico*, vol. 18, no. 69, 1960–1, pp. 59–64.

Diapsalmata, trans. by Javier Armada, Buenos Aires: Aguilar 1961.

Obras y Papeles de Kierkegaard [Kierkegaard's Works and Papers], vols. 1–9, trans. and ed. by Demetrio Gutiérrez Rivero, Madrid: Guadarrama 1961–9:

— vol. 1, *Ejercitación del Cristianismo* [*Practice in Christianity*] (1961).

— vol. 2, *Dos diálogos sobre el primer amor y el matrimonio* ["Two Dialogues on the First Love and Marriage"] (translation of "The Esthetic Validity of Marriage" and "Some Reflections on Marriage in Answer to Objections by a Married Man" from *Stages on Life's Way*) (1961).

— vol. 3, *Los lirios del campo y las aves del cielo. Trece discursos religiosos* [The Lilies in the Field and the Birds of the Air. Three Devotional Discourses] (1963).

— vol. 4, *Las obras del amor I. Meditaciones cristianas en forma de discursos. Primera Parte* [Works of Love I. Christian Meditations in the Form of Discourses. Part One] (translation of *Works of Love*, First Series) (1965).

— vol. 5, *Las obras del amor II. Meditaciones cristianas en forma de discursos. Segunda Parte* [Works of Love II. Christian Meditations in the Form of Discourses. Part Two] (translation of *Works of Love*, Second Series) (1965).

— vol. 6, *El concepto de la angustia* [*The Concept of Anxiety*] (1965) (republished, Barcelona: Orbis 1984, and Madrid: Hyspamérica 1985).

— vol. 7, *La enfermedad mortal (o de la desesperación y el pecado)* [*The Sickness unto Death* (or Despair and Sin)] (1969) (republished, Madrid: Sarpe 1984, and Madrid: Alba 1998).

— vol. 8, *Estudios estéticos, I: Diapsalmata y el erotismo musical* [Esthetical Studies I: Diapsalmata and the Musical-Erotic] (1969) (republished, Málaga: Ágora 1996).

— vol. 9, *Estudios estéticos, II: De la tragedia y otros ensayos* [Esthetical Studies II: On Tragedy and Other Essays] (translation of "The Tragic in Ancient Drama Reflected in the Tragic in Modern Drama," "Silhouettes," "The Unhappiest One," "The First Love," and "Rotation of Crops"] (1969) (published also, Málaga: Ágora 1998).

Los estadios eróticos inmediatos o lo erótico musical ["The Immediate Erotic Stages or the Musical-Erotic"], trans. by Javier Armada, Buenos Aires: Aguilar 1967.

La dificultat d'ésser cristià [The Difficulty of Being a Christian], trans. from French (*La difficulté d'être Chrétien. Présentation et choix de textes*, ed. by Jacques Colette, Paris: Éditions du Cerf 1964) by Mariona Serra de Sala, Barcelona: Ariel 1968.

Diario de un seductor ["The Seducer's Diary"], trans. from French by Jacinto León Ignacio, Barcelona: Ediciones 29 1971 (republished, Barcelona: Río Nuevo 1997).

Evangelio de los sufrimientos [The Gospel of Suffering] (translation of "The Gospel of Suffering" from *Upbuilding Discourses in Various Spirit*], trans. by Alejo Oria León, Mexico City: Ediciones Paulinas 1973.

La preocupación de la indecisión, de la inconstancia y del desaliento ["The Care of Indecisiveness, Vacillation, and Disconsolateness" (from *Christian Discourses*)], *Cuadernos monásticos* vol. 9, no. 29, 1974, pp. 325–40.

In vino veritas. La repetición ["In vino veritas," *Repetition*], trans. by Demetrio Gutiérrez Rivero, Madrid: Guadarrama 1975.

Temor y temblor [*Fear and Trembling*], trans. by Vicente Simón Merchán, Madrid: Editora Nacional 1975 (republished, Madrid: Tecnos 1987; Barcelona: Altaya, 1995, and Madrid: Alianza 2001).

Temor y temblor. Diario de un seductor [*Fear and Trembling.* "The Seducer's Diary"], trans. by Demetrio Gutiérrez Rivero, Madrid: Guadarrama 1976 (*Fear and Trembling* republished, Barcelona: Labor 1992; "The Seducer's Diary" reissued with an introduction by José María Valverde, Barcelona: Destino 1988).

Cartas del noviazgo ["Letters from the Engagement"], trans. from French (*Lettres des fiançailles*, Paris: Falaize 1956) by Carlos Correas, Buenos Aires: Siglo Veinte 1979.

La pureza de corazón es querer una sola cosa [Purity of the Heart is to Will One Thing] (translation of "On the Occasion of a Confession"), trans. from English by Leo Farré, Buenos Aires: La Aurora 1979.

Diario de un seductor ["The Seducer's Diary"], trans. by Ramón Alvarado Cruz, Mexico City: Juan Pablo 1984.

La espera de la fe. Con ocasión del año nuevo ["The Expectancy of Faith" (translation of parts of *Two Upbuilding Discourses*, 1843)], trans. (from English and French) by S.I.E.K. in collaboration with Catalina García Martínez, Mexico City: Mixcoac 1992.

La repetició [*Repetition*], trans. by Begonya Sáez Tajafuerce, Barcelona: Edicions 62 1992.

In vino veritas, trans. by Anna Pascual, Barcelona: Llibres de l'índex 1993.

"La immutabilidad de Dios," "La neutralidad armada," "La dialéctica de la comunicación ética y ético-religiosa" (Excerpts from *The Changelessness of God, Armed Neutrality*, and "The Dialectic of Ethical and Ethical-Religious Communication. A Little Sketch" (in *Pap.* VIII–2 B 79–89, pp. 143–90 / *JP* 1, 648–57)), trans. by Francesc Torralba, in *Amor y diferencia. El misterio de Dios en Kierkegaard*, Barcelona: PPU, 1993, pp. 313–25.

Discursos Cristians [*Christian Discourses*], trans. by Francesc Torralba, Barcelona: Proa–Enciclopèdia Catalana 1994.

Seduzitzailearen egunkaria ["The Seducer's Diary"], trans. by J.M. Mendizábal, Bilbao: Klasikoak 1994.

Tratado de la desesperación [*The Sickness unto Death*], trans. (from German) by Juan Enrique Holstein, Barcelona: Edicomunicación 1995.

Pregàries [Prayers], trans. by Francesc Torralba, Barcelona: Publicacions Abadia de Montserrat 1996.

Migajas filosóficas o Un poco de filosofía [*Philosophical Fragments*], trans. by Rafael Larrañeta, Madrid: Trotta 1997 (reissued as *Escritos. Migajas filosóficas o un poco de filosofía*, Madrid: Trotta 2001).

La repetición [*Repetition*], trans. by K.A. Hjelmström, Buenos Aires: Psiqué 1997.

Diario de un seductor ["The Seducer's Diary"], trans. from French by Omar Barroso, Buenos Aires: Leviatán 1998.

"Una primera i darrera explicació" ["A First and Last Explanation"], trans. by Begonya Sáez Tajafuerce, *Enrahonar*, no. 29, 1998, ed. by Begonya Sáez Tajafuerce, Barcelona: Universitat Autònoma de Barcelona 1998 (special issue: *Monograph on Kierkegaard*), pp. 159–62.

"Sobre el concepto de ironía" [On the Concept of Irony] (a fragment from Darío González' translation of *The Concept of Irony*, published in 2000), *Revista de Occidente*, vol. 221, 1999, pp. 72–86.

Escritos de Søren Kierkegaard, I. De los papeles de alguien que todavía vive. Sobre el concepto de ironía [Kierkegaard's Writings, vol. 1, *From the Papers of One Still Living, The Concept of Irony*], trans. by Darío González and Begonya Sáez Tajafuerce, ed. by Rafael Larrañeta, Darío González and Begonya Sáez Tajafuerce, Madrid: Trotta 2000.

La época presente ["The Present Age"], trans. by Manfred Svensson Hagvall, Santiago de Chile: Editorial Universitaria 2001.

Cómo juzga Cristo el cristianismo oficial [*What Christ Judges of Official Christianity*], trans. by Andrés Roberto Albertensen et al., *Cuadernos de Teología*, vol. 21, 2002, pp. 357–64.

Diario de un seductor ["The Seducer's Diary"], trans. by Francesc Lluís Cardona, Barcelona: Edicomunicación 2003.

"La definición socrática del pecado" ["The Socratic Definition of Sin" (from *The Sickness unto Death*)], trans. by Luis Guerrero and "Un vistazo a un esfuerzo contemporáneo en la literatura danesa" ["A Glance at a Contemporary Effort in Danish Literature" (from *Concluding Unscientific Postscript*], trans. by Leticia Valádez, in Luis Guerrero, *La verdad subjetiva: Søren Kierkegaard como escritor* [Subjective Truth. Søren Kierkegaard as an Author], Mexico City: Universidad Iberoamericana 2004, pp. 145–56 and pp. 185–245.

II. Spanish Secondary Literature on Kierkegaard

Abbagnano, Nicola, *Introducción al existencialismo* (*Introduzione all'esistenzialismo*) [Introduction to Existentialism], Mexico City: FCE 1955 [Milano 1942], see pp. 37–9.

Abellán, José Luis, "Influencias filosóficas en Unamuno" [Unamuno's Philosophical Influences], *Insula*, no. 181, 1961, p. 11.

Aizpún de Bobadilla, Teresa, "Kierkegaard. ¿Una filosofía de la trascendencia?" [Kierkegaard. A Philosophy of Transcendence?], in *El hombre: Inmanencia y Trascendencia*, vols. 1–2, ed. by Rafael Alvira, Pamplona: Universidad de Navarra 1991, vol. 1, pp. 771–8.

— *Kierkegaards Begriff der Ausnahme. Der Geist als Liebe*, Munich: Akademischer Verlag 1992.

— "Cómo puede un pagano vencer el mundo? Observaciones sobre los *Tres discursos edificantes* de 1843" [How can a Pagan Defeat the World? Remarks on *Three Upbuilding Discourses* (1843)], *Tópicos. Revista de Filosofía*, vol. 3, no. 5, 1993 (Mexico City: Universidad Panamericana), pp. 217–33.

— "Dialéctica y Libertad" [Dialectic and Freedom], *Tópicos. Revista de Filosofía*, vol. 4, no. 7, 1994 (Mexico City: Universidad Panamericana), pp. 33–43.

— "La libertad en *El concepto de la angustia*" [Freedom in *The Concept of Anxiety*], in *El Concepto de la Angustia: 150 años después* [*The Concept of Anxiety*: 150 Years Later], ed. by María García Amilburu, Seville: Universidad de Sevilla 1995 (*Thémata*, vol. 15), pp. 55–65.

Alcoberro i Pericay, Ramon, "Søren Kierkegaard (1813–1855). Una introducció" [Søren Kierkegaard (1813–1855). An Introduction], in www.alcoberro.info/kierke.htm n.d.

Alcorta y Echeverría, José Ignacio, "Ética kierkegaardiana y ética heideggeriana" [Kierkegaardian Ethics and Heideggerian Ethics], *Lo ético en el existencialismo*, 1951, pp. 65–78.

— "El constitutivo ontológico del existencialismo" [The Ontological Constituent Element of Existentialism], *Revista de Filosofía* vol. 15, no. 56, 1956, pp. 5–33.

Alvira, Rafael, "Sobre el comienzo radical. Consideraciones acerca de *El concepto de la angustia* de S.A. Kierkegaard" [On the Radical Beginning. Considerations on Kierkegaard's *The Concept of Anxiety*], in *El Concepto de la Angustia: 150 años después* [*The Concept of Anxiety*: 150 Years Later], ed. by María García Amilburu, Seville: Universidad de Sevilla 1995 (*Thémata*, vol. 15), pp. 31–42.

Amorós, Cèlia, *Søren Kierkegaard o la subjetividad del caballero. Un estudio a la luz de las paradojas del patriarcado* [Søren Kierkegaard or the Gentleman's Subjectivity. A Study in the Light of Patriarchy's Paradoxes], Barcelona: Anthropos 1987.

— "Søren Kierkegaard a la luz de las paradojas del patriarcado" [Søren Kierkegaard in the Light of Patriarchy's Paradoxes], in *Los Antihegelianos: Kierkegaard y Schopenhauer* [The Antihegelians: Kierkegaard and Schopenhauer], ed. by Javier Urdanibia, Barcelona: Anthropos 1990, pp. 109–40.

Artola, José María, "Situación y sentido del pensamiento hegeliano en la actualidad" [The Current Situation and the Meaning of Hegelian Thought], *Estudios Filosóficos*, vol. 22, 1973, pp. 349–83.

Ballestero, Manuel, "Kierkegaard, sujeto y realidad" [Kierkegaard, Subject and Actuality], in *Crítica y marginales. Compromiso y trascendencia del símbolo literario* [Criticism and Marginalia: Compromise and the Transcendence of the Literary Symbol], Barcelona: Barral 1974, pp. 33–44.

Baraldi, Sonia, "Del estadio estético en Kierkegaard" [On the Aesthetic Stage in Kierkegaard], *Alcalá*, no. 66, 1955, p. 13.

Baroja, Pío, *Las horas solitarias* [The Lonely Hours], Madrid: Rafael Caro Raggio 1918, see pp. 37–41.

— *El gran torbellino del mundo* [The Great Whirl of the World], Madrid: Caro Raggio 1926, see pp. 118–20; pp. 130–1; pp. 142–3; p. 236.

Barreiro, Xosé Luís, "Søren Kierkegaard y las fases de la personalidad" [Søren Kierkegaard and the Stages of Personality], *Compostellanum*, vol. 15, no. 3, 1970, pp. 387–419.

Barreiro, Xosé Luis and Óscar Parcero Oubiña, "A palabra e o silencio (II): Kierkegaard ou o eloxio do silencio" [The Word and Silence (II): Kierkegaard or the Praise of Silence], in *O Legado das luces* [The Legacy of the Enlightenment], ed. by Martín González and Luís R. Camarero, Santiago de Compostela: Universidade de Santiago de Compostela 2002, pp. 178–211.

Barrio Maestre, José María, "Kierkegaard y el escándalo moderno ante la fe" [Kierkegaard and the Modern Offense before Faith], *Folia Humanística*, vol. 26, no. 304, 1988, pp. 351–7.

Beldarrain, J.M., "La fe o la paradoja del absoluto en Kierkegaard" [Faith or the Paradox of the Absolute in Kierkegaard], *Ensayos*, vol. 49, 1967, pp. 35–8.

Bernaola, P., "La moral existencial de Søren Kierkegaard" [Søren Kierkegaard's Existential Ethics], *Ensayos*, vol. 49, 1967, pp. 20–3.

Bilbeny, Norbert, "Kierkegaard," in *Historia de la Ética*, vols. 1–3, ed. by Victoria Camps, Barcelona: Crítica 1992, vol. 2, pp. 522–46.

El Búho Filósofo, "Kierkegaard," in www.publicaciones.mundivia.es/smoreno (*Lycëum. Biografías*) n.d.

Calderer, Lluís, "Kierkegaard a Catalunya" [Kierkegaard in Catalonia], *El pou de lletres*, vol. 6, 1997, p. 48.

Canals Vidal, Francisco, "Kierkegaard," in *Textos de los grandes filósofos: Edad Contemporánea* [Texts of the Great Philosophers. The Contemporary Age], Barcelona: Herder 1974, pp. 29–61.

Cañas, José Luis, *Søren Kierkegaard. Entre la inmediatez y la relación* [Søren Kierkegaard. Between Immediacy and Relation], Madrid: Trotta 2003.

de Candamo, Luis G., "La influencia de lo circunstante en el pensamiento agónico de Kierkegaard" [The Influence of the Circumstantial in Kierkegaard's Agony of Thought], *El Español*, vol. 4, no. 144, 1945, p. 11.

Capanaga, Victorino, "Kierkegaard y el P. Abraham de Santa Clara" [Kierkegaard and Father Abraham of Santa Clara], *Mayéutica*, vol. 2, no. 4, 1976, pp. 61–6.

Careaga Guzmán, Virginia, *Kierkegaard: Ingenuidad y paradoja* [Kierkegaard: Ingenuity and Paradox], Ph.D. Thesis, San Sebastián: Universidad del País Vasco 1986.

— "De lo real a lo posible o de lo posible a lo real" [From the Real to the Possible or from the Possible to the Real], *Ágora*, no. 8, 1989 (Santiago de Compostela: Universidade de Santiago de Compostela), pp. 93–105.

— "El método de la evocación o la experiencia de lo arbitrario" [The Method of Evocation or the Experience of the Arbitrary], *Arc Voltaic*, no. 18, 1990, pp. 18–9.

Carrasco de la Vega, Rubén, "Origen del existencialismo: Alma y doctrina de Kierkegaard" [The Origin of Existentialism: The Soul and Doctrine of Kierkegaard], *Kollasuyo*, no. 10, 1951, pp. 50–61.

— "Eksistentialismens oprindelse: Sjælen i Kierkegaards lære" [The Origin of Existentialism: The Soul in Kierkegaard's Theory], *Exil*, vol. 3, 1968, pp. 1–10.

Carrillo Canán, Alberto, "Kierkegaard's Amphibolous Conjunction of Joy and Sorrow and his Literary Theory," *A Parte Rei*, no. 9, 2000 pp. 1–9.

Casariego Córdoba, Pedro, *El hidroavión de K* [K's Seaplane], Madrid: Ave del paraíso 1994.

Cassini de Vázquez, Maria Cristina, "Kierkegaard, el caballero de la fe" [Kierkegaard the Knight of Faith], *Sapienta*, no. 27, 1972, pp. 273–84.

Castilla del Pino, Carlos, "El concepto de gravedad en Kierkegaard" [The Concept of Earnestness in Kierkegaard], *Actas luso–españolas de neurología y psiquiatría*, vol. 2, 1950, pp. 33–7.

Castrosín, Carlos F., "El efecto Kierkegaard–Pennebaker" [The Kierkegaard–Pennebaker Effect], *Artífex*, Segunda Época, vol. 4, 2000.

Chacel, Rosa, "Kierkegaard y el pecado" [Kierkegaard and Sin"], *Sur*, no. 162, 1948 (Buenos Aires), pp. 71–96.

— *La Confesión* [The Confession], Barcelona: Edhasa 1971, see pp. 9–44.

Ciarlo, H.O., "La noción de instante y presencia en Kierkegaard" [The Notion of the Moment and Presence in Kierkegaard], *Philosophía*, 1961, pp. 34–43.

Collado, Jesús Antonio, *La existencia religiosa en Kierkegaard y su influencia en el pensamiento de Unamuno* [The Religious Existence in Kierkegaard and its Influence in Unamuno's Thought], Ph.D. Thesis, Facultad de Filosofía y Letras, Madrid 1961.

— *Kierkegaard y Unamuno. La existencia religiosa* [Kierkegaard and Unamuno. The Religious Existence], Madrid: Gredos 1962.

— "Notas de una existencia: Søren Kierkegaard" [Notes of an Existence: Søren Kierkegaard], *Atlántida*, vol. 2, 1964, pp. 198–204.

— "Unamuno y el existencialismo de Søren Kierkegaard" [Unamuno and Søren Kierkegaard's Existentialism], *Revista de la Universidad de Madrid*, vol. 13, nos. 49–50, 1964, pp. 145–61.

Colomer, Eusebi, "El postidealismo: Kierkegaard, Feuerbach, Marx, Nietzsche, Dilthey, Husserl, Scheler, Heidegger" [Postidealism: Kierkegaard, Feuerbach, Marx, Nietzsche, Dilthey, Husserl, Scheler, Heidegger], in *El pensamiento alemán de Kant a Heidegger* [German Thought from Kant to Heidegger], vols. 1–3, Barcelona: Herder, 1986–90, vol. 3 (1986), pp. 27–90.

Conde, R., "Kierkegaard y el existencialismo" [Kierkegaard and Existentialism], *Convivium*, vol. 2, no. 1 (Barcelona: Universitat de Barcelona) 1957, pp. 195–204.

Cruells, Antoni, "En torno a un fragmento del Diario de Søren Kierkegaard" [On a Fragment of Søren Kierkegaard's Diary], *Estudios Franciscanos*, vol. 80, 1979, pp. 91–100.

Daniel-Ropa, H. [Henry Jules Charles Petiot], "Un Pascal protestante: Søren Kierkegaard" [A Protestant Pascal: Søren Kierkegaard], *Folia humanística*, vol. 3, no. 29, 1965, pp. 385–90.

Díaz, Carlos, *Entre Atenas y Jerusalén. Los caminos de E. Brunner, H.U. von Balthasar, Xavier Zubiri, K. Wojtyla, G. Rovirosa, S. Kierkegaard* [Between Athens and Jerusalem. The Ways of E. Brunner, H.U. von Balthasar, Xavier Zubiri, K. Wojtyla, G. Rovirosa, S. Kierkegaard], Madrid: Sociedad de Educación de Atenas 1994.

— "La angustia de Kierkegaard y la nuestra" [Kierkegaard's Anxiety and Ours], in *El Concepto de la Angustia: 150 años después* [*The Concept of Anxiety*: 150 Years Later], ed. by María García Amilburu, Seville: Universidad de Sevilla 1995 (*Thémata*, vol. 15), pp. 123–46.

Dolby Múgica, María del Carmen, "San Agustín y Kierkegaard: dos filósofos religiosos" [Saint Augustine and Kierkegaard: Two Religious Philosophers], *Revista Agustiniana*, vol. 36, no. 111, 1995, pp. 791–807.

Drudis, Raimundo, "Las traducciones alemanas de Kierkegaard" [The German Translations of Kierkegaard], *Arbor*, vol. 33, no. 122, 1956, pp. 266–8.

Echegaray-Inda, Guillermo, *Debate sobre el yo. Hegel y Kierkegaard* [Debate on the Self. Hegel and Kierkegaard], Ph.D. Thesis, Universidad de Navarra, Pamplona 1992.

Estelrich i Artigues, Joan, "El sentiment tràgic de Søren Kierkegaard" [The Tragic Sense of Søren Kierkegaard], *La Revista*, vol. 4, nos. 74–9, 1918–19, pp. 4–7; pp. 354–7; pp. 376–8; pp. 392–3; pp. 406–9; pp. 425–8.

— "Kierkegaard dins del pensament nòrdic" [Kierkegaard in Nordic Thought], *La revista*, vol. 5, nos. 81–3, 1919, pp. 35–8; pp. 48–50; pp. 64–8.

— "Kierkegaard i Unamuno" [Kierkegaard and Unamuno], *La Revista*, vol. 5, no. 84, 1919, pp. 83–4.

— "Søren Kierkegaard," in his *Entre la vida i els llibres* [Between Life and Books], Barcelona: Llibreria Catalonia 1926, pp. 63–218.

— "Kierkegaard y Unamuno" [Kierkegaard and Unamuno], *Gaceta Literaria*, vol. 4, no. 78, 1930.

— "Experiència i elogi de la solitud. El retorn a Kierkegaard" [Experience and Praise of Solitude. Return to Kierkegaard], in *La nostra Terra* [Our Land], Mallorca 1936.

— "Kierkegaard en España" [Kierkegaard in Spain], *Destino*, August 9, 1947, p. 9.

Farré, Luis, "Unamuno, William James y Kierkegaard" [Unamuno, William James and Kierkegaard], *Cuadernos Hispanoamericanos*, no. 57, 1954, pp. 279–99 and no. 58, 1954, pp. 64–88.

— "Unamuno, William James y Kierkegaard" [Unamuno, William James and Kierkegaard] and "Hegel, Kierkegaard y dos españoles: Ortega y Gasset y Unamuno" [Hegel, Kierkegaard and Two Spaniards: Ortega y Gasset and

Unamuno], in *Unamuno, William James, Kierkegaard y otros ensayos* [Unamuno, William James, Kierkegaard and Other Essays], Buenos Aires: La Aurora 1967, pp. 17–97 and pp. 151–60.

Fernández, Clemente, "Kierkegaard (1813–1855)," in *Los Filósofos Modernos*, vols. 1–2, Madrid: Editorial Católica 1970, vol. 2, pp. 65–87.

Fernández Manzano, Juan A., "La lupa de Kierkegaard" [Kierkegaard's Magnifying Glass], in *La Ética, aliento de lo eterno. Homenaje al profesor Rafael A. Larrañeta Olleta* [Ethics, Breath of the Eternal, Homage to Professor Rafael A. Larrañeta Olleta], ed. by Luis Méndez Francisco, Salamanca and Madrid: Aletheia-Universidad Complutense 2003, pp. 517–24.

Ferrater Mora, Josep, "Kierkegaard, Søren Aabye," in *Diccionario de filosofía*, Mexico City: Atlante 1941 (republished, Buenos Aires: Editorial Sudamericana 1951, pp. 521–2; revised in Josep Ferrater Mora and Josep Mª Terricabras, *Diccionario de filosofía*, vols. 1–4, Barcelona: Ariel 1994, vol. 3, pp. 2012–17).

Ferrer Bonifaci, Consuelo, *Kierkegaard y el amor* [Kierkegaard and Love], Barcelona: Herder 1963.

Fontán Jubero, Pedro, "Søren Kierkegaard," in *Los existencialismos: Claves para su comprensión* [The Existentialists: Keys to Understanding], Madrid: Cincel 1985, pp. 39–56.

Franco Barrio, Jaime, "Un ejemplo de 'filosofía crítica' en el siglo XIX: Kierkegaard contra el hegelianismo" [An Example of "Critical Philosophy" in the Nineteenth Century: Kierkegaard against Hegelianism], *Studia Zamorensia*, vol. 6, 1985, pp. 155–72.

— *Kierkegaard frente al hegelianismo en el contexto de la filosofía decimonónica* [Kierkegaard against Hegelianism in the Context of Nineteenth Century Philosophy], Ph.D. Thesis, Universidad de Salamanca, Salamanca 1986.

— "Kierkegaard en el *Brand* de Ibsen" [Kierkegaard in Ibsen's *Brand*], *Estudios Agustinianos*, vol. 25, no. 1, 1990, pp. 47–87.

— *Kierkegaard frente al hegelianismo* [Kierkegaard in the face of Hegelianism], Valladolid: Universidad de Valladolid 1996.

Frutos Cortés, Eugenio, "La enseñanza de la verdad en Kierkegaard" [The Teaching of Truth in Kierkegaard], *Revista de Filosofía*, no. 9, 1950, pp. 91–8.

Funke, Gerhard, "Kierkegaard como pensador existencial" [Kierkegaard as Existential Thinker], *Atlántida*, vol. 5, no. 27, 1967, pp. 234–55.

García Amilburu, María, "La existencia humana en Kierkegaard" [Human Existence in Kierkegaard], in *El hombre: Inmanencia y Trascendencia* [Man: Immanence and Transcendence], vols. 1–2, ed. by Rafael Alvira, Pamplona: Universidad de Navarra 1991, vol. 2, pp. 863–80.

— *La existencia en Kierkegaard* [Existence in Kierkegaard], Pamplona: EUNSA 1992.

— "Kierkegaard y la comunicación indirecta. Algunos comentarios a *La Alternativa*" [Kierkegaard and Indirect Communication. Some Commentaries to *Either/Or*], *Tópicos. Revista de Filosofía*, vol. 3, no. 5, 1993 (Mexico City: Universidad Panamericana), pp. 113–39.

— (ed.), *El Concepto de la Angustia: 150 años después* [*The Concept of Anxiety*: 150 Years Later], Seville: Universidad de Sevilla 1995 (*Thémata*, vol. 15).

García Bacca, Juan David, "Kierkegaard y la filosofía contemporánea española" [Kierkegaard and Contemporary Spanish Philosophy], *Cuadernos americanos*, vol. 151, no. 2, (Mexico City) 1967, pp. 94–105.
García Chicón, Agustín, *La autenticidad como sustancia de la verdad. Influencia de Kierkegaard en Unamuno* [Authenticity as Substance of the Truth. Kierkegaard's Influence on Unamuno], Málaga: D. Juan de Austria 1987.
García González, Juan A., "Kierkegaard en Polo" [Kierkegaard in Polo], *Studia Poliana*, no. 6, 2004, pp. 85–98.
Gelabert, Martín, "Dimensión hermenéutica de la doctrina luterana de la justificación" [The Hermeneutic Dimension of the Lutheran Doctrine of Justification], in *El método en teología* [Method in Theology], Valencia: Facultad de Teología San Vicente Ferrer 1981, pp. 237–49.
— "El dogma como seguimiento. Reflexiones en torno a una polémica de Kierkegaard con Lutero" [Dogma as Path. Reflections on Kierkegaard's Polemic with Luther], *Estudios del Vedat*, vol. 11, 1981, pp. 219–38.
Giordani, Mário Curtis, "Kierkegaard, pensador religioso" [Kierkegaard, Religious Thinker], *Vozes*, no. 56, 1962, pp. 335–49.
Gómez de Liaño, Ignacio, "El instante decisivo" [The Decisive Moment], in *El Idioma de la Imaginación* [The Language of the Imagination], Madrid: Taurus 1982, pp. 413–42.
Goñi Zubieta, Carlos, "La ciència contra l'ètica i la fe en Søren Kierkegaard" [Science against Ethics and Faith in Søren Kierkegaard], *Ilerda Humanitats*, no. 48, 1990, pp. 85–9.
— *Tiempo y eternidad en Søren Kierkegaard* [Time and Eternity in Søren Kierkegaard], Ph.D. Thesis, Universitat de Barcelona, Barcelona 1994.
— *El valor eterno del tiempo: Introducción a Kierkegaard* [The Eternal Value of Time: Introduction to Kierkegaard], Barcelona: PPU 1996.
— "La comunicación de la 'verdad subjetiva' en Søren Kierkegaard" [The Communication of "Subjective Truth" in Søren Kierkegaard], *Espíritu*, vol. 46, no. 115, 1997, pp. 85–93.
— "Sócrates y Kierkegaard" [Socrates and Kierkegaard], *Espíritu*, vol. 50, no. 123, 2001, pp. 75–99.
González, Carlos N., *El problema de la comunicación en S. Kierkegaard* [The Problem of Communication in S. Kierkegaard], Ph.D. Thesis, Pontifica Universitas Gregoriana, Vatican City 1988.
González Álvarez, Ángel, "Kierkegaard y el existencialismo" [Kierkegaard and Existentialism], in his *El tema de Dios en la filosofía existencial* [The Idea of God and Existential Philosophy], Madrid: Instituto Luis Vives de filosofía 1945, pp. 67–102.
— "Kierkegaard y el existencialismo" [Kierkegaard and Existentialism], *Cisneros*, vol. 11, 1946, pp. 29–38.
González Caminero, Nemesio, "Miguel de Unamuno, precursor del existencialismo" [Miguel de Unamuno, Forerunner of Existentialism], *Pensamiento*, vol. 6, 1949, pp. 455–71.
González de Cardedal, Olegario, "Kierkegaard y el cristianismo en España" [Kierkegaard and Christianity in Spain], *Saber leer*, vol. 108, 1997, pp. 6–7.

— *La entraña del cristianismo* [The Entrails of Christianity], Salamanca: Secretariado Trinitario 1997.

González Porto, Bompiani, "Kierkegaard," in *Diccionario de autores*, vols. 1–3, Barcelona: Montaner y Simón 1963, vol. 2, pp. 497–501.

González Uribe, H., "Tres modelos de interioridad en la filosofía contemporánea: Kierkegaard, Marcel y Peter Wust" [Three Models of Inwardness in Modern Philosophy: Kierkegaard, Marcel and Peter Wust], *Revista de Filosofía*, vol. 20, nos. 58–9, 1987, pp. 91–104.

Gullón, Ricardo, "Imágenes del otro" [Images of the Other], *Revista Hispánica Moderna*, vol. 31 (New York: Columbia University), 1966, pp. 210–21.

Gurméndez, Carlos, "La resurrección de Kierkegaard en su propio país" [Kierkegaard's Resurrection in his own Country], *El País*, February 12, 1984, p. 6.

— "Los abismos de la angustia: de Kierkegaard a Bergamín" [Abysses of Anxiety: from Kierkegaard to Bergamín], in *La constitución social de la subjetividad* [The Social Constitution of Subjectivity], ed. by Eduardo Crespo and Carlos Soldevilla, Madrid: Catarata 2000, pp. 99–111.

Igual V., "Determinación del 'Yo' y su desesperación. Nota-Comentario a *La enfermedad mortal* de Kierkegaard" [Determination of the Self and its Despair. Note-Commentary to Kierkegaard's *The Sickness unto Death*], *Estudios del Vedat*, no. 4, 1975, pp. 345–57.

Jarauta Marión, Francisco, "Kierkegaard y Schleiermacher. Nota sobre su concepción de lo religioso" [Kierkegaard and Schleiermacher. Note on their Religious Conception], *Razón y Fábula*, nos. 33–4 (Bogotá: Universidad de los Andes), 1973, pp. 46–59.

— "Søren Kierkegaard, pensador subjetivo religioso" [Søren Kierkegaard, Subjective Religious Thinker], *Logos*, vol. 6 (Cali: Universidad del Valle), 1973, pp. 25–48.

— "La relación Kierkegaard–Schelling" [The Kierkegaard–Schelling Relation], *Eco*, no. 159 (Bogotá) 1974, pp. 279–92.

— "El Problema fundamental del 'Post-scriptum' de Søren Kierkegaard" [The Philosophical Problem of Søren Kierkegaard's *Postscript*], *Stromata*, vol. 31, nos. 3–4 (Buenos Aires) 1975, pp. 299–311.

— "Kierkegaard frente a Hegel" [Kierkegaard against Hegel], *Pensamiento*, vol. 31, no. 121, 1975, pp. 387–406.

— *Kierkegaard: los límites de la dialéctica del individuo* [Kierkegaard: the Limits of the Individual's Dialectics], Cali: Universidad del Valle 1975.

— "Nota sobre la recepción de Schelling por Kierkegaard" [Note on Kierkegaard's Reception of Schelling], in *Filosofía, Sociedad e Incomunicación. Homenaje a Antonio García Martínez* [Philosophy, Society and Isolation. Homage to Antonio García Martínez], ed. by José Luis L. Arangueren et al., Murcia: Universidad 1983, pp. 175–83.

Lago Bornstein, Juan Carlos, "Unamuno y Kierkegaard: dos espíritus hermanos" [Unamuno and Kierkegaard: Two Brother Spirits], *Anales del Seminario de Metafísica*, vol. 21, 1986, pp. 59–71.

Landsberg, Pablo Luis, "Reflexiones sobre Unamuno" [Reflections on Unamuno], *Cruz y Raya*, no. 31, 1935, pp. 7–54.

Larrañeta Olleta, Rafael, "La existencia como encrucijada dialéctica entre la filosofia y la fe. Un estudio sobre Søren Kierkegaard" [Existence as Dialectical Crossroad between Philosophy and Faith. A Study on Søren Kierkegaard], *Estudios Filosóficos*, no. 24, 1975, pp. 337–81 and no. 25, 1976, pp. 17–70.

— *Feuerbach y Kierkegaard. Significado teológico de dos interpretaciones críticas y antihegelianas de la religión* [Feuerbach and Kierkegaard. The Theological Meaning of Two Critical and Antihegelian Interpretations of Religion], Salamanca: Ciencia Tomista 1976.

— *La interioridad apasionada. El concepto de verdad y amor en la obra de Søren Kierkegaard* [Passionate Inwardness. The Concept of Truth and Love in the Work of Søren Kierkegaard], Ph.D. Thesis, Universidad de Salamanca, Salamanca 1988.

— *La interioridad apasionada. Verdad y amor en S. Kierkegaard* [Passionate Inwardness. Love and Truth in S. Kierkegaard], Salamanca: San Esteban-Universidad Pontificia 1990.

— "Kierkegaard, crítico de la modernidad" [Kierkegaard, Critic of Modernity], in *Crisis de la modernidad* [The Crisis of Modernity], Salamanca: Sociedad Castellano-Leonesa de Filosofía 1991, pp. 145–9.

— "Kierkegaard y Heidegger. La verdad de la filosofía" [Kierkegaard and Heidegger. Philosophy's Truth], in *Acercamiento a la obra de Martin Heidegger* [Approach to the Work of Martin Heidegger], ed. by Mariano Álvarez Gómez, Salamanca: Sociedad Castellano-Leonesa de Filosofía 1991, pp. 27–46.

— "Kierkegaard: Tragedia o Teofanía. Del sufrimiento inocente al dolor de Dios" [Kierkegaard: Tragedy or Theophany. From Innocent Suffering to the Grief of God], in *El Concepto de la Angustia: 150 años después* [*The Concept of Anxiety*: 150 Years Later], ed. by María García Amilburu, Seville: Universidad de Sevilla 1995 (*Thémata*, vol. 15), pp. 67–77.

— "Nietzsche y Kierkegaard: vuelta al origen" [Nietzsche and Kierkegaard: Back to the Origins], in *Conocer a Nietzsche* [Knowing Nietzsche], Salamanca: Sociedad Castellano-Leonesa de Filosofía 1996, pp. 259–71.

— "El verdadero rostro de Kierkegaard" [Kierkegaard's Real Face], *Revista de Filosofía*, vol. 10, no. 18, 1997, pp. 83–112.

— *Kierkegaard*, Madrid: Ediciones del Orto 1997.

— "Razón y religión en Søren Kierkegaard" [Reason and Religion in Søren Kierkegaard], *Contrastes*, vol. 3, 1997–8, pp. 147–67.

— "Hermenéutica del mito de la pena. Una lectura ricoeuriana de Hegel y Kierkegaard" [Hermeneutics of the Myth of Punishment. A Ricoeurian Reading of Hegel and Kierkegaard], *Contrastes*, vol. 4, 1999, pp. 273–83.

— "Seminario internacional sobre Kierkegaard" [International Seminar on Kierkegaard], *Contrastes*, vol. 4, 1999, pp. 231–4.

— "El poder revelador y liberador de la nada. Conato de retorno al Maestro Eckhart partiendo de Kierkegaard y Heidegger" [The Revealing and Liberating Power of Nothingness. An Attempt to Return to Meister Eckhart departing from Kierkegaard and Heidegger], in *Ética y Sociología. Estudio en memoria del profesor José Todolí O.P.* [Ethics and Sociology. Study in the Memory of Professor José Todolí O.P.], ed. by Luis Méndez Francisco, Madrid and Salamanca: Universidad Complutense de Madrid–San Esteban 2000, pp. 603–24.

— "La verdadera realidad en el 'Efterskrift' de Kierkegaard" [True Actuality in Kierkegaard's *Postscript*], *Il Singolo*, 2000, pp. 105–24.

— "Novedades kierkegaardianas en España" [Kierkegaardian News in Spain], *Estudios Filosóficos*, vol. 49, no. 141, 2000, pp. 329–32.

— *La lupa de Kierkegaard* [Kierkegaard's Magnifying Glass], Salamanca: San Esteban 2002.

Larrauri, Maite, "El teatro del devenir" [The Theatre of Becoming], in *Los Antihegelianos: Kierkegaard y Schopenhauer* [The Antihegelians: Kierkegaard and Schopenhauer], ed. by Javier Urdanibia, Barcelona: Anthropos 1990, pp. 64–80.

Llevadot, Laura, "L'educació de si mateix: Kierkegaard i l'art de la comunicació ètica" [The Education of Oneself: Kierkegaard and the Art of Ethical Communication], in *Un món de valors* [A World of Values], ed. by Josep Pallach, Girona: Institut de Ciències de la Educació 2003, pp. 65–79.

López Aranguren, José Luis, "Angustia, existencia y vitalidad" [Anxiety, Existence and Vitality], *Revista de la Universidad de Buenos Aires*, no. 7, 1948 (Buenos Aires).

— "Sobre el talante religioso de Miguel de Unamuno" [On the Religious Disposition of Miguel de Unamuno], *Arbor* vol. 11, no. 36, 1948, pp. 485–503.

— "Teología luterana y filósofos de nuestro tiempo" [Lutheran Theology and Contemporary Philosophers], *Escorial*, no. 56, 1949, pp. 59–82.

— "Exposición de Kierkegaard" [Exposition of Kierkegaard], *Cuadernos Hispanoamericanos*, no. 22, 1951, pp. 41–7.

— "Lutero en Kierkegaard" [Luther in Kierkegaard], in *Catolicismo y Protestantismo como formas de existencia*, Madrid: Revista de Occidente 1952, pp. 61–78.

— "El misterio de la Melancolía" [The Mystery of Melancholy], in *El descubrimiento de la intimidad y otros ensayos*, 3rd ed., Madrid: Aguilar 1958 [1952], pp. 137–55.

— "Luteranismo de Kierkegaard" [Kierkegaard's Lutheranism], in *Obras*, Madrid: Plenitud 1965, pp. 328–40 [*El protestantismo y la moral*, Madrid: Sapientia 1954].

López Quintás, Alfonso, "Los tres estadios en el camino de la vida, según Søren Kierkegaard" [The Three Stages on Life's Way, according to Søren Kierkegaard], in *Estrategia del lenguaje y manipulación del hombre*, Madrid: Narcea 1979, pp. 48–84.

— "Confrontación de la figura del hombre 'burlador' (Tirso), el 'estético' (Kierkegaard), el 'absurdo' (Camus)" [Comparison of the Figures of the "Trickster" (Tirso), the "Aesthetic" (Kierkegaard) and the "Absurd" (Camus) Man"], *Estudios*, vol. 37, nos. 132–5, 1981, pp. 337–80.

Maceiras Fafián, Manuel, *Schopenhauer y Kierkegaard. Sentimiento y pasión* [Schopenhauer and Kierkegaard. Feeling and Passion], Madrid: Cincel 1985.

Marías, Julián, *Miguel de Unamuno*, Madrid: Espasa-Calpe 1943, see p. 14; p. 22; pp. 24–5; p. 35; pp. 188–9.

Martínez Marzoa, Felipe, "Kierkegaard," in *Historia de la Filosofía*, vols. 1–2, Madrid: Istmo, 1994, vol. 2, pp. 225–7.

Mauri Álvarez, Margarita, "Søren Kierkegaard: las características de la vida ética" [Søren Kierkegaard: the Characteristics of Ethical Life], *Folia humanística*, vol. 31, no. 331, 1993, pp. 150–75.

Méndez Francisco, Luis (ed.), *La Ética, aliento de lo eterno. Homenaje al profesor Rafael A. Larrañeta Olleta* [Ethics, Breath of the Eternal, Homage to Professor Rafael A. Larrañeta Olleta], Salamanca and Madrid: Aletheia-Universidad Complutense 2003.

Morón Arroyo, Ciriaco, "Unamuno y Hegel," in *Miguel de Unamuno*, ed. by Antonio Sánchez Barbudo, Madrid: Taurus 1974, pp. 151–79.

Moscardo Ramis de Ayreflor, M. Francisca, *El tema religioso en la obra de S. Kierkegaard. Humanismo y cristianismo* [The Religious Topic in the Work of S. Kierkegaard. Humanism and Christianity], Ph.D. Thesis, Palma de Mallorca: Universitat de les Illes Balears 1990.

Narvarte, Cástor, "La fe cristiana contra la razón: Kierkegaard" [Christian Faith against Reason: Kierkegaard], in *Nihilismo y violencia. Ensayos sobre filosofía contemporánea* [Nihilism and Violence. Essays on Contemporary Philosophy], vols. 1–2, Donostia: Saturrarán 2003, vol. 1, pp. 189–321.

Navarra Ordoño, Andreu, "Unamuno, Nietzsche y Kierkegaard," *Babab*, no. 10, 2001.

Negre Rigol, Montserrat, "Fundamentación ontológica del sujeto en Kierkegaard" [Ontological Foundations of the Subject in Kierkegaard], *Anuario Filosófico*, vol. 21, no. 1, 1988, pp. 51–72.

— "El sueño y la vigilia. Reflexiones en torno al yo y el arte" [Sleep and Wakefulness. Reflections on the Self and Art], in *Pensar la vida cotidiana* [Thinking Daily Life], ed. by Carlos Baliñas and Marcelino Agís, Santiago de Compostela: Universidade de Santiago de Compostela 2001, pp. 177–86.

Ocaña García, Marcelino, "La razón del sí mismo kierkegaardiano en la sin–razón de la fe" [The Reason of the Kierkegaardian Self in the Non–Reason of Faith], *Aporía*, vol. 5, nos. 17–18, 1982, pp. 61–78.

— "Sujeto y Subjetividad en S. Kierkegaard" [Subject and Subjectivity in S. Kierkegaard], in *Anales del Seminario de Historia de la Filosofía*, vol. 5, 1985, pp. 59–80.

d'Ors, Eugeni, "Els llibres: el fullet de la Neotípia" [Books: Neotípia's Leaflet], *La veu de Catalunya*, December 21, 1908 (republished, *Obra catalana completa (Glosari 1906–1910)*, Barcelona: Selecta 1950, p. 900).

— "Albir i decisió" [Judgement and Decision], *La veu de Catalunya*, October 6, 1909 (republished, *Obra catalana completa (Glosari 1906–1910)*, Barcelona: Selecta 1950, p. 1140).

— "Bones coses" [Good Things], *La veu de Catalunya*, May 4, 1909 (republished, *Obra catalana completa (Glosari 1906–1910)*, Barcelona: Selecta 1950, p. 1023).

— "Elogi del Sant Rosari" [Eulogy of the Holy Rosary], *La veu de Catalunya*, December 7, 1909 (republished, *Obra catalana completa (Glosari 1906–1910)*, Barcelona: Selecta 1950, p. 1199).

— "Ètica" [Ethics], *La veu de Catalunya*, November 27, 1909 (republished, *Obra catalana completa (Glosari 1906–1910)*, Barcelona: Selecta 1950, p. 1187).

— "Imperialisme i lliberalisme" [Imperialism and Liberalism], *La veu de Catalunya*, July 10, 1909 (republished, *Obra catalana completa (Glosari 1906–1910)*, Barcelona: Selecta 1950, p. 1085).

— "No un alçament: una ascensió" [Not an Elevation: An Ascension], in *La veu de Catalunya*, May 7, 1910 (republished, *Glosari 1910–1911*, Barcelona: Quaderns crema 2003, p. 139).

— "Èxit" [Success], *La veu de Catalunya*, March 27, 1911 (republished, *Glosari 1910–1911*, Barcelona: Quaderns crema 2003, p. 560).

— "La festa dels manyans" [The Locksmiths' Party], *La veu de Catalunya*, December 1, 1911 (republished, *Glosari 1910–1911*, Barcelona: Quaderns crema 2003, p. 805).

— "La Sra. Verdaguer i Callés, noucentista" [Mrs. Verdaguer i Callés, Noucentist], *La veu de Catalunya*, December 14, 1911 (republished, *Glosari 1910–1911*, Barcelona: Quaderns crema 2003, p. 817).

Ortega y Gasset, José, *La idea de principio en Leibniz y la evolución de la teoría deductiva* [The Idea of Principle in Leibnitz and the Evolution of Deductive Theory], Buenos Aires: Emecé 1958, see p. 368; pp. 370–3; p. 389.

— *Prólogo para alemanes* [Prologue for Germans], Madrid: Taurus 1958 (published also, Madrid: Revista de Occidente 1974, pp. 58–60).

Padilla, Tarcisio M., "Kierkegaard y la 'philosophie de l'esprit'" [Kierkegaard and the "Philosophie de l'Esprit"], *Estudios*, vol. 20, 1964, pp. 377–96.

Palao, Antonio, "El absurdo de la fe" [The Absurdity of Faith], in *Los Antihegelianos: Kierkegaard y Schopenhauer* [The Antihegelians: Kierkegaard and Schopenhauer], ed. by Javier Urdanibia, Barcelona: Anthropos 1990, pp. 100–8.

Palomo-Lamarca, Antonio, "Existential Knots: Laing's Anti–Psychiatry and Kierkegaard's Existentialism," *A parte Rei*, no. 25, pp. 1–7.

Paucker, E. Krane, "Kierkegaardian Dread and Despair in Unamuno's 'El que se enterró,'" *Cuadernos de la Cátedra Miguel de Unamuno*, nos. 16–17, 1966–7, pp. 75–91.

Pegueroles, Joan, "Otra verdad, otra razón en Newman y Gadamer, Kierkegaard y Blondel" [Another Truth, Another Reason in Newman and Gadamer, Kierkegaard and Blondel], *Espíritu*, vol. 47, no. 117, 1998, pp. 37–46.

— "El concepto de Verdad en el 'Postscriptum' de Kierkegaard" [The Concept of Truth in Kierkegaard's *Postscript*], *Espíritu*, vol. 48, no. 120, 1999, pp. 199–204.

— "Amor, sufrimiento y alegría: Dios en el *Diario* de Kierkegaard" [Love, Suffering and Happiness: God in Kierkegaard's Diary], *Pensamiento*, vol. 56, no. 216, 2000, pp. 477–89.

— "El instante y el tiempo, el instante y la repetición, en el pensamiento de Kierkegaard" [The Moment and Time, the Moment and Repetition in Kierkegaard's Thought], *Espíritu*, vol. 49, no. 122, 2000, pp. 197–202.

— "La libertad y el bien, la libertad y la verdad, en *El Concepto de la Angustia* de Kierkegaard" [Freedom and the Good, Freedom and Truth in Kierkegaard's *The Concept of Anxiety*], *Espíritu*, vol. 49, no. 121, 2000, pp. 77–83.

— "La verdad del sujeto y de la existencia en el *Postscriptum* de Kierkegaard" [The Truth of the Subject and Existence in Kierkegaard's *Postscript*], *Espíritu*, vol. 50, no. 123, 2001, pp. 49–58.

— "La insoportable grandeza del hombre en el cristianismo, según Kierkegaard. Algunos textos del Diario" [The Unbearable Magnanimity of Man in Christianity, according to Kierkegaard. Some Texts from the Diary], *Espíritu*, vol. 51, no. 125, 2002, pp. 5–9.

— "La verdad objetiva y la verdad subjetiva en el *Postscriptum* de Kierkegaard" [Objective and Subjective Truth in Kierkegaard's *Postscript*], *Espíritu*, vol. 51, no. 126, 2002, pp. 273–6.

— "La relación del hombre con el Bien eterno en el *Postscriptum* de Kierkegaard" [Man's Relation to the Eternal Good in Kierkegaard's *Postscript*], *Espíritu*, vol. 52, no. 127, 2003, pp. 29–38.

Peñalver Gómez, Patricio, "Pseudonimia y responsabilidad" [Pseudonymity and Responsibility], *Postdata*, vol. 20, 1999.

— "Kierkegaard," in *La filosofía del siglo XIX*, ed. by José Luis Villacañas, Madrid: Trotta 2001, pp. 113–61.

Perarnau Vidal, Dolors, *El punto de vista sobre mi actividad como escritor*: tan sólo un punto de vista" [*The Point of View for My Work as an Author*: Only a Point of View], *Kierkegaardiana*, vol. 23, 2004, pp. 96–112.

Plazaola, Juan, "Estética y religión en Kierkegaard" [Aesthetics and Religion in Kierkegaard], *Estudios*, vol. 32, 1974, pp. 301–19.

Polo, Leonardo, "Kierkegaard, crítico de Hegel: la dialéctica como tedio y desesperación" [Kierkegaard, Critic of Hegel: Dialectic as Boredom and Despair], in *Hegel y el posthegelianismo* [Hegel and the Posthegelianism], 2nd ed., Pamplona: EUNSA 1999 [Peru: Universidad de Piura 1985], pp. 101–74.

— "Consideraciones en torno a lo ético y lo religioso en *Temor y Temblor*" [Considerations of the Ethical and the Religious in *Fear and Trembling*], *Tópicos. Revista de Filosofía* (Mexico City: Universidad Panamericana), vol. 3, no. 5, 1993, pp. 163–81.

Pons Juanpere, Joan Manuel, "El momento de la repetición (A propósito de la teoria de la conciencia en S. Kierkegaard)" [The Moment of Repetition (Speaking of the Theory of Conscience in S. Kierkegaard)], in *Los Antihegelianos: Kierkegaard y Schopenhauer* [The Antihegelians: Kierkegaard and Schopenhauer], ed. by Javier Urdanibia, Barcelona: Anthropos 1990, pp. 81–99.

Portabella Durán, P., "Kierkegaard," in *Psicología de Don Juan. Práctica del enamoramiento* [The Psychology of Don Juan. The Practice of the Lover], Barcelona: Zeus 1965.

Pòrtulas, Jaume, "Joan Estelrich o les retòriques de l'humanisme" [Joan Estelrich and Rhetoric of Humanism], *Els Marges*, no. 70, 2002, pp. 24–34.

Ramírez Marco, Antonio, *Individualidad y Soledad en S. Kierkegaard* [Individuality and Solitude in S. Kierkegaard], Ph.D. Thesis, Universidad de Murcia, Murcia 1996.

Ramos Varela, Antonio, "Notas en torno a Søren Kierkegaard: el concepto de la angustia y la categoría psicológica de la ambigüedad" [Notes on Søren Kierkegaard: the Concept of Anxiety and the Pyschological Category of Ambiguity], *Boletín de la Universidad de Santiago de Compostela*, vol. 5, no. 17, 1933, pp. 155–66.

Riezu, Jorge, "Kierkegaard y la ética de situación" [Kierkegaard and Situation Ethics], *Estudios filosóficos*, vol. 13, no. 33, 1964, pp. 219–52.

Roberts, Gemma, "El *Quijote*, clavo ardiente de la fe de Unamuno" [The *Quijote*, Burning Nail of Unamuno's Faith], *Revista Hispánica Moderna* (New York), vol. 32, no. 1, 1966, pp. 17–24.

— "Un modo de la existencia religiosa en *Paz en la guerra:* Una coincidencia con Kierkegaard" [A Way of Religious Existence in *Paz en la guerra:* A Coincidence with Kierkegaard], *Journal of Spanish Studies: Twentieth Century* (Kansas City), vol. 7, 1979, pp. 329–36.

— *Unamuno: afinidades y coincidencias kierkegaardianas* [Unamuno: Kierkegaardian Similarities and Coincidences], Colorado: Society of Spanish and Spanish–American Studies 1986.

Rodríguez Doval, Fernando, "El concepto de amor en el pensamiento y obra de Søren Kierkegaard" [The Concept of Love in Kierkegaard's Thought and Work], *Arbil*, no. 42, n.d.

Rodríguez Rosado, Juan José, *El tema de la nada en la filosofía existencial* [The Question of Nothingness in Existential Philosophy], Madrid: Escorial 1966, see pp. 19ff.

— "Teodicea y Nihilismo" [Theodicy and Nihilism], *Anuario Filosófico*, vol. 6, 1973, pp. 241–57.

— "La angustia existencial: 'Kierkegaard'" [The Existential Anxiety: "Kierkegaard"], in his *La aventura de existir*, Pamplona: EUNSA, 1976, pp. 38–43.

Rof Carballo, Xoán, "O problema do seductor en Kierkegaard, Proust e Rilke" [The Question of the Seducer in Kierkegaard, Proust and Rilke], *Cuadernos Hispanoamericanos*, vol. 35, nos. 102–3, 1958, pp. 5–30.

Rohatyn, Dennis A., "Kierkegaard sobre el argumento ontológico" [Kierkegaard on the Ontological Argument], *Pensamiento*, vol. 33, 1977, pp. 205–11.

— "Kierkegaard y sus críticos" [Kierkegaard and His Critics], *Folia Humanística*, vol. 24, 1986, pp. 317–36.

Rollan Sagrario, María del, "De la fe angustiada a las ansias de amor. Søren Kierkegaard y San Juan de la Cruz" [From Anxious Faith to the Longing for Love. Søren Kierkegaard and San Juan de la Cruz], *Diálogo Ecuménico*, no. 22, 1987, pp. 223–45.

Román, Miguel Ángel, "Kierkegaard: la paradoja como mediación" [Kierkegaard: The Paradox as Mediation], *Sappiens.com*, January 2004, pp. 1–24.

Sáez Tajafuerce, Begonya, "Autorrealización y temporalidad en *El concepto de la angustia*" [Self–Fulfilment and Temporality in *The Concept of Anxiety*], in *El Concepto de la Angustia: 150 años después* [*The Concept of Anxiety*: 150 Years Later], ed. by María García Amilburu, Seville: Universidad de Sevilla 1995 (*Thémata*, vol. 15), pp. 43–53.

— *Søren Kierkegaard: la seducció ètica* [Søren Kierkegaard: the Ethical Seduction], Ph.D. Thesis, Universitat Autònoma de Barcelona, Barcelona 1997.

— (ed.), *Enrahonar*, no. 29, 1998 (Barcelona: Universitat Autònoma de Barcelona, special issue on Kierkegaard).

— "Kierkegaard: den *etiske* forførelse" [Kierkegaard: The *Ethical* Seduction], in *Studier i Stadier*, ed. by Joakim Garff, Tony Aagaard Olesen and Pia Søltoft, Copenhagen: C.A. Reitzel 1998, pp. 88–101.

— "Lectures de Kierkegaard" [Readings of Kierkegaard], *Enrahonar*, no. 29, 1998, pp. 9–16.

— "Realidad y racionalidad kierkegaardianas: la curvatura ética de la subjetividad" [Kierkegaardian Reality and Rationality: the Ethical Curvature of Subjectivity], *Daimon*, no. 16, 1998, pp. 171–8.

— "Søren Kierkegaard's Ethical Seduction: 'Yours, yours, I am yours, your curse,'" *Ukrainska Kierkegaardiana* (Lviv), vol. 1 1998, pp. 104–14.

— "Works of Love: Modernity or Antiquity?" *Kierkegaard Studies. Yearbook*, 1998, pp. 60–76.

— "*A Literary Review*: A Rhetorical Experiment or 'Watchman, Hallo!'" *Kierkegaard Studies. Yearbook*, 1999, pp. 50–70.

— "Rhetoric in *Works of Love* or No Sooner Said than Done," in *Works of Love*, ed. by Robert L. Perkins, Macon, Georgia: Mercer University Press 1999 (*International Kierkegaard Commentary*, vol. 16), pp. 305–37.

— "'We want to see action!' On Kierkegaard's Ethical Interpretation," *Kierkegaardiana*, vol. 20, 1999, pp. 97–110.

— "Kierkegaard Seduction, or the Aesthetic actio(nes) in distans," *Diacritics*, vol. 30, no. 1, 2000 (Baltimore: John Hopkins University), pp. 78–88.

— "Principia Translationis," *Kierkegaard Studies. Yearbook*, 2000, pp. 383–95.

— "Søren Kierkegaard, el lletraferit" [Søren Kierkegaard, Man of Letters], in *Filosofia iArxiu*, 2000, pp. 39–49.

— "Palabra de Job" [Job's Word], in *La Ética, aliento de lo eterno. Homenaje al profesor Rafael A. Larrañeta Olleta* [Ethics, Breath of the Eternal, Homage to Professor Rafael A. Larrañet Olleta], ed. by Luis Méndez Francisco, Salamanca and Madrid: Aletheia–Universidad Complutense 2003, pp. 335–41.

Salamone, Maria Antonietta, "La interioridad apasionada, Verdad y amor en Søren Kierkegaard" [Passionate Inwardness. Love and Truth in Søren Kierkegaard], in *La Ética, aliento de lo eterno. Homenaje al profesor Rafael A. Larrañeta Olleta* [Ethics, Breath of the Eternal, Homage to Professor Rafael A. Larrañeta Olleta], ed. by Luis Méndez Francisco, Salamanca and Madrid: Aletheia-Universidad Complutense 2003, pp. 493–506.

San Miguel, José R., "En torno a Kierkegaard: Posibilidad y sentido de una teología en el existencialismo" [On Kierkegaard: Possibility and Sense of a Theology in Existentialism], *Crisis* vol. 4, no. 16, 1957, pp. 433–45.

Sánchez Barbudo, Antonio, "La intimidad de Unamuno: Relaciones con Kierkegaard y W. James" [Unamuno's Intimacy: Relations to Kierkegaard and W. James], *Occidental* (New York), no. 7, 1949, pp. 10–3.

— "La formación del pensamiento de Unamuno. Una experiencia decisiva: La crisis de 1897" [The Development of Unamuno's Thought. A Decisive Experience: The Crisis of 1897], *Hispanic Review*, vol. 18, 1950 (Pennsylvania), pp. 218–43.

— "Unamuno y Kierkegaard" [Unamuno and Kierkegaard] and "Diferencia entre Unamuno y Kierkegaard" [The Difference between Unamuno and Kierkegaard], in his *Estudios sobre Unamuno y Machado*, Madrid: Guadarrama 1959, pp. 65–79 and pp. 189–93.

Serrano, Susan, *The Will as Protagonist: The Role of the Will in the Existentialist Writings of Miguel de Unamuno: Affinities and Divergencies with Kierkegaard and Nietzsche*, Seville: Padilla Libros 1996.

Shein, L. J., "El concepto kierkegaardiano de temor en relación con el yo" [Kierkegaard's Concept of Dread in Relation to the Self], *Folia Humanística*, vol. 15, no. 172, 1977, pp. 297–306.

Sotiello, Gabriel de, "Cristianismo y mundanidad. Algunos aspectos del pensamiento religioso de Kierkegaard" [Christianity and Worldliness. Some Aspects of Kierkegaard's Religious Thought], *Naturaleza y Gracia*, no. 3, 1956, pp. 93–118.

Suances Marcos, Manuel, *Søren Kierkegaard, tomo I: Vida de un filósofo atormentado* [Søren Kierkegaard, vol. I: Life of a Tormented Philosopher], Madrid: UNED 1997.

— *Søren Kierkegaard, tomo II: Trayectoria de su pensamiento filosófico* [Søren Kierkegaard, vol. II: Trajectory of His Philosophical Thought], Madrid: UNED 1998.

— "El irracionalismo existencial de Søren Kierkegaard" [Søren Kierkegaard's Existential Irrationalism], in *El irracionalismo*, vols. 1–2, ed. by Manuel Suances Marcos and Alicia Villar Ezcurra, Madrid: Síntesis 2000, vol. 2, pp. 81–164.

— "El problema kierkegaardiano de 'la espina clavada en la carne'" [The Kierkegaardian Problem of "The Thorn in the Flesh"], *El Garabato*, no. 12, 2000 (Mexico City), pp. 18–20.

— *Søren Kierkegaard: III Estructura de su pensamiento religioso* [Søren Kierkegaard: III The Structure of His Religious Thought], Madrid: UNED 2003.

— "La solidaridad en el pensamiento de Kierkegaard" [Solidarity in Kierkegaard's Thought"], *Volubilis*, vol. 11, 2003, pp. 178–87.

— "El fundamento de la solidaridad en Kierkegaard" [Foundations of Solidarity in Kierkegaard], in *Pensar la Solidaridad*, ed. by Alicia Villar Ezcurra et. al., Madrid: Universidad Pontificia de Comillas 2004, pp. 287–344.

Tornos, Andrés M., "Sobre Unamuno y Kierkegaard" [On Unamuno and Kierkegaard], *Pensamiento*, vol. 18, 1962, pp. 131–46.

Torralba, Francesc, *Dios, individuo y libertad. La lírica–dialéctica de Kierkegaard* [God, Individual and Freedom. Kierkegaard's Lyrics–Dialectics], Ph.D. Thesis, Universitat de Barcelona, Barcelona 1992.

— "El individuo como testimonio de la verdad" [The Individual as Witness to the Truth], *Analogía* (Mexico City), vol. 1, 1992, pp. 41–60.

— "Kierkegaard en el universo de las máscaras" [Kierkegaard in the Universe of the Masks], *Espíritu*, no. 106, 1992, pp.153–66.

— "Las raíces kantianas de la ontología de J. Climacus" [The Kantian Roots of J. Climacus' Ontology], *Studium*, vol. 32, 1992, pp. 419–30.

— *Punt d'inflexió. Lectura de Kierkegaard* [Point of Inflection. A Reading of Kierkegaard], Lleida: Pagès Editors 1992.

— *Amor y diferencia. El misterio de Dios en Kierkegaard* [Love and Difference. The Mystery of God in Kierkegaard], Barcelona: PPU 1993.

— "La esencia de la música según Kierkegaard" [The Essence of Music according to Kierkegaard], *Estudios Filosóficos*, no. 120, 1993, pp. 363–80.

— "Les arrels bíbliques del pensament kierkegaardià" [Biblical Roots of Kierkegaardian Thought], *Butlletí de l'Associació Bíblica de Catalunya*, no. 44, 1993, pp. 19–25.

— "Necesidad, posibilidad y libertad. Comentario a Kierkegaard" [Necessity, Possibility and Freedom. Commentary to Kierkegaard], *Paideia*, no. 14, 1993, pp. 65–71.

— "Santo Tomás y Kierkegaard ante el dilema abrahámico" [Saint Thomas and Kierkegaard before Abraham's Dilemma], *Pensamiento*, vol. 50, no. 196, 1994, pp. 75–94.

— "Cuando la oración se hace lírica. La espiritualidad de Kierkegaard" [When Prayer becomes Lyrical. Kierkegaard's Spirituality], *Phase*, no. 210, 1995, pp. 499–512.

— "Cristologia de Kierkegaard" [Kierkegaard's Christology], *Revista catalana de Teologia* vol. 20, no. 1, 1995, pp. 103–53.

— "Igualdad (Ligelighed) y diferencia (Forskel). En torno a la comunidad fraternal de Søren Kierkegaard" [*Ligelighed* and *Forskel*. On Søren Kierkegaard's Fraternal Community], *Sapientia* vol. 50, nos. 195–6, 1995 (Buenos Aires), pp. 59–78.

— "Kierkegaard: L'escriptura al servei del cristianisme" [Kierkegaard: Writing in the Service of Christianity], *Questions de Vida Cristiana*, vol. 181, 1996, pp. 38–49.

— "Kierkegaard desfet en paràgrafs" [Kierkegaard Cut up into Paragraphs], *El pou de lletres*, vol. F6, 1997, pp. 45–7.

— "Kierkegaard: Ironia i subjectivitat" [Kierkegaard: Irony and Subjectivity], *El pou de lletres*, vol. F6, 1997, pp. 43–4.

— "Teologia de l'angoixa. Kierkegaard i Urs von Balthasar" [Theology of Anxiety. Kierkegaard and Urs von Balthasar], in *Fe i teologia en la història. Estudis en honor del prof. Dr. Evangelista Vilanova* [Faith in Theology and History. Studies in Honor of Prof. Dr. Evangelista Vilanova], ed. by Joan Busquets and Maria Martinell, Barcelona: Abadia de Montserrat 1997, pp. 449–56.

— "El camí de la infantesa: Teresa de Lisieux, Kierkegaard e Nietzsche" [The Path of Childhood: Teresa de Lisieux, Kierkegaard and Nietzsche], in *Teresa de Lisieux: Déu en la vida de cada dia* [Teresa de Lisieux: God in Everyday Life], ed. by Agustí Borrell, Barcelona: Abadia de Montserrat 1998, pp. 173–95.

— "Kierkegaard, el heredero moderno de la mayéutica socrática" [Kierkegaard, the Modern Inheritor of the Socratic Maieutic], *Espíritu*, vol. 47, no. 117, 1998, pp. 55–69.

— "Lectura de la postmodernitat amb Kierkegaard" [Reading of Postmodernism with Kierkegaard], *Urc*, vol. 12, 1998, pp. 47ff.

— *Poética de la libertad. Lectura de Kierkegaard* [Poetics of Freedom. A Reading of Kierkegaard], Madrid: Caparrós 1998.

— "AntiClimacus: El desgarro del yo" [Anti-Climacus: the Split of the Self], *Tres al cuarto*, no. 6, 1999, pp. 41–4.

— "Comunicació (Meddelelse), primitivitat (Primitivitet) i reduplicació (Fordoblelse). Lectura de *La dialèctica de la comunicació ètica i ètico-religiosa* (1847) de S. Kierkegaard" [*Meddelelse, Primitivitet* and *Fordoblelse*. A Reading of Søren

Kierkegaard's "The Dialectic of Ethical and Ethical-Religious Comunication (1847)" (in *Pap.* VIII–2 B 79–89)], *Comprendre*, vol. 1, no. 2, 1999, pp. 19–40.

— "El lenguaje de la fe y del culto. A vueltas con Kierkegaard y Wittgenstein" [The Language of Faith and Worship. Going on about Kierkegaard and Wittgenstein], *Phase* vol. 39, no. 232, 1999, pp. 327–42.

— "Individualidad versus globalización. De nuevo, Kierkegaard" [Individuality versus Globalization. Again, Kierkegaard], *El garabato*, no. 12, 2000 (Mexico City), pp. 6–7.

— "Déu i l'eclipsi de les icones. Dues postil·les a Kierkegaard" [God and the Eclipse of Icons. Two Postscripts to Kierkegaard], *Ars Brevis*, vol. 8, 2002, pp. 203–15.

— "Kierkegaard," in *Història del pensament cristià. Quaranta figures* [History of Christian Thought. Forty Figures], ed. by Pere Lluís Font, Barcelona: Proa 2002, pp. 747–76.

— *Kierkegaard en el laberinto de las máscaras* [Kierkegaard in the Labyrinth of Masks], Madrid: Fundación Emmanuel Mounier 2003.

Torres Queiruga, Andrés, "A revelación como maiéutica histórica" [Revelation as Historical Maieutic], in his *A revelación de Deus na realización do home* [The Revelation of God in the Realization of Man], Vigo: Galaxia 1985.

— "Deus e a Historia Bíblica. Do Terror de Isaac ó Abbá de Xesús" [God and Biblical History. From Isaac's Terror to Jesus' Abba], in his *Do Terror de Isaac ó Abbá de Xesús* [From Isaac's Fright to Jesus's "Abba"], Vigo: SEPT 1999.

Unamuno y Jugo, Miguel de, "El 'alma' de Manuel Machado" [Manuel Machado's "Soul"], *Heraldo de Madrid*, March 19, 1901 (reissued in *Libros y autores españoles contemporáneos (1898–1936)*, in *Obras completas*, vols. 1–16, Madrid: Afrodisio Aguado 1951–60, vol. 5, 1952, pp. 194 passim).

— "Los naturales y los espirituales" [Naturals and Spirituals] (1905), in *Ensayos* [Essays], vols. 1–2, Madrid: Aguilar 1945 vol. 1, pp. 625–43.

— "Sobre la erudición y la crítica" [On Erudition and Criticism] (1905), in *Ensayos*, vols. 1–2, Madrid: Aguilar 1945, vol. 1, pp. 701–22.

— "Soledad" [Solitude] (1905), in *Ensayos*, vols. 1–2, Madrid: Aguilar 1945, vol. 1, pp. 681–99.

— "El secreto de la vida" [The Secret of Life] (1906), in *Ensayos*, vols. 1–2, Madrid: Aguilar 1945, vol. 1, pp. 817–30.

— "Ibsen y Kierkegaard" [Ibsen and Kierkegaard], in *Los Lunes de El Imparcial*, 1907 (reissued in *Mi religión y otros ensayos breves*, Madrid: Biblioteca Renacimiento 1910, pp. 67–75).

— "Verdad y vida" [Truth and Life] (1908), in *Ensayos*, vols. 1–2, Madrid: Aguilar 1945, vol. 2, pp. 373–80.

— "Un filósofo del sentido común" [A Philosopher of Common Sense] (1910), in *Ensayos*, vols. 1–2, Madrid: Aguilar 1945, vol. 2, p. 1075–83.

— "Sobre la tumba de Costa" [On Costa's Tomb] (1911), in *Ensayos*, vols. 1–2, Madrid: Aguilar 1945, vol. 1, pp. 909–25.

— *Soliloquios y conversaciones* [Essays and Soliloquies], in *Ensayos*, vols. 1–2, Madrid: Aguilar 1945, vol. 2, p. 530; p. 583; pp. 660–1 [Madrid: Renacimiento 1911].

— "Contra esto y aquello" [Against This and That], in *Ensayos*, vols. 1–2, Madrid: Aguilar 1945, vol. 2, p. 1080; p. 1107; p. 1147 [Madrid: Renacimiento 1912].
— *Del sentimiento trágico de la vida en los hombres y en los pueblos* [The Tragic Sense of Life in Men and Nations], Madrid: Renacimiento 1912, see p. 7; pp. 111–13; pp. 117–18; p. 124; p. 154; pp. 176–7, p. 197; p. 253; p. 280; p. 318.
— *Sensaciones de Bilbao* [Sensations from Bilbao], in *Obras completas*, vols. 1–16, Madrid: Afrodisio Aguado 1951–60, vol. 1, 1951, see p. 817 [Bilbao: Editorial Vasca 1922].
— *L'agonie du christianisme* [The Agony of Christianity], trans. from an unpublished Spanish text by Jean Cassou, Paris: F. Rieder 1925 (republished in *Ensayos*, vols. 1–2, Madrid: Aguilar 1945, vol. 1, see p. 943).
— "Forord" [Preface], in *Den tragiske Livsfølelse hos Mennesker og Folkeslag* [Danish translation of *Del sentimiento trágico de la vida*], Copenhagen: Haase 1925, pp. 5–6.
— *San Manuel Bueno, mártir, y tres historias más* [Saint Manuel Bueno, Martyr], Madrid: Espasa-Calpe 1933 (published also, Madrid: Espasa-Calpe 1942, see p. 90).
— "A Federico Urales" [Letter to Federico Urales], in Federico Urales, *Evolución de la filosofía en España* [The Development of Spanish Philosophy], vols. 1–2, Barcelona: Revista Blanca 1934, vol. 2, pp. 205–9.
— "Carta a Clarín" [Letter to Clarín], in *Epistolario a Clarín*, Madrid: Escorial 1941.
Urbina, Pedro Antonio, *Søren Kierkegaard: el seductor* [Søren Kierkegaard: The Seducer], Seville: Universidad de Sevilla 1975.
Urdanibia, Javier (ed.), "Introducción: Dos Antihegelianos. De Estética Y Ascética" [Two Antihegelians. On Aesthetics and Asceticism], in his (ed.), *Los Antihegelianos: Kierkegaard y Schopenhauer* [The AntiHegelians: Kierkegaard and Schopenhauer], Barcelona: Anthropos 1990, pp. 9–33.
— "La proximidad de lo lejano" [The Proximity of the Distant], in his (ed.), *Los Antihegelianos: Kierkegaard y Schopenhauer* [The AntiHegelians: Kierkegaard and Schopenhauer], Barcelona: Anthropos 1990, pp. 37–63.
— *Los Antihegelianos: Kierkegaard y Schopenhauer* [The AntiHegelians: Kierkegaard and Schopenhauer], Barcelona: Anthropos 1990.
Urdanoz, Teófilo, "Kierkegaard," in *Siglo XIX: Socialismo, materialismo y positivismo*, Madrid: Editorial Católica 1975 (Guillermo Fraile and Teófilo Urdanoz, *Historia de la filosofía* vols. 1–8, Madrid: Editorial Católica, 1966–85, vol. 5, 1975), pp. 422–81.
Urmeneta, Fermín de, "Glosas al centenario de Kierkegaard" [Glosses to Kierkegaard's Centenary], *Las Ciencias*, vol. 21, no. 2, 1956, pp. 273–8.
— "Sobre estética Kierkegaardiana" [On Kierkegaardian Aesthetics], *Revista de Ideas Estéticas* vol. 30, no. 119, Instituto Diego Velázquez, Madrid 1972, pp. 233–6.
Uscatescu, Jorge, "Kierkegaard e Unamuno o l'interiorità segreta" [Kierkegaard and Unamuno or the Secret Inwardness], *Città di Vita* (Florence), vol. 5, 1978, pp. 347–62.
— "Unamuno y Kierkegaard" [Unamuno and Kierkegaard], *ABC*, August 18, 1978.

— "Encuentro con Kierkegaard" [Encounter with Kierkegaard], *El País*, September 21, 1979.
— "Unamuno y Kierkegaard o la interioridad secreta" [Unamuno and Kierkegaard or the Secret Inwardness], *Arbor*, vol. 103, nos. 403–4, 1979, pp. 25–40.
— "Kierkegaard et Unamuno ou l'interiorité secrète" [Kierkegaard and Unamuno or the Secret Inwardness], in *Kierkegaard Serie Obliques*, Paris: Luxe, 1981, pp. 104–17.
— *Agustín, Nietzsche, Kierkegaard. Nuevas lecturas de filosofía y filología* [Augustine, Nietzsche, Kierkegaard. New Readings of Philosophy and Philology], Madrid: Forja 1983.
— "Unamuno y Kierkegaard. Medio siglo después de la muerte de Unamuno, 1936–1986" [Unamuno and Kierkegaard. Half a Century After Unamuno's Death, 1936–1986], *Filosofia Oggi* (Geneve), vol. 9, nos. 3–4, 1986, pp. 475–86.
— "Unamuno y Kierkegaard" [Unamuno and Kierkegaard], *Cuadernos Hispanoamericanos*, nos. 440–1, 1987, pp. 283–93.
Valádez, Leticia, "La crítica a la mundanidad en *El concepto de la angustia*" [The Critic of Worldliness in *The Concept of Anxiety*], in *El Concepto de la Angustia: 150 años después* [*The Concept of Anxiety*: 150 Years Later], ed. by María García Amilburu, Seville: Universidad de Sevilla 1995 (*Thémata*, vol. 15), pp. 99–108.
Vall i Solaz, F. Xavier, "Aproximació a la influència de l'existencialisme en la literatura catalana de postguerra" [Approximation to Existentialism's Influence on Postwar Catalan Literature], in *Els anys de la postguerra a Catalunya (1939–1959)*, Barcelona: Abadia de Montserrat 1994 (*Cicle de conferències fet al CIC de Terrassa*, curs 1987–8), pp. 59–72.
— "L'existencialisme als Països Catalans abans de la postguerra" [Existentialism in the Catalan Countries before the Postwar Era], *Revista de Catalunya* no. 112, Segona etapa, 1996, pp. 156–64.
— "Joan Fuster i l'existencialisme" [Joan Fuster and Existentialism], in Claude Benoit et al., *Les literatures catalana en francesa al llarg del segle XX. Les littératures catalane et française au XXème siècle* [Catalan Literature in French in the Twentieth Century], Barcelona: Abadia de Montserrat 1997 (Primer congrés internacional de literatura comparada, València 15–18 abril 1997), pp. 367–84.
— "Llorenç Villalonga i l'existencialisme" [Llorenç Villalonga and Existentialism], *Els Marges*, no. 62, 1998, pp. 105–16.
Valverde, José María, "Kierkegaard: correctivo del Cristianismo, adversario de la Cristiandad" [Kierkegaard: Christianity's Corrective, Christendom's Opponent], in *La entrada en el siglo XX* in *Historia de la literatura universal*, vols. 1–10, ed. by Martín de Riquer and José María Valverde, Barcelona: Planeta 1984–6, vol. 8, 1986, pp. 94–105 and pp. 126–33.
— "Algo más de Kierkegaard" [Something else of Kierkegaard], *Saber leer*, no. 68, 1993, pp. 1–2.
— "Kierkegaard: la dificultad del cristianismo" [Kierkegaard: The Difficulty of Christianity], in *Filosofía de la religión. Estudios y textos* [Philosophy of Religion. Studies and Texts], ed. by Manuel Fraijó, Madrid: Trotta 1994, pp. 265–90.
Vasseur, Álvaro Armando, *Soren Kierkegaard*, Madrid: Editorial América 1918.

— "La potencia trágica. Don Javier de Urrazuno" [The Tragic Power. Don Javier de Urrazuno], in *Gloria. Aventuras peregrinas*, Madrid: Editorial América 1919, pp. 229–43.

Vázques, Mária Cristina Cassins de, "Kierkegaard, el caballero de la fe" [Kierkegaard, the Knight of Faith], *Sapienta*, no. 27, 1972, pp. 273–84.

Vermal Beretta, J.L., "La crítica de la concepción idealista del sujeto en *La enfermedad mortal* de Kierkegaard" [The Critic of the Idealistic Conception of the Subject in Kierkegaard's *The Sickness unto Death*], *Sa Taula*, nos. 7–8, Palma de Mallorca: Universitat de les Illes Balears 1987, pp. 205–12.

Vidal Auladell, Felip, "Sentido y proyección comunitaria del caballero abrahámico en Kierkegaard" [The Memory and Communitarian Projection of the Abrahamic Knight in Kierkegaard], *A Parte Rei*, no. 25, pp. 1–3.

Vidiella, Jorge, *De Kierkegaard a Sartre. El existencialismo* [From Kierkegaard to Sartre. Existentialism], Barcelona: Bruguera 1963.

Villacañas, José Luis, "Kierkegaard, filósofo de la comunicación" [Kierkegaard, Philosopher of Communication], in *Historia de la filosofía contemporánea*, Madrid: Akal 1997, pp. 61–80.

Xirau, Ramon, "Kierkegaard o de la pasión por la existencia" [Kierkegaard or the Passion for Existence], in *Introducción a la Historia de la Filosofía*, 3rd ed., México City: UNAM 1971, pp. 332–40 [1964].

Xirau, Ramón, Alastair McKinnon and Basilio Rojo, "Mesa Panel sobre Temor y Temblor" [Panel Board on *Fear and Trembling*], *Tópicos. Revista de Filosofía*, vol. 3, no. 5, Mexico: Universidad Panamericana 1993 (special issue on Kierkegaard, *Las publicaciones de Søren Kierkegaard de 1843*), pp. 183–97.

Zanovello, Nevio, "Cristiandad y Cristianismo en Kierkegaard" [Christendom and Christianity in Kierkegaard], *Religión y Cultura*, no. 22, 1976, pp. 113–41.

— "El subjetivismo ético–religioso de S. Kierkegaard" [The Ethical-Religious Subjectivism of S. Kierkegaard], *Religión y Cultura*, vol. 25, no. 111, 1979, pp. 463–476.

III. Secondary Literature on Kierkegaard's Reception in Spain

Bacca, Juan David García, "Kierkegaard y la filosofía contemporánea española" [Kierkegaard and Contemporary Spanish Philosophy], *Quadernos Americanos*, no. 151, 1967, pp. 94–105.

Estelrich i Artigues, Joan, "Bibliografia de S. Kierkegaard" [S. Kierkegaard Bibliography], *La Revista*, vol. 5, no. 85, 1919, pp. 106–8.

Franco Barrio, Jaime, "Kierkegaard en español" [Kierkegaard in Spanish], *Azafea*, no. 2, 1989, pp. 211–34.

González, Darío, "Sur quelques moments de la réception de *Frygt og Bæven* et *Gjentagelsen* en espagnol" [On Some Moments of the Spanish Reception of *Fear and Trembling* and *Repetition*], *Kierkegaard Studies. Yearbook*, 2002, pp. 353–63.

Larrañeta, Rafael, "Recepción y actualidad de Kierkegaard en España" [The Reception and Topicality of Kierkegaard in Spain], *Estudios Filosóficos*, vol. 37, no. 105, 1988, pp. 317–46.

— "Novedades kierkegaardianas en España" [Kierkegaard Novelties in Spain], *Estudios filosóficos*, vol. 49, 2000, pp. 329–32.

Sáez Tajafuerce, Begonya, "Recent Spanish and Italian Literature on *Works of Love*," *Kierkegaard Studies. Yearbook*, 1998, pp. 199–212.

Valls, Álvaro L.M., "*The Concept of Anxiety* in Spanish and Portuguese" in *Kierkegaard Studies. Yearbook*, 2001, pp. 335–40.

Italy:
From a Literary Curiosity to a Philosophical Comprehension

Ingrid Basso

I.

"Nobody or almost nobody in Italy knows S. Kierkegaard apart from the name. Still, this vigorous and singular preacher of deeper lives and more certain choices could be an educator for us as he was for his fellow Danes."[1] Preceded by these words, Kierkegaard, in 1906, made his entry into the Italian cultural world, through the mediation of the Danish scholar and philosopher Harald Høffding (1843–1931), whose brief essay on Kierkegaard as "a descendant of Hamlet" was published in the the Italian review *Leonardo*. Founded in Florence only three years before by the men of letters Giovanni Papini (1881–1956) and Giuseppe Prezzolini (1882–1982), *Leonardo* set itself the aim of opposing what it called "academicism." As Eugenio Garin, one of the most important scholars of humanistic thought in Italy supposes, it was in all probability Papini who wrote these words which introduce Høffding's essay.[2] At that time indeed, Papini was in touch with the Danish scholar Knud Ferlov (1881–1977). Thanks to the latter, the Italian translation of Kierkegaard's "The Unhappiest One," from *Either/Or*, also appeared in *Leonardo* in 1907.[3]

Nevertheless, as Garin informs us,[4] Høffding's article—as well as the chapter on Kierkegaard in his *History of Modern Philosophy*, which was translated into Italian in the same year[5]—was not exactly the first appearance of Kierkegaard in Italy. The first treatment of the Danish philosopher dates back to 1904, even if it was only

---

[1]   See the Introduction to Harald Høffding's article, "Un discendente di Amleto. Søren Kierkegaard," *Leonardo*, vol. 3. no. 6, 1906, pp. 65–79.
[2]   Eugenio Garin, "Kierkegaard in Italia," *Rivista Critica di Storia della Filosofia*, vol. 28, 1973, p. 453.
[3]   "Il più infelice," trans. by Knud Ferlov, *Leonardo*, vol. 5, no. 3, 1907, pp. 246–77. In 1910, the same translation was republished together with the translation of "In vino veritas" and "Diapsalmata," in *"In vino veritas," con l'aggiunta de "Il più infelice" e "Diapsalmata,"* trans. by Knud Ferlov, Lanciano: Carabba 1910.
[4]   Garin, "Kierkegaard in Italia," see pp. 453–4.
[5]   Høffding, *Storia della filosofia moderna*, trans. by P. Martinetti, Milan: Bocca 1906, pp. 230–9.

published in 1906. It was an essay with which the scholar Giovanni Calò (1882–1970) won the competition announced by the "Reale Accademia di Scienze Morali e Politiche" of the "Società Reale" in Naples. The competition was for an essay on ethical individualism in the nineteenth century: the winners were Giovanni Calò and another scholar, Giovanni Vidari (1871–1934).[6] Calò knew Kierkegaard's works through the first German translations by Schrempf and through the contributions of Høffding. It is interesting to note the report that the philosopher Filippo Masci wrote for the Academy about Calò's essay:

> The common feature in this direction [i.e., the ethical individualism that was the topic of the competition] is the interiority of the individual life. Among the philosophers, Kierkegaard excels, among the poets, Ibsen. Anti-Hegelian and anti-determinist, the former conceives the individual as isolated, as someone who obtains the rules of his action from himself, who is *ironical* towards other individuals, because his ideal is imperfectly communicable. He is a kind of Leibnitzian monad without the pre-established harmony, and only religion—which sets the finite spirit in relation with the infinite one—can unite him with others, by giving a universal content to morality....[7]

The knowledge of the existence of this text is remarkable for several reasons. First, it shows that there was an acquaintance with Kierkegaard in Italy before 1906, but at the same time it confirms the mediating role of Høffding in it, or at least the role of the German cultural milieu.[8] Second, it shows how from the beginning the figure of Kierkegaard was connected with a kind of individualistic philosophical perspective, as it was in all the early readings of the Dane's philosophy in Italy, at least until the end of the 1930s. At that point, Kierkegaard was associated with the existentialist perspectives of Luigi Pareyson (1918–91), Enzo Paci (1911–76) or Nicola Abbagnano (1901–90), as we shall see.

Another aspect that must be noted is that, unlike the Leonardians' "Scapigliatura"-milieu, that of Naples was an academic sphere. Finally, one can remark that at the

---

[6] Giovanni Calò, *L'individualismo etico nel secolo XIX*, Naples: Tipografia della Regia Università 1906, (originally published as an article in *Atti della Reale Accademia di Scienze Morali e Politiche di Naples*, on Kierkegaard see Chapter 4, pp. 156–70: *La diffusione dell'idealismo Romentico nei paesi scandinavi:...Søren Aabye Kierkegaard...*, in particular from p. 161. On Kierkegaard's influence on Ibsen's work see also pp. 171–80; Giovanni Vidari, *L'individualismo nelle dottrine morali del secolo 19.*, Milan: U. Hoepli 1909.

[7] Filippo Masci, *Relazione del socio Filippo Masci su concorso a premii del 1904*, Naples: Tipografia della della R. Università 1905, p. 24.

[8] Franca Castagnino, *Gli studi italiani su Kierkegaard 1906–1966* (Rome: Ed. dell'Ateneo 1972, pp. 6–8), questions, among the other things, the possibility of knowledge of Kierkegaard in Italy before Høffding's article in *Leonardo*. Her starting point is the assertion of Ettore Bignone in *Le Cronache Letterarie*, no. 4, 1910, who says that the only Italian scholars who knew Søren Kierkegaard were those who had been "made curious about him by the histories of modern philosophy written by Høffding and Ueberweg, and looked up something more about him through the German translations...." That would imply that one could have heard of the Danish philosopher even before 1906. However, again Castagnino adds, we do not have any documents that attest to this, and if this were the case, the *Leonardo* review would have noticed it.

very beginning of Kierkegaard's reception in Italy, the first consideration of him was not as an esthete or a man of letters—as it would be immediately afterwards—but, actually, as a philosopher: "Among the *philosophers*, Kierkegaard excels, among the *poets*, Ibsen." But then, precisely the parallel between Kierkegaard and Ibsen became extremely significant among those first critics who were interested in Kierkegaard from a literary point of view.

We can read in one of the first articles on Kierkegaard's reception in Italy, written by Nicola Abbagnano in 1950, "In Italy the first manifestations of interest in Kierkegaard had a literary character, and they arose from the desire to understand the work of some foreign artists, particularly Ibsen."[9] The first reason for this attitude was probably that the first translations of *Either/Or* presented the work in many fragments, and so it was impossible to grasp the purpose of the text as a whole. For this reason, the "*poetical works*"—to use Høffding's words[10]—were given priority. The first of Kierkegaard's writings that saw the light in Italy, as we said, were "The Unhappiest One" in 1907, "The Seducer's Diary,"[11] translated in 1910 by Luigi Redaelli, "In vino veritas"[12] from *Stages on Life's Way*, translated in 1910 by Knud Ferlov together with "The Unhappiest One" again and the "Diapsalmata," and "The Esthetic Validity of Marriage"[13] in 1912 by Gualtiero Petrucci, and "The Immediate Erotic Stages or the Musical-Erotic"[14] in 1913 again by Gualtiero Petrucci. As Franca Castagnino wrote in her detailed critical study on Kierkegaard reception in Italy until 1966,[15] it was as if the aim of these translations was just to give scattered impressions so that the reading public could gain a sense of the complexity of Kierkegaard's thought, without clarifying its terms. The figure of Kierkegaard that emerges from these first translations is that of a problematic and melancholy thinker (for Høffding and Ferlov), an individualist and pseudo-decadent esthete (for Redaelli, who completely neglects to define Kierkegaard's ethical point of view from a speculative and theological perspective, and for Gualtiero Petrucci who attacks Kierkegaard's individualism and intellectualism in particular). Then Ettore Bignone (1879–1953), who wrote some articles on the Danish thinker in 1910,[16] speaks about his ethical individualism and connects it with Romanticism. Finally, Kierkegaard is included by the famous Sicilian writer Giuseppe Antonio Borgese (1882–1952) in the literary

---

[9] Nicola Abbagnano, "Kierkegaard in Italy," *Meddelelser fra Søren Kierkegaard Selskabet*, vol. 2, nos. 3–4, 1950, p. 49.
[10] Høffding, "Un discendente di Amleto. Søren Kierkegaard," p. 68.
[11] *Il diario del seduttore*, trans. by Luigi Redaelli, Turin: Fratelli Bocca 1910.
[12] *In vino veritas*, con l'aggiunta de *Il più infelice* e *diapsalmata*, trans. by Knud Ferlov, Lanciano: R. Carabba 1910.
[13] *Il valore estetico del matrimonio*, trans. by Gualtiero Petrucci, Naples: F. Perrella e C. 1912.
[14] *L'erotico nella musica*, trans. by Gualtiero Petrucci, Geneva: A.F. Formiggini 1913.
[15] Castagnino, *Gli studi italiani su Kierkegaard 1906–1966*, p. 10.
[16] Ettore Bignone, "Søren Kierkegaard," *Le cronache letterarie*, no. 4, 1910, p. 1; Bignone, "Søren Kierkegaard. II. La filosofia dell stadio estetico," *Le cronache letterarie*, no. 9, 1910, p. 3.

field of autobiographical and introspective narrative.[17] Among other things, it is interesting to make a comparison—as Alessandro Cortese (b. 1940) does—between this Italian interpretative tendency and the German ones, carried out at the same time by Georg Lukács (1885–1971), who spent most of 1911 in Florence. In precisely this year, he published his collection of essays entitled *Soul and Form*, in which the important essay "Kierkegaard und Regine Olsen" also appears.[18] Also, we cannot forget Georg Brandes' (1842–1927) influence either in Denmark or in Germany, and thus indirectly in Italy: he asserted that the most interesting things in Kierkegaard were his aesthetic works.[19]

Carl Koch's essay of 1908 is just an isolated case of entire "Brandesian" tendency of this period—as Cortese is used to call it in contrast to the religious or "Martensenian" tendency.[20] His article "Søren Kierkegaard"—which reproduced a part of his essay of 1898[21]—appears in the Italian review *Il Rinnovamento*.[22] Its approach to Kierkegaard's work has a religious nature that focuses especially on the last part of the Dane's life, that is, his struggle against the Church. After this, from 1914 to the beginning of the 1930s there was in Italy a relative stagnation in Kierkegaardian studies.

---

[17] Giuseppe Antonio Borgese, "Don Giovanni in Danimarca," in his *La vita e il libro. Saggi di letteratura e cultura contemporanea*, Turin: Bocca, 1910–13, vol. 2, pp. 231–41. On the quoted judgements see also Castagnino, *Gli studi italiani su Kierkegaard 1906–1966*, pp. 10–1; Alessandro Cortese, "Kierkegaard," in *Questioni di storiografia filosofica dalle origini all'800*, vols. 1–6, ed. by Vittorio Mathieu, Brescia: La scuola 1975–78, vol. 3, pp. 603–4; Salvatore Spera, "Storia della critica: 5. Area italiana," in his *Introduzione a Kierkegaard*, Rome and Bari: Laterza 1983, see p. 163.

[18] See Georg Lukács' essay collection, *Die Seele und die Formen*, Berlin: Fleischer 1911; in English as "The Foundering of Form against Life. Sören Kierkegaard and Regina Olsen," in *Soul and Form*, trans. by Anna Bostock, Cambridge, Massachusetts: MIT Press 1974, pp. 28–41. The essay was first published in the Hungarian literary periodical *Nyugat* (no. 6, 1910) and shortly after reprinted in Lukács' essay collection, entitled *A lélek és a formák. Kísérletek* [Soul and Form. Experiments], Budapest: Franklin 1910. See also Garin, "Kierkegaard in Italia," p. 453. About Lukács' stay in Florence see also Árpád Kadarkay, *Georg Lukács. Life, Thought, and Politics*, Cambridge MA and Oxford: Blackwell 1991, pp. 113–4.

[19] Georg Brandes gave his public lectures on Kierkegaard in Copenhagen in 1877 before he left for Berlin, and in the same year, he published his monograph entitled *Søren Kierkegaard: En kritisk Fremstilling i Grundrids* (Copenhagen: Gyldendal 1877), which was translated into German in 1879.

[20] See Cortese, "Kierkegaard," p. 603.

[21] Carl Koch, *Søren Kierkegaard: tre Foredrage*, Copenhagen: Det Schønbergske Forlag 1898.

[22] See Karl Koch, "Søren Kierkegaard," trans. by Ragnhild Lund, *Il Rinnovamento*, vol. 3, 1908, pp. 27–42.

II.

What we might call the second phase of the first period in these studies began with the philosopher Antonio Banfi's (1886–1957) translation from German of *The Moment* in 1931.[23] There are various interpretations about the Italian interest in Kierkegaard's polemics in these years, but almost all of them trace this interest back to the Italian philosophical and political situation of the 1930s. Abbagnano, for instance, speaks about the "dissatisfaction produced by the idealistic form of culture, which was totally incapable of answering certain fundamental exigencies of man...."[24] Here he refers first to the neo-Hegelian or idealistic turn effected in Italian philosophy by Giovanni Gentile (1875–1944) and then to his adherence to fascist politics.

In the same vein Eugenio Garin (1909–2004) speaks openly about the translation of *The Moment* as a kind of comment on the agreement between Mussolini and Pope Pius XI (1857–1939), which was ratified by the *Patti Lateranensi* in 1929.[25] Garin mentions the name of the journalist, theologian and philosopher Giuseppe Gangale (1898–1978), who had recently converted to Protestantism. He wrote the first preface to Banfi's translation and collaborated with him on several publishing initiatives. Gangale, a member of the Baptist Church and since 1922 the leading force of the weekly *Conscientia*, had assumed a more and more anti-fascist position, and during his collaboration with *Conscientia*, Banfi also wrote about Kierkegaard in some articles from 1926.

The Moment was the only work by Kierkegaard which was translated in full in Italy and which had a second and third edition. The image of Kierkegaard derived from this work was that of a revolutionary and individualist spirit, who attacked the institution of the Church. Nevertheless, Banfi's reading of Kierkegaard also signals the appearance of the first existentialist wave in Italy. After the First World War, this current reflected the awareness of the crises caused by the collapse of liberal culture which had shown the tragic nature of human existence. In this sense Kierkegaard became, together with Nietzsche—as Jaspers asserted—one of the most significant philosophers. So, one can say that the world knew Kierkegaard through the mediation of "crisis-thought," which had its major voices in Jaspers and Heidegger, and, on the theological side, in Barth. This is what is called the German "Kierkegaard renaissance," which was the result of Schrempf's translation (1909–12) of Kierkegaard's works. The limitations of this translation will be shown later.[26]

---

[23] *L'Ora. Atti d'accusa al cristianesimo del Regno di Danimarca*, trans. from German (the edition of Hermann Gottsched and Christoph Schrempf) by Antonio Banfi, Milan and Rome: Edit. Doxa 1931. This translation does not reproduce the whole text, and it is referred to as tendentious by the translator of the last edition of it, Alberto Gallas, *L'istante*, Geneva: Marietti 2002, p. 8.

[24] See Abbagnano, "Kierkegaard in Italy," p. 50.

[25] Garin, "Kierkegaard in Italia," pp. 454–5. About the relationship between Banfi's translation and the Italian political situation, see also Ettore Rocca, "Kierkegaard in the Italian Language," *Søren Kierkegaard Newsletter*, no. 40, 2000, p. 18.

[26] About this question, see Walter Rest, "Die kontroverstheologische Relevanz Sören Kierkegaards," *Chatolica*, 1951, pp. 87ff. On this point see Giuseppe Mario Pizzuti, "L'equivoco della 'Kierkegaard Renaissance,'" in his *Tra Kierkegaard e Barth: l'ombra di*

In any case, *Existenzialphilosophie*'s reading of Kierkegaard had its origin in a perspective and need different from that of Kierkegaard. Consequently, there has been talk about a "hermeneutic dystonia" or distortion from which all the misunderstandings and strained interpretations were derived. Moreover, it is also necessary to note that this reading did not consider the whole of Kierkegaard's work. This is especially true of his journals and notebooks, which were neglected. As was said, the reading of the Danish philosopher's thought in Italy would be influenced by the German "Kierkegaard renaissance." It is in precisely this tradition that Banfi's reading finds its place, using Kierkegaard in the direction of a new "humanism."

III.

The second half of the 1930s signals the beginning of the Italian "Kierkegaard renaissance." In 1935 Walter Lowrie, the former rector of St. Paul's American Church in Rome, defined the state of Kierkegaard studies in Italy as "insular." He exhorts Italian Kierkegaard scholars to give up Ibsen and Brandes' misunderstanding of Kierkegaard's thought and to see in Kierkegaard a stimulus for an inner revival of Catholicism itself.[27]

In the same year, Karl Löwith's article, "The Conclusion of Classical Philosophy with Hegel and Its Dissolution in Marx and Kierkegaard," appeared in the *Giornale Critico della Filosofia Italiana*.[28] This work shows how different Kierkegaard's thought was from German philosophy. Löwith shows that *Existenzphilosophie* had used Kierkegaard's thought in order to criticize the idealistic perspective and to found, in this way, a new philosophical view based on the "situation" of man in the world. But at the same time Löwith sees in Kierkegaard the origin of existentialism's negative attitude. So Italian existentialism accepted the Kierkegaardian critique of Hegel in order to oppose idealism, that is, Gentile's actualism. However, unlike German existentialism, the Italian variety found in Kierkegaard a way to overcome the negativity of the German "Kierkegaard renaissance."[29] To this tradition belong Lombardi and especially Abbagnano with his theory of a "positive existentialism."

Franco Lombardi (1906–89) wrote in 1936 the first complete Italian monograph on Kierkegaard.[30] A former professor at Marburg University, he intended to interpret Kierkegaard in the sense of a new humanism. A Feuerbach scholar,[31] Lombardi

---

Nietzsche. La crisi come odissea dello spirito, preface by Cornelio Fabro, Venosa: Edizioni Osanna Venosa 1986, pp. 21–100. On Jaspers' reading of Kierkegaard, see also Filippo Costa's translation and critical essay in Karl Jaspers, *La fede filosofica di fronte alla rivelazione*, Milan: Longanesi 1970 and the "Poscritto" (1955) to Umberto Galimberti's translation of Karl Jaspers' *Filosofia*, Turin: UTET 1978. Thse books are all quoted by Giuseppe Mario Pizzuti in his *Invito al pensiero di Kierkegaard*, Milan: Mursia 1995, pp. 214–22.

[27] See Walter Lowrie, "Søren Kierkegaard," *Religio*, vol. 11, 1935, pp. 1–15.
[28] See Karl Löwith, "La conchiusione della filosofia classica con Hegel e la sua dissoluzione in Marx e Kierkegaard," *Giornale Critico della Filosofia Italiana*, no. 16, 1935, pp. 342–71.
[29] On this point see Castagnino, *Gli studi italiani su Kierkegaard 1906–1966*, pp. 15ff.
[30] Franco Lombardi, *Kierkegaard*, Florence: La Nuova Italia 1936.
[31] See also Lombardi's monograph entitled *Feuerbach*, Florence: La Nuova Italia 1935.

developed a concept of existence based on Feuerbachian categories. He tends to reduce Kierkegaard's philosophy to a form of anti-Hegelianism and to relegate his view of the inwardness of faith to a kind of philosophical irrationalism. Indeed, he goes as far as to speak of Kierkegaard's "irrationalistic individualism." Moreover Lombardi considers Kierkegaard's journals and notebooks to be merely autobiographical documents and thus bases his reading solely on the pseudonymous works, such as *The Concept of Anxiety*, *The Sickness unto Death*, *Either/Or*, and *Stages on Life's Way*. Finally, because of the painful Kierkegaardian view of life, he finds in him just a "Sunday companion,"[32] who has to be abandoned during the practicalities of daily life. Later, Cornelio Fabro (1911–95)—the most significant Italian Kierkegaard scholar—acknowledged that Lombardi's monograph was his first point of contact with the Danish philosopher, but at the same time he severely criticized the "pioneer of Kierkegaardian studies in Italy," accusing him of following Höffding and Brandes' positivistic "deviant line," like that of Schrempf.[33] By contrast, in 1974 Cortese would appreciate how Lombardi still placed Kierkegaard in the Hegelian orbit, because of his "Hegelian" linguistic and conceptual horizon: in Cortese's opinion, this should at least contribute to a different positive consideration of Hegelian idealism.[34]

Despite the fact that he never wrote a monograph on Kierkegaard, Nicola Abbagnano is another of the most significant commentators on Kierkegaard within the horizon of Italian existentialism. His speculative reading of the concept of possibility in Kierkegaard's works is to be found primarily in his *History of Philosophy*.[35] Abbagnano's *positive existentialism* intends to compare Kant and Kierkegaard in a complementary fashion:

> the characteristic of Kierkegaard's personality and work is to have made the attempt to trace the entire understanding of human existence back to the category of *possibility*, and to have shown the negative and paralyzing nature of possibility itself. Kant already recognized the *real* or *transcendental possibility* as the basis of any human power, but he showed the positive nature of this possibility that makes it a real human capacity.[36]

Abbagnano shows that both the left wing of existentialism (the early Heidegger, Jaspers, and Sartre) or the right one (Marcel, Lavelle, Le Senne) are grounded on a negative foundation, even though they are opposites. While the first negates existence as possibility by showing the "impossibility of the possible," the second views the possible as "potential," that is, as a necessity. In both cases human freedom

---

[32] Lombardi, *Kierkegaard*, p. 9.
[33] See Cornelio Fabro's Introduction (vol. 1, paragraph 19) to his translation of Kierkegaard's *Papers: Diario*, vols. 1–3, Brescia: Ed. Morcelliana 1948–51 (vol. 1, 1948 (1834–48); vol. 2, 1949 (1848–52); vol. 3, 1951 (1852–55). See his polemics about the second edition of Lombardi's work in 1967, in Fabro, "Kierkegaard in Italia," *Il Veltro*, vol. 225, nos. 1–3, 1981, pp. 81ff.; and Lombardi's answer in *Il Veltro*, vol. 26, nos. 1–2, 1982, pp. 92–4.
[34] See Cortese, "Kierkegaard," p. 605.
[35] See Nicola Abbagnano, "Kierkegaard," in *Storia della Filosofia*, Turin: UTET 1946–50, vol. 2, part 2: "Il Romenticismo," pp. 179–93.
[36] Ibid., § 598.

is negated. By following the Kierkegaardian demonstration of the "non-necessity" of history in the "Interlude" of the *Philosophical Fragments*, Abbagnano intends to emphasize the "enormous power of liberation that the Kierkegaardian category of possibility possesses."[37]

In the same years the above-mentioned Luigi Pareyson also became interested in Kierkegaard's philosophy. Driven by theological interests, he came to it through the studies of Jean Wahl. Pareyson reads Kierkegaard in the direction of a philosophy of existence turned toward salvaging transcendence; he proceeds on the way of a new humanism, but converted into a form of a "Christian personalism,"[38] which finds a place within the Catholic perspective.

By contrast, one can talk about "phenomenological existentialism" in the case of Enzo Paci, who connects Kierkegaard with Husserl, avoiding in this way the possibility of an irrationalist reading of Kierkegaard's philosophy. In this sense, what he openly asserts in one of his essays in 1953 is emblematic: "Kierkegaard's work starts with a phenomenology of a will to concealment: it is this will that causes anxiety. This anxiety cannot be understood if, at its very beginning, it does not act with a secret intentionality that goes through various phenomenological stages, arriving at the end at love."[39] Paci means that in the whole of Kierkegaard's work the negative is just a "proof by contradiction" of the positive. He continues to refer to Kierkegaard when he, in 1951, founded the philosophical review *Aut-Aut*, which is still today one of the most important philosophical periodicals in Italy.

In 1940 there appeared the translation of *The Concept of Anxiety* by Michele Federico Sciacca (1918–75), based on a German translation.[40] But this work did not reproduce the whole of Kierkegaard's text: it was just a selection that excluded the polemic against Hegel and several footnotes in which Kierkegaard defended his own position against the accusations of Pelagianism. The resulting work was thus mutilated both from a philosophical and a theological point of view.[41] The first

---

[37] Abbagnano, "Kierkegaard in Italy," p. 52.

[38] For Luigi Pareyson in this period see "Note sulla filosofia dell'esistenza," *Giornale Critico della Filosofia Italiana*, vol. 19, 1938, pp. 407–38 and "Nota Kierkegaardiana," *Annali della R. Scuola Normale Superiore di Pisa*, vol. 8, 1939, pp. 53–68 (entitled "Søren Kierkegaard e l'esistenzialismo," republished in *Studi sull'esistenzialismo*, Florence: Sansoni 1943, pp. 59–80).

[39] Enzo Paci, "Ironia, demoniaco ed eros in Kierkegaard," *Archivio di filosofia*, 1953 (*Kierkegaard e Nietzsche*), pp. 71–113 (the same article also in his *Relazioni e significati. Kierkegaard e Thomas Mann*, Milan: Lampugnani Nigri and Vicenza: C. Stocchero, 1965, vol. 2, quotation at p. 7). See also Paci, "Studi su Kierkegaard," *Studi filosofici*, vol. 1, nos. 2–3, 1940, pp. 279–91 (the same writing also as "Personalità ed esistenza nel pensiero di Kierkegaard," in his *Pensiero, esistenza e valore*, Milan and Messina: Principato 1940, pp. 77–97); See also Enzo Paci, *L'esistenzialismo*, Padua: CEDAM 1943.

[40] *Il concetto dell'angoscia*, trans. and ed. by Michele Federico Sciacca, Milan: F.lli Bocca 1940 (2nd ed., 1944; 3rd ed., 1950). (This work is a translation from the German, *Sämtliche Werke*, ed. by Hermann Gottsched and Christoph Schrempf, Jena: Diederichs 1922–3.)

[41] In 1936, in the Appendix of Armando Carlini's "L'angoscia e il peccato. L'angoscia e l'istante," in *Il mito del realismo*, Florence: Sansoni 1936, pp. 59–67, some passages from *The Concept of Anxiety* had already appeared, translated by Carlini himself from the French

full translation of *The Concept of Anxiety*, by Meta Corssen,[42] appeared only two years later. Sciacca basically condemned Kierkegaard's thought for his morbidity.[43] Banfi's follower, Remo Cantoni (1914–78) represents in this context the best of the "humanistic" readings of Kierkegaard: he shows Kierkegaard as a restless "two-faced Janus" who hesitates between an ethical and an aesthetic perspective. Finally, he settles on a religious point of view but in this way loses historicity. As Castagnino points out,[44] Cantoni's work represents a kind of synthesis in Kierkegaardian studies in Italy from 1910 to 1946.[45] However, Cornelio Fabro later accused Italian existentialism of having ignored Kierkegaard, referring especially to a survey of existentialism in Italy conducted by the periodical *Il Primato* in 1943. There Fabro claimed all the contributors, in particular Paci and Abbagnano in their opening papers, failed to give the Danish philosopher the credit he deserved.[46]

By contrast, in his monograph on existentialism in 1953 and then in various articles,[47] Pietro Prini (b. 1915) emphasizes Kierkegaard's "irrationalism" as a new philosophical method: he defines this method as a *"theologia sperimentalis"* or "theological autobiography." Prini's tendency goes in the direction of a Christian spiritualism, influenced by Haecker's Kierkegaard reading, even if he continues to present a Romantic image of the Danish philosopher and claims his religiosity is ambiguous.

---

edition, *Le concept de l'angoisse*, by Knud Ferlov and J.J. Gateau (Paris: Gallimard 1935). This text also considered the German one by Schrempf (Jena: Diederichs 1913). Carlini showed for the first time the peculiarity of Kierkegaard's concept of anxiety in comparison with Heidegger, (see also Cortese, "Kierkegaard," pp. 607–8).

[42] *Il concetto dell'angoscia. Una semplice psicologica sul problema del peccato originale*, trans. by Meta Corssen, Florence: Sansoni 1942.

[43] For Michele Federico Sciacca see "L'esperienza etico-religiosa di Søren Kierkegaard," *Logos*, vol. 20, 1937, pp. 121–8; "Søren Kierkegaard il poeta della solitudine eroica," in his *La filosofia oggi*, Milan and Rome: Bocca 1945; "Kierkegaard il filosofo del 'salto,'" in *Rivista dei Giovani*, no. 5, 1947, pp. 25–8; and *L'estetismo, Kierkegaard, Pirandello*, Milan, Marzorati 1974.

[44] See Castagnino, *Gli studi italiani su Kierkegaard 1906–1966*, pp. 28–9.

[45] See especially Remo Cantoni, *La coscienza inquieta. Søren Kierkegaard*, Milan: Mondadori 1949.

[46] See "Il Primato," *L'esistenzialismo in Italia*, nos. 1–6, January–March 1943 (contributions by A. Carlini, U. Spirito, A. Guzzo, P. Carabellese, C. Pellizzi, G. Della Volpe, G. Luporini and G. Gentile). Cornelio Fabro's notices in "Linee fondamentali di ermeneutica kierkegaardiana," in "Introduzione" to his own Italian translation of S. Kierkegaard, *Opere*, Florence: Sansoni 1972, pp. LXV–LXVI; "Kierkegaard in Italia," *Veltro*, vol. 25, nos. 1–3, 1981, pp. 80–1. See also Cornelio Fabro, "L'esistenzialismo kierkegaardiano," in *Storia della filosofia*, ed. by Fabro, Rome: Colletti 1954, pp. 773–856 (2nd ed. of 1959, vols. 1–2, see vol. 2, *La Kierkegaard Renaissance*, pp. 839–918, see also "Bibliografia," in vol. 2, pp. 959–63).

[47] See in particular Pietro Prini, "Kierkegaard testimonio della verità sofferente è una biografia dell'esistenzialismo Romentico," in his *L'esistenzialismo*, Rome: Studium 1953, pp. 11–30 and "Kierkegaard e la filosofia come giornale intimo," *Archivio di filosofia*, 1959, pp. 73–90 (published also in his *Esistenzialismo*, Rome: Edizioni Studium 1971, pp. 10–53).

IV.

But the real turning point in the Italian Kierkegaard reception is represented by Cornelio Fabro's translation of the journals and notebooks between 1948 and 1951. Based on the first Danish edition of *Søren Kierkegaards Papirer*,[48] it was at that time the most complete edition in translation, surpassing those of Haecker in German, Dru in English, and Tisseau in French. Moreover, even today it is second only to the Hongs' edition (the third edition in 12 volumes dates back to 1980–83 and, unlike the first, also includes a few extracts from sections B and C of the journals and papers).[49] In the introduction to the first edition of his translation, Fabro describes in this way the criterion he chose in order to select Kierkegaard's passages: "I gave precedence to the doctrinal and edifying texts, keeping in the background the autobiographical ones, but without totally sacrificing the aesthetic texts, respecting, what I believe is the real proportion of Kierkegaard's work and spirit."[50] In this way, Fabro opened a new period of Kierkegaard studies, which brought to an end a phase of vague and mediated works, and moved toward a new critical and philological one.

Fabro's publication of the *Diario* started the dispute against existentialism together with the Kierkegaard renaissance, of which he intended to show the faults and the "falsifications," as he writes. He openly declares that he become interested in Kierkegaard "in order to understand his theory of truth, that is, his reaction to idealism and decadent Christianity that, since my first contact with existentialism, I felt had been distorted by the Kierkegaard renaissance."[51] In this way Fabro starts the apologia for Kierkegaard as religious writer, and, certain about the positivity of his message, he connects it with Catholicism, following Lowrie's advice on this point, and then, going further than Przywara, he talks about a Kierkegaardian Catholicism. Fabro's apologetic intention was further motivated by the resistance that he found amongst Italian Catholic intellectuals. Between 1948 and 1949 he published a series of articles in order to refute the notion that there was any contact between Kierkegaard's thought and atheistic existentialism.[52] Then, in 1950 Pope Pius XII (1876–1958) published the Encyclical *Humani Generis*, which condemned idealism, materialism, and existentialism as atheist theories, together with any religious current which founds itself only on an inner feeling of faith, excluding every role of the human intelligence in order to demonstrate the existence of God and the basis of

---

[48] *Søren Kierkegaards Papirer*, vols. 1–11, ed. by P.A. Heiberg, V. Kuhr and E. Torsting, Copenhagen: C.A. Reitzel 1909–48.

[49] On the Italian reception of Kierkegaard's papers and journals, see Andrea Scaramuccia, "The Italian Reception of Kierkegaard's Journals and Papers," *Kierkegaard Studies. Yearbook*, 2003, pp. 366–72.

[50] See Fabro's introduction to Søren Kierkegaard, *Diario*, 3rd revised and enlarged ed., vols. 1–12, Brescia: Morcelliana 1980–83, vol. 1, p. 127.

[51] Ibid., pp. 126–7.

[52] See, for example, Cornelio Fabro, "Kierkegaard poeta-teologo dell'Annunciazione," *Humanitas*, vol. 3, 1948, pp. 1025–34; "La religiosità di Kierkegaard nel suo 'Diario,'" *Humanitas*, vol. 3, 1948, pp. 209–16; "Critica di Kierkegaard all'Ottocento," in *Atti del XV congresso nazionale di filosofia 1948*, Messina: D'Anna 1949, pp. 375–85.

Christian faith.[53] In the same year, Fabro made a collection of Kierkegaard's texts taken from the journals and notebooks and the *Upbuilding Discourses* and entitled it *Prayers*.[54]

In the same period A. Miggiano and Kirsten Montanari Guldbrandsen's translation of *Practice in Christianty* also appeared,[55] a work in which Kierkegaard stressed the value of Christianity not as a doctrine but as inner faith. Shortly after this two articles in *La Civiltà Cattolica* and *L'Osservatore Romano* openly attacked Kierkegaard's thought for denying the sacraments and not accepting the Church.[56] As a Thomist scholar,[57] Fabro intended to combine the principles of the classical Greek perspective with the needs of modern thought, and in this way he found in Kierkegaard's anti-idealistic polemics the necessary elements needed to oppose both the philosophy of immanence and atheist modernism.[58]

The first complete syntheses of Fabro's perspective appeared in "Kierkegaard and Marx," in *Atti del congresso internazionale di filosofia 1946*,[59] in which he actually reversed the last twenty years of reading Kierkegaard. The disciple and scholar of Fabro, Giuseppe Mario Pizzuti (b. 1945)—who founded in the late 1980s together with Fabro himself, the first, Italian Søren Kierkegaard Research Center in Potenza—presents a detailed description of the main interpretative lines of Fabro's reading of Kierkegaard in his article "Cornelio Fabro, Translator and Interpreter of Kierkegaard in Italy."[60] Fabro emphasized that Kierkegaard's criticism of modern immanentism was a criticism of the "essentialistic" tendency of modern rationalism. One must read Kierkegaard's stress on concrete actuality, not in the sense of empirical reality, but in the sense of an individual decision toward freedom that is incompatible with the "System." This also implies a *soteriological* dimension of the truth, and this

---

[53] See Pope Pius XII, "Humanis generis. De nonnullis falsis opinionibus quae catholicam doctrinam minantur," *Civiltà Cattolica*, vol. 28, no. 3, 1950, p. 466.

[54] See *Preghiere*, ed. by Cornelio Fabro, Brescia: Morcelliana 1951 (selected texts of Kierkegaard).

[55] *Scuola di cristianesimo*, trans. by Agostino Miggiano and Kirsten Montanari Guldbrandsen, Milan: Ed. Di Comunità 1950.

[56] See Pietro Parente, "Il vero volto di Kierkegaard," *L'Osservatore Romano*, vol. 11, no. 3, 1952, p. 3; Salvatore Fruscione, "Kierkegaard di fronte all'esistenza di Dio," *La civiltà cattolica*, vol. 102, 1951, pp. 618–31.

[57] See Cornelio Fabro, *La nozione metafisica di partecipazione secondo San Tommaso*, Turin: Società Editrice Italiana 1939.

[58] See also, later, Cornelio Fabro, *Introduzione all'ateismo moderno*, 2nd ed, Rome: Studium 1969 [1961].

[59] Cornelio Fabro, "Kierkegaard e Marx," in *Atti del congresso internazionale di filosofia 1946*, Milan: Castellani 1947, vol. 1 (*Il materialismo storico*), pp. 3–16 (the same writing later as the first chapter in his *Tra Kierkegaard e Marx. Per una definizione dell'esistenza*, Florence: Vallecchi 1952, pp. 9–39 (republished in Rome: Edizioni Logos 1978)). On this point see especially Castagnino, *Gli studi italiani su Kierkegaard 1906–1966*, pp. 32ff.

[60] See Giuseppe Mario Pizzuti, "Cornelio Fabro, traduttore e interprete di Kierkegaard in Italia," *Humanitas*, no. 2 (new series), 1984, pp. 192–219. See also Flavio Capucci, "Cornelio Fabro interprete di Kierkegaard," *Studi Cattolici*, no. 256, 1982, pp. 364–7; Giuseppe Mario Pizzutti, "Un filosofo inattuale. Cornelio Fabro nel suo ottantesimo genetliaco," *Humanitas*, no. 5 (new series), 1991, pp. 680–93.

is the point that most separates Kierkegaard from existentialism. Fabro then places the Danish philosopher in the line of Greek (Aristotelian), Christian (Scholastic), metaphysical realism, and this permits him to identify in Kierkegaard a precise and peculiar form of rationality that leads to a positive solution in the relationship between faith and reason: Kierkegaard wanted to defend the absolute transcendence of Christianity against the abuses of idealistic reason, but this does not mean that the work of reason is totally excluded from the object of faith. The object of the faith is the absurd, the paradox, only for those who see this object from the outside, that is, for those who do not have faith. This means that the absurd has an existential, but not an essential, origin. In this sense, the thesis of the subjectivity of the truth as "objective uncertainty, held fast through appropriation with the most passionate inwardness"[61] is the most complete expression of Kierkegaard's theoretical and spiritual agenda, and Fabro talks about a kind of theoretical "trans-evaluation" of Hegelian philosophy from within itself. Moreover, Fabro saw the reason for what he called the "inconclusiveness" of Kierkegaard's thought in the absence of a Catholic comprehension of the mystery of the Incarnation, in an incomplete definition of the metaphysical doctrine of being, as well as in the lack of a positive role for the Church.

The other basis of Fabro's reading is the accent put on the edifying production[62] and then on the duplicity of communication in Kierkegaard. In 1953 he published his translation of *The Concept of Anxiety* and *The Sickness unto Death*,[63] which he associates with indirect communication and places within the group of the pseudonymous works. Then he points to anxiety as the philosophical point of departure, which is subordinated to the theological one, expressed in *The Sickness unto Death*. Finally, with his translation of the entire *Concluding Unscientific Postscript* and *Philosophical Fragments* in 1962,[64] he thought that Kierkegaard's Christology would appear in all its clarity and be beyond any misunderstanding by existentialism or the Catholic milieu.

In fact, Cantoni and Pareyson also approached Kierkegaard's thought after this period differently.[65] In 1963 Dino Donadoni published a selection of *Christian*

---

[61] See *SKS* 7, 186 / *CUP1*, 203.

[62] See *Gli atti dell'amore*, Milan: Rusconi 1983.

[63] *Il concetto dell'angoscia. La malattia mortale*, trans. by Cornelio Fabro, Florence: Sansoni 1953.

[64] *Briciole di filosofia ovvero una filosofia in briciole* e *Postilla conclusiva non scientifica alle "Briciole di filosofia*,*"* vols. 1–2, trans. by Cornelio Fabro, Bologna: Zanichelli 1962. A complete collection of Fabro's translations of Kierkegaard's main writings appeared later in 1972, entitled *Opere*, Florence: Sansoni 1972. In particular on Fabro's translation of the *Postscript* and *Philosophical Fragments*, see Simonella Davini, "Cornelio Fabro and the Italian Reception of *Philosophical Fragments*," in *Kierkegaard Studies. Yearbook*, 2004, pp. 356–69.

[65] See Remo Cantoni, "Kierkegaard Søren Aabye. Polemica antihegeliana," in *Filosofia della storia e senso della vita*, Milan: La goliardica 1965; Luigi Pareyson, "Kierkegaard e la poesia d'occasione," *Rivista di Estetica*, vol. 10, 1965, pp. 248–55; Luigi Pareyson, *L'etica di Kierkegaard nella prima fase del suo pensiero: corso di filosofia morale dell'anno*

Discourses,[66] and after that Catholic thinkers also started to shift over to Fabro's position.[67] In any case, one saw that Fabro's reading had already prevailed when he published his *Kierkegaard Studies* in 1957, a collection of essays in which appeared the names of the most important Italian and international Kierkegaard scholars of that time.[68] A new series of specialist studies on the Scandinavian line was inaugurated in Denmark by Niels Thulstrup (1924–88), with whom Fabro was in contact. The 1960s were characterized by Fabro's "monopoly" on Kierkegaard studies, as Ettore Rocca (b. 1965) writes in his article on Kierkegaard's reception in Italy.[69]

However, Italy was not lacking critics who were opposed to Fabro's Catholic reading of Kierkegaard: the publication of the second edition of Lombardi's monograph in 1967, for instance, occasioned a discussion between Fabro and Lombardi.[70] But already earlier, even during the existentialist discussion of Kierkegaard's thought, Salvatore Navarria had rejected the possibility of a Catholic interpretation, even if he was one of the first scholars to emphasize Kierkegaard's religious dimension as fundamental and his call to authentic Christianity. But Furio Jesi's monograph on Kierkegaard[71] also has to be mentioned. Unlike the general tendency of the moment, he takes a look at Kierkegaard from a secular point of view.

V.

At the end of the 1960s, a new generation of Kierkegaard translators and scholars appeared, of which the most prominent are the above-mentioned Cortese and Salvatore Spera. To the former—who declares himself to be educated in the classical-metaphysical tradition[72]—we owe the first and only Italian translation of the whole of *Either/Or*.[73] A meticulous and precise philologist, often critical of Fabro, Cortese prefers to conduct his research through articles, notes, reviews, or commentaries to the translations, rather than through systematic monographs. By 1967 he had already translated *The Battle between the Old and the New Soap-Cellars*,[74] and later several of Kierkegaard's minor

---

accademico 1964–1965, Turin: G. Giappichelli 1965; Luigi Pareyson, *L'etica di Kierkegaard nella Postilla*, Turin: G. Giappichelli 1971.

[66]   *Discorsi cristiani*, trans. and ed. by Dino T. Donadoni, Turin: Borla 1963.

[67]   See Domenico Farias, "La cultura tra invidia e comunione: Kierkegaard e Dante," *Rivista di Filosofia Neo-Scolastica*, vol. 55, 1963, pp. 317–42; Piero Sessa, "La persona di Cristo nel pensiero di Søren Kierkegaard," *La Scuola Cattolica*, vol. 93, 1965, pp. 223–38.

[68]   *Studi Kierkegaardiani*, ed. by Cornelio Fabro, Brescia: Morcelliana 1957.

[69]   See Rocca, "Kierkegaard in the Italian Language," p. 19.

[70]   See the polemics in their aforementioned articles appeared which in the review *Il Veltro* in 1981 and 1982.

[71]   Furio Jesi, *Kierkegaard*, Fossano: Esperienze 1972. (This monograph has been recently reissued in 2001 by Boringhieri, Turin.)

[72]   See Cortese, "Kierkegaard," pp. 632–3.

[73]   *Enten-Eller: un frammento di vita*, trans. by Alessandro Cortese, vols. 1–5, Milan: Adelphi 1976–89.

[74]   *La lotta tra il vecchio e il nuovo negozio del sapone*, trans. and ed. by Alessandro Cortese, Padua: Liviana 1967. See also "Che cosa giudica Cristo del cristianesimo ufficiale," trans. by Alessandro Cortese, in *Contributi dell'Istituto di filosofia dell'Università Cattolica*

works which he considered interesting in order to set the philosopher's activity in its historical context. In 1982 Cortese was the organizer of an international congress on Kierkegaard, held at the Catholic University of Milan,[75] which brought together several of the most important Kierkegaard scholars of the time.

Similarly, Spera studied in depth some novel aspects of Kierkegaard's work, such as the socio-political one[76] or the theological issues in connection with the Danish and German philosophical and theological milieu of the time.[77] In 1979 Alessandro Klein (b. 1944) wrote his monograph on Kierkegaard's anti-rationalism,[78] taking in this sense a different direction from Fabro's position. In 1981, Giorgio Penzo published *Friedrich Gogarten. The Problem of God between Historicism and Existentialism*,[79] in which Kierkegaard is considered again in relation to the "crisis-thought" of the period after the First World War. Penzo takes up Troelsch's image of Gogarten as *ein Apfel vom Baume Kierkegaards*, and he makes a comparison between the two thinkers, finding in them the same existential and ontological reading of Luther's thought.

In 1984 the review *Humanitas*, together with the Pro Civitate Christiana Library, organized a Conference on Kierkegaard in Assisi, whose proceedings were published in 1985 and later taken up and discussed by Bruno Belletti in an article in 1986.[80]

In 1988, as was mentioned, the first Italian Søren Kierkegaard Research Center was born in Potenza, at the initiative of Cornelio Fabro and Giuseppe Mario Pizzuti, in order to give to the Italian Kierkegaard scholars a place where they could meet with one another. The C.I.S.K. (Centro Italiano di Studi Kierkegaardiani) published its statute in the first number of what was to be its review, entitled *Nuovi Studi Kierkegaardiani*, where it was expressly stated that the focus of the newborn Centre

---

del S. Cuore di Milan, Milan: Vita e Pensiero 1972, vol. 2, pp. 57–64 and in the same collection also "È vero che il vescovo Mynster fu un 'Sandhedsvidne' [testimone della verità], uno 'de rette Sandhedsvidner' [gli autentici testimoni della verità]?," vol. 2, pp. 52–6.

[75]   See *Kierkegaard oggi. Atti del Convegno dell'11 novembre 1982, Università Cattolica del Sacro Cuore, Milan, Aula degli atti accademici Pio XI*, ed. by Alessandro Cortese, Milan: Vita e pensiero 1986.

[76]   See Salvatore Spera, "Kierkegaard e la crisi europea del 1848," *Archivio di Filosofia*, nos. 2–3, 1978, pp. 385–407 and *Kierkegaard politico*, Rome: Istituto di studi filosofici 1978.

[77]   See Salvatore Spera, "Il divenire cristiano come imitazione del Cristo sofferente in Søren Kierkegaard," *Bollettino Stauros*, no. 2, 1976; *Il pensiero del giovane Kierkegaard. Indagini critiche sulla filosofia della religione e studi sugli aspetti inediti del pensiero kierkegaardiano*, Padua: CEDAM 1977; "Aspetti del demoniaco in una prospettiva di filosofia della religione," *Aquinas*, vol. 21, 1978, pp. 382–99; "L'influsso di Schelling sulla formazione del giovane Kierkegaard," *Archivio di Filosofia*, no. 1, 1976, pp. 73–108.

[78]   See Alessandro Klein, *Antirazionalismo di Kierkegaard*, Milan: Mursia 1979.

[79]   Giorgio Penzo, *Friedrich Gogarten. Il problema di Dio tra storicismo ed esistenzialismo*, Rome: Città nuova 1981.

[80]   See *Kierkegaard. Esistenzialismo e dramma della persona. Atti del convegno di Assisi (29 nov.–1 dic. 1984)*, Brescia: Morcelliana 1985; Bruno Belletti, "Per una ripresa critica del pensiero di Kierkegaard. Gli atti di un recente convegno di Assisi 29 novembre–1 dicembre 1984," *Humanitas*, vol. 41, no. 1, 1986, pp. 72–9.

would be on philological, critical, and historiographic matters.[81] Among the founding members, one reads the names of Spera, Gaetano Mollo (b. 1947), Sergio Marini (b. 1952), and Mario Gigante. The second number of the *Nuovi Studi Kierkegaardiani* was to be published in 1993.[82] Fabro died two years later, and then for a number of reasons the center ceased to exist.

In 1996 there was an international congress on the topic *Kierkegaard: Philosophy and Theology of the Paradox*, organized by the Institute of Theological Sciences of Trento, December 4–6. The organizers were Michele Nicoletti and Giorgio Penzo (1925–2006). Among the Italian Kierkegaard experts present were Virgilio Melchiorre (b. 1931), Umberto Regina (b. 1937), Anna Giannatiempo Quinzio, and Giuseppe Modica.

Melchiorre, in particular, a Kierkegaard scholar since the 1950s, belongs to the classical tradition and basically shows how the existential reading of Kierkegaard is connected with the metaphysical one. In this way, he analyzes the ontological structure of the human being from a phenomenological point of view and shows the metaphysical transcendence of the foundation of this structure. Then, Umberto Regina, also a scholar of Nietzsche and Heidegger, focuses especially on the problem of human finitude that he interprets in the sense of a possible openness for consciousness. Finally, the approach of Giuseppe Modica to Kierkegaard starts from an ethical-religious point of view, while Anna Giannatiempo Quinzio especially analyzes how the esthetic finds a place in the relationship between the ethical and the religious.

VI.

Now, what one may regard as the new generation of Kierkegaard scholars appeared in 1989 with the translation of *The Concept of Irony* by Dario Borso,[83] who also later published other minor works by Kierkegaard, which had not yet been published in Italy before, such as *Prefaces* in 1990,[84] *Two Ages* in 1994 (a partial translation of *A Literary Review*),[85] *A Literary Review* in 1995,[86] and later *Two Upbuilding Discourses*, *Three Upbuilding Discourses*, and *Four Upbuilding Discourses* of 1843.[87]

---

[81] See Giuseppe Mario Pizzuti, "Il Centro Italiano di Studi Kierkagaardiani," in *Nuovi Studi Kierkegaardiani*, ed. by Giuseppe Mario Pizzuti, Potenza: Centro Italiano di Studi Kierkegaardiani, vol. 1, 1989, pp. 213–9.

[82] *Nuovi Studi Kierkegaardiani. Bollettino del Centro Italiano di Studi Kierkegaardiani*, March 1993, ed. by Giuseppe Mario Pizzuti.

[83] *Sul concetto di ironia in riferimento costante a Socrate*, trans. by Dario Borso, Milan: Guerini e Associati 1989 (2nd ed., Milan: Biblioteca Universale Rizzoli 1995).

[84] *Prefazioni. Lettura ricreativa per determinati ceti a seconda dell'ora e della circostanza*, trans. by Dario Borso, Milan: Guerini e Associati 1990 (2nd ed., Milan: Biblioteca universale Rizzoli 1996).

[85] *Due epoche*, partial trans. by Dario Borso, Viterbo: Stampa Alternativa 1994.

[86] *Una recensione letteraria*, trans. by Dario Borso, Milan: Guerini 1995.

[87] *Discorsi edificanti 1843* (*Due discorsi edificanti*, *Tre discorsi edificanti*; *Quattro discorsi edificanti*), trans. and ed. by D. Borso, Casale Monferrato: Piemme 1998.

Also in the 1990s, we should mention the studies and translations of Simonella Davini, who has focused especially on the aesthetic issues in Kierkegaard's work.[88] In the same years, Ettore Rocca translated and edited the most recent Italian version of *The Sickness unto Death*, making significant changes vis-à-vis the older translations. He collaborates as a resident researcher at the Søren Kierkegaard Research Centre at Copenhagen University. His interests in Kierkegaard are, in particular, the relation between aesthetics and theology. He has argued for, among other things, the presence in Kierkegaard of a "second aesthetic," which is an aesthetic rooted in the religious.[89]

It is precisely this new generation of Kierkegaard scholars—among whom one may mention also Massimo Iiritano and Isabella Adinolfi—who founded in 2000 the Italian Society for Kierkegaard Studies (S.I.S.K.), in order to promote the study of Kierkegaard in this country. Among its activities, there is a biannual international congress: the first one took place at Venice University, December 14–16, 2000, with the topic "The Religious in Kierkegaard."[90] Many of the most important Kierkegaard scholars of that moment in Italy and abroad participated, including Virgilio Melchiorre—the current president of the society—Giorgio Penzo, Umberto Regina, Anna Giannatiempo Quinzio, Aurelio Rizzacasa (b. 1940),[91] and Giuseppe Modica. The S.I.S.K. also publishes every year a number of its review, focusing each time on a different topic. The journal is called *NotaBene. Quaderni di Studi Kierkegaardiani*, and its first three numbers have appeared.[92] A second congress was organized in October 2002 at the monastery of Bose (Biella, Piemonte) on the topic of "The Edifying in Kierkegaard." Finally, the most recent international congress on Kierkegaard's philosophy, organized by Umberto Regina in collaboration with

---

[88] See *Johannes Climacus o De omnibus dubitandum est. Un racconto*, trans. by Simonella Davini, Pisa: ETS 1995; *In vino veritas*, trans. and ed. by Dario Borso and Simonella Davini, Milan: G. Tranchida 1996; "La sapienza segreta," trans. by Simonella Davini, in *Seconda navigazione. Annuario di filosofia 2002*, Milan: Mondadori 2002, pp. 217–54. Among the theoretical work see in particular Simonella Davini, *Il circolo del salto. Kierkegaard e la ripetizione*, Pisa: Edizioni ETS 1996.

[89] See in particular Ettore Rocca, "La seconda estetica di Kierkegaard," *Il Pensiero*, no. 1, 2000, pp. 85–97; "Kierkegaard's Second Aesthetic," *Kierkegaard Studies. Yearbook*, 1999, pp. 278–92 and *Tra estetica e teologia. Studi kierkegaardiani*, Pisa: ETS 2004.

[90] See *Il religioso in Kierkegaard. Atti del convegno di studi organizzato dalla Società italiana per gli Studi Kierkegaardiani tenutosi dal 14 al 16 dicembre 2000 a Venezia*, ed. by Isabella Adinolfi, Brescia: Morcelliana 2002. About the congress see Franco Macchi, "La ripresa degli studi kierkegaardiani in Italia e il convegno su "Il religioso Kierkegaard" Venezia 14–16 dicembre 2000," *Protestantesimo*, vol. 56, no. 2, 2001, pp. 124–31.

[91] See Aurelio Rizzacasa, *Kierkegaard. Storia ed esistenza*, Rome: Studium 1984; *Il tema di Lessing: è possibile provare una verità eterna a partire da un fatto storico?* San Paolo: Cinisello Balsamo 1996.

[92] See *Leggere oggi Kierkegaard*, ed. by Isabella Adinolfi, Rome: Città nuova 2000 (*NotaBene. Quaderni di Studi Kierkegaardiani*, vol. 1); *Kierkegaard e la letteratura*, ed. by Massimo Iritano and Inge Lise Rasmussen, Rome: Città nuova 2002 (*NotaBene. Quaderni di Studi Kierkegaardiani*, vol. 2) and *L'arte dello sguardo: Kierkegaard e il cinema*, ed. by Isabella Adinolfi, Rome: Città nuova 2003 (*NotaBene. Quaderni di Studi Kierkegaardiani*, vol. 3).

the S.I.S.K., was held at the University of Verona in December 2003, on the topic "Kierkegaard as Contemporary. Repetition, Repentance, Forgiveness."

One may describe the present tendency of Kierkegaard studies in Italy as bound to historical and philological rigor as concerns the translations, and a close collaboration (particularly among the new generation of scholars) with the international milieu, especially the Danish one based around the Søren Kierkegaard Research Centre in Copenhagen. This has resulted in a profitable exchange which will hopefully bring an approach to Kierkegaard's philosophy that is, as far as possible, devoid of prejudices and misconceptions.

Bibliography

I. Italian Translations of Kierkegaard's Works

"Il più infelice" ["The Unhappiest One"], trans. (from *SV1*) by Knud Ferlov, *Leonardo*, vol. 5, no. 3, 1907, pp. 246–77.

Il diario del seduttore ["The Seducer's Diary"], trans. and introduction by Luigi Redaelli, Turin: Fratelli Bocca 1910 (several later editions).

In vino veritas, con l'aggiunta del *più infelice* e *diapsalmata* ["In vino veritas," together with "The Unhappiest One" and "Diapsalmata"], trans. (from *SV1*) by Knud Ferlov, Lanciano: R. Carabba 1910 (several later editions).

Il valore estetico del matrimonio ["The Esthetic Validity of Marriage"], trans. and ed. by Gualtiero Petrucci, Naples: F. Perrella e C. 1912.

L'erotico nella musica ["The Immediate Erotic Stages"], trans. by Gualtiero Petrucci, Genova: A.F. Formiggini 1913.

L'Ora. Atti d'accusa al cristianesimo del Regno di Danimarca [*The Moment*], vols. 1–2, trans. by Antonio Banfi, Milan and Rome: Doxa 1931 (2nd ed. in one volume (nos. 1–9, 1855), with an introduction by Mario Dal Pra, Milan: Bocca 1951).

"Kierkegaard. Con una scelta di passi nuovamente tradotti" [Kierkegaard, with a New Translation of a Series of Passages], trans. by Franco Lombardi, in *Appendice: Kierkegaard su Kierkegaard. Testimonianze e frammenti* [Appendix: Kierkegaard on Kierkegaard. Testimonies and Fragments] (extracts from the journals and papers), Florence: La Nuova Italia 1936, pp. 255–322 (2nd enlarged ed., entitled *Søren Kierkegaard. Con una antologia dagli scritti e una bibliografia sistematica* [Søren Kierkegaard. With an Anthology and a Systematic Bibliography], Florence: Sansoni 1967.)

"L'angoscia e il peccato. L'angoscia e l'istante" [Anxiety and Sin. Anxiety and the Moment] (extracts from *The Concept of Anxiety*), trans. by Armando Carlini, in *Il mito del realismo* [The Myth of Realism], Florence: Sansoni 1936, pp. 59–67.

Il concetto dell'angoscia [*The Concept of Anxiety*], trans. and ed. by Michele Federico Sciacca (translation from Gottsched and Schrempf's German edition, *Sämtliche Werke* (Jena: Diederichs 1922–23)), Milan: F.lli Bocca 1940 (2nd ed., 1944; 3rd revised ed., 1950).

Il concetto dell'angoscia. Una semplice ricerca psicologica sul problema del peccato originale [*The Concept of Anxiety. A Simple Psychologically Orienting Deliberation on the Dogmatic Issue of Hereditary Sin*], trans. by Meta Corssen, Florence: Sansoni 1942.

"Il valore dell'angoscia morale; la fede come salvezza dall'angoscia" [The Value of Moral Anxiety; Faith as Salvation from Anxiety (extracts from *The Concept of Anxiety*)], in Nicola Abbagnano, *Pagine di scrittori morali moderni* [Pages by Modern Moral Writers], Turin: Paravia 1943, pp. 257–69.

Aut-aut. Estetica ed etica nella formazione della personalità [*Either/Or.* "The Balance between the Esthetic and the Ethical in the Development of the Personality"], trans. from Danish by Kirsten Montanari Guldbrandsen and Remo Cantoni, Milan: M.A. Denti 1944 (several later editions).

Don Giovanni. La musica di Mozart e l'Eros [Don Giovanni. Mozart's Music and the Erotic], trans. from Danish by Kirsten Montanari Guldbrandsen and Remo Cantoni, introduction by Remo Cantoni, Milan: M.A. Denti 1944 (several later editions).

Gli uccelli dell'aria e i gigli del campo [*The Birds of the Air and the Lilies of the Field*], trans. and introduction by G.D.M. (Nazzareno Padellaro), Rome: La Bussola 1945.

I gigli dei campi e gli uccelli del cielo [*The Lilies of the Field and the Birds of the Air*], trans. by Eugenio Augusto Rossi, Milan: F. lli Bocca 1945.

La ripetizione. Saggio d'esperienza psicologica [*Repetition. An Essay in Experimental Psychology*], trans. by Enrichetta Valenziani, Milan: F. lli Bocca 1945.

La malattia mortale. Svolgimento psicologico cristiano di Anti Climacus [*The Sickness unto Death. A Christian Psychological Exposition for Edification and Awakening*], trans. by Meta Corssen, Preface by Paolo Brezzi, Milan: Ed. Di Comunità 1947. (Several later editions. In the 3rd revised edition (1965) passages from journals and papers from 1849, entitled as "Climacus e Anticlimacus"; "Lettera Al Professor Rasmus Nielsen e Riguardo a lui. (Da una brutta copia di una lettera datata 4 agosto 1849 a R.N.)"; "Nota dell Editore alla *Malattia mortale*" [Climacus and Anticlimacus; A Letter to Professor Rasmus Nielsen and about Him (from a rough copy of a letter to R.N. dated August 4, 1849); A Note on *The Sickness Unto Death* by the Editor].)

Lo specchio della parola [The Mirror of the Word] (translation of *For Self-Examination: Recommended to the Present Age*), trans. by Enrichetta Valenziani and Cornelio Fabro, with an essay by Lev Šestòv, entitled "Kierkegaard et la philosophie existentielle. Vox clamantis in deserto" [*Kierkegaard and the Existential Philosophy. Vox clamantis in deserto*] (Paris: Vrin 1936)], Florence: F. Fussi 1948.

Timore e tremore. Lirica dialettica [*Fear and Trembling. A Dialectical Lyric*], trans. by Franco Fortini and Kirsten Montanari Guldbrandsen, Preface by Jean Wahl, Milan: Ed. Di Comunità 1948 (several later editions).

Diario [Diary], trans. by Cornelio Fabro, vols. 1–3, Brescia: Morcelliana 1948–51 (2nd revised ed., vols. 1–2, 1962–3; 3rd revised and enlarged ed., vols. 1–12, 1980–3).

"Pagine di Kierkegaard dal 'Diario' della maturità" [Kierkegaard's Pages from the Diary of Maturity], trans. by Cornelio Fabro, *Humanitas*, 1950, no. 5, pp. 1–11.

Scuola di cristianesimo [*Practice in Christianity*], trans. by Agostino Miggiano and Kirsten Montanari Guldbrandsen, Milan: Ed. Di Comunità 1950 (several later editions).

Preghiere [Prayers], ed. by Cornelio Fabro, Brescia: Morcelliana 1951 (several later editions).

Antologia kierkegaardiana [Kierkegaard Anthology] (extracts from the journals and papers), ed. by Cornelio Fabro, Turin: S.E.I. 1952 (reprinted in 1967).

Ritratto della malinconia [Portrait of Melancholy] (selected passages from Kierkegaard's writings), trans. and ed. by Romena Guarnieri, Brescia: Morcelliana 1952 (several later editions).

Il concetto dell'angoscia. La malattia mortale [*The Concept of Anxiety. The Sickness unto Death*], trans. (from *SV2*) by Cornelio Fabro (from the second edition of *Samlede Værker*, 1920ff.), Florence: Sansoni 1953 (several later editions).

Il concetto dell'angoscia [*The Concept of Anxiety*], trans., abbreviated and ed. by Enzo Paci (based on the French translation by Ferlov-Gateau, Paris: Gallimard 1935, the German translation by Schrempf, Jena: Diedrichsen 1923, the Italian translation by Meta Corssen, Florence: Sansoni 1942 and compared to Fabro's translation, Florence: Sansoni 1953), Turin: Paravia 1954.

La ripresa. Tentativo di psicologia sperimentale di Constantin Constantius [*Repetition. An Essay in Experimental Psychology by Constantin Constantius*], trans. by Angela Zucconi, Milan: Ed. Di Comunità 1954 (several later editions).

Diario del seduttore ["The Seducer's Diary"], trans. by Attilio Veraldi, introduction by Remo Cantoni, Milan: Rizzoli 1955 (several later editions).

"La dialettica della comunicazione etica ed etico-religiosa" [The Dialectic of Ethical and Ethical-Religious Communication] (translations from *Pap.* VIII–2, B 78–89, pp. 143-90), ed. by Cornelio Fabro, in *Studi kierkegaardiani* [Kierkegaard Studies], Brescia: Morcelliana 1957, pp. 359–414.

L'esistenzialismo. Una antologia dagli scritti di Kierkegaard, Heidegger, Jaspers, Marcel, Sartre, Abbagnano [Existentialism. An Anthology of the Writings by Kierkegaard, Heidegger, Jaspers, Marcel, Sartre, Abbagnano], ed. by Pietro Chiodi, Turin: Loescher 1957 (several later editions).

Breviario [Breviary] (translation of the anthology *Kierkegaard-Brevier* (ed. by Peter Schäfer and Max Bense, Leipzig: Insel Verlag 1937)), trans. and ed. by Domenico Tarizzo and Pucci Panzieri, Milan: Il Saggiatore 1959 (several later editions).

"Il giglio e l'uccello" [The Bird and the Lily] (in *Appendice* [Appendix] to Pius Aimone Reggio, *La gioia*) [originally as *Vergiss die Freude nicht*, Freiburg: Herder 1956], trans. by Luciana Bulgheroni Spallino, Milan: Ediz. Corsia dei Servi 1960.

La sinistra hegeliana [The Left Hegelians] (selected texts ed. by Karl Löwith), Italian trans. by Claudio Cesa (passages from Kierkegaard's journals and papers), pp. 449–50; "Un manifesto" letterario [A Literary Manifesto], pp. 451–9; "Gli scritti su se stesso [Writings on Himself], pp. 460–8; and "L'unica cosa che è necessaria," [The Only Necessary Thing], pp. 469–78, Bari: Laterza 1960.

Briciole di filosofia ovvero una filosofia in briciole and *Postilla conclusiva non scientifica alle "Briciole di filosofia"* [*Philosophical Fragments or a Fragment of Philosophy* and *Concluding Unscientific Postscript to Philosophical Fragments*], vols. 1–2, ed. by Cornelio Fabro, Bologna: Zanichelli 1962.

Discorsi cristiani [*Christian Discourses*], trans. and ed. by Dino T. Donadoni, Turin: Borla 1963.

"Risoluzione e frammento sui Quattro stadi della vita (da II A 118–121; I C 226)," [Resolution and Fragment on the Four Stages of Life], trans. by Alessandro Cortese

Italy: From a Literary Curiosity to a Philosophical Comprehension 101

(in an Appendix of the article: "Kierkegaard e Sartre. Appunti di metodologia" [Kierkegaard and Sartre. Notes of Methodology], *Filosofia e Vita*, vol. 7, no. 22, 1965, pp. 46–9.

La difficoltà di essere cristiani [The Difficulty of Being Christians] (a selection from the *Upbuilding Discourses*), trans. and ed. by Jacques Colette, Alba: Paoline 1967 (2nd ed., 1970).

La lotta tra il vecchio e il nuovo negozio del sapone [*The Battle between the Old and the New Soap-Cellars*], trans. and ed. by Alessandro Cortese, Padua: Liviana 1967.

L'inquietudine della fede [The Anxiety of Faith], ed. by di Massimo Tosco, Turin: Gribaudi 1968.

La comunicazione della singolarità [The Communication of Singularity], ed. by Mauro La Spisa, Naples: Istituto Editoriale del Mezzogiorno 1969 (2nd revised ed., Palermo: Herbita 1982).

È magnifico essere uomini [It is wonderful to be Human (translation of *What we learn from the Lilies of the Field and the Birds of the Air*)], trans. by Luigi Rosadoni, Turin: Gribaudi Turin 1971 (2nd ed., 1990).

Esercizio del cristianesimo [*Practice in Christianity*], trans. and ed. by Cornelio Fabro, Rome: Editrice Studium 1971 (in the Appendix (pp. 327–41), "La "neutralità armata," ossia la mia posizione come scrittore cristiano nella cristianità" [*Armed Neutrality. My Position as a Religious Author in "Christendom" and My Strategy*], trans. by Cornelio Fabro).

Vangelo delle sofferenze [The Gospel of Sufferings], trans. by Cornelio Fabro, Fossano: Esperienze 1971.

"Che cosa giudica Cristo del cristianesimo ufficiale" [How Christ Judges the Official Christianity], trans. by Alessandro Cortese, *Contributi dell'Istituto di filosofia dell'Università Cattolica del S. Cuore di Milan*, vol. 2, 1972, pp. 57–64.

"È vero che il vescovo Mynster fu un 'Sandhedsvidne' ['testimone della verità'], uno 'de rette Sandhedsvidner' ['gli autentici testimoni della verità']?" [*Was Bishop Mynster "a Witness to the Truth," One of "the True Witnesses to the Truth"— is this the Truth?*], trans. by Alessandro Cortese, *Contributi dell'Istituto di filosofia dell'Università Cattolica del S. Cuore di Milan*, vol. 2, 1972, pp. 52–6.

La neutralità armata e il piccolo intervento [Armed Neutrality and the Little Intervention], ed. by Mariano Cristaldi and Gregor Malantschuk, trans. by Nicola De Domenio and Pina Zaccarin-Lauritzen, Messina: A.M. Sortino 1972.

Opere [Works], trans. and ed. by Cornelio Fabro, Florence: Sansoni 1972, includes parts of *Either/Or* ("Diapsalmata," "The Tragic in Ancient Drama Reflected in the Tragic in Modern Drama"), *Fear and Trembling*, *The Concept of Anxiety*, *Philosophical Fragments*, *Concluding Unscientific Postscript to Philosophical Fragments*, *The Sickness unto Death*, *Practice in Christianity*, *Gospel of Sufferings*, *For Self-Examination: Recommended to the Present Age*, and *The Changelessness of God*.

Puoi soffrire con gioia [You Can Suffer with Joy], ed. by Luigi Rosadoni, Turin: Gribaudi 1972.

Peccato, perdono, misericordia [Sin, Forgiveness and Mercy], trans. by di Laura Vagliasindi, Turin: Gribaudi 1973.

Diario [Diary], abridged edition by Cornelio Fabro, Milan: Biblioteca Universale Rizzoli 1975 (several later editions).

Dell'autorità e della rivelazione. Libro su Adler [*On Authority and Revelation. The Book on Adler*], trans. and ed. by Cornelio Fabro, Padua: Gregoriana 1976.

Enten-Eller: un frammento di vita [*Either/Or. A Fragment of Life*], vols. 1–5, trans. by Alessandro Cortese, Milan: Adelphi 1976–89.

"Pure una difesa delle alte qualità della donna" ["Another Defense of Woman's Great Abilities"], trans. by Salvatore Spera in his *Il pensiero del giovane Kierkegaard. Indagini critiche sulla filosofia della religione e studi sugli aspetti inediti del pensiero kierkegaardiano* [The Thought of the Young Kierkegaard. Critical Researches on Philosophy of Religion and Studies on Some Unknown Aspects of Kierkegaard's Thought], Padua: CEDAM 1977, pp. 150–3.

Il problema della fede [The Problem of Faith] (an anthology of Kierkegaard's writings), trans. and ed. by Cornelio Fabro, Brescia: La Scuola 1978.

"La nostra letteratura giornalistica" [Our Journalistic Literature], trans. by Salvatore Spera in "Appendice," in his *Kierkegaard politico* [Kierkegaard Politician], Rome: Istituto di Studi Filosofici 1978, pp. 98–119.

"Lettere a Regine" [Letters to Regine], trans. by Vanina Sechi, *Comunità*, no. 179, 1978, pp. 379–405.

Scritti sulla comunicazione [Writings on Communication], trans. and ed. by Cornelio Fabro, vols. 1–2, Rome: Logos 1979–82:

— vol. 1, contains "La dialettica della comunicazione etica ed etico-religiosa" ["The Dialectic of Ethical and Ethical Religious Communication"]; "Sulla mia attività letteraria" [*On My Activity as a Writer*]; "Il punto di vista della mia attività letteraria" [*The Point of View for My Work as an Author*].

— vol. 2, contains "Due piccole dissertazioni etico-religiose" ["Two Minor Ethical-Religious Essays"]; "La neutralità armata" [*Armed Neutrality*]; "La risposta al 'pastore di campagna' " [The Answer to the Country Pastor]; "Testi complementari sulla comunicazione" [Complementary Texts on Communication].

In vino veritas: un ricordo riferito da William Afham ["In vino veritas." A Recollection Related by William Afham], ed. by Domenico Pertusati, introduction by Nicola Abbagnano, Rapallo: Ipotesi 1982.

Pensieri che feriscono alle spalle e altri discorsi edificanti ["Thoughts that Wound from Behind—For Upbuilding"], trans. and ed. by Cornelio Fabro, Padua: EMP 1982, includes "Il pungolo nella carne" ["The Thorn in the Flesh"]; "Tre discorsi per la comunione del venerdì" ["Three Discourses at the Communion on Fridays"]; "Due discorsi per la comunione del venerdì" ["Two Discourses at the Communion on Fridays"]; "Un discorso edificante: 'La peccatrice' " ["An Upbuilding Discourse: The Woman Who Was a Sinner"].

Gli atti dell'amore [*Works of Love*], trans. and ed. by Cornelio Fabro, Milan: Rusconi 1983 (2nd ed., Milan: Bompiani 2003, includes Danish parallel text and editorial updating by Giuseppe Girgenti).

In vino veritas, ed. by Icilio Vecchiotti, Rome–Bari: Universale Laterza 1983 (several later editions).

"Indirizzo 'al benevolo lettore' " ["Lectori Benevolo" from *Stages on Life's Way*], trans. by Alessandro Cortese, in *Kierkegaard oggi. Atti del Convegno dell'11 novembre 1982* [Kierkegaard Today. Proceedings of the Congress November 11, 1982], Università Cattolica del Sacro Cuore, Milan, Aula degli atti accademici Pio XI, Milan: Vita e Pensiero 1986, pp. 145–50.

"*L'Istante*, n.1, 24 maggio 1855" [*The Moment*, no. 1, May 24, 1855], trans. by Alessandro Cortese, in *Kierkegaard oggi. Atti del Convegno dell'11 novembre 1982*, [Kierkegaard Today. Proceedings of the Congress November 11, 1982], Università Cattolica del Sacro Cuore, Milan, Aula degli atti accademici Pio XI, Milan: Vita e Pensiero 1986, pp. 152–71.

Briciole filosofiche [*Philosophical Fragments*], trans. by Salvatore Spera, Brescia: Queriniana 1987 (several later editions).

"Johannes Climacus ovvero 'De omnibus dubitandum est.' Un racconto" [*Johannes Climacus or De Omnibus Dubitandum Est. A Narrative*], trans. and ed. by Cornelio Fabro, in *Nuovi Studi Kierkegaardiani* [New Kierkegaard Studies], ed. by Giuseppe Mario Pizzuti, Potenza: Centro Italiano di Studi Kierkegaardiani 1989, pp. 165–211.

Sul concetto di ironia in riferimento costante a Socrate [*The Concept of Irony with Constant Reference to Socrates*], trans. by Dario Borso, Milan: Guerini e Associati 1989 (2nd ed., Milan: Biblioteca Universale Rizzoli 1995).

"La crisi e una crisi nella vita di un'attrice" [*The Crisis and a Crisis in the Life of an Actress*], trans. and ed. by Inge Lise Rasmussen Pin, in *Maschere Kierkegaardiane* [Kierkegaardian Masks], ed. by Leonardo Amoroso, Turin: Rosemberg & Sellier 1990, pp. 201–32.

Prefazioni. Lettura ricreativa per determinati ceti a seconda dell'ora e della circostanza [*Prefaces: Light Reading for Certain Classes as the Occasion may Require*], trans. by Dario Borso, Milan: Guerini e Associati 1990 (2nd ed., Milan: Biblioteca Universale Rizzoli 1996).

La ripetizione [*Repetition*], trans. by Dario Borso, Milan Guerini e Associati 1991 (several later editions).

Filosofia e paradosso [Philosophy and Paradox] (selected writings), ed. by Anna Giannatiempo Quinzio, Turin: SEI 1993.

Per provare sé stesso. Giudica da te! [*For Self-Examination—Judge For Yourselves!*], ed. by Maria Laura Sulpizi, Florence: Ponte alle Grazie 1993.

Stadi sul cammino della vita [*Stages on Life's Way*], ed. by Ludovica Koch, trans. by Anna Maria Segala and Anna Grazia Calabrese, Milan: Rizzoli 1993 (2nd ed., Milan: Biblioteca Universale Rizzoli 2001).

Due epoche [*Two Ages* (partial translation)], trans. by Dario Borso, Viterbo: Stampa Alternativa 1994.

Il concetto dell'angoscia [*The Concept of Anxiety*], ed. by Bruno Segre, Milan: E. Opportunity Books 1994.

Il mio punto di vista [*The Point of View for My Work as an Author*], trans. by Lidia Mirabelli, Vimercate: La Spiga 1994.

Accanto a una tomba ["At a Graveside"], trans. and ed. by Roberto Garaventa, Genova: Il Melangolo 1995.

Aforismi e pensieri [Aphorisms and Thoughts], trans. by Silvia Giulietti, ed. by Massimo Baldini, Rome: Tascabili economici Newton 1995.

Diario di un seduttore [*The Seducer's Diary*], trans. from German and ed. by Alessandro Quattrone, Bussolengo: Demetra 1995.

Johannes Climacus o De omnibus dubitandum est. Un racconto [*Johannes Climacus or The Omnibus Dubitandum Est. A Narrative*], trans. by Simonella Davini, Pisa: ETS 1995.

Opere [Works], vols. 1–3, with an opening essay by Sergio Quinzio, trans. and ed. by Cornelio Fabro, bibliographical updating by Anna Giannatiempo Quinzio, Casale Monferrato: Piemme 1995;

— vol. 1, includes *Sulla mia attività di scrittore* [*On My Activity as a Writer*]; *Il punto di vista sulla mia attività di scrittore* [*The Point of View for My Work as an Author*]; *Aut-Aut* (*Diapsalmata* e *Il riflesso del tragico antico nel tragico moderno*) [*Either/Or* ("Diapsalmata" and "The Tragic in Ancient Drama Reflected in the Tragic in Modern Drama")]; *Timore e tremore* [*Fear and Trembling*]; *Il concetto dell'angoscia* [*The Concept of Anxiety*]

— vol. 2, includes *Briciole di filosofia* [*Philosophical Fragments*]; *Postilla conclusiva non scientifica alle "Briciole di filosofia"* [*Concluding Unscientific Postscript to "Philosophical Fragments"*]

— vol. 3, includes *La malattia mortale* [*The Sickness unto Death*]; *Esercizio del cristianesimo* [*Practice in Christianity*]; *Vangelo delle sofferenze* [*The Gospel of Sufferings*]; *Per l'esame di se stessi raccomandato ai contemporanei* [*For Self-Examination: Recommended to the Present Age*]; *L'immutabilità di Dio* [*The Changelessness of God*].

Una recensione letteraria [*A Literary Review*], trans. by Dario Borso, Milan: Guerini & Associati 1995.

Diapsalmata, from *Aut-Aut* ["Diapsalmata" from *Either/Or*], ed. by Bruno Segre, Milan: Opportunity Books 1996.

In vino veritas, ed. by Dario Borso and Simonella Davini, Milan: G. Tranchida 1996.

Breviario [Breviary] (passages selected from various works and journals in Cornelio Fabro's translation), ed. by Dario Antiseri, Milan: Rusconi 1997.

"Guardate gli uccelli del cielo" (da *Il giglio nel campo e l'uccello nel cielo. Tre discorsi religiosi*) [Look at the Birds of the Air (from *The Lily of the Field and the Bird of the Air. Three Religious Discourses*)], trans. and presented by Ettore Rocca, *MicRomeega*, no. 1997, pp. 175–90.

L'attrice. Opera pseudonima di Kierkegaard (1848), Inter et Inter [The Actress. A Pseudonymous Work by Kierkegaard (1848), Inter et Inter], ed. by Alessandro Cortese, Treviso: Antilia 1997.

"Una fugace osservazione su un particolare nel Don Giovanni" [A Cursory Observation Concerning a Detail in Don Giovanni], trans. by Marcello Gallucci and U. Hammer Mikkelsen, in *Musicus discologus—Musiche e scritti per il 70° anno di Carlo Marinelli* [Musicus discologus—Tunes and Writings for Carlo Marinelli's 70th Birthday], ed. by Giuliano Macchi, Marcello Gallucci and Carlo Scimone, Vibo Valentia: Monteleone 1997, pp. 203–19.

Discorsi edificanti 1843 (*Due discorsi edificanti*, *Tre discorsi edificanti*; *Quattro discorsi edificanti*) [*Upbuilding Discourses 1843* (Two Upbuilding Discourses;

Three Upbuilding Discourses; Four Upbuilding Discourses)], trans. and ed. by Dario Borso, Casale Monferrato: Piemme 1998.
Il giglio nel campo e l'uccello nel cielo. Discorsi 1849–1851 ("Il sommo sacerdote"— "Il pubblicano"—"La peccatrice." Tre discorsi per la comunione del venerdì; Un discorso edificante; Due discorsi per la comunione del venerdì) [*The Lily in the Field and the Bird of the Air. Discourses 1849–1851* ("The High Priest"; "The Tax Collector"; "The Woman Who Was a Sinner; Two Discourses at the Communion on Fridays")], trans. and ed. by Ettore Rocca, Rome: Donzelli 1998.
Mozart. L'erotico nella musica. Dalle "Nozze di Figaro" al "Don Giovanni" [Mozart. The Musical-Erotic. From *Nozze di Figaro* to *Don Giovanni*], Foggia: Bastogi Editrice Italiana 1998.
Dalle carte di uno ancora in vita [*From the Papers of One Still Living*], trans. by Dario Borso, Brescia: Morcelliana 1999.
La malattia per la morte [*The Sickness unto Death*], trans. and ed. by Ettore Rocca, Rome: Donzelli 1999.
Esercizio di cristianesimo [*Practice in Christianity*], trans. by Cornelio Fabro, introduced and ed. by Salvatore Spera, Casale Monferrato: Piemme 2000.
"Esercizi di cristianesimo (Due sermoni inediti per la comunione del venerdì: 18 giugno 1847 e 27 agosto 1847, Vor Frue Kirke)" [Practice in Christianity. Two Unpublished Discourses at the Communion on Fridays: June 18, 1847 and August 27, 1847, Vor Frue Kirke], trans. and ed. by Ettore Rocca, *MicRomeega*, no. 2, 2000, pp. 97–108.
"L'arte di raccontare storie ai bambini" [The Art of Telling Stories to the Children (a passage of 1837 from BB:37)], trans. and ed. by Ettore Rocca, *MicRomeega*, no. 5, 2000, pp. 236–45.
"S. Kierkegaard, Post-Scriptum a *Enten-Eller*" [Post-Scriptum to *Either/Or*], trans. by Andrea Scaramuccia, in *NotaBene. Quaderni di Studi Kierkegaardiani*, vol. 1, *Leggere oggi Kierkegaard* [Reading Kierkegaard Today], ed. by Isabella Adinolfi, Rome: Città nuova 2000, pp. 191–210.
"Preghiere di Soren Kierkegaard" [Søren Kierkegaard's Prayers], in Mario Carrera, *Un'alba di luce. Via Crucis per condividere il dramma della sofferenza* [A Dawn of Light. *Via Crucis* to Share the Tragedy of Suffering], Milan: Paoline 2001.
L'attrice di Inter e Inter (1848); Due discorsi edificanti del maggio 1843 [*The Actress by Inter and Inter (1848); Two Upbuilding Discourses of May 1843*], in *Carte personali e opere pubbliche di S. Kierkegaard* [Søren Kierkegaard's Personal Papers and Public Works], ed. by Alessandro Cortese, Genova: Marietti 2002.
"La sapienza segreta (*Predica dimissoria* 1844)" [The Secret Wisdom. Dimissory Sermon], trans. by di Simonella Davini, in *"Seconda navigazione" Annuario di filosofia 2002*, Milan: Mondadori 2002, pp. 217–54.
L'istante [*The Moment*], trans. and ed. by Alberto Gallas, Genova: Marietti 2002.
Antologia dal Diario [Anthology from Kierkegaard's Diary], in *Il mistero della Passione* [The Mystery of Passion], ed. by Tito Di Stefano, Padua: Messaggero 2003.
"Il mito di Faust. Appunti e annotazioni dei *Papirer* (vols. 1 e 12)" [The Myth of Faust. Notes and Annotations from *Papirer* (vols. 1 and 12)], trans. by Carola Scanavino, in *L'arte dello sguardo: Kierkegaard e il cinema* [The Art of Looking:

Kierkegaard and the Cinema], ed. by Isabella Adinolfi, Rome: Città nuova 2003 (*NotaBene. Quaderni di Studi Kierkegaardiani*, vol. 3), pp. 183–207.

II. Secondary Literature on Kierkegaard in Italy

Abbagnano, Nicola, "Kierkegaard," in his *Storia della Filosofia* [History of Philosophy], Turin: UTET 1946–50, vol. 2, part 2 ("Il Romanticismo"), pp. 179–93 (in the 3rd edition of 1963, vol. 3, Chapter 8, pp. 181–99).
— "Filosofia della possibilità. Kant e Kierkegaard" [Philosophy of Possibility. Kant and Kierkegaard], in his *Esistenzialismo positivo* [Positive Existentialism], 2nd ed., Turin: Taylor 1948, pp. 31–3.
— "Kierkegaard e il sentiero della possibilità" [Kierkegaard and the Path of Possibility], in *Studi Kierkegaardiani* [Kierkegaard Studies], ed. by Cornelio Fabro, Brescia: Morcelliana 1957, pp. 9–28.
Acone, G., "L'opposizione kierkegaardiana a Hegel" ["Kierkegaard's Opposition to Hegel"], *Rivista di Studi Salernitani*, no. 1, 1968, pp. 189–205.
Adinolfi Bettiolo, Isabella, *Poeta o testimone? Il problema della comunicazione del cristianesimo in Søren Aabye Kierkegaard* [Poet or Witness? The Problem of the Communication of Christianity in Søren Aabye Kierkegaard], Genova: Marietti 1991.
— "Oltre l'etica: il rapporto tra morale e sovramorale in Søren Kierkegaard" [Beyond Ethics: the Relation between Moral and Supra-Moral in Søren Kierkegaard], in *L'etica e il suo Altro* [Ethics and its Other], ed. by Carmelo Vigna, Milan: F. Angeli 1994, pp. 150–88.
— "Kierkegaard: libertà e ragione" [Kierkegaard: Freedom and Reason], in *La libertà del bene* [The Freedom of the Good], ed. by Carmelo Vigna, Milan: Vita e Pensiero 1998, pp. 319–50.
— *Il cerchio spezzato: linee di antropologia in Pascal e Kierkegaard* [The Broken Circle: Anthropological Outlines in Pascal and Kierkegaard], Rome: Città nuova 2000.
— "Søren Kierkegaard e Woody Allen: l'umorismo come comunicazione indiretta della 'contraddizione priva di dolore' " [Søren Kierkegaard and Woody Allen: Humor as Indirect Communication of the "Painless Contradiction"], in *Leggere oggi Kierkegaard* [Reading Kierkegaard Today], ed. by Isabella Adinolfi, Rome: Città nuova 2000 (*NotaBene. Quaderni di Studi Kierkegaardiani*, vol. 1), pp. 147–62.
— " 'Djävlens öga': variazioni bergmaniane su temi kierkegaardiani" [Djävlens öga: Bergmanian Variations on Kierkegaardian Themes], in *L'arte dello sguardo: Kierkegaard e il cinema* [The Art of Looking: Kierkegaard and the Cinema], ed. by Isabella Adinolfi, Rome: Città nuova 2003 (*NotaBene. Quaderni di Studi Kierkegaardiani*, vol. 3), pp. 43–57.
Aliotta, Antonio, *Critica dell'esistenziaismo* [Critique of Existentialism], Rome: Cremonese 1951 (2nd ed., 1957).
Amoroso, Leonardo, "L'esistenza sorniona e il suo discorso. L'arte della comunicazione in Søren Kierkegaard" [The Sly Existence and Its Discourse. The

Art of Communication in Søren Kierkegaard], *Studi Filosofici e Pedaogici*, no. 2, 1977, pp. 101–36.

— *Maschere kierkegaardiane* [Kierkegaardian Masks], Turin: Rosemberg and Sellier 1990.

Armellini, Rina Anna, "Genesi ed evoluzione dell'angoscia esistenzialista" (profili di Kierkegaard, Dostoevskij, Sartre e Camus) [Genesis and Development of Existentialistic Anxiety (Profiles of Kierkegaard, Dostoyevsky, Sartre and Camus)], *Centro di Cultura* (Special number of the review *La Sorgente*), 1950.

Armetta, Francesco, *Storia e idealità in Kierkegaard* [History and Ideality in Kierkegaard], [S.l.]: Dialogo 1972.

Armieri, Salvatore, *Søren Kierkegaard e il cristianesimo* [Søren Kierkegaard and Christianity], Lugano: Edizioni del Cenobio 1956.

Baccarini, Emilio, "Esistenza ed etica. Letture ebraiche di Kierkegaard" [Ethics and Existence. Hebraic Readings of Kierkegaard], in *Kierkegaard. Esistenzialismo e dramma della persona. Atti del convegno di Assisi (29 nov.–1 dic. 1984)* [Existentialism and the Situation of the Individual. Proceedings of Congress in Assisi, November 29–December 1, 1984], Brescia: Morcelliana 1985, pp. 131–46.

Bach, Giovanni, "Note sulla cultura scandinava" [Notes on Scandinavian Culture], *Archivio di storia della filosofia*, no. 1, 1932, pp. 61–72.

Balbino, Giulian, "Søren Kierkegaard," in his *Il cammino del pensiero* [The Way of Thought], foreword by Fausto Sartorelli, Florence: Le Monnier 1962, pp. 626–8.

Banfi, Antonio, "Il problema dell'esistenza" [The Problem of Existence], *Studi Filosofici*, 1941, pp. 170–92.

— "Filosofia e teologia della crisi. I. Kierkegaard" [Philosophy and Theology of Crisis. I. Kierkegaard], in *Filosofi contemporanei* [Contemporary Philosophers], ed. by Remo Cantoni, Milan–Florence: Parenti 1961, pp. 255–62.

Battaglia, Felice, "Kierkegaard fra il singolo e Dio" [Kierkegaard between the Singular Individual and God], in his *Il problema della morale nell'esistenzialismo* [The Moral Problem in Existentialism], Bologna: Zuffi 1946, pp. 9–81.

— "Etica e religione nel 'Diario' di Kierkegaard" [Ethics and Religion in Kierkegaard's "Diary"], in *Studi Kierkegaardiani* [Kierkegaard Studies], ed. by Cornelio Fabro, Brescia: Morcelliana 1957, pp. 29–65.

Bausola, Adriano, "Sul rapporto Schelling–Kierkegaard" [On the Schelling–Kierkegaard Relation], in F.W.J. Schelling, *Filosofia della Rivelazione* [Philosophy of Revelation], trans. by Adriano Bausola, Milan: Rusconi 1997, pp. LXXIX–LXXXIII.

Bazzi, T. and R. Giorda, "L'angoscia: ambiguità del termine (comunicazione e angoscia)" [Anxiety: the Ambiguity of the Word (Communication and Anxiety)], *Rassegna di Pedagogia*, vol. 41, nos. 2–3, 1983, pp. 122–9.

Belletti, Bruno, "Appunti su Peter Wust lettore di Kierkegaard" [Notes on Peter Wust. Reader of Kierkegaard], in *Kierkegaard. Esistenzialismo e dramma della persona. Atti del convegno di Assisi (29 nov.–1 dic. 1984)* [Existentialism and the Situation of the Individual. Proceedings of the Congress in Assisi, November 29–December 1, 1984], Brescia: Morcelliana 1985, pp. 225–33.

Bellezza, Vito Antonio, "Nota sull'esistenzialismo italiano" (analisi critica degli scritti di Cornelio Fabro) [Note on Italian Existentialism (critical analysis of Cornelio Fabro's Writings)], *Archivio di Filosofia*, vol. 15, nos. 1–2, 1946, pp. 143–62.

— "La lotta al teocentrismo nell'esistenzialismo kierkegaardiano" [The Fight against the Theocentrism in Kierkegaard's Existentialism], *Archivo di Filosofia*, no. 18, 1949, pp. 49–59.

— "Lo specchio della parola di Kierkegaard" [The Mirror of Kierkegaard's Word], *Archivio di filosofia*, no. 18, 1949, pp. 120–3.

— "Recenti critiche dell'esistenzialismo" [Recent Criticism of Existentialism], *Rassegna di filosofia*, vol. 2, no. 1, 1952, pp. 119–39.

— "Il singolo e la comunità nel pensiero di Kierkegaard" [The Individual and the Community in Kierkegaard's Thought], *Archivio di filosofia (Kierkegaard e Nietzsche)*, 1953, pp. 133–89.

Bellisario, Vincenzo, "Il dramma di Kierkegaard" [The Drama of Kierkegaard], *Rivista di Filosofia Neo-Scolastica*, no. 34, 1942, pp. 127–36.

Benzo, Massimo, "Kierkegaard e la denuncia del dramma della filosofia hegeliana nel *Libro su Adler*" [Kierkegaard and the Denunciation of the Drama of Hegelian Philosophy in *The Book on Adler*], *Per la Filosofia*, no. 35, 1995, pp. 88–95.

Bertin, G.M., "Comico, ironia e umorismo nel pensiero di Kierkegaard" [The Comic, Irony and Humor in Kierkegaard's Thought], in *Pedagogia tra tradizione e innovazione. Studi in onore di A. Agazzi* [Pedagogy between Tradition and Innovation. Studies in Honour of A. Agazzi], Milan: Vita e Pensiero 1979, pp. 361–82.

Bettiolo, Isabella Adinolfi, "La dialettica della fede in Pascal e Kierkegaard" [The Dialectic of Faith in Pascal and Kierkegaard], in *Kierkegaard: filosofia e teologia del paradosso, Atti del Convegno tenuto a Trento il 4–6 dicembre 1996* [Kierkegaard: Philosophy and Theology of Paradox. Proceeding of the Congress of Trento, December 4–6, 1996], ed. by Michele Nicoletti and Giorgio Penzo, Brescia: Morcelliana 1999, pp. 223–50.

Bianchi, Cirillo, "Cristo scandalo della ragione e oggetto della fede secondo Kierkegaard" [Christ as Scandal of Reason and Object of Faith in Kierkegaard], *Rivista Rosminiana*, no. 68, 1974, pp. 316–21.

Bignone, Ettore, "Søren Kierkegaard," *Le cronache letterarie*, no. 4, 1910, p. 1.

— "Søren Kierkegaard. II. La filosofia dello stadio estetico" [Søren Kierkegaard. II. The Philosophy of the Aesthetic Stage], *Le Cronache Letterarie*, no. 9, 1910, p. 3.

Bobbio, Norberto, "Kierkegaard e noi" [Kierkegaard and We], *Comunità*, no. 4, 1950, pp. 54ff.

Bochi, Giulia, *Pecato e fede. Motivi pietistici nel pensiero di Kierkegaard* [Sin and Faith. Pietistic Motifs in Kierkegaard's Thought], Faenza: Tipografia Lega 1957.

Bonagiuso, G., "Dalla morte: il silenzio e la parola. Kierkegaard e Rosenzweig" [From Death: Silence and the Word. Kierkegaard and Rosenzweig], in *Il religioso in Kierkegaard. Atti del convegno di studi organizzato dalla Società Italiana per gli Studi Kierkegaardiani tenutosi dal 14 al 16 dicembre 2000 a Venezia* [The Religious in Kierkegaard. Proceedings of the Congress organized by The Italian

Society for Kierkegaard Studies in Venice, December 14–16, 2000], ed. by Isabella Adinolfi, Brescia: Morcelliana 2002, pp. 393–409.
— "La donna che camminava con Dio. Una lettura filosofica per "Breaking the Waves" di Lars von Trier" [The Woman Who Walked with God. A Philosophical Reading of Lars von Trier's "Breaking the Waves"], in *L'arte dello sguardo: Kierkegaard e il cinema* [The Art of Looking: Kierkegaard and the Cinema], ed. by Isabella Adinolfi, Rome: Città nuova 2003 (*NotaBene. Quaderni di Studi Kierkegaardiani*, vol. 3), pp. 81–99.
Borgese, Giuseppe Antonio, "Don Giovanni in Danimarca" [Don Juan in Denmark], in his *La vita e il libro. Saggi di letteratura e cultura contemporanea* [The Life and the Book. Essays on Literature and Contemporary Culture], Turin: Bocca 1910–3, vol. 2, pp. 231–41.
Borgia, Salvatore, "Il riscatto del singolo nella dialettica qualitativa di Kierkegaard" [The Redemption of the Singular Individual in Kierkegaard's Qualitative Dialectics], in his *Sapere assoluto e verità soggettiva* [Absolute Knowledge and Subjective Truth], Galatina: Editrice Salentina 1971, pp. 45–254.
Borso, Dario, "Due note kierkegaardiane" [Two Kierkegaardian Notes], *Rivista di Storia della Filosofia*, no. 49, 3, 1994, p. 547–58.
Bottani, Livio, "Noia, acedia ed epoché" [Tediousness, Sloth and *epoché*], *Sapienza*, 1991, pp. 113–91.
— "Malinconia e nichilismo. I: Dalla ferita mortale alla ricomposizione dell'infranto" [Melancholy and Nihilism. I. From the Mortal Wound to the Recomposition of the Broken], *Filosofia*, vol. 43, no. 2, 1992, pp. 269–93.
Brancatisano, Fortunato, "Angoscia e inquietudine in Kierkegaard" [Anxiety and Worry in Kierkegaard], *Noesis*, no. 1, 1946, pp. 291–316.
Brandalise, A., "Stato d'animo. Sguardo e cinematografia a proposito di Kierkegaard" [Mood. Look and Cinematography about Kierkegaard], in *L'arte dello sguardo: Kierkegaard e il cinema* [The Art of Looking: Kierkegaard and the Cinema], ed. by Isabella Adinolfi, Rome: Città nuova 2003 (*NotaBene. Quaderni di Studi Kierkegaardiani*, vol. 3), pp. 115–20.
Bucceri, Stefania, "Kierkegaard e Dostoevskij di fronte al problema del male nel mondo" [Kierkegaard and Dostoyevsky Confronted by the Problem of the Evils of the World], in *Atti del Congresso Internazionale di Filosofia 1946* [Proceedings of the International Congress of Philosophy 1946], Milan and Rome 1947, vol. 2 (*L'esistenzialismo*).
Buonaiuti, Ernesto, "Ancora Kierkegaard" [Kierkegaard Again], *Religio*, no. 13, 1937, pp. 366–7.
— "Carlo Barth e la teologia della crisi" [Karl Barth and the Theology of Crisis], *La Nuova Europa*, no. 2, 1945.
Burghi, Giancarlo, "Conversazione con Cornelio Fabro" [Conversation with Cornelio Fabro], *Aquinas*, vol. 39, no. 3, 1996, pp. 459–74.
Caccia, Gabriele, *La fede ed il suo oggetto nell'"Esercizio del cristianesimo" di Søren Kierkegaard* [Faith and Its Object in Søren Kierkegaard's *Practice in Christianity*], Rome: Tipografia poliglotta della Pontificia Università Gregoriana 1992.

Calò, Giovanni, *La diffusione dell'idealismo Romentico nei paesi scandinavi: ...Søren Aabye Kierkegaard...* [The Diffusion of Romantic Idealism in the Scandinavian Countries: ... Søren Aabye Kierkegaard ...], in his *L'individualismo etico nel secolo XIX* [Ethical Individualism in the Nineteenth Century], Naples: Tipografia della Regia Università 1906, see pp. 161–80 (offprint from vol. 37 (1906) of *Atti della Reale Accademia di Scienze Morali e Politiche di Naples* [Proceedings of the Royal Academy of Moral and Political Sciences of Naples], prize-winning paper for the Academy in 1904).

Calogero, G., "Frammenti pedagogici di Søren Kierkegaard" [Pedagogical Fragments by Søren Kierkegaard"], *I Problemi della Pedagogia*, vol. 23, no. 17, 1971, pp. 10–23.

Calvi, Guido, *Il singolo e la comunità in Søren Kierkegaard* [The Individual and the Community in Søren Kierkegaard], Rome: ITAL, edizioni italiane 1983.

Cannistra, S., "Storia e fede nell'*Interludio* delle *Briciole filosofiche* di S. Kierkegaard" [History and Faith in the *Interlude* of S. Kierkegaard's *Philosophical Fragments*], *Teresianum*, vol. 43, no. 1, 1992, pp. 241–50.

Cantillo, Giuseppe, "Kierkegaard e la filosofia dell'esistenza di Karl Jaspers" [Kierkegaard and the Philosophy of Existence of Karl Jaspers], in *Kierkegaard: filosofia e teologia del paradosso, Atti del Convegno tenuto a Trento il 4–6 dicembre 1996* [Kierkegaard: Philosophy and Theology of Paradox. Proceeding of the Congress of Trento December 4–6, 1996], ed. by Michele Nicoletti and Giorgio Penzo, Brescia: Morcelliana 1999, pp. 265–78.

Cantoni, Remo, *Crisi dell'uomo. Il pensiero di Dostoevskij* [The Crisis of the Human Being. Dostoyevsky's Thought], Milan: Mondadori 1948.

— *La coscienza inquieta. Søren Kierkegaard* [The Anxious Consciousness. Søren Kierkegaard], Milan: Mondadori 1949 (2nd revised ed., Milan: Il Saggiatore 1976).

— "Umanesimo vecchio e nuovo" [Old and New Humanism], *Il Pensiero Critico*, no. 1, 1950, pp. 1–19.

— "La figura del *Freigeist* in Nietzsche" [The Figure of the *Freigeist* in Nietzsche], *Archivio di filosofia* (*Kierkegaard e Nietzsche*), 1953, pp. 239ff.

— "L'eredità spirituale di Søren Kierkegaard" [The Spiritual Heir of Søren Kierkegaard], in *Studi Kierkegaardiani* [Kierkegaard Studies], ed. by Cornelio Fabro, Brescia: Morcelliana 1957, pp. 95–104.

— "Kierkegaard Søren Aabye. Polemica antihegeliana" [Kierkegaard Søren Aabye. Anti-Hegelian Polemics], in his *Filosofia della storia e senso della vita* [The Philosophy of History and the Meaning of Life], Milan: La goliardica 1965, pp. 371ff.

Cantoro, Umberto, *Variazioni sull'angoscia di Kierkegaard* [Variations on Kierkegaard's Anxiety], Padua: Liviana 1948.

Capone Braga, Gaetano, "Il valore dell'argomento ontologico secondo il Kierkegaard" [The Value of the Ontological Argument in Kierkegaard], *Sophia*, no. 22, 1954, pp. 148–51.

Capucci, Flavio, "La rilettura di un filosofo religioso: interpretazione di Kierkegaard" [The Rereading of a Religious Philosopher: Interpretation of Kierkegaard], *Studi Cattolici*, no. 136, 1972, pp. 411–19.

Cappuccio, Sofia, "Le dimensioni dello spirito umano nell'esistenzialismo di Kierkegaard e di G. Marcel" [The Dimensions of the Human Spirit in Kierkegaard and G. Marcel's Existentialism], in *Storia e Valori. Convegno di Naples (16–17 ottobre 1990)* [History and Values. Proceedings of the Congress in Naples (October 16–17, 1990)], Naples: Loffredo 1992, pp. 157–63.

Caputo, Annalisa, "Esistenza. Categorie filosofiche del novecento" [Existence. Philosophical Categories of the Twentieth Century], *Paradigmi*, vol. 20, no. 59, 2002, pp. 291–302.

Carlini, Armando, "Il problema dell'interiorità nel Kierkegaard e nello Heidegger. Kierkegaard: I. L'angoscia e il peccato. II. L'angoscia e l'istante" [The Problem of Inwardness in Kierkegaard and Heidegger: I. Anxiety and Sin. II: Anxiety and Moment], in his *Il mito del realismo* [The Myth of Realism], Florence: Sansoni 1936, pp. 57–67.

Carrano, Antonio, "Tempo erotico e limite del tempo in Kierkegaard" [Erotic Time and Limit of Time in Kierkegaard], *Il Cannocchiale*, nos. 1–3, 1981, pp. 167–79.

— "Verità e scrittura in Søren Kierkegaard" [Truth and Writing in Kierkegaard], *Il Cannocchiale*, nos. 1–2, 1987, pp. 91–116.

Casellato, Sante, *Di alcune considerazioni intorno alla verità e all'errore* [Some Considerations on Truth and Error], Padua: CEDAM 1958.

Casini, Leonardo, "Il Diario di Søren Kierkegaard" [Søren Kierkegaard's Diary], *Humanitas*, vol. 39, no. 6, 1984, pp. 937–40.

— "Kierkegaard e il cristianesimo contemporaneo" [Kierkegaard and Contemporary Christianity], in *Kierkegaard. Esistenzialismo e dramma della persona. Atti del convegno di Assisi (29 nov.–1 dic. 1984)* [Existentialism and the Situation of the Individual. Proceedings of the Congress in Assisi, November 29 –December 1, 1984], Brescia: Morcelliana 1985, pp. 147–60.

— "Singolo, genere umano e storia universale. Un confronto tra Feuerbach e Kierkegaard" [Singular Individual, Humankind and Universal History. A Comparison of Feuerbach and Kierkegaard], *Filosofia e Teologia*, vol. 4, no. 2, 1990, pp. 317–28.

Castagnino, Franca, *Ricerche non scientifiche su Søren Kierkegaard* [Unscientific Researches on Søren Kierkegaard], foreword by Antimo Negri, Rome: Cadmo 1977.

Castellana, Wanda, "La crisi del modello hegeliano in Søren Kierkegaard" [The Crisis of the Hegelian Model in Søren Kierkegaard], in *Saggi e ricerche di filosofia* [Philosophical Essays and Research], ed. by Ada Lamacchia, Lecce: Milella 1973, pp. 41–57.

Castelli, Enrico, *Esistenzialismo teologico* [Theological Existentialism], Rome: Abete 1966.

— "Søren Kierkegaard suscitatore di realtà eterne e invisibili" [Søren Kierkegaard Evoker of Eternal and Invisible Realities], *La Civiltà Cattolica*, vol. 127, no. 2, 1976, pp. 456–63.

Castoro, Eliseo, *Esistenza in preghiera sulle orme di Kierkegaard* [Praying Existence in Kierkegaard's Footsteps], Casale Monferrato: Piemme 2001.

Casuscelli, Paolo, "Musica e linguaggio? Kierkegaard e Don Giovanni" [Music and Language? Kierkegaard and Don Juan], *Rivista di Estetica*, vol. 26, no. 23, 1986, pp. 51–62.

Cenacchi, G., "Kierkegaard: fenomenologia del peccato e filosofia esistenziale in *Il concetto dell'angoscia*" [Kierkegaard: Phenomenology of Sin and Existential Philosophy in *The Concept of Anxiety*], in *Nuovi Studi Kierkegaardiani. Bollettino del Centro Italiano di Studi Kierkegaardiani* [New Kierkegaard Studies. Bulletin of the Italian Center for Kierkegaard Studies], ed. by Giuseppe Mario Pizzuti, vol. 1, March 1993, pp. 25–40.

Cerasi, E., "Singolo o comunità? Per un confronto tra Kierkegaard e Barth" [Singular Individual or Community? For a Comparison Between Kierkegaard and Barth], in *L'arte dello sguardo: Kierkegaard e il cinema* [The Art of Looking: Kierkegaard and the Cinema], ed. by Isabella Adinolfi, Rome: Città nuova 2003 (*NotaBene. Quaderni di Studi Kierkegaardiani*, vol. 3), pp. 143–58.

Cerrigone, Mario Enrico, "Il demoniaco in Kierkegaard" [The Demonic in Kierkegaard], *Divus Thomas*, vol. 105, no. 2, 2002, pp. 59–87.

Chiesa, Mario, "Cinque esistenzialisti. (Kierkegaard, Dostoevskij, Barth, Marcel, Berdiaeff)" [Five Existentialists. (Kierkegaard, Dostoyevsky, Barth, Marcel, Berdiaeff)], *Rivista Rosminiana*, no. 44, 1950, pp. 67–74.

Ciaravolo, P., "Insorgenza e ambiguità del concetto di singolo in S. Kierkegaard" [Emergence and Ambiguity of the Concept of the Singular Individual in S. Kierkegaard], *Contributo*, no. 1, 1981, pp. 21–36.

Collenea Isernia, G., "La difficile rivoluzione di Søren Kierkegaard" [The Hard Revolution of Søren Kierkegaard], *Città Vita*, no. 1, 1972, pp. 91–100.

Colombo, G., "Il Cristianesimo di Kierkegaard e la modernità" [Kierkegaard's Christianity and Modernity], *Per la Filosofia*, no. 38, 1996, pp. 50–57.

— "La salvezza nell'essere che è parola e azione. Riflessioni *sull'Esercizio del Cristianesimo* di S. Kierkegaard" [The Salvation in Being which is Word and Action. Reflexions on Kierkegaard's *Practice in Christianity*], *Per la Filosofia*, no. 40, 1997, pp. 61–9.

Colombo, Yoseph, "Il dramma di Abramo nel tormentato pensiero di Kierkegaard" [Abraham's Drama in Kierkegaard's Tormented Thought], in *Annuario di Studi Ebraici*, ed. by Elio Toaf, 1969, pp. 89–108.

— "Il dramma di Abramo visto da Søren Kierkegaard" [Abraham's Drama Seen by Kierkegaard], *La Rassegna Mensile d'Israele*, no. 3, 1970, pp. 122–39.

Colosio, I., "Il Cristianesimo radicale di Kierkegaard nella sua ultima polemica contro la chiesa costituita" [Kierkegaard's Radical Christianity in his Late Polemics against the Established Church], *Rivista di Ascetica e Mistica*, no. 5, 1968, pp. 517–27.

— "Il Cristianesimo come antiborghesia nell'ultima polemica di Kierkegaard contro la chiesa di stato" [Christianity as Anti-Bourgeoisie in Kierkegaard's Late Polemics against the State Church], in *La borghesia e la sua crisi nella cultura contemporanea italiana e tedesca nel quadro dell'unità culturale europea. Atti del VIII Convegno Internazionale di studi italo-tedeschi, Merano 1971* [The Bourgeoisie and Its Crisis in Italian and German Contemporary Culture, within the Frame of European Cultural Unity. Proceedings of the VIIIth International Congress of Italian–German Studies, Meran 1971], pp. 445–53.

Contri, G.B., "Kierkegaard. Il Vangelo della sofferenza. Dolor diabolicus" [Kierkegaard. The Gospel of Suffering. Dolor diabolicus], *Il Nuovo Areopago*, no. 2, 1995, pp. 59–70.

Corsano, Antonio, "Dimensioni del fatto religioso" [The Dimension of the Religious Fact], *Giornale Critico della Filosofia Italiana*, no. 51, no. 4, 1972, pp. 516–24.

Cortese, Alessandro, "Recentes traductions italiennes de Søren Kierkegaard" [Recent Italian Translations of Søren Kierkegaard], *Kierkegaardiana*, vol. 5, 1964, pp. 123–9.

— "In margine all'estetica di Kierkegaard" [Marginal Notes on Kierkegaard's Aesthetics], *Nuova Presenza*, no. 17, 1965, pp. 10–22.

— "Kierkegaard–Sartre: appunti di metodologia" [Kierkegaard–Sartre: Methodological Notes], *Filosofia e Vita*, no. 6, 1965, pp. 31–49.

— "L'Organico culturale: paragrafi Kierkegaardiani" [The Cultural Structure: Kierkegaardian Paragraphs], *Vita e Pensiero*, vol. 48, no. 2, 1965, pp. 132–44.

— "Søren Aabye Kierkegaard. Abbozzo sulla sua vita" [Søren Aabye Kierkegaard. A Sketch of His Life], *Vita e Pensiero*, vol. 48, no. 1, 1965, pp. 38–54.

— "Filosofia, pena e tempo. La coscienza della pena in Kierkegaard" [Philosophy, Pain and Time. The Awareness of Pain in Kierkegaard], in *Archivio di Filosofia* (*Il mito della Pena*), Padua: CEDAM 1967 (*Atti del Colloquio internazionale Rome 7–12 gennaio 1967* [Proceedings of the International Congress in Rome January 7–12, 1967]), pp. 469–81.

— "Il pastore Adler: Della libertà religiosa in Kierkegaard" [Pastor Adler: On Religious Freedom in Kierkegaard], *Archivio di Filosofia*, 1968, pp. 630–46 (published also in *Il pastore A.P. Adler o della libertà religiosa in Kierkegaard* [Pastor Adler or On Religious Freedom in Kierkegaard], Milan: Vita e Pensiero 1969 (*Contributi dell'Istituto di Filosofia*, vol. 1), pp. 81–113).

— "La domanda su Kierkegaard: (*La lotta tra il vecchio ed il nuovo negozio del sapone*)" [The Question on Kierkegaard: (The Competition between Rival Soap Sellers)], *Archivio di Filosofia*, no. 1, 1968, pp. 143–58.

— "Del nome di Dio come l'edificante in Søren Kierkegaard" [The Name of God as the Edifying in Søren Kierkegaard], *Archivio di Filosofia* (*L'analisi del linguaggio teologico. Il nome di Dio*), nos. 2–3, 1969, pp. 539–50.

— "Dell'Infallibilità come Messaggio di Cristo in Søren Kierkegaard" [On Infallibility as Message of Christ in Søren Kierkegaard], *Archivio di Filosofia*, nos. 2–3, 1970, pp. 603–13 (published also in *L'infallibilità: l'aspetto filosofico e teologico. Atti del Convegno internazionale tenuto a Rome nel 1970* [Infallibility: The Philosophical and the Theological Aspect. Proceedings of the International Congress in Rome 1970], Milan: Vita e Pensiero 1972 (*Contributi dell'Istituto di Filosofia*, vol. 2), pp. 30–64).

— "Kierkegaard oggi: tra nichilismo e rinascita della filosofia" [Kierkegaard Today: between Nihilism and the Rebirth of Philosophy], *Itinerari*, no. 3, 1980, pp. 45–88.

— "Kierkegaard oggi" [Kierkegaard Today], *Rivista di Filosofia Neo-Scolastica*, vol. 75, no. 3, 1983, pp. 500–10.

Costa, Filippo, "Intra-soggetto ed inter-soggetto in Kierkegaard" [Intra-Subject and Inter-Subject in Kierkegaard], *Giornale di Metafisica*, vol. 25, no. 1, 2003, pp. 9–28.
— *Ermeneutica ed esistenza. Saggio su Kierkegaard* [Hermeneutics and Existence. An Essay on Kierkegaard], Pisa: ETS 2003.
Costa, Giuseppe, "Personalità religiose moderne" [Modern Religious Personalities], *Bilychnis*, nos. 8–9, 1930, pp. 117–19.
Costantini, A., "Concetto di peccato in Kierkegaard" [The Concept of Sin in Kierkegaard], *Rivista di Teologia Morale*, vol. 14, no. 56, 1982, pp. 553–68.
Cotta, Sergio, "Sur la signification eschatologique du droit" [On the Eschatological Meaning of Law], *Rivista Internazionale di Filosofia del Diritto*, no. 48, 1971, pp. 209–19.
Cristaldi, Giuseppe, *Il senso della fede in Kierkegaard* [The Meaning of Faith in Kierkegaard], Milan: Servizio librario dell'ISU dell'Università Cattolica del Sacro Cuore 1983.
Cristaldi, Mariano, "Materialismo storico ed esistenzialismo: Kierkegaard e Marx" [Historical Materialism and Existentialism: Kierkegaard and Marx], *Humanitas*, no. 4, 1949, pp. 1043–6.
— "Kierkegaard, Feuerbach, Marx e la dialettica" [Kierkegaard, Feuerbach, Marx and Dialectics] and "Struttura del paradosso kierkegaardiano" [The Structure of the Kierkegaardian Paradox], in his *Filosofia e Metafisica: studi sull'antimetafisicismo contemporaneo* [Philosophy and Metaphysics: Studies on Contemporary Anti-Metaphysics], Catania: Tip. Etna 1957, pp. 61–104 and pp. 105–27 respectively (republished as an appendix to his *Problemi di storiografia kierkegaardiana* [Problems of Kierkegaardian Historiography], Giannotta: Catania 1973, pp. 137–96).
— *Problemi di storiografia kierkegaardiana* [Problems of Kierkegaardian Historiography], Catania: Giannotta 1973.
— "Søren Kierkegaard: la rivelazione sofferente" [Søren Kierkegaard: The Suffering Revelation], in *Kierkegaard. Esistenzialismo e dramma della persona. Atti del convegno di Assisi (29 nov.–1 dic. 1984)* [Existentialism and the Situation of the Individual. Proceedings of the Congress in Assisi, November 29–December 1, 1984], Brescia: Morcelliana 1985, pp. 105–28.
Cristaldi, R.V., "Kierkegaard o della testimonianza impossibile" ["Kierkegaard or the Impossible Testimony"], *Teoresi*, 1977, pp. 233–46.
Cristellon, Luca, "Silenzio e comunicazione nel pensiero di Kierkegaard" [Silence and Communication in Kierkegaard's Thought], in *Nuovi Studi Kierkegaardiani. Bollettino del Centro Italiano di Studi Kierkegaardiani* [New Kierkegaard Studies. Bulletin of the Italian Center for Kierkegaard Studies], ed. by Giuseppe Mario Pizzuti, vol. 1, March 1993, pp. 41–56.
— "L'interpretazione del paradosso kierkegaardiano in Theodor Haecker" [The Interpretation of the Kierkegaardian Paradox in Theodor Haecker], in *Kierkegaard: filosofia e teologia del paradosso, Atti del Convegno tenuto a Trento il 4–6 dicembre 1996* [Kierkegaard: Philosophy and Theology of the Paradox. Proceedings of the Congress of Trento, December 4–6, 1996], ed. by Michele Nicoletti and Giorgio Penzo, Brescia: Morcelliana 1999, pp. 301–26.

Curi, Umberto, *Filosofia del Don Giovanni: alle origini di un mito moderno* [The Philosophy of Don Juan: on the Origins of a Modern Myth], Milan: B. Mondadori 2002.

D'Agostino, Francesco, "La fenomenologia dell'uomo giusto: un parallelo tra Kierkegaard e Platone" [The Phenomenology of the Just Man: a Comparison between Kierkegaard and Plato], *Rivista Internazionale di Filosofia del Diritto*, no. 49, 2, 1972, pp. 153–72.

— "Considerazioni sul problema del divenire in Søren Kierkegaard" [A Consideration of the Problem of Becoming in Søren Kierkegaard], *La Cultura*, no. 16, 1978, pp. 409–43.

Dalladonne, A., "*L'Esercizio del Cristianesimo* nel *Diario* di S. Kierkegaard" [*Practice in Christianity* in Kierkegaard's Diary], *Renovatio*, no. 4, 1985, pp. 407–28.

— "La dottrina kierkegaardiana del Singolo come critica cristiana del collettivismo giudaico" [Kierkegaard's Doctrine of the Singular Individual as Christian Criticism of Jewish Collectivism], in *Nuovi Studi Kierkegaardiani. Bollettino del Centro Italiano di Studi Kierkegaardiani* [New Kierkegaard Studies. Bulletin of the Italian Center for Kierkegaard Studies], ed. by Giuseppe Mario Pizzuti, vol. 1, March 1993, pp. 57–74.

D'Angelo, Antonello, "La dialettica della ripresa in Søren Kierkegaard" [The Dialectics of Repetition in Søren Kierkegaard], *La Cultura*, no. 20, 1982, pp. 110–55.

Davini, Simonella, *Il circolo del salto. Kierkegaard e la ripetizione* [The Circle of the Leap. Kierkegaard and Repetition], Pisa: Edizioni ETS 1996.

— "Sapere, passione, verità nell'interpretazione kierkegaardiana dello scetticismo antico" [Knowledge, Passion, Truth in Kierkegaard's Interpretation of Ancient Scepticism], in *Leggere oggi Kierkegaard* [Reading Kierkegaard Today], ed. by Isabella Adinolfi, Rome: Città nuova 2000 (*NotaBene. Quaderni di Studi Kierkegaardiani*, vol. 1), pp. 61–78.

— *Arte e critica nell'estetica di Kierkegaard* [Art and Criticism in Kierkegaard's Aesthetics], Palermo: Centro Internazionale Studi di Estetica 2003 (*Aesthetica preprint*).

De Feo, Nicola Massimo, "La dialettica dell'inversione" [The Dialectics of the Inversion], in his *L'ontologia fondamentale. Kierkegaard, Nietzsche, Heidegger* [Fundamental Ontology. Kierkegaard, Nietzsche, Heidegger], Milan: Silva 1964, pp. 19–38.

— "L'uomo-dio nel cristianesimo di Kierkegaard" [The Man-God in Kierkegaard's Christianity], *Giornale Critico della Filosofia Italiana*, no. 44, 1965, pp. 369–85.

Della Volpe, Galvano, *Appunti sulla filosofia contemporanea. I. (Banfi, Bariè, Carabellese, Kierkegaard)* [Notes on Contemporary Philosophy. I. (Banfi, Bariè, Carabellese, Kierkegaard)], Rocca di San Casciano: Tipografia Cappelli 1937, pp. 61–76.

De Natale, Ferruccio, *Esistenza, filosofia, angoscia: tra Kierkegaard e Heidegger* [Existence, Philosophy and Anxiety: between Kierkegaard and Heidegger], Bari: Adriatica Editrice 1995.

— (ed.), *Tra linguaggi e silenzi: riflessioni filosofiche* [Between Languages and Silences: Philosophical Reflections], Bari: Adriatica Editrice 2004.

De Paz, Alfredo, *Europa Romentica: fondamenti e paradigmi della sensibilità moderna* [Romantic Europe: Grounds and Paradigms of the Modern Sensibility], Naples: Liguori 1994.

De Rosa, Gabriele, "Il vescovo luterano Mynster, S. Alfonso de' Liguori e Kierkegaard" [The Lutheran Bishop Mynster, S. Alfonso de' Liguori and Kierkegaard"], in *Veritatem in caritate. Studi in onore di Cornelio Fabro* [*Veritatem in caritate.* Studies in Honor of Cornelio Fabro], ed. by Giuseppe Mario Pizzuti, Potenza: Ermes 1991, pp. 275 (also published in *Ricerche di storia sociale e religiosa*, vol. 21, no. 41, 1992, pp. 7–21).

— "Cornelio Fabro fra S. Tommaso, Kierkegaard e la morte a Pompei" [Cornelio Fabro between St. Thomas, Kierkegaard and Death in Pompey], *Ricerche di Storia Sociale e Religiosa*, no. 48, 1995, pp. 165–70.

De Ruggiero, Guido, "Kierkegaard," in *Filosofi del Novecento* [Philosopher of the Twentieth-Century], Appendix to his *La Filosofia Contemporanea* [Contemporary Philosophy], Bari: Laterza 1933.

— "La filosofia dell'esistenza" [The Philosophy of Existence], *Rivista di Filosofia*, no. 33, 1942, pp. 4–42.

Diddi, Roul, "Il momento etico nel pensiero di Kierkegaard" [The Ethical Moment in Kierkegaard's Thought], *Pagine Nuove*, vol. 2, no. 6, 1948, pp. 248–51.

Di Giamberardino, Oscar, "Kierkegaard iniziatore dell'esistenzialismo" [Kierkegaard Founder of Existentialism], in his *Dall'esistenzialismo alla filosofia della sensibilità* [From Existentialism to Philosophy of Sensibility], Padua: CEDAM 1951, pp. 7–28.

Di Monte, Italo, "Kierkegaard tra idealità e realtà. La dialettica della fede contro i falsi fideismi. Noterelle polemiche" [Kierkegaard between Ideality and Reality. The Dialectic of Faith Against the False Fideisms. Short Polemical Notes], in *Nuovi Studi Kierkegaardiani* [New Kierkegaard Studies], ed. by Giuseppe Mario Pizzuti, Potenza: Centro Italiano di Studi Kierkegaardiani 1988, pp. 101–15.

Di Stefano, Tito, "La sofferenza di Cristo nella teologia della croce di S. Kierkegaard" [The Suffering of Christ in Kierkegaard's Theology of the Cross], in *La sapienza della Croce oggi: atti del Congresso internazionale, Rome 13–18 ottobre 1975* [The Wisdom of the Cross Today: Proceedings of the International Congress in Rome, October 13–18, 1975], Turin: Leumann, Elle Di Ci 1976, vol. 3, pp. 68–75.

— *Il paradigma della verità esistenziale secondo S. Kierkegaard* [The Paradigm of Existential Truth in Kierkegaard], Perugia: Galeno 1985.

— *La libertà rischio della verità. Il problema di Lessing. La soluzione di Kierkegaard* [Freedom as Risk of the Truth. The Problem of Lessing. Kierkegaard's Solution], Città di Castello: Galeno 1985.

— *Søren Kierkegaard: dalla situazione dell'angoscia al rischio della fede* [Søren Kierkegaard: from the Situation of the Anxiety to the Risk of Faith], Assisi: Cittadella 1986.

— "Il ruolo dell'etica nella struttura dell'esistenza secondo S. Kierkegaard" [The Role of Ethics in the Structure of Existence in S. Kierkegaard], *Antonianum*, vol. 71, no. 1, 1996, pp. 105–13.

Dottori, Riccardo, "La testimonianza di Kierkegaard" [Kierkegaard's Testimony], *Archivio di Filosofia* (*Informazione e testimonianza*), no. 3, 1972, pp. 55–66.

Dottorini, D., "Il pensiero dello spettro. Note sul rapporto tra Kierkegaard e il cinema" [The Thought of the Spectre. Notes on The Relation between Kierkegaard and the Cinema], in *L'arte dello sguardo: Kierkegaard e il cinema* [The Art of Looking: Kierkegaard and the Cinema], ed. by Isabella Adinolfi, Rome: Città nuova 2003 (*NotaBene. Quaderni di Studi Kierkegaardiani*, vol. 3), pp. 101–13.

Ducci, Edda, *La maieutica kierkegaardiana* [Kierkegaardian Maieutics], Turin: Società Editrice Internazionale 1967.

Erri De, Luca, "Avventura del nome" [The Adventure of the Name], in *Kierkegaard e la letteratura* [Kierkegaard and Literature], ed. by Massimo Iritano and Inge Lise Rasmussen, Rome: Città Nuova 2002 (*NotaBene. Quaderni di Studi Kierkegaardiani*, vol. 2), pp. 11–12.

Faber, Bettina, *La contraddizione sofferente: la teoria del tragico in Søren Kierkegaard* [The Suffering Contradiction: The Theory of the Tragic in Søren Kierkegaard], Padua: Il poligrafo 1998.

— "L'inattualità del religioso in Kierkegaard" [The Untimeliness of the Religious in Kierkegaard], in *Il religioso in Kierkegaard. Atti del convegno di studi organizzato dalla Società Italiana per gli Studi Kierkegaardiani tenutosi dal 14 al 16 dicembre 2000 a Venezia* [The Religious in Kierkegaard. Proceedings of the Congress organized by The Italian Society for Kierkegaard Studies in Venice, December 14–16th, 2000], ed. by Isabella Adinolfi, Brescia: Morcelliana 2002, pp. 283–303.

Fabris, Adriano "La filosofia, la malattia, la morte. A proposito della 'Malattia per la morte' di Søren Kierkegaard" [Philosophy, Sickness, Death. About Kierkegaard's *Sickness Unto Death*], in *L'arte dello sguardo: Kierkegaard e il cinema* [The Art of Looking: Kierkegaard and the Cinema], ed. by Isabella Adinolfi, Rome: Città nuova 2003 (*NotaBene. Quaderni di Studi Kierkegaardiani*, vol. 3), pp. 137–42.

Fabro, Cornelio, *Introduzione all'esistenzialismo* [Introduction to Existentialism], Milan: Vita e Pensiero 1943, on Kierkegaard see pp. 24–44.

— "Centenari kierkegaardiani" [Kierkegaard's Centenaries], *Osservatore Romeno*, June 18, 1944, p. 3.

— "Kierkegaard e Marx" [Kierkegaard and Marx], in *Atti del congresso internazionale di filosofia 1946* [Proceedings of the International Congress of Philosophy 1946], Milan and Rome 1947, vol. 1 (*Il materialismo storico* [Historical Materialism]), pp. 3–16. (The same article is also the first chapter of Cornelio Fabro, *Tra Kierkegaard e Marx. Per una definizione dell'esistenza* [Between Kierkegaard and Marx. For a Definition of the Existence], Florence: Vallecchi 1952, pp. 9–39.)

— "Kierkegaard in inglese" [Kierkegaard in English], *Euntes Docete*, no. 1, 1948, pp. 163–6.

— "Kierkegaard poeta-teologo dell'Annunciazione" [Kierkegaard as Poet-Theologian of Annunciation], *Humanitas*, no. 3, 1948, pp. 1025–34.

— "La religiosità di Kierkegaard nel suo *Diario*" [Kierkegaard's Religiousness in his Diary], *Humanitas*, no. 3, 1948, pp. 209–16.

— "Critica di Kierkegaard all'Ottocento" [Kierkegaard's Criticism of the Nineteenth Century], in *Atti del XV Congresso Nazionale di Filosofia 1948* [Proceedings of the XVth National Congress of Philosophy 1948], Messina: G.D.'Anna 1949, pp. 375–85.

— "Esistenzialismo teologico" [Theological Existentialism], in *L'esistenzialismo* [Existentialism], Florence: Città di Vita 1950, pp. 15–40 (reprint in Cornelio Fabro, *Tra Kierkegaard e Marx. Per una definizione dell'esistenza* [Between Kierkegaard and Marx. For a Definition of Existence], Florence: Vallecchi 1952, pp. 9–39).

— "Rassegna dell'esistenzialismo" [A Review of Existentialism], *Divus Thomas*, no. 27, 1950, pp. 265–73.

— "L'Assoluto nel tomismo e nell'esistenzialismo" [The Absolute in Thomism and in Existentialism], *Salesianum*, no. 13, 1951, pp. 185–201 (also published in his *L'Assoluto nell'esistenzialismo* [The Absolute in Existentialism], Catania: Miano 1954, pp. 67–104).

— "Recenti studi danesi su Kierkegaard" [Recent Danish Studies on Kierkegaard], in *Rassegna di Filosofia*, no. 1, 1952, pp. 347–54 (republished also in his *Note di bibliografia kierkegaardiana* [Notes of Kierkegaardian Bibliography], in *Studi kierkegaardiani* [Kierkegaard Studies], ed. by Cornelio Fabro, Brescia: Morcelliana 1957, pp. 417–38).

— "La dialettica della libertà e l'Assoluto. Per un confronto tra Kierkegaard ed Hegel" [The Dialectics of Freedom and the Absolute. A Comparison of Kierkegaard and Hegel], *Archivio di Filosofia* (*Kierkegaard e Nietzsche*) 1953, pp. 45–69.

— "L'esistenzialismo kierkegaardiano" [Kierkegaard's Existentialism], in *Storia della filosofia* [History of Philosophy], ed. by Cornelio Fabro, Rome: Colletti 1954, pp. 773–856 (2nd ed., vols. 1–2, 1959 as "L'esistenzialismo kierkegaardiano" and "La Kierkegaard renaissance" [Kierkegaard's Existentialism" and "The Kierkegaard Renaissance"], vol. 2, pp. 839–918 (see also "Bibliografia," vol. 2, pp. 959–63).

— "Attualità e ambiguità nell'opera kierkegaardiana" [Actuality and Ambiguity in Kierkegaard's Work], *Orbis Litterarum*, no. 10, 1955, pp. 66–74 (with the title "L'ambiguità del cristianesimo kierkegaardiano" [The Ambiguity of Kierkegaard's Christianity] reprinted in his *Dall'essere all'esistente* [From Being to the Existent], Brescia: Morcelliana 1957, pp. 277–333).

— "La dialettica della fede nell'idealismo trascendentale" [The Dialectics of Faith in Transcendental Idealism], *Archivio di Filosofia*, no. 2, 1955, pp. 116–23.

— "Kierkegaard," in *Vite di pensatori* [Lives of Thinkers], Milan and Rome: RAI 1956, pp. 34–5.

— "Kierkegaard e il cattolicesimo" [Kierkegaard and Catholicism], *Divus Thomas*, no. 59, 1956, pp. 67–70.

— "Kierkegaard e San Tommaso" [Kierkegaard and St. Thomas], *Sapienza*, no. 9, 1956, pp. 292–308.

— "Sant'Agostino e l'esistenzialismo" [St. Augustine and Existentialism], in *Sant'Agostino e le grandi correnti della filosofia contemporanea.—Atti del congresso italiano di filosofia agostiniana. Rome 20–23 ottobre 1954* [St. Augustine and the Great Currents of the Contemporary Philosophy.—Proceedings of the Italian Congress of Augustinian Philosophy. Rome, October 20–23, 1954], Rome: Tolentino 1956, pp. 141–66 (on Kierkegaard see pp. 156–66).

— "Estetica mozartiana nell'opera di Kierkegaard" [Mozart's Aesthetics in Kierkegaard's Work], in *Atti del III congresso internazionale di estetica. Venezia 3–5 settembre 1956* [Proceedings of the Third International Congress of Aesthetics. Venice, September 3–5, 1956], Istituto di estetica dell'Università di Turin: Ed. della Rivista di Estetica, 1957, pp. 706–10.

— "Kierkegaard," in *Enciclopedia filosofica* [Encyclopaedia of Philosophy], Florence: Sansoni 1957, vol. 2 (ER–LE) columns 1699–1713.

— "La 'comunicazione della verità' nel pensiero di Kierkegaard" [The "Communication of the Truth" in Kierkegaard's Thought], in *Studi Kierkegaardiani* [Kierkegaard Studies], ed. by Cornelio Fabro, Brescia: Morcelliana 1957, pp. 125–63.

— "La fenomenologia della fede. Ambiguità della fede in Søren Kierkegaard" [The Phenomenology of Faith. Ambiguity of Faith in Søren Kierkegaard], *Archivio di Filosofia*, nos. 1–2, 1957, pp. 187–97.

— "Kierkegaard e Karl Barth" [Kierkegaard and Karl Barth], *Studi Francescani*, no. 55, 1958, pp. 155–8.

— "Il problema del peccato nell'esistenzialismo" [The Problem of Sin in Existentialism], in *Il peccato* [The Sin], Rome: Ares 1959, pp. 712–25.

— "Influssi cattolici sulla spiritualità kierkegaardiana" [Catholic Influences on Kierkegaardian Spirituality], *Humanitas*, no. 7, 1962, pp. 501–7.

— "Le prove dell'esistenza di Dio in Kierkegaard" [The Proofs of the Existence of God in Kierkegaard], *Humanitas*, no. 17, 1962, pp. 97–110 (Italian translation of Fabro's writing published under the French title "L'existence de Dieu dans l'œuvre de Kierkegaard" [The Existence of God in Kierkegaard's Work], in *L'existence de Dieu* [The Existence of God], Paris: Casterman, pp. 37–47).

— "Kierkegaard e la donna" [Kierkegaard and the Woman], *Mater Ecclesiae*, no. 2, 1967, pp. 240–4.

— "Kierkegaard e San Tommaso" [Kierkegaard and St. Thomas], *Mater Ecclesiae*, no. 1, 1967, pp. 152–60.

— "Il Cristianesimo come contemporaneità e impegno essenziale" [Christianity as Contemporaneity and Essential Engagement], in *Il Cristianesimo nella società di domani* [Christianity in the Future Society], ed. by Pietro Prini, Rome: Edizioni Abete 1968, pp. 49–80.

— "Kierkegaard e la teologia dialettica" [Kierkegaard and Dialectical Theology], in his *L'uomo e il rischio di Dio* [The Human Being and the Risk of God], Rome: Editrice Studium 1969, pp. 446–8.

— "La missione di Kierkegaard" [The Mission of Kierkegaard], *Ethica*, no. 8, 1969, pp. 169–80.

— "I caratteri dell'amore cristiano secondo Kierkegaard" [The Characteristics of Christian Love in Kierkegaard], *Ecclesia Mater*, no. 1, 1970, pp. 50–5.

— "Inediti kierkegaardiani" [Kierkegaard's Unpublished Works], *Humanitas*, no. 7, 1970, pp. 707–11.

— "Kierkegaard critico di Hegel" [Kierkegaard as Critic of Hegel], in *Incidenza di Hegel. Studi raccolti in occasione del II centenario della nascita del filosofo* [The Influence of Hegel. Studies Collected on the Occasion of the Second Centenary of Hegel's Birth], ed. by Fulvio Tessitore, Naples: Morano 1970, pp. 499–563.

— "Kierkegaard e la Madonna" [Kierkegaard and the Virgin Mary], *Ecclesia Mater*, no. 2, 1971, pp. 132–44.

— "Il conforto del Paradiso in Søren Kierkegaard" [The Consolation of Heaven in Kierkegaard], *Ecclesia Mater*, no. 3, 1971, pp. 226–34.

— "La libertà umana e l'eternità dell'inferno in Søren Kierkegaard" [Human Freedom and the Eternity of Hell in Søren Kierkegaard], *Ecclesia Mater*, no. 2, 1971, pp. 143–6.

— "Pensieri sulla morte in Søren Kierkegaard" [Thoughts on Death in Søren Kierkegaard], *Ecclesia Mater*, no. 1, 1971, pp. 43–47.

— "Cristologia kierkegaardiana" [Kierkegaardian Christology], *Divinitas*, vol. 16, no. 1, 1972, pp. 130–5.

— "La sofferenza di Cristo nella teologia di Søren Kierkegaard" [The Suffering of Christ in Kierkegaard's Theology], *Tabor*, nos. 11–12, 1972, pp. 330–2.

— "Sull'essenza della testimonianza cristiana" [On the Essence of Christian Testimony], *Archivio di Filosofia*, (*Informazione e testimonianza*), no. 3, 1972, pp. 39–54.

— "L'attività oratoria, dottrinale e pastorale di un vescovo luterano dell'Ottocento: J.P. Mynster" [The Oratorical, Doctrinal and Pastoral Activity of a Lutheran Pastor in the Nineteenth Century: J.P. Mynster], *Ricerche di Storia Sociale e Religiosa*, no. 1, 1973, pp. 41–108.

— "Spunti cattolici nel pensiero di Søren Kierkegaard" [Catholic Ideas in Søren Kierkegaard's Thought], *Doctor Communis*, no. 4, 1973, pp. 251–80.

— "La dialettica della situazione nell'etica di Søren Kierkegaard" [The Dialectics of the Situation in Søren Kierkegaard's Ethics], in *L'etica della situazione* [The Ethics of Situation], ed. by Pietro Piovani, Naples: Guida 1974, pp. 73–96.

— "La *pistis* aristotelica nell'opera di Søren Kierkegaard" [The Aristotelian *Pistis* in Søren Kierkegaard's Work], *Proteus*, no. 5, 1974, pp. 3–24.

— "Kierkegaard e la dissoluzione idealistica della libertà" [Kierkegaard and the Idealistic Dissolution of Freedom], in *Problemi religiosi e filosofia* [Religious Problems and Philosophy], ed. by Albino Babolin, Padua: Editrice La garangola 1975, pp. 99–122 (republished in *Scritti di filosofia in onore di Cleto Carbonara* [Philosophical Writings in Honor of Cleto Carbonara], ed. by Università dgli Studi di Napoli, Facoltà di Lettere e Filosofia, Naples: Giannini Editore, pp. 304–22).

— "La fondazione metafisica della libertà di scelta in S. Kierkegaard" [The Metaphysical Foundation of Choice in S. Kierkegaard], in *Studi di filosofia in onore di Gustavo Bontadini* [Philosophical Studies in Honor of Gustavo Bontadinj], vols. 1–2, Milan: Vita e Pensiero 1975, vol. 2, pp. 86–116.

— "Kierkegaard. Cristianesimo tragico o drammatico?" [Kierkegaard. Tragic or Dramatic Christianity?], *Humanitas*, no. 7, 1976, pp. 532–7.

— "Egli imparò l'obbedienza da ciò che soffrì" [He Learned Obedience by Suffering], *Ecclesia Mater*, no. 1, 1977, pp. 11–3.

— "La dialettica d'intelligenza e volontà nella costituzione dell'atto libero" [The Dialectics of the Intelligence and the Will in the Constitution of the Free Act], *Doctor Communis*, no. 2, 1977, pp. 163–91.

— "La dialettica qualitativa di Søren Kierkegaard" [The Qualitative Dialectics of Søren Kierkegaard], in *Dialettica e religione. Atti del 2° Convegno di Studi di*

Filosofia della Religione [Dialectics and Religion. Proceedings of the 2nd Congress of Studies in Philosophy of Religion], ed. by Albino Babolina, Perugia: Benucci 1977, pp. 1–50.

— "Sorpresa e attesa cristiana della morte in Kierkegaard" [The Christian Surprise and the Wait for Death in Kierkegaard], *Nuova Rivista di Ascetica e Mistica*, no. 3, 1977, pp. 297–310.

— "Il problema della chiesa in Newman e Kierkegaard" [The Problem of the Church in Newman and Kierkegaard], *Newman Studien*, no. 10, 1978, pp. 120–39.

— "La critica di Kierkegaard alla dialettica hegeliana nel *Libro su Adler*" [Kierkegaard's Criticism of the Hegelian Dialectic in *The Book on Adler*], *Giornale Critico della Filosofia Italiana*, no. 9, 1978, pp. 1–32.

— "Preghiera e dialettica dell'esistenza in Kierkegaard" [Prayer and the Dialectics of Existence in Kierkegaard], in his *La preghiera nel pensiero moderno* [Prayer in Modern Thought], Rome: Edizioni di Storia e Letteratura 1979, pp. 363–96.

— "Dialettica della libertà e necessità nella storia in Kierkegaard e Tolstoj" [The Dialectics of Freedom and the Necessity of History in Kierkegaard and Tolstoy], in *Tolstoj oggi* [Tolstoy Today], ed. by Sante Graciotti and Vittorio Strada, Florence: Quaderni di S. Giorgio 1980, pp. 111–28.

— "Circa l'ispirazione cristiana dell'opera di Kierkegaard. In margine ad una nota di Franco Lombardi" [About the Christian Inspiration of Kierkegaard's Work. Marginal Notes to a Note by Franco Lombardi], in *Scritti in onore di Nicola Petruzzellis* [Writings in Honor of Nicola Petruzzellis], ed. by Università dgli Studi di Napoli, Facoltà di Lettere e Filosofia, Naples: Giannini 1981, pp. 105–12.

— "La dialettica della prima e seconda immediatezza nella soluzione-dissoluzione dell'Assoluto hegeliano" [The Dialectic of the First and the Second Immediacy in the Solution-Dissolution of the Hegelian Absolute], *Aquinas*, 1981, pp. 245–78.

— "La negazione assurda" [Absurd Negation], *Quadrivium*, no. 4, 1981, pp. 434–88.

— "Convergenze tomistiche nell'opera di Søren Kierkegaard nel centenario dell'Enciclica *Aeterni Patris*" [Thomistic Convergences in Søren Kierkegaard's Work in the Centenary of the Encyclical *Aeterni Patris*], in *Atti dell'VIII Congresso Tomistico Internazionale* [Proceedings of the VIIIth International Thomistic Congress], vol. 8, *S. Tommaso nella storia del pensiero* [St. Thomas in the History of Thought], Città del Vaticano: Pontificia Accademia di S. Tommaso e di Religione Cattolica 1982, pp. 191–208.

— "L'angoscia esistenziale come tensione di essere-nulla, uomo-mondo nella prospettiva di Heidegger e Kierkegaard" [Existential Anxiety as Tension between Being and Nothing, Human Being and World in Kierkegaard's Perspective and Heidegger's], *Le Panarie*, no. 55, 1982, pp. 79–94.

— "Negatività e dialettica nell'opera di Søren Kierkegaard e di Karl Barth" [Negativity and Dialectics in the Work of Søren Kierkegaard and Karl Barth], in *Annali del Liceo Gian Giacomo Adria* [Yearbook of the Liceo Gian Giacomo Adria], Mazara del Vallo 1982, pp. 1–42.

— "Dall'ammirazione alla riprovazione della linea di Spinoza–Lessing nell'evoluzione del pensiero di S. Kierkegaard" [From Admiration to Criticism of the Spinoza–Lessing Line in the Development of S. Kierkegaard's Thought], *Studi Urbinati*, 1983, pp. 9–39.

— "La comunicazione nella dialettica esistenziale di S. Kierkegaard" [Communication in the Existential Dialectics of S. Kierkegaard], in *Conoscenza e comunicazione nella filosofia moderna e contemporanea* [Knowledge and Communication in Modern and Contemporary Philosophy], ed. by Edda Ducci and Mario Sina, Rome: Studium 1983 (*Quaderni dell'Istituto Universitario pareggito di Magistero "Maria F.F. Assunta,"* vol. 1), pp. 33–46.

— "La sicurezza del numero come oppio del popolo nell'ultimo Kierkegaard" [The Certainty of Number as the Opium of the People in the Late Kierkegaard], *Humanitas*, vol. 38, no. 2, 1983, pp. 214–26.

— *Riflessioni sulla libertà* [Reflections on Freedom], Rimini: Maggioli 1983.

— "Kierkegaard e Lutero: incontro-scontro" [Kierkegaard and Luther: Encounter], *Humanitas*, vol. 39, no. 1, 1984, pp. 5–12.

— "Kierkegaard e la Chiesa di Danimarca" [Kierkegaard and the Church of Denmark], in *Nuovi Studi Kierkegaardiani* [New Kierkegaard Studies], ed. by Giuseppe Mario Pizzuti, Potenza: Centro Italiano di Studi Kierkegaardiani 1988, pp. 117–23.

— "Ragione e fede in Rasmus Nielsen" [Reason and Faith in Rasmus Nielsen], in *Nuovi Studi Kierkegaardiani. Bollettino del Centro Italiano di Studi Kierkegaardiani* [New Kierkegaard Studies. Bulletin of the Italian Center for Kierkegaard Studies], ed. by Giuseppe Mario Pizzuti, vol. 1, March 1993, pp. 11–24.

— "Il pentimento cristiano nella dialettica esistenziale di S. Kierkegaard" [Christian Repentance in Kierkegaard's Existential Dialectics], in *NotaBene. Quaderni di Studi Kierkegaardiani*, vol. 1, *Leggere oggi Kierkegaard* [Reading Kierkegaard Today], ed. by Isabella Adinolfi, Rome: Città nuova 2000, pp. 167–77.

Faggi, Vico, *Kierkegaard: due radiodrammi* [Kierkegaard: Two Radio Plays], foreword by Adriano Guerrini, Savona: Sabatelli 1984.

Faggin, S., "Kierkegaard e Kafka. Materiali per un'ermeneutica esistenziale" [Kierkegaard and Kafka. Materials for an Existential Hermeneutics], in *Kierkegaard e la letteratura* [Kierkegaard and Literature], ed. by Massimo Iritano and Inge Lise Rasmussen, Rome: Città nuova 2002 (*NotaBene. Quaderni di Studi Kierkegaardiani*, vol. 2), pp. 139–42.

Farias, Domenico, "La cultura tra invidia e comunione: Kierkegaard e Dante" [Culture between Envy and Communion: Kierkegaard and Dante], *Rivista di Filosofia Neo-Scolastica*, no. 55, 1963, pp. 317–42.

Farina, M., "Più profonda è l'angoscia, più grande è l'uomo: considerazioni sulla sofferenza nella lettura del *Diario* di S. Kierkegaard" [Deeper is Anxiety, Greater is the Man: Considerations on Suffering in S. Kierkegaard's Diary], *Per la Filosofia*, no. 36, 1996, pp. 62–9.

Fazio, Mariano, "Il singolo kierkegaardiano: una sintesi in divenire" [The Kierkegaardian Singular Individual: A Becoming Synthesis], *Acta Philosophica*, vol. 5, no. 2, 1996, pp. 221–49.

— *Un sentiero nel bosco: guida al pensiero di Kierkegaard* [A Path in the Wood: a Guide to Kierkegaard's Thought], Rome: Armando 2000.

Ferrarotti, Franco, "Riflessioni preliminari sul concetto di singulus in Søren Kierkegaard" [Preliminary Reflections on the Concept of "Singulus" in Søren Kierkegaard], in *Kierkegaard: filosofia e teologia del paradosso, Atti del Convegno tenuto a Trento il 4–6 dicembre 1996* [Kierkegaard: Philosophy and Theology of the Paradox. Proceedings of the Congress of Trento, December 4–6, 1996], ed. by Michele Nicoletti and Giorgio Penzo, Brescia: Morcelliana 1999, pp. 155–62.

Fioravanti, A., "L'indicibile come paradosso: il volto di Bergman attraverso l'analisi di Gilles Deleuze" [The Unspeakable as Paradox: Bergman's Face through Gilles Deleuze's Analysis], in *L'arte dello sguardo: Kierkegaard e il cinema* [The Art of Looking: Kierkegaard and the Cinema], ed. by Isabella Adinolfi, Rome: Città nuova 2003 (*NotaBene. Quaderni di Studi Kierkegaardiani*, vol. 3), pp. 59–70.

Forte, Bruno, *Fare teologia dopo Kierkegaard* [*Making Theology after Kierkegaard*], Brescia: Morcelliana 1997.

— "Fare teologia dopo Kierkegaard" [Doing Theology after Kierkegaard], in *Kierkegaard: filosofia e teologia del paradosso, Atti del Convegno tenuto a Trento il 4–6 dicembre 1996* [Kierkegaard: Philosophy and Theology of the Paradox. Proceedings of the Congress of Trento, December 4–6, 1996], ed. by Michele Nicoletti and Giorgio Penzo, Brescia: Morcelliana 1999, pp. 31–52.

— "Pensare l'interruzione: Kierkegaard ai teologi" [Thinking the Interruption: Kierkegaard to the Theologians], in *Leggere oggi Kierkegaard* [Reading Kierkegaard Today], ed. by Isabella Adinolfi, Rome: Città nuova 2000 (*NotaBene. Quaderni di Studi Kierkegaardiani*, vol. 1), pp. 135–45.

— " 'Il settimo sigillo' di Ingmar Bergman. Nota teologica" ["The Seventh Seal" by Ingmar Bergman. A Theological Note], in *L'arte dello sguardo: Kierkegaard e il cinema* [The Art of Looking: Kierkegaard and the Cinema], ed. by Isabella Adinolfi, Rome: Città nuova 2003 (*NotaBene. Quaderni di Studi Kierkegaardiani*, vol. 3), pp. 39–41.

Fortunato, Marco, "Irragione, dolore e protesta in Kierkegaard" [Irrationality, Suffering and Kierkegaard's Protest], in *Il religioso in Kierkegaard. Atti del convegno di studi organizzato dalla Società Italiana per gli Studi Kierkegaardiani tenutosi dal 14 al 16 dicembre 2000 a Venezia* [The Religious in Kierkegaard. Proceedings of the Congress organized by The Italian Society for Kierkegaard Studies in Venice, December 14–16, 2000], ed. by Isabella Adinolfi, Brescia: Morcelliana 2002, pp. 259–70.

— "Kierkegaard 'contro' il cinema e alcuni argomenti in difesa dell'arte cinematografica" [Kierkegaard "against" Cinema and Some Arguments in Defence of Cinematographic Art], in *L'arte dello sguardo: Kierkegaard e il cinema* [The Art of Looking: Kierkegaard and the Cinema], ed. by Isabella Adinolfi, Rome: Città nuova 2003 (*NotaBene. Quaderni di Studi Kierkegaardiani*, vol. 3), pp. 121–33.

Franchi, Alfredo, "La tradizione filosofica moderna d'ispirazione immanentistica: analisi di alcuni brani" [The Immanentist-Inspired Tradition of Modern Philosophy: Analysis of Some Passages], *Sapienza*, no. 38, 1985, pp. 63–72.

— "Kierkegaard irrazionalista? Filosofi e filosofie nella interpretazione del filosofo danese" [Kierkegaard Irrationalist? Philosophers and Philosophies in the Interpretation of the Danish Philosopher], *Sapienza*, no. 43, 1990, pp. 271–91.

— "Tra malinconia e riso. La crisi dell'uomo contemporaneo" [Between Melancholy and Laughter. The Crisis of Contemporary Man], *Sapienza*, vol. 46, no. 3, 1993, pp. 263–86.

— "La crisi dell'uomo contemporaneo. Osservazioni sulla figura dell'esteta tra Ottocento e Novecento" [The Crisis of Contemporary Man. Remarks on the Figure of the Esthete in the Nineteenth and Twentieth Centuries], *Sapienza*, 1999, vol. 52, no. 3, pp. 281–315.

Francia, Ennio, "Preludio su Kierkegaard" [Prelude to Kierkegaard], *Frontespizio*, no. 3, 1938, pp. 188–99.

— "Il significato di Søren Kierkegaard" [The Meaning of Søren Kierkegaard], *Studium. Rivista Universitaria*, vol. 31, 1935, pp. 334–41.

Franco, Vittoria, *Etiche possibili: il paradosso della morale dopo la morte di Dio* [Possible Ethics: The Paradox of Morality after the Death of God], Rome: Donzelli 1996.

Franzini, Elio, "Kierkegaard e il senso del tragico" [Kierkegaard and the Sense of the Tragic], in *Tragico e modernità. Studi sulla teoria del tragico da Kleist ad Adorno* [The Tragic and Modernity. Studies on the Theory of the Tragic from Kleist to Adorno], ed. by Fuvio Carmagnola, Milan: Franco Angeli Editore 1985, pp. 68–85.

Fruscione, Salvatore, "Kierkegaard di fronte all'esistenza di Dio" [Kierkegaard on the Existence of God], *La Civiltà Cattolica*, no. 102, 1951, pp. 618–31.

Gabetti, Giuseppe, "Søren Aabye Kierkegaard," in *Enciclopedia italiana* [Italian Encyclopaedia], Rome: Istituto della Enciclopedia Italiana, Treccani 1933, vol. 20, pp. 193–4.

Gaeta, G., "Kierkegaard: cristianità come *ordine stabilito* e la contemporaneità con Cristo" [Kierkegaard: Christianity as *Established Order* and Contemporaneity with Christ], in *Il Cristianesimo nella Storia* [Christianity in History], vol. 5, no. 3, 1984, pp. 563–76.

Gallas, Alberto, "Contemporaneità e critica della cristianità stabilita in Søren Kierkegaard" [Contemporaneity and Criticism of the Established Christianity in Søren Kierkegaard], in *La cattura della fine: variazioni dell'escatologia in regime di cristianità* [Capturing the End: Variations on the Eschatology within Christianity], ed. by Giuseppe Ruggieri, Genova: Marietti 1992, pp. 225–70.

Gallino, Guglielmo, "Kierkegaard e l'ironia socratica" [Kierkegaard and Socratic Irony], *Filosofia,*" vol. 45, no. 2, 1994, pp. 143–61.

— "Kierkegaard. La Seduzione, l'Interiorità, l'Ironia" [Kierkegaard. Seduction, Inwardness, Irony], *Filosofia*, vol. 45, no. 3, 1994, pp. 291–328.

Gardini, Michele, "L'uomo è un rapporto: l'antropologia di Kierkegaard in margine a un giudizio Heideggeriano" [The Human Being is a Relation: Kierkegaard's Anthropology compared to a Heideggerian Judgment], *Discipline filosofiche*, vol. 12, no. 1, 2002, pp. 351–82.

Gargano, M., "Cristianesimo tragico, cristianesimo ludico: i due volti della fedeltà al Dio dialettico" [Tragic Christianity, Playful Christianity: the Two Faces of Fidelity to the Dialectical God], *Du*, vol. 42, no. 1, 1991, pp. 61–83.

Garin, Eugenio, *Cronache di filosofia italiana (1900–1943)* [Accounts of Italian Philosophy (1900–1943)], Bari: Laterza, 1955, see p. 24; p. 26; p. 512; pp. 515–19.

Garrera, Gianni, "Musicalità dell'intelligenza demoniaca" [The Musical Essence of the Demonic Intelligence], in *Leggere oggi Kierkegaard* [Reading Kierkegaard Today], ed. by Isabella Adinolfi, Rome: Città nuova 2000 (*NotaBene. Quaderni di Studi Kierkegaardiani*, vol. 1), pp. 87–100.

Gavazzeni, Gianandrea, "Kierkegaard, il Don Giovanni e la musica" [Kierkegaard, Don Juan and the Music], *Rassegna d'Italia*, vol. 2, no. 2, 1947, pp. 54–6.

Gherardini, B., "La teologia della croce di Kierkegaard" [The Theology of the Cross in Kierkegaard], *Studi Cattolici*, nos. 198–9, 1977, pp. 496–501.

Giampiccoli, Guglielmo, "Kierkegaard e Leopardi" [Kierkegaard and Leopardi], *Gioventù Cristiana*, nos. 2–3, 1940, pp. 80–3.

Giannatiempo Quinzio, Anna *Il "cominciamento" in Hegel* [The "Starting Point" in Hegel], foreword by di Antimo Negri, Rome: Storia e Letteratura 1983.

— *L'estetico in Kierkegaard* [Aesthetics in Kierkegaard], Naples: Liguori 1992.

— "Notabene cristiano: il fatto storico che Dio è esistito" [Christian Notabene: the Fact that God has Existed], in *Leggere oggi Kierkegaard* [Reading Kierkegaard Today], ed. by Isabella Adinolfi, Rome: Città nuova 2000 (*NotaBene. Quaderni di Studi Kierkegaardiani*, vol. 1), pp. 101–14.

— "Il malinteso tra speculazione e cristianesimo. Critica delle prove tradizionali dell'esistenza di Dio" [The Misunderstanding between Speculation and Christianity. The Criticism of the Traditional Proofs of God's Existence], in *Il religioso in Kierkegaard. Atti del convegno di studi organizzato dalla Società Italiana per gli Studi Kierkegaardiani tenutosi dal 14 al 16 dicembre 2000 a Venezia* [The Religious in Kierkegaard. Proceedings of the Congress organized by The Italian Society for Kierkegaard Studies in Venice, 14–16, December 2000], ed. by Isabella Adinolfi, Brescia: Morcelliana 2002, pp. 200–18.

Giannini, Florio, "Pregare il Padre celeste con Kierkegaard" [Praying to the Heavenly Father with Kierkegaard], *Il Dialogo*, 2003.

Gigante, Mario, Il messaggio esistenziale di Kierkegaard e la filosofia hegeliana" [The Existential Message of Kierkegaard and Hegelian Philosophy], *Asprenas*, no. 17, 1970, pp. 392–412.

— *Religiosità di Kierkegaard* [Religiousness in Kierkegaard], Naples: Morano 1972.

— *Il matrimonio nel giovane Kierkegaard* [Marriage in the Young Kierkegaard], Salerno: Istituto Superiore di Scienze Religiose 1982.

Givone, Sergio, "Aut Hegel Aut Kierkegaard," in *Cristo nel pensiero contemporaneo* [Christ in Contemporary Thought], ed. by Gino Ciolini et al., Palermo: Augustinus 1988, pp. 43–51.

— "A partire da Kierkegaard" [Starting from Kierkegaard], in *Leggere oggi Kierkegaard* [Reading Kierkegaard Today], ed. by Isabella Adinolfi, Rome: Città nuova 2000 (*NotaBene. Quaderni di Studi Kierkegaardiani*, vol. 1), pp. 79–86.

Glässer, G., "L'irrazionalismo religioso di Søren Kierkegaard. La dottrina del salto qualitativo" [The Religious Irrationalism of Søren Kierkegaard. The Doctrine of the Qualitative Leap], *Bilychnis*, no. 15, 1926, pp. 99–112.

Gneo, Corrado, "L'opzione radicale come fondamento dell'essere e Duns Scoto" [The Radical Option as Ground of Being in Duns Scotus], *Aquinas*, no. 14, 1971, pp. 125–32.

Goggi, G., "Il 'Non-io' di Fichte e l' 'ignoto' di Kierkegaard. Analogie" [Fichte's "Not-I" and Kierkegaard's Unknown. Analogies], in *Il religioso in Kierkegaard. Atti del convegno di studi organizzato dalla Società Italiana per gli Studi Kierkegaardiani tenutosi dal 14 al 16 dicembre 2000 a Venezia* [The Religious in Kierkegaard. Proceedings of the Congress organized by The Italian Society for Kierkegaard Studies in Venice, December 14–16, 2000], ed. by Isabella Adinolfi, Brescia: Morcelliana 2002, pp. 421–35.

Goisis, G., " 'L'istante.' Kierkegaard e l'attacco alla 'cristianità costituita,' " [*The Moment.* Kierkegaard and the Attack Against the Established Christianity], in *Il religioso in Kierkegaard. Atti del convegno di studi organizzato dalla Società Italiana per gli Studi Kierkegaardiani tenutosi dal 14 al 16 dicembre 2000 a Venezia* [The Religious in Kierkegaard. Proceedings of the Congress organized by The Italian Society for Kierkegaard Studies in Venice, December 14–16, 2000], ed. by Isabella Adinolfi, Brescia: Morcelliana 2002, pp. 219–43.

Gozzini, Mario, "La tragedia dell'io in Søren Kierkegaard" [The Tragedy of the Self in Søren Kierkegaard], *L'Ultima*, nos. 34–5, 1948 and nos. 37–8, 1949.

Guanti, Giovanni, "La musica come metafora teologica in Agostino e in Kierkegaard" [Music as Theological Metaphor in Augustine and Kierkegaard], *Rivista di Estetica*, nos. 26–7, 1987, pp. 153–69.

— "Tempo musicale e tempo storico in Agostino e in Kierkegaard" [Musical Time and Historical Time in Augustine and Kierkegaard], *Rivista di Estetica*, vol. 30, no. 36, 1990, pp. 95–141.

Guzzo, Augusto, *Gli Entretiens di Copenhagen su Kierkegaard* [Copenhagen "Entretiens" on Kierkegaard], Turin: Edizioni di Filosofia 1967.

Henrici, Peter [Blondel, Maurice], "Per una filosofia cristiana della prassi" [For a Christian Philosophy of Praxis], *Gregorianum*, no. 53, 1972, pp. 717–30.

— "Di fronte a Marx, Kierkegaard e Nietzsche" [Facing Marx, Kierkegaard and Nietzsche], in his "Maurice Blondel di fronte alla filosofia tedesca" ["Maurice Blondel in Front of German Philosophy], *Gregorianum*, no. 56, 1985, pp. 615–38.

Heschel, Abraham Joshua, "Il chassidismo e Kierkegaard" [Chassidism and Kierkegaard], *Conoscenza Religiosa*, no. 3, 1971, pp. 337–53.

Iiritano, Massimo, "Il paradosso kierkegaardiano come 'emergenza'" storica ed esistenziale" [The Kierkegaardian Paradox as Historical and Existential Emergence], *Aquinas*, vol. 40, no. 3, 1997, pp. 499–507.

— *Disperazione e fede in Søren Kierkegaard: una lotta di confine* [Despair and Faith in Søren Kierkegaard: A Border Struggle], introduction by Anna Giannatiempo Quinzio, Soveria Mannelli: Rubbettino 1999.

— "La "sesta parte del mondo": la disperazione del moderno tra estetico e religioso in Kierkegaard [The "Sixth Part of the World": Kierkegaard and the Despair of Modernity between the Aesthetical and the Religious], in *Leggere oggi Kierkegaard* [Reading Kierkegaard Today], ed. by Isabella Adinolfi, Rome: Città nuova 2000 (*NotaBene. Quaderni di Studi Kierkegaardiani*, vol. 1), pp. 45–60.

— "Introduzione," in *Kierkegaard e la letteratura* [Kierkegaard and Literature], ed. by Massimo Iritano and Inge Lise Rasmussen, Rome: Città nuova 2002 (*NotaBene. Quaderni di Studi Kierkegaardiani*, vol. 2), pp. 77–81.

— "La lacerazione dell'io tra disperazione e fede" [The Tearing of the Self between Despair and Faith], in *Il religioso in Kierkegaard. Atti del convegno di studi organizzato dalla Società Italiana per gli Studi Kierkegaardiani tenutosi dal 14 al 16 dicembre 2000 a Venezia* [The Religious in Kierkegaard. Proceedings of the Congress organized by The Italian Society for Kierkegaard Studies in Venice, December 14–16, 2000], ed. by Isabella Adinolfi, Brescia: Morcelliana 2002, pp. 271–82.

— "Amore e paradosso. Una lettura kierkegaardiana del 'Gertrud' di Dreyer" [Love and Paradox. A Kierkegaardian Reading of "Gertrud" by Dreyer], in *L'arte dello sguardo: Kierkegaard e il cinema* [The Art of Looking: Kierkegaard and the Cinema], ed. by Isabella Adinolfi, Rome: Città nuova 2003 (*NotaBene. Quaderni di Studi Kierkegaardiani*, vol. 3), pp. 15–38.

Impara, Paolo, *Kierkegaard interprete dell'ironia socratica* [Kierkegaard as Commentator of Socratic Irony], Rome: Armando 2000.

Innamorati, Marco, *Il concetto di Io in Kierkegaard* [The Concept of the Self in Kierkegaard], Rome: Edizioni dell'Ateneo 1991.

Jaworski, Marian, "Dio e l'esistenza umana" [God and Human Existence], *Acta Philosophica*, vol. 5, no. 1, 1996, pp. 95–101.

Jesi, Furio, *Kierkegaard*, Fossano: Esperienze 1972 (2nd ed., ed. by Andrea Cavalletti, Turin: Bollati Boringhieri 2001).

Klein: Alessandro, *Antirazionalismo di Kierkegaard* [Kierkegaard's Antirationalism], Milan: Mursia 1979.

— "La critica di Kierkegaard a Hegel" [Kierkegaard's Criticism of Hegel], in *Kierkegaard. Esistenzialismo e dramma della persona. Atti del convegno di Assisi (29 nov.–1 dic. 1984)* [Existentialism and the Situation of the Individual. Proceedings of the Congress in Assisi, November 29–December 1, 1984], Brescia: Morcelliana 1985, pp. 23–37.

Lamanna, Eustachio Paolo, "Søren Kierkegaard," in *Storia della filosofia* [History of Philosophy], Florence: Le Monnier 1936, vol. 2.

Lancellotti, Mario, "Kierkegaard: tragico e dialettica" [Kierkegaard: The Tragic and Dialectics], *Il Veltro*, no. 22, 1978, pp. 525–32.

— "Kierkegaard 1843: morfologia dell'arte e dialettica" [Kierkegaard 1843: Morphology of Art and Dialectics], in his *Filosofie sintetiche del linguaggio: Kierkegaard, Croce, Cassirer, Heidegger* [Synthetic Philosophies of Language: Kierkegaard, Croce, Cassirer, Heidegger], Rome: Bulzoni 1982, pp. 11–62.

Lazzarini, Renato, "Logica esistenzialistica e logica agonistica in Kierkegaard" [Existential Logic and Agonistic Logic in Kierkegaard], in *Atti del Congresso Internazionale di Filosofia 1946* [Proceedings of the International Congress of Philosophy 1946], ed. by Enrico Castelli, Milan and Rome: Castellani & C., 1948, vol. 2 (*L'esistenzialismo*), pp. 313–19.

Liber Academiae Kierkegaardiensis Annuarius, vol. 1, 1977–78 and vols. 2–4 1979–81, ed. by Alessandro Cortese, Milan: Vita e Pensiero 1980 and 1982 respectively.

Licciardello, P. Nicola, "Itinerari dell'esistenzialismo Romantico: Søren Kierkegaard" [Itineraries in Romantic Existentialism: Søren Kierkegaard"], *Teoresi*, no. 15, 1960, pp. 25–42.

Limentani, Ludovico, "Søren Kierkegaard. Polemica antihegeliana" [Søren Kierkegaard. Anti-Hegelian Polemics], in his *Il pensiero moderno. Storia della filosofia da R. Descartes a H. Spencer* [Modern Thought. The History of Philosophy from R. Descartes to H. Spencer], Milan: Società Editrice Anonima Dante Alighieri 1930, pp. 542–9.

Liotta, R., "L'educazione della possibilità in Søren Kierkegaard" [The Education of the Possibility in Søren Kierkegaard], *Prospettive Pedagogiche*, no. 3, 1968, pp. 204–13.

Llevadot, Laura, "Il tempo della ripetizione: l'istante" [The Time of Repetition: The Moment], *La Società degli Individui*, no. 19, 2004, pp. 23–35.

Lombardi, Franco, *Kierkegaard*, Florence: La Nuova Italia 1936 (2nd revised and enlarged ed., Florence: Sansoni 1967).

— "Alcune riflessioni su Kierkegaard ed altre poche cose" [Some Considerations on Kierkegaard and a Few Other Things], *Archivio di Filosofia* (*Kierkegaard e Nietzsche*), 1953, pp. 105–13.

— "Kierkegaard oggi" [Kierkegaard Today], *Il Cannocchiale*, no. 1, 1968, pp. 47–65.

Lombardi, Riccardo, "Il momento religioso nel pensiero kierkegaardiano" [The Religious Moment in Kierkegaard's Thought], *La Civiltà Cattolica*, no. 2258, 1944, pp. 87–98.

— "Søren Kierkegaard precursore dell'esistenzialismo" [Søren Kierkegaard, Forerunner of Existentialism], *La Civiltà Cattolica*, no. 2256, 1944, p. 366–76.

— "Søren Kierkegaard un pensatore triste" [Søren Kierkegaard: an Unhappy Philosopher], *La Civiltà Cattolica*, no. 2254, 1944, pp. 247–55.

Luisi, Giuseppe M., "Etica, ontologia, antropologia" [Ethics, Ontology, Anthropology], *Giornale Critico della Filosofia Italiana*, no. 48, 1969, pp. 561–82.

Lunardi, Lorenzo, *La dialettica in Kierkegaard* [Dialectics in Kierkegaard], Padua: Liviana 1982.

Macchi, Franco, "Con Kierkegaard oltre Kierkegaard" [With Kierkegaard, Beyond Kierkegaard], in *Il religioso in Kierkegaard. Atti del convegno di studi organizzato dalla Società Italiana per gli Studi Kierkegaardiani tenutosi dal 14 al 16 dicembre 2000 a Venezia* [The Religious in Kierkegaard. Proceedings of the Congress organized by The Italian Society for Kierkegaard Studies in Venice, December 14–16, 2000], ed. by Isabella Adinolfi, Brescia: Morcelliana 2002, pp. 361–76.

Magnino, Bianca, "Enrico Ibsen e Søren Kierkegaard" [Henrik Ibsen and Søren Kierkegaard], *Nuova Antologia*, series 7, no. 258 (336), 1928, pp. 298–311.

— "Il problema religioso di Søren Kierkegaard" [The Religious Problem of Søren Kierkegaard], *Giornale Critico della Filosofia Italiana*, no. 11, 1938, pp. 215–39.

Maiorani, Arianna, "Blixen e Kierkegaard: dialogo sul seduttore" [Blixen and Kierkegaard: Dialogue on the Seducer], *Intersezioni*, vol. 20, no. 1, 2000, p. 43–57.

Majoli, Bruno, "La critica ad Hegel in Schelling e Kierkegaard" [The Criticism of Hegel in Schelling and Kierkegaard], *Rivista di Filosofia Neo-Scolastica*, no. 46, 1954, pp. 222–63.

Mancinelli, P. "Homo absconditus homo revelatus: su alcune tracce kierkegaardiane in René Girard" [Homo absconditus homo revelatus: On Some Kierkegaardian Traces in René Girard], in *Kierkegaard e la letteratura* [Kierkegaard and

Literature], ed. by Massimo Iritano and Inge Lise Rasmussen, Rome: Città nuova 2002 (*NotaBene. Quaderni di Studi Kierkegaardiani*, vol. 2), pp. 127–37.

Mancini, Italo, *Filosofi esistenzialisti* [Existentialist Philosophers], Urbino: Argalia Editore 1964 (*Pubblicazioni dell'Università di Urbino. Serie di Lettere e Filosofia*, vol. 18.

Mangiagalli, M., "Il tempo dell'autenticità" [The Time of Authenticity], *Sapienza*, vol. 53, no. 1, 2000, pp. 69–86.

Manzia, Carlo, "Il problema della fede in Kierkegaard" [The Problem of Faith in Kierkegaard], in *Problemi scelti di teologia contemporanea* [Selected Problems of Contemporary Theology] (*Relazioni lette nella sezione di teologia del Congresso internazionale per il IV centenario della Pontificia Università Gregoriana, 13–17 ottobre 1953* [Papers read during the theological section at the international Congress for the centenary of the Pontifical Gregorian University of Rome, October 13–17, 1953]), in *Analecta Gregoriana*, vol. 68, 1954, pp. 123–32.

Marchesi, Angelo, "Due scelte di fronte a Cristo: Kierkegaard e Nietzsche" [Two Choices in Front of Christ], in *Il Cristo dei filosofi, Atti del XXX Convegno di Gallarate 1975* [The Christ of the Philosophers, Proceedings of the XXXth Congress of Gallarate 1975], Brescia: Morcelliana 1976, pp. 149–66.

— *L'uomo contemporaneo: smarrimenti e recupero* [Contemporary Man: Disorientations and Rehabilitation], Milan: Vita e Pensiero 1977.

Mariani, Eliodoro, *Analisi esistenziale e pre-comprensione della fede: da Kierkegaard ad Heidegger e Bultmann, le premesse filosofiche della demitizzazione* [Existential Analysis and Pre-Comprehension of Faith: From Kierkegaard to Heidegger and Bultmann, the Philosophical Premises of Demythologization], Rome: Istituto Pedagogico Pontificio Ateneo Antonianum 1980.

Marini, Sergio, "Soggettività ed educazione in Kierkegaard" [Subjectivity and Education in Kierkegaard], in *Il problema dell'antropologia. Atti del 23. Convegno di assistenti universitari di filosofia, Padova 1979* [The Problem of Anthropology. Proceedings of the 24th Congress of University Assistants, Padua 1979], Padua: Gregoriana 1980, pp. 81–95.

— "Il 'divenire' e il 'possibile' nelle 'Briciole di filosofia' di Søren Kierkegaard" [Becoming and Possibility in Søren Kierkegaard's *Philosophical Fragments*], *Humanitas*, vol. 36, 1981, pp. 325–44.

— "Il 're dei ladri.' Appunti su una figura del 'Diario' di Kierkegaard" [The "King of Thieves." Notes on a figure of Kierkegaard's Diary], *Humanitas*, vol. 36, 1981, pp. 826–35.

— "Il rifiuto kierkegaardiano dell'argomento ontologico" [The Kierkegaardian Refutation of the Ontological Argument], *Humanitas*, vol. 38, no. 3, 1983, pp. 343–57.

— "La presenza di Kierkegaard nel pensiero di Wittgenstein" [The Presence of Kierkegaard in the Thought of Wittgenstein], *Rivista di Filosofia Neo-Scolastica*, no. 2, 1986, pp. 211–26.

Masi, Giuseppe, *La determinazione della possibilità dell'esistenza in Kierkegaard* [The Definition of the Possibility of Existence in Kierkegaard], Bologna: C. Zuffi Editore 1949.

— "Storicità e cristianesimo in Kierkegaard" [Historicity and Christianity in Kierkegaard], *Archivio di Filosofia* (*Kierkegaard e Nietzsche*), no. 2, 1953, pp. 115–32.

— "Il significato dell'amore in Kierkegaard" [The Meaning of Love in Kierkegaard], in *Studi Kierkegaardiani* [Kierkegaard Studies], ed. by Cornelio Fabro, Brescia: Morcelliana 1957, pp. 203–42.

— *Disperazione e speranza. Saggio sulle categorie kierkegaardiane* [Despair and Hope. Essay on Kierkegaard's Categories], Padua: Gregoriana 1971.

Mazzatosta, Terese Maria, "Educazione e seduzione in Kierkegaard" [Education and Seduction in Kierkegaard], *Problemi di Pedagogia*, vol. 29, nos. 1–2, 1983, pp. 1–8.

Mazzù, Domenica, "Il tema kierkegaardiano dell'identità e la polemica antihegeliana" [The Kierkegaardian Theme of Identity and Anti-Hegelian Polemics], *Incontri Culturali*, no. 7, 1974, pp. 257–67.

Melchiorre, Virgilio, "Kierkegaard e il fideismo" [Kierkegaard and Fideism], *Rivista di Filosofia Neo-Scolastica*, no. 45, 1953, pp. 143–76.

— "Il principio di analogia come categoria metafisica nella filosofia di Kierkegaard" [The Principle of Analogy as a Metaphysical Category in Kierkegaard's Philosophy], in *Giornale Critico della Filosofia Italiana*, no. 34, 1955, pp. 56–66.

— "Metafisica e storia in Søren Kierkegaard" [Metaphysics and History in Søren Kierkegaard], *Sapienza*, no. 8, 1955, pp. 203–21.

— "Possibilità e realtà nell'estetica di Kierkegaard" [Possibility and Actuality in Kierkegaard's Aesthetics], in his *Arte ed esistenza* [Art and Existence], Florence: Philosophia, 1956, pp. 203–21.

— "Kierkegaard ed Hegel. La polemica sul punto di partenza" [Kierkegaard and Hegel. Polemics about the Point of Departure], in *Studi Kierkegaardiani* [Kierkegaard Studies], ed. by Cornelio Fabro, Brescia: Morcelliana 1957, pp. 243–66.

— "La dialettica della 'ripresa' in Søren Kierkegaard [The Dialectic of "Repetition" in Søren Kierkegaard], in *Kierkegaard oggi. Atti del Convegno dell'11 novembre 1982, Università Cattolica del Sacro Cuore, Milan* [Kierkegaard Today. Proceedings of the Congress of November 11, 1982, Università Cattolica del Sacro Cuore, Milan], ed. by Alessandro Cortese, Milan: Vita e pensiero 1986, pp. 88–118.

— *Saggi su Kierkegaard* [Essays on Kierkegaard], Genova Marietti 1987 (2nd revised and enlarged ed., 1998).

— *Figure del sapere* [Figures of Knowing], Naples: Vitale 1994.

— "Esperienza religiosa e filosofia in Kierkegaard" [Religious Experience and Philosophy in Kierkegaard], in *Filosofia ed esperienza religiosa: a partire da Luigi Pareyson. VI colloquio su filosofia e religione (Macerata, 7–9 ottobre 1993)* [Philosophy and Religious Experience: Starting with Luigi Pareyson. IVth Congress on Philosophy and Religion (Macerata, October 7–9, 1993)], ed. by Giovanni Ferretti, Macerata: Giardini 1995, pp. 97–140.

— "Il paradosso come passione del pensiero. Saggio su Kierkegaard" [The Paradox as Passion of Thought. Essay on Kierkegaard], in *Kierkegaard: filosofia e teologia del paradosso, Atti del Convegno tenuto a Trento il 4–6 dicembre 1996* [Kierkegaard: Philosophy and Theology of Paradox. Proceedings of the Congress of Trento, December 4–6, 1996], ed. by Michele Nicoletti and Giorgio Penzo, Brescia: Morcelliana 1999, pp. 69–90.

— *Gli stadi di vita in Søren Kierkegaard. Schemi e materiali di lavoro* [The Stages of Life in Søren Kierkegaard. Schemes and Work Materials], Milan: ISU Università Cattolica 2000.

— "Il cristianesimo in Kierkegaard" [Christianity in Kierkegaard], in *Leggere oggi Kierkegaard* [Reading Kierkegaard Today], ed. by Isabella Adinolfi, Rome: Città nuova 2000 (*NotaBene. Quaderni di Studi Kierkegaardiani*, vol. 1), pp. 27–44.

— "Una circolarità ermeneutica. Tra fede cristiana e filosofia" [A Hermeneutical Circularity. Between Christian Faith and Philosophy], *Il religioso in Kierkegaard. Atti del convegno di studi organizzato dalla Società Italiana per gli Studi Kierkegaardiani tenutosi dal 14 al 16 dicembre 2000 a Venezia* [The Religious in Kierkegaard. Proceedings of the Congress organized by The Italian Society for Kierkegaard Studies in Venice, December 14–16, 2000], ed. by Isabella Adinolfi, Brescia: Morcelliana 2002, pp. 133–5.

Mennini, Sandra M., "La vera fede soprannaturale, virtù indispensabile alla formazione del missionario: il concetto di scandalo in S.A. Kierkegaard" [The Real Supernatural Faith, Essential Virtue in the Education of the Missionary: the Concept of Scandal in S.A. Kierkegaard], in *La Formazione del Missionario oggi: atti del Simposio internazionale di missiologia, 24–28 ottobre 1977* [The Education of the Missionary Today: Proceedings of the International Symposium, October 24–28, 1977], Brescia: Paideia Editrice 1978, pp. 245–58.

Mesnard, Pierre, "Spigolame filosofico al congresso kierkegaardiano di Copenhague" [Philosophical "Gleaning" at the Kierkegaard Congress in Copenhagen], in *Studi Kierkegaardiani* [Kierkegaard Studies], ed. by Cornelio Fabro, Brescia: Morcelliana 1957, pp. 267–82.

Miano, Vincenzo, "Filosofi cristiani di fronte all'ateismo" [Christian Philosophers in the Face of Atheism], in *L'ateismo contemporaneo* [Contemporary Atheism], ed. by Facoltà Filosofica della Pontificia Università Salesiana di Rome, Turin: S.E.I. 1969, vol. 3, pp. 127–35.

Micheletti, M., "Wittgenstein, Kierkegaard e il 'problema di Lessing'" [Wittgenstein, Kierkegaard and the "Problem of Lessing"], in *Kierkegaard e la letteratura* [Kierkegaard and Literature], ed. by Massimo Iritano and Inge Lise Rasmussen, Rome: Città nuova 2002 (*NotaBene. Quaderni di Studi Kierkegaardiani*, vol. 2), pp. 143–54.

Miegge, Giovanni, "Kierkegaard e la Chiesa" [Kierkegaard and the Church], *Gioventù Cristiana*, no. 10, 1931, pp. 75–7.

— "Diritto e società in Kierkegaard e Dostoevskij" [Law and Society in Kierkegaard and Dostoyevsky], *Rivista Internazionae di Filosofia del Diritto*, no. 38, 1961, pp. 474–90.

— "Kierkegaard. Il cristianesimo e la storia" [Kierkegaard. Christianity and History], *Protestantesimo*, no. 19, 1964, pp. 23–32 (republished as "Kierkegaard e la storia" [Kierkegaard and History], in his *Il protestante nella storia* [The Protestant in History], Turin: Claudiana, pp. 137–54.

Milan, Andrea, "Il 'divenire di Dio' in Hegel, Kierkegaard e San Tommaso d'Aquino" [The "Becoming of God" in Hegel, Kierkegaard and St. Thomas Aquinas], in *San Tommaso e il pensiero moderno: saggi* [St. Thomas and Modern Thought: Essays], ed. by Pontificia Accademia Romena di S. Tommaso d'Aquino, Rome: Città nuova 1974, pp. 284–94.

— "Deus immutabilis: l'infinita differenza qualitativa e l'immutabilita di Dio in Kierkegaard" [Deus immutabilis: The Infinite Qualitative Difference and the Changelessness of God in Kierkegaard], in *Parola e spirito: studi in onore di Settimio Cipriani* [Word and Spirit: Studies in Honor of Settimio Cipriani], ed. by Cesare Casale Marcheselli, Brescia: Paideia Editrice 1982, vol. 2, pp. 1451–77.

Modica, Giuseppe, *Fede, libertà, peccato: figure ed esiti della "prova" in Kierkegaard* [Faith, Freedom, Sin: Figures and Results of the "Proof" in Kierkegaard], Palermo: Palumbo 1992.

— "Kierkegaard e l'estetica del Don Giovanni. Postille" [Kierkegaard and the Aesthetics of Don Juan. Marginal Notes], *Giornale di Metafisica*, vol. 17, no. 3, 1995, pp. 379–92.

— "Alterità e paradosso in Kierkegaard" [Alterity and Paradox in Kierkegaard], *Giornale di Metafisica*, vol. 20, nos. 1–2, 1998, pp. 61–86.

— "Alterità e paradosso in Kierkegaard" [Alterity and Paradox in Kierkegaard], in *Kierkegaard: filosofia e teologia del paradosso, Atti del Convegno tenuto a Trento il 4–6 dicembre 1996* [Kierkegaard: Philosophy and Theology of the Paradox. Proceedings of the Congress of Trento, December 4–6, 1996], ed. by Michele Nicoletti and Giorgio Penzo, Brescia: Morcelliana 1999, pp. 163–84.

— "*Ordet* di Dreyer. Percorsi kierkegaardiani" [*The Word* by Dreyer. Kierkegaard's Routes], *Giornale di Metafisica*, vol. 23, no. 1, 2001, pp. 5–34 (published also in *Il religioso in Kierkegaard. Atti del convegno di studi organizzato dalla Società Italiana per gli Studi Kierkegaardiani tenutosi dal 14 al 16 dicembre 2000 a Venezia* [The Religious in Kierkegaard. Proceedings of the Congress organized by The Italian Society for Kierkegaard Studies in Venice, December 14–16, 2000], ed. by Isabella Adinolfi, Brescia: Morcelliana 2002, pp. 320–47.

Mollo, Gaetano, "Fede e ragione: un raffronto tra san Bonaventura e Søren Kierkegaard" [Faith and Reason: a Comparison of St. Bonaventure and Søren Kierkegaard], in *San Bonaventura maestro di vita francescana e di sapienza cristiana: atti del congresso internazionale per il 7. centenario di san Bonaventura da Bagnoregio, Rome, 19–26 settembre 1974* [St. Bonaventure, Master of Franciscan Life and Christian Wisdom: Proceedings of the International Congress for the 7th Centenary of St. Bonaventure from Bagnoregio, Rome, September 19–26, 1974], ed. by Alfonso Pompei, Rome: Pontificia Facoltà Teologica San Bonaventura, in *Miscellanea Francescana*, vol. 75, no. 1, 1975, pp. 721–32.

— "La passione della croce come culmine dialettico della fede in Søren Kierkegaard" [The Passion of the Cross as the Dialectical Acme of Faith in Søren Kierkegaard], in *La sapienza della Croce oggi: atti del Congresso internazionale, Rome, 13–18 ottobre 1975* [The Wisdom of the Cross Today: Proceedings of the International Congress, Rome, October 13–18, 1975], Turin: Leumann, Elle Di Ci 1976, vol. 3, pp. 144–56.

— "Mondo della cultura e carattere. Un confronto tra Hegel e Kierkegaard" [The World of the Culture and Character. A Comparison of Hegel and Kierkegaard], in *Il problema della cultura. Atti del 21. Convegno di assistenti universitari di filosofia Padova 1976* [The Problem of Culture. Proceedings of the 21st Congress of University Philosophy Assistants in Padua, 1976], Padua: Gregoriana 1977, pp. 65–76.

— "Soggettività ed educazione in Kierkegaard" [Subjectivity and Education in Kierkegaard], *Il problema dell'antropologia. Atti del 24. Convegno di Assistenti Universitari di Filosofia* [The Problem of the Anthropology. Proceedings of the 24th Congress of University Philosophy Assistants in Padua], Padua: Gregoriana 1980, pp. 81–95.

— *Al di là dell'angoscia, l'educazione etico-religiosa in S. Kierkegaard* [Beyond Anxiety, Ethical-Religious Education in S. Kierkegaard], S. Assisi: Maria degli Angeli, Porziuncola 1988.

— "Estetica ed etica in Kierkegaard" [Aesthetics and Ethics in Kierkegaard], *Per la Filosofia*, no. 24, 1992, pp. 52–61.

— "L'educazione etico-religiosa in S. Kierkegaard" [Ethical-Religious Education in S. Kierkegaard], *Pedagogia e Vita*, no. 4, 1997, pp. 36–54.

Mondin, Battista, "La teologia esistenziale di S. Kierkegaard" [The Existential Theology of S. Kierkegaard], *Sapienza*, vol. 49, no. 4, 1996, pp. 397–416.

Montanari, Primo, "Intorno alle *Briciole di filosofia* e *Postilla non scientifica* di Kierkegaard" [On Kierkegaard's *Philosophical Fragments* and *Postscript*], *Studia Patavina*, no. 12, 1965, pp. 143–5.

Morandi, F., "Rileggendo Kierkegaard un secolo dopo" [Reading Kierkegaard after a Century], in *Nuovi Studi Kierkegaardiani. Bollettino del Centro Italiano di Studi Kierkegaardiani* [New Kierkegaard Studies. Bulletin of the Italian Center for Kierkegaard Studies], ed. by Giuseppe Mario Pizzuti, vol. 1, March 1993, pp. 101–7.

Morando, Dante, "Kierkegaard padre dell'esistenzialismo" [Kierkegaard as the Father of Existentialism], *Rivista Rosminiana*, no. 2, 1942, pp. 50–7.

— "Søren Kierkegaard padre dell'esistenzialismo" [Søren Kierkegaard as the Father of Existentialism], in his (ed.) *Saggi sull'esistenzialismo teologico* [Essays on Theological Existentialism], Brescia: Morcelliana 1949, pp. 17–41.

— "I maestri dell'esistenzialismo" [The Masters of Existentialism], in *L'esistenzialismo* [Existentialism], Florence: Città di Vita 1950, pp. 99–116.

Moretti, Giancarlo, "Delitto, peccato e punizione nel *Don Giovanni* di Mozart e Da Ponte (Kierkegaard)" [Crime, Sin and Punishment in Mozart and Da Ponte's *Don Juan* (Kierkegaard)], *Filosofia Oggi*, vol. 14, no. 4, 1991, pp. 521–30.

Morigi, S., "Nervature kierkegaardiane nel pensiero francese del Novecento: da Gabriel Marcel a Denis de Rougemont e René Girard" [Kierkegaardian Structures in Twentieth-Century French Thought: from Gabriel Marcel to Denis de Rougemont and René Girard], in *Kierkegaard e la letteratura* [Kierkegaard and Literature], ed. by Massimo Iritano and Inge Lise Rasmussen, Rome: Città nuova 2002 (*NotaBene. Quaderni di Studi Kierkegaardiani*, vol. 2), pp. 101–25.

Morra, Gianfranco, "La sospensione della morale secondo S.A. Kierkegaard" [The Suspension of Ethics in S.A. Kierkegaard], *Ethica*, no. 1, 1962, pp. 121–37.

— "Chi sono gli pseudonimi di Kierkegaard" [Who are Kierkegaard's Pseudonyms?], *Ethica*, no. 11, 1972, pp. 41–50.

Muccio, Antimo, *Cenni dell'esistenzialismo del Kierkegaard e la persona umana* [An Outline of Kierkegaard's Existentialism and the Human Being], Aversa: Arti grafiche f. lli Macchione 1968, pp. 35.

Mura, Gaspare, *Angoscia ed esistenza: da Kierkegaard a Moltmann, Giobbe e la sofferenza di Dio* [Anxiety and Existence: from Kierkegaard to Moltmann, Job and the Suffering of God], Rome: Città nuova 1982.

Nardi, Lorenzo, *Kierkegaard e il cristianesimo tragico* [Kierkegaard and Tragic Christianity], Rome: Cremonese 1976.

Navarria, Salvatore, *Søren Kierkegaard e l'irrazionalismo di Karl Barth* [Søren Kierkegaard and the Irrationalism of Karl Barth], Palermo: Palumbo 1943.

Nepi, Paolo, "Dallo stadi etico al paradosso" [From the Ethical Stage to the Paradox], in *Kierkegaard. Esistenzialismo e dramma della persona. Atti del convegno di Assisi (29 nov.–1 dic. 1984)* [Existentialism and the Situation of the Individual. Proceedings of the Congress in Assisi, November 29–December 1, 1984], Brescia: Morcelliana 1985, pp. 161–8.

— *L'"Esercizio del cristianesimo" di Kierkegaard e il Cristo dei filosofi* [Kierkegaard's *Practice in Christianity* and the Christ of the Philosophers], Turin: Paravia 1992.

Nicoletti, Michele, "Un frutto dall'albero di Kierkegaard" [A Fruit from Kierkegaard's Tree], *Nottola*, no. 4, 1982, pp. 77–9.

— *La dialettica dell'Incarnazione: soggettività e storia nel pensiero di Søren Kierkegaard* [The Dialectics of the Incarnation: Subjectivity and History in Søren Kierkegaard's Thought], Bologna: Dehoniane 1983 (reprint, Trento: Istituto di Scienze Religiose 1984).

— "Kierkegaard e la 'teologia politica' " [Kierkegaard and Theological Politics], in *Kierkegaard. Esistenzialismo e dramma della persona. Atti del convegno di Assisi (29 nov.–1 dic. 1984)* [Existentialism and the Situation of the Individual. Proceedings of the Congress in Assisi, November 29–December 1, 1984], Brescia: Morcelliana 1985, pp. 169–81.

— "Genialità, scacco del pensiero e terapia. Il paradosso kierkegaardiano tra dimensioni teoretiche e aspetti pratici" [Brilliance, Setback of Thought and Therapy. The Kierkegaardian Paradox between Theoretical Dimensions and Practical Aspects], in *Kierkegaard: filosofia e teologia del paradosso, Atti del Convegno tenuto a Trento il 4–6 dicembre 1996* [Kierkegaard: Philosophy and Theology of the Paradox. Proceedings of the Congress of Trento, December 4–6, 1996], ed. by Michele Nicoletti and Giorgio Penzo, Brescia: Morcelliana 1999, pp. 53–68.

Nobile Ventura, A., "Kierkegaard. L'angoscia come apertura alla fede" [Kierkegaard. Anxiety as an Opening to Faith], *Idea*, no. 12, 1974, pp. 47–8.

Oggioni, Emilio, *L'esistenzialismo* [Existentialism], Bologna: Patron 1956.

Orlando, Pasquale, "L'immutabilità di Dio. Il pensiero di S. Tommaso di fronte ad Hegel e a Kierkegaard" [The Changelessness of God. St. Thomas' Thought compared to Hegel and Kierkegaard], *Doctor Communis*, vol. 40, no. 3, 1987, pp. 278–84.

Ottonello, Pier Paolo, "Søren Kierkegaard," in *Grande Antologia Filosofica* [Great Philosophical Anthology], Milan: Marzorati 1971, vol. 18, pp. 1169–88.

— *Kierkegaard e il problema del tempo* [Kierkegaard and the Problem of Time], Genova: Tilgher 1972.

— *Struttura e forma del nichilismo europeo* [The Structure and Form of European Nihilism], vol. 2, *Da Lutero a Kierkegaard* [From Luther to Kierkegaard], L'Aquila–Rome: Japadre 1988.

Paci, Enzo, "Studi su Kierkegaard" [Studies on Kierkegaard], *Studi Filosofici*, vol. 1, nos. 2–3, 1940, pp. 279–91 (reprinted as "Personalità ed esistenza nel pensiero di Kierkegaard" [Personality and Existence in Kierkegaard's Thought] in his *Pensiero, esistenza e valore* [Thought, Existence, Value], Milan and Messina: Principato 1940, pp. 77–97).

— *L'esistenzialismo* [Existentialism], Padua: CEDAM 1943.

— "Ironia, demoniaco ed eros in Kierkegaard" [Irony, the Demonic and Eros in Kierkegaard], in *Archivio di Filosofia* (*Kierkegaard e Nietzsche*), 1953, pp. 71–113 (reprinted in his *Relazioni e significati. II. Kierkegaard and Thomas Mann* [Relations and Meanings. II. Kierkegaard and Thomas Mann], Milan: Lampugnani Nigri, and Vicenza: C. Stocchero 1965, pp. 8–45).

— "Kierkegaard e la dialettica della fede" [Kierkegaard and the Dialectic of Faith], *Archivio di Filosofia* (*Kierkegaard e Nietzsche*), 1953, pp. 9–44 (reprinted as "La dialettica della fede" [The Dialectic of Faith] in his *Relazioni e significati. II. Kierkegaard and Thomas Mann* [Relations and Meanings. II. Kierkegaard and Thomas Mann], Milan: Lampugnani Nigri, and Vicenza: C. Stocchero 1965, pp. 80–119).

— *L'esistenzialismo* [Existentialism], Turin: Edizioni Radio Italiana 1953, see the Introduction and pp. 87–180.

— "Angoscia e fenomenologia dell'eros" [Anxiety and Phenomenology of Eros], *Aut-Aut*, no. 24, 1954, pp. 468–85 (reprinted in his *Relazioni e significati. II. Kierkegaard e Thomas Mann* [Relations and Meanings. II. Kierkegaard and Thomas Mann], Milan: Lampugnani Nigri, and Vicenza: C. Stocchero 1965, pp. 197–213).

— "Angoscia e relazione in Kierkegaard" [Anxiety and Relation in Kierkegaard], *Aut-Aut*, no. 23, 1954, pp. 363–76 (also in his *Relazioni e significati. II. Kierkegaard and Thomas Mann* [Relations and Meanings. II. Kierkegaard and Thomas Mann], Milan: Lampugnani Nigri, and Vicenza: C. Stocchero 1965, pp. 184–96).

— "Il cammino della vita" [Life's Way], *Aut-Aut*, no. 20, 1954, pp. 111–26.

— "Il significato dell'Introduzione kierkegaardiana al *Concetto dell'angoscia*" ["The Meaning of Kierkegaard's Introduction to *The Concept of Anxiety*"], *Rivista di Filosofia*, no. 45, 1954, pp. 392–8 (reprinted as "La psicologia e il problema dell'angoscia" [The Psychology and the Problem of Anxiety] in his *Relazioni e significati. II. Kierkegaard and Thomas Mann* [Relations and Meanings. II. Kierkegaard and Thomas Mann], Milan: Lampugnani Nigri, and Vicenza: C. Stocchero 1965, pp. 176–83).

— "Kierkegaard contro Kierkegaard" [Kierkegaard against Kierkegaard], *Aut-Aut*, no. 22, 1954, pp. 269–301 (reprinted as "Estetica ed etica" [*Aesthetics and Ethics*] in his *Relazioni e significati. II. Kierkegaard and Thomas Mann* [Relations and

Meanings. II. Kierkegaard and Thomas Mann], Milan: Lampugnani Nigri, and Vicenza: C. Stocchero 1965, pp. 47–79).

— "Ripetizione, ripresa e rinascita in Kierkegaard" [Repetition, Resumption and Rebirth in Kierkegaard], *Giornale Critico della Filosofia Italiana*, no. 33, 1954, pp. 313–40 (reprinted as "Ripetizione e ripresa: il teatro e la sua funzione catartica" [Repetition and Resumption: the Theatre and its Cathartic Function] in his *Relazioni e significati. II. Kierkegaard and Thomas Mann* [*Relations and Meanings. II. Kierkegaard and Thomas Mann*]: Lampugnani Nigri, and Vicenza: C. Stocchero 1965, pp. 120–50].

— "Storia ed apocalisse in Kierkegaard" [History and Apocalypse in Kierkegaard], *Archivio di Filosofia* (*Apocalisse e insecuritas*), 1954, pp. 141–62 (reprinted as "Storia ed apocalisse" [History and Apocalypse] in his *Relazioni e significati. II. Kierkegaard and Thomas Mann* [Relations and Meanings. II. Kierkegaard and Thomas Mann], Lampugnani Nigri, and Vicenza: C. Stocchero 1965, pp. 151–75).

— "Su due significati del concetto dell'angoscia in Kierkegaard" [On the Twofold Meaning of *The Concept of Anxiety* in Kierkegaard], *Orbis litterarum*, no. 10, 1955, pp. 196–207 (reprinted as "L'intenzionalità e l'amore" [Intentionality and Love] in his *Relazioni e significati. II. Kierkegaard and Thomas Mann* [Relations and Meanings. II. Kierkegaard and Thomas Mann], Milan: Lampugnani Nigri, and Vicenza: C. Stocchero 1965, pp. 214–28).

— *Kierkegaard e Thomas Mann 4.* [Kierkegaard and Thomas Mann 4.], Milan: Bompiani, Dipartimento di filosofia dell'Università degli studi 1991.

Palermo, S., "La scena e il prisma. Teatro e cinema come immagini concettuali in Kierkegaard e Benjamin" [The Scene and the Prism. Theatre and Cinema as Conceptual Images in Kierkegaard and Benjamin], in *Kierkegaard e la letteratura* [Kierkegaard and Literature], ed. by Massimo Iritano and Inge Lise Rasmussen, Rome: Città nuova 2002 (*NotaBene. Quaderni di Studi Kierkegaardiani*, vol. 2), pp. 83–99.

Papuzza, C., "Angoscia e trascendenza in Kierkegaard" [Anxiety and Transcendence in Kierkegaard], *Il Dialogo*, no. 1, 1970, pp. 41–6.

Parente, Pietro, "Il vero volto di Kierkegaard " [The Real Face of Kierkegaard], *L'Osservatore Romano*, vol. 11, no. 3, 1952, p. 3.

Paresce, E., "Hume, Hamann, Kierkegaard e la filosofia della credenza" [Hume, Hamann, Kierkegaard and the Philosophy of Belief], *Rivista Internazionale di Filosofia del Diritto*, vol. 26, series 3, no. 4, 1949, pp. 357–75.

Pareyson, Luigi, "Note sulla filosofia dell'esistenza" [Notes on the Philosophy of Existence], *Giornale Critico della Filosofia Italiana*, no. 19, 1938, pp. 407–38.

— "Nota Kierkegaardiana" [A Kierkegaardian Note], *Annali della R. Scuola Normale Superiore di Pisa*, no. 8, 1939, pp. 53–68.

— *La filosofia dell'esistenza e Carlo Jaspers* [The Philosophy of Existence and Karl Jaspers], Naples: Loffredo 1940.

— *Studi sull'esistenzialismo* [Studies on Existentialism], Florence: Sansoni 1943 (see "La dissoluzione dello hegelismo e l'esistenzialismo" [The Dissolution of Hegelianism and Existentialism], pp. 69–78; and "Søren Kierkegaard e l'esistenzialismo" [Søren Kierkegaard and Existentialism], pp. 79–110).

- *Esistenza e persona* [Existence and Person], Turin: Taylor 1950, see "Due possibilità: Kierkegaard e Feuerbach" [Two Possibilities: Kierkegaard and Feuerbach], pp. 11–46 and "Esistenzialismo ed umanesimo" [Existentialism and Humanism], pp. 69–78.
- "Kierkegaard e la poesia d'occasione" [Kierkegaard and Occasional Poems], *Rivista di Estetica*, no. 10, 1965, pp. 248–55.
- *L'etica di Kierkegaard nella prima fase del suo pensiero* [Kierkegaard's Ethics in the First Phase of His Thought], Turin: G. Giappichelli 1965.
- *L'etica di Kierkegaard nella Postilla* [Kierkegaard's Ethics in the *Postscript*], Turin: G. Giappichelli 1971.
- *Kierkegaard e Pascal* [Kierkegaard and Pascal], ed. by Sergio Givone, vol. 13 (1999) of his *Opere complete* [Complete Works], vols. 1–20, Milan: Mursia 1998ff.

Pastore, Annibale, "Il messaggio di Søren Kierkegaard" [Søren Kierkegaard's Message], *Logos*, nos. 1–2, 1943 (republished in *La volontà dell'assurdo* [The Will of the Absurd], Milan: Bolla 1948, pp. 49–58).
- "Kierkegaard. Pensare il paradosso" [Kierkegaard. Thinking the Paradox], in *In Lotta con l'Angelo. La filosofia degli ultimi due secoli di fronte al Cristianesimo* [Fighting against the Angel. The Last Two Centuries of Philosophy in the Face of Christianity], ed. Claudio Ciancio, Giovanni Ferretti, Annamaria Pastore, and Ugo Perone, Turin: SEI 1989, pp. 114–28.

Pellegrini, Alessandro, "Il *sistema* e gli eretici" [The *System* and the Heretics], *Archivio di Storia della Filosofia Italiana*, no. 4, 1935, pp. 159–65.

Pellegrini, Giovanni, "Kafka lettore di Kierkegaard. Analisi di una interpretazione" [Kafka as Reader of Kierkegaard. Analysis of an Interpretation], *Tempo Presente*, no. 172, 1995, pp. 52–8.
- "Colpa e peccato in Kierkegaard e Nietzsche" [Fault and Sin in Kierkegaard and Nietzsche], *Il Cannocchiale*, no. 3, 1997, pp. 101–25.
- "Abramo, l'argomentazione e l'incantesimo: Kafka interprete di Kierkegaard" [Abraham, the Argumentation and the Spell: Kafka Commentator of Kierkegaard], *Il Cannocchiale*, no. 3, 1999, pp. 69–110.
- *La legittimazione di sé: Kafka interprete di Kierkegaard* [Self-Legitimation: Kafka Commentator of Kierkegaard], Turin: Trauben 2001.

Pellegrino, A., "Paradosso della fede e paradosso della modernità: Franz Overbeck e Søren Kierkegaard" [Paradox of Faith and Paradox of Modernity: Franz Overbeck and Søren Kierkegaard], in *Kierkegaard e la letteratura* [Kierkegaard and Literature], ed. by Massimo Iritano and Inge Lise Rasmussen, Rome: Città nuova 2002 (*NotaBene. Quaderni di Studi Kierkegaardiani*, vol. 2), pp. 155–86.

Penelhum, Terence, "Ateismo, scetticismo e fideismo" [Atheism, Scepticism and Fideism], *Rivista di Filosofia Neo-Scolastica*, vol. 86, no. 1, 1994, pp. 134–53.

Penzo, Giorgio, *Friedrich Gogarten. Il problema di Dio tra storicismo ed esistenzialismo* [Friedrich Gogarten. The Problem of God between Historicism and Existentialism], Rome: Città nuova 1981.
- "Un nuovo studio italiano su Kierkegaard" [A New Italian Research on Kierkegaard], in *Nuovi Studi Kierkegaardiani. Bollettino del Centro Italiano di Studi Kierkegaardiani* [New Kierkegaard Studies. Bulletin of the Italian Center

for Kierkegaard Studies], ed. by Giuseppe Mario Pizzuti, vol. 1, March 1993, pp. 115–19.

— "Il paradosso come verità esistenziale in Kierkegaard" [The Paradox as Existential Truth in Kierkegaard], in *Kierkegaard: filosofia e teologia del paradosso, Atti del Convegno tenuto a Trento il 4–6 dicembre 1996* [Kierkegaard: Philosophy and Theology of the Paradox. Proceedings of the Congress of Trento, December 4–6, 1996], ed. by Michele Nicoletti and Giorgio Penzo, Brescia: Morcelliana 1999, pp. 13–30.

— *Kierkegaard: la verità eterna che nasce nel tempo* [Kierkegaard: The Eternal Truth which is Born in Temporality], Padua: Messaggero 2000.

— "Kierkegaard: il divino cristiano e il negativo" [Kierkegaard: the Christian Divine and the Negative], in *Il religioso in Kierkegaard. Atti del convegno di studi organizzato dalla Società Italiana per gli Studi Kierkegaardiani tenutosi dal 14 al 16 dicembre 2000 a Venezia* [The Religious in Kierkegaard. Proceedings of the Congress organized by The Italian Society for Kierkegaard Studies in Venice, December 14–16, 2000], ed. by Isabella Adinolfi, Brescia: Morcelliana 2002, pp. 101–33.

Perini, G., "Søren Kierkegaard: il coraggio di dire *io*" [Søren Kierkegaard and the Courage to Say *I*], *Idea*, no. 1, 1970, pp. 41–8.

— "Søren Kierkegaard: ricostruire il cristiano" [Søren Kierkegaard: Rebuilding the Christian], *Idea*, no. 11, 1971, pp. 19–26.

— "Søren Kierkegaard: ricostruire l'uomo" [Søren Kierkegaard: Rebuilding Man], *Idea*, nos. 6–7, 1971, pp. 23–8.

— "Søren Kierkegaard: smaltire la sbornia dei sogni" [Søren Kierkegaard: Sobering up of Dreams], *Idea*, no. 5, 1971, pp. 13–17.

— "Il *Diario* di Kierkegaard in italiano. Nuova edizione" [Kierkegaard's *Diary* in Italian. The New Edition], *Divus Thomas*, vol. 87, nos. 1–2, 1984, pp. 87–98.

Perini, Roberto, *Soggetto e storicità. Il problema della soggettività finita tra Hegel e Kierkegaard* [The Subject and Historicity. The Problem of Finite Subjectivity in Hegel and Kierkegaard], Naples: Edizioni Scientifiche Italiane 1995.

Perlini, Tito, *Che cosa ha veramente detto Kierkegaard* [What Kierkegaard really Said], Rome: Ubaldini 1968.

— "Kierkegaard in Šestov," in *Il religioso in Kierkegaard. Atti del convegno di studi organizzato dalla Società Italiana per gli Studi Kierkegaardiani tenutosi dal 14 al 16 dicembre 2000 a Venezia* [The Religious in Kierkegaard. Proceedings of the Congress organized by The Italian Society for Kierkegaard Studies in Venice, December 14–16, 2000], ed. by Isabella Adinolfi, Brescia: Morcelliana 2002, pp. 39–69.

Perris, Carlo, "Psicopatologia ed esistenzialismo. Il problema della vita in Kierkegaard e la valutazione critica dei rapporti tra psicopatologia della clinica e filosofia esistenziale" [Psychopathology and Existentialism. The Problem of Life in Kierkegaard and the Critical Judgment of the Relations between Clinical Psychopathology and Existential Philosophy], in *Studi Kierkegaardiani* [Kierkegaard Studies], ed. by Cornelio Fabro, Brescia: Morcelliana 1957, pp. 283–322.

Pieretti, Antonio, "Per una semantica dell'angoscia" [About a Semantics of Anxiety], in *Kierkegaard. Esistenzialismo e dramma della persona. Atti del convegno di Assisi (29 nov.–1 dic. 1984)* [Existentialism and the Situation of the Individual. Proceedings of the Congress in Assisi, November 29–December 1, 1984], Brescia: Morcelliana 1985, pp. 93–104.

Pinto, V., "L'esperienza cristiana della verità. Appunti per un confronto tra Heidegger e Kierkegaard" [The Christian Experience of Truth. Some Notes for a Comparison between Heidegger and Kierkegaard], *Atti Accademia di Scienze Morali e Politiche di Naples*, vol. 100, 1990, pp. 283–308.

Pizzorni, Reginaldo M., "Dio fondamento ultimo della morale e del diritto" [God as the First Ground of Morality and Law], *Sapienza*, vol. 49, no. 4, 1996, pp. 435–48.

Pizzuti, Giuseppe Mario, "A proposito di una nuova edizione del *Diario* di Kierkegaard" [About a New Edition of Kierkegaard's *Diary*], *Humanitas*, vol. 36, no. 5, 1981, pp. 736–40.

— "Perché Kierkegaard lasciò Regina. Note sul rapporto tra esemplarità e dialettica nell'estetica kierkegaardiana" [Why Kierkegaard Left Regine. Notes on the Relationship between Exemplariness and Dialectics in Kierkegaard's Aesthetics], *Filosofia*, no. 33, 1982, pp. 463–71.

— "Kierkegaard e Regina. Metafisica della crisi e dialettica dell'eccezione" ["Kierkegaard and Regine. Metaphysics of Crisis and Dialectics of the Exception"], *Atti Accademia di Scienze Morali e Politiche di Naples*, vol. 93, 1983, pp. 325–46.

— "Inattualità di Kierkegaard" [Kierkegaard's Untimeliness], in *Kierkegaard. Esistenzialismo e dramma della persona. Atti del convegno di Assisi (29 nov.–1 dic. 1984)* [Existentialism and the Situation of the Individual. Proceedings of the Congress in Assisi, November 29–December 1, 1984], Brescia: Morcelliana 1985, pp. 183–202.

— "La dialettica dell'edificante nella polemica antihegeliana di S. Kierkegaard" [The Dialectics of the Edifying in Kierkegaard's Anti-Hegelian Polemics], in *Atti dell'Accademia di Scienze Morali e Politiche di Naples*, 1985, pp. 1–18.

— *Tra Kierkegaard e Barth: l'ombra di Nietzsche. La crisi come odissea dello spirito* [Between Kierkegaard and Barth: The Shadow of Nietzsche. The Crisis as Odyssey of the Spirit], foreword by Cornelio Fabro, Venosa: Edizioni Osanna Venosa 1986.

— "Esemplarità di Abramo. Trascendenza e trascendentalità della libertà nell'opera di S. Kierkegaard e di Karl Barth" [Abraham's Exemplariness. Transcendence and Transcendentality of Freedom in Kierkegaard's Work], in *Nuovi Studi Kierkegaardiani* [New Kierkegaard Studies], ed. by Giuseppe Mario Pizzuti, Potenza: Centro Italiano di Studi Kierkegaardiani 1988, pp. 23–52.

— "Kierkegaard e Mozart. Sulle ragioni di una confessione autobiografica" [Kierkegaard and Mozart. On the Reasons for an Autobiographical Confession], in *Nuovi Studi Kierkegaardiani* [New Kierkegaard Studies], ed. by Giuseppe Mario Pizzuti, Potenza: Centro Italiano di Studi Kierkegaardiani 1988, pp. 125–34.

— "Sulle tracce del soggetto. Fenomenologia e dialettica della soggettività in Kierkegaard" [On the Subject's Trail. Phenomenology and the Dialectics of Subjectivity in Kierkegaard], *Filosofia e Teologia*, vol. 3, no. 3, 1989, pp. 533–45.
— "Morte o aurora della filosofia? Sull'u-topia del pensare dopo Kierkegaard e Nietzsche" [Death or Dawn of Philosophy? On the U-topia of Thinking after Kierkegaard and Nietzsche], *Velia*, no. 1, 1990, pp. 109–46.
— "Fede filosofica e rivelazione: trascendenza e comunicazione. Convergenza e distonie nel rapporto Jaspers–Kierkegaard" [Philosophical Faith and Revelation: Transcendence and Communication. Convergences and Dissonances in the Relationship between Kierkegaard and Jaspers], *Velia*, no. 4, 1991, pp. 45–59.
— "Gli pseudonimi di Kierkegaard" [Kierkegaard's Pseudonyms], *Annuario Filosofico*, no. 7, 1991, pp. 369–93.
— "Un filosofo inattuale. Cornelio Fabro nel suo ottantesimo genetliaco" [An Untimely Philosopher. Cornelio Fabro on His Eightieth Birthday], *Humanitas*, vol. 46, no. 5, 1991, pp. 680–93.
— "Suggestioni e referenze kierkegaardiane dell'esperienza di Dio nella biografia speculativa di Karl Barth e di Karl Jaspers" [Kierkegaard's Suggestions and References on the Experience of God in the Speculative Biography of Karl Barth and Karl Jaspers], in *Teologia razionale, filosofia della religione, linguaggio su Dio* [Rational Theology, Philosophy of Religion, Language on God], ed. by Marcello Sanchez Sorondo, Rome: Università Pontificia Lateranense, Herder 1992, pp. 299–335.
— "Genesi e fenomenologia dell'uomo-massa nell'opera di Søren Kierkegaard" [Genesis and Phenomenology of Mass-Man in Søren Kierkegaard's Work] (I), in his (ed.) *Nuovi Studi Kierkegaardiani. Bollettino del Centro Italiano di Studi Kierkegaardiani* [New Kierkegaard Studies. Bulletin of the Italian Center for Kierkegaard Studies], vol. 1, March 1993, pp. 86–100.
— *Kierkegaard: una biografia intellettuale. Il discorso cifrato di uno psicologo estetizzante* [Kierkegaard: An Intellectual Biography. The Coded Discourse of a Psychologist Posing as an Esthete], Potenza: Edizioni Ermes 1993.
— "Una rivista kierkegaardiana" [A Kierkegaardian Review], in his (ed.) *Nuovi Studi Kierkegaardiani. Bollettino del Centro Italiano di Studi Kierkegaardiani* [New Kierkegaard Studies. Bulletin of the Italian Center for Kierkegaard Studies], vol. 1, March 1993, pp. 7–10.
— "Anti-Climacus. Dialettica e struttura dell'ultimo pseudonimo di kierkegaaard" [Anti-Climacus. Dialectics and Structure of the Last Pseudonym of Kierkegaard], *Annuario Filosofico*, no. 11, 1995, pp. 225–70.
— *Invito al pensiero di Kierkegaard* [Introduction to Kierkegaard's Thought], Milan: Mursia 1995.
Polizzi, Paolo, *Kierkegaard, ovvero Della dialettica della scelta* [Kierkegaard or The Dialectics of Choice], ed. by Centro studi G. Toniolo di Palermo, Palermo: S.F. Flaccovio 1991.
Ponzio, Augusto, *Filosofia del linguaggio* [Philosophy of Language], Bari: Adriatica 1985.

Possenti, Vittorio, *La filosofia dopo il nichilismo: sguardi sulla filosofia futura* [Philosophy after Nihilism: A Look at the Philosophy of the Future], Soveria Mannelli: Rubettino 2001.

— "Kierkegaard e Dostoevskij. Nella filosofia futura" [Kierkegaard and Dostoyevsky. In the Philosophy of the Future], in *Il religioso in Kierkegaard. Atti del convegno di studi organizzato dalla Società Italiana per gli Studi Kierkegaardiani tenutosi dal 14 al 16 dicembre 2000 a Venezia* [The Religious in Kierkegaard. Proceedings of the Congress organized by The Italian Society for Kierkegaard Studies in Venice, December 14–16, 2000], ed. by Isabella Adinolfi, Brescia: Morcelliana 2002, pp. 71–100.

Preti, Giulio, "Kierkegaard, Feuerbach e Marx" [Kierkegaard, Feuerbach and Marx], *Studi Filosofici*, no. 10, 1949, pp. 187–208.

Prezzo, Rosella, "Gli stili di Kierkegaard" [Kierkegaard's Styles], *Aut-Aut*, no. 1, 1994, pp. 195–207.

Prini, Pietro, *Kierkegaard testimonio della verità sofferente è e una biografia dell'esistenzialismo Romantico* [Kierkegaard as Witness of the Suffering Truth and a Biography of Romantic Existentialism], in his *L'esistenzialismo* [Existentialism], Rome: Studium 1953, pp. 11–30.

— "Le tre età dell'esistenzialismo" [The Three Ages of Existentialism], *Studi Francescani*, no. 55, 1958, pp. 159–75.

— "Kierkegaard e la filosofia come giornale intimo" [Kierkegaard and Philosophy as Intimate Journal], *Archivio di Filosofia*, 1959, pp. 73–90 (republished in his *Esistenzialismo* [Existentialism], Rome: Studium 1971, pp. 10–53).

— "Kierkegaard e la filosofia come giornale intimo" [Kierkegaard and Philosophy as Intimate Journal], in *Kierkegaard. Esistenzialismo e dramma della persona. Atti del convegno di Assisi (29 nov.–1 dic. 1984)* [Existentialism and the Situation of the Individual. Proceedings of the Congress in Assisi, November 29 –December 1, 1984], Brescia: Morcelliana 1985, pp. 13–21.

— "La teologia sperimentale di Søren Kierkegaard" [Søren Kierkegaard's Experimental Theology], in his *Storia dell'esistenzialismo. Da Kierkegaard a oggi* [History of Existentialism. From Kierkegaard Until Today], Rome: Studium 1989, pp. 13–46.

Quinzio, Sergio, "Kierkegaard, il cristiano moderno" [Kierkegaard, the Modern Christian], in *Leggere oggi Kierkegaard* [Reading Kierkegaard Today], ed. by Isabella Adinolfi, Rome: Città nuova 2000 (*NotaBene. Quaderni di Studi Kierkegaardiani*, vol. 1), pp. 179–89.

Regina, Umberto, *La costruzione dell'interiorità in Kierkegaard dalla ripetizione esistenziale al salto del paradosso* [The Construction of Kierkegaard's Inwardness from the Existential Repetition to the Leap of Paradox], Venezia: La Baùta 1995.

— "La visione esistenziale della natura in Kierkegaard, Nietzsche, Heidegger" [The Existential View of Nature in Kierkegaard, Nietzsche, and Heidegger], in *La concezione della natura nella scienza attuale, nella poesia, nella filosofia. Convegno di Naples (26–27 ottobre 1994)* [The Idea of Nature in Contemporary Science, Poetry and Philosophy. Congress in Naples (October 26–27, 1994)], Naples: Loffredo 1995, pp. 151–66.

— "Filosofia e religione nella formazione della coscienza europea" [Philosophy and Religion in the Building of the European Consciousness], *Philo-Logica*, vol. 5, no. 9, 1996, pp. 47–59.
— *La differenza Amata e il Paradosso cristiano: gli "Stadi sul cammino della vita" di Søren Kierkegaard* [The Beloved Difference and the Christian Paradox: Kierkegaard's *Stages on Life's Way*], Verona: CUSL 1997.
— "La finitudine dell'uomo, l'onnipotenza di Dio e il senso dell'essere. Da Kierkegaard a Heidegger" [The Finitude of the Human Being, the Omnipotence of God and the Sense of Being. From Kierkegaard to Heidegger], in *Kierkegaard: filosofia e teologia del paradosso, Atti del Convegno tenuto a Trento il 4–6 dicembre 1996* [Kierkegaard: Philosophy and Theology of the Paradox. Proceedings of the Congress of Trento, December 4–6, 1996], ed. by Michele Nicoletti and Giorgio Penzo, Brescia: Morcelliana 1999, pp. 280–91.
— "Oltre la modernità ripercorrendo la via esistenziale da Kierkegaard al secondo Heidegger" [Beyond Modernity, Going Along the Existential Path from Kierkegaard to the Second Heidegger], *Acta Philosophica*, vol. 8, no. 2, 1999, pp. 223–50.
— "L'attualità dell' 'edificante' per poter ancora sperare" [The Actuality of the "Edifying" in order to Hope Again], in *NotaBene. Quaderni di Studi Kierkegaardiani*, vol. 1, *Leggere oggi Kierkegaard* [Reading Kierkegaard Today], ed. by Isabella Adinolfi, Rome: Città nuova 2000, pp. 127–34.
— "Il rafforzamento dell'uomo interiore in Søren Kierkegaard" [The Strengthening of the Inner Man in Søren Kierkegaard], in *Progresso del Mezzogiorno* [The Progress of the Mezzogiorno], vol. 25, nos. 1–2, 2001 (*Atti del convegno nazionale su: L'anima umana: sua origine, sua natura, sue facoltà, suo destino, Naples 24–25 ottobre 2000* [Proceedings of the National Congress on the Human Soul: Its Origins, Its Nature, Its Faculties, Its Destiny, Naples, October 24-25, 2000]), Naples: Loffredo 2001, pp. 121–40.
— "Dal padre nei cieli prende nome ogni paternità" [After the Father in Heaven is Named Every Paternity], in *Il religioso in Kierkegaard. Atti del convegno di studi organizzato dalla Società Italiana per gli Studi Kierkegaardiani tenutosi dal 14 al 16 dicembre 2000 a Venezia* [The Religious in Kierkegaard. Proceedings of the Congress organized by The Italian Society for Kierkegaard Studies in Venice, December 14–16, 2000], ed. by Isabella Adinolfi, Brescia: Morcelliana 2002, pp. 305–17.
Ricca, Paolo, "Kierkegaard e Lutero" [Kierkegaard and Luther], in *Kierkegaard. Esistenzialismo e dramma della persona. Atti del convegno di Assisi (29 nov.–1 dic. 1984)* [Existentialism and the Situation of the Individual. Proceedings of the Congress in Assisi, November 29–December 1, 1984], Brescia: Morcelliana 1985, pp. 38–66.
Riconda, Giuseppe, "L'eredità di Kierkegaard e la teologia dialettica nel suo significato speculativo" [Kierkegaard's Heritage and Dialectical Theology in its Speculative Meaning], *Filosofia*, no. 25, 1974, pp. 215–32.
Rinaldi, Francesco, "Della presenza schellinghiana nella critica di Kierkegaard a Hegel" [About Schelling's Influence on Kierkegaard's Criticism of Hegel], *Studi Urbinati*, no. 43, 1969, pp. 243–62.

Rizzacasa, Aurelio, *Kierkegaard. Storia ed esistenza* [Kierkegaard. History and Existence], Rome: Studium 1984.

— "Søren Kierkegaard: la dinamica del rapporto esistenza-storia nelle riflessioni del 'Diario'" [Søren Kierkegaard: the Dynamic of the Relationship between Existence and History in the "Diary"], in *Kierkegaard. Esistenzialismo e dramma della persona. Atti del convegno di Assisi (29 nov.–1 dic. 1984)* [Existentialism and the Situation of the Individual. Proceedings of the Congress in Assisi, November 29 – December 1, 1984], Brescia: Morcelliana 1985, pp. 213–24.

— *Il tema di Lessing: è possibile provare una verità eterna a partire da un fatto storico?* [The Theme of Lessing: Is it Possible to Demonstrate an Eternal Truth from a Historical Fact?], Cinisello Balsamo: San Paolo ed. 1996.

Rocca, Ettore, "Kierkegaard: comunicazione diretta e indiretta. Un'analisi" [Kierkegaard: Direct and Indirect Communication], in *Senso e storia dell'estetica* [Sense and History of Aesthetics], ed. by Pietro Montanari, Parma: Pratiche 1995, pp. 389–402.

— "Kierkegaard predicatore del venerdì" [Kierkegaard, Friday Preacher], *MicRomega. Almanacco di Filosofia*, no. 2, 2000, pp. 97–9.

— "La memoria, il silenzio e lo straniero: Søren Kierkegaard, Primo Levi e i campi di sterminio" [Memory, Silence and the Foreigner: Søren Kierkegaard, Primo Levi and the Death Camps], in *Leggere oggi Kierkegaard* [Reading Kierkegaard Today], ed. by Isabella Adinolfi, Rome: Città nuova 2000 (*NotaBene. Quaderni di Studi Kierkegaardiani*, vol. 1), pp. 115–25.

— "La seconda estetica di Kierkegaard" [Kierkegaard's Second Aesthetics], *Il Pensiero*, no. 1, 2000, pp. 85–97.

— "Quando il malato è l'uomo occidentale e il medico si chiama Kierkegaard" [When the Patient is the Western Man and the Doctor is Called Kierkegaard], *L'Arco di Giano. Rivista di Medical Humanities*, 2000, no. 24, pp. 153–65.

— "Un Kierkegaard sorprendente" [A Surprising Kierkegaard], *MicRomega*, no. 5, 2000, pp. 236–8.

— "Kierkegaard" in *Dal senso comune alla filosofia. Profili* [From Common Sense to Philosophy. Profiles], ed. by Guido Boffi, Clotilde Calabi, Elisabetta Cattaneo et al., Florence: Sansoni 2001, vol. 2, pp. 298–306.

— "L'Antigone di Kierkegaard o della morte del tragico" [Kierkegaard's Antigone or the Death of the Tragic], in *Antigone e la filosofia. Hegel, Kierkegaard, Hölderlin, Heidegger, Bultmann* [Antigone and Philosophy. Hegel, Kierkegaard, Hölderlin, Heidegger, Bultmann], ed. by Pietro Montani, Rome: Donzelli 2001, pp. 73–84.

— "La parola della fede o se Abramo è un uomo" [The Word of Faith or if Abraham is a Man], in *Strutture dell'esperienza. III. Mente, linguaggio, espressione* [The Structure of Experience. III. Death, Language, Expression], Milan: Mimesis 2001 (*Annuario di Itinerari Filosofici*, vol. 5), pp. 141–9.

— *Tra estetica e teologia. Studi kierkegaardiani* [Between Aesthetics and Theology. Kierkegaard Studies], Pisa: ETS 2004.

Rollier, Mario Alberto, "*L'Ora* di Søren Kierkegaard" [Søren Kierkegaard's *The Moment*], *Gioventù cristiana*, no. 10, 1931, pp. 73–5.

Romeno, Bruno, *Il senso esistenziale del diritto nella prospettiva di Kierkegaard* [The Existential Meaning of Law in Kierkegaard's Perspective], Milan: Giuffrè 1973.

Rosati, M., "Poter–essere–se–stessi e essere soggetti morali. J. Habermas tra Kierkegaard e Kant" [Being–Able–to–be–Oneself and Being a Moral Subject. J. Habermas between Kierkegaard and Kant], *Rassegna Italiana di Sociologia*, vol. 44, no. 4, 2003, pp. 493–513.

Rosso, L., "Il pungolo della carne in Kierkegaard" [The Thorn in the Flesh in Kierkegaard], *Idea*, nos. 6–7, 1974, pp. 41–4.

Salami, S., "Amore nella verità. Gli *Atti dell'Amore* di Kierkegaard" [Love within the Truth. Kierkegaard's *Works of Love*], *Pedagogia e Vita*, no. 5, 1984, pp. 523–40.

Salmona, Bruno, "La socialità nel *Diario* di Kierkegaard" [Sociality in Kierkegaard's *Diary*], *Sapienza*, no. 11, 1958, pp. 409–23.

Santucci, Antonio, *Esistenzialismo e filosofia italiana* [Existentialism and Italian Philosophy], Bologna: Il Mulino 1959.

Schoepflin, Maurizio, "Dall'ammirazione all'imitazione di Cristo" [From Admiration to the Imitation of Christ], in *Kierkegaard. Esistenzialismo e dramma della persona. Atti del convegno di Assisi (29 nov.–1 dic. 1984)* [Existentialism and the Situation of the Individual. Proceedings of the Congress in Assisi, November 29 –December 1, 1984], Brescia: Morcelliana 1985, pp. 203–11.

Sciacca, Giuseppe Maria, *L'esperienza religiosa e l'io in Hegel e Kierkegaard* [The Religious Experience and the Self in Hegel and Kierkegaard], G.B. Palermo: Palumbo 1948.

— *La filosofia dell'esistenza e Søren Kierkegaard* [The Philosophy of Existence and Søren Kierkegaard], Palermo: Lilia 1949.

— "Significato dell'irrazionalismo di Kierkegaard" [The Meaning of Kierkegaard's Irrationalism], in *Atti del XV Congresso Nazionale di fiosofia 1948* [Proceedings of the XVth National Congress of Philosophy 1948], Messina–Florence: D'anna 1949, pp. 643–52.

Sciacca, Michele Federico, "L'esperienza etico-religiosa di Søren Kierkegaard" [The Ethical-Religious Experience of Søren Kierkegaard], *Logos*, no. 20, 1937, pp. 121–8.

— "Søren Kierkegaard il poeta della solitudine eroica" [Søren Kierkegaard, the Poet of Heroic Solitude] in his *La filosofia oggi* [Philosophy Today], Milan and Rome: Bocca, 1945, vol. 1, pp. 104–28 (5th revised ed., Milan: Marzorati 1970, vol. 1, pp. 109–33).

— "Kierkegaard il filosofo del *salto*" [Kierkegaard, the Philosopher of the *Leap*], *Rivista dei Giovani*, no. 5, 1947, pp. 25–8.

— *L'estetismo, Kierkegaard, Pirandello* [Estheticism, Kierkegaard, Pirandello], Milan: Marzorati 1974.

Sciamannini, Raniero, "La morale esistenzialistica" [Existentialist Ethics], in *L'esistenzialismo* [Existentialism], Florence: Città di Vita 1950, pp. 75–83.

Sefanini, Luigi, "L'estetica dell'esistenzialismo" [The Esthetics of Existentialism], in *L'esistenzialismo* [Existentialism], Florence: Città di Vita 1950, pp. 4–56.

Sequeri, Pierangelo, *Fede e sapere in Kierkegaard* [Faith and Knowledge in Kierkegaard], in *Il religioso in Kierkegaard. Atti del convegno di studi organizzato dalla Società Italiana per gli Studi Kierkegaardiani tenutosi dal 14 al 16 dicembre 2000 a Venezia* [The Religious in Kierkegaard. Proceedings of the Congress organized by The Italian Society for Kierkegaard Studies in Venice, December 14–16, 2000], ed. by Isabella Adinolfi, Brescia: Morcelliana 2002, pp. 165–83.

Serra, Antonio, "Istanze pedagogiche nel pensiero di Søren Kierkegaard" [Pedagogical Issues in Søren Kierkegaard's Thought], *Rivista Rosminiana*, no. 71, 1977, pp. 133–49.

— "Eros ed estetismo nell'opera conviviale di Kierkegaard" [Eros and Aestheticism in Kierkegaard's Convivial Writing], *Giornale di Metafisica*, no. 3, 1981, pp. 327–46.

Sessa, Piero, "La persona di Cristo nel pensiero di Søren Kierkegaard" [The Person of Christ in Søren Kierkegaard's Thought], *La Scuola Cattolica*, no. 93, 1965, pp. 223–38.

Sesta, Luciano, "Fede e paradosso in Kierkegaard" [Faith and Paradox in Kierkegaard], *Giornale di Metafisica*, vol. 22, nos. 1–2, 2000, pp. 327–35.

— "Onnipotenza divina, creazione dal nulla e libertà umana in Søren Kierkegaard" [Divine Omnipotence, Creation ex nihilo and Human Freedom in Søren Kierkegaard], in *Il religioso in Kierkegaard. Atti del convegno di studi organizzato dalla Società Italiana per gli Studi Kierkegaardiani tenutosi dal 14 al 16 dicembre 2000 a Venezia* [The Religious in Kierkegaard. Proceedings of the Congress organized by The Italian Society for Kierkegaard Studies in Venice, December 14–16, 2000], ed. by Isabella Adinolfi, Brescia: Morcelliana 2002, pp. 379–92.

Sfriso, Maurizio, "Cristianesimo e Cristianità in S. Kierkegaard" [Christianity and Christendom in S. Kierkegaard], *Città di Vita*, vol. 52, no. 3, 1997, pp. 297–309.

— "La filosofia dell'esistenza di Kierkegaard e la crisi della soggettività" [The Philosophy of Existence of Kierkegaard and the Crisis of the Subjectivity], *Rivista Rosminiana di Filosofia e di Cultura*, vol. 92, nos. 3–4, 1998, pp. 275–92.

— "Rosmini e Kierkegaard" [Rosmini and Kierkegaard], *Rivista Rosminiana di Filosofia e di Cultura*, vol. 94, nos. 3–4, 2000, pp. 239–62.

— "Hegel e Kierkegaard. Per quale realtà?" [Hegel and Kierkegaard. To Which Actuality?], *Filosofia Oggi*, vol. 26, no. 1, 2003, pp. 42–68.

Sgalambro, Manlio, "Estetica e materialismo in Kierkegaard" [Aesthetics and Materialism in Kierkegaard], *Tempo Presente*, no. 9, 1964, pp. 69–72.

Sibilio, F. Romeno, "Il rapporto al padre: Kierkegaard" [The Relation to the Father: Kierkegaard], *Ricerche Metodologiche*, no. 1, 1969, pp. 14–24.

Siclari, Alberto, *L'Ascetica dell'uomo comune: Cristianesimo e cultura nel "Diario" di Søren Kierkegaard* [The Asceticism of the Common Man: Christianity and Culture in Søren Kierkegaard's *Diary*], Milan: ISU Università Cattolica, 1989.

— "La comunicazione di Søren Kierkegaard e le sue modalità" [Søren Kierkegaard's Communication and its Modalities], *Philo-Logica*, vol. 4, no. 8, 1995, pp. 63–96.

— "Kierkegaard e i doveri della singolarità" [Kierkegaard and the Duties of Singularity], *La Società degli Individui*, no. 3, 1998, pp. 33–51.

— "Per una teologia della crisi: tempo ed eternità in Kierkegaard" [For a Theology of the Crisis: Time and Eternity in Kierkegaard], *Annali di Scienze Religiose*, no. 6, 2001, pp. 15–56.

— "Le opere e la misericordia negli *Atti dell'amore* di Kierkegaard" [Works and Mercy in Kierkegaard's *Works of Love*], *La Società degli Individui*, vol. 6, no. 18, 2003, pp. 103–18.

Silvestri, F., "Ontologia del divenire e necessità di una scelta trascendentale. Kierkegaard e Hegel" [The Ontology of Becoming and the Necessity of a Transcendental Choice. Kierkegaard and Hegel], *Atti dell'Accademia di Scienze Morali e Politiche di Naples*, vol. 108, no. 1, 1997, pp. 311–25.

Sini, Anna Maria, "Søren Kierkegaard," in *Grande Dizionario Enciclopedico*, Turin: UTET 1986, vol. 6.

— "L'itinerario fondamentale della libertà in Søren Kierkegaard" [The Essential Itinerary of Freedom in Søren Kierkegaard], in *Nuovi Studi Kierkegaardiani* [New Kierkegaard Studies], ed. by Giuseppe Mario Pizzuti, Potenza: Centro Italiano di Studi Kierkegaardiani 1988, pp. 53–79.

Slataper Camusso, Giulia, "Romanticismo come letterarietà: approssimazione all'estetismo kierkegaardiano" [Romanticism as Literariness: Approximation to Kierkegaard's Aestheticism], in *Atti del Congresso Internazionale di filosofia 1946* [Proceedings of the International Congress of Philosophy 1946], Milan and Rome: Castellani 1947, vol. 2 (*L'esistenzialismo* [Existentialism]) pp. 453–5.

Socrate, Sergio Marini, "Socrate 'quel Singolo.' A proposito di alcune annotazioni del 'Diario' kierkegaardiano [Socrates "that Individual." About some Notes from Kierkegaard's "Diary"], in *Nuovi Studi Kierkegaardiani. Bollettino del Centro Italiano di Studi Kierkegaardiani* [New Kierkegaard Studies. Bulletin of the Italian Center for Kierkegaard Studies], ed. by Giuseppe Mario Pizzuti, vol. 1, March 1993, pp. 75–85.

Sogni, Cesare, *Pensare la morte nel discorso "Vicino a una tomba" di S. Kierkegaard* [Thinking Death in Kierkegaard's Discourse "At a Graveside"], Gallarate: published by the author 2000.

Sorrentino, S., "Verità e salvezza. Kierkegaard e Nietzsche di fronte al Cristianesimo" [Truth and Salvation. Kierkegaard and Nietzsche in the Face of Christianity], in *Veritatem in caritate. Studi in onore di Cornelio Fabro* [*Veritatem in caritate*. Studies in Honor of Cornelio Fabro], ed. by Giuseppe Mario Pizzuti, Potenza: Ermes 1991, pp. 259–72.

Spera, Salvatore, "Il mito di Faust. Aspirazioni letterarie, riflessioni filosofiche, preoccupazioni religiose del giovane Kierkegaard" [The Myth of Faust. Literary Ambitions, Philosophical Reflections], *Archivio di Filosofia*, 1974, pp. 309–40 (reprinted as chapter 1 of his *Il giovane Kierkegaard. Indagini critiche sulla filosofia della religione e studi sugli aspetti inediti del pensiero kierkegaardiano* [The Young Kierkegaard. Critical Investigations on the Philosophy of Religion and Studies on Unknown Aspects of Kierkegaard's Thought], Padua: CEDAM 1977).

— "Il divenire cristiano come imitazione del Cristo sofferente in Søren Kierkegaard" [Christian Becoming as Imitation of the Suffering Christ in Søren Kierkegaard], *Bollettino Stauros*, no. 2, 1976.

— "L'influsso di Schelling sulla formazione del giovane Kierkegaard" [Schelling's Influence on the Young Kierkegaard's Education], *Archivio di Filosofia*, no. 1, 1976, pp. 73–108.

— *Il pensiero del giovane Kierkegaard. Indagini critiche sulla filosofia della religione e studi sugli aspetti inediti del pensiero kierkegaardiano* [The Young Kierkegaard. Critical Investigations on the Philosophy of Religion and Studies on Unknown Aspects of Kierkegaard's Thought], Padua: CEDAM 1977.

— "Aspetti del demoniaco in una prospettiva di filosofia della religione" [Some Aspects of the Demonic from the Perspective of Philosophy of Religion], *Aquinas*, no. 21, 1978, pp. 382–99.

— *Kierkegaard politico* [The Political Kierkegaard], Rome: Istituto di studi filosofici 1978.

— "Kierkegaard e la crisi europea del 1848" [Kierkegaard and the European Crisis of 1848], *Archivio di Filosofia*, nos. 2–3, 1978, pp. 385–407.

— *Introduzione a Kierkegaard* [Introduction to Kierkegaard], Rome–Bari: Laterza 1983.

— "Kierkegaard e Schleiermacher" [Kierkegaard and Schleiermacher], *Archivio di Filosofia*, 1984, pp. 435–63.

— "Le carte schleiermacheriane di Kierkegaard" [Kierkegaard's Papers on Schleiermacher], *Aquinas*, no. 27, 1984, pp. 287–316.

— "Ambiguità e inconclusività della politica nel pensiero di Kierkegaard" [Ambiguity and Inconclusiveness of Politics in Kierkegaard], in *Kierkegaard. Esistenzialismo e dramma della persona. Atti del convegno di Assisi (29 nov.–1 dic. 1984)* [Existentialism and the Situation of the Individual. Proceedings of the Congress in Assisi, November 29–December 1, 1984], Brescia: Morcelliana 1985, pp. 67–91.

— "Paradosso cristiano e scandalo della cristianità" [Christian Paradox and the Scandal of Christianity], in *Kierkegaard: filosofia e teologia del paradosso, Atti del Convegno tenuto a Trento il 4–6 dicembre 1996* [Kierkegaard: Philosophy and Theology of the Paradox. Proceedings of the Congress of Trento, December 4–6, 1996], ed. by Michele Nicoletti and Giorgio Penzo, Brescia: Morcelliana 1999, pp. 185–202.

Stanco, F.M.T., *Il tema dell'angoscia in Kierkegaard* [The Theme of Anxiety in Kierkegaard], Naples: Ferraro 1977.

Stefani, P., "Risonanze filosofiche del Qohelet" [Philosophical Resonances of Qohelet], *Humanitas*, vol. 50, no. 3, 1995, pp. 393–409.

Stefanini, Luigi, "L'estetica di Kierkegaard" [Kierkegaard's Ethics], in his *Esistenzialismo ateo ed esistenzialismo teistico* [Atheistic and Theistic Existentialism], Padua: CEDAM 1952, pp. 354–61 (reprinted as "L'esteticità come antitesi di eternità e realtà in Søren Kierkegaard" [The Aestheticism as Antithesis of Eternity and Actuality in Søren Kierkegaard], in his *Arte e critica* [Art and Criticism], Milan: Principato 1953, pp. 75–84).

Stella, Fernando, "Kierkegaard: un uomo in presenza di Dio" [Kierkegaard: A Man in the Presence of God], *Raccolta di Studi e Ricerche*, no. 2, 1978, pp. 331–41.

Svartholm, Nils, "Søren Kierkegaard e la fisica moderna" [Søren Kierkegaard and Modern Physics], *L'Umana Avventura*, no. 12, 1989, pp. 61–3.

Terzi, Carlo, *Il Kierkegaard di Régis Jolivet* [Régis Jolivet's Kierkegaard], Turin: Edizioni di Filosofia 1967.

Tilliette, Xavier, "La cristologia di Kierkegaard nelle *Briciole filosofiche*" [Kierkegaard's Christology in *Philosophical Fragments*], in *Kierkegaard: filosofia e teologia del paradosso, Atti del Convegno tenuto a Trento il 4–6 dicembre 1996* [Kierkegaard: Philosophy and Theology of the Paradox. Proceedings of the Congress of Trento, December 4–6, 1996], ed. by Michele Nicoletti and Giorgio Penzo, Brescia: Morcelliana 1999, pp. 119–26.

Tomasoni, Francesco, "La morte come paradosso tra Feuerbach e Kierkegaard" [Death as Paradox in Feuerbach and Kierkegaard], in *Kierkegaard: filosofia e teologia del paradosso, Atti del Convegno tenuto a Trento il 4–6 dicembre 1996* [Kierkegaard: Philosophy and Theology of the Paradox. Proceedings of the Congress of Trento, December 4–6, 1996], ed. by Michele Nicoletti and Giorgio Penzo, Brescia: Morcelliana 1999, pp. 251–64.

Tomassone, L., "La critica di Kierkegaard alle filosofie della storia" [Kierkegaard's Criticism of the Philosophies of History], *Protestantesimo*, vol. 41, no. 3, 1986, pp. 129–41.

Tortora, Giuseppe, "Kierkegaard and Schopenhauer on Hegelianism," *Metalogicon*, no. 1, 1994, pp. 69–84.

Trenti, Z., "Il rinnovamento del linguaggio religioso e le sue matrici esistenziali" [The Renewal of Religious Language and Its Existential Matrices], *Orientamenti Pedagogici*, vol. 34, no. 203, 1987, pp. 895–909.

Tricomi, Flavia, "Søren Kierkegaard e la morale kantiana" [Søren Kierkegaard and Kantian Ethics], in *A partire da Kant. L'eredità della "Critica della ragion pratica"* [Beginning from Kant. The Heritage of the *Critique of Practical Reason*], ed. by Adriano Fabris and Luca Baccelli, Milan: Franco Angeli 1989, pp. 199–201.

Tunisini Bertozzi, Rita, *La spina nella carne. Søren Kierkegaard: dramma in due atti* [The Thorn in the Flesh. Søren Kierkegaard: A Drama in Two Acts], Forlì: Forum 1975.

Tuono, Marco, "La metafora della rinascita in una teologia capovolta. Suggestioni antropologiche del pensiero di Kierkegaard nella 'Metamorfosi' di Kafka" [The Metaphor of Rebirth in an Overturned Theology. Anthropological Suggestions of Kierkegaard's Thought in Kafka's "Metamorphosis"], in *Il religioso in Kierkegaard. Atti del convegno di studi organizzato dalla Società Italiana per gli Studi Kierkegaardiani tenutosi dal 14 al 16 dicembre 2000 a Venezia* [The Religious in Kierkegaard. Proceedings of the Congress organized by The Italian Society for Kierkegaard Studies in Venice, December 14–16, 2000], ed. by Isabella Adinolfi, Brescia: Morcelliana 2002, pp. 437–45.

Vaccaro, Gian Battista, "Il Kierkegaard di Adorno e la critica dell'ontologia esistenziale" [Adorno's Kierkegaard and the Criticism of Existential Theology], *Annali della Facoltà di Lettere e Filosofia, Università di Siena*, 1989, pp. 67–89.

Valenziano, Crispino, "Limiti della cristologia kierkegaardiana" [The Limits of Kierkegaard's Christology], *Giornale di Metafisica*, no. 20, 1965, pp. 20–9.

Valori, Paolo, "Husserl e Kierkegaard" [Husserl and Kierkegaard], *Archivio di Filosofia* (*Kierkegaard e Nietzsche*), 1953, pp. 191–200.

Vecchi, Giovanni, "Il problema dell'arte nell'esistenzialismo di Kierkegaard" [The Problem of Art in Kierkegaard's Existentialism], *Rivista di Filosofia Neo-Scolastica*, no. 38, 1946, pp. 61–9.

Vecchio, M. Dal, "L'amore di Dio secondo Kierkegaard" [God's Love in Kierkegaard], in *Il religioso in Kierkegaard. Atti del convegno di studi organizzato dalla Società Italiana per gli Studi Kierkegaardiani tenutosi dal 14 al 16 dicembre 2000 a Venezia* [The Religious in Kierkegaard. Proceedings of the Congress organized by The Italian Society for Kierkegaard Studies in Venice, December 14–16, 2000], ed. by Isabella Adinolfi, Brescia: Morcelliana 2002, pp. 411–20.

Vela, Raffaele, "Kierkegaard e la verità esistenziale" ["Kierkegaard and the Existential Truth"], *Vita Sociale*, no. 23, 1966, pp. 231–9.

Velocci, Giovanni, *Filosofia e fede in Kierkegaard* [Philosophy and Faith in Kierkegaard], Rome: Città nuova 1976.

— *La donna in Kierkegaard* [The Woman in Kierkegaard], L'Aquila: Japadre 1980.

Vettori Vittorio, "Giovanni Gentile tra Kierkegaard e Marx" [Giovanni Gentile between Kierkegaard and Marx], *Città di Vita*, no. 9, 1954, pp. 685–91.

Vircillo, Domenico, "Ambiguità e fede in Kierkegaard, Nietzsche e Kafka" [Ambiguity and Faith in Kierkegaard, Nietzsche and Kafka], *Sapienza*, no. 26, 1973, pp. 27–69.

Zanovello, N., "La soggettività della verità in Kierkegaard" [The Subjectivity of the Truth in Kierkegaard], *Rivista Rosminiana di Filosofia e di Cultura*, no. 73, 1979, pp. 47–56.

Zarone, G., "*Itinerarium in fidem*. Pascal–Agostino–Kierkegaard," *Filosofia e Teologia*, 1997, pp. 527–44.

Zecchi, Stefano, "Il paradosso della rinascita. Tra Kierkegaard e Husserl" [The Paradox of the Rebirth. Between Kierkegaard and Husserl], *Aut-Aut*, nos. 214–15, 1986, pp. 97–110.

Zizi, Paolo, *Ontologia della libertà. (Tra Kierkegaard–Heidegger–Fabro)* [The Ontology of Freedom. (Between Kierkegaard, Heidegger, and Fabro)], Sassari: Edizioni Unidata 1987.

III. Secondary Literature on Kierkegaard's Reception in Italy

Abbagnano, Nicola, "Kierkegaard in Italy," *Meddelelser fra Søren Kierkegaard Selskabet*, vol. 2, nos. 3–4, 1950, pp. 49–53.

Ballezza, Vito A., "Traduzioni di Kierkegaard" [Translations of Kierkegaard], *Italia che Scrive*, no. 32, 1949, pp. 1–2.

Belletti, Bruno, "Per una ripresa critica del pensiero di Kierkegaard. Gli atti di un recente convegno di Assisi 29 novembre–1 dicembre 1984" [For a Critical Renewal of Kierkegaard's Thought. About the Proceedings of a Recent Congress in Assisi, November 29–December 1, 1984], *Humanitas*, vol. 41, no. 1, 1986, pp. 72–9.

Capucci, Flavio, "Cornelio Fabro interprete di Kierkegaard" [Cornelio Fabro as Commentator of Kierkegaard], *Studi Cattolici*, no. 256, 1982, pp. 364–7.

Castagnino, Franca, *Gli studi italiani su Kierkegaard 1906–1966* [Italian Studies on Kierkegaard 1906–1966], Rome: Ed. dell'Ateneo 1972.

Cortese, Alessandro, "Una nuova bibliografia kierkegaardiana (Complète la S.K. International Bibliografi par una Integrazione alle edizioni italiane e agli studi in lingua italiana et un Supplemento pour 1956–août 1962)" [A New Kierkegaard Bibliography (completing the Søren Kierkegaard International Bibliography with the Integration of the Italian Editions and Italian Secondary Literature, and a Supplement for the years 1956–August 1962)], *Rivista di Filosofia Neo-Scolastica*, no. 55, 1963, pp. 98–108.

— "Récentes traductions italiennes de Soren Kierkegaard," *Kierkegaardiana*, vol. 5, 1967, pp. 107–30.

— "Kierkegaard," in *Questioni di storiografia filosofica dalle origini all'800* [Problems of Philosophical Historiography from the Origins to the Nineteenth Century], ed. by V. Mathieu, Brescia: La Scuola 1975, vol. 3, pp. 471–717, see especially pp. 601–33.

— *Criteri dell'edizione* [Criteria of the Edition], Milan: Adelphi, 1976, vol. 1, pp. 11–19.

— "Italy," in *The Legacy and Interpretation of Kierkegaard*, ed. by Niels Thulstrup and Marie Mikulová Thulstrup, Copenhagen: C.A. Reitzel 1981 (*Bibliotheca Kierkegaardiana*, vol. 8), pp. 135–60.

Davini, Simonella, "Cornelio Fabro and the Italian Reception of *Philosophical Fragments*," *Kierkegaard Studies. Yearbook*, 2004, pp. 356–69.

Davini, Simonella, Ettore Rocca and Ivan Z. Sørensen, "Bibliografia delle traduzioni italiane degli scritti di S. Kierkegaard (1907–2000)" [Bibiography of the Italian Translations of S. Kierkegaard's Writings (1907–2000)], ed. by Isabella Adinolfi, Rome: Città nuova 2000 (*NotaBene. Quaderni di Studi Kierkegaardiani*, vol. 1), pp. 211–24.

Fabro, Cornelio, "Note di bibliografia kierkegaardiana" [Notes for a Kierkegaardian Bibliography], in *Studi kierkegaardiani* [Kierkegaard Studies], ed. by Cornelio Fabro, Brescia: Morcelliana 1957.

— "Linee fondamentali di ermeneutica kierkegaardiana" [Fundamental Outlines of a Kierkegaardian Hermeneutics], in the Introduction to his Italian translation of S. Kierkegaard, *Opere* [Writings], Florence: Sansoni 1972, pp. LIV–LXIX (on the Italian reception, see especially pp. LXV–LXIX).

— "Kierkegaard in Italia" [Kierkegaard in Italy], *Il Veltro*, vol. 25, nos. 1–3, 1981, pp. 79–89.

Garin, Eugenio, "Kierkegaard in Italia" [Kierkegaard in Italy], *Rivista Critica di Storia della Filosofia*, no. 28, 1973, pp. 452–6.

Giannatiempo Quinzio, Anna, "Søren Kierkegaard," in *Grande antologia filosofica* [Great Philosophical Anthology], vols. 1–35, Milan: Marzorati 1971–85, vol. 34 (vol. 3 in *Aggiornamento bibliografico* [Bibliographical Updating], vols. 1–3 (vols. 32–34)], pp. 237–50.

Lancellotti, Mario, "Ritorno di Kierkegaard" [The Return of Kierkegaard], *Il Veltro*, vol. 21, nos. 3–4, 1977, pp. 290–6.

Lombardi, Franco, "Kierkegaard in Italia" [Kierkegaard in Italy], *Il Veltro*, vol. 26, nos. 1–2, 1982, pp. 92–4.

Macchi, Franco, "La ripresa degli studi kierkegaardiani in Italia e il convegno su *Il religioso in Kierkegaard*, Venezia 14–16 dicembre 2000" [The Resumption of Kierkegaard Studies in Italy and the Congress on *The Religious in Kierkegaard*

in Venice, December 14–16, 2000], *Protestantesimo*, vol. 56, no. 2, 2001, pp. 124–31.
Marini, Sergio, "Schede di bibliografia kierkegaardiana in lingua italiana 1967–1986" [Bibliographical Reports on Kierkegaard in Italian Language 1967–1986], in *Nuovi Studi Kierkegaardiani* [New Kierkegaard Studies], ed. by Giuseppe Mario Pizzuti, Potenza: Centro Italiano di Studi Kierkgardiani 1989, pp. 81–97.
— "Schede di bibliografia kierkegaardiana in lingua italiana 1987–1991" [Bibliographical Reports on Kierkegaard in Italian Language 1987–1991], in *Nuovi Studi Kierkegaardiani, Bollettino del Centro Italiano di Studi Kierkegaardiani* [New Kierkegaard Studies. Bulletin of the Italian Center for Kierkegaard Studies], ed. by Giuseppe Mario Pizzuti, 1993, pp. 109–14.
Ottonello, Pier Paolo, "Gli studi kierkegaardiani in Italia nell'ultimo ventennio" [Kierkegaard Studies in Italy in the Last Twenty Years], *Cultura e Scuola*, no. 28, 1968, pp. 127–38.
Penzo, Giorgio, "Presenza di Kierkegaard" [The Presence of Kierkegaard], *Humanitas*, no. 3 (nuova serie), 1984, pp. 461–4.
Pizzuti, Giuseppe Mario, "Cornelio Fabro, traduttore e interprete di Kierkegaard in Italia" [Cornelio Fabro as Translator and Commentator of Kierkegaard in Italy], *Humanitas*, no. 39, 2, 1984, pp. 192–220.
— "Recenti studi italiani su Kierkegaard" [Recent Italian Studies on Kierkegaard], in *Filosofia*, no. 35, 1984, pp. 127–38.
— "L'equivoco della 'Kierkegaard Renaissance' " [The Misinterpretation of the "Kierkegaard Renaissance"], in his *Tra Kierkegaard e Barth: l'ombra di Nietzsche. La crisi come odissea dello spirito* [Between Kierkegaard and Barth: the Shadow of Nietzsche. The Crisis as Odyssey of the Spirit], foreword by Cornelio Fabro, Venosa: Edizioni Osanna Venosa 1986, pp. 21–100.
— "Kierkegaard. La critica" [Kierkegaard and the Criticism], in his *Invito al pensiero di Kierkegaard* [Introduction to Kierkegaard's Thought], Milan: Mursia 1993, pp. 211–39.
Rocca, Ettore, "Kierkegaard in the Italian Language," *Søren Kierkegaard Newsletter*, no. 40, 2000, pp. 18–19.
— "The Secondary Literature on *The Concept of Anxiety*: the Italian Contribution, *Kierkegaard Studies. Yearbook*, 2001, pp. 330–4.
Scaramuccia, Andrea, "The Italian Reception of Kierkegaard's Journals and Papers," *Kierkegaard Studies. Yearbook*, 2003, pp. 366–72.
Spera, Salvatore, *Storia della critica: 5. Area italiana* [History of Criticism], in his *Introduzione a Kierkegaard* [Introduction to Kierkegaard], Rome–Bari: Laterza 1983, pp. 163–9.

PART II

Central Europe

Hungary:
The Hungarian Patient

András Nagy

No one in Hungary can pronounce Kierkegaard's name properly, except those few who speak Danish; thus Kierkegaard remains phonetically unattainable for scholars, writers, and students, who call him KEER-KA-GARD, even with a heavy "d" at the end. The reluctance to learn the proper pronounciation may originate from its closeness to the Hungarian *kergekór*; with the change of only two consonants, the word means a dangerous disease that sheep can transmit to humans, which ends with one loosing one's mind and "whirling around." Writers like to play on the closeness of the sound of the words.[1] Sometimes, this feature surfaces even in everyday conversations as well.

This is not the only "morbid" aspect of Kierkegaard's paradoxical presence in Hungary. Many countries and nations may claim how much the reception of his thinking was shaped or even distorted by history, particularly in Central and Eastern Europe. Yet, Hungary may be the only country where Kierkegaard, even if indirectly and briefly, actually helped to "shape" history since his name, his arguments, and his conclusions were in the minds, the dialogues, and the political activity of young intellectuals at the beginning of the twentieth century.[2]

A further ambiguity of Hungarian Kierkegaard reception is the lack of systematic theological and philosophical studies before the second half of the nineteenth century. When later—before the turn of the twentieth century, and between the two World Wars—conditions were favorable for significant intellectual progress, history soon came to disappoint people's hopes and efforts. However, neither the lack of systematic studies nor the later ban on his entire *oeuvre* meant that his influence was absent. On the contrary, Kierkegaard's writing and thinking significantly influenced several Hungarian intellectuals, artists, and theologians throughout the last 150 years.

There is still a lot of philological work to be done to attain an adequate picture of Kierkegaard's "hidden" presence that anticipated the explicit references to him, the Hungarian translations of his works, and the later studies about him and his

---

[1] See Péter Esterházy, *Bevezetés a szépirodalomba* [Introduction to the Belles Lettres], Budapest: Magvető Kiadó 1986, see for example, p. 26; p. 721.
[2] György Lukács and his circle, see András Nagy, "Abraham the Communist," in *Kierkegaard—The Self in Society*, ed. by George Pattison and Steven Shakespeare, London: Macmillan 1998, pp. 196–220.

thinking. It is important to note that in the multi-faceted reception of Kierkegaard in Hungary, literature played an eminent role. For his first readers, Kierkegaard was a writer, something familiar for Hungarian intellectuals, since, in accordance with its role and nature, Hungarian literature tried to include, or even act as a substitute for, the discussion and interpretation of important philosophical and theological questions, providing a field of experience for ideas that were not discussed in a systematic or scholarly manner. The receptivity for Kierkegaard in Hungary was also due to the closeness of those sources that were important both for the Danish thinker and for many Hungarian writers: German Romanticism, Hegel's philosophy, as well as other things, like ancient Greek drama, or the appreciation of folk tales. Later many authors inspired by him were also widely read and greatly appreciated in Hungary: Russian writers and thinkers as well as Ibsen. While Ibsen denied his own Kierkegaardian inspiration, the dilemmas, ideas, and "masks" of the Danish thinker were already applauded on Hungarian stages, long before his name was pronounced (probably incorrectly).

The reception of Kierkegaard can be divided into several, sometimes overlapping chapters, primarily following certain temporal reference points, as history determined the phases of when and how his thinking was "absorbed" in Hungary.

I. Kierkegaard's Younger Hungarian Contemporaries

It is still to be determined if there were any Hungarians who sat beside the Danish thinker in Schelling's classroom, or if his name and thinking were mentioned during the trip Hans Christian Andersen (1805–75) took across Hungary. Some of Andersen's tales were edited and published in Hungary by Júlia Szendrey (1828–68), the widow of the greatest Hungarian poet Sándor Petőfi (1823–49), but at that time Kierkegaard's name was not mentioned or at least not registered. However, the other significant poet of the time, Mihály Vörösmarty (1800–55), Petőfi's senior by two decades, authored a famous philosophical poem "Thoughts at the Library,"[3] and he may have been receptive to some Kierkegaardian ideas, as one literary historian suggests.[4]

Based on the same logic and following the subtle reception of philosophical thinking in Hungary, the same historian emphasized the possible influence of Kierkegaard on *The Tragedy of Man*,[5] a great philosophical drama of Imre Madách (1823–64), in which the human will is confronted by history, as humanity's fate. The play is constructed according to the logic of the Hegelian thesis–antithesis–synthesis structure, but concludes in the "ambiguity of fulfilment," very much resembling the

---

[3] Mihály Vörösmarty, "Gondolatok a könyvtárban" (1844), in *Vörösmarty összes költeményei* [Vörösmarty's Collected Poems], ed. by Pál Gyulai, Budapest: Franklin-Társulat ca. 1920.

[4] Pál Belohorszky, "Madách és Kierkegaard [Madách and Kierkegaard]," *Irodalomtörténet*, no. 4, 1971, p. 894. The author here refers also to another poem of Mihály Vörösmarty, "A merengőhöz" [To the Reflective One] (1843).

[5] Imre Madách, *Az ember tragédiája. Drámai költemény*, ed. by János Arany, Budapest: Athenaeum 1862 (the drama was written in 1859–60).

Danish genius. The imaginary trip through history, taken by the protagonists, could likewise follow the Kierkegaardian "stages," ending in a Kierkegaardian anxiety, when facing the ultimate dilemmas of human existence.[6] A closer analysis might focus on certain similarities between the biography of the Hungarian author and that of Kierkegaard, as the literary historian emphasizes. Similar parallels and transparencies can be also seen in some writings of the ironic and critical storytelling genius Kálmán Mikszáth (1847–1910). However, his inspiration may be due to an indirect Kierkegaardian influence, through Russian literature, that played an increasingly important role in Hungary from the second half of the nineteenth century.[7]

Minor figures from the extremely rich Hungarian literature of that period could well have been receptive to Kierkegaard's thoughts and to his personality, also as interpreted by Georg Brandes (1842–1927), whose name and works were also known and read in circles of intellectuals and artists in this country.

II. Kierkegaard and Early Hungarian Existentialism

It was the French philosopher Lucien Goldmann (1913–70) who called the Hungarian philosopher György Lukács' (1885–1971) "The Metaphysics of the Tragedy"[8] from 1911 the first existentialist essay, the first to make the distinction between the authentic and the empirical life.[9] According to Goldmann's logic, this text could have been influential even for Martin Heidegger,[10] paradoxically enough, along with another work by the Hungarian philosopher, which was written quite soon after the essay mentioned but already from a Marxist position: *History and Class Consciousness*.[11] Both works were preceded by the young Hungarian thinker's review, "Thoughts on Henrik Ibsen," published in 1906 and conceived years before, in which Kierkegaard was already praised as the one who could "best express the extremes."[12]

---

[6] Belohorszky, "Madách és Kierkegaard," p. 895.
[7] See also Pál Belohoroszky, "Dosztojevszkij és Kierkegaard" [Dostoyevsky and Kierkegaard], *Új Írás*, no. 6, 1981, p. 80.
[8] György Lukács, "A tragédia metafizikája," in *Ifjúkori művek* [Juvenal Works], ed. by Árpád Tímár, Budapest: Magvető Kiadó 1977, pp. 492–518 (in English as "The Metaphysics of Tragedy," in *Soul and Form*, Cambridge, Mass.: MIT Press 1974, pp. 152–74). (The essay was first published in German as "Die Metaphysik der Tragödie," *Logos. Internationale Zeitschrift für Philosophie der Kultur*, 1911.)
[9] See Lucien Goldmann, *Kierkegaard vivant*, Paris: Gallimard 1966, pp. 125–64.
[10] See Lucien Goldmann, *Lukács et Heidegger*, Paris: Denoel and Gothier 1973, p. 115.
[11] György Lukács, *Geschichte und Klassenbewusstsein. Studien über marxistishe Dialektik*, Berlin: Malik-Verlag 1923 (in English as *History and Class Consciousness*, London: Merlin Press 1971).
[12] György Lukács, "Gondolatok Ibsen Henrikről," in *Ifjúkori művek*, ed. by Árpád Tímár, p. 92 (in English as "Thoughts on Henrik Ibsen," in *The Lukács Reader*, ed. by Arpad Kadarkay, Oxford and Cambridge, Mass.: Blackwell 1995, pp. 97–112). (The essay was first published in the sociological periodical *Huszadik Század*, in August 1906.)

The early reference to the Danish thinker was also inspired by the Austrian philosopher and writer Rudolph Kassner (1873–1959). Lukács often quoted Kierkegaard's works and ideas together with other Scandinavian writers such as August Strindberg (1849–1912), Jens Peter Jacobsen (1847–85), and Henrik Pontoppidan (1857–1943). Henrik Ibsen's (1828–1906) influence, however, was overwhelming for the young Lukács, as it was for his friends and colleagues, who later became significant artists, thinkers, and dramaturges. At the age of eighteen, "George von Lukács"[13] asked his millionaire father to treat him to a trip to Norway (as a birthday present), to visit and talk to the living genius. Later though, as he moved farther from theater, and maybe from Ibsen as well, Lukács got closer to Kierkegaard, as if Oslo were on the way to Copenhagen. In 1910, he wrote his famous essay "The Foundering of Form against Life: Sören Kierkegaard and Regina Olsen."[14] It was inspired by his Kierkegaardian love affair, focusing also on the dilemma, described thoroughly in the text: "Perhaps something in him knew that happiness—if it was attainable—would have made him lame and sterile for the rest of his life."[15]

The most important question of Lukács' essay was the "life value of gesture," as he put it:

> Perhaps the gesture—to use Kierkegaard's dialectics—is the paradox, the point in which reality and possibility intersect, matter and air, the finite and infinite, life and form...the gesture is the leap by which the soul passes from one into the other, the leap by which it leaves the always relative facts of reality to reach the eternal certainty of forms. In a word, the gesture is the unique leap by which the absolute is transformed into life, into possibility."[16]

At this time Lukács was involved with "his Regine Olsen," a talented painter and disturbed soul: Irma Seidler. Yet, he soon "sacrificed her," the dearest, as it was written, on the altar of his spiritual duty, to remain faithful to his melancholy. Miss Seidler, having been left by Lukács, soon married one of her colleagues, but unlike her Danish "model," after a brief and unhappy marriage, she tried to re-establish her relationship with Lukács, in vain. On a warm spring night, she committed suicide.[17]

---

[13] The family obtained a "noble" rank (baronship); the young Lukács used the "von" in his name.

[14] György Lukács, "Sören Kierkegaard és Regine Olsen," in *Ifjúkori művek*, ed. by Árpád Tímár, pp. 287–303" (in English as "The Foundering of Form against Life. Sören Kierkegaard and Regina Olsen," in *Soul and Form*, pp. 28–41). The essay was first published in the Hungarian literary periodical *Nyugat* (no. 6, 1910), and shortly after reprinted in Lukács' essay collection, entitled *A lélek és a formák. Kísérletek* [Soul and Form. Experiments], Budapest: Franklin 1910. The periodical *Nyugat* was the most significant forum for progressive writers and poets of literature in the Hungarian Golden Age.

[15] Lukács, "Sören Kierkegaard és Regine Olsen," p. 294.

[16] Ibid., p. 288.

[17] See also, Ágnes Heller, "Lukács György és Seidler Irma" [György Lukács and Irma Seidler], in her *Portrévázlatok az etika történetéből* [Portrait Sketches from the History of Ethics], Budapest: Gondolat 1976, pp. 385–422. See also my essay-novel on the affair, András Nagy, *Kedves Lukács* [Dear Lukács], Budapest: Magvető Kiadó 1984.

Deeply shocked by the final loss of the one once closest to him, Lukács understood, yet again in Kierkegaardian terms, why human sacrifice was needed and explained this with borrowed terminology in a dialogue, in which he "attempted" to come to terms with his heavy responsibility in Irma Seidler's premature death.[18]

It was not the only essay on Kierkegaard that was inspired by Irma Seidler, but there was a whole series of essays dedicated to her that were published throughout the years. In 1910, Lukács collected these essays in the above mentioned book, *Soul and Form. Experiments*,[19] which was soon to bring him considerable success. The book was introduced by a letter, explaining his philosophical vocation and referring to Kierkegaard (along with Plato and Montaigne), as the one who provided a model for Lukács' own work, by means of his imaginative journals and stories. Lukács also added bitterly that any given age can only produce one genius like Kierkegaard but is unable to understand and appreciate him.[20]

Russian literature, mainly the works of Dostoyevsky and Tolstoy as well as Russian religious philosophy, which was growing out of it, represented the other philosophical and literary tradition to which Hungarian artists and intellectuals (including Lukács and his circle) were very receptive. This fact would soon also shape his interpretation of Kierkegaard.[21] When reviewing the collection of Solovyov's essays in 1915, Lukács emphasizes the strong influence of Kierkegaard.[22] Being deeply influenced, even "mesmerized" by the "holy Russian literature," he soon decides to describe the whole "theoretical universe" of Dostoyevsky as the frames of his very own *Weltanschauung*. The ambitious project would be interrupted after the introduction (which was separately published as *The Theory of the Novel*[23]); the drafts would only appear posthumously.[24]

---

[18] See György Lukács, "A lelki szegénységről," in *Ifjúkori művek*, ed. by Árpád Tímár, pp. 537–52 (in English as "On Poverty of Spirit," in *The Lukács Reader*, ed. by Arpad Kadarkay, pp. 42–57).

[19] Lukács, *A lélek és a formák. Kísérletek*.

[20] See György Lukács, "Az esszé lényegéről és formájáról. Levél a kísérletről" [On Essence and Form of the Essay. Letter about the Experiment], in his *Ifjúkori művek*, ed. by Árpád Tímár, p. 306 (the essay was first published in Lukács' essay collection *A lélek és a formák. Kísérletek*).

[21] On Kierkegaard's influence on Russian literature, see also András Nagy, "Kierkegaard in Russia," in *Kierkegaard Revisited*, ed. by Jon Stewart and Niels Jørgen Cappelørn, Berlin and New York: Walter de Gruyter 1997 (*Kierkegaard Studies Monograph Series*, vol. 1), pp. 107–38.

[22] György Lukács, "Vlagyimir Szolovjov, Válogatott művek, 1. kötet" [Vladimir Solovyev, Selected Works, vol. 1], in *Ifjúkori művek*, ed. by Árpád Tímár, pp. 622–3.

[23] György Lukács, "Die Theorie des Romans. Ein geschichtsphilosophischer Versuch über die Formen der großen Epik," *Zeitschrift für Aesthetik und Allgemeine Kunstwissenschaft*, vol. 11, nos. 3–4, 1916, pp. 1–89 (in English as *The Theory of the Novel. A Historico–Philosophical Essay on the Forms of Great Epic Literature*, Cambridge, Mass.: MIT Press 1971).

[24] György Lukács, *Dostojewski, Notizen und Entwürfe* [Dostoyevsky, Notes and Sketches], ed. by J. Kristóf Nyíri (on the basis of Lukács' *Nachlaß*), Budapest: Akadémiai Kiadó 1985.

The Kierkegaardian interpretation and set of references in the projected work are of major importance since several parallels are described in the writings of Dostoyevsky and Kierkegaard and briefly elaborated in the notes. The drafts were never worked out systematically or summarily as originally planned because history played a more and more important role, with the nearly metaphysical shock of the First World War. Lukács at that time moved to Heidelberg, to search for a new, spiritual and intellectual home, close to thinkers like Max Weber, Ernst Troeltsch, Karl Jaspers, and Ernst Bloch—and many others—while he continued his studies on Kierkegaard's criticism of Hegel, a project he still recalled nostalgically fifty years later.[25] He was even considering a German academic career at the University of Heidelberg, with a *Habilitation* based on the same topic, Kierkegaard's critique of Hegel.[26]

He was soon rejected by the university, and so later he spent more and more time in Hungary, and established the so-called Sunday Circle, a gathering place for young intellectuals (many of whom later gained international recognition),[27] to discuss the issues inspired by his "twin-saints," Dostoyevsky and Kierkegaard. At this time, another aspect emerges in Lukács' orientation which soon becomes dominant in the argumentation of the critics of his thinking: his recognized Jewish identity and consciousness. As his close friend, the famous poet and playwright, later film aesthete and scriptwriter, Béla Balázs (1884–1949) put it: Lukács "discovered" the Jew in himself,[28] and paradoxically enough, the interest in Jewish mysticism and messianism also prepared the road for understanding Kierkegaard. Lukács discussed his essay with Martin Buber, who praised it as "exceptionally clear and solid in its formulation, delineation and cohesiveness," and thanked Lukács for "discussing an issue so important for [him] in such a dignifying manner."[29]

When his academic career failed and the "time of complete sinfulness"[30] was tragically shaping history, Lukács' focus moved from Kierkegaard to another critic of Hegel, namely Marx. When asked in an interview in 1918 who the most influential author was for him, he still laid stress on Kierkegaard's role, who, he

---

[25] See György Lukács, *Curriculum vitae*, ed. by János Ambrus, Budapest: Magvető Kiadó 1982, p. 266.

[26] See György Lukács, *Megélt gondolkodás. Életrajz magnószalagon*, Budapest: Magvető Kiadó 1989, pp. 9–39 (in English as *Record of a Life: An Autobiographical Sketch*, London: Verso 1983).

[27] Participants were Karl Mannheim, Arnold Hauser, Charles de Tolnay, Frederick Antal, Karl Polányi and several others, the young Béla Bartók performed some of his new pieces at the circle. See, *A vasárnapi kör* [The Sunday Circle], ed. by Éva Karádi and Erzsébet Vezér, Budapest: Gondolat 1980.

[28] About the whole process, see Béla Balázs, *Napló* [Journals], Budapest: Magvető Kiadó 1982.

[29] Buber's letter to Lukács, in *Lukács György levelezése 1902–1917*, ed. by Éva Fekete and Éva Karádi, Budapest: Magvető Kiadó 1981, p. 351 (in English as *Selected Correspondence 1902–1920*, trans. by Judith Marcus and Zoltan Tar, New York: Columbia University Press 1986).

[30] The terminology was borrowed from Fichte, and Lukács used it to characterize his own age.

said, "accompanied me from the very beginning in my intellectual development." But another name is also emphasized: "I have read him this time also as something with an enduring value: Marx."[31] In 1918, he wrote an essay, judging the ethical problem of Bolshevism as unsolvable,[32] and the same month—"from one Sunday to another"—Lukács joined the Hungarian Communist Party. This "leap of faith" remains inexplicable with reasoning and logic, and, as such, would determine his entire life, and partly his country's as well.

III. Kierkegaard Reception in Scholarly Frames

The tradition of interpreting Kierkegaard à la Lukács and his circle was suspended by the sudden "conversion" by Lukács himself and then by the short communist intermezzo in 1919. After the fall of the Hungarian Soviet Republic, many of its representatives left the country or were silenced. Kierkegaard certainly was innocent in everything that happened politically, yet it is hard to trace his intellectual and spiritual footprints in Hungary during that decade.

The sole exception is László Ravasz (1882–1975), a Protestant bishop and influential thinker, pastor, politician, who wrote an article on Kierkegaard as early as 1914, that was later followed by two translated sermons, first published in 1929.[33] Interest in Kierkegaard in the first two decades of the twentieth century was due to some intellectuals with lively international contacts and with a certain radical bent in their thinking. This later turned into political radicalism and as such was compromised. Meanwhile, the Jewish background of many of these important figures was, for the official intellectuals of the 1930s, somewhat unpleasant and easy to "blame."

The next phase of Kierkegaard's reception in Hungary was shaped mainly by theologians and philosophers, some of whom held significant university and academic positions, but who were often limited with respect to their originality. Kierkegaard's writings were still interpreted through German translations and analyses, with the consequence that neither the literary richness of Kierkegaard's language nor its polemical independence from the German philosophical tradition could be wholly observed.

Yet in the 1930s, the very same decade in which Adorno's (1903–69) and Lev Shestov's (1866–1938) important books on Kierkegaard were published,[34] five

---

[31] György Lukács, "Könyvek könyve" [Book of the Books], in *Ifjúkori művek*, ed. by Árpád Tímár, p. 767.

[32] György Lukács, "A bolsevizmus mint erkölcsi probléma," in *Forradalomban* [In Revolution], Budapest: Magvető Kiadó 1987, pp. 36–41 (in English as "Bolshevism as an Ethical Problem," in *The Lukács Reader*, ed. by Arpad Kadarkay, pp. 216–22). (First published in *Szabadgondolat*, 1918, pp. 228–32).

[33] László Ravasz, *Egység a különbségben* [Unity in Difference], Budapest: Sylvester 1929.

[34] Theodor W. Adorno, *Kierkegaard. Konstruktion des Ästhetischen*, Tübingen: Mohr 1933 (in English as *Kierkegaard, Construction of the Aesthetic*, trans. by Robert Hullot-Kentor, Minneapolis: University of Minnesota Press 1989); Lev Shestov, *Kierkegaard and*

volumes appeared in Hungary, focusing on the Danish thinker. The most influential one was probably the work of the young, but already well-established, university professor, Béla Brandenstein (1901–89). Having obtained many important positions during his lifetime and become totally forgotten later, Brandenstein published his *Kierkegaard* in 1934,[35] a work which was the first general attempt to introduce his thinking to the Hungarian public, with an interpretative analysis of the *oeuvre*. Biography and descriptive bibliography were interwoven, highlighting the humorous, clownish, sometimes even morbid features of the protagonist—partly in a way that avoided a deeper understanding of his theological and philosophical originality. Brandenstein's renewed attempts to open up the deeper side of the writings from a psychological angle made several shortcuts in the interpretation. Thus, the Regine Olsen story, the social background of the family, and Kierkegaard's relationship to his father were described to explain the complexity and "polyphony" of the *oeuvre*. The emphasis on Kierkegaard's excentrism also allows the author to omit any analysis of controversies in contemporary philosophy, which is summarized simply as an anti-Hegelian attack. *The Point of View for My Work as an Author* was mainly quoted as the "key" for the entire body of writings, in which *Either/Or* and the *Upbuilding Discourses* were discussed. But Kierkegaard's attack on "Christendom" was only vaguely mentioned.

At the end of the 1930s, a more significant book was written by the theologian Sándor Koncz (1913–83),[36] focusing on "post-World War theology," with an interpretation of Kierkegaard. In this way, Karl Barth's dialectical theology was finally introduced in Hungary—in a Kierkegaardian context. The author was also familiar with the works of Jaspers and Heidegger, who were not commonly known names in Hungarian intellectual circles in the 1930s. However, in the year of the work's publication (1938) the focus of interest definitely moved away from theological and philosophical problems, as the *Anschluß* took place "next door" and the "nazification" of Hungarian political life became more and more evident.

Kierkegaard's writings "exercised on the German youth a more profound and a more serious impact than that of Nietzsche,"[37] writes László Széles, summarizing his experiences in the Third Reich, in his *The Basic Lines of Kierkegaard's Thinking*. According to Széles' explanation, Kierkegaard's "critical philosophy" focuses on "existential thinking" with discussions of despair, choice, and loneliness.[38] The author refers to Jaspers, as a follower of the Danish thinker, but also to Heinrich Rickert (1863–1936), one of the founders of the neoKantian school in Germany, who did not consider Kierkegaard's works scientific and for this reason did not engage in theoretical debates with his thinking.

---

the Existential Philosophy, from Russian trans. by Elinor Hewitt, Athens: Ohio University Press 1969 (originally as *Киргегард и экзистенциальная философия. Глас вопиющего в пустыне*, Paris: Sovremenniye zapiski i Dom Knigi 1939).

[35]   Béla Brandenstein, *Kierkegaard*, Budapest: Franklin 1934.
[36]   Sándor Koncz, *Kierkegaard és a világháború utáni teológia* [Kierkegaard and Post-War Theology], Miskolc: Fekete P. 1938.
[37]   László Széles, *Kierkegaard gondolkodásának alapvonalai* [The Basic Lines of Kierkegaard's Thinking], Budapest: Sárkány 1933, p. 6.
[38]   Ibid., pp. 15–32.

The other book dealing with Kierkegaard from another aspect is Sándor Tavaszy's (1888–1951) *Kierkegaard's Personality and Thinking*, inspired by the fashionable Spenglerian views and influenced by Schleiermacher as well.[39] Tavaszy's emphasis on Kierkegaard's biography reframes the philosophical dilemmas, focusing mainly and again on its anti-Hegelian features, which the author considers as the major achievement of Kierkegaard's thinking. Tavaszy lived in Transylvania, where the Hungarian artistic and intellectual traditions had been very strong, even though after 1918 the area was under Rumanian rule. In this context, the theoretical dialectics of reality and existence, as described in the book, could and did have another—slightly political—meaning.

On the Hungarian side of the border, the Protestant pastor Lajos Zsigmond Szeberényi (1890–1941) published in 1929 his translations of Kierkegaard's treatises,[40] and a few years later a book entitled *Kierkegaard's Life and Works*.[41] The goal of the work was to offer a general guide to the writings of the Danish thinker, paradoxically enough, from the point of view of the Protestant Church. Kierkegaard's attack on Christendom in this interpretation was a "sad detour," a "breaking with his whole past."[42] By contrast, Kierkegaard's denial of intellectualism in his explanation may inspire and encourage both Christians and atheists. Szeberényi emphasizes the difficulties in translating Kierkegaard, which is also obvious when one reads his Hungarian version of the sermons. According to his analysis, the *oeuvre* may be read from a psychological point of view, which explains various theological and philosophical problems—for example, the father's curse of God concludes in the melancholy of the son and everything that comes with it.

In spite of the publication of five books in Hungarian on Kierkegaard, his primary texts remained largely untranslated, only appearing in the form of quotations, overgrown and debated by commentaries. While Protestant theologians seemed to understand the originality of the Danish thinker, the official *Hungarian Lexicon for Church History* does even not mention his name,[43] although even minor Hungarian pastors are listed on its pages. The prestigious *Catholic Lexicon* has an entry on him, which emphasizes his role as a critic of the Danish National Church and thus describes him as refusing the "misery of Protestantism." It notes that the adherents of the Danish Church will realize only "after their death how much Lutheranism is mistaken." However, it is conceded that Kierkegaard knows about the "psychology of religion."[44]

---

[39] Sándor Tavaszy, *Kierkegaard személyisége és gondolkodása* [Kierkegaard's Personality and Thinking], Kolozsvár 1934.

[40] *Önvizsgálat. Ajánlva a kortársaknak. Isten változatlansága* [*For Self-Examination. Recommended to the Present Age* and *The Changlessness of God*], trans. by Lajos Zsigmond Szeberényi, Békéscsaba: Evangélikus Egyházi Könyvkereskedés 1929.

[41] Lajos Zsigmond Szeberényi, *Kierkegaard élete és munkái* [Kierkegaard's Life and Works], Békéscsaba: Evangélikus Egyházi könyvkereskedés 1937.

[42] Ibid., p. 113.

[43] *Magyarországi protestáns egyháztörténeti Lexicon*, ed. by Sándor Ladányi, 3rd revised ed., Budapest: Református Egyház Zsinati Irodájának Sajtóosztálya 1977.

[44] *Katholikus Lexikon*, vols. 1–4, ed. by Béla Bangha, Budapest: Magyar Kultúra 1931, vol. 3, p. 67.

IV. Kierkegaard's "Literary Presence" before the Second World War in Hungary

The famous writers of the literary magazine *Nyugat* were sensitive and open to philosophical dilemmas, both the members of the so-called "Golden" and "Silver" generation. The most important poet of the first period, Endre Ady (1877–1919), may have been inspired by the Danish genius,[45] while his friend and rival, Mihály Babits (1883–1941), mentioned Kierkegaard's name when writing *The History of European Literatures*—though only when referring to Ibsen's extravagant pastor, Brand.[46]

It is still an open question if Babits had more knowledge of contemporary interpretations of Kierkegaard than the brief reference suggests. Philological research may unearth details about his relationship with Vilmos Szilasi (1889–1966), who was once close to Lukács, and later an assistant of Husserl and colleague of Heidegger, and who also corresponded with Babits about important philosophical problems. Other great writers, who were well read and certainly influenced by pre-Second-World-War philosophy, were open to existentialism, like Dezső Kosztolányi (1885–1936) and Attila József (1905–37)—yet the Kierkegaardian impact on these thinkers is still hypothetical. Factual confirmation would be needed to answer questions of origination and inspiration posed by their poetry. Meanwhile, writers from neighbouring countries who were influenced by Kierkegaard, such as Rilke and Kafka, were known in Hungary—but the only example of Kierkegaard's explicit presence is in an essay of the somewhat isolated and yet very original thinker Béla Hamvas (1897–1968). His essay, entitled "Kierkegaard in Sicily" is a masterfully written imagined journey of the Danish thinker to the island in the Mediterranean—a rich and emphatic portrait that focuses on the life we live, instead of the many lives we would want to live. And yet it praises the inner victory of the autonomous individual, even when defeated from the "outside."[47]

V. Marxist Interpretations

Hamvas was certainly "defeated" by the outside world after the communist takeover of Hungary in 1948. The sensitive and educated intellectual could only find a job as an unskilled worker at an aluminum plant in the countryside—as a consequence of the polemical writings of another Kierkegaard scholar, György Lukács. However, the Marxist interpretation was dramatically shaped by history from 1918 to 1989, which started with (1) the "radical" understanding of Kierkegaardian paradoxes and giving Marxist answers to the questions posed, and which later concluded in (2) the total rejection of Kierkegaard's views as "inhuman," "idiotic," and "parasitic," slowly

---

[45] See Tibor Gintly, "Ady és Kierkegaard" [Ady and Kierkegaard], *Iskolakultúra*, no. 9, 1998, pp. 37–47.

[46] Mihály Babits, *Az európai irodalom története*, Budapest: Szépirodalmi Kiadó 1979, p. 423.

[47] Béla Hamvas, "Kierkegaard Szicíliában" [Kierkegaard in Sicily], in *Esszépanoráma*, vols. 1–3, ed. by Zoltán Kenyeres, Budapest: Széepriodalmi Kiadó 1978, vol. 3, pp. 92–104.

softening into (3) a "critical reception" of Kierkegaardian ideas, so important in the dissolution of the Marxist *Weltanschauung*.

(1) It took Lukács nearly a decade after finishing his essay on Kierkegaard, inspired by the Danish thinker's unhappy love, to find the deeper meaning of the gesture he praised and described in his text. Later he referred to Kierkegaard as the one who helped him "to lose God,"[48] so the choice he was facing could only be a secular one. The nature and concept of secularized faith, as a product of historical choices was described in a documentary novel, explaining the train of thought of young intellectuals, including Lukács and his circle—and with several references to Kierkegaard. "To believe is different from to know; to believe means just a consciously irrational mentality that one follows when facing one's life"—as the author, Ervin Sinkó (1898–1967) writes, reconstructing their debates in the Budapest House of Soviets. "Hamlet can't act, because he only knows and doesn't believe. Lenin and Trotsky excellently recognized the revolutionary situation, but they could have been just sitting in a library." However, the author's conclusions go further: "where to live means to die for something—and to die for something means [not only] to live, but [also] to kill someone else."[49]

This dangerous conclusion that Lukács himself shared was "beyond tragedy," as described in Agamemnon's sacrifice, in opposition to Abraham's, and beyond understanding for those, who do not believe. The years of the First World War gave a new meaning to the dilemmas described by Johannes de silentio in *Fear and Trembling*. Lukács understood this to mean that "on the basis of a mystical morality one must become a cruel politician and thus violate the absolute commandment: 'Thou shall not kill!' "[50] When joining the Communist Party and even the Hungarian Red Army as a political commissar, he really sacrificed everything: his intellect, his morality, his social privileges, and his purity. He described his situation as one who could only choose between sins and the measure of our choice is the sacrifice: "But only the murder of those can be tragically moral who know, definitely and clearly know that killing is absolutely not allowed."[51] But one major difference became obvious when quoting the sacrifice of Abraham for political reasons: the object of the sacrifice was lost forever; in the secularized—historically shaped—universe there was no longer anyone to save "Isaac."

Later in life, Lukács returned again and again to the same situation: to the sacrifice the dearest. The return to this motif is surprising after his Marxist conversion; it is as if he were looking for explanations regarding the logic that became so fatally determinant for his entire life. This was profoundly influential for many of his followers, for young Marxist intellectuals, receptive to this logic even after the

---

[48] Lukács, *Curriculum vitae*, p. 281.
[49] Ervin Sinkó, *Optimisták* [The Optimists], Budapest: Magvető Kiadó 1965, p. 691.
[50] Lukács' letter to Paul Ernst, May 4, 1915, in *Lukács György levelezése*, p. 595.
[51] György Lukács, "Taktika és etika," in *Forradalomban*, p. 132 (first published in the essay collection, entitled *Taktika és ethika*, Budapest: Közoktatásiügyi Népbiztosság Kiadása 1919, pp. 5–13. (For an English translation see *Tactics and Ethics. Political Essays 1919–1929*, vols. 1–2, trans. from German by Michael McColgan, New York: Harper & Row 1972–75).

Second World War. This became a starting point for a new world-view and was used as a plea to avoid the "repetition" of the nightmares which Europe went through twice in the twentieth century (and in which Hungary was always on the losing side).

(2) After the fall of the first communist republic in Hungary in 1919, many of the leaders of the "Council of Soviets," including Lukács, left the country for Vienna, and later moved to Berlin. At the time Lukács' concept of history was not only influenced but also determined by Hegel; decades later, he emphasized that he arrived at Hegel from Kierkegaard.[52] Living in Berlin in the 1920s and 1930s, during the radicalization of the political and intellectual climate, soon convinced the communist Lukács that the development of modern "bourgeois" philosophy was heading toward fascism. This was the experience of many left-wing intellectuals, who left the German capital after 1933, the year of the Nazi takeover—when Lukács' *The Destruction of Reason*, the Marxist analysis of contemporary Western philosophy, was probably conceived. The book, besides other things, was designed to give his "theoretical accounting concerning Kierkegaard."[53]

The influential book was written in the years before settling in Moscow, where Lukács moved from Berlin and stayed until the end of the Second World War. In his close intellectual environment there, the atmosphere of Stalinism was dominant, while on the other side of the continent and in his homeland, the growing influence of Nazism was determinant. The book became a kind of "manual" for Marxist readers about bourgeois thinking. It was published and republished in different parts of Europe, in several translations and with some modifications, particularly after the death of Stalin. Kierkegaard, once so important for Lukács, was given an entire chapter, which was used to describe modern bourgeois thinking as a "forerunner of contemporary imperialism."[54]

The segment dealing with the great Danish thinker is one of the longest and most closely argued. Relatively speaking, he received a better treatment than Lukács' contemporaries, many of whom he knew personally from his Heidelberg years. In this context, Kierkegaard's "intellectual honesty" is mentioned several times. However, he is still described as a right-wing critic of Hegel (as opposed to the left-wing criticism of Marx), heading towards "existential nihilism," whose development in the dissolution of Hegelianism ended in "radical irrationalism," in the "negation of history," in "denying dialectics and thus, progress itself," and concluding in a "philosophy of despair." Even his religion, for Lukács, was no more than a poetically described atheism: "Kierkegaard did not want to admit that his religion is only a rescue for shipwrecked, decadent aesthetes." But even this form of religion is needed "for the ruling class, since this way they may neutralize criticism, revolt, anger, etc. by integrating them into a new, desperate form of belief."[55]

---

[52] Lukács, "Utam Marxhoz" [Road to Marx], in *Curriculum vitae*, pp. 227–38.

[53] György Lukács, *Az ész trónfosztása. Az irracionalista filozófia kritikája*, Budapest: Magvető Kiadó 1978 [1954], p. 17 (in English as *The Destruction of Reason*, London: Merlin Press 1980).

[54] Ibid., pp. 227–79.

[55] Ibid., p. 263.

Kierkegaard's philosophical independence, as Lukács and his Stalinist followers emphasize, was based on the capital provided by his father. Meanwhile, he shared "with Romanticism the life-basis of reactionary parasite intellectuals," to establish an "art of living." Kierkegaard made efforts "to try to rescue religion from aestheticism," and thus he represents "the Ash Wednesday of the Romantic carnival, just as Heidegger represents [the Ash Wednesday] of imperialist parasitism, following the pre-war carnival of Simmel and Bergson."[56]

Even if Lukács refers repeatedly to the honesty and also to the moral superiority of Kierkegaard, compared with his "imperialist epigones," such as Jaspers, Camus, or Heidegger, nevertheless, it is to Heidegger, who "in his existential free choice chose Nazism,"[57] that Lukács attributes the Kierkegaard renaissance, from the 1930s on, with his "imperialist hatred of Marxism-Leninism." Yet, at the very center of his rejection of Kierkegaard, the determinant figure of Abraham recurs, as Lukács wants to revisit the question of the suspension of ethics, the superiority of individual choice against the universal:

> To raise the most exemplary case of Kierkegaard, when Abraham sacrifices Isaac, what makes him different from a tragic (and, as such aesthetic and ethical) hero is precisely the absolute, theoretical immeasurability of his acts, and his real, decisive experiences remain theoretically incommunicable. By this, however, we state the total erosion of the universal ethics (and not the dialectical negation) in the religious sphere.[58]

If one reads between the lines, these words can be understood as a "self-critique" by Lukács, for whom such logic seemed to be valid. He erased his own ethics and chose the irrational or, as he describes it now, "the end of ethics."

In spite of this extremely harsh criticism, Kierkegaard was at least present, and the strong polemics, paradoxically, emphasized his significance. By comparison, in the *Philosophical Lexicon*, written by Soviet philosophers and published in a faithful translation in Hungary in 1953, in which eight pages quote Stalin, there is not even a single entry on Kierkegaard.[59] Even years later, for Soviet ideologues, Kierkegaard seemed to be more a mental case than a thinker.[60]

1948 was the year when the "Stalinization" of Hungarian philosophical life started, with the involvement of Lukács—who later himself became a victim of the same process. However heavy-handed and even brutal Lukács was, his "victims" got a slightly better verbal treatment than those of his colleagues, like László Rudas (1885–1950), József Szigeti (1892–1973), or László Mátrai (1909–83), scholars of that time with significant university positions. Mátrai characterized Kierkegaard's views as "solipsism," a reinterpretation of only "old dogmas" sometimes several

---

[56] Ibid., p. 261.
[57] Ibid., p. 274.
[58] Ibid., p. 262.
[59] *Filozófiai Lexikon*, ed. by Mark Moiseerich Rozental and Pavel Yudin, from Russian trans. by Béla Tábor and Stefánia T. Mándy, Budapest: Szikra 1953.
[60] David I. Zaslavsky, "Yurodstvo i yurodnie v sovremennoy burzhoaznoy filosofi" [Idiocy and Idiots in Contemporary Bourgeois Philosophy], *Voprosy Filosofii*, no. 5, 1954, pp. 138–51.

thousand years old, thoughts taken "from the dust"; in his view, the only excuse for the appreciation of such thinking could be the shock of the recent World War.[61] However, such views are basically false, dangerous, and clear obstacles to progress. And there was no tolerance for those who tried to slow down the march toward communist victory. But Kierkegaard remained in the picture, and he did not disappear from the collective memory.

During the softening of hard-core Stalinism at the time of the "fermentation" of the 1956 revolution, one landmark was the so-called "Philosophy Debate" at the Petőfi Circle, the gathering point of young intellectuals in need of real philosophical polemics. Lukács, back again on stage agreed with the "rehabilitation" of great thinkers of the nineteenth and twentieth century, but only from a Marxist position. His role in the revolutionary government of Imre Nagy (1896–1958) soon discredited him again from Hungarian scholarly life for the coming years; however, he had time and peace enough to think over some of the problems which he touched upon before and during 1956. On the other end of the theoretical landscape, the evangelical bishop Lajos Ordass (1901–78), who was sentenced for participating in the revolution, could use his years in prison to translate Kierkegaard's sermons and to think about him from this extreme position.[62] Kierkegaard may have been right: the present age does not need geniuses but martyrs—several thinkers were ready to follow this road.

(3) In 1963, Kierkegaard could finally be mentioned and analyzed in a university textbook in a less militant manner.[63] This was the very year of the general amnesty for the participants of the revolution. At the same time, young philosophers (including a member of the "Lukács School") put together a general introduction entitled *Trends in Contemporary Bourgeois Philosophy*,[64] and for the "general characterization," Kierkegaard was needed. Though existentialism could lead to fascism, as it was explained, this was not necessarily the case since some anti-fascists and even Marxists were also members of the same philosophical tradition. In the biography of Kierkegaard, as well as in the analysis of this thinking, his importance is emphasized, sometimes indirectly and hidden between the lines.

In 1965, a carefully selected anthology was published containing some short texts of Kierkegaard's works, together with other great thinkers of existentialism.[65] In the ideologically argued preface, written by a famous Marxist mandarin, it was explained why Kierkegaard was attractive to many thinkers and artists in the West;

---

[61] László Mátrai, *Haladás és fejlődés. Filozófiai tanulmányok* [Progress and Development. Philosophical Studies], Budapest: Irodalmi és művészeti Intézet 1947, pp. 47–51.

[62] Vilmos Vajta, *Hit és élet összecsengése: Kierkegaard, Ordass Lajos tolmácsolásában* [The Harmony of Life and Faith: Kierkegaard in Lajos Ordass' Interpretation], Keszthely: Ordass Baráti kör 1990. See also László Donáth, "Hite által még holta után is beszél" ["He died, but through his faith he still speaks"], in *Kierkegaard Budapesten* [Kierkegaard in Budapest], ed. by András Nagy, Budapest: Fekete Sas 1994, pp. 276–87.

[63] See *Mai nyugati filozófia* [Contemporary Western Philosophy], ed by Istvánné Simonovits, Budapest: Tankönyvkiadó 1963.

[64] György Márkus and Zádor Tordai, *Irányzatok a mai polgári filozófiában*, Budapest: Gondolat 1964.

[65] Béla Köpeczi (ed.), *Az egzisztencializmus* [Existentialism], Budapest: Gondolat 1965.

it is important to come to terms with his *oeuvre* even if his "teachings" (qualified by quotation marks) are obscure, confused, and contradictory. The interest in his works is also a clear sign of the crisis in bourgeois philosophy: the escape into irrationalism is characteristic of the decadent social class in the twentieth century. In the appreciation of his works, the misery of bourgeois thinking is expressed, though the literary and aesthetic inspiration from his writings is important for modern art.

In the 1960s, the first texts of Kafka, Rilke, and Camus were translated and published in Hungarian; this also proved important for the reception of Kierkegaard's thinking. As the attention of the intellectual audience was very much focused on recently banned and still barely tolerated writers, the strong Marxist criticism could not disturb his influence—on the contrary. Mediation through literature is always penetrating. The former "Kierkegaardian classics" were also republished in this decade: Ibsen, Strindberg—and some years later the *oeuvre* of Dostoyevsky was analyzed in a very original and polemical monograph, with a whole chapter on Kierkegaard, concluding with his influence on Russian religious philosophy.[66]

In the course of the 1960s, Hungarian writers became receptive to the Danish thinker; Béla Hamvas wrote his poetic and original works, freely interpreting Kierkegaard (and other thinkers) though these remained unpublished and were distributed only in typewritten copies. The greatest Catholic poet, János Pilinszky (1921–81), was profoundly inspired by the Danish writer, albeit through French existentialism. Young writers, growing up in this decade, also became receptive to Kierkegaard, sometimes attending the same university courses with the "Lukács Nursery"—the younger generation of the followers of the great thinker, already in preparation for the role they would come to play in the coming years.

Compared with the politically dominant Soviet analyses, for example, that of Piama Pavlovna Gaidenko (b. 1934),[67] the Hungarian criticism of Kierkegaard now became softer. It did not call him "half-forgotten," and the interpretation did not go so far as to say: "Reason is the murderer of human liberty, of human personality—states Kierkegaard."[68] The Soviet author, who was published as a "model" in Budapest, still referred to Dostoyevsky and Shestov and emphasized Kierkegaard's influence on Heidegger and Jaspers, while the conclusion of her study included the resolution of the Twenty-Second Congress of the Communist Party of the USSR.

Kierkegaard's slow "rehabilitation" in philosophy can be best traced in different dictionaries and encyclopaedias. For example, the same authors who left Kierkegaard out in 1953, eleven years later dedicated thirty-four lines to him, characterizing him as a mystic, who could afford to publish his works thanks to the rich inheritance from his father, and who criticized Hegel from the point of view of extreme subjectivism, and otherwise was devoted to despair, anxiety, and hatred of the masses. "Nowadays imperialists need the antihuman views of Kierkegaard," they state at the end of the

---

[66] Ferenc Fehér, *Az antinómiák költője* [The Poet of Antinomies], Budapest: Magvető Kiadó 1972.
[67] Published also in Hungary, see Piama Pavlovna Gaidenko, *Az egzisztencializmus és a kultúra. M. Heidegger filozófiájának bírálata* [Existentialism and Culture. A Critique of M. Heidegger's Philosophy], trans. by József S. Nyírő, Budapest: Kossuth 1966.
[68] Ibid., p. 17.

entry.[69] In 1970, there is a whole page on him in the second edition of the *Little Philosophical Lexicon*.[70] Soon even some appreciation is given to him, albeit only as a writer, in the *Encyclopedia of World Literatures*. The excuses for this include his activity as "working for a progressive newspaper like *Fædrelandet*," and his doctoral thesis was "like that of Marx, a critique of Hegel."[71]

At the end of the 1960s, the first volume of Kierkegaard's selected writings was published,[72] with a long (75-page) preface by a devoted and disciplined Marxist, to disinfect the dangerous thoughts, which were being let out of the intellectual quarantine. Parts of *The Concept of Irony, Either/Or, Repetition, Fear and Trembling, The Concept of Anxiety*, and *Concluding Unscientific Postscript* were translated, even if somewhat heavy-handedly. The preface also contained a description of the Hungarian Kierkegaard reception, and finally focused on his influence beyond existentialism, on thinkers like Barth, Tillich, and Banhoffer (*sic*). Even though there was all the usual Marxist analysis to shape the understanding, a bibliography and an index of subjects were also attached. The same volume was republished in 1982, in the changing intellectual climate of Hungary, with significant success.

At the end of Lukács' life, his struggle with Kierkegaard was still not over. He had to settle accounts with the Danish thinker, by whom he was once so paradoxically influenced, and a whole generation of philosophers followed his interpretation. His *Ontology of Social Being*,[73] the most ambitious work he left unfinished when he died at the age of eighty-six, contains a chapter on existentialism; and everything he writes about Kierkegaard can be understood as a conclusion after sacrificing his life on the altar of an "omnipotent theory," a sacrifice for secularized redemption and its institution: the Communist Party. Writing now about Abraham, Lukács emphasizes that the individual-personal relationship with God has nothing to do with institutions. Later he explains that atheism, as it is represented in Kierkegaard, is the world of present-day Christianity. Then he refers to the Grand Inquisitor, arguing that to follow Jesus' life would destroy the Church itself, an easy metaphor for the institution he once believed in unconditionally.

It was too late—too late for him, not for Kierkegaard. In the same year Lukács died, a larger study on Kierkegaard appeared by Ervin Rozsnyai (b. 1926), whose goal was to demonstrate Kierkegaard's thinking as an example: "where are those

---

[69] See a new and revised edition of the *Filozófiai Lexikon* [Philosophical Lexicon], ed. by Mark Moiseerich Rozental and Pavel Yudin, Budapest: Szikra 1953. This edition, entitled *Filozófia Kislexikon* [Little Philosophical Lexicon], was translated by Péter Józsa et al. and edited by Györgyné Vári, Budapest: Kossuth 1964.

[70] *Filozófiai Kislexikon*, 2nd revised ed., ed. by Györgyné Szigeti et al., from Russian trans. by István Csibra et al., Budapest: Kossuth Kiadó 1972, pp. 190–1.

[71] *Virágirodalmi lexikon* [Encyclopedia of World Literatures], ed. by István Király et al., Budapest: Akadémiai Kiadó 1979.

[72] *Sören Kierkegaard írásaiból* [From Søren Kierkegaard's Writings], trans. by Tivadar Dani et al., ed. by Béla Suki, Budapest: Gondolat 1969.

[73] See Lukács, *A társadalmi lét ontológiájáról*, vols. 1–3, Budapest: Magvető Kiadó 1976, vol. 2, pp. 639–41 (in English as *Ontology of Social Being*, trans. from German by David Fernbach, vols. 1–3, London: Merlin Press 1978–80).

dead ends that prove that the road of history parallels that of Marx?"[74] Kierkegaard is to show there is no "way out"; his influence is similar to that of a medieval epidemic. In Rozsnyai's interpretation, the basic question of the Danish thinker is "to exist or to think."[75] The most determinant experience for Kierkegaard, according to his interpretation, was the disappearance of his social class, and this was the motif of his defence of the "counter-revolution" after 1848. This was something dangerously familiar for Hungarian ears, since it was only seven or eight years after the "counter-revolutionaries" (as the revolution of 1956 was called in the communist era) were let out of prison; the rhetoric is still frightening.

In the 1970s, the first texts were finally translated and published: first "The Immediate Erotic Stages" from the first part of *Either/Or*, entitled "Mozart's Don Juan,"[76] then the whole of *Either/Or*.[77] The thick book would soon disappear from library shelves (being stolen rather than borrowed). This work was followed by a substantial postscript, explaining how Kierkegaard describes the phenomenon of alienation, even if he did not see any way out of it. Ultimately, his work is seen as one of the two consistent reactions to the phenomenon of bourgeois alienation, along with that of Marx. But whereas Marx tries to "transcend" this state, Kierkegaard does not; whereas Marx revolts, Kierkegaard resigns; and while Marx looks for the possibility of change (through the force of a social class, etc.), Kierkegaard gives up with the conclusion that our relation to the world has to be changed, as opposed to Marx's answer, that we should change the world. The essay closes with the judgement: either Kierkegaard—or Marx.[78] A choice that time made for Hungary.

However, the author of this postscript, Ágnes Heller (b. 1929), a close student of Lukács and a protagonist of the Marxist renaissance—soon to be rejected by the ideologues of the Hungarian Communist Party and forced to leave Hungary—prepared the road for the interpretation of Kierkegaard in the years to come. She also focused on the young Lukács' reception of Kierkegaard and thus contributed to revealing her master's early existential sensitivity.[79] It was supported by the unexpected revelation: Lukács's old suitcase was discovered in a safe in a bank in Heidelberg, where he kept his early writings, diaries, correspondence, drafts of works, etc. just before his fatal "conversion" to Marxism. These works document his preparations for his "road to Marx," that soon seemed to be a dead end, however, a very important one.

Only one text by Kierkegaard was translated in the 1980s, *Fear and Trembling*, done masterfully by the poet Péter Rácz (albeit from German) and published with

---

[74] Ervin Rozsnyai, *Filozófiai arcképek* [Philosophical Portraits], Budapest: Magvető Kiadó 1971, p. 9.
[75] Ibid., p. 10.
[76] *Mozart Don Juanja* [Mozart's Don Juan] (translation of "The Immediate Erotic Stages or the Musical-Erotic"), trans. by László Lontay, Budapest: Európa Kiadó 1972.
[77] *Vagy-vagy* [*Either/Or*], trans. by Tivadar Dani, Budapest: Gondolat 1978.
[78] Ágnes Heller, "A szerencsétlen tudat fenomenológiája" [The Phenomenology of the Unhappy Consciousness], in *Vagy-vagy*, 1978, pp. 1017–79.
[79] See Ágnes Heller's above mentioned work, *Portrévázlatok az etika történetéből*.

a long postscript by the literary historian Péter Balassa.[80] By this time Balassa was already far from Marxism and receptive to the multifaceted influence that Kierkegaard had on European and Russian thinking and literature. However, these were the years before the dissolution of the Soviet empire when intellectual fermentation was of great importance and Kierkegaard exerted an eminent, albeit grassroot, influence in it. University courses were finally allowed, theological thinking progressed, publications of his works in foreign languages were more or less available in libraries, and interpretations included the *oeuvre* of Sartre, Jaspers, and Heidegger—authors "capriciously" tolerated or banned in the final years of communism.

VI. Kierkegaard and the Embarrassment of Freedom

There is a Hungarian expression referring to the "embarrassment of richness," that was experienced to some degree by the sudden arrival of freedom in 1989—and by the inspiring social, intellectual, and political confusion it created. At this time Kierkegaard was not wholly or deeply understood by scholars, students, and intellectuals in Hungary since many of the previous misunderstandings from the preceding decades still remained. The political changes seemed to be at the center of attention, but, as Kierkegaard understood, neither freedom nor political changes can answer important individual dilemmas.

The most important task, once the Wall came down, was to publish the works in Hungarian translation, finally with no censorial obstacles, and focusing on the original Danish text. However, the need to read Kierkegaard was more powerful than the appreciation of carefully worked out editions; so quite soon after the political changes, Kierkegaard's works started to appear. First, his once-published sermons were reprinted,[81] then the three most important, heretofore untranslated books, *Repetition*,[82] *The Concept of Anxiety*,[83] and *The Sickness unto Death*.[84] Based on the ambiguous Hungarian tradition, prefaces or postscripts were included in the editions, in some cases a "glossary" was also provided to explain the special terminology which the Danish thinker used. The basis of the texts was still mainly the German edition, though the translators (the writer Péter Rácz and the philosopher Zoltán Gyenge) also consulted the Danish original to produce the final version, and even smaller publishers were interested in investing in the Danish writer.

Unfortunately, no planned "strategy" of publication was considered or followed while the Danish critical edition, *Søren Kierkegaards Skrifter*, was not yet available. Soon the translations were based on the original, and the editions were carefully worked out. Major and highly specialized publishers printed them: *Practice in Christianity* was part of a series of philosophical books by a professional and

---

[80] *Félelem és reszketés* [*Fear and Trembling*], trans. by Péter Rácz, postscript by Péter Balassa (pp. 221–73), Budapest: Európa Kiadó 1986.
[81] "Minden javunkra van—ha szeretjük Istent" ["All Things Must Serve Us for Good—When We Love God"], trans. by Lajos D. Ordass, *Lelkipásztor*, nos. 7–8, 1992, pp. 219–23.
[82] *Az ismétlés*, trans. by Zoltán Gyenge, Budapest: Ictus 1993.
[83] *A szorongás fogalma*, trans. by Péter Rácz, Budapest: Göncöl 1993.
[84] *A halálos betegség*, trans. by Péter Rácz, Budapest: Göncöl 1993.

prestigious publisher,[85] while the *Berlin Notes* were also produced by an excellent editor—albeit still translated from German.[86] *From the Papers of One Still Living* and *The Concept of Irony* were the first texts to be part of a planned series of Kierkegaard's works,[87] finally based on *Søren Kierkegaards Skrifter*, the critical edition of the Søren Kierkegaard Research Centre in Copenhagen, with the application of the entire scholarly apparatus of that edition and in collaboration with an editorial board.

Throughout the same years earlier publications (even the once "censored" selections and rather unprofessionally translated versions) were reprinted and sold: from time to time also profit-oriented publishers came onto the "market" with texts that were out-of-print before—most recently with "The Seducer's Diary," where it is hard to identify what the textual basis for the translation was.[88] These witness the constant interest in Kierkegaard's works, while several philosophical and theological journals published some of the more important shorter works of the Danish thinker, or segments of larger texts.

While in the early 1990s the opposition to Marxism played an eminent role, together with the "rehabilitation" of existentialism, later the continuity of theological thinking inspired new publications and reflections. At the same time, the focus of interest started to move toward previously unexamined questions in the history of philosophy, together with the new trends in interpreting Kierkegaard: hermeneutics, postmodern analysis, etc. The sudden simultaneity of interpretations often created interesting or even humorous episodes: contradicting tendencies arrived at the same time, fresh or rather "half-baked" ideas were presented as final conclusions, and Kierkegaard seemed to be a perfect subject for all these approaches, based on his originality, his pseudonyms, his irony, with his overwhelming influence in Hungary.

Once the works started to appear, it became important that a language be established that could be used for dialogues on Kierkegaard, to help Hungarian thinkers to be integrated into international Kierkegaard scholarship. The first attempt to be engaged in the international Kierkegaardian conversation was a whole "week" in Budapest in 1992, dedicated wholly to the Danish genius, when the euphoric atmosphere of the fresh political changes renewed the interest in earlier lesser known or less tolerated thinkers. "Kierkegaard in Budapest" was multicultural event, with concerts, cabaret, exhibitions, theatre performances, and publications. At the core of the festival was a five-day long series of dialogues, approaching Kierkegaard's *oeuvre* and personality from different angles: psychology, theology, philosophy, history of influence. Internationally known scholars were invited to take part in

---

[85] *A keresztény hit iskolája* [Practice in Christianity] (a selection from *Practice in Christianity*), trans. by Zoltán Hidas, Budapest: Atlantisz 1998.

[86] *Berlini töredék. Jegyzetek Schelling 1841/42 előadásairól* [Berlin Fragments. Notes to Schelling's Lectures of 1841–42] (translation of the *Notes to Schelling's Berlin Lectures*), trans. by Zoltán Gyenge, Budapest: Osiris-Gond-Cura Alapítvány 2001.

[87] *Egy még élő ember írásaiból. Az irónia fogalmáról* [*From the Papers of One Still Living. The Concept of Irony*], trans. by Gábor Miszoglád and Anita Soós, Pécs: Jelenkor 2004.

[88] *A csábító naplója. Mesék az emberi szívről* ["The Seducer's Diary." Tales of the Heart], trans. by Irini Angelisz, Szada: Kassák 2004.

the conversations, to deliver lectures and to attend the discussions.[89] Psychology in Hungary was a particularly important approach, based on the overwhelming influence of the Budapest school of psychoanalysis; other great thinkers focused on special philosophical questions, unknown—or undiscussed—before. It was also of great importance that theologians and practicing pastors could be involved in the dialogues, as systematic theological thinking was much needed in those years, and with Kierkegaard the limitations of the existing theological tradition in Hungary also became highly visible. When philosophy was in the focus, many representatives of the "Lukács School" (or rather "Nursery") spoke; however, the younger generation's radical reading of Kierkegaard was also represented. The lectures and discussions on the influence of the Danish thinker helped those present to understand the long-lasting effects of his originality that also shaped Russian, Scandinavian, German, and Hungarian thinkers and artists. The last day was used to "wrap up" the conclusions and help to think about future Hungarian Kierkegaard scholarship.

Characteristic of Hungary of the early 1990s, one lecturer, a highly original philosopher, arrived from the Parliament (in the break between two sessions) to talk about Kierkegaard,[90] while the mayor of Budapest (a famous ex-dissident and an admirer of the Danish thinker) sponsored the opening event: a concert version of *Don Giovanni* in a ruined church in the outskirts of Buda. Heavy media coverage followed the events—some of them focusing on Kierkegaard's opinion of democracy, something hard to understand in a country for so long time deprived of it. This week was unforgettable, the atmosphere and spirit were unique—conferences in the later years focused more on more professional aspects and special topics.

In 1999, "Crossroads in Kierkegaard's Thinking" was the title of an international conference organized by the Aesthetics Department of the University of Budapest (or more exactly the Eötvös Loránd University) and co-sponsored by the Søren Kierkegaard Research Centre in Copenhagen. The emphasis was on the possible "intersections" of the *oeuvre*, still of great importance for the Hungarian intellectual context. Famous foreign scholars, together with representatives of Hungarian Kierkegaard research joined in the discussions and gave talks at the University of Budapest. Present at the conference were Hungarian scholars living outside of the capital, and even outside of the country.[91]

The next conference was organized in the western part of Hungary: Veszprém was the host town for the gathering of Kierkegaard scholars in Hungary, focusing on his irony, humor, and also on the influence which he may have had inside Hungary and also abroad. Lectures of both conferences were published,[92] while in another center of Kierkegaard scholarship, in Debrecen (in eastern Hungary) a special

---

[89] Among the participants were Alastair McKinnon, Julia Watkin, Joakim Garff, George Pattison, Henri-Bernard Vergote, Helmut Vetter and others. The lectures were published in *Kierkegaard Budapesten*, ed. by András Nagy.

[90] Miklós Tamás Gáspár; unfortunately his talk was not printed in the volume since it was mainly improvised and never put down on paper.

[91] The lectures were published in the philosophical periodical *Magyar Filozófiai Szemle* in 2003 and in 2004; for details see the bibliography.

[92] The Veszprém conference's lectures were published in the philosophical periodical *Pro Philosophia Füzetek*, Veszprém 2001; for details see the bibliography.

anthology was published, "masquerading" as a magazine dedicated to him.[93] In this collection of writings Kierkegaard's works were published together with those of Derrida, Agacinski, Ricoeur, Lévinas, and others, to open up the interpretation of his works in the very contemporary philosophical context.

Besides these events and publications, other important "crossroads" of Kierkegaard research should be followed when considering Hungarian scholarship: the Catholic University of Piliscsaba (close to Budapest) should be mentioned, due to the devoted work of István Czakó, while in southern Hungary the University of Szeged is famous for the Kierkegaard lectures given by Zoltán Gyenge. The other charming university town in the south-west of Hungary, Pécs, also attracts the interest of those willing to learn about Kierkegaard, since, at the Janus Pannonius University, János Weiss and other scholars offer courses on Kierkegaard. Moreover, the publishing house Jelenkor that issued the first volume of the new edition of Kierkegaard's works in Hungarian translation, together with Joakim Garff's biographical novel on Kierkegaard, is also located in the city.

There are also several Hungarian scholars in Transylvania working on Kierkegaard's texts, often together with Rumanian colleagues. The research in Hungary, even if with many local focuses, is somewhat centralized in Budapest, where both the Scandinavian Institute and the Institute of Science of Art and Media Studies often have seminars on Kierkegaard in their curriculum. Many experts and professors are affiliated with the latter institute: Ágnes Heller, Sándor Radnóti, Béla Bacsó, Géza Fodor and others are eminent scholars in the field, while there are philosophers from the same university also doing research on Kierkegaard: György Tatár and István Fehér M. The confessional academies are also of great importance: Protestant, Evangelical, and also the Jewish University; for example, Gyula Rugási's works are outstanding in this respect. Meanwhile the Institute of Philosophy at the Academy of Science should also be noted as a basis of future research.

At the turn of the millennium, a Kierkegaard Society was organized to integrate Hungarian scholarship and to offer a meeting place for those interested. Then in 2001 the Kierkegaard Cabinet was established and registered as a foundation, soon to start working as a resource center, offering access to a special library, organizing lectures, putting together a database, and establishing professional contacts for researchers inside and outside the country.[94]

The "flow" of studies and articles on Kierkegaard—as seen from the bibliography—has not yet concluded in the production of extensive monographs or major analyses on the Danish thinker. For the time being, the discourse is more important; probably later the achievements will also be clearly visible. The most

---

[93] *Vulgo*, nos. 3–5, 2000.
[94] The Kierkegaard Cabinet's official founder is Péter Nádas (b. 1942) the great writer, and is located at Budapest University. Among the guests invited were Niels Jørgen Cappelørn, Jon Stewart, Bruce Kirmmse, George Pattison, Cynthia Lund, and many other scholars. The special library was donated by the Søren Kierkegaard Research Centre at the University of Copenhagen and by the Hong Kierkegaard Library at St. Olaf College, Northfield, Minnesota, USA. For more information on the Kierkegard Cabinet, see http://emc.elte.hu/~hargitai/kirke/indexe.html.

recent years of Kierkegaard studies suggest that things are "back to normal," while Hungary, now a part of the European Union, can provide a greater opportunity for scientific collaborations, for joint projects, and for participation in international research groups. The "Hungarian patient" may be even cured; the stubborn tradition of melancholy, the strong attraction to morbidity, the special interest in the extreme interpretation of Kierkegaard may only be episodes of our past, soon forgetten. If Hungary were to be "normal," would it help Kierkegaard research, or would the often morbid interest be gone forever? Until now the country has survived all its tragedies and difficulties—will it survive peace and satisfaction? Or following the young Lukács' concern, by then will creativity itself disappear? And what if Kierkegaard would become "only" a subject for scholarly analysis and interpretation? Shall we get closer to him—or would the fatal misunderstandings and heated misinterpretations be somehow more "authentic?"

How did Kierkegaard put it? Christ didn't sweat blood on the cross in order for Privatdozents to carve out their *Habilitation*. Or is that our future?

Bibliography

By Judit Bartha

I. Hungarian Translations of Kierkegaard's Works

Önvizsgálat. Ajánlva a kortársaknak. Isten változatlansága [*For Self-Examination. Recommended to the Present Age. The Changlessness of God*], trans. by Lajos Zsigmond Szeberényi, Békéscsaba: Evangélikus Egyházi Könyvkereskedés 1929 (2nd ed., Budapest: Új Mandátum 1993, after this, several later editions).

Sören Kierkegaard írásaiból [From Søren Kierkegaard's Writings], trans. by Tivadar Dani et al., ed. by Béla Suki, Budapest: Gondolat 1969 (2nd ed., 1982; 3rd ed., 1994).

Mozart Don Juanja [Mozart's Don Juan] (translation of "The Immediate Erotic Stages or the Musical-Erotic"), trans. by László Lontay, Budapest: Európa Kiadó 1972 (2nd ed., 1993).

Vagy-vagy [*Either/Or*], trans. by Tivadar Dani, Budapest: Gondolat 1978 (several later editions, latest, Budapest: Osiris 2005).

Félelem és reszketés [*Fear and Trembling*], trans. by Péter Rácz, postscript by Péter Balassa Budapest: Európa Kiadó 1986 (several later editions, latest, Budapest: Göncöl 2004).

"Minden javunkra van—ha szeretjük Istent" ["All Things Must Serve Us for Good—When We Love God"], trans. by Lajos Ordass, *Lelkipásztor*, nos. 7–8, 1992, pp. 219–23.

A halálos betegség [*The Sickness unto Death*], trans. by Péter Rácz, Budapest: Göncöl 1993.

"A kereszténység elsajátítása" [The Acquisition of Christianity] (an extract from *Practice in Christianity*), trans. by Gábor Miszoglád, *Pannonhalmi Szemle*, no. 1, 1993, pp. 35–42.

"Lesz feltámadásuk a halottaknak, mind igazaknak mind hamisaknak" ["There Will Be the Resurrection of the Dead, of the Righteous—and of the Unrightous"], trans. by Anna Molnár, *Gond*, no. 4, 1993, pp. 3–11.

A szorongás fogalma [*The Concept of Anxiety*], trans. by Péter Rácz, Budapest: Göncöl 1993.

Az ismétlés [*Repetition*], trans. by Zoltán Gyenge, Budapest: Ictus 1993.

Építő keresztény beszédek [Upbuilding Christian Tales] (a selection from *Christian Discourses*), trans. by Zoltán Bohács et al., ed. by Kocziszky Éva, Budapest: Hermeneutikai Kutatóközpont 1995.

Filozófiai morzsák [*Philosophical Fragments*], trans. by Zoltán Hidas, Budapest: Göncöl 1997.

A keresztény hit iskolája [School of Christian Faith] (a selection from *Practice in Christianity*), trans. by Zoltán Hidas, Budapest: Atlantisz 1998.

"Ki a szerzője a Vagy-vagynak" ["Who Is the Author of *Either/Or*"], trans. by Gábor Gulyás, *Vulgo*, nos. 3–5, 2000, pp. 274–6.

"Magyarázat és egy kicsit több" ["An Explanation and a Little More"], trans. by Gulyás Gábor, *Vulgo*, nos. 3–5, 2000, pp. 277–8.

Szerzői tevékenységemről [*On My Work as an Author*], trans. by Zoltán Hidas, ed. by Gábor Gulyás, Debrecen: Latin betűk 2000.

Berlini töredék. Jegyzetek Schelling 1841/42 előadásairól [Berlin Fragments. Notes to Schelling's Lectures of 1841–42] (translation of the *Notes to Schelling's Berlin Lectures*), trans. by Zoltán Gyenge, Budapest: Osiris-Gond-Cura Alapívány 2001.

A csábító naplója. Mesék az emberi szívről ["The Seducer's Diary." Tales of the Heart], trans. by Irini Angelisz, Szada: Kassák 2004.

Egy még élő ember írásaiból. Az irónia fogalmáról [*From the Papers of One Still Living. The Concept of Irony*], trans. by Gábor Miszoglád and Anita Soós, Pécs: Jelenkor 2004.

Naplójegyzetek AA–DD [*Journals AA–DD*], trans. by Anita Soós, Pécs: Jelenkor 2006.

II. Secondary Literature on Kierkegaard in Hungary

Antal, Éva, "Szókratész halott—és élvezi. A szókratészi irónia bestialitásáról" [Socrates Has Died—And He Enjoys It], *Vulgo*, nos. 3–5, 2000, pp. 206–11.

Bacsó, Béla, "Ismételhető-e az ismétlés?" [Can Repetition Be Repeated?], *Gond*, no. 4, 1993, pp. 21–5 (republished in *Kierkegaard Budapesten*, ed. by András Nagy, pp. 87–96).

— *Határpontok. Hermeneutikai esszék* [Border Lines. Hermenutical Essays] Budapest: Twins Kiadó 1994 (on Kierkegaard, see pp. 64–70).

— "Kierkegaard-ról" [On Kierkegaard], *Élet és irodalom*, March 9, 2001.

— "A szorongás mint egzisztens kategória" [Fear as an Existential Category] in his *Írni és felejteni. Filozófiai és művészetelméleti írások* [Writing and Forgetting. Writings on Philosophy and Theory of Art], Budapest: Kijárat 2001, pp. 26–38 (republished, *Magyar Filozófiai Szemle*, nos. 1–2, 2003, pp. 173–83; in German as "Angst als existentielle Kategorie," *Prima Philosophia*, vol. 13, no. 1, 2000, pp. 37–42).

Balassa, Péter, "Utószó Ábrahám hallgatásához" [Postscript to Abraham's Silence], in *Félelem és reszketés* [*Fear and Trembling*], 1986, pp. 221–73 (republished in *Majdnem és talán* [Almost and Perhaps], Budapest: T-Twins, Lukács Archívum 1995, pp. 63–89).

— "Kierkegaard—Bergman—Pilinszky," *Beszélő*, no. 50, 1992, pp. 39–41 (republished in *Kierkegaard Budapesten*, ed. by András Nagy, pp. 352–61 and in

Majdnem és talán [Almost and Perhaps], Budapest: T-Twins. Lukács Archívum 1995, pp. 90–7).
— "Kierkegaard és Bergman" [Kierkegaard and Bergman], *Pannonhalmi Szemle*, vol. 1, no. 1, 1993. pp. 45–53.
Bali, Brigitta, "Az 'épületes gondolat' maszk mögötti arca Kierkegaard *Vagy-vagy*-ának álarcosbálján [The Face behind the Mask of the "Upbuilding Thought" in the Carnival of Kierkegaard's *Either/Or*], *Filozófiai Figyelő*, no. 3, 1988, pp. 147–51.
Bartha, Judit, "Az esztétikai inkognitó pluralitása. Kierkegaard korai pszeudonim műveiről" [The Plurality of the Aesthetic Incognito. On Kierkgaard's Early Pseudonymous Wrirtings], *Gond*, nos. 27–8, 2001, pp. 133–52.
— "Alteregó-centrumok polifóniája. Kierkegaard és Hoffmann" [Polyphony of Alterego Centers. Kierkegaard and Hoffmann], *Pro Philosophia Füzetek*, no. 28, 2001, pp. 61–70.
Bazsányi, Sándor, "'Hiszen nem ti vagytok, akik beszéltek.' A retorika kommunikációs modelljének esztétikai fordulata Søren Kierkegaard 'Ha Istent szeretjük, minden a javunkra kell, hogy váljon' című épületes keresztény beszédben" ["For it is not you who speaks, but the Holy Spirit." Aesthetical Alteration of the Communicative Model of Rhetoric in Kierkegaard's Christian Discourse "All Things Must Serve Us for Good—*When* We Love God"], *Vulgo*, nos. 3–5, 2000, pp. 259–72.
Belohorszky, Pál, "Madách és Kierkegaard" [Madách and Kierkegaard], *Irodalomtörténet*, no. 4, 1971, pp. 886–96.
— "Dosztojevszkij és Kierkegaard," *Új Írás*, vol. 21, no. 6, 1981, pp. 73–86.
— "Dostoevskij i Kierkegaard," *Studia Slavica Academiae Scientiarum Hungaricae*, vol. 32, 1986, pp. 181–201.
Bogdán, Ágnes, "Kierkegaards kinesiske æskesil. Om pseudonymernes rolle i den litterære produktion," *Skandinavisztikai Füzetek/Papers in Scandinavian Studies*, no. 8, 1998, pp. 25–39.
— "Csak abból táplálkozz, ami egészséges benned. A 19. sz. második felének halálos betegsége" [Nourish Yourself Only from Your Healthy Parts. The Sickness unto Death of the Second Part of the Nineteenth Century], *Pro Philosophia Füzetek*, no. 28, 2001, pp. 159–74.
Bohár, András, "Kierkegaard és az avanrgárd lehetséges kapcsolatai" [Possible Connections between Kierkegaard and the Avant-garde], *Pro Philosophia Füzetek*, no. 28, 2001, pp. 120–32.
Bókay, Antal, "Az ismétlés: a lélek titkos törvénye" [The Repetition as the Soul's Secret Low], in *Kierkegaard Budapesten*, ed. by András Nagy, pp. 33–51.
Bölcskey, Gusztáv, "Kierkegaard egyház- és kereszténységkritikája" [Kierkegaard's Church and Critique of Christianity], in *Kierkegaard Budapesten*, ed. by András Nagy, pp. 311–20 (reprinted in *Debreceni Református Akadémia Theologia Évkönyve*, Debrecen 1992–93, pp. 67–85).
Brandenstein, Béla, *Kierkegaard*, Budapest: Franklin Társulat 1934 [2nd ed., Budapest: Kairosz 2005].
Czakó, István, "Abramo come paradigma del credente nel libro *Timore e tremore* di Søren Kierkegaard" [Abraham as Paradigm of Believer in Kierkegaard's *Fear and Trembling*, *Folia theologica*, no. 8, 1997, pp. 199–226.

— "Das Problem des Glaubens und der Geschichte in der Philosophie Kierkegaards und Karl Jaspers," *Kierkegaard Studies. Yearbook*, 2000, pp. 373–82.

— "Søren Kierkegaard hitkoncepciója a fundamentálteológia tükrében" [Søren Kierkegaard's Conception of Faith as Reflected in the Fundamental Theology], *Pannonhalmi szemle*, vol. 8, no. 1, 2000, pp. 17–26.

— *Hit és egzisztencia* [Faith and Existence], Budapest: L'Harmattan 2001.

— "Kierkegaard Feuerbach-recepciójának alapvonalai a filozófiai forráskutatás és a szöveganalízis tükrében," *Pro Philosophia Füzetek*, no. 25, 2001, pp. 85–99 (in German as "Kierkegaards Feuerbach-Bild im Lichte seiner Schriften," *Kierkegaard Studies. Yearbook*, 2001, pp. 396–413).

— "Reflexiók Friedrich Schleiermacher valláskoncepciójára Sören Kierkegard feljegyzéseiben" [Reflections on Friedrich Schleiermacher's Concept of Religion in Kierkegaard's Notebooks and Journals], *Pro Philosophia Füzetek*, no. 28, 2001, pp. 133–42.

— "Bibliai elbeszélés és filozófiai interpretáció: a Ter 22,1–19 'lírai-dialektikus' olvasata Søren Kierkegaard *Félelem és reszketés* című művében" [Biblical Narration and Philosophical Interpretation: The "lyric-dialectic" reading of Gen 22,1–19 in Søren Kierkegaard's *Fear and Trembling*], *Tanítvány*, vol. 9, no. 1, 2003, pp. 3–21.

— "Élet és elmélet az egzisztencia évszázadában" [Life and Theory in the Century of Existence], *Pro Philosophia Füzetek*, no. 32, 2003, pp. 131–6.

— "Hit és történelem viszonya Kierkegaard és Karl Jaspers gondolkodásában" [The Relation between Faith and History in Kierkegaard's and Karl Jasper's Thought], *Magyar Filozófiai Szemle*, no. 3, 2003, pp. 359–71.

— "Az ártatlanság dialektikája: Kierkegaard és Hegel a bűnbeesésről" [The Dialectic of Innocence: Kierkegaard and Hegel on the Fall], in *Lábjegyzetek Platónhoz: A bűn*, ed. by András Dékány and Sándor Laczkó, Szeged: Pro Philosophia Szegediensi Alapítvány: Librarius 2004, pp. 169–79.

— "Das Unbekannte. Die Aufhebung der klassischen *theologia naturalis* in der negativen Theologie des Johannes Climacus," *Kierkegaard Studies. Yearbook*, 2004, pp. 235–49.

— "Das Zeitalter der 'Reflexion' und 'Nivellierung': Kierkegaards *Eine literarische Anzeige* als kritische Diagnose," in *Schleiermacher und Kierkegaard: Subjektivität und Wahrheit: Akten des Schleiermacher-Kierkegaard-Kongresses in Kopenhagen, Oktober 2003. Subjectivity and Truth: Proceedings from the Schleiermacher–Kierkegaard Congress in Copenhagen October, 2003*, ed. by Niels Jørgen Cappelørn et al., Berlin and New York: Walter de Gruyter 2006 (*Kierkegaard Studies. Monograph Series*, vol. 11), pp. 635–53.

— "A szabad Ismeretlen: a természetes istenismeret problematikája Karl Rahner és Søren Kierkegaard valláskoncepciójában" [The Free Unknown: the Problem of Natural Knowledge of God in the Conception of Religion of Karl Rahner and Søren Kierkegaard], in *In memoriam Karl Rahner*, Budapest: Vigilia 2006, pp. 112–29.

— "A választás választása: Søren Kierkegaard szabadságértelmezésének alapvonalai" [Choosing the Choice: Outlines of Søren Kierkegaard's Conception of Freedom], *Vigilia*, vol. 71, no. 5, 2006, pp. 331–41.

Csejtei, Dezső, *Filozófiai etűdök a végességre. Schopenhauer, Kierkegaard és Nietzsche a halálról* [Philosophical Studies about the Finitude. Schopenhauer, Kierkegaard and Nietzsche on Death], Veszprém: Veszprémi Humán Tudományokért Alapítvány 2001.
— "A hit lovagja spanyol földön. Kierkegaard–Unamuno párhuzamok," *Magyar Filozófiai Szemle*, nos. 1–2, 2003, pp. 81–99 (in English as "The Knight of Faith on Spanish Land. Kierkegaard and Unamuno," *Letras Peninsulares*, vol. 13, nos. 2–3, 2000–01, pp. 707–23).
Csige, Ilona, "A szabadság dilemmái Kierkegaard *Vagy-vagy* című művében" [The Dilemmas of Freedom in Kierkegaard's *Either/Or*], *Stúdium*, no. 14, 1983, pp. 77–100.
Dévény, Istán, "A költő és a filozófus. Pilinszky és Kierkegaard" [The Poet and the Philosopher. Pilinszky and Kierkegaard], *Jelenkor*, no. 9, 1994. pp. 788–96 and no. 4, 1995, pp. 345–55.
— *Sören Kierkegaard*, Máriabesenyő-Gödöllő: Attraktor 2003.
Donáth, László, " 'Hite által még holta után is beszél' " ["He died, but through his faith he still speaks"], in *Kierkegaard Budapesten*, ed. by András Nagy, pp. 276–87.
Erdélyi, Ildikó, "A csábítás lélektana" [The Psychology of the Seduction], in *Kierkegaard Budapesten*, ed. by András Nagy, pp. 69–84.
Fehér M., István, "Schelling, Kierkegaard, Heidegger—rendszer, szabadság, gondolkodás. A poszthegelianus filozófia néhány közös motívuma és filozófiai témája," trans. by László Vásárhelyi Szabó, *Pro Philosophia Füzetek*, nos. 11–12, 1997, pp. 3–20 (in German as "Schelling, Kierkegaard, Heidegger hinsichtlich System, Freiheit und Denken. Gemeinsame Motive und Philosopheme der nachhegelschen Philosophie," in *Zeit und Freiheit. Schelling, Schopenhauer, Kierkegaard, Heidegger. Akten der Fachtagung der Internationalen Schelling-Gesellschaft, Budapest, 24. bis 27. April 1997*, ed. by István Fehér M. and Wilhelm G. Jacobs, Budapest: Éthos könyvek 1999, pp. 17–36).
Garaczi, Imre, "Élet és filozófia Kierkegaard-nál" [Life and Philosophy in Kierkegaard], *Pro Philosophia Füzetek*, no. 28, 2001, pp. 153–8.
Gáspár, Csaba László, "Vallás, filozófia, technika. Kierkegaard olvasása közben" [Religion, Philosophy, Technology. While Reading Kierkegaard], *Buksz*, no. 3, 1999, pp. 296–302.
Gerlóczi, Ferenc, "A szorongás költője. Az új Kierkegaard-divat" [The Poet of Anxiety. The New Kierkegaard-Mode], *HVG*, no. 20, 1998, pp. 83–4.
Gintly, Tibor, "Ady és Kierkegaard" [Ady and Kierkegaard], *Iskolakultúra*, no. 9, 1998, pp. 37–47.
Gulyás, Gábor, "Kierkegaard teste" [Kierkegaard's Body], *Gond*, nos. 18–9, 1999, pp. 199–232.
— "Kísértetek testedzése. Haláltánc" [Ghosts' Exercise. Dance of Death], *Vulgo*, nos. 3–5, 2000, pp. 212–8.
— "A filozófia ritka pillanatai. Zoltán Gyenge, *Kierkegaard és a német idealizmus*; Zoltán Gyenge, *Az egzisztencia évszázada*" [Rare Moments of Philosophy. Zoltán Gyenge, *Kierkegaard and German Idealism*; Zoltán Gyenge, *The Century of Existence*], *Vulgo*, no. 1, 2002, pp. 245–52.

Gyenge, Zoltán, "Megjegyzések a *Félelem és reszketés* magyar kiadásához [Some Remarks to the Hungarian Edition of *Fear and Trembling*], *Filozófiai Figyelő*, no. 3, 1988, pp. 152–7.
— "A megértett idő" [The Time is Ripe], *Existentia*, nos. 1–4, 1992, pp. 417–33.
— "Hit és egzisztencia. Gondolatok a kierkegaard-i egzisztencia-fogalom kapcsán" [Faith and Existence. On Kierkegaard's Concept of Existence], *Gond*, no. 4, 1993, pp. 12–20.
— "Hegel és Kierkegaard" [Hegel and Kierkegaard], in *Majdnem nem lehet másként. Tanulmányok Vajda Mihály 60. Születésnapjára* [It Can Hardly Be Otherwise. Studies on the Occasion of Mihály Vajda's 60th Birthday], ed. by Ferenc Fehér, András Kardos and Sándor Radnóti, Budapest: Cserépfalvi 1995, pp. 190–8.
— "Az örökké élő egzisztencia" [The Forever Existing Existence], *Eszterházy Károly Tanárképző Főiskola tudományos közleményei. Tanulmányok a filozófia köréből*, vol. 22, 1995, pp. 47–80.
— *Kierkegaard és a német idealizmus* [Kierkegaard and German Idealism], Szeged: Ictus, 1996.
— "Az irónia fogalma" [The Concept of Irony], *Gond*, no. 17, 1998, pp. 202–12.
— "Az egzisztencia golgotája" [The Golgotha of Existence], in *Diotima. Heller Ágnes 70. születésnapjára* [Diotima. On the Occasion of Ágnes Heller's 70th Birthday], ed. by András Kardos et.al., Budapest: Osiris-Gond 1999 pp. 186–91.
— "Az incognito" [The Incognito], *Gond*, nos. 18–19, 1999, pp. 13–9.
— "A személytelen személyesség. A hegeli rendszerfilozófia hatása Kierkegaard filozófiájára" [The Impersonal Personality. The Influence of Hegel's Systematic Philosophy on Kierkegaard's Philsophy], *Pro Philosophia Füzetek*, no. 23, 2000, pp. 31–6.
— *Az egzisztencia évszázada* [The Century of Existence], Veszprém: Veszprémi HTA 2001.
— "A 19. század új mitológiája. A mese szerepe Søren Kierkegaard filozófiájában" [The New Mythology of the Nineteenth Century. The Role of the Fairy Tale in Kierkegaard's Philosophy], *Pro Philosophia Füzetek*, no. 28, 2001, pp. 15–27.
— "Az egzisztencia valósága. Kierkegaard létanalízise" [The Truth of Existence. Kierkegaard's Existence Analysis], *Magyar Filozófiai Szemle*, nos. 1–2, 2003, pp. 201–16.
— "Még egyszer az irónia fogalmáról. Soós Anita, *'Ha egy arcot sokáig és figyelmesen nézel,'* Budapest: HASS 2002" [Once Again on the Concept of Irony. [Review of] Anita Soós' [Ph.D. Thesis published as] *"Ha egy arcot sokáig és figyelmesen szemlélünk..."* [If We Watch a Face Long and Carefully Enough ...], Budapest: HASS 2002], *Pro Philosophia Füzetek*, no. 32, 2003, pp. 123–9.
Hamvas, Béla, "Kierkegaard Szicíliában" [Kierkegaard in Sicily], in *Esszépanoráma*, vols. 1–3, ed. by Zoltán Kenyeres, Budapest: Szépriodalmi Kiadó 1978, vol. 3, pp. 92–104.
Heller, Ágnes, "Kierkegaard és a modern zene" [Kierkegaard and Modern Music], in *Érték és történelem*, Budapest: Magvető Kiadóp 1969, pp. 321–65.
— "A kierkegaardi esztétika és a zene" [Kierkegaard's Aesthetics and Music], *Magyar Filozófiai Szemle*, vol. 9, no. 1, 1965, pp. 48–74.

— "A stádiumok között" [Between Stages], *Pro Philosophia Füzetek*, no. 28, 2001, pp. 1–14.
— *Személyiségetika* [The Ethic of Personality], Budapest: Osiris 1999.
— "Two Episodes from the Shakespeare–Kierkegaard Relationship," in *Kierkegaard Studies. Yearbook*, 2000, pp. 361–72.
— "A szerencsétlen tudat fenomenológiája" [The Phenomenology of the Unhappy Consciousness], in *Vagy-vagy* [*Either/Or*], 1994, pp. 623–58 (published also in the first Hungarian edition of *Either/Or* of 1978, pp. 1017–79 and in *Magyar Filozófiai Szemle*, nos. 3–4, 1971, pp. 364–94).
Hermann, István, "Szorongás és tragikum. Sören Kierkegaard tragikumelmélete" [Anxiety and Tragedy. Søren Kierkegaard's Concept of Tragedy], *Világosság*, no. 5, 1972, pp. 293–8.
Hidas, Zoltán, "Az egyes és az őhozzá intézett kérdés. Kierkegaard és Buber" [The Single Individual and the Question You Want to Ask this Person. Kierkegaard and Buber], *Pannonhalmi Szemle*, no. 3, 1996, pp. 41–7.
Imre, László, "Kierkegaard és az orosz szimbólizmus" [Kierkegaard and Russian Symbolism], *Studium*, vol. 2, 1971, pp. 117–21.
Iványi, Gábor, "Menj el!" [Go Away!], in *Kierkegaard Budapesten*, ed. by András Nagy, pp. 273–5.
Joós, Ernő, *Isten és lét: körséta Heidegger, Kierkegaard, Nietzsche és más filozófusok társaságában* [God and Existence: Walking About with Heidegger, Kierkegaard Nietzsche and Other Philosophers], Sárvár: Sylvester János Könyvtár 1994.
Kalmár, Zoltán, "Egy tintahal monogramjai" [The Monogram of a Cuttlefish], *Pro Philosophia Füzetek*, no. 28, 2001, pp. 81–7.
Kaposi, Márton, "Az álnév elrejtő és feltáró szerepe Kierkegaard munkásságában" [The Hiding and Revealing Role of the Pseudonyms in Kierkegaard's Works], *Pro Philosophia Füzetek*, no. 28, 2001, pp. 71–9.
Kardos, András, "A metafizika tragédiája, avagy miért nem írt drámát Sören Kierkegaard?" [The Tragedy of Metaphysics, Or Why Kierkegaard Did not Write Tragedy], *Gond*, no. 4, 1993, pp. 26–32 (republished in *Kierkegaard Budapesten*, ed. by András Nagy, pp. 149–63).
Kardos Daróczi, Gábor, "Az önmagát értelmező mű mint az interpretáció kierkegaard-i alternatívája" [The Self-Interpreting Work as an Alternative of Interpreting Kierkegaard], *Holmi*, no. 1, 1994, pp. 89–105 (republished in *Kierkegaard Budapesten*, ed. by András Nagy, pp. 191–223).
Kiss, Pál, "Az idő, örökkévalóság és történelem problémája Kierkegaard és Barth alapján" [The Problems of Time, Eternity and History in Kierkegaard and Barth], *Sárospataki Füzetek*, no. 1, 1997, pp. 60–6.
Kocziszky, Éva, "Don Juan. Vázlat az érzéki csábításról" [Don Juan. A Draft of the Sensuous Seduction], *Világosság*, no. 1, 1989, pp. 34–42.
— "Mit tanulhatunk a madaraktól és a liliomoktól?" [What Can We Learn from the Birds and the Lily], *Gond*, no. 4, 1993 (*Kierkegaard-tanulmányok*, vol. 1), pp. 37–51.
Koncz, Sándor, *Kierkegaard és a világháború utáni teológia* [Kierkegaard and Post-War Theology], Miskolc: Fekete P. 1938.
Köpeczi, Béla (ed.), *Az egzisztencializmus* [Existentialism], Budapest: Gondolat 1965.

Lőrinczné Thiel, Katalin, "A kierkegaard-i hatás néhány vonatkozása Hamvas Bélánál" [Some Aspects of Kierkegaard's Influence on Béla Hamvas], *Eszterházy Károly Tanárképző Főiskola Tudományos Közleménye. Tanulmányok a társadalomelmélet köréből*, vol. 20, 1991, pp. 31–8.

— "A hit problematikája egy egzisztencia-filozófiai megközelítésben" [The Problem of Faith Approached from the Philosophy of Existence], *Jelen-lét*, no. 2, 1993, pp. 12–7.

Loboczky, János, "A zene és a zenei Kierkegaard-nál" [Music and the Musical in Kierkegaard], *Pro Philosophia Füzetek*, no. 28, 2001, pp. 112–8.

Lukács, György, *Az ész trónfosztása. Az irracionalista filozófia kritikája*, Budapest: Magvető Kiadó 1954 (in English as *The Destruction of Reason*, trans. by Peter Palmer, London: Merlin Press 1980).

— *A lélek és a formák. Kísérletek*, Budapest: Franklin 1910 (in English as *Soul and Form*, trans. by Anna Bostock, Cambridge, Mass.: MIT Press 1974).

— *A polgári filozófia válsága* (in German as *Existentialismus oder Marxismus*, Berlin: Aufbau Verlag 1951, Budapest: Hungária 1947).

— *Gegen den mißverstandenen Realismus. Die Gegenwartsbedeutung des kritischen Realismus*, Hamburg: Claassen 1958.

Márkus, György and Zádor Tordai, *Irányzatok a mai polgári filozófiában* [Trends in Contemporary Bourgeois Philosophy], Budapest: Gondolat 1964.

Masát, András, "Kierkegaard Ibsen drámáiban" [Kierkegaard in Ibsen's Dramas], in *Kierkegaard Budapesten*, ed. by András Nagy, pp. 331–46.

Mátrai, László, *Haladás és fejlődés. Filozófiai tanulmányok* [Progress and Development. Philosophical Studies], Budapest: Irodalmi és művészeti Intézet 1947.

Mesterházy, Balázs, "A szétcsúszás alakzatai két 19. századi szövegben" [The Formations of Sliding in Two Texts from the Nineteenth Century], *Literatúra*, no. 3, 1998, pp. 241–63.

Micskey, Kálmán, "Kierkegaard teológiájához" [On Kierkegaard's Theology], in *Kierkegaard Budapesten*, ed. by András Nagy, pp. 321–7.

Miszoglád, Gábor, "Milyen nyelven beszél hozzánk Kierkegaard?" [In Which Language does Kierkegaard Talk to Us?], *Pro Philosophia Füzetek*, no. 28, 2001, pp. 29–32.

— "Rendszer—refrén—aforizmák. A diapszalmata szerepe Kierkegaard műveiben" [System—Refrain—Aphorism. The Role of the Diapsalmata in Kierkegaard's Works], *Pannonhalmi Szemle*, no. 3, 1996 pp. 63–7.

Nagy, András, "The Hungarian Kierkegaard," *Søren Kierkegaard Newsletter*, no. 24, 1991, pp. 10–3.

— "A csábító naplója. Kierkegaard Budapesten" [The Seducer's Diary. Kierkegaard in Budapest], *168 óra*, no. 49, 1992, pp. 24–5.

— (ed.) *Kierkegaard Budapesten* [Kierkegaard in Budapest], Budapest: Feete Sas 1994.

— "Kierkegaard in Russia. The Ultimate Paradox: Existentialism at the Crossroads of Religious Philsophy and Bolshevism," in *Kierkegaard Revisited*, ed. by Niels Jørgen Cappelørn and Jon Stewart, Berlin and New York: Walter de Gruyter 1997 (*Kierkegaard Studies. Monograph Series*, vol. 1), pp. 107–38.

— "Abraham the Communist," in *Kierkegaard—The Self in Society*, ed. by George Pattison and Steven Shakespeare, London: Macmillan 1998, pp. 196–220.
— *Főbenjárás. Kierkegaard, Mahler, Lukács. Esszék* [Parapethetics. Kierkegaard. Mahler, Lukács. Essays], Budapest: Fekete Sas 1998 (on Kierkegaard, see pp. 11–151).
— "The Mount and the Abyss. The Literary Reading of *Fear and Trembling*," *Kierkegaard Studies. Yearbook*, 2002, pp. 227–46.
— *Kis angyaltan. Kísérlet a leíró angelológiában* [Little Angel-Encyclopaedia. An Attempt at a Descriptive Angelology], Budapest: Liget 2003 (on Kierkegaard, see pp. 201–77).
Németh G., Béla, "Kierkegaard utóhatása—vallásos újjászültés?" [Kierkegaard's Aftermath—A Religious Revival], in *Kierkegaard Budapesten*, ed. by András Nagy, pp. 362–71.
Neumer, Katalin, "Nyelv és választás. Kierkegaard írásainak nyelv-és irodalomelméleti vonatkozásairól" [Language and Choice. Kierkegaard's Writings with Reference to the Theory of Literature and Language], *Magyar Filozófiai Szemle*, no. 3 1986, pp. 407–17.
— (ed.), *Nyelvfilozófia Locke-tól Kierkegaard-ig* [Philosophy of Language from Locke to Kierkegaard], Budapest: Gondolat 2004.
Nun, Katalin, "Korszakok. Thomasine Gyllembourg és Kierkegaard," *Tekintet*, no. 6, 2003, pp. 89–111 (in English as "Thomasine Gyllembourg's *Two Ages* and Her Portrayal of Everyday Life," in *Kierkegaard and His Contemporaries. The Culture of Golden Age Denmark*, ed. by Jon Stewart, New York and Berlin: Walter de Gruyter 2003 (*Kierkegaard Studies. Monograph Series*, vol. 10), pp. 272–97).
Pálfalusi, Zsolt, "A bolond és a bűn. Kierkegaard a komolyságról" [The Idiot and the Crime. On Kierkegaard's Earnestness], *Gond*, nos. 8–9, 1994–95, pp. 55–84.
Pasqualetti, Zsófia, *The Demon's Silence. A démon hallgatása. Gondolatok Kierkegaard rajzaihoz. Some Ideas about Kierkegaard's Drwaings*, Budapest: Fekete Sas 1993 (Hungarian and English).
Pintér, Tibor, "Kierkegaard és Mozart 'Don Giovanni'-ja: Egy mítosz mítosza" [Kierkegaard and Mozart's *Don Giovanni*: The Myth of a Myth], *Magyar Filozófiai Szemle*, nos. 1–2, 2003, pp. 147–52.
Pólik, József, "Kísérlet egy utazó portréjának rekonstrukciójára" [An Attempt at the Reconstruction of a Traveller], *Gond*, nos. 15–16, 1998, pp. 302–26.
— "Mission Impossible avagy egy 'besúgó' mártíriuma" [Mission Impossible or a 'Spy's' Martyrdom], *Vulgo*, nos. 3–5, 2000, pp. 508–16.
Popovics, Zoltán, " 'Hemiplegia.' Maurice Blanchot Kierkegaard-ról és a szorongásról" ["Hemiplegia." Maurice Blanchot on Kierkegaard and Anxiety], *Pro Philosophia Füzetek*, no. 32, 2003, pp. 1–17.
Rácz, Péter, "Belépés a kapcsolatba. Kierkegaard Budapesten, avagy filozófiájának hatása Martin Buberre" [Entering the Contact. Kierkegaard in Budapest or the Influence of his Philosophy on Martin Buber], *Liget*, no. 1, 1995, pp. 10–15.
Radnóti, Sándor, "Kierkegaard és Schlegel" [Kierkegaard and Schlegel], in *Kierkegaard Budapesten*, ed. by András Nagy, pp. 97–102.

Rozsnyai, Ervin, *Filozófiai arcképek. Descartes, Vico, Kierkegaard* [Philosophical Portraits. Descartes, Vico, Kierkegaard], Budapest: Magvető Kiadó 1971.

Rugási, Gyula, "A pillanat foglya. Kierkegaard megváltásfilozófiájáról" [The Prisoner of the Moment. Kierkegaard's Philosophy of Redemption], *Vulgo*, nos. 3–5, 2000, pp. 228–52.

Sarkadi Nagy, Pál, "Az időszerű Kierkegaard" [The Current Kierkegaard], *Theológiai Szemle*, nos. 11–2, 1963, pp. 350–4.

Soós, Anita, "A narráció mint a csábítás eszköze Søren Kierkegaard *Az ismétlés* című művében," *Pro Philosophia Füzetek*, no. 23, 2000, pp. 37–48 (in German as "Narration als Mittel der Verführung in Søren Kierkegaards Wiederholung," *Skandinavisztikai Füzetek/Papers in Scandinavian Studies*, no. 8, 1998, pp. 41–50).

— " 'Maszkodról ismerlek fel.' A kierkegaard-i irónia az álneves írásokban" ["I Recognize You from Your Mask." Kierkegaardian Irony in the Pseudonymous Writings], *Pro Philosophia Füzetek*, no. 28, 2001, pp. 45–59.

— *"Ha egy arcot sokáig és figyelmesen szemlélünk..."* ["If We Watch a Face Long and Carefully Enough..."] Budapest: HASS 2002.

— "Narráció—Csábítás—Értelmezés. Sören Kierkegaard *A csábító naplója, Az ismétlés* és a *Bűnös—Nem bűnös* című műveinek egybevetése" [Narration—Seduction—Interpretation. Comparison of Kierkegaard's "The Seducer's Diary," *Repetition* and "Guilty/Not Guilty"], *Magyar Filozófiai Szemle*, nos. 1–2, 2003, pp. 125–36.

Suki, Béla, "Isten nélküli vallásosság avagy a paradox kereszténység. Gondolatok Sören Kierkegaard nézeteiről" [Religiosity without God or the Paradox of Christianity. Thoughts about Kierkegaard's Views], *Világosság*, no. 6, 1965, pp. 328–33.

— Preface to *Sören Kierkegaard írásaiból* [From Søren Kierkegaard's Writings], trans. by Tivadar Dani et al., 1969, pp. 5–74.

Szeberényi, Lajos Zsigmond, *Kierkegaard élete és munkái* [Kierkegaard's Life and Works], Békéscsaba: Evangélikus Egyházi könyvkereskedés 1937.

Széles, László, *Kierkegaard gondolkozásának alapvonalai* [The Basic Lines of Kierkegaard's Thought], Budapest: Sárkány 1933.

Szennay, András, "Sören Kierkegaard és a kereszténység" [Søren Kierkegaard and Christianity], *Vigília*, no. 5, 1963, pp. 299–302.

Szigeti, József, *Útban a valóság felé. Tanulmányok* [On the Way to the Light. Essays], Budapest: Hungária 1948.

Szilágyi, Ákos "A *Vagy-Vagy* szerelemfilozófiája [The Philosophy of Love of *Either/Or*], *Valóság*, no. 12, 1978, pp. 14–22.

Szűcs, Ferenc, "A XX. századi teológia kezdetei és Kierkegaard. Kierkegaard és Barth Károly" [The Beginning of Twentieth-Century Theology and Kierkegaard. Kierkegaard and Karl Barth], *Gond*, no. 4, 1993, pp. 33–6 (republished in *Kierkegaard Budapesten*, ed. by András Nagy, pp. 304–10).

Tatár, György, "A híd túl messze van" [A Bridge Too Far], *2000*, nos. 4–5, 1999, pp. 95–8.

Tavaszi Sándor: *Kierkegaard személyisége és gondolkodása* [Kierkegaard's Personality and Thought], Cluj-Kolozsvár: Erdélyi Múzeum-Egyesület 1930.

— *A lét és valóság. Az exisztenciálizmus filozófiájának alapproblémái* [Existence and Truth. The Fundamental Problems of the Philosophy of Existence], Cluj–Kolozsvár: Erdélyi Muzeum-Egyesület 1933.
— *Kierkegaard gondolkozásának alapvonalai* [The Basic Lines of Kierkegaard's Thought], Budapest 1934.
Thiel, Katalin, "A hit lovagja és a 'várakozó.' Kierkegaard hatása Hamvas Bélára" ["The Knight of Faith" and "Someone Waiting." Kierkegaard's Influence on Béla Hamvas], *Pro Philosophia Füzetek*, no. 28, 2001, pp. 143–51.
— *Maszkjáték. Hamvas Béla Kierkegaard és Nietzsche tükrében* [Playing with Masks. Béla Hamvas in the Mirror of Kierkegaard and Nietzsche], Veszprém: Veszprémi Humán Tudományokért Alapítvány 2002.
Tóta, Benedek, "Ismétlés: Kísérlet Kierkegaard nyomán" [Repetition: An Attempt in the Footsteps of Kierkegaard], *Pannonhalmi Szemle*, vol. 1, no. 1, 1993, pp. 54–9.
Török, Endre, "Dosztojevszkij és Kierkegaard. 'Istennel szemben soha sincs igazunk,' " [Dostoyevsky and Kierkegaard. "In Relation to God We Are Always in the Wrong"], in *Kierkegaard Budapesten*, ed. by András Nagy, pp. 347–51 (republished, *Pannonhalmi Szemle*, vol. 1, no. 1, 1993, pp. 43–5).
Vajda, Mihály, "Kétségbeesés és gond. Késői kora-Heideggeriánus széljegyzetek Kierkegaard *Die Krankheit zum Tode* című könyvéhez" [Despair and Anxiety. Late Notes in the Spirit of the Early Heidegger to Kierkegaard's *The Sickness unto Death*], *Hiány*, no. 3, 1993, pp. 24–8 (republished in *Kierkegaard Budapesten*, ed. by András Nagy, pp. 372–89).
— "Filozófia mint elbeszélés. Emlékezet és ismétlés" [Philosophy as Narration. Recollection and Repetition], *Pro Philosophia Füzetek*, no. 23, 2000, pp. 19–29.
Vajta, Vilmos, *Hit és élet öszszecsengése: Kierkegard* [sic!] *Ordass Lajos tolmácsolásában* [The Harmony of Life and Faith: Kierkegaard in Lajos Ordass' Interpretation], Keszthely: Ordass Baráti kör 1990.
Valastyán, Tamás, "Az inkognitó, a griff és a töredék. Az aforisztikus és metaforikus beszédmódokról és azok koraromantikus vonatkozásairól—Kierkegaard, Derrida, F. Schlegel" [Incognito, Grasp and Fragment. The Aphoristic and the Metaphorical Way of Speaking and their Connections to the Early Romanticism—Kierkegaard, Derrida, F. Schlegel], *Pro Philosophia Füzetek*, no. 28, 2001, pp. 33–44.
Vikár, György, "A Don Juan-tanulmány mint egy élettörténeti válság megoldási kísérlete" [The Don Juan Essay as an Attempt to Solve an Existential Crisis], in *Kierkegaard Budapesten*, ed. by András Nagy, pp. 21–32.
V. Szabó, László, "Kierkegaard és Hermann Hesse" [Kierkegaard and Hermann Hesse], *Pro Philosophia Füzetek*, no. 28, 2001, pp. 98–110.
Weiss, János, "Kierkegaard, a bohóc és Ludwig Tieck" [Kierkegaard, the Clown and Ludwig Tieck], *Pro Philosophia Füzetek*, no. 28, 2001, pp. 89–96.

III. Secondary Literature on Kierkegaard's Reception in Hungary

Gyenge, Zoltán, "Kierkegaard-Forschung in Ungarn. Vergangenheit und Gegenwart," *Kierkegaard Studies. Yearbook*, 2000, pp. 341–61.

Matkó, László, "Örökkévalóság pillanata. Sören Kierkegaard hatása Erdélyben és Magyarországon" [The Moment of Eternity. Søren Kierkegaard's Influence in Hungary and Transylvania], *M. híd*, no. 2, 1991, p. 19, and no. 3, 1991, pp. 10–1.

Németh G., Béla, "Kierkegaard utóhatása—vallásos újjászületés?" [Kierkegaard's Impact—A Religious Rebirth?], in *Kierkegaard Budapesten*, ed. by András Nagy, pp. 362–71.

Slovakia:
A Joint Project of Two Generations

Roman Králik

"My friends scorn me;
my eye pours out tears to God."
Job 16:20

The present article focuses on the reception of Kierkegaard's intellectuel heritage in Slovakia with special attention to the broader context of Slovak history. Until 1918 Slovakia was part of the Austro-Hungarian Empire, and from 1918 to 1939 and 1945 to 1992 it was part of Czechoslovakia. It is also important to note that in the years 1948–89 Czechoslovakia was formally part of the Eastern Bloc which had a significant effect on the freedom of thought and practice regarding religion and philosophy. These domains were strongly regulated by the state. It is obvious that the philosophical monoculture of Communist Czechoslovakia did not favor public discourse about Christian thinkers such as Kierkegaard, and it naturally followed that there was little interest or incentive to translate or research his works.

Although most of the research of Kierkegaard's thought in Slovakia is relatively new, there are two scholars with roots in Slovakia who have achieved international recognition: Jaroslav Pelikán (1923–2006)[1] and Martin Matuštík (b. 1957).[2] This fact was highlighted also by Abrahim Khan in an interview given to the Slovak TV station TA3 in February 2007.

I. Brief Characteristics of Kierkegaard's Reception in Different Historical Periods

When analyzing the reception of Kierkegaard's thought in Slovakia, it is important to point out the crucial role of the linguistic proximity between the Slovak and the Czech languages. It is historical fact that the Slovak general and academic public

---

[1] Cf. Jaroslav Pelikan, *From Luther to Kierkegaard: A Study in the History of Theology*, St. Louis: Concordia 1950; *Fools for Christ: Essays on the True, the Good, and the Beautiful*, Philadelphia: Muhlenberg Press 1955.
[2] Cf. *Kierkegaard in Post/Modernity*, ed. by Martin J. Matuštík and Merold Westphal, Bloomington and Indianapolis: Indiana University Press 1995; Martin Matustik, *Post-National Identity: Habermas, Kierkegaard, and Havel*, New York: The Guilford Press 1993.

used to encounter Kierkegaard primarily through Czech translations and also through Czech research.

Historically, the first mention of Kierkegaard that was accessible to Slovak-speaking readers appeared in František Ladislav Rieger's *Encyclopedia* in 1865.[3] The entry was published only ten years after Kierkegaard's death and long before the upswing of French, American, or Japanese research.

The Danish thinker was also mentioned in the influential *Otto's Encyclopedia* in 1899,[4] but there is no evidence of philosophical or theological research about Kierkegaard's legacy in Slovakia at the turn of the century. One of the probable reasons for the lack of attention is the fact that Kierkegaard was presented as a critic of the Church which might have been perceived negatively by the predominantly clerical Slovak intelligentsia.

Similarly, in the years prior to the foundation of Czechoslovakia in 1918, as well as in later years, there is no evidence of interest in Kierkegaard in Slovak philosophical or theological circles. In the Czech lands the situation was slightly better, mainly due to the influence of Karl Barth[5] on the renowned Czech theologian Josef Lukl Hromádka (1889–1969). A similar influence was exerted by Paul Tillich on the theologian Zdeněk Trtík (1914–83),[6] but neither of these connections had any apparent impact on the situation in Slovakia.

After the incorporation of Czechoslovakia into the Eastern Bloc in 1948 the situation in philosophy worsened significantly. Natural development was halted by ideological monopolization. The years of Communist rule can be in many ways considered a period of stagnation in philosophical research. Up until 1978 when interest in Kierkegaard experienced a certain revival, Czechoslovakia had been lagging behind its western counterparts. Exceptions to the rule were the well-known articles by Josef Lukl Hromádka[7] and Marie Mikulová Thulstrup (b. 1923)[8] in Czech. In these years theology students had access to Kierkegaard through the popular study of Josef Smolík (b. 1922), entitled *Contemporary Attempts at the Interpretation of the Gospel*.[9] International research remained, however, largely inaccessible to Czech and Slovak scholars, and libraries lacked Kierkegaard's works and their translations.

---

[3] František Ladislav Rieger, "Kierkegaard Søren," in *Slovník naučný*, vols. 1–11, Prague: I.L. Kober 1860–74, vol. 4, p. 652.

[4] František Xaver Šalda, "Kierkegaard," in *Ottův slovník naučný: illustrovaná encyklopedie obecných vědomostí*, vols. 1–28, Prague: J. Otto 1888–1909, vol. 14 (1899), pp. 208–11.

[5] Cf. Karl Barth, *Der Römerbrief*, Munich: Chr. Kaiser 1922, p. XIII.

[6] Zdeněk Trtík, *Vztah já–ty a křesťanství* [The I–Thou Relation and Christianity], Prague: Blahoslav 1948; Trtík, *Moderní teologie* [Modern Theology], Prague: ČCS 1951.

[7] Josef Lukl Hromádka, "Søren Kierkegaard," *Křesťanská revue*, vol. 22, no. 8, 1955, pp. 243–7.

[8] Marie M. Thulstrupová, *Kierkegaard s jiné stránky* [Kierkegaard from Another Point of View], *Křesťanská revue*, vol. 30, no. 9, 1963, pp. 203–6.

[9] Josef Smolík, *Současné pokusy o interpretaci evangelia* [Contemporary Attempts at the Interpretation of the Gospel], 2nd ed., Prague: Oikoymenh 1993.

In 1949 a unique article appeared by Rudolf Koštiaľ (1913–91) in the Slovak journal *Tvorba* entitled *Søren Kierkegaard*.[10] In 1955 the Slovak thinker Ľudovít Fazekaš (b. 1929), who claimed to be influenced by Kierkegaard, wrote a study about the Danish philosopher. For political reasons it could not be published and appeared only in 2002.[11] The same fate concerned the study written by Jozef Ondrej Markuš (1901–93) which was published in 2007.

The situation began to change in 1978 when the Slovak Lutheran theologian Karol Nandrásky (b. 1927) started to publish his articles in the Lutheran periodical *Cirkevné listy* [Ecclesial Journal].[12] The attention of Karol Nandrásky was drawn to Kierkegaard by his teacher László Remete (1910–45)—a Hungarian-speaking Lutheran pastor—who suffered the same fate as Kaj Munk due to his anti-Nazi activities. László Remete was so strongly inspired by Kierkegaard that "within a couple of weeks he appropriated the basics of Danish grammar and read with the help of a dictionary some of Kierkegaard's non-translated writings."[13]

The years following the Velvet revolution in 1989 were characteried by an increased interest in philosophy and theology. New universities were established and new fields of study were introduced that had been ignored in the previous decades due to ideological bias. Kierkegaard ceased to be just a critic of bourgois society and an irrationalist. In 1992 Dušan Ondrejovič (b. 1930) published his *Theological Encyclopedia*,[14] which introduced Kierkegaard to the students of theology.[15] Also new theological and philosophical journals were founded, showing renewed interest in research on Kierkegaard's thought.

The general public in Slovakia started to rediscover Kierkegaard through the Czech translations of his works produced by Marie Mikulová Thulstrup as well as through studies about Kierkegaard published in Czech.[16] It was only later that the first monographs and translations were published in Slovak and that conferences

---

[10] Rudolf Koštiaľ, "Søren Kierkegaard," *Tvorba*, vol. 8, no. 8, 1949, pp. 114–6.

[11] Ľudovít Fazekaš, "Ideály proti klamu zmyslov (S.A. Kierkegaard a jeho Okamih)" [Ideals against the Deception of Senses (S.A. Kierkegaard and his Moment)], in *Štafeta svedkov. Život kresťanských služobníkov*, Banská Bystrica: KETM 2002, pp. 69–85.

[12] Cf. Karol Nandrásky: "Prorocký mysliteľ dánskeho národa" [The Prophetic Thinker of the Danish Nation], *Cirkevné listy*, vol. 92, no. 6, 1978, pp. 90–4; "O dojmoch z Dánska vo forme listu S. Kierkegaardovi" [On my Impressions from Denmark in the Form of a Letter to S. Kierkegaard], *Cirkevné listy*, vol. 96, no. 10, 1982, pp. 154–5.

[13] Karol Nandrásky, *László Remete–človek, ktorý prekračoval hranice* [László Remete– The Man who Crossed the Boundaries], Bratislava: 2006, p. 15.

[14] Dušan Ondrejovič, *Teologická Encyklopédia*, Bratislava: Univerzita Komenského v Bratislave 1992, pp. 55–7.

[15] A similar role was played by the Lutheran pastor Dušan Chovanec. Cf. Dušan Chovanec, "Cesta k Bohu" [The Way to God], in *Zápas Sørena Kierkegaarda*, ed. by Roman Králik, Nitra: FF UKF 2006, p. 143.

[16] Among the most important studies published in Czech in the 1990s were the following: Patrick Gardiner, *Kierkegaard*, Prague: Argo 1997; Romano Guardini, *Těžkomyslnost a její smysl* [Melancholy and its Meaning], Olomouc: Votobia 1995; Peter P. Rohde, *Kierkegaard*, Olomouc: Votobia 1995; Lev I. Shestov, *Kierkegaard a existenciální filosofie* [Kierkegaard and the Existential Philosophy], Prague: OIKOYMENH 1997.

were organized in Slovakia. An important event was the appearance of an influential philosophical work, *The Metamorphoses of the Post-Classical Philosophy* in 1994,[17] in which Kierkegaard is treated in greater detail. Due to Dušan Ondrejovič an entry on Kierkegaard was included also in the work *A Little Anthology from the Works of Philosophers*, published in 1998.[18]

The first monograph on Kierkegaard written by a Slovak scholar was the study *Søren A. Kierkegaard: A Philosophical-Critical Analysis of his Works*,[19] which was written by František Sirovič (b. 1920) and appeared in 2004. Two years later it was followed by Roman Králik's (b. 1973) monograph *The Problem Called Kierkegaard*.[20] In the recent years several studies dealing with Kierkegaard's thought were published in the prestigious philosophical journal *Filozofia*.[21]

In the 1990s and at the beginning of the new millennium the older generation of researchers, composed mainly of Lukáč Ján Veverka (b. 1931), Dušan Ondrejovič, Karol Nandrásky, and Ľudovít Fazekaš, started to cooperate with the emerging new generation represented by Peter Šajda (b. 1977),[22] Milan Petkanič (b. 1974),[23] Roman Králik,[24] and Andrej Démuth (b. 1974). The result of this cooperation was a number of conferences and publications that were aimed at a better acquaintance of the general and academic public with the intellectual heritage of the Danish philosopher.

---

[17] František Mihina, "Søren Kierkegaard a jeho revolta" [Søren Kierkegaard and his Revolt], in *Metamorfózy poklasickej filozofie*, ed. by František Mihina and Vladimír Leško, Prešov: FF UPJŠ 1994, pp. 193–218. This book has proved to be very successful and has appeared in five editions so far.

[18] *Malá antológia z diel filozofov II*, ed. by Ladislav Kiczko and Dušan Ondrejovič, Bratislava: Slovenské pedagogické nakladateľstvo 1998. An Entry on Kierkegaard appeared also in *Religionistika a náboženská výchova. Terminologický a výkladový slovník*, ed. by Ján Komorovský, Bratislava: F.R./G. spol. 1997, vol. 3, pp. 179–80.

[19] František Sirovič, *Søren A. Kierkegaard: Filozoficko-kritická analýza diela* [Søren A. Kierkegaard: a Philosophical-Critical Analysis of his Works], Nitra: Spoločnosť Božieho Slova 2004.

[20] Roman Králik, *Problém zvaný Kierkegaard* [The Problem Called Kierkegaard], Bratislava: Roman Králik 2006.

[21] Peter Šajda, "Náčrt kritiky Kierkegaardovho konceptu lásky v diele M. Bubera, T.W. Adorna a K.E. Løgstrupa" [An Outline of the Critique of Kierkegaard's Concept of Love by M. Buber, T.W. Adorno and K.E. Løgstrup], *Filozofia*, vol. 58, no. 7, 2003, pp. 484–93; "Náčrt kontrapozície preferenčnej a nepreferenčnej lásky v diele Sørena Kierkegaarda" [An Outline of the Counterposition of Preferential and Non-Preferential Love in the Works of Søren Kierkegaard], *Filozofia*, vol. 62, no. 2, 2007, pp. 110–21.

[22] See also Peter Šajda, *Koncept lásky v diele Majstra Eckharta a Sørena Kierkegaarda* [The Concept of Love in the Works of Meister Eckhart and Søren Kierkegaard], Ph.D. Thesis, Comenius University, Bratislava 2007.

[23] See also Milan Petkanič, *Pojem vášne u Kierkegaarda* [The Concept of Passion in Kierkegaard], Ph.D. Thesis, Comenius University, Bratislava 2007.

[24] See also Králik, *Søren Aabye Kierkegaard (1813–1855). Život, viera a teológie* [Søren Aabye Kierkegaard (1813–1855). Life, Faith and Theology], Ph.D. Thesis, Charles University, Prague 2006.

II. Translations

The first translations of Kierkegaard's works into Slovak were produced by the renowned translator from Scandinavian languages Milan Žitný (b. 1948). *The Seducer's Diary* was published in 2003,[25] followed by *Fear and Trembling* in 2005,[26] and "The Balance between the Esthetic and the Ethical in the Development of the Personality" in 2006.[27] The latter comprised also "Ultimatum" and "The Upbuilding That Lies in the Thought That in Relation to God We Are Always in the Wrong" from *Either/Or*, Part 1. A Czech translation of "The Unchangeableness of God" from *The Moment* produced by Marie Mikulová Thulstrup was published in Slovakia in 2007.[28] Before the translations of Milan Žitný the only published pieces of Kierkegaard's *oeuvre* in Slovak were his prayers.[29]

III. Conferences, Lecture Series, and Publications

The first conference on Søren Kierkegaard in the history of Slovakia and Czechoslovakia took place May 14–16, 1993 at the Technical University in Zvolen. It was organized in connection with the 180th anniversary of the philosopher's birth, and it was attended by a number of scholars from both Slovakia and abroad.[30] The lectures delivered at the conference appeared later as articles in a collective volume with the title *Kierkegaard's Days*.[31]

The conference was organized and led by Lukáč Ján Veverka, who summed up the aim of the event in his address: "This event could be the first step to initiate the publishing of at least the most fundamental works of this admirably original, self-educated, lone and absolutely authentic genius. This event should enable us in the

---

[25] *Zvodcov denník* ["The Seducer's Diary"], trans. by Milan Žitný, Bratislava: Kalligram 2003.
[26] *Strach a chvenie* [*Fear and Trembling*], trans. by Milan Žitný, Bratislava: Kalligram 2005.
[27] *Rovnováha medzi estetickým a etickým pri utváraní osobnost* ["The Balance between the Esthetic and the Ethical in Development of the Personality"], trans. by Milan Žitný, Bratislava: Kalligram 2006.
[28] Kierkegaard research in Slovakia owes a lot to Marie Mikulová Thulstrup, as her translations and studies constituted an important inspiration for a number of Slovak philosophers and theologians. The author of this article has been in written contact with her for seven years, and during that time Marie Mikulová Thulstrup has actively supported several activities in Slovakia linked to the research and popularization of Kierkegaard's thought.
[29] Dick Helander, *Modlitby Pánových svedkov* [Prayers of Lord's Witnesses], Bratislava: Vesna 1991, p. 223; p. 251; p. 273; p. 309.
[30] The lecturers were given by Mária Adamcová, Jaroslav Adamík, Stanislav Hubík, Eva Kačmáriková, Milan Kapusta, Tomáš Kalenka, Peter Korcsog, Peter Krchnák, Boris Kusenda, Oldřiška Luptáková, Miriam Martinkovičová, Janka Morongová, Marián Palenčár, Zlatica Plašienková, Ivo Rolný, Søren Sørensen, Lukač Ján Veverka, and Jozef Vysopal.
[31] *Kierkegaardove dni*, ed. by Peter Krchnák, Zvolen: KSV FE TU 1993.

years to come to understand Kierkegaard as he was, as well as to understand the conditions of his intellectual development."[32]

In 2005, in order to commemorate the 150th anniversary of Kierkegaard's death, the Philosophical Faculty of the Trnava University, Schola Philosophica, and the Slovak Philosophical Association at the Slovak Academy of Sciences organized a series of lectures with the intention of presenting the philosophical heritage of the Danish philosopher to students of philosophy, as well as to a more general public. The project was the second arrangement of this kind—the first one being dedicated to Immanuel Kant—and the lectures were later published in the form of articles in *The Postscript to Kierkegaard* in 2006.[33] The participants in this project included renowned philosophers, theologians, and translators,[34] as well as young (post) doctoral students and researchers.[35]

In connection with the presentation of the monograph entitled *The Problem Called Kierkegaard*, written by Roman Králik,[36] a series of lectures was initiated on July 12, 2006 with the aim of presenting Kierkegaard's thought to the general public. These lectures were later published as an appendix to the above-mentioned monograph under the title *The Struggle of Søren Kierkegaard*.[37] The lecture series was inaugurated by H.E. Jørgen Munk Rasmussen, the Danish Ambassador to Slovakia, and Mr. Tibor Baran, the mayor of the city of Šaľa. Among the authors contributing to the collective volume of the project were several Kierkegaard researchers from abroad,[38] as well as a number of scholars from Slovakia.[39]

On February 23, 2007 an international conference entitled *Søren Kierkegaard: A Theologian, Philosopher and Thinker* was organized by the Department of General and Applied Ethics at the Philosophical Faculty of Constantine the Philosopher University in Nitra.[40] The conference was attended by the leadership of the University, H.E. Jørgen Munk Rasmussen, the Danish Ambassador to Slovakia, as

---

[32] Ján Lukáč Veverka, "Podstata autencitity filozofie Sørena Kierkegaarda a jej význam pre životnú orientáciu človeka v súčasnosti" [The Essence of the Authenticity of Søren Kierkegaard's Philosophy and its Meaning for the Human's Life Orientation Today], in *Kierkegaardove dni*, Zvolen: Technická univerzita vo Zvolene 1993, p. 23.

[33] *Postskriptum ku Kierkegaardovi*, ed. by Andrej Démuth, Pusté Úľany: Schola Philosophica 2006.

[34] František Sirovič, Marie Mikulová Thulstrup, Václav Umlauf, and Milan Žitný.

[35] Andrej Démuth, Renáta Kišoňová, Roman Králik, Milan Petkanič, Peter Šajda, Ladislav Tkáčik, Anton Vydra, Martin Vydra, and Michal Žitňanský.

[36] Roman Králik, *Problém zvaný Kierkegaard*, Bratislava: Roman Králik 2006.

[37] *Zápas Sørena Kierkegaarda*, ed. by Roman Králik, Nitra: FF UKF 2006.

[38] Catalina E. Dobre (Romania), Jiří Olšovský (Czech Republic), Rafael Garcia Pavón (Mexico).

[39] Dušan Chovanec, Cyril Diatka, Andrej Démuth, Ľudovít Fazekaš, Dalimír Hajko, Roman Králik, Peter Šajda, Lukáč Ján Veverka, and Anton Vydra.

[40] The conference was organized by Cyril Diatka and Roman Králik. It was held under the patronage of Rector of Constantine the Philosopher University in Nitra Prof. Dr. Ľubor Vozár, His Excellency the Danish Ambassador in the Slovak Republic Jørgen Munk Rasmussen, Dean of Faculty of Arts Prof. Dr. Zdenka Gadušová. Among the scholars at the conference were Prof. Dr. Zdenka Gadušová, the Dean of Faculty of Arts UKF in Nitra; Prof. Eva Malá, the Prorector of UKF in Nitra; Prof. Abraham H. Khan (Canada), Prof. Ján Liguš, and Prof. Bernard Garaj.

well as by Kierkegaard scholars from Slovakia and abroad. The event exceeded the previous ones in extent, as 36 studies by authors from 10 countries were sent to the organizing committee. Among the papers to be published in a collective volume is the so far unpublished Czech translation of *The Unchangeableness of God* by Marie Mikulová Thulstrup, as well as contributions by internationally renowned scholars, such as Abrahim Khan and C. Stephen Evans.[41] Some of the articles focusing on Kierkegaard's *Purity of Heart* will be published in a separate volume that is supposed to constitute the first part of the planned ten-volume series *Acta Kierkegaardiana* that has been inspired by the *Bibliotheca Kierkegaardiana* project.[42]

The above-mentioned event was also a kind of a tribute to three important personalities who significantly co-shaped the theology and philosophy of the twentieth century and contributed to the spreading of Kierkegaard's intellectual heritage: Jaroslav Pelikán, Jan Milič Lochman, and Julia Watkin.[43]

In connection with this conference, Abrahim Khan, from Toronto University, visited the Kierkegaard Collection in the city of Šaľa and gave an interview about Kierkegaard and Kierkegaard-linked activities to the national news channel TV3.

IV. The Kierkegaard Collection and the Kierkegaard Society in Slovakia

Important milestones in the modern history of Kierkegaard research in Slovakia were the establishing of the Kierkegaard Collection in 2005, and the founding of the Kierkegaard Society in Slovakia in 2007. The idea of setting up the Kierkegaard Collection originated in 2004 and was inspired by Cynthia Lund from the Hong Kierkegaard Library at St. Olaf College.[44]

Unofficially, the Kierkegaard Collection was started in 2000 when Marie Mikulová Thulstrup together with the publishing house C.A. Reitzel donated a complete edition of *Bibliotheca Kierkegaardiana*, as well as all Kierkegaard's works

---

[41] Among the participants from abroad were Junius Stenseth (USA), Rafael García Pavón (Mexico), Elisabete Sousa (Portugal), Catalina Elena Dobre (Romania), Stefania Lubańska (Poland), Laura Llevadot Pascual (Spain), Jaro Křivohlavý, Ján Liguš and Noemi. Bravená (Czech Republic). The participants from Slovakia included: Marcel Cibík, Cyril Diatka, Andrej Demúth, Ludovít Fazekaš, Dalimír Hajko, Milan Jozek, Jarmila Jurová, Mária Klobušická, Peter Kondrla, Peter Korený, Jana Kotrusová, Roman Králik, Jozef Ondrej Markuš, Adrián Michalík, Karol Nandrásky, Dušan Ondrejovič, Marcel Papp, Milan Petkanič, Štefan Rácz, Lucia Rákayová, Dominik Roman, Peter Šajda, Lukáč Ján Veverka, and Miroslav Zumrík.

[42] Cf. *Bibliotheca Kierkegaardiana*, vols. 1–16, ed. by Niels Thulstrup and Marie Mikulová Thulstrup, Copenhagen: C.A. Reitzel 1978–88.

[43] The author of this article was in written contact with all three mentioned thinkers.

[44] I was awarded the Jonathan Stenseth Memorial Fellowship for the years 2004 and 2007, which enabled me to study at the Hong Kierkegaard Library at St. Olaf College, Northfield, Minnesota. This was a formative experience that prompted me to consider the setting up of a specialized Kierkegaard collection in Slovakia. The Hong Kierkegaard Library was also an important donor of books. Other donors included Junius Stenseth—who donated some of Jonathan Stenseth's books—as well as R.G. Pavón, M. Caraza, D. Olson, and D. Prowe. These donations led to an ever firmer decision on my part to establish the Kierkegaard Collection at the City Library in Šaľa.

in Czech translation, and Marie Mikulová Thulstrup's monograph, *Kierkegaard and the History of Christian Spirituality*.[45] Also a number of renowned Kierkegaard scholars—mainly from the Anglophone world—supplied the Kierkegaard Collection with their books and articles.[46]

Immediately after its official opening, the Kierkegaard Collection attracted the interest of the local media. The establishing of the Kierkegaard Collection was, however, presented also in one of the most prestigious philosophical journals in the Czech Republic *Filozofický časopis*,[47] as well as in the Czech theological journal *Theologická reflexe*.[48] In the United States a report about the Kierkegaard Collection appeared in the *Søren Kierkegaard Newsletter*.[49]

Since 2006 a vital cooperation has been going on between the Kierkegaard Collection and the Royal Danish Embassy in Slovakia. The Embassy of Denmark supported the Collection financially, and H.E. Jørgen Munk Rasmussen was personally present at two presentations of books on Kierkegaard that took place in Šaľa, where the Collection is situated. He was also present at the Open Day of Slovak–Danish Culture and Friendship in Šaľa—which included a joint presentation of Søren Kierkegaard and Hans Christian Andersen—and provided patronage for the international conference *Søren Kierkegaard: A Theologian, Philosopher and Thinker* that took place in 2007 in Nitra.

The idea of founding the Kierkegaard Society in Slovakia originates from 2006 and came from Peter Šajda.[50] It was officially established in February 2007, and its purpose is to further research, as well as to promote Kierkegaard's intellectual legacy in Slovakia and in the region of Central Europe by means of seminars, lecture series, and publications.[51]

Since most Kierkegaard research in Slovakia has been done in the last two decades, it is the aim of the Kierkegaard Society in Slovakia, as well as of other researchers, to combine the efforts of the older and the younger generation of Kierkegaard scholars. It is also necessary to expand cooperation with Kierkegaard bodies abroad, in order to transcend the limitations characteristic of a small country's possibilities. An important challenge remains with the translation of a greater number of Kierkegaard's works into the Slovak language.

---

[45] Marie Mikulová Thulstrupová, *Kierkegaard a dějiny křesťanské zbožnosti*, Brno: CDK 2005.

[46] Among the donors were Robert L. Perkins, Julia Watkin, C. Stephen Evans, Bruce H. Kirmmse, Abrahim H. Khan, Robert C. Roberts, Alastair McKinnon, Amy L. Hall, Jun Hashimoto, and Martin B. Matuštík.

[47] Roman Králik, "Kierkegaard na Slovensku," *Filosofický časopis*, vol. 53, no. 6, 2005, p. 977.

[48] Roman Králik, "Kierkegaard na Slovensku," *Theologická reflexe*, vol. 11, no. 2, 2005 p. 220.

[49] Roman Králik, "Kierkegaard Collection in Slovakia," *Søren Kierkegaard Newsletter*, no. 50, 2006, p. 3.

[50] Peter Šajda made brief research stays at the Søren Kierkegaard Research Center in Copenhagen in 2003, 2005, and 2006. He drew inspiration also from the Kierkegaard Cabinet in Budapest, which was introduced to him by the Hungarian Lutheran theologian Szilvia Rozs-Nagy.

[51] The founding members of the Kierkegaard Society in Slovakia were Roman Králik (Chairperson), Peter Šajda (Vice-Chairperson), and Lukáč Ján Veverka.

Bibliography

I. Slovak Translations of Kierkegaard's Works

"Modlitba" [A Prayer], trans. by Andrej Hajduk, *Cirkevné listy*, vol. 102, no. 10, 1989, p. 151.
"Počúvať" [To Listen], trans. by Andrej Hajduk, *Cirkevné listy*, vol. 102, no. 7, 1989, p. 3.
"To je láska" [This is Love], trans. by Andrej Hajduk, *Cirkevné listy*, vol. 103, no. 1, 1990, p. 4.
"Napokon stíchnem" [I Will Grow Silent], trans. by František Sirovič, *Katolícke noviny*, vol. 107, no. 40, 1992, p. 3.
Zvodcov denník ["The Seducer's Diary"], trans. by Milan Žitný, Bratislava: Kalligram 2003.
Strach a chvenie [*Fear and Trembling*], trans. by Milan Žitný, Bratislava: Kalligram 2005.
Rovnováha medzi estetickým a etickým pri utváraní osobnosti ["The Balance between the Esthetic and the Ethical in the Development of the Personality"], trans. by Milan Žitný, Bratislava: Kalligram 2006.
"Boží nezměnitelnost" [God's Unchangeableness], trans. by Marie Mikulová Thulstrupová, in *Čistota srdca* [*Purity of Heart*], ed. by Roman Králik and Cyril Diatka, Nitra: FF UKF 2007 (*Acta Kierkegaardiaana*, vol. 1), pp. 13–28.
Buď – alebo [*Either/Or*], trans. by Milan Žitný, Bratislava: Kalligram 2007.

II. Secondary Literature on Kierkegaard in Slovakia

Adamcová, Mária, "S. Kierkegaard o vede a filozofii" [S. Kierkegaard on Science and Philosophy], in *Kierkegaardove dni*, ed. by Peter Krchnák, Zvolen: KSV FE TU Zvolen 1993, pp. 50–5.
Adamec, Róbert, "Fresky na stenách srdca: meditácie nad 'Skutkami lásky' od S. Kierkegaarda" [The Frescos on the Walls of the Heart: Meditations on S. Kierkegaard's "Works of Love"], *Tvorba*, vol. 11 (20), nos. 1–2, 2001, pp. 65–9.
— "Bieda tradicionalizmu" [The Misery of Traditionalism], *Tvorba*, vol. 15 (24), no. 4, 2005, pp. 29–31.
Bošmanský, Karol, "Náhľad na svet a na človeka. František Sirovič: Søren A. Kierkegaard: filozoficko–kritická analýza diela" [A View of the World and of the Human. František Sirovič: Søren A. Kierkegaard: a Philosophical-Critical Analysis of his Works], *Katolícke noviny*, no. 31, 2004, p. 20.

— "Søren Kierkegaard (1813–1855)," *Duchovný Pastier*, vol. 85, no. 8, 2004, pp. 506–13.

— "Søren A. Kierkegaard—filozof a osobnosť" [Søren A. Kierkegaard—a Philosopher and a Personality], *Acta Facultatis Theologicae Universitatis Comenianae Bratislaviensis*, vol. 5, no. 3, 2005, pp. 14–21.

Čapková, Anna, "'Zvodca' Kierkegaard v našich hľadaniach" ["The Seducer" Kierkegaard in our Search], *Tvorba*, vol. 15 (24), no. 4, 2005, pp. 16–17.

Chovanec, Dušan, "Cesta k Bohu" [The Way to God], in *Zápas Sørena Kierkegaarda*, ed. by Roman Králik, Nitra: FF UKF 2006, pp. 143–5.

Démuth, Andrej, "Kierkegaardov strach, chvenie a pojem úzkosti" [Kierkegaard's *Fear, Trembling* and *The Concept of Anxiety*], in *Postskriptum ku Kierkegaardovi*, ed. by Andrej Démuth, Pusté Úľany: Schola Philosophica 2006, pp. 90–7.

— "Søren Kierkegaard—inšpirátor Heideggerovho myslenia" [Kierkegaard—the Inspirer of Heidegger's Thinking], in *Zápas Sørena Kierkegaarda*, ed. by Roman Králik, Nitra: FF UKF 2006, pp. 146–9.

Diatka, Cyril, "Cesta k sebe samému. Úvahy podnietené S. Kierkegaardom" [The Way to Oneself. Reflections Inspired by S. Kierkegaard], in *Zápas Sørena Kierkegaarda*, ed. by Roman Králik, Nitra: FF UKF 2006, pp. 150–2.

Dobre, Catalina E. and Pavón, Rafael G., "Søren Kierkegaard and the Moods of the Existence—Summary," in *Zápas Sørena Kierkegaarda*, ed. by Roman Králik, Nitra: FF UKF 2006, pp. 153–5.

Farkašová, Etela, "Splácanie kultúrnej podlžnosti" [Acquittal of a Cultural Debt], *Knižná revue*, vol. 14, no. 8, 2004, p. 7.

Fazekaš, Ľudovít, "Ideály proti klamu zmyslov (S.A. Kierkegaard a jeho Okamih)" [Ideals against the Deception of Senses (S.A. Kierkegaard and his Moment)], in *Štafeta svedkov. Život kresťanských služobníkov*, Banská Bystrica: KETM 2002, pp. 69–85.

— "Kierkegaard ako kresťan" [Kierkegaard as a Christian], in *Zápas Sørena Kierkegaarda*, ed. by Roman Králik, Nitra: FF UKF 2006, pp. 114–9.

Gluchman, Vasil, "Medzinárodné sympózium o Kierkegaardovi" [International Symposium on Kierkegaard], *Filozofia*, vol. 47, no. 9, 1992, p. 566.

Hajko, Dalimír, "Søren Kierkegaard a literatúra ľudskej existencie" [Søren Kierkegaard and the Literature on Human Existence]. *Romboid*, vol. 25, no. 2, 1990, pp. 71–82.

— "Boh a existencia u Sørena Kierkegaarda" [God and Existence in Søren Kierkegaard], *Slovenské pohľady*, vol. 4, no. 12, 1993, pp. 82–7.

— "Søren Kierkegaard v reflexii indickej filozofie" [Søren Kierkegaard in the Reflections of Indian Philosophy], in *Zápas Sørena Kierkegaarda*, ed. by Roman Králik, Nitra: FF UKF 2006, pp. 133–42.

Hubík, Stanislav, "Kierkegaard a doba postmoderní" [Kierkegaard and the Postmodern Age], in *Kierkegaardove dni,* ed. by Peter Krchnák, Zvolen: KSV FE TU 1993, pp. 56–65.

Jahelka, Tomáš, "Kierkegaardov rytier viery a jeho absurdný paradox" [Kierkegaard's Knight of Faith and his Absurd Paradox], *Tvorba*, vol. 15 (24), no. 4, 2005, pp. 13–5.

Kačmáriková, Eva, "Søren Kierkegaard—filozof existencie života" [Søren Kierkegaard—Philosopher of the Existence of Life], in *Kierkegaardove dni*, ed. by Peter Krchnák, Zvolen: KSV FE TU 1993, pp. 25–30.

Kasáč, Zdenko, Príspevok k poznaniu tvorby Hermanna Hesseho [A Contribution to Acquaintance with the Oeuvre of Hermann Hesse], *Filologická revue*, vol. 2, no. 2, 1999, pp. 79–80.

Kišoňová, Renáta, "Curriculum vitae et vitae opus", in *Postskriptum ku Kierkegaardovi*, ed. by Andrej Démuth, Pusté Úľany: Schola Philosophica 2006, pp. 10–19.

— "Zvodcov denník alebo Kierkegaardov vzťah k žene" ["The Seducer's Diary" and Kierkegaard's Relation to a Woman], in *Postskriptum ku Kierkegaardovi*, ed. by Andrej Démuth, Pusté Úľany: Schola Philosophica 2006, pp. 106–10.

Klimeková, Anna. "Otec existencializmu" [The Father of Existentialism], *Literárny týždenník*, vol. 9, no. 13, 1996, p. 12.

Králik, Roman, "Søren Kierkegaard a jeho láska. Šalamúnov sen" [Søren Kierkegaard and his Love. The Dream of Salomon], *Cirkevné listy*, vol. 114 (125), no. 12, 2001, pp. 180–3.

— "Søren Kierkegaard: Tři páteční pozvání k Večeři Páně" [Søren Kierkegaard: *Three Discourses on Imagined Occasions*], *Theologická revue*, vol. 72, no. 3, 2001, pp. 345–7.

— "Kierkegaard a Tillich—teológovia na hranici" [Kierkegaard and Tillich—Theologians on the Border], *Cirkevné listy*, vol. 115 (126), no. 8, 2002, pp. 122–6.

— "Kierkegaard jako křesťan" [Kierkegaard as a Christian], *Český zápas*, vol. 82, no. 8, 2002, p. 6.

— "Kierkegaardova viera. Cestou svetla" [Kierkegaard's Faith. On the Path of Light], *Časopis Evanjelickej a. v. cirkvi na Slovensku venovaný záujmom evanjelizácie*, vol. 13, no. 8, 2002, p. 9.

— "Søren Kierkegaard: Skutky lásky aneb několik křesťanských úvah ve formě proslovů" [Søren Kierkegaard: *Works of Love*], *Theologická revue*, vol. 73, no. 1, 2002, p. 101–3.

— "Modlitba a jej význam u S. Kierkegaarda" [Prayer and its Meaning in S. Kierkegaard], *Cirkevné listy*, vol. 116 (127), nos. 7–8, 2003, pp. 22–4.

— "Kierkegaard a jeho modlitby" [Kierkegaard and his Prayers], *Modlitba ako výskumný fenomén duchovný (teologický), pedagogický, jazykovokomunikačný, literárny, literárnohistorický a etnologický* (ed. by Viera Kovácová), vol. 4, nos. 2–3, 2004, pp. 67–76.

— "Bádanie o diele a živote Sørena Kierkegaarda v súčasnosti" [The Research of Søren Kierkegaard's Life and Work Today], *Cirkevné listy*, vol. 118 (129), no. 9, 2005, pp. 20–2.

— "K dosavadnímu bádání o díle a životě Sørena Kierkegaarda" [On the History of the Research of Søren Kierkegaard's Work and Life], in *Postskriptum ku Kierkegaardovi*, ed. by Andrej Démuth, Pusté Úľany: Schola Philosophica 2006, pp. 20–7.

— "Kierkegaard Collection in Slovakia," *Søren Kierkegaard Newsletter*, no. 50, 2006, p. 8.

— "Kierkegaard v našej knižnici" [Kierkegaard in our Library], *Slovo Šaľanov*, vol. 11, no. 4, 2006, p. 18.
— "Kierkegaard v súčasnosti" [Kierkegaard Today], *Český zápas*, vol. 86, no. 21, 2006, p. 3.
— "The Preacher Without a Pulpit—S. Kierkegaard," *Universitatea Dunărea de Jos Filosofie*, no. 6, 2006, pp. 5–10.
— *Problém zvaný Kierkegaard* [The Problem Called Kierkegaard], Bratislava: Roman Králik 2006.
— " 'Problém zvaný Kierkegaard' alebo Kierkegaard ako náboženský mysliteľ" ["The Problem Called Kierkegaard" or Kierkegaard as a Religious Thinker], in *Postskriptum ku Kierkegaardovi*, ed. by Andrej Démuth, Pusté Úľany: Schola Philosophica 2006, pp. 126–33.
— "The Social Dimension of Kierkegaard's Ethics: Kierkegaard's Understanding of the Term 'Neighbour,' " *Mozaik*, no. 17, 2006, pp. 24–5.
— *Søren Aabye Kierkegaard (1813–1855). Život, víra a teologie* [Søren Aabye Kierkegaard (1813–1855). Life, Faith and Theology], Ph.D. Thesis, Charles University, Prague 2006.
— "Søren Kierkegaard and His Prayers," in *Dreaming our Neighbour*, ed. by Szabolcs Nagypál et al., Warsaw: BGÖI: WSCF-CESR 2006, pp. 101–10.
— "Vztah státu a církve u Sørena Kierkegaarda" [The Relation between Church and State in Søren Kierkegaard], *Český zápas*, vol. 86, no. 32, 2006, pp. 1–3.
— *Zápas Sørena Kierkegaarda* [The Struggle of Søren Kierkegaard], Nitra: FF UKF Nitra 2006 (Part 1, pp. 1–106 by Roman Králik; Part 2, pp. 107–66 by other scholars).
Králik, Roman and Veverka, Lukáč Ján, "Kierkegaard and His Legacy For the Present," in *Zápas Sørena Kierkegaarda*, ed. by Roman Králik, Nitra: FF UKF 2006, pp. 164–6.
Krchnák, Peter, "Ľudské bytie ako bytie pre druhých a s druhými" [Human Being as Being for Others and with Others], in *Kierkegaardove dni*, ed. by Peter Krchnák, Zvolen: KSV FE TU 1993, pp. 117–22.
— (ed.), *Kierkegaardove dni*, Zvolen: KSV FE TU 1993.
Křivohlavý, Jaro, "Problém zvaný Kierkegaard" [The Problem Called Kierkegaard], *Český zápas*, no. 34, 2006, p. 3.
Markuš, Jozef Ondrej, "Søren Kierkegaard. Úryvky z jeho života a životného diela" [Søren Kierkegaard. Fragments from his Life and his Life *Oeuvre*] in *Čistota srdca* [*Purity of Heart*], ed. by Roman Králik and Cyril Diatka, Nitra: FF UKF 2007 (*Acta Kierkegaardiaana*, vol. 1), pp. 145–57.
Matuštík, Martin J., "Kierkegaard a existenciálna revolúcia" [Kierkegaard and the Existential Revolution], *Kultúrny život*, vol. 25, no. 26, 1991, pp. 6–7.
Michelko, Roman F., "Zvodcov denník v kontexte Kierkegaardovej tvorby" ["The Seducer's Diary" in the Context of Kierkegaard's Production], *Dotyky*, vol. 18, no. 1, 2006, pp. 36–7.
Mihina, František, "Søren Kierkegaard a jeho revolta" [Søren Kierkegaard and His Revolt], in *Metamorfózy poklasickej filozofie*, ed. by František Mihina and Vladimír Leško, Prešov: FF UPJŠ 1994, pp. 193–218.

Mikulová Thulstrupová, Marie, "Kierkegaard a církev v jeho době" [Kierkegaard and the Church of his Time], in *Postskriptum ku Kierkegaardovi*, ed. by Andrej Démuth, Pusté Úľany: Schola Philosophica 2006, pp. 118–25.

Morávek, Július, "Výnimočná zbierka kníh" [An Exceptional Collection of Books], *Slovo Šaľanov*, vol. 11, no. 3, 2006, p. 31.

Nandrásky, Karol, "Prorocký mysliteľ dánskeho národa" [The Prophetic Thinker of the Danish Nation], *Cirkevné listy*, vol. 92, no. 6, 1978, pp. 90–4.

— "O dojmoch z Dánska vo forme listu S. Kierkegaardovi" [On My Impressions from Denmark in the Form of a Letter to S. Kierkegaard], *Cirkevné listy*, vol. 96, no. 10, 1982, pp. 154–5.

Olšovský, Jiří, "Březina a Kierkegaard" [Březina and Kierkegaard], in *Zápas Sørena Kierkegaarda*, ed. by Roman Králik, Nitra: FF UKF 2006, pp. 121–9.

Palenčár, Marián, "Poznámky k problému úzkosti" [Comments on the Problem of Anxiety], in *Kierkegaardove dni*, ed. by Peter Krchnák, Zvolen: KSV FE TU Zvolen 1993, pp. 35–40.

Petkanič, Milan, "Passion and Age—Kierkegaard's Diagnosis of The Present Age," *Human Affairs*, vol. 14, no. 2, 2004, pp. 165–82.

— "Bytie človeka ako existencia" [The Being of the Human as Existence], in *Člověk—příroda—kultura*, ed. by Emil Višňovský and Josef Krob, Brno: Masarykova univerzita v Brně 2005, pp. 77–86.

— "Myslenie a existencia (vo filozofii Sørena Kierkegaarda)" [Thinking and Existence (in the Philosophy of Søren Kierkegaard)], in *Ľudská prirodzenosť a kultúrna identita*, ed. by Blanka Šulavíková and Emil Višňovský, Bratislava: Iris 2006, pp. 187–225.

— "Pojem vášne v Kierkegaardovej kritike súčasnosti" [The Concept of Passion in Kierkegaard's Critique of the Present Age], in *Postskriptum ku Kierkegaardovi*, ed. by Andrej Démuth, Pusté Úľany: Schola Philosophica 2006, pp. 73–81.

— *Pojem vášne u Kierkegaarda* [The Concept of Passion in Kierkegaard], Ph.D. Thesis, Comenius University, Bratislava, 2007.

Plašienková, Zlatica and Luptáková, Oldřiška, "Filozofické a ekonomické aspekty humanizácie a 'kvality života'" [Philosophical and Economic Aspects of Humanization and 'Quality of Life'], in *Kierkegaardove dni,* ed. by Peter Krchnák, Zvolen: KSV FE TU 1993, pp. 93–8.

Rákayová, Lucia, "Otec existencializmu, otčim postmoderny?" [The Father of Existentialism, a Stepfather of Postmodernism?], *Kultúrny život*, vol. 2, no. 19, 2001, p. 11.

Rolný, Ivo, "S. Kierkegaard a F. Nietzsche, hlasy volající na poušti" [S. Kierkegaard and F. Nietzsche, Voices in the Desert], in *Kierkegaardove dni,* ed. by Peter Krchnák, Zvolen: KSV FE TU Zvolen 1993, pp. 41–9.

Šabík, Vincent, "Prípad Kierkegaard" [The Case of Kierkegaard], *Revue svetovej literatúry*, vol. 25, no. 7, 1989, pp. 149–66.

— "Søren Kierkegaard alebo paradox zmyslu" [Søren Kierkegaard or the Paradox of Meaning], *Literárny týždenník*, vol. 5, no. 12, 1992, p. 3; p. 5.

Šajda, Peter, "Are Ecumenical Novel-Writers the Hope of Συμπαρανεκρωμενοι? A Study in Andersen's and Kierkegaard's Discussion on the Importance of a Life-

View in a Novel," in *The River Book. Identity, Culture and Responsibility*, ed. by Suzanna Vergouwe et al., Bialystok: BGÖI & WSCF-CESR 2003, pp. 78–92.

— "Erotika, manželstvo a pustý ostrov alebo asymetria lásky u Sørena Kierkegaarda" [Erotics, Marriage and a Deserted Island, or the Asymmetry of Love in Søren Kierkegaard], *Verbum*, vol. 14, nos. 3–4, 2003, pp. 31–45.

— "Náčrt kritiky Kierkegaardovho konceptu lásky v diele M. Bubera, T.W. Adorna a K.E. Løgstrupa" [An Outline of the Critique of Kierkegaard's Concept of Love by M. Buber, T.W. Adorno and K.E. Løgstrup], *Filozofia*, vol. 58, no. 7, 2003, pp. 484–93.

— "Buď–alebo a iné klobúky: pseudonymy Sørena Kierkegaarda" [*Either/Or* and other Hats: The Pseudonyms of Søren Kierkegaard], *Slovenské pohľady*, vol. 4, no. 2, 2004, pp. 47–54.

— "Fixation as a Source of Unbalance in Relationships. Illustrated with Søren Kierkegaard's Theory of Personality Development Stages," in *Medi(t)ations, (Re)conciliations. Conflict Resolution and European Integration*, ed. by Rebecca Blocksome et al., Bratislava: BGÖI & WSCF-CESR 2004, pp. 156–67.

— "Majster Eckhart sa plaví do Dánska. Krátka úvaha o súčinnosti myšlienok Majstra Eckharta a Sørena Kierkegaarda" [Meister Eckhart's Travel to Denmark. A Short Reflection on the Synergy of the Ideas of Meister Eckhart and Søren Kierkegaard], in *Zápas Sørena Kierkegaarda*, ed. by Roman Králik, Nitra: FF UKF 2006, pp. 156–63.

— "Štrasburská hus v Kodani. Náčrt pojmu irónie u Sørena Kierkegaarda" [A Strassburg Goose in Copenhagen. An Outline of the Concept of Irony in Søren Kierkegaard], in *Postskriptum ku Kierkegaardovi*, ed. by Andrej Démuth, Pusté Úľany: Schola Philosophica 2006, pp. 57–64 (published also in *Ostium*, nos. 2–3, 2006, pp. 57–64).

— *Koncept lásky v diele Majstra Eckharta a Sørena Kierkegaarda* [The Concept of Love in the Works of Meister Eckhart and Søren Kierkegaard], Ph.D. Thesis, Comenius University, Bratislava 2007.

— "Náčrt kontrapozície preferenčnej a nepreferenčnej lásky v diele Sørena Kierkegaarda" [An Outline of the Counterposition of Preferential and Non-Preferential Love in the Works of Søren Kierkegaard], *Filozofia*, vol. 62, no. 2, 2007, pp. 110–21.

— "Meister Eckhart: The Patriarch of German Speculation who was a *Lebemeister*: Meister Eckhart's Silent Way into Kierkegaard's Corpus," in *Kierkegaard and the Patristic and Medieval Traditions*, ed. by Jon Stewart, Aldershot: Ashgate 2008 (*Kierkegaard Research: Sources, Reception and Resources*, vol. 4), pp. 237–53.

— "Tauler: A Teacher in Spiritual Dietethics: Kierkegaards's Reception of Johannes Tauler," in *Kierkegaard and the Patristic and Medieval Traditions*, ed. by Jon Stewart, Aldershot: Ashgate 2008 (*Kierkegaard Research: Sources, Reception and Resources*, vol. 4), pp. 265–87.

Sirovič, František, *Søren A. Kierkegaard: Filozoficko-kritická analýza diela*. [Søren A. Kierkegaard: a Philosophical-Critical Analysis of his Works], Nitra: Spoločnosť Božieho Slova 2004.

— "Historicko-špekulatívne východiská Kierkegaardovho antihegelizmu" [Historical-Speculative Bases of Kierkegaard's Anti-Hegelianism], in *Postskriptum ku Kierkegaardovi*, ed. by Andrej Démuth, Pusté Úľany: Schola Philosophica 2006, pp. 38–47.

Sivčák, Ondrej, "Kierkegaardovo mesto—Šaľa" [Šaľa—Kierkegaard's City], *Nitrianske noviny. Noviny juhozápadu*, vol. 15, no. 33, 2006, p. 9.

— "V Šali predstavia dánsku kultúru" [In Šaľa there will be a Presentation of Danish Culture], *Nitrianske noviny. Noviny juhozápadu*, vol 15, no. 44, 2006, p. 9.

Sklenka, Imrich, "Nie je reč ako reč: od Kierkegaarda po Bartha" [Language, but what Kind? From Kierkegaard to Barth], *Knihy a spoločnosť*, vol. 2, no. 9, 2005, p. 3.

Šlosiar, Ján, "Existenciálna komunikácia s blížnym" [Existential Communication with the Neighbour], *Cirkevné listy*, vol. 108, nos. 7–8, 1995, pp. 108–9.

— "Fenomén úzkosti v sebapoznaní človeka u Kierkegaarda a Sartra" [The Phenomenon of Anxiety in the Self-Knowledge of the Human in Kierkegaard and Sartre], in *Človek medzi životom a smrťou*, ed. by Miroslava Nemčeková, Martin: JLF UK 1996, pp. 251–8.

Somolayová, Ľubica, "Manipulácia ako estetika zvádzania" [Manipulation as the Aesthetics of Seduction], *Revue aktuálnej kultúry*, vol. 10, no. 5, 2005, p. 48.

Teplan, Dušan, "Prednášky o (ne)rozume" [Lectures on (un-)Reason], *Os*, vol. 7, no. 12, pp. 55–7.

Tkáčik, Ladislav, "Etické u Kierkegaarda" [The Ethical in Kierkegaard], in *Postskriptum ku Kierkegaardovi*, ed. by Andrej Démuth, Pusté Úľany: Schola Philosophica 2006, pp. 111–7.

Umlauf, Václav, "Sympatický Kierkegaard" [The Amiable Kierkegaard], in *Postskriptum ku Kierkegaardovi*, ed. by Andrej Démuth, Pusté Úľany: Schola Philosophica 2006, pp. 48–56.

Vanovič, Július, *Cesta samotárova* [A Solitary's Way], Martin: Matica slovenská 1994.

Veverka, Lukáč Ján, "Podstata autencitity filozofie Sørena Kierkegaarda a jej význam pre životnú orientáciu človeka v súčasnosti" [The Essence of the Authenticity of Søren Kierkegaard's Philosophy and its Meaning for the Human's Life Orientation Today], in *Kierkegaardove dni*, ed. by Peter Krchnák, Zvolen: KSV FE TU 1993, pp. 15–24.

— "Kierkegaard ako filozof" [Kierkegaard as a Philosopher], in *Zápas Sørena Kierkegaarda*, ed. by Roman Králik, Nitra: FF UKF 2006, pp. 110–3.

— "Téma Søren Kierkegaard" [The Theme: Søren Kierkegaard], *Cirkevné listy*, no. 5, 2006, pp. 17–8.

Vydra, Anton, "Fascinovaný tvárou muža" [Fascinated by a Man's Face], in *Zápas Sørena Kierkegaarda*, ed. by Roman Králik, Nitra: FF UKF 2006, pp. 130–2.

— "Okamih u Sørena Kierkegaarda" [Søren Kierkegaard's Moment], in *Postskriptum ku Kierkegaardovi*, ed. by Andrej Démuth, Pusté Úľany: Schola Philosophica 2006, pp. 65–72.

Vydra, Martin, "Kto je jedinec?" [Who is the Individual?], in *Postskriptum ku Kierkegaardovi*, ed. by Andrej Démuth, Pusté Úľany: Schola Philosophica 2006, pp. 82–9.

Vysopal, Jozef, "Søren Kierkegaard—osobnosť" [Søren Kierkegaard—Personality], in *Kierkegaardove dni*, ed. by Peter Krchnák, Zvolen: KSV FE TU 1993, pp. 31–4.

Žitný, Milan, "Kierkegaard v preklade" [Kierkegaard in Translation], *Tvorba T*, vol. 10, no. 1, 1991, pp. 25–6.

— "K niektorým litarárnym aspektom Kierkegaardovho diela" [On some Literary Aspects of Kierkegaard's Works], in *Postskriptum ku Kierkegaardovi*, ed. by Andrej Démuth, Pusté Úľany: Schola Philosophica 2006, pp. 28–39.

III. Secondary Literature on Kierkegaard's Reception in Slovakia

Králik, Roman, "Kierkegaard na Slovensku" [Kierkegaard in Slovakia], *Filosofický časopis*, vol. 53, no. 6, 2005, p. 977.
— "Kierkegaard na Slovensku" [Kierkegaard in Slovakia], *Theologická reflexe*, vol. 11, no. 2, 2005, p. 220.
— "Kierkegaard 'prišiel' na Slovensko" [Kierkegaard 'came' to Slovakia], *Evanjelický posol spod Tatier*, vol. 96, nos. 50–1, 2006, p. 10.
Šabík, Vincent, "Slováci a Kierkegaard" [The Slovaks and Kierkegaard], *Slovenské pohľady*, vol. 4, no. 9, 2004, pp. 120–2.

The Czech Republic:
Kierkegaard as a Model for the Irrationalist Movements

Helena Brezinova

This article is an attempt both to present a complete list of translations of Søren Kierkegaard's works in Czech and to summarize all existing secondary literature on the Danish philosopher written in Czech or by Czech scholars. Since the Czech Republic was established in its present form on January 1, 1993, this article will include translations and secondary literature published in the existing Czech Republic and its predecessors: Bohemia, which was a part of the Austro-Hungarian Empire until 1918, and Czechoslovakia, which existed until 1993.

I. Kierkegaard's Reception in Czech

If one looks up the entries on Kierkegaard in the Czech National Library, one will not find a long list. Neither the list of primary literature nor the catalogue of secondary literature on the philosopher will be particularly extensive. Generally, one can say that the era of the Czechoslovakian Communist regime (1945–89) severely hindered Kierkegaard's reception. The highly religious philosopher, who was the object of a massive revival by Western existentialism in the post-war era, was by no means popular with the Communist regime. It is symptomatic that only Kierkegaard's more "secular" works were published in the period from 1945 to 1989: "The Seducer's Diary" and an extract from *A Literary Review*. And symptomatically, the very rare secondary literature on Kierkegaard written by Western philosophers that the Czech National Library bought during this period is mostly listed under keywords such as anthropology, morality, philosophy, or ethics.

Since the fall of Communism, the interest in publishing Kierkegaard has intensified and some new translations, articles, and books have been released; however, the possibilities for the Czech readers to familiarize themselves with Kierkegaard's writings are still extremely limited unless they read Danish, German, or English.

The only near-satisfactory overview of Kierkegaard translations in Czech to date is to be found in the *Dictionary of Scandinavian Authors*,[1] where the entry

---

[1] *Slovník severských spisovatelů*, ed. by Dagmar Hartlová et al., Prague: Libri 1996 (2nd revised ed., 2004).

on Kierkegaard was written by Martin Humpál, the Head of the Department of Scandinavian Studies at the Charles University in Prague.

II. Translations before 1948

Moderní revue, a progressive and influential cultural magazine appearing in Prague at the turn of the twentieth century regularly published articles on Scandinavian literature and culture. One of the contributors, Arnošt Procházka, was among the first to introduce Kierkegaard to the Czech audience. In 1906, he selected and translated a one-page passage from Kierkegaard and issued it with the title "Man—Woman. Woman is the Embodiment of Egoism."[2]

Hugo Kosterka, the co-founder of *Moderní revue* and a prolific translator of Scandinavian languages, published in this magazine his own translation of selected passages from the *Stages on Life's Way*. Following Kierkegaard, he named the text "In vino veritas," and it appeared as a serial in 1913.[3] Kosterka published a series of works under the title *Symposion—Books of Modern Age*, where the collected articles from "In vino veritas" were published in book form.[4]

"The Seducer's Diary"—the most-often translated work of Kierkegaard into Czech to date—was first published in 1910 by Josef Heim.[5] Milada Lesná-Krausová, the daughter of Arnošt Kraus, the most renowned Czech Scandinavist of the first half of the twentieth century, translated Kierkegaard's pamphlet *The Moment* into Czech in 1911.[6] These translations were pioneering attempts to introduce Kierkegaard to the Czech audience.

III. Translations during the Communist Era (1948–89)

As mentioned above, the Communist regime was not very sympathetic to Kierkegaard and the number of translations during this period was extremely limited. Kierkegaard was considered a protagonist of ultra-religious philosophy, something that could not appeal to a regime trying to ban all religion. Another obstacle to Kierkegaard's Czech reception was the fact that Kierkegaard's main philosophical opponent, Hegel, who according to Marxist-Leninist doctrine was the forerunner of Marx, was held in ideological esteem. According to the *Illustrated Encyclopaedia*, created by the Czech Academy of Sciences in 1980, Kierkegaard "annuled the Hegelian incorporation of man into the process of evolution,"[7] but the historical process of

---

[2] "Žena—muž. Žena coby ztělesnění egoismu" [Man—Woman. Woman is the Embodiment of Egoism], trans. by Arnošt Procházka, *Moderní revue*, no. 9, 1906, pp. 221–2.

[3] "In vino veritas" (excerpts from *Stages on Life's Way*), trans. by Hugo Kosterka, *Symposion*, 1913, pp. 1–88.

[4] Hugo Kosterka, *Symposion—Knihy nové doby*, Prague: Hugo Kosterka 1914.

[5] *Svůdcův deník*, trans. by Josef Heim, Prague: Adámek 1910.

[6] *Okamžik* [*The Moment*], trans. by Milada Krausová-Lesná, Prague: Laichter 1911.

[7] *Ilustrovaný encyklopedický slovník*, vols. 1–3, Prague: Academia 1980–2, vol. 2 (1981).

evolution was a sacred mantra of political scientists and historians in the country between 1948 and 1989.

Another aspect played an important role in the deplorable reception the Danish philosopher received: the massive post-war popularity of Kierkegaard with existentialist philosophers unfortunately occurred at the very same time that the Communist Party seized power in Czechoslovakia. And to the utterly collectivist system where all the parts were only allowed to exist in order to function for the benefit of the whole, Kierkegaard's radical subjectivism and his demands on the individual were an anathema.

A pregnant illustration of Kierkegaard's reception in Communist Czechoslovakia is shown by the publishing history of the renowned literary critic Václav Černý (1905–87). In the winter semester 1947–48 Černý gave a series of lectures on existentialism at the Charles University in Prague. The auditorium was packed to capacity, and his class attracted the notice of the general public. In his first lecture, called "Forerunners," Černý introduces Kierkegaard in approximately ten pages and writes, for example, that his "philosophy is a philosophy of the individual in two senses: it is based on the statement that there cannot be any other philosophy than that of the individual, and, at the same time, it is a pure expression of Kierkegaard's personal lot, the passionate idealizing of the subjective experience of sin; it is a kind of philosophical expressionism."[8] Černý's lectures were published in book form in January 1948 and within a week the book was sold out.[9] Soon afterwards a reprint appeared and a third extended edition was about to be published. In February, however, the Communist putsch came, and the rest of the reprint was seized from the bookstores; the book was banned and removed from all public libraries. This is hardly surprising given that existentialism was a school particularly hated and banned by Moscow.

Kierkegaard's position in the Communist era can be demonstrated by a simple comparison of two encyclopedias. In 1899, *Otto's Encyclopedia* dedicated a whole three and one-half pages to Kierkegaard, and its profound entry informs us—among other things—that the Czechs traditionally became acquainted with the philosopher through early German translations.[10] Conversely, the six-volume *Little Czechoslovakian Encyclopedia* dedicates a "whole" 10 cm of print to Kierkegaard's works.[11] It concludes, "The way Kierkegaard philosophized became the model for all the irrationalist movements of the late bourgeois philosophy."[12] The terms "irrationalist" and "bourgeois" were, of course, words of contempt in the communist ideology.

---

[8] Václav Černý, *První a druhý sešit o existencialismu* [The First and Second Book on Existentialism], Prague: Mladá fronta 1992, p. 23.
[9] Černý, *První sešit o existencialismu* [The First Book on Existentialism], Prague: Václav Petr 1948.
[10] *Ottův slovník naučný: illustrovaná encyklopedie obecných vědomosti*, vols. 1–28, Prague: J. Otto 1888–1909, vol. 14 (1899).
[11] *Malá československá encyklopedie*, vols. 1–6, Prague: Academia 1984–7, vol. 3 (1986).
[12] Ibid.

In fact, not one work by Kierkegaard was translated as a whole during this period but only some selected passages or excerpts. Around the time of the so-called Prague Spring in the end of 1960s, in the short period of democratization and liberalization of Czech political and cultural life, the best translations of Kierkegaard to date began to appear. Unfortunately, this process had just begun, only to be brutally stopped by the tanks of the Warsaw Pact armies that invaded Czechoslovakia on August 21, 1968.

Miloslav Žilina, a renowned Czech Scandinavist, translated selected passages from *A Literary Review*, which appeared in 1969 under the title *The Present Age*.[13] And a very sound translation of "The Seducer's Diary" was published in 1970 with a profound afterword by Ladislav Hejdánek, a Czech philosopher and theologian.[14] This edition was reprinted in 1994. Quite paradoxically though, it was during this very period that the most credible and solid translations of Kierkegaard were created. In fact, the editorial work and publishing culture was of a very high quality in this country until 1989.

IV. Translations after the Fall of Communism in 1989

The new democracy in the country brought a renewed interest in Kierkegaard. But simultaneously, editorial practices and publishing ethics worsened. Specifically, the transitional period of the early 1990s was marked by sloppy editorial work and a general slapdash attitude in the publishing sector. A number of improperly edited and unreliable translations of Kierkegaard appeared. Unfortunately, this is the case of the most prolific contemporary Kierkegaard translator into Czech, Marie Mikulová-Thulstrupová. Her translations by no means live up to the academic standards of scholarship needed for research and criticism, especially due to their terminological inaccuracy. Nor can they satisfy the common reader because Mikulová-Thulstrupová's Czech is awkward, and many nuances are lost in her version. This fact is especially lamentable, for it is quite certain that no Czech publishing house in the near future will publish the titles already published in her translation.

V. Secondary Literature on Kierkegaard in Czech

The secondary literature on Kierkegaard shared the same fate as his translations. Nearly all attempts to introduce Kierkegaard's works to the Czech audience and to do research on him, which were admittedly quite sketchy up until then anyway, stopped almost completely in 1948. Critical interest in Kierkegaard began around 1900. The first of the more comprehensive articles on Kierkegaard was written by the leading Czech Scandinavist Arnošt Kraus in 1900,[15] and four years later, Georg

---

[13] *Současnost*, trans. by Miloslav Žilina, Prague: Votobia 1969.
[14] *Svůdcův deník* ["The Seducer's Diary"], trans. by Radko Kejzlar, Prague: Odeon 1970.
[15] Arnošt Vilém Kraus, "Søren Kierkegaard," *Česká mysl*, vol. 1, no. 5, 1900, pp. 321–9 and vol. 1, no. 6, 1900, pp. 435–43.

Brandes' (1842–1927) monograph on Kierkegaard was translated into Czech by Anežka Schulzová.[16]

Generally, we must acknowledge that the Czech literary and philosophical scene have been completely lacking scholars specialized in Kierkegaard. In recent years, however, one Czech doctoral dissertation on Kierkegaard has appeared[17] and there have been several articles written by Czech scholars on the philosopher. At the same time, a couple of foreign Kierkegaard monographs have been translated into Czech.[18] The scholars of this country who work with Kierkegaard for the most part use the German translations or, more rarely, the French or English.

No Kierkegaard society or Kierkegaardian resource center has ever been founded in the Czech Republic, and to date there have no been conferences on the works of the philosopher. In short, there still remains much to do in Czech Kierkegaard research.

---

[16]   Georg Brandes, *Søren Kierkegaard*, trans. by Anežka Schulzová, Prague: Jos. Pelcl 1904 (originally in Danish as *Søren Kierkegaard: En kritisk Fremstilling i Grundrids*, Copenhagen: Gyldendalske Boghandels Forlag 1877).

[17]   Jan Kranát, *Kierkegaardův paradox* [Kierkegaard's Paradox], Ph.D. Thesis, Charles University, Prague 2000. This work is an attempt to interpret Kierkegaard's philosophy not as a refutation of German idealism but as its culmination. It has affinities with the postulates by W. Schulze on the end of speculative idealism.

[18]   Romano Guardini, *Těžkomyslnost a její smysl* [The Meaning of Melancholy], from German trans. by František Pastor, Stará Říše na Moravě: Marta Florianová 1932 (2nd ed., Olomouc: Votobia 1995; originally in German as "Vom Sinn der Vernunft," *Die Schildgenossen*, no. 8, 1928, pp. 103–25); Nikolaj A. Berdajev, *O otroctví a svobodě člověka* [On Slavery and Freedom of Man], Prague: Oikumené 1997 (originally in Russian as *О рабстве и свободе человека. Опыт персоналистической метафизики*, Paris: YMCA-Press [1939]; in English as Nikolai Berdyaev, *Slavery and Freedom*, trans. by R.M. French, London: G. Bles 1939 and New York: Scribner's 1939); Lev Isaakovič Šestov, *Kierkegaard a existenciální filosofie* [Kierkegaard and the Existential Philosophy], Prague: Oikoymenh 1997 (originally in Russian as *Киргегард и экзистенциальная философия (Глас вопиющего в пустыне)* [Kierkegaard and the Existential Philosophy (Vox clamantis in deserto)], Paris: Sovremennije zapiski i Dom Knigi 1939; in English as Lev Shestov, *Kierkegaard and the Existential Philosophy*, trans. by Elinor Hewitt, Athens: Ohio University Press 1969); Peter P. Rohde, Kierkegaard, from German trans. by Jiří Horák, Olomouc: Votobia 1995 (originally in German as *Søren Kierkeaard in Selbstzeugnissen und Bilddokumenten*, Hamburg: Rowohlt 1959).

Bibliography

I. Czech Translations of Kierkegaard's Works

"Žena—muž. Žena coby ztělesnění egoismu" [Man—Woman. Woman is the Embodiment of Egoism], trans. by Arnošt Procházka, *Moderní revue*, no. 9, 1906, pp. 221–2.

Svůdcův deník ["The Seducer's Diary"], trans. by Josef Heim, Prague: Adámek 1910.

Okamžik [*The Moment*], trans. by Milada Krausová-Lesná, Prague: Laichter 1911.

"In vino veritas" (excerpts from *Stages on Life's Way*), trans. by Hugo Kosterka, *Symposion*, 1913, pp. 1–81.

In vino veritas (excerpts from *Stages on Life's Way*), trans. by Hugo Kosterka, Prague: Hugo Kosterka 1914.

Svůdcův deník ["The Seducer's Diary"], trans. by Karel Sudějovský, Prague: Sfinx 1920.

Chvalořeč na Abrahama, otce národů a otce víry [Praise for Abraham, the Father of the Nations and the Father of Faith], trans. by Jaroslav Šimsa, Prague: YMCA 1939.

Současnost [The Present Age] (extracts from *A Literary Review*), trans. by Miloslav Žilina, Prague: Votobia 1969.

Svůdcův deník ["The Seducer's Diary"], trans. by Radko Kejzlar, Prague: Odeon 1970.

Čistota srdce aneb chtít jen jedno (a selection from the *Upbuilding Discourses in Various Spirits*), trans. by Josef Veselý, Prague: Ústřední církevní nakladatelství 1989.

Bázeň a chvění [*Fear and Trembling*], trans. by Marie Mikulová-Thulstrupová, Prague: Svoboda-Libertas 1993.

Svůdcův deník ["The Seducer's Diary"], trans. by Radko Kejzlar, Prague: Mladá fronta 1994.

Současnost [The Present Age] (extracts from *A Literary Review*), trans. by Miloslav Žilina, Prague: Votobia 1996.

Filosofické drobky, aneb Drobátko filosofie [*Philosophical Fragments or A Fragment of Philosophy*], trans. by Marie Mikulová-Thulstrupová, Olomouc: Votobia 1997.

Skutky lásky: několik křestanských úvah ve formě proslovů [*Works of Love*], trans. by Marie Mikulová-Thulstrupová, Brno: CDK 2000.

Tři páteční pozvání k Večeři Páně [*Three Discourses at the Communion on Fridays*], trans. by Robert Novotný, Prague: Kalich 2000.

Nácvik křesťanství. Suďte sami! [*Practice in Christianity. Judge for Yourself!*], trans. by Marie Mikulová-Thulstrupová, Brno: CDK 2002.

Má literární činnost (selected passages from *The Point of View for My Work as an Author*), trans. by Marie Mikulová-Thulstrupová, Brno: CDK 2003.

Okamžik [*The Moment*], trans. by Milada Krausová-Lesná, Prague: Kalich 2005.

Opakovárú: pokus v oblasti experimentující psychologie od Constantina Constantia [*Repetition. A Venture in Experimental Psychology by Constantin Constantinus*], trans. by Zdeněk Zacpal, Prague: Vyšehrad 2006.

II. Secondary Literature on Kierkegaard in the Czech Republic

Benyovszky, Ladislav, "Ego cogito" a transcendence pobytu. O Kierkegaardově vypracování problému subjektivity ve srovnání s Descartem ["Ego cogito" and the Transcendence of Dasein: On Kierkegaard's Elaboration of the Problem of Subjectivity in Comparison with Descartes], *Acta oeconomica pragensia*, no. 6, 1995, pp. 44–64.

— "Negativita a vrženost. O Kierkegaardově kritice Hegelova pojmu negativita" [Negativity and Thrownness: On Kierkegaard's Criticism of Hegel's Negativity], *Filosofický časopis*, no. 3, 1997, pp. 357–71.

— "Transcendence a úzkost" [Transcendence and Anxiety: On Kierkegaard's Conception of Anxiety], *Lidé města*, no. 8, 2002, pp. 3–12.

Černý, Václav, *První sešit o existencialismu* [The First Book on Existentialism], Prague: Václav Petr 1948 (in 1992 republished as *První a druhý sešit o existencialismu* [The First and Second Book on Existentialism], Prague: Mladá fronta 1992]).

Fiala, Václav, *Trojzvuk* [The Triplicity: Søren Kierkegaard, Edvard Grieg, Jean Sibelius], Prague: František Borový 1945.

Heidrich, Oldrich, "Søren Aabye Kierkegaard," *Masarykuv slovnir naučný*, no. 3, 1927, pp. 984–5.

Hromádka, Josef Lukl, "Søren Aabye Kierkegaard," *Ottuv slovnik naučný*, vol. 3, no. 1, 1934, pp. 506–7.

— "Søren Kierkegaard," in *Křesťanská revue* [Christian Revue], Prague: Oikumené-Akademická YMCA 1955, pp. 243–7.

Humpál, Martin, "Why a Dialectician Is Not a Philosopher: The Poetics of Dialectics in Kierkegaard's *Frygt og Baeven*," *Scandinavian Studies*, vol. 73, no. 4, 2001, pp. 493–506.

— "Søren Kierkegaard," in *Slovník severských spisovatelů* [Dictionary of Scandinavian Authors], Prague: Libri 2004, pp. 260–2.

Kranát, Jan, *Kierkegaardův paradox* [Kierkegaard's Paradox], Ph.D. Thesis, Charles University, Prague 2000.

Kraus, Arnošt Vilém, "Søren Kierkegaard," *Česká mysl*, vol. 1, no. 5, 1900, pp. 321–9 and vol. 1, no. 6, 1900, pp. 435–43.

Mikulová Thulstrup, Marie, "Kierkegaard as an Edifying Christian Author," in *Kierkegaard's View of Christianity*, ed. by Niels Thulstrup and Marie Mikulová-

Thulstrup, Copenhagen: C.A. Reitzel 1978 (*Bibliotheca Kierkegaardiana*, vol. 1), pp. 179–82.
— "Studies of Pietists, Mystics, and Church Fathers," in *Kierkegaard's View of Christianity*, ed. by Niels Thulstrup and Marie Mikulová-Thulstrup, Copenhagen: C.A. Reitzel 1978 (*Bibliotheca Kierkegaardiana*, vol. 1), pp. 60–80.
— "Præsentation af kristne mystikere i faglitteraturen, Kierkegaard kendte," *Kierkegaardiana*, vol. 11, 1980, pp. 55–92.
— "Pietism," in *Kierkegaard and Great Traditions*, ed. by Niels Thulstrup and Marie Mikulová-Thulstrup, Copenhagen: C.A. Reitzel 1981 (*Bibliotheca Kierkegaardiana*, vol. 6), pp. 173–222.
— "Baader," in *Kierkegaard's Teachers*, ed. by Niels Thulstrup and Marie Mikulová-Thulstrup, Copenhagen: C.A. Reitzel 1982 (*Bibliotheca Kierkegaardiana*, vol. 10), pp. 170–7.
— "Plato's Vision and its Interpretations," in *Kierkegaard's Classical Inspiration*, ed. by Niels Thulstrup and Marie Mikulová-Thulstrup, Copenhagen: C.A. Reitzel 1985 (*Bibliotheca Kierkegaardiana*, vol. 14), pp. 63–103.
— *Kierkegaard a dějiny křesťanské zbožnosti* [Kierkegaard and the History of Christian Piety], Brno: CDK 2005.
Olšovský, Jiří, *Kierkegaard—niternost a existence: úvod do Kierkegaardova myšlení* [Kierkegaard—The Inner and the Existence: Introduction to Kierkegaard's Thinking], Prague: Akropolis 2005.
Šalda, František Xaver, *Okamžik a věčnost: Dvě stati z Časových i nadčasových* [The Moment and Eternity: Two Essays on the Temporal and the Timeless], Prague: Společnost F.X. Šaldy 1992.
Svobodová, Zdeňka, "Kierkegaard a Mozart" [Kierkegaard and Mozart], in *Křesťanská revue*, Prague: Oikumené—Akademická YMCA 1956, pp. 39–41.
Umlauf, Václav, *Hermeneutická interpretace* [Hermeneutical Interpretation], Brno: Centrum pro studium demokracie a kultury 2005.

III. Secondary Literature on Kierkegaard's Reception in the Czech Republic

None.

Poland:
A Short History of the Reception of Kierkegaard's Thought

Antoni Szwed

I. The Early Kierkegaard Reception

In Poland, unlike in Germany and France, an interest in Søren Kierkegaard appeared relatively late and in an indirect way. In Germany Martin Heidegger and Karl Jaspers (apart from a considerable group of Protestant theologians) had drawn ideas and notions from the already existing comprehensive German translations of Kierkegaard's works. The same thing was the case with Jean Paul Sartre in France. To a certain degree, their existential philosophies assimilated some of Kierkegaard's categories and ideas. In Poland, however, things were different. The interest in the philosophical and theological reflection of the "father of existentialism" appeared almost at the same time as the interest in Heidegger, Jaspers, Sartre, and Marcel; and for many years (after the Second World War), we looked at Kierkegaard through the eyes of his later followers and philosophical relatives. In such a situation, one can talk of intellectual mediation in reference to Kierkegaard.

At the beginning of the twentieth century, the most important of Kierkegaard's works were edited in the twelve-volume German translation. This edition was prepared by Christoph Schrempf and was a reliable basis for detailed investigations.[1] At that time in Poland only "The Seducer's Diary" was translated,[2] in addition to a few passages from *Either/Or*, *Fear and Trembling*, and *The Moment*, published by Maks Bienenstock (1881–1918) in Lvov.[3] This selection of texts was hardly representative of the thought of the Danish philosopher as a whole. For this reason, in the years 1918–39 it did not exercise any great influence on Polish literature.

---

[1] Søren Kierkegaard, *Gesammelte Werke*, trans. and ed. by Hermann Gottsched and Christoph Schrempf, vols. 1–12, Jena: Diederichs 1909–22.
[2] *Dziennik uwodziciela* ["The Seducer's Diary"], trans. by Jan August Kisielewski, Warsaw 1899; "Dziennik uwodziciela" ["The Seducer's Diary"], trans. by Stanisław Lack, *Życie*, nos. 8–22, 1899 (2nd ed., Lwów 1907).
[3] *Wybór pism: Albo-albo, Bojaźni i drżenia, Chwili* [Selected writings: *Either/Or*, *Fear and Trembling*, *The Moment*], trans. and ed. by Maks Bienenstock, Lvov: Księgarnia Polska B. Połonieckiego 1914.

The first concise references and scattered comments appeared only thirty years later. Their authors did not use the original Danish texts but read German translations and comprehensive foreign studies. In the *Illustrated Encyclopaedia* we can find that Kierkegaard was the author of *Either/Or*, and that he was dealing with the psychology of sin, conversion and faith.[4]

Stefan Kołaczkowski (1887–1940) in his "Danish Literature" calls Kierkegaard "one of the deepest moralists of Europe and an exponent of extreme religious subjectivism."[5] Paweł Hulka-Laskowski (1881–1946) published his article on Kierkegaard in the periodical *Wiadomości Literackie*.[6] He expresses a deep amazement that such a profoundly religious thinker could have aroused such an interest in Germany and France in such an irreligious epoch (the 1930s). According to his opinion, it is impossible to understand how it could happen that this "not widely read" writer can remain up-to-date. The issues he is dealing with should— according to all signs on heaven and earth—belong to the past. The Catholic priest, professor Józef Pastuszka (1897–1989), in the *Present Tendencies in the Philosophy of Religion*, mentions briefly some motifs of the Danish philosopher. He emphasizes the seriousness of Christianity based on paradoxes, the depth of human existential issues, simultaneously seeing in them "religious pessimism" which involves an anti-intellectualism in the sphere of faith.[7]

The first meaningful article was written by the Protestant clergyman, professor Rudolf Kesselring (ca. 1880–ca. 1945).[8] The author underlines the originality and importance of Kierkegaard's thought. He makes a note of its predominant influence on contemporary Protestant theology and especially on dialectical theology and the theology of crisis. According to Kesselring, Kierkegaard's individuality is "exceedingly complicated and enigmatic." It is difficult to find "any rectitude and clarity" in it, a fact characteristic of some other great thinkers. But, for him, Kierkegaard is a pattern of absolute honesty and sincerity. Making objections to the Danish Church and its priests, he does so with a Christian humility, induced by deep personal religiosity. He wanted Christianity to be treated seriously. But there are also critical accents. Kesselring criticizes Kierkegaard's excessive emphasis on suffering in Christianity, his own painful martyrdom, though this agrees with his opinion that Protestantism became "diluted" and secularized Christianity in a

---

[4] *Ilustrowana encyklopedia*, vols. 1–6, ed. by Stanisław Lam, Warsaw: Trzaska, Evert i Michalski 1927–37, vol. 2 (1932), p. 912.

[5] Stefan Kołaczkowski, "Literatura duńska—S. Kierkegaard" [Danish Literature— S. Kierkegaard], in *Wielka Literatura Powszechna* [Great Works of World Literature], vols. 1–4, ed. by Stanisław Lam, Warsaw: Trzaska, Evert i Michalski 1930–34, vol. 3 (1932), pp. 627–9.

[6] Paweł Hulka-Laskowski, "Sören Kierkegaard," *Wiadomości Literackie*, no. 4, 1935, p. 2.

[7] Józef Pastuszka, *Współczesne kierunki filozofii religii*, Warsaw: skł. gł. Księg. św. Wojciecha 1932, pp. 112–14; p. 121.

[8] Rudolf Kesselring, "Sören Kierkegaard. Indywidualizm religijny Kierkegaarda i jego wpływ na współczesną teologię ewangelicką" [Søren Kierkegaard. Kierkegaard's Religious Individuality and his Influence on Contemporary Lutheran Theology], in *Rocznik Teologiczny*, vols. 1–4, Warsaw: Wydział Teologji Ewangelickiej 1936–39, vol. 1 (1936), pp. 101–33.

way that deprived it of an "anxiety of heart" as in Augustine or Luther. Kesselring underlines the importance of a return to a vivid faith in Christ and points to the Kierkegaardian theology of the Cross. At the same time, he sees the need to reject what he regards as "petrified" theological formulas. Kesselring notes, however, the strange relation of Kierkegaardian "erotica"—contained in the aesthetic writings—to Christian mysticism. It becomes—in his opinion—a sign of Kierkegaard's "abnormal emotionality." In spite of certain psychopathic features of "suppressed sexuality" in him, this does not affect his reflection on the depth of Christianity. It is valid, for example, for the notion of the Revelation. "The Revelation of God," Kesselring writes, "is not identical with a most important historical date, or only historic fact....For Kierkegaard, the Revelation is first of all an experience of God, relying on the fact that temporality has possibility in some exceptional cases to join itself with eternity."[9]

The absence of a deeper interest in Kierkegaard's thought before the Second World War has many reasons. Geographically Denmark and Poland are close to each other, but culturally they are quite distant. Not being in exactly the same geographical region and having different historical fates made any cultural exchange in practice impossible. One of the main obstacles is also the extreme lack of linguistic resemblance. For a Pole a concrete Danish word does not create any field of meaningful association if his knowledge of English or German is not advanced. One obstacle in studying this language is a complete shortage of media and large Danish–Polish and Polish–Danish dictionaries. For this reason, translators often make use of "indirect" dictionaries like: Danish–German or Danish–English. The presence of Danish philology is something rare at Polish universities in contrast to, for example, Swedish philology. Hence, very few people in Poland know Danish. Yet among them, there are small groups of translators who have advanced knowledge of Kierkegaard's writings. Not without significance for the appreciation of his thought is the fact that the Danish "Socrates" was a Protestant, belonging to the Lutheran Confession. In the period before the Second Vatican Council, relations between Catholic and Protestant Churches were cool. The time was not favorable—at least in the first period—for the propagation of Protestant thought in a Catholic country.

Finally, perhaps the most important reason for the lack of interest in Kierkegaard during this period is the fact that in Poland from 1918 to 1939, unlike France and Germany, there were no representatives of existentialism. Contemporary Polish philosophical schools and groups were dealing with logic, philosophy of science, neoThomism, and phenomenology. Those philosophical currents did not have anything to do with the problems explored by Kierkegaard. Even contemporary interest in Hegelian philosophy was not direct but rather associated with leftist Marxism. A Hegelian interpretation of Christianity and a possible reaction to it were not in a field of interests of Polish scholarship. Even if among the Polish intelligentsia at that time a crisis of confidence in the Church, a crisis of faith, was felt, it was rather connected with a positivistic belief in progress and the power of scientific rationalism, and was not rooted in existential and subjective problems.

---

[9] Ibid., p. 126.

After the end of the Second World War, twenty years passed before the first translations of entire works by Kierkegaard began to appear. Yet earlier some Catholic scholars attempted to grasp a Kierkegaardian sense of religiosity and Christianity. They included Franciszek Sawicki (1877–1952), Father Antoni Warkocz (1908–92), Hanna Malewska (1911–83), Father Józef Pastuszka (1897–1989), and Father Wincenty Granat (1900–79). In their comments they treated the author of *Either/Or* favorably, presenting a sufficiently detailed introduction of most of the important threads of Kierkegaard's anthropological and theological thought and restricting themselves to a prudent and carefully weighed criticism of the depicted content. One exception was the somewhat emotional article by Father Warkocz entitled, "Brightnesses and Shadows in Kierkegaard's Existentialism," which was written from the standpoint of narrow-minded Catholic orthodoxy.[10] The author did not hold back from criticizing Kierkegaard for an extreme subjectivism in the recognition of truth, a rejection of scientific cognition, and for the impossibility of a reconciliation of individual existence with society. He did not deny that Kierkegaard had an authentic faith, though he did not see the possibility of confessing it after the rejection of basic Christian notions and categories.

Sawicki, a more moderate author, is univocally positive towards Kierkegaard.[11] He calls him a "brilliant, deep and clever thinker," who, though philosophically related to Nietzsche, with regard to Christianity, is "worlds apart" from the German philosopher. According to Sawicki, one can see in Kierkegaard an unusual desire for cognition, someone for whom even religion is an interesting philosophical problem. But there is a reason for this. To indicate a way to Christianity to his contemporaries, the Danish thinker had to "begin" from paganism and direct eroticism ("The Seducer's Diary"). His way of thinking is "remarkably dialectical." He puts together theses and antitheses, often aiming to synthesize conflicting views. "Hence," Sawicki writes, "it is difficult to establish what his real and final opinion is."[12] As a result, his thought is often interpreted "too one-sidedly." Sawicki enumerates those threads in his writings, in which "a distinct inclination and sympathy for Catholicism is disclosed."[13] Often enough this opinion is shared by other Catholic scholars.

A post-war article by Pastuszka entitled "Life's Attitudes according to S. Kierkegaard,"[14] which was written in a modern philosophical language, gives the first reliable account of the main threads of Kierkegaard's thought. Writing about the method of Kierkegaard's philosophy, Pastuszka emphasizes the differences between Hegel's system and the Kierkegaardian philosophy of existence, but at the same time notes that the philosopher from Copenhagen does not condemn "all philosophy," seeing its source not in wonder or admiration as the ancient Greeks did, but in despair

---

[10] Albert Warkocz, "Blaski i cienie egzystencjalizmu Kiekegaarda" [Brightnesses and Shadows in Kierkegaard's Existentialism], *Ateneum kapłańskie*, vol. 5, no. 52, 1950, pp. 365–80.

[11] Franciszek Sawicki, "P. Kierkegaard," *Przegląd Powszechny*, vol. 2, no. 225, 1948, pp. 81–91.

[12] Ibid., p. 85.

[13] Ibid.

[14] Józef Pastuszka, "Postawy życiowe według S. Kiekegaarda," *Rocznik Filozoficzny*, vol. 4, 1958, pp. 105–25.

and fear. This philosophy has to serve the concrete man by dissolving his existential problems. From a temporal standpoint and eternal synthesis, Pastuszka clearly reconstructs three stages of existence, i.e., the aesthetic, ethical, and religious stages, analyzing separately religiosity A (so-called Socratic religiosity) and religiosity B (Christianity). He points out the paradox of both forms of religiosity and affirms that in religiosity A God's perception is reduced to a pure experience "in the moments of self-reflection." Pastuszka concludes that in philosophy (religiosity A) "every man is a believer," and in connection with it "atheists do not exist."[15]

Wincenty Granat appreciates Kierkegaard's existentialism in the light of the Catholic doctrine of mercy and sin.[16] Furthermore, he suggests that the whole literary, philosophical and theological activity of the Danish thinker in fact contains comprehensive comments on St. Paul's Letters. Subjective truth has a tight relationship with justificatory faith, which believes in permanently defeating sin, thanks to the remission of sins, caused by Christ. Granat clearly distinguishes Kierkegaard's existentialism, directed towards Christ and his mercy that overcomes sin, from the atheistic existentialism of Sartre and the agnostic ontology of Martin Heidegger.

II. The History of the Translations of Kierkegaard's Works into Polish

A crucial event for Kierkegaard's reception in Poland was the first Polish edition of *Fear and Trembling* and *The Sickness unto Death*.[17] These translations were done by the well-known and distinguished poet Jarosław Iwaszkiewicz (1894–1980). Living in Copenhagen as a cultural attaché of the Polish Embassy, he not only acquainted himself with with Danish language but also became an admirer of the literary art of the outstanding Danish writer. From a literary perspective, this was a very successful translation, and, as a result, *Fear and Trembling* is the most often cited of Kierkegaard's works in Polish philosophical literature. Ten years later *Either/Or* appeared on the book market.[18] And this time the first ("more literary") volume was translated by Jarosław Iwaszkiewicz, while the second ("more philosophical") one was done by Karol Toeplitz (b. 1936), philosopher and disciple of the internationally recognized scholar Leszek Kołakowski (b. 1927). Professor Toeplitz made a precise, straightforward translation and determined most of the Kierkegaardian categories in the Polish language. Beginning with his doctoral thesis on the subject of faith in Kierkegaard's work, he devoted himself during his entire life to detailed studies and the very successful popularization of Kiekegaard in Poland. The fruit of his studies

---

[15] Ibid., p. 117.
[16] Wincenty Granat, "Egzystencjalizm w świetle nauki o łasce i grzechu" [Existentialism in the Light of the Doctrines of Grace and Sin], in *Roczniki Teologiczno-Kanoniczne* [Theological and Canonical Yearbooks], ed. by Piotr Kałura and Ludwik Krupa, Lublin: KUL 1956, pp. 191–229.
[17] *Bojaźń i drżenie. Choroba na śmierć*, trans. by Jarosław Iwaszkiewicz, Warsaw: PWN 1966 (2nd ed., 1982).
[18] *Albo-Albo*, trans. by Jarosław Iwaszkiewicz (vol. 1) and Karol Toeplitz (vol. 2), Warsaw: PWN 1976 (2nd ed., 1982).

was, among other things, the monograph *Kierkegaard*[19] and numerous articles, which began a new epoch in Polish research. Toeplitz's articles are cited by almost everyone writing about Kierkegaard in Poland. He also translated *Philosophical Fragments* and the ten leaflets entitled *The Moment*.[20]

In the 1990s and at the beginning of present century some new translations were completed. In 1992, Bronisław Świderski (b. 1946) published *Repetition* in Polish.[21] A few years later, in the second enlarged edition (2000), he added *Prefaces* and Kierkegaard's correspondence with Professor Heiberg.[22] This last edition was based on the new critical Danish edition, *Søren Kierkegaards Skrifter*, produced by the Søren Kierkegaard Research Centre in Copenhagen. In 1996, Alina Djakowska gave to the Polish reader a translation of *The Concept of Anxiety*.[23] This work was translated anew by Antoni Szwed on the basis of *Søren Kierkegaards Skrifter*.[24] Three years later a translation of *The Concept of Irony* by Djakowska appeared on the market.[25] In 2000 and 2001 two books were added: *Journals* (a comprehensive selection of Kierkegaard's journal entries), and *Practice in Christianity*.[26] One should also mention that a large number of short fragmentary excerpts exist. They were translated both from Danish and from other languages (mainly German) by various translators. Until recent years, there was no strategic plan for the translation of Kierkegaard's works. In general, translators chose those works according to their personal preferences; they recognized them as worthy of quick publication. Yet in 2003, a special team was appointed whose objective is the systematic translation into Polish of those works not yet available. These translations will be done on the basis of *Søren Kierkegaards Skrifter*.

---

[19] Karol Toeplitz, *Kierkegaard* (a monograph about Kierkegaard, it includes extracts from primary texts as well), Warszawa: Wiedza Powszechna 1975 (2nd ed., 1980).

[20] *Okruchy filozoficzne. Chwila*, trans. by Karol Toeplitz, Warsaw: PWN 1988.

[21] *Powtórzenie. Próba psychologii eksperymentalnej przez Constantina Constantinusa* [*Repetition. A Venture in Experimental Psychology by Constantin Constantinus*], trans. by Bronisław Świderski, Warsaw: Aletheia 1992.

[22] *Powtórzenie. Przedmowy. List otwarty Constantina Constantiusa do Pana Profesora Heiberga* [*Repetition. Prefaces. Open Letter to Professor Heiberg from Constantin Constantinus*], trans. by Bronisław Świderski, Warsaw: W.A.B. 2000.

[23] *Pojęcie lęku: psychologicznie orientujące proste rozważanie o dogmatycznym problemie grzechu pierworodnego przez Virgiliusa Haufniensis* [*The Concept of Anxiety. A Simple Psychologically Orienting Deliberation on the Dogmatic Issue of Hereditary Sin by Vigilius Haufniensis*], trans. by Alina Djakowska, Warsaw: Aletheia 1996.

[24] *Pojęcie lęku. Proste rozważania o charakterze psychologicznym, odniesione do dogmatycznego problemu grzechu pierworodnego autorstwa Vigiliusa Haufniensisa* [*The Concept of Anxiety. A Simple Psychologially Orienting Deliberation on the Dogmatic Issue of Hereditary Sin by Vigilius Haufniensis*], trans. by Antoni Szwed, Kęty: Antyk 2000 (2nd ed., Warsaw: De Agostini 2002).

[25] *O pojęciu ironii z nieustającym odniesieniem do Sokratesa* [*The Concept of Irony. With Continual References to Socrates*], trans. by Alina Djakowska, Warsaw: KR 1999.

[26] *Dziennik (wybór)* (a selection from the journals), trans. by Antoni Szwed, Lublin: TNKUL 2000; *Wprawki do chrześcijaństwa Anti-climacusa wydane przez P. Kierkegaarda* [*Practice in Christianity by Anti-Climacus edited by S. Kierkegaard*], trans. by Antoni Szwed, Kęty: Antyk 2002 (2nd ed., Warsaw: De Agostini 2004).

III. How to Read Kierkegaard?

Since the beginning of the 1990s, attention has been paid that one of the most difficult problems for every scholar: to find an interpretative key to the whole of Kierkegaard's thought. People realized that there was no such one work which could be acknowledged as representative for Kierkegaard's thinking as a whole. In other words, none of his books on their own would be enough for an understanding of the entirety of his thought. Even such important works as *Either/Or* or *Concluding Unscientific Postscript* do not play that role but are only stages (very essential ones, of course) in the development of Kierkegaard's philosophy. The Dane performed a conscious disintegration of any homogenous form of reading, treating each published book as a kind of mental experiment. He assigned separate fictitious authors (so-called pseudonymous authors) to his works, creating the literary illusion that the authors of the pseudonymous works are fundamentally different from his own person. It is easy to see that on any given issue (for example that of faith) the opinions of the pseudonymous authors differ considerably and in extreme cases are mutually exclusive. Similar divergences arise between the pseudonyms and Kierkegaard himself as an author. In such a situation, a reasonable question arises: whether it is possible, generally speaking, to give a coherent interpretation of the *corpus scriptorum* and to attain one general meaning of everything that Kierkegaard wrote.

Opinions are divided. Alina Djakowska suggests that it is not possible.[27] She claims that there do not exist direct personal statements by Kierkegaard about the whole work. Nowhere does he express his own opinions in a way which could serve as a kind of personal diary. Djakowska assumes a very broad understanding of the pseudonyms. Pseudonyms call into being theatrical masks, multi-level curtains, which in a complicated way harmonize with themselves. This is also true for Kierkegaard as an author. Even where Kierkegaard signs his own name (for example in the upbuilding discourses and the majority of the journals), as an author, he does not distinguish himself fundamentally from other fictitious authors. He also participates in the game. They all serve to create a "constellation of glances with equal rights." They move into play certain psychological observations and perform spiritual experiments for cognitive purposes.

In Djakowska's opinion, the use of the whole pseudonymous construction is an operation which makes impossible any final or adequate interpretation of the whole of Kierkegaard's work. It is rather a movement of thought, a parade of moods, and a sequence of pictures, and one does not know where they start or end. There is no map of the pseudonymous works, but it remains—as Djakowska describes it—only "a swamp," in which it is easily to lose one's way. In other words, Kierkegaard nowhere expresses something directly "from himself" but uses indirect communication, drawing different kinds of existential possibilities and poetical pictures of being.

---

[27] See Alina Djakowska, "Dyskurs pseudonimów" [The Pseudonyms' Discourse], *Archiwum Historii Filozofii i Myśli Społecznej*, no. 37, 1992, pp. 117–9; Djakowska, "Jestem Pseudonimem" [I am Pseudonym], in *Tożsamości Kierkegaarda* [Kierkegaard's Identities], ed. by Alina Djakowska, Artur Przybysławski and Aldona Schiffmann, Kraków: Aureus 1999 (special number of the Journal *Principia*, vol. 23), pp. 79–94.

Thus, it makes no sense to seek any cohesion of opinions between Kierkegaard and the pseudonymous authors. We have a collection of texts of which we are not able to say a single word. Collectively, the pseudonymous authors have no teleology, no common aim. Their autonomic discourse of pseudonymous authors shows itself as an impersonal transfer which simultaneously determines the range of speech possibility. By contrast, the consistent rejection of the pseudonyms, or indirect utterance, leads to silence.

Antoni Szwed is of a somewhat different opinion.[28] The fictitious author depicts a possible work and a poetically outlined personality. Its hypothetical existence expresses the implementation of a definite idea. A pseudonymous configuration is not accidental, but it creates enough which is clearly sketched with regard to final aim and hierarchy. This final existential aim is, for Kierkegaard, "to become Christian." Assumed ideas determine a full palette of different potential ways of life which constitute a kind of prelude for the highest way of life, which is the existence of a Christian, an imitator of Christ, the God-Man. The Danish philosopher constructs a multi-level anthropology which is based on an increasing degree of internal, personal freedom. To these subjective constructions correspond stages, sub-stages, and inter-stages of human existence. They outline—quite hypothetically (poetically)—the spiritual development of the individual. That game of pseudonyms has its own internal teleology, fixed by the highest idea—the idea of Jesus Christ, the Redeemer, and the pattern to imitate by all human beings. The dialectical realization of this idea leads, according to Kierkegaard, to the full spiritual liberation of man and to existence in truth. Any attempt to answer the basic question, "What does it mean to become a Christian?" determines the general sense of the work. This philosophical-theological work is intended to be valid not only for every reader but also for Kierkegaard alone as a concrete individual.

Alex Fryszman also discusses the issue of the pseudonyms, but for him the origin of them in Kierkegaard is not of any particular interest.[29] Fryszman seeks the existence of the author in general. He refers to Michaił Bachtin, the Russian theoretician of literature, according to whom "the identity of human subjectiveness can be expressed exclusively through story-telling."[30] "Division into author and hero exists in every speech act. This speech act does not know the division but only cries and screams of pain."[31] Each of us is an author, who, when telling a story, creates a distance from himself, from his own lived identity. Bachtin's statement, which has an anthropological and not a literary character, underlines Fryszman's view. Each of us can choose different roles and different authors, who we want to be. That

---

[28] See Antoni Szwed, *Miedzy wolnością a prawdą egzystencji. Studium myśli S. Kierkegaarda* [Between Freedom and the Truth of Existence. A Study of S. Kierkegaard's Thought], Kraków: Universitas 1991 (2nd ed., Kęty: Antyk 1999); "Przedmowa tłumacza" [Translator's Foreword], in *Dziennik* [Journals], Lublin: TNKUL 2001, pp. 5–38.

[29] See Alex Fryszman, "Być może Bachtin? Kierkegaard versus Bachtin" [Bachtin Perhaps? Kierkegaard versus Bachtin], *Teksty Drugie*, no. 1, 1996, pp. 139–48.

[30] Ibid., p. 140.

[31] Ibid.

pseudonymous distance in Kierkegaard is not anything extraordinary, but a natural state of man, who narrates himself.

In a similar spirit to Fryszman, Edward Kasperski expresses his view that in Kierkegaard, more than in other authors, one cannot separate the means of expression (literary forms) from the content.[32] The authorship is of a dialogical character, and its concrete compositions have a polyphonic structure. Kierkegaard gives up traditional philosophical discourse based on rules of internal logical cohesion and direct speech. He transforms philosophical and philosophical-theological discourses into artistic and para-artistic utterances in which new rules and new poetics are obligatory. His work is not the authoritative form or articulation of the author's thought. It grows out of the conviction that, with respect to individual human existence, one cannot speak from one point of view and with one kind of speech. Here, the language of art is the only adequate form of communication, albeit not an objective or scientific one.

Bronisław Świderski is convinced that in the epoch of "self"-worship, Kierkegaard introduces fictitious authors in order to belittle his own "self."[33] Those fictitious subjects respond to each other mutually, as if to put the actual creator aside, keeping him in the background. No fictitious "self" is at the base of system, and it is not identical with some transcendental "self"; it does not even have features of concrete historic peoples. They are completely separate from the social context and are reduced to the anonymous "little me." What is a pseudonym?

> It is existential activity, being before word. At the beginning, it is silence. It means treating things in their negativity, the creation of ironical distance to oneself alone, "almost disappearance." Positivity comes into being with this movement simultaneously, and as a result of the retreat a space appears before our eyes, to which the pseudonym can invite guests.[34]

Different scholars (for example, Kasperski),[35] underline that Kierkegaard's authorship is principally based on irony as a basic dialogical rule. In Kierkegaard irony or the absolute negation of all finite things appears at the so-called intermediary stage between the aesthetic and the ethical stage, but irony is also a general method of his thinking. In the temporary role of a pseudonymous author together with his idea and "view of life" (*Livs-Anskuelse*), Kierkegaard has written a possibility of entirely negating them. That real subject, which gives existence to fictitious authors, has the power and privilege to deny the importance of their narration. He does not express himself directly; he is silent, but he speaks simultaneously, when, in replacing the negated fictitious entities, the author presents the next one. Thus, he

---

[32] See Edward Kasperski, "Kierkegaard o komunikacji" [Kierkegaard on Communication], in *Dialog i dialogizm. Idee, formy, tradycje* [Dialogue and Dialogism. Ideas, Forms, and Traditions], Warsaw: Elipsa 1994, pp. 11–147; *Kierkegaard. Antropologia i dyskurs o człowieku* [Kierkegaard. Anthropology and Discourse on Man], Pułtusk: WHS 2003.
[33] See Bronisław Świderski, "Ludzie wolą być Żydami" [People would much more prefer to be Jewish], *Tygodnik Powszechny*, no. 33, 2004, Supplement; "Dar" [Gift], in *Powtórzenie. Przedmowy* [Repetition. Prefaces], pp. 343–68.
[34] Ibid.
[35] See Kasperski, "Kierkegaard o komunikacji."

expresses himself indirectly but by means of statements of posited and cancelled fictitious authors.

Now it is generally admitted that the vast majority of Kierkegaard's works are an attempt at indirect communication in relation to the reader. They do not contain a direct account of philosophical anthropology, in which human nature or human essence, fixed by several ontological rules, would be objectively expressed. In Kierkegaard's anthropology one finds the irremovable tension between who man is, and who he should be. In this thinking a certain idea of man is pointed out, which is perceived by the concrete individual as an internal aim in relation to which he should exist. Indirect communication is the art of suggestion, poetically introduced majeutic endeavors—communication of the ethical, and witness of faith—religious communication. This kind of communication has definite existential results, and not merely the simple acceptance of the same communicated content. Some works (for example, *The Concept of Anxiety*) appear to be a direct communication of content. This outwardly theoretical style of communication does not have a syllogistic character, however, but only a figurative and even metaphorical one. It is the transposition of existential qualities and man's states into the ideality of notions that in so-called resubjectivisation (for example, Toeplitz)[36] have to be appropriated in an individual way.

IV. More Important Issues Treated by Polish Scholars

Every scholar knows that Kierkegaard's philosophy, although it constitutes a contrast to Hegel's system, nonetheless remains an integrated thought. This means that in this philosophy there really does not exist any detailed problem which could be analyzed in separation from other things. Each concretization of one of them requires a demonstration in a well-ordered and systematic way, even if as general background or in outline; all the rest, treated together, determine definite philosophy, man, or philosophical anthropology. A systematic account of such anthropology is a difficult undertaking, and it requires considerable effort. On Polish ground, a successful attempt is represented by Edward Kasperski's monograph.[37]

Kasperski takes into account a considerable number of the most important foreign works, written mainly in the 1990s. This work, based on Kierkegaard's fundamental ontological statements and on a solid familiarity with the works of the Dane, shows the whole complexity of issues connected with spirit and its existence, existential ethics, the paradoxical idea of faith, tensions between faith and reason, indirect communication, irony and humor.

The other attempt of Kierkegaardian anthropology in reference to Kant's philosophy can be found in Hubert Mikołajczyk's work.[38] One of its main conclusions

---

[36] See Karol Toeplitz, "Egzystencjalna resubiektywizacja" [Existential Resubjectivization], in *Egzystencjalizm jako zjawisko kulturowe* [Existentialism as a Cultural Phenomenon], Gdańsk: AM 1983, pp. 56–70.

[37] Kasperski, *Kierkegaard. Antropologia i dyskurs o człowieku*.

[38] Hubert Mikołajczyk, "Søren Kierkegaard—absolutyzacja istnienia ludzkiego" [Søren Kierkegaard—Absolutism of Human Being], *Słupskie Prace Humanistyczne*, no. 6a, 1985, pp. 179–96.

is that "from the standpoint of Kierkegaard's anthropology, speaking of God means the same as speaking of man. God is an internal dimension of man...man's self-realization is the condition of absolute experience simultaneously."[39] Mikołajczyk brings Kierkegaard's position close to Feuerbach's anthropology. The works of Karol Toeplitz and Antoni Szwed also treat the foundations of Kierkegaard's anthropology.[40]

V. The Most Recent Polish Scholarship

In the last decades, Polish scholars have taken up a series of detailed issues: Kierkegaard's philosophical opposition to the Hegelian system, the possibility of Christian existentialism, the problem of individual existence in the relation to freedom and existential truth, the communication of ethical and religious contents, the relations of reason to faith, the paradox of Christianity, and the dialectics of faith and despair.

(1) Kierkegaard's controversy with Hegel has often been discussed. It was shown that there was dissimilarity in their philosophies, while simultaneously it was pointed out that the Danish philosopher to a considerable degree took over Hegel's categories and many of his logical structures. He disputed with the author of the *Phenomenology of Spirit* with great passion, rejected the system, but simultaneously remained under the great influence of Hegel (Iwaszkiewicz, Kasperski).[41] Even the basic scheme of three stages has its prototype in Hegel's logical-ontological schemes, where the becoming of historical consciousnesses was replaced by the "leap" in the development of individual existence. But at the same time, it has been underlined that the fundamental difference between the two philosophies is in the impossibility of an adequate description of the movement of existence by Hegel's "static" logical categories; existence is a phenomenon, which denies the hitherto described type of rationality. According to Kierkegaard, all Hegelian mediations create only apparent movement, which has nothing to do with the actual movement of existence.

Tadeusz Płużański does not think, however, that the position of the Dane contributes anything new to philosophy.[42] He writes: "Even if one assumes that the Kierkegaardian critic was not quite groundless, his success comes at such a horrendous price that it is to acknowledge it as deep and painful defeat."[43] After the rejection of all mediations, the individual, extracted from the social and natural environment, becomes condemned to loneliness, in which faith and despair alone are dominant. Reacting to the extreme rationalization of Christianity, Kierkegaard

---

[39] Hubert Mikołajczyk, *Kierkegaard, Kant a antropologia filozoficzna* [Kierkegaard, Kant and Philosophical Anthropology], Słupsk: WSP 1990, p. 92.
[40] See Toeplitz, *Kierkegaard*; Szwed, *Między wolnością a prawdą egzystencji*.
[41] See Jarosław Iwaszkiewicz, "Nad Kierkegaardem" [About Kierkegaard], *Twórczość*, no. 5, 1966, pp. 34–49; Kasperski, *Kierkegaard. Antropologia i dyskurs o człowieku*.
[42] Tadeusz Płużański, "Kierkegaard contra Hegel; Kierkegaard—Mounier," in *Paradoks w nowożytnej filozofii chrześcijańskiej* [The Paradox in Contemporary Christian Philosophy], Warsaw: PWN 1970, pp. 58–123; pp. 190–202.
[43] Ibid., p. 121.

wanted "to move its irrationalization as far as possible." But the assault on Hegel had a wider range. It concerned also the Hegelian philosophy of history. A history does not contain in itself such necessities as Hegel ascribed to it (Jerzy Niecikowski).[44] Kierkegaard had an aversion to all-inclusive rationality, consciously transferred to the ground of theology and the doctrine of the Church. Sharp criticism of institutional Christianity, direct communication of the content of the Holy Scripture, and dogmatic truths—these were, so to speak, a prolongation of Hegel's panlogism (Toeplitz).[45] Kierkegaard's thought matured in the shadow of Hegelian construction. "If Hegel did not exist, maybe there would be no Kierkegaard, and…his work would not have reached the intensity and depth that it did."[46]

(2) Does not Kierkegaard's attack on the system, his declaration for a vivid faith against Christian speculation, therefore cancel the possibility of a consistent Christian existentialism? Toeplitz proves that it is not possible to reconcile doctrinal Christianity and existential thought.[47] Existential subjectivity cancels religious essentiality, which no Christian confession can ever accept. The aforementioned author affirms—making use of Pope Pius XII's statements on contemporary existential currents—that the synthesis of existentialism with Christianity is not possible at all. "The more the existential elements, the less the Christian ones and vice versa. Either faith or knowledge, either Christianity or existential attitude,"[48] writes Toeplitz, making the observation that if in fact a Christian existentialism were to appear, it would be a sign of compromise and internal weakness. It cannot appear in a "pure" form.

This essential difficulty raised by Toeplitz can be overcome to a certain degree, provided that the relation, religious essentialism vis-á-vis concrete existence, is considered in the light of indirect communication and not direct communication. In indirect communication, the objective content is given for subjective assimilation. According to Kierkegaard's thought, it is possible to authorize such an existential "passage" from religiosity A to religiosity B, i.e., from negative religiosity to the positive religion (Christianity).[49] Wiesław Gromczyński sees this problem from a slightly different point of view.[50] He proposes to acknowledge Kierkegaard's Christian existentialism as a historic fact and to limit himself to the question: how is such a philosophical construction possible, which avoids Sartre's dichotomy: either God exists and the freedom of man does not exist, or man is free and then God does not exist. Gromczyński tries to show that Kierkegaard avoids this dichotomy, thanks

---

[44] Jerzy Niecikowski, "Stirner, Kierkegaard—krytycy Hegla" [Stirner, Kierkegaard—Critics of Hegel], *Archiwum Historii Filozofii i Myśli Społecznej*, no. 13, 1967, pp. 141–71.
[45] See Toeplitz, "Egzystencjalna resubiektywizacja."
[46] Kasperski, *Kierkegaard. Antropologia i dyskurs o człowieku*.
[47] Karol Toeplitz, "O możliwości i niemożliwości istnienia 'chrześcijańskiego egzystencjalizmu' " [About the Possibility and Impossibility of Existence of a "Christian existentialism"], *Studia Filozoficzne*, no. 7, 1983, pp. 3–26.
[48] Ibid., p. 24.
[49] See Szwed, *Miedzy wolnością a prawdą egzystencji*.
[50] Wiesław Gromczyński, "O możliwości chrześcijańskiego egzystencjalizmu" [About the Possibility of Christian Existentialism], *Studia Filozoficzne*, no. 6, 1984, pp. 89–107.

to the introduction of the idea of the God-Man. Christology is an indispensable component of his existentialism. God Jesus gives a condition of faith, and he alone is a Giver of truth of subjective character. Man, who desires to live in truth, needs God, but for God to appear to man as Absolute requires the creative freedom of man. Christology explains how Christian existentialism is possible.

(3) The Kierkegaardian criticism of the Hegelian rationalization of Christianity, with its stress on the manifold paradoxes of human existence, leads some scholars to ask the question: was Kierkegaard an irrationalist? Toeplitz gives an affirmative answer, because what is most essential in Kierkegaard's thought—faith, the paradox of the God-Man, authenticity and the truth of Holy Scripture—is not submitted to rational demonstration.[51] Mystery is the heart of religion and Christianity, which falls outside all rationalization. Toeplitz believes Kierkegaard introduces so many irrational elements into religious Christianity that they ultimately cause its destruction.[52] Gromczyński does not agree with the opinion that Christianity alone is in itself irrational and that the God-Man is a logical contradiction.[53] Kierkegaard, when he writes that the Christian believes against reason, shows not the abstract contradiction between the idea of the God-Man and the mind, but rather the Christian survival of the Absolute, relying on the paradox that an infinite God appeared as a humble man. While it is true that one cannot reconcile faith with reason, it does not follow that faith requires a total negation of reason. The Danish philosopher criticizes effusive spirituality, which escapes from reason. His thought in a quite rational way leads to the limits of reason and rationally prepares the individual to take the existential leap of faith. His argument for the absurdity of faith does not claim either the logical or the actual impossibility of God's incarnation. The idea of the absurdity of faith serves to disclose a pure *eidos* of faith, free from elements introduced from outside, thanks to science, philosophy, theology, ecstasies, effusive bursts of passion and romantic moods. Those arguments do not justify describing Kierkegaard's position as irrational.

(4) Further development of this discussion is consideration about the absolute Paradox (i.e., Jesus Christ) and the paradoxes of Christian existence. Some notes appear in the margins of different presentations of Kierkegaard's statements. Father Stanisław Kowalczyk believes that in Kierkegaard, in spite of a distinct connection with Tertullian's words *credo quia absurdum*, faith is located *super rationem* and not *contra rationem*.[54] Faith refers to a different, higher rationality, which rises above

---

[51] Karol Toeplitz, "Nad Kierkegaardem i egzystencjalizmem" [About Kierkegaard and Existentialism], in *Okruchy filozoficzne. Chwila* [*Philosophical Fragments. The Moment*], pp. vii–lxvi.

[52] Karol Toeplitz, "Kierkegaard jako krytyk Kościoła" [Kierkegaard as a Church Critic], *Euhemer*, no. 3, 1971, pp. 79–93.

[53] Wiesław Gromczyński, "Czy Kierkegaard był irracjonalistą? Kilka uwag o porównaniu Kierkegaarda z Pascalem" [Was Kierkegaard irrationalist? Several Remarks on Comparison between Kierkegaard and Pascal], in *Tożsamości Kierkegaarda*, ed. by Alina Djakowska et al., pp. 157–70.

[54] See Stanisław Kowalczyk, "Søren Kierkegaard: Paradoksy wiary" [Søren Kierkegaard: Paradoxes of Faith], in his *Bóg w myśli współczesnej. Problematyka Boga i religii u czołowych myślicieli współczesnych* [God in Contemporary Thinking. The Problematics of God and

human rationality (see also Stefania Lubańska).[55] The absurdity of faith is a sign of the limitation of human reason, although—according to Kowalczyk—Kierkegaard "too strongly stressed the existential-ethical element to the disadvantage of the doctrinal-explicative one."[56] Submitting to Kant's agnosticism, he questioned the possibility of finding traces of God's activity in the world.

Originally, the paradoxes of religiosity A and B are not theoretical problems, but they appear as the intellectual answer of the individual in so-called infinite passion, whose aim and object is comprehended as absolute.[57] Faith is the culminating act of existence, referred directly to the Absolute and, as such, is related to existential anthropology. Faith is not a phenomenon, which appears ordinarily, but something rare and difficult to attain. It is pain and suffering. "Believing Faith" (Kasperski's term) is a rescue against despair and an exit beyond the rational-sensual circle of immanence towards the Absolute. This is a happy passion for which the object is a paradox. The anthropology of faith is strictly connected with the anthropology of the sinner. Among the commentators, there appear here two different readings of Kierkegaard's intentions. According to Kasperski, eternal happiness is the final prize for faith; according to Szwed, eternal happiness is tantamount to a fullness of freedom, which the individual achieves thanks to faith.

In a comprehensive way, Lubańska deals with faith and despair in a comparative study of Pascal's and Kierkegaard's philosophy.[58] Despair is the opposition to faith, which she understands as a psychical state, an "internal split," but also as a conflict of two wills. Analyzing different kinds of despair, Lubańska dedicates special attention to despair, understood in a strictly religious sense as sin.

(5) Being convinced that every individual acquires objective contents in his own way, Kierkegaard underlined many times the meaning of ethical and religious communication as indirect. The differences between direct and indirect communication have been made the object of detailed analysis.[59] Commentators

---

Religion in Leading Contemporary Thinkers], Wrocław: Wyd. Wrocławskiej Księgarni Archidiecezjalnej 1979, pp. 371–91; Stanisław Kowalczyk, "Bóg w myśli współczesnej" [God in Contemporary Thought], in his *Bóg w myśli współczesnej. Problematyka Boga i religii u czołowych myślicieli współczesnych* [God in Contemporary Thinking. The Problematics of God and Religion in Leading Contemporary Thinkers], Wrocław: Wyd. Wrocławskiej Księgarni Archidiecezjalnej 1982, pp. 105–25.

[55] Stefania Lubańska, *Pascal i Kierkegaard-filozofowie rozpaczy i wiary* [Pascal and Kierkegaard—Philosophers of Faith and Despair], Kraków: Universitas 2001.

[56] Kowalczyk, "Søren Kierkegaard: Paradoksy wiary," pp. 374–8.

[57] Kasperski, *Kierkegaard. Antropologia i dyskurs o człowieku*; Szwed, *Między wolnością a prawdą egzystencji*.

[58] Lubańska, *Pascal i Kierkegaard-filozofowie rozpaczy i wiary*.

[59] See Wiesław Gromczyński, "Dialektyka komunikacji etycznej wedle Kierkegaarda [Dialectics of Ethical Communication according to Kierkegaard], *Studia Filozoficzne*, no. 11, 1980, pp. 99–114; Kasperski, "Kierkegaard o komunikacji"; Jacek Aleksander Prokopski, "Kierkegaard o bezpośredniej i pośredniej komunikacji religijnej" [Kierkegaard on Direct and Indirect Religious Communication], *Zeszyty Naukowe KUL*, nos. 3–4, 2000; Antoni Szwed, "Komunikacja pośrednia jako podstawowa metoda filozofii egzystencji Kierkegaarda" [Indirect Communication as a Fundamental Method of Kierkegaard's Existential Philosophy],

paid attention to the fact that the latter is an art of the development of ethical and religious skills in the other person. Indirect communication in the sphere of ethics is a form of maieutics, known from antiquity; in the sphere of religion (Christianity) it is the testimony of faith. This kind of communication has a relationship with the so-called edifying elements, a certain kind of existential persuasion, which appears in the majority of Kierkegaard's writings. Written in the second person, these texts provide the opportunity to intensify the activity of the reader, which is to make definite considerations and to undertake definite existential decisions in his own life. The objective content of the Christian revelation gains the binding power for the individual only when it becomes subjectivized, and appears as the reply to consciousness of sin, the need for reconciliation with God. The dignity of the Holy Scripture and the authority of Church do not have their own power of influence if the individual does not acquire subjectively the objective religious content and if he does not become "contemporary" with Jesus Christ.

(6) During the last thirty years, many articles (and several books) have been written in which many of Kierkegaard's categories were analyzed in more a philosophical sense, and the ideological dimension, i.e., in reference to Marxism, and the psychological dimension become less prominent. Serious analyses of the most important categories of Kierkegaard's existential philosophy were given, which created the groundwork for further investigations. What is at stake here are categories of the human spirit as an existing subject, mutual relationships between transcendence and immanence (Janina Jakubowska),[60] the category of qualitative dialectics together with categories such as choice, repetition, the qualitative leap, subjectivization, and resubjectivisation.[61] Complex existential phenomena such as inward freedom,[62] anxiety,[63] and boredom[64] were made the object of detailed investigations.

Finally, it is worth noting some Polish intellectuals who appealed to the great Dane in their philosophical and literary activity. The internationally famous writer Witold Gombrowicz (1904–69) was the one of those who strongly sympathized with the different trends of European existentialism. Towards the end of his life, he recapitulated his vivid interest in Kierkegaard's thought, giving mini-lectures on its

---

in *Tożsamości Kierkegaarda*, ed. by Alina Djakowska et al., pp. 171–84; Karol Toeplitz, "Dialektyka jakościowa Sørena Kierkegaarda" [Søren Kierkegaard's Qualitative Dialectics], *Studia Filozoficzne*, no. 2, 1980, pp. 69–81.

[60]   See Janina Jakubowska, "Dialektyka transcendencji i immanencji. Od Kierkegaarda do Robinsona" [The Dialectics of the Transcendence and Immanence. From Kierkegaard to Robinson], *Studia Filozoficzne*, no. 5, 1971, pp. 136–52.

[61]   See Toeplitz, "Egzystencjalna resubiektywizacja"; "Dialektyka jakościowa Sørena Kierkegaarda."

[62]   See Andrzej Niemczuk, *Wolność egzystencjalna. Kant i Kierkegaard* [Existential Freedom. Kant and Kierkegaard], Lublin: Wyd. Uniwersytetu Marii Curie–Skłodowskiej 1995; Szwed, *Miedzy wolnością a prawdą egzystencji*.

[63]   See Alex Fryszman, "Pojęcie lęku" [The Concept of Anxiety], *Znak*, no. 12, 1996, pp. 136–42.

[64]   See Michal P. Markowski, "Nuda i tożsamość" [Boredom and Identity], in *Tożsamości Kierkegaarda*, ed. by Alina Djakowsa et al., pp. 43–56.

main features.[65] Gombrowicz juxtaposes the extremely abstract thinking of Hegel's philosophy to the Kierkegaardian description of real individual becoming. The latter is able to grasp the phenomenon of concrete human life and to accompany the individual inwardly. Kierkegaard, the father of European existentialism, proposes such a reflection which permits the individual to narrate his own life history from the inside with some general categories. These do not constitute a logical system but help to promote individual thinking. External, abstract theories and concepts do not get in touch with reality; they are, so to speak, "from another world." In the opinion of Gombrowicz, the splendid development of twentieth–century existentialism would not be possible without the mediation of Husserl's phenomenology. At its starting point, phenomenology overcame the strongly established conviction that nineteenth-century objectivism is the highest achievement of philosophical thinking. Independently of Husserl's aims, detailed investigation of human consciousness and advanced studies on the subjective sphere of man opened the door to different existential, subjective trends in contemporary philosophy. According to Gombrowicz, existentialism, initiated by Kierkegaard, constitutes a suitable method for providing a deeper understanding of the complex relation between different kinds of theisms (including Christianity) and contemporary atheisms.

The other Polish thinker who readily referred to Kierkegaard was a Catholic priest Joseph Tischner (1931–2000). This outstanding philosophical essayist and commentator of the "Solidarity" movement in Poland was never a Kierkegaard researcher. Yet he was strongly under the influence of Kierkegaard's manner of thought, sharpness, and accuracy of expression. Tischner highly appreciated Kierkegaard as a great writer and stylist. He often quoted "The Seducer's Diary," *Either/Or*, and *The Sickness unto Death*. He saw "The Seducer's Diary" as a psychologically penetrating description. For many years, Tischner was concerned with a *Philosophie der Begegnung* and philosophy of dialogue, and from this point of view he read "The Seducer's Diary." He was also under the influence of the brilliant presentation of sensorial beauty (in *Either/Or*), which can be fully expressed only by poetic art and not by philosophical discourse. Beauty, he wrote, following Kierkegaard, is absolute in its essence but simultaneously extremely fragile and fleeting. A poet rather than the philosopher can grasp beauty when it reveals itself in an instant.[66] Kierkegaard does not separate sense data into the simplest primary elements of observation, like philosophers such as Descartes, Locke, or Husserl, but he shows them as a qualitative new synthesis which never comes into being as a straight sum of those primitive elements. This qualitative synthesis shows that "the other is beautiful." The beauty of the other (for example, the other person) is a joyful enchantment, but simultaneously its loss brings suffering. To discover beauty is at the same time to resign from any possession of it. In Kierkegaard, beauty is not the appearance of a

---

[65] Witold Gombrowicz, "Egzystencjalizm" [Existentialism], in Francesco M. Cataluccio and Jerzy Illg, *Gombrowicz filozof*, Kraków: Znak 1991, pp. 128–40.

[66] Joseph Tischner, *Filozofia Dramatu* [Philosophy of Drama], Paris: Éd. du Dialogue 1990, pp. 99–102.

dead object, but something like light that "gives life and takes it." Beauty happens outside words and forces one to silence.[67]

Kierkegaard (along with Pascal and Nietzsche) was a favorite writer of Alexander Wat (1900–67), the Polish futurist and later well-known critic of communism. In his early youth Wat read *Either/Or* in a German translation, but not as an admirer of Danish existentialism. He treated Kierkegaard's writings as excellent intellectual exercises and very sophisticated literature.[68]

Most recently, the philosopher and theater director Włodzimierz Herman, who has lived in Denmark since 1968, prepared a theatrical adaptation of Kierkegaard's main views in dialogue form, performed by two actors.[69] This performance was held in Poznań and Szczecin and met with great applause by the Polish audience.

One index of the increasing interest in Kierkegaard's thought in Poland is the fact that to date three conferences dedicated to him have been held. The first conference was organized by the Danish Cultural Institute and the Department of Scandinavian Studies and Philosophy and was held at Gdańsk University in Gdańsk in 1997. The second conference, entitled "A jednak nie mogę powiedzieć 'ja' " [And yet I cannot say "I"], was organized by the Institute of Art of the Polish Academy of Sciences and was held in Warsaw in May 1998. The most recent conference was the Kraków Conference, which was dedicated to Kierkegaard's category of despair. This conference, held in Kraków, in April 2004, was organized by the Pontifical Academy in Kraków and the Danish Consulate in Kraków.

In the near future one can look forward to further investigations on Kierkegaard's thought in connection with the new translations of his works into Polish. A time of great and important debate on religious and existential subjects will certainly come, and Søren Kierkegaard will doubtless play an inspiring role in it.

---

[67]   Ibid., pp. 106–8.
[68]   Alexander Wat, *Mój wiek* [My Age], London: Plolonia Book Fond 1981.
[69]   "Kierkegaard. Kabaret literacko filozoficzny na podstawie tekstów filozofa, przygotował Włodzimierz Herman [Kierkegaard. Literary and Philosophical Cabaret on the Basis of the Texts of the Philosopher, prepared by Włodzimierz Herman], *Pogranicza*, no. 3, 2000, pp. 115–20.

Bibliography

I. Polish Translations of Kierkegaard's Works

"Dziennik uwodziciela" ["The Seducer's Diary"], trans. by Jan August Kisielewski, Warsaw 1899.
"Dziennik uwodziciela," ["The Seducer's Diary"], trans. by Stanisław Lack, *Życie*, nos. 8–22, 1899 (2nd ed., Lvov 1907).
Wybór pism: Albo–albo, Bojaźni i drżenia, Chwili [Selected Writings: *Either/Or* (pp. 1–75), *Fear and Trembling* (pp. 77–201), *The Moment* (pp. 203–29)], trans. and ed. by Maks Bienenstock, Lwów: Księgarnia Polska B. Połonieckiego 1914.
"Trwoga i drżenie" [Fear and Trembling] (a selection from texts of Kierkegaard), trans. by Maks Bienenstock, *Wielka Literatura Powszechna*, vol. 6, 1934.
"Bądź wola Twoja" [Be Your Will] (An extract from *Practice in Christianity*), trans. by Jacek Woźniakowski, *Znak*, no. 67, 1960, pp. 52–4.
"Ukryte życie miłości" [The Secret Life of Love], trans. by Jacek Susuł, *Znak*, no. 67, 1960, pp. 41–51.
"Co jest budującego w myśli, że wobec Boga nigdy nie mamy racji" ["The Upbuilding That Lies in the Thought That in Relation to God We Are Always in the Wrong"] (an extract from the "Ultimatum," *Either/Or*, part 2), trans. by Hedda Bartoszek, in *Filozofia egzystencjalna* [Existential Philosophy], ed. by Leszek Kołakowski and Krzysztof Pomian, Warsaw: PWN 1965, pp. 59–73.
"Jednostka i tłum" ["The Single Individual," Supplement, *On My Work as an Author*], trans. by Andrzej Ściegienny, in *Filozofia egzystencjalna* [Existential Philosophy], ed. by Leszek Kołakowski and Krzysztof Pomian, Warsaw: PWN 1965, pp. 51–8.
Bojaźń i drżenie. Choroba na śmierć [*Fear and Trembling. The Sickness unto Death*], trans. by Jarosław Iwaszkiewicz, Warsaw: PWN 1966 (2nd ed., 1982).
"Diapsalmata" (an extract from the "Diapsalmata"), trans. by Jarosław Iwaszkiewicz, *Twórczość*, no. 10, 1967, pp. 51–67.
"Listy" [Letters], trans. by Maria Kurecka, *Twórczość*, no. 3, 1967, pp. 66–76.
"Stadia erotyki bezpośredniej, czyli erotyka muzyczna" ["The Immediate Erotic Stages or The Musical-Erotic"], trans. by Antoni Buchner, *Res Facta*, no. 40, 1970.
"Dziennik uwodziciela" ["The Seducer's Diary"], trans. by Jarosław Iwaszkiewicz, *Twórczość*, no. 10, 1974, pp. 8–56 and no. 12, 1974, pp. 11–56.
"Co jest przedmiotem wiary? Krytyka heglizmu" [What is Object of Faith? Critique of Hegelianism] (an extract from *Concluding Unscientific Postscript*, Part Two, Conclusion), trans. by Karol Toeplitz, in *Kierkegaard*, 1975, pp. 270–6.

"Czy biskup Mynster był świadkiem prawdy jednym z autentycznych świadków prawdy i czy to jest prawdą?" ["Was Bishop Mynster a 'Truth Witness,' One of 'the Authentic Truth-Witnesses'—Is *This the Truth?*"], trans. by Karol Toeplitz, in *Kierkegaard*, 1975, pp. 300–4.

"Dialektyka komunikowalności" [Dialectics of Communication] (translation of "The Possibility of Offense is to Deny Direct Communication" (in *SV 1* XII, 130–4 / *PC*, 139–44)), trans. by Karol Toeplitz, in *Kierkegaard*, 1975, pp. 263–9.

Kierkegaard (a monograph about Kierkegaard, which includes extracts from primary texts as well, the concrete fragments are presented below), trans. and ed. by Karol Toeplitz, Warsaw: Wiedza Powszechna 1975 (2nd ed., 1980).

"O powszechnym znaczeniu ironii. Ironia Sokratesa" [About the General Meaning of Irony. The Socratic Irony] (extracts from *The Concept of Irony*), trans. by Karol Toeplitz, in his *Kierkegaard*, 1975, pp. 198–205.

"O różnicy między religijnością A i B" [About the Difference between Religiosity A and B] (extracts from *Concluding Unscientific Postscript*), trans. by Karol Toeplitz, in *Kierkegaard*, 1975, pp. 277–82.

"O znaczeniu Kościoła dla prawdy w chrześcijaństwie" [About the Meaning of the Church for the Christian Truth] (extracts from *Concluding Unscientific Postscript*), trans. by Karol Toeplitz, in *Kierkegaard*, 1975, pp. 228–40.

"Pojęcie lęku" ["The Concept of Anxiety"] (extracts from *The Concept of Anxiety*), trans. by Karol Toeplitz, in *Kierkegaard*, 1975, pp. 222–6.

"Problem uczniów z drugiej ręki" [The Issue of Second-Hand Disciples], trans. by Karol Toeplitz, in *Kierkegaard*, 1975, pp. 305–12.

"Sen Salomona" [Solomon's Dream] (extracts from *Stages on Life's Way*), trans. by Karol Toeplitz in *Kierkegaard*, 1975, pp. 206–8.

"W związku z nowym wydaniem Wprawek w chrześcijaństwie ["For the New Edition of *Practice in Christianity*"] (in *SV 1* XIV, 80–1 / *M*, 69–70), trans. by Karol Toeplitz, in *Kierkegaard*, 1975, pp. 298ff.

Albo–Albo [*Either/Or*], trans. by Jarosław Iwaszkiewicz (vol. 1) and Karol Toeplitz (vol. 2), Warsaw: PWN 1976 (2nd ed., 1982).

"Jak wioślarz w łodzi" [Like an Oarsman in a Boat] (extracts from *Christian Discourses*), trans. by Andrzej Więckowski, *Znak*, no. 12, 1978, pp. 1565–7.

"Uzbrojona neutralność" ["Armed Neutrality"], trans. by Karol Toeplitz, in *Wybór Tekstów Filozoficznych*, Warszawa: SGGW-AR 1978, pp. 21–37.

"Co to jest prawda?" [What is Truth?] (an extract from *Practice in Christianity*, No. III and V), trans. by Karol Toeplitz, in *Kierkegaard*, 1980, pp. 291–8.

"Jedna teza, tylko jedna teza" ["A Thesis—Just One Single One"] (from *The Moment*), trans. by Karol Toeplitz, in *Kierkegaard*, 1980, pp. 286–7.

"Notatki z Dziennika" [Entries from the Journals], trans. by Karol Toeplitz, in *Kierkegaard*, 1980, pp. 312–16.

"Postulat naśladowania" [Demand of Imitation] (extracts from *Judge for Yourself! For Self–Examination Recommended to the Present Age*), trans. by Karol Toeplitz, in *Kierkegaard*, 1980, pp. 273–85.

"Systemu odzwierciedlającego rzeczywistość nie można stworzyć [A System of Existence Cannot Be Given] (an extract from *Concluding Unscientific Postscript*), trans. by Karol Toeplitz, in *Kierkegaard*, 1980, pp. 241–50.

"Wprowadzenie chrystianizmu do świata chrześcijańskiego. Wiedza i historia a chrystologia" [Introduction of Christianity into the Christian World. Knowledge, History and Christology] (extracts from *Practice in Christianity*), trans. by Karol Toeplitz, in *Kierkegaard*, 1980, pp. 241–52.

"Z Dzienników 1847–1854" [Extracts from the Journals, 1847–1854], trans. by Bronisław Świderski, *Kultura*, no. 11, 1985, pp. 125–9.

Okruchy filozoficzne. Chwila [*Philosophical Fragments. The Moment*], trans. by Karol Toeplitz, Warsaw: PWN 1988.

"Uzbrojona neutralność" ["Armed Neutrality"], trans. by Karol Toeplitz, *W Drodze*, nos. 7–8, 1991, pp. 55–64.

"O Lutrze, luteranizmie i protestantyzmie" [About Luther, Lutheranism and Protestantism] (extracts from the journals), trans. by Antoni Szwed, *Znak*, no. 7, 1992, pp. 90–5.

Powtórzenie. Próba psychologii eksperymentalnej przez Constantina Constantinusa [*Repetition. A Venture in Experimental Psychology by Constantin Constantinus*], trans. by Bronisław Świderski, Warsaw: Aletheia 1992.

"Przekład wybranych fragmentów z Dzienników Sørena Kierkegaarda" [Translation of Selected Entries from the Journals of Søren Kierkegaard], trans. by Alina Djakowska, *Archiwum Historii Filozofii i Myśli Społecznej*, no. 37, 1992, pp. 120–7.

"Pojęcie niewinności i lęku" [The Concepts of Innocence and Anxiety] (extracts from *The Concept of Anxiety*), trans. by Antoni Szwed, *Logos i Ethos*, no. 2, 1993, pp. 171–7.

"O niewidzialnej jedności żartu i powagi, eksperymencie i zaczynaniu od nicości [About the Invisible Unity of Jest and Seriousness, Experiment and Starting from Nothingness] (extracts from *Stages on Life's Way*, *Prefaces*, *Concluding Unscientific Postscript*, and the *Journals*), trans. by Alina Djakowska, *Społeczeństwo Otwarte*, no. 9, 1996, pp. i–xii.

Pojęcie lęku: psychologicznie orientujące proste rozważanie o dogmatycznym problemie grzechu pierworodnego przez Vigiliusa Haufniensis [*The Concept of Anxiety. A Simple Psychologially Orienting Deliberation on the Dogmatic Issue of Hereditary Sin by Vigilius Haufniensis*], trans. by Alina Djakowska, Warsaw: Aletheia 1996.

"Ryzyko, prawda subiektywna i dialektyka komunikacji, przekład wybranych fragmentów z pism Sørena Kierkegaarda" [The Risk, Subjective Truth and Dialectics of Communication. Translation of Selected Entries from Søren Kierkegaard's Writings] (extracts from *The Concept of Irony*, *Concluding Unscientific Postscript*, *Stages on Life's Way*, *Christian Discourses*, and the journals), trans. by Alina Djakowska, *Społeczeństwo Otwarte*, nos. 7–8, 1996, pp. i–xii.

"Wstęp do Kończącego Nienaukowego Dopisku" [Introduction to *Concluding Unscientific Postscript*], trans. by Bronisław Świderski, *ResPublica Nowa*, no. 5, 1998, pp. 87–91.

O pojęciu ironii z nieustającym odniesieniem do Sokratesa [*The Concept of Irony. With Continual Reference to Socrates*], trans. by Alina Djakowska, Warsaw: KR 1999.

Dziennik (wybór) [Journals. A Selection], trans. by Antoni Szwed, Lublin: TNKUL 2000.

"List Constantina Constantiusa do Pana Profesora Heiberga..." [Open Letter to Professor Heiberg...from Constantin Constantinus], in *Powtórzenie. Próba psychologii eksperymentalnej przez Constantina Constantiusa* [*Repetition. Prefaces. Open Letter to Professor Heiberg from Constantin Constantinus*], trans. and ed. by Bronisław Świderski, Warsaw: W.A.B. 2000, pp. 33–43.

Pojęcie lęku. Proste rozważania o charakterze psychologicznym, odniesione do dogmatycznego problemu grzechu pierworodnego autorstwa Vigiliusa Haufniensisa [*The Concept of Anxiety. A Simple Psychologially Orienting Deliberation on the Dogmatic Issue of Hereditary Sin by Vigilius Haufniensis*], trans. by Antoni Szwed, Kęty: Antyk 2000 (2nd ed., Warsaw: De Agostini 2002).

Powtórzenie. Przedmowy. List otwarty Constantina Constantiusa do Pana Profesora Heiberga [*Repetition. Prefaces. Open Letter to Professor Heiberg from Constantin Constantinus*], trans. by Bronisław Świderski, Warsaw: W.A.B. 2000.

Wprawki do chrześcijaństwa Anti-climacusa wydane przez P. Kierkegaarda [*Practice in Christianity by Anti-Climacus Edited by S. Kierkegaard*], trans. by Antoni Szwed, Kęty: Antyk 2002 (2nd ed., Warsaw: De Agostini 2004).

Modlitwy [Prayers], trans. by Jacek A. Prokopski, Szczecin: Nowa Krytyka 2003 (2nd ed., 2005).

O trudnościach bycia chrześcijaninem (antologia) [About the Difficulties of Being Christian. An Anthology] (a selection of texts from previous translations), ed. by Kamil Frączek, Kraków: Wydawnictwo M 2004.

II. Secondary Literature on Kierkegaard in Poland

Balcerzan, Edward, "Perpektywy poetyki odbioru" [Perspectives of the Poetics of Reception], in *Problemy socjologii literatury*, ed. by Janusz Sławiński, Wrocżław 1971, pp. 79–95.

Bocheński, Józef Maria, "Subiektywne myślenie Kierkegaarda" [The Subjective Thinking of Kierkegaard], in *Współczesne metody myślenia*, Poznań: W Drodze 1992, pp. 31–2.

Chojecki, Andrzej, "A jednak nie mogę powiedzieć: ja" [And yet I Cannot Say: I], in *Tożsamości Kierkegaarda*, ed. by Alina Djakowska et al., pp. 137–44.

Chojnacki, Hieronim, "Uwodzicielstwo estetyczne" [Aesthetical Seduction], in *Tożsamości Kierkegaarda*, ed. by Alina Djakowska et al., pp. 145–55.

Djakowska, Alina, "Dyskurs pseudonimów" [The Pseudonyms' Discourse], *Archiwum Historii Filozofii i Myśli Społecznej*, no. 37, 1992, pp. 117–9.

— "Marginalia," in *Pojęcie lęku* [*The Concept of Anxiety*], Warsaw: Aletheia 1996, pp. 195–208.

— "O słowach, które się ruszają" [About Words, Which are Moving Themselves], in *O pojęciu ironii* [*The Concept of Irony*], Warsaw: KR 1999, pp. 321–33.

— "Jestem Pseudonimem" [I am Pseudonym], in *Tożsamości Kierkegaarda*, ed. by Alina Djakowska et al., pp. 79–94.

Djakowska, Alina, Artur Przybysławski and Aldona Schiffmann (eds.), *Tożsamości Kierkegaarda* [Kierkegaard's Identities], Kraków: Aureus 1999 (special number of the journal *Principia*, vol. 23).
Filek, Jacek, *Ontologizacja odpowiedzialności. Analityczne i historyczne wprowadzenie w problematykę* [The Ontologization of Responsibility. Analytical and Historical Introduction in Problem] Kraków: Wyd. Baran i Suszczyński 1996, pp. 45–59.
— *Filozofia odpowiedzialności XX wieku* [The Philosophy of Responsibility in the Twentieth Century], Kraków: ZNAK 2003 (see pp. 19–21).
Fryszman, Alex, "Dialog w teatrze powtórzenia" [Dialogue in the Theatre of Repetition], *Zeszyty Literackie*, no. 47, 1993.
— "Być może Bachtin? Kierkegaard versus Bachtin" [Bachtin Perhaps? Kierkegaard versus Bachtin], *Teksty Drugie*, no. 1, 1996, pp. 139–48.
— "Pojęcie lęku" ["The Concept of Anxiety"], in *Znak*, no. 12, 1996, pp. 136–42.
— "Komizm i tragizm ofiary" [The Comic and the Tragic Nature of the Victim], in *Tożsamości Kierkegaarda*, ed. by Alina Djakowska et al., pp. 95–116.
Gombrowicz, Witold, "Egzystencjalizm" [Existentialism], in Francesco M. Cataluccio and Jerzy Illg, in *Gombrowicz filozof*, Kraków: Znak 1991, pp. 128–40.
Gorski, Artur, "Z dziennika uwodziciela" ["The Seducer's Diary"], *Zycie*, no. 3, 1899.
— "Søren Kierkegaard: Albo-albo" [Søren Kierkegaard: *Either/Or*], *Ateneum*, vol. 102, no. 3, 1901, pp. 602–25.
Granat, Wincenty, "Egzystencjalizm w świetle nauki o łasce i grzechu" [Existentialism in the Light of the Doctrines of Grace and Sin], in *Roczniki Teologiczno-Kanoniczne*, ed. by Piotr Kałura and Ludwik Krupa, Lublin: KUL 1956, pp. 191–229.
Gromczyński, Wiesław, "Wprowadzenie do 'filozofii' Kierkegaarda [Introduction to Kierkegaard's "Philosophy"], *Studia Filozoficzne*, no. 4, 1975, pp. 115–44.
— "Aktualność Kierkegaarda" [The Importance of Kierkegaard], *Człowiek i Światopogląd*, nos. 2–3, 1979, pp. 24–43.
— "Dialektyka komunikacji etycznej wedle Kierkegaarda [The Dialectics of Ethical Communication According to Kierkegaard], *Studia Filozoficzne*, no. 11, 1980, pp. 99–114.
— "O możliwości chrześcijańskiego egzystencjalizmu" [About the Possibility of Christian Existentialism], *Studia Filozoficzne*, no. 6, 1984, pp. 89–107.
— "Czy Kierkegaard był irracjonalistą? Kilka uwag o porównaniu Kierkegaarda z Pascalem" [Was Kierkegaard an Irrationalist? Several Remarks on the Comparison between Kierkegaard and Pascal], in *Tożsamości Kierkegaarda*, ed. by Alina Djakowska et al., pp. 157–70.
Hulka–Laskowski, Paweł, "Sören Kierkegaard," *Wiadomości Literackie*, no. 4, 1935, p. 2.
Ilustrowana encyklopedia, [Illustrated Encyclopaedia], vols. 1–6, ed. by Stanisław Lam, Warsaw: Trzaska, Evert i Michalski 1927–37, vol. 2 (1932), p. 912.
Iwaszkiewicz, Jarosław, "Nad Kierkegaardem" [About Kierkegaard], *Twórczość*, no. 5, 1966, pp. 34–49.

— "Od tłumacza" [From the Translator], in *Bojaźń i drżenie. Choroba na Śmierć*, Warsaw: PWN 1969, pp. ix–xxxix (republished in Iwaszkiewicz, *Szkice o literaturze skandynawskiej*, pp. 198–226).
— "Od tłumacza" [From the Translator], in *Albo-Albo*, vols. 1–2, Warsaw: PWN 1976, vol. 1, pp. vii–xii (republished in Iwaszkiewicz, *Szkice o literaturze skandynawskiej*, pp. 350–4).
— *Szkice o literaturze skandynawskiej* [Drafts on Scandinavian Literature], Warsaw: Czytelnik 1977.
Jakubowska, Janina, "Dialektyka transcendencji i immanencji. Od Kierkegaarda do Robinsona" [The Dialectics of the Transcendence and Immanence. From Kierkegaard to Robinson], *Studia Filozoficzne*, no. 5, 1971, pp. 136–52.
— "Człowiek i wspólnota we współczesnej myśli protestanckiej. Kierkegaard–Tillich–Bonhoeffer" [Man and Community in Contemporary Protestant Thinking. Kierkegaard–Tillich–Bonhoeffer], *Filozoficzne problemy współczesnego chrześcijaństwa* [Philosophical Problems of Contemporary Christianity], vol. 5, 1973, pp. 213–43.
— "Søren Kierkegaard-dialektyka 'bytu wobec Boga' " [Søren Kierkegaard— The Dialectics of "Being before God"], in her *Pawła Tillicha sakralizacja rzeczywistości* [Sacralization of the Reality of Paul Tillich], Warsaw: PWN 1975, pp. 29–34.
Janion, Maria, *Romantyzm, rewolucja, marksizm* [Romanticism, Revolution, Marxism], Gdansk: Wydawnictwo Morskie 1972 (*Colloquia Gdańskie*).
— *Kobiety i duch inności* [Women and the Spirit of Otherness], Warsaw: Sic! 1996, pp. 126–30.
Jaranowski, Marcin, "Richard Rorty a wiara religijna" [Richard Rorty and Religious Belief], *Znak*, no. 1, 2001, pp. 65–85.
Jędraszewski, Marek, "Przyciągnij nas do siebie" [Attract Us to Yourself], in his *Filozofia i modlitwa* [Philosophy and Prayer], Poznań: W Drodze 1986, pp. 82–94.
Karski, Karol, *Teologia protestancka XX wieku* [Protestant Theology in the Twentieth Century], Warsaw 1967 passim.
Kasperski, Edward, "Kierkegaard jako krytyk literacki" [Kierkegaard as a Literary Critic], *Miesięcznik Literacki*, no. 9 1988, pp. 59–68.
— "Poeta antypoeta Kierkegaard" [Poet Anti-Poet Kierkegaard], *Poezja*, no. 3, 1989, pp. 61–72.
— "Kierkegaard o komunikacji" [Kierkegaard on Communication], in his *Dialog i dialogizm. Idee—formy— tradycje* [Dialogue and Dialogism. Ideas, Forms, and Traditions], Warsaw: Elipsa 1994, pp. 11–147.
— "Poznanie i sztuka egzystowania u Kierkegaarda" [Cognition and Existential Art in Kierkegaard], in *Tożsamości Kierkegaarda*, ed. by Alina Djakowska et al., pp. 117–36.
— *Kierkegaard. Antropologia i dyskurs o człowieku* [Kierkegaard. Anthropology and Discourse on Man], Pułtusk: WHS 2003.
Kaszyński, Stefan Hubert, "O duńskiej nowelistyce" [On Danish Short Story Writing], in *Anegdoty losu. Antologia nowel i opowiadań duńskich* [Fate Anecdote. Anthology of Short Stories and Danish Stories], Poznań: Wydawnictwo Poznańskie 1976, pp. 5–19.

— *Zarys historii literatury duńskiej* [Outline of the History of Danish Literature], Poznań: Uniwersytet im. Adama Mickiewicza 1976.

— "Kierkegaard Søren Aabye," in *Słownik pisarzy skandynawskich* [Dictionary of Scandinavian Writers], ed. by Zenona Ciesielski, Warsaw: Wiedza Powszechna 1991, pp. 58–61.

— "Literatura duńska" [Danish Literature], in *Dzieje literatur europejskich* [History of European Literatures], vols. 1–3, ed. by Władysława Floryana, Warsaw: PWN 1979–89, vol. 2 (1982), pp. 177–9.

Kaszyński, Stefan Hubert and Maria Krysztofiak, *Dzieje literatury duńskiej* [History of the Danish Literature], Poznań: WAM 1985 (*Seria Filologia Skandynawska*, vol. 3).

Kesselring, Rudolf, "Søren Kierkegaard. Indywidualizm religijny Kierkcgaarda i jego wpływ na współczesną teologię ewangelicką" [Søren Kierkegaard. Kierkegaard's Religious Individuality and his Influence on Contemporary Lutheran Theology], in *Rocznik Teologiczny*, vols. 1–4, Warsaw: Wydział Teologji Ewangelickiej 1936–39, vol. 1 (1936), pp. 101–33.

Klentak-Zabłocka, Małgorzata, "Spotkanie na skraju przepaści. Kafka i Kierkegaard" [Meeting on the Edge of Abyss. Kafka and Kierkegaard], *Literatura na Świecie*, no. 6, 1986, pp. 256–62.

— "Etyka ofiary. O recepcji Kierkegaarda we wczesnych pismach Lukacsa" [Ethics of the Victim. About Kierkegaard's Reception in the Early Writings of Lukács], *AUNC*, vol. 262, 1993, pp. 33–47.

Kołaczkowski, Leszek, "Filozofia egzystencji i porażka egzystencji" [The Philosophy of Existence and the Defeat of Existence], in *Filozofia egzystencjalna* [Existential Philosophy], ed. by Leszek Kołakowski and Krzysztof Pomian, Warsaw: PWN 1965, pp. 7–27.

— Søren Kierkegaard. Biografia i bibliografia" [Søren Kierkegaard. Biography and Bibliography] in *Filozofia egzystencjalna* [Existential Philosophy], ed. by Leszek Kołakowski and Krzysztof Pomian, Warsaw: PWN 1965, pp. 49–51.

— "Kierkegaard" in *Słownik filozofów* [Dictionary of Philosophers], ed. by Irena Krońska, Warsaw: PWN 1966, pp. 306–8.

Kołaczkowski, Stefan, "Literatura duńska—S. Kierkegaard" [Danish literature— S. Kierkegaard], in *Wielka Literatura Powszechna* [Great Works of World Literature], vols. 1–4, ed. by Stanisław Lam, Warsaw: Trzaska, Evert i Michalski 1930–34, vol. 3, 1932, pp. 627–9.

Kossak, Jerzy, "Kierkegaard i Jaspers" [Kierkegaard and Jaspers], *Zeszyty Teoretyczne Argumentów*, vol. 1, no. 24, 1966, pp. 49–64.

— "Prorok zagubionych–Søren Kierkegaard, oraz Chrześcijańscy i laiccy kontynuatorzy Kierkegaarda" [Prophet of Loses, and Christian and Lay Followers of Kierkegaard], in *Egzystencjalizm w filozofii i literaturze* [Existentialism in Philosophy and Literature], Warsaw: Książka i Wiedza 1976, pp. 66–82.

Kowalczyk, Stanisław, *Podstawy światopoglądu chrześcijańskiego* [Foundations of a Christian Philosophy of Life], Warsaw: Ośrodek Dokumentacji i Studiów Społecznych 1979.

— "Søren Kierkegaard: Paradoksy wiary" [Søren Kierkegaard: Paradoxes of Faith], in his *Bóg w myśli współczesnej. Problematyka Boga i religii u czołowych myślicieli współczesnych* [God in Contemporary Thinking. The Problematics of God and Religion at Leading Contemporary Thinkers], Wrocław: Wyd. Wrocławskiej Księgarni Archidiecezjalnej 1979, pp. 371–91.

— "Bóg w myśli współczesnej" [God in Contemporary Thought], in his *Bóg w myśli współczesnej. Problematyka Boga i religii u czołowych myślicieli współczesnych* [God in Contemporary Thinking. The Problematics of God and Religion in Leading Contemporary Thinkers], Wrocław: Wyd. Wrocławskiej Księgarni Archidiecezjalnej 1982, pp. 105–25.

Krzysztofiak-Kaszyńska Maria, *Dansk litteratur. Tekster til undervisningsbrug. Wypisy z historii literatury duńskiej. Wprowadzenie do historii literatury duńskiej* [Extracts from the History of Danish Literature. Introduction to the History of Danish Literature], Poznań: Uniwersytet im. Adama Mickiewicza w Poznaniu 1982, pp. 5–22 (on Kierkegaard, see pp. 11–13; Original texts: Extracts from "The Unhappiest One," pp. 162–70 and "Diapsalmata," pp. 170–87.)

Kwiatkowski, Stanisław, "Egzystencjalne uwarunkowania potrzeby myślenia: Kierkegaard, Nietzsche" [Existential Conditions of the Need for Thought: Kierkegaard, Nietzsche, Heidegger], *Studia Filozoficzne*, no. 4, 1987, pp. 51–65.

Lubańska, Stefania, *Pascal i Kierkegaard-filozofowie rozpaczy i wiary* [Pascal and Kierkegaard—Philosophers of Faith and Despair], Kraków: Universitas 2001.

Malewska, Hanna, "Søren Kierkegaard," *Znak*, no. 1, 1946, pp. 110–2.

Marias, Julian, "Gatunki literackie w filozofii" [Literary Genres in Philosophy], *Pamiętnik Literacki*, no. 2, 1979, pp. 309–20.

Markowski, Michal P., "Nuda i tożsamość" [Boredom and Identity], in *Tożsamości Kierkegaarda*, ed. by Alina Djakowska et al., pp. 43–56.

Mikołajczyk, Hubert, "Søren Kierkegaard—absolutyzacja istnienia ludzkiego" [Søren Kierkegaard—The Absolutism of the Human Being], *Słupskie Prace Humanistyczne*, no. 6a, 1985, pp. 179–96.

— *Kierkegaard, Kant a antropologia filozoficzna* [Kierkegaard, Kant and Philosophical Anthropology], Słupsk: WSP 1990.

— *Antropologia Kierkegaarda w świetle Kantowskiej filozofii praktycznej* [Kierkegaard's Anthropology in the light of Kantian Practical Philosophy], Słupsk: WSP 1995.

Miś, Andrzej, "Egzystencjalizm Sørena Kierkegaarda" [Søren Kierkegaard's Existentialism], in his *Filozofia współczesna: główne nurty* [Contemporary Philosophy], Warszawa: Scholar, 1995, pp. 67–74.

Moryń, Mariusz, "Kierkegaard, Søren," in *Słownik filozofów: filozofia powszechna* [Dictionary of Philosophers], ed. by Bolesław Andrzejewski, Poznań: Dom Wydawniczy Rebis 1996, pp. 133–6.

Niecikowski, Jerzy, "Stirner, Kierkegaard—krytycy Hegla" [Stirner, Kierkegaard—Critics of Hegel], *Archiwum Historii Filozofii i Myśli Społecznej*, no. 13, 1967, pp. 141–71.

Niemczuk, Andrzej, *Wolność egzystencjalna. Kant i Kierkegaard* [Existential Freedom. Kant and Kierkegaard], Lublin: Wyd. Uniwersytetu Marii Curie-Skłodowskiej 1995.

Palacz, Ryszard, "Søren A. Kierkegaard, czyli zagadka Sfinksa" [Søren A. Kierkegaard or The Sphinx Enigma], in his *Klasycy filozofii* [Classics of Philosophy], Warsaw: Krajowa Agencja Wydawnicza 1988, pp. 200–5.

Pastuszka, Józef, *Współczesne kierunki w filozofji religji* [Present Tendencies in the Philosophy of Religion], Warsaw: skł. gł. Księg. św. Wojciecha 1932, pp. 112–14; p. 121.

— "Postawy życiowe według S. Kiekegaarda" [Life Attitude According to S. Kierkegaard], *Rocznik Filozoficzny*, vol. 4, 1958, pp. 105–25.

— "Marksizm—egzystencjalizm—myśl chrześcijańska" [Marxism—Existentialism—Christian Thinking], *Studia Filozoficzne*, no. 5, 1971, pp. 153–72.

Płużański, Tadeusz, "Kierkegaard contra Hegel," *Człowiek i światopogląd*, no. 6, 1969.

— "Kierkegaard contra Hegel; Kierkegaard— Mounier," in *Paradoks w nowożytnej filozofii chrześcijańskiej* [The Paradox in Contemporary Christian Philosophy], Warsaw: PWN 1970, pp. 58–123; pp. 190–202.

— *Kierkegaardowska koncepcja człowieka* [The Kierkegaardian Conception of Man], Warsaw: Bibl. St. Społ. WSNS 1973.

— *Paradoks w nowożytnej filozofii* [Paradox in the Modern Philosophy], Warsaw: PWN 1970.

Pomian, Krzysztof, "Egzystencjalizm i filozofia współczesna" [Existentialism and Contemporary Philosophy], in *Filozofia egzystencjalna* [Existential Philosophy], ed. by Leszek Kołakowski and Krzysztof Pomian, Warsaw: PWN 1965, pp. 29–48.

— "Niewczesność i współczesność Kierkegaarda" [Inopportunity and the Present Age of Kierkegaard], in his *Człowiek pośród rzeczy. Szkice historycznofilozoficzne* [A Man among Things. Outlines in the History of Philosophy], Warsaw: Czytelnik 1973, pp. 100–19.

Pospiszyl, Kazimierz, *Tristan i Don Juan, czyli odcienie miłości mężczyzny w kulturze europejskiej* [Tristan and Don Juan as the Shades of Man's Love in European Culture], Warsaw: Iskry 1986.

Prokopski, Jacek Aleksander, "Dialektyczna wirtuozeria pseudonimów według S. Kierkegaarda" [Dialectic Virtuosity of the Pseudonyms according to S. Kierkegaard], *Heksis*, nos. 1–2, 1999, pp. 92–102.

— "Søren Kierkegaard—wiara egzystencjalna" [Søren Kierkegaard—Existential Faith], *Myśl Protestancka*, no. 1, 1999, pp. 20–30.

— "Szkic o egzystencjalnej obecności wiary u S. Kierkegaarda" [Draft on the Existential Presence of Faith at S. Kierkegaard], *Wrocławski Przegląd Teologiczny*, no. 2, 1999, pp. 77–91.

— "Kierkegaard o bezpośredniej i pośredniej komunikacji religijnej" [Kierkegaard on Direct and Indirect Religious Communication], *Zeszyty Naukowe KUL*, nos. 3–4, 2000, pp. 55–65.

— "Paradoks Chrystusa w filozofii Kierkegaarda" [The Paradox of Christ in Kierkegaard's Philosophy], *Myśl Protestancka*, no. 1, 2000, pp. 31–4.

— "Søren Kierkegaard—nadracjonalny paradoks wiary" [Søren Kierkegaard—Superrational Paradox of Faith], *Nowa Krytyka*, no. 11, 2000, pp. 183–200.

— "Kilka uwag o irracjonalnym unicestwieniu u S. Kierkegaarda" [A Few Remarks on Irrational Annihilation in S. Kierkegaard], *Myśl Protestancka*, no. 1, 2001, pp. 47–55.

— *Søren Kierkegaard: dialektyka paradoksu wiary* [Søren Kierkegaard. The Dialectics of the Paradox of Faith], Wrocław: Arboretum 2002.

— *O rozmowie Kierkegaarda z Panem Bogiem* [On the Discourse of Kierkegaard with God], Szczecin: Nowa Krytyka 2003.

Puszko, Hanna, "Søren Kierkegaard," in her *Być Stendhalem i Spinozą* [To be Stendhal and Spinoza], Warsaw: Scholar 1997, pp. 100–2.

Rogalski, Aleksander, "Søren Kierkegaard—poeta i chrześcijanin" [Søren Kierkegaard—Poet and Christian], in his *Myśl i wyobraźnia. Szkice do portretów* [Thought and Immagination. Sketches to Portraits], Warsaw: Pax 1977, pp. 100–2.

— *Tryptyk miłosny: Sören Kierkegaard—Regine Olsen, Franz Kafka—Felice Bauer, Émile Verhaeren —Marthe Massin* [Amorous Triptych], Warsaw: Państ. Instytut Wydawniczy 1977 (on Kierkegaard, see pp. 19–193).

Rowiński, Cezary, "Kierkegaard—Don Kichot filozoficzny" [Kierkegaard—Philosophical Don Quixote], *Miesięcznik Literacki*, no. 9, 1986, pp. 107–22.

Sarnowski, Stanisław, "Kierkegaard: absolutyzacja istnienia ludzkiego" [Kierkegaard: Absolutism of Human Being], in *Zmierzch absolutu?* [Absolut Decline?], Warsaw 1974, pp. 46–52.

Sawicki, Franciszek, "P. Kierkegaard," *Przegląd Powszechny*, vol. 2, no. 225, 1948, pp. 81–91.

Siemek, Jerzy, "Czytając Kierkegaarda" [Reading Kierkegaard], *Polityka*, no. 20, 1970.

Siemianowski, Andrzej, "Między zracjonalizowana wiarą a irracjonalizmem" [Between Rationalized Faith and Irrationalism], in *Odczytywanie myśli Pascala*, ed. by Andrzej Siemianowski [Reading out of Pascal's Thought], Poznań: Wyd. Fundacji Humaniora 1997, pp. 17–19.

Siemianowski, Antoni, "O stawaniu się sobą, Filozofia S. Kierkegaarda" [On Becoming Himself according to S. Kierkegaard], *W Drodze*, no. 11, 1975, pp. 7–30.

Strózewski, Włdisław, "O Kierkegaardzie" [About Kierkegaard], *Znak*, no. 67, 1960, pp. 126–32.

Świderski, Bronisław, "Postawić na Powtórzenie" [To Bet on "Repetition"], in *Próba psychologii eksperymentalnej przez Constantina Constantinusa* [*Repetition. A Venture in Experimental Psychology by Constantin Constantinus*], Warsaw: Aletheia 1992, pp. 9–16.

— "Kierkegaard jako powieściopisarz" [Kierkegaard as a Novelist], *Teksty*, no. 2, 1994, pp. 169–75.

— "Melancholia jest trójkątem" [Melancholy is a Triangle], *ResPublica Nowa*, no. 6, 1994, pp. 20–2.

— "Kierkegaardowska teoria komunikacji" [The Kierkegaardian Theory of Communication], in his *Gdańsk i Ateny. O demokracji bezpośredniej w Polsce* [Gdańsk and Ateny. About Direct Democracy in Poland], Warsaw: PAN 1996, pp. 129–34.

— "Żyć z Kierkegaardem po polsku" [To Live with Kierkegaard in a Polish Way], *ResPublica Nowa*, no. 5, 1997, pp. 51–6.
— "Przedmowa do Wstępu do Kończącego Nienaukowego Dopisku" [Foreword to the Introduction of *Concluding Unscientific Postscript*], *ResPublica Nowa*, no. 5, 1998, pp. 86ff.
— "Hurra! Nareszcie jedna Europa!" [Hurray! At Last One Europe] (Omówienie [Discussion] of *A Literary Review*), *ResPublica Nowa*, no. 3, 1999, p. 126.
— "Replika Kierkegaarda" [Kierkegaard's Replica], in *Tożsamości Kierkegaarda*, ed. by Alina Djakowska et al., 1999, pp. 57–78.
— "Dar" [Gift], in *Powtórzenie. Przedmowy. List otwarty Constantina Constantiusa do Pana Profesora Heiberga* [*Repetition. Prefaces. Open Letter to Professor Heiberg from Constantin Constantinus*], Warsaw: W.A.B. 2000, pp. 343–68.
— "Ludzie wolą być Żydami" [People would much more prefer to be Jewish], *Tygodnik Powszechny*, no. 33, 2004, Supplement.
— "Blizni—to ty?" [My Neighbour—Is it You?], *Przeglad Polityczny*, no. 70, 2005, pp. 2–20.
Swieżawski, Stefan, *Rozum i tajemnica* [Reason and Mystery], Kraków: ZNAK 1960.
Szwed, Antoni, "Jak czytać Kierkegaarda" [How to Read Kierkegaard], *Tygodnik Powszechny*, no. 25, 1989, p. 1.
— "Biblia i Wiara według Kierkegaarda" [The Bible and Faith According to Kierkegaard], *Znak*, no. 3, 1991, pp. 71–9.
— *Miedzy wolnością a prawdą egzystencji: studium myśli S. Kierkegaarda* [Between Freedom and the Truth of Existence. A Study of S. Kierkegaard's Thought], Kraków: Universitas 1991 (2nd ed., Kęty: Antyk 1999).
— "O niemożliwości dowodów na istnienie Boga według Kierkegaarda" [About the Possibility and Impossibility of Proofs Concerning God's Existence According to Kierkegaard], *Analecta Cracoviensia*, vol. 22, 1991, pp. 49–60.
— "Kierkegaarda fenomenologia doświadczenia wolności" [Kierkegaard's Phenomenology of the Experience of Freedom], *Logos i Ethos*, no. 2, 1992, pp. 156–60.
— "O metodzie filozofii S. Kierkegaarda" [About the Philosophical Method of S. Kierkegaard], *Logos i Ethos*, no. 2, 1992, pp. 39–45.
— "Wolność i wiara w filozofii S. Kierkegaarda" [Freedom and Faith in S. Kierkegaard's Philosophy], *Logos i Ethos*, no. 3, 1993, pp. 179–84.
— S. Kierkegaarda próba przezwyciężenia estetycznego chrześcijaństwa" [S. Kierkegaard's Attempt to Overcome Aesthetic Christianity], *Ethos*, vol. 40, 1997, pp. 169–78.
— "Komunikacja pośrednia jako podstawowa metoda filozofii egzystencji Kierkegaarda" [Indirect Communication as a Fundamental Method of Kierkegaard's Existential Philosophy], in *Tożsamości Kierkegaarda*, ed. by Alina Djakowska et al., pp. 171–84.
— "Kierkegaard," Entry in *Encyklopedia Katolicka* [Catholic Encyclopaedia], vols. 1–10, ed. by Feliks Gryglewicz et al., Lublin: TNKUL, 1995–2004, vol. 8 (2000), pp. 1410–11.

— "Przedmowa tłumacza" [Translator's Foreword], in *Pojęcie lęku. Proste rozważania o charakterze psychologicznym, odniesione do dogmatycznego problemu grzechu pierworodnego autorstwa Vigiliusa Haufniensisa* [*The Concept of Anxiety. A Simple Psychologially Orienting Deliberation on the Dogmatic Issue of Hereditary Sin by Vigilius Haufniensis*], trans. by Antoni Szwed, Kęty: Antyk 2000, pp. 3–10.

— "Przedmowa tłumacza" [Translator's Foreword], in *Dziennik* [Journals], Lublin: TNKUL 2001, pp. 5–38.

— "U źródeł powagi egzystencji w myśli Kierkegaarda" [The Source of Existential Seriousness in Kierkegaard's Thought], in *Jest-że dla prawdy przyszłość jaka? Prace dedykowane Profesorowi Karolowi Toeplitzowi*, ed. by Adam A. Korzus [Is there a Fututre for the Truth? Works Dedicated to Prof. Karol Toeplitz], Toruń: Wyd. Adam Marszałek 2001, pp. 128–41.

— "O komunikacji pojęcia powagi egzystencji" [About the Communication of the Concept of Existential Seriousness], in *Człowiek i polityka, Księga jublileuszowa z okazji 65. urodzin Profesora Jerzego Gałkowskiego*, ed. by Jan Kłos and Andrzej Noras [Man and Politics. Jubilee Book on the 65th Anniversary of Prof. Jerzy Gałkowski Birthday], Lublin: KUL 2002, pp. 253–9.

— "Przedmowa tłumacza" [Translator's Foreword], in *Wprawki do chrześcijaństwa Anti–climacusa wydane przez P. Kierkegaarda* [*Practice in Christianity by Anti–Climacus Edited by S. Kierkegaard*], trans. by Antoni Szwed, Kęty: Antyk 2002, pp. 5–14.

Tatarkiewicz, Władysław, "Søren Kierkegaard," in *Historia filozofii* [A History of Philosophy], vols. 1–3, Warsaw: PWN 1970, vol. 3, pp. 63–8.

Terlecki, Tymon, *Egzystencjalizm chrześcijański* [Christian Existentialism], Londyn: Oficyna Poetów i Malarzy 1958.

— *Krytyka personalistyczna. Egzystencjalizm chrześcijański* [Personalistic Critique. Christian Existentialism], Kraków: Znak 1987.

Toeplitz, Karol, "Kierkegaard a Luter i Reformacja" [Kierkegaard, Luther and the Reformation], *Gdańskie Zeszyty Humanistyczne* (*Seria Filozofia*), vol. 1, 1965, pp. 97–140 (republished, *Rocznik Teologiczny Chrześcijańskiej Akademii Teologicznej*, no. 2, 1993, pp. 77–17)

— "Konflikt Abrahama, próba egzystencjalizacji religii prawa" [Abraham's Problem: An Attempt to Create an Existential Religion of Law], *Gdańskie Zeszyty Humanistyczne* (*Seria Filozofia*), no. 2, 1966, pp. 29–71.

— "Jednostka a społeczeństwo w filozofii Kierkegaarda" [The Individual and Society in Kierkegaard's Philosophy], *Gdańskie Zeszyty Humanistyczne* (*Seria Filozofia*), no. 3, 1967, pp. 85–97.

— *Wiara i wybór moralny u S. Kierkegaarda, rozprawa doktorska* [Faith and Moral Choice in S. Kierkegaard's Doctoral Dissertation], Warsaw: Uniwersytet Warszawski 1967.

— "Teoria osobowości estetycznej wg S. Kierkegaarda" [The Theory of the Aesthetic Personality According to Kierkegaard], *Gdańskie Zeszyty Humanistyczne* (*Seria Filozofia*), no. 1, 1968.

— "Irracjonalizm przeciwko racjonalizmowi. Kierkegaard przeciwko Heglowi" [Irrationalism contra Rationalism. Kierkegaard contra Hegel], *Studia Filozoficzne*, no. 4, 1970, pp. 78–98.

— "Egzystencjalizm religijny" [Religious Existentialism], *Euhemer*, no. 2, 1971, pp. 105–10.

— "Kierkegaard jako krytyk Kościoła" [Kierkegaard as a Church Critic], *Euhemer*, no. 3, 1971, pp. 79–93.

— "Problem egzystencji i esencji w filozofii S. Kierkegaarda" [The Problem of Existence and Essence in Kierkegaard's Philosophy], *Archiwum Historii Filozofii i Myśli Społecznej*, no. 17, 1971, pp. 351–81.

— *Kierkegaard* (a monograph about Kierkegaard, which includes extracts from primary texts as well), Warsaw: Wiedza Powszechna 1975 (2nd ed., 1980).

— "Bądź własnym. Sędzią posłowie tłumacza t. 2 Albo-albo" [Be Your Own Judge. Translator's epilogue to *Either/Or*, vol. 2], *Życie Literackie*, no. 41, 1977.

— "Bajka o śniegu, czyli recenzja z książki *Albo–albo*" [Fairy Tale on Snow or a Review of *Either/Or*], *Życie Literackie*, no. 1366, 1978.

— "Dialektyka jakościowa Sørena Kierkegaarda" [Søren Kierkegaard's Qualitative Dialectics], *Studia Filozoficzne*, no. 2, 1980, pp. 69–81.

— "Bibliografia światowa opracowań Kierkegaarda" [World Bibliography of Kierkegaard's Elaborations], *Studia Filozoficzne*, no. 3, 1981, pp. 157–76.

— "Dialektyka jakościowa" [Qualitative Dialectics], in his *Egzystencjalizm jako zjawisko kulturowe* [Existentialism as a Cultural Phenomenon], Gdańsk: AM 1983, pp. 34–55.

— "Egzystencjalna resubiektywizacja" [Existential Resubjectivization], in *Egzystencjalizm jako zjawisko kulturowe* [Existentialism as a Cultural Phaenomenon], Gdańsk: AM 1983 pp. 56–70.

— "O możliwości i niemożliwości istnienia 'chrześcijańskiego egzystencjalizmu'" [About the Possibility and Impossibility of the Existence of a "Christian Existentialism"], *Studia Filozoficzne*, no. 7, 1983, pp. 3–26.

— "F. Kafki i J.P. Sartre'a reinterpretacja 'Konfliktu Abrahama' " [F. Kafka and J.P. Sartre's Reinterpretation of the "Abraham Conflict"], *Gdańskie Zeszyty Humanistyczne*, vol. 2, no. 28, 1985, pp. 41–55.

— "Nad Kierkegaardem i egzystencjalizmem" [About Kierkegaard and Existentialism], in *Okruchy filozoficzne. Chwila* [*Philosophical Fragments. The Moment*], Warsaw: PWN 1988, pp. vii–lxvi.

— "...Sola scriptura" [By Scripture Alone], *Rocznik Filozoficzny*, vol. 23, no. 1, 1990, pp. 235–45.

— "Teologiczne źródła filozofii egzystencjalnych" [Theological Sources of Existential Philosophies], *Rocznik Teologiczny Chrześcijańskiej Akademii Teologicznej*, no. 2, 1991.

Warkocz, Albert, "Søren Kierkegaard czyli genera egzystincjalizme" [Søren Kierkegaard and the Origin of Existentialism], *Nauka i Sztuka*, vol. 4, no. 3, 1948, pp. 25–37.

— "Blaski i cienie egzystencjalizmu Kiekegaarda" [Brightnesses and Shadows in Kierkegaard's Existentialism], *Ateneum kapłańskie*, vol. 5, no. 52, 1950, pp. 365–80.

III. Secondary Literature on Kierkegaard's Reception in Poland

Chojnacki, Hieronim, "Bibliografia polska Sørena Kierkegaarda [Polish Bibliography of Søren Kierkegaard], in *Tożsamości Kierkegaarda*, ed. by Alina Djakowska et al., pp. 185–92.
— "Kierkegaard in Poland since 1965," *Kierkegaard Studies. Yearbook*, 2001, pp. 341–51.
Djakowska, Alina and Alex Fryszman, "Drei Stadien in der polnischen Rezeption von *Furcht und Zittern* und *Die Wiederholung*," *Kierkegaard Studies. Yearbook*, 2002, pp. 310–30.

PART III

Eastern Europe

Russia:
Kierkegaard's Reception through Tsarism, Communism, and Liberation

Darya Loungina

Russian readers have had over ten different encounters with Søren Kierkegaard, and each time he appeared not as an old acquaintance but as a new person. This stranger did not make a very prominent initial appearance; he spoke either in a very simple or in a very sophisticated manner, often contradicted himself and was hard to listen to. Failure to understand him gave rise to embarrassment. Trying to overcome this embarrassment, people hastened to find some justification for him, though more often than not they ended up condemning him. After people formed an opinion about him, he was forgotten. Later he appeared again, and even today the process of getting acquainted with him has not still been completed.

I. The Beginning: Two Centuries Ago

The first encounter took place in 1878 by sheer coincidence. The name Søren Kierkegaard was mentioned in a letter received by Ivan Goncharov (1812–91) from his long-time correspondent Peter Emmanuel Hansen (1846–1930).[1] Hansen was born in Copenhagen, but in 1871 his fortunes brought him to Omsk, Siberia, where he started working as the head of a telegraph school and, in his spare time, made his first steps in translation. Regardless of how far away Hansen was from Denmark, the figure of Søren Kierkegaard always lingered in his memory—not the actual image but the mental picture, which had been passed on to young Hansen by the actors of the Royal Theater, who had known Kierkegaard personally. Goncharov directed Hansen, in his enthusiasm for Kierkegaard, to Leo Tolstoy (1828–1910). Thus the first texts of the Danish thinker in Russian were prepared especially for Tolstoy

---

[1] *Переписка Ивана Гончарова* [Correspondence of Ivan Goncharov], ed. by M.P. Alekseev, Moscow: Nauka 1961 (*Литературный архив*, vol. 6), p. 73. Hansen wrote: "There is a Danish writer [Søren Kierkegaard], who speaks much more eloquently and convincingly, and if I translate for you different passages from his works, I, perhaps, could convince you! He was a *dialectician!* 'The devil himself cannot argue with him,' someone said about him, and you would love him!"

himself, who had a great influence on Hansen and whose story *The Death of Ivan Ilyich* (1891) had been previously translated by Hansen.

By 1917 when Hansen had to leave Russia and return home to Copenhagen, he had translated a dozen separate works by Kierkegaard. Six of them were ready for publication as early as 1885, including "In vino veritas,"[2] "The Immediate Erotic Stages or The Musical-Erotic,"[3] and selected journal entries from the period of the *Corsair* affair (1847), which were also translated for Tolstoy.[4] In addition, in 1885 Hansen informed Tolstoy that he had translated *For Self-Examination*, but his manuscript probably did not reach the addressee since Tolstoy, to Hansen's disappointment, made no comments on it.

Hansen had been given a chance to publish three other extracts from Kierkegaard's texts. These are "The Balance between the Esthetic and the Ethical in the Development of the Personality," which Hansen translated completely under the title "The Harmonious Development of the Esthetic and the Ethical in a Human Personality"[5]; then "Diapsalmata," translated by Hansen *in toto* and entitled, "An Aesthete's Aphorisms."[6] After this, Hansen translated "The Diary of a Seducer." These texts were published together in an anthology entitled *Pleasure and Debt.*[7]

In addition to these, Hansen translated other texts by Kierkegaard as well; however, these remained unfinished and have been kept in his archive in his house in St. Petersburg. These texts include most of *Repetition*,[8] a highly abridged translation of *Fear and Trembling*,[9] fragments from " 'Guilty?'/'Not Guilty?,' " and fragments from "The Aesthetic Validity of Marriage" together with other scattered excerpts.[10]

The responses to these first Russian translations of Kierkegaard were few and superficial. There were only two notices of them in the mass media. Even making

---

[2] This and the following manuscript are preserved in the library of the Yasnaya Polyana (Tolstoy's manor near Tula).

[3] Entitled by Hansen as "Don Juan in Music and Literature."

[4] "Отрывки из *Дневника* 1847 г (с "оценками" и пометками Льва Толстого)" [extracts from the Journals of 1847 (with "marks" and marginal notes by Leo Tolstoy)], trans. by Peter Hansen, *Вестник религиозного христианского движения*, no. 148 (Paris), 1986, pp. 55–81.

[5] "Гармоническое развитие в человеческой личности эстетических и этических начал" [The Harmonious Development of the Aesthetic and the Ethical in a Human Personality], *Северный вестник*, nos. 1, 3, 4, 1885, pp. 109–52.

[6] "Афоризмы эстетика" [An Aesthete's Aphorisms], *Вестник Европы*, no. 3, 1886, pp. 108–15.

[7] *Наслаждение и долг* [Pleasure and Debt], St. Petersburg: Izdaniye M.M. Lederle and Co. 1894.

[8] This translation of Hansen was later completed and published as *Повторение* [Repetition], Moscow: Labyrinth 1997, by Darya Loungina.

[9] These extracts (sixty pages) were later published in New York (Chalidze Publications 1982) entitled *Страх и трепет* [Fear and Trembling].

[10] Leonid Tchertkov mentions also fragments of "Rotation of Crops," "The Lily in the Field and the Bird of the Air" and some others, which I, however, did not see with my own eyes, see Леонид Чертков [Leonid Tchertkov], "Серен Киркегор в русской литературе" [Søren Kierkegaard in Russian Literature], *Вестник религиозного христианского движения*, no. 148 (Paris), 1986, pp. 33–4.

allowances for the journalistic, non-philosophical milieu of this reception, which always tends to go for the hot and scandalous interpretations, the responses of the Russian journalists cannot help but amaze us by their comic inadequacy not just with respect to Kierkegaard himself but even with respect to the elementary message of Hansen's prefaces to his publications. The journalists did not trouble themselves with such details as Hansen's warnings about Kierkegaard's indirect method of communication. The Russian critics refused to take Kierkegaard's use of pseudonyms seriously. There were a variety of reasons for this literary blindness. The first respondent Timophey Ivanovich Butkevitch (1854–1925),[11] a professor at Kharkov Theological Seminary, made no secret about what he regarded as Kierkegaard's sole preoccupation: the pursuit of the soul's salvation. He informed readers that Kierkegaard, as a judge, a married man, a respectable parishioner, etc., preached salvation by means of good resolutions and the performing of good deeds. At least it is clear why the ecclesiastical press regarded Kierkegaard favorably, in contrast to the journal *The Russian Welfare*,[12] whose anonymous reviewer was obliged to read not only "The Balance" but also "The Seducer's Diary." Here the reviewer felt the need to seek the explanation for the author's strange duality. The lack of clarity and the complexity of the composition of *Pleasure and Debt* could have prejudiced the malevolent review from the start. The respondent decided that Kierkegaard must have been Judge William, "a common German burgher…very neat, very tidy and moderate, self-satisfied, well-nourished and loyal," but hypocritical, since it must have been a very two-faced preacher who would have set people right in such a conniving way. Since *Pleasure and Debt*, as in the case of Butkevich's reading, was expected to be beneficial to the public, the reviewer wrote as though he were indifferent to the fact that *Either/Or* was a literary work rather than a complicated attempt at moral edification.

The second group of responses was inspired not by Hansen's translations but by interest in the figure of Kierkegaard, who was increasingly winning popularity in Europe. In 1894 Hansen wrote an extended biographical article on Kierkegaard for the famous *Encyclopedia Brockhaus-Efron*.[13] But despite his efforts, the Russian journalists drew on the French sources. Since each edition followed its own trend, it is no surprise that their conclusions about Kierkegaard were diametrically opposed to one another. The responses belonged to the magazines *Mir Bozhiy*,[14] *Russkiy*

---

[11] Тимофей Буткевич [Timophey Butkevich], "Датский философ Серен Киркегор как проповедник ифических начал в развитии личности" [The Danish Philosopher Søren Kierkegaard as a Preacher of the Ethical Principles in the Composition of a Personality], *Вера и разум*, no. 16, 1886, pp. 182–225.

[12] Анонимно [Anonymous], "Рецензия на *Наслаждение и долг*" [Review of "Pleasure and Debt"], *Русское богатство*, no. 6, 1894, pp. 80–1.

[13] Петр Ганзен [Peter Hansen], "Киркегор" [Kierkegaard], in *Энциклопедический словарь Брокгауза-Ефрона* [Encyclopedia Brockhaus-Efron], vols. 1–43, St. Petersburg: I.A. Efron 1890–1907, vol. 15 (1895), pp. 124–7.

[14] [Борис О.] Э [фруси] [[Boris O.] E[ffrusi], "Датский философ Серен Киркегаард" [The Danish Philosopher Søren Kierkegaard], *Мир Божий*, no. 7, 1894, pp. 211–12.

Vestnik[15] and the newspaper *Odesskiye Novosti*.[16] In *Russkiy Vestnik*, which was famous for its conservatism, Kierkegaard was stigmatized as the spiritual father of Henrik Ibsen (1828–1906) and modernism on the whole, the latter being marked by "artificiality, pretentiousness and mannerism." The author's point of view was very superficial, not rising above the level of sensational, silly impressions, and, as was common at that time, he tried to give a psychopathological analysis of modernism, using the motif of health against decadence. Kierkegaard fit into this "abnormal phenomenon" very well since he had done nothing but "make people feel like fish out of water."

The *Odesskiye Novosti* correspondent Isaak Vladimirovich Shklovsky (1865–1935) was a former member of the terrorist group *Narodnaya Volya* and a prisoner who had been exiled to Odessa. Shklovsky, writing under the pseudonym Dioneo, sympathized with Kierkegaard because of his scandalous reputation. He liked Kierkegaard's eccentricity, which he classified under the rubric "the cult of passions and the romanticism of the soul."[17] Shklovsky penned the only favorable review of Kierkegaard.

The third review was just plain comic. Boris Osipovich Effrusi, a contributor in *Mir Bozhiy*, was in charge of the entertainment column. He put his account of Kierkegaard's life between the notes "The Status of Women Workers in Great Britain" and "On the Troubles in the Spread of Infectious Diseases." Effrusi regarded Kierkegaard as a phenomenon to be observed with a naturalist's eye; fortunately, he formed no judgment. Such was the first layer of reception of Kierkegaard in Russia. When his mediators, i.e., the translator and the journalists, mentioned him they inevitably squeezed his image into the available schemes in accordance with the purposes of their journals.

Almost simultaneously with the first reception there was another reception of Kierkegaard by the people of a more comparable level who were more likely to actually understand him. But each of them had already been carried away with his own mission, so that they were ready to perceive the news of Kierkegaard only as news of a fellow thinker. For example, there was Konstantin Dmitrievich Kavelin (1818–85), who immediately recognized in Kierkegaard "a writer of genius" and who tried to help Hansen get his first translations published in the *Vestnik Yevropy*. There was also Nikolay Nikolayevich Strakhov (1828–96). Last but not least there was Leo Tolstoy, who one would have reasonably expected to fully grasp the value of Kierkegaard. But Tolstoy could only appreciate like-minded thinkers; being occupied with his own endeavors, he sought the same in Kierkegaard and did not recognize him as a companion. By the time he encountered Kierkegaard, the famous author was consumed by his own quest, and, because he could not assimilate Kierkegaard into that quest, he was rather dismissive of him. As was noted, he only took notice of Kierkegaard after Hansen promised that he would

---

[15] Аноним [Anonymous], "Предшественник Ибсена" [Ibsen's Forerunner], *Русский вестник*, no. 8, 1901, pp. 567–73.

[16] Дионео [Исаак Шкловский] [Dioneo, [Isaak Shklovsky]], "Датский моралист" [The Danish Moralist], *Одесские новости*, November 25, 1894.

[17] Ibid., p. 5.

re-translate *For Self-Examination* "in conformity with the spiritual interests of the Russian people." Tolstoy recommended Hansen to his publisher Ivan Gorbunov-Posadov, but their negotiations reached a deadlock when Hansen refused to follow Tolstoy's recommendations about making Kierkegaard more accessible. Hansen never wrote a popular book on Kierkegaard, and Tolstoy was of the opinion that a propaedeutic of this kind was necessary since "Kierkegaard did not make his great and often brilliant and beautiful thoughts clear to the reader." In short, "his speech was obscure."[18] Kavelin also advised Hansen to write a book on Kierkegaard. He warned, "otherwise, for the Russian readers ignorant of German philosophy, to say nothing of the Danish, the subtle discourse of the Danish writer is very likely to disappear without a trace."[19] Using even stronger language, Strakhov complained in his letter to Tolstoy from 1890:

> To read him [sc. Kierkegaard in Hansen's translation] was beyond my powers. So I got the book in German—I thought it might help, but it did not! The translator, his great admirer, also confessed in the Preface that he could not guarantee that he had understood everything correctly. But how could it happen that such an obscure writer could win such fame and find so many followers?[20]

In all likelihood, Tolstoy, judging by his marginalia, read attentively only Kierkegaard's journals from 1847. Those were for the most part directly communicated notes, which Tolstoy interpreted as if they had been written in his favorite Buddhist–Schopenhauerian didactical style and which, in his turn, he marked in the margins with his grades of "fours" and "fives" signifying "good" and "excellent." According to Hansen's testimony during his visit to Tolstoy in 1890, he considered Kierkegaard "young and therefore too perky."[21]

However, Hansen did not give up his attempt to excite Tolstoy's interest. He had no sooner left Yasnaya Polyana than Tolstoy received as a gift from Hansen copies of *Either/Or* and *Stages on Life's Way* along with Kierkegaard's portrait. To express his gratitude Tolstoy answered that he would like to learn to read Danish but had no time to do so.[22] Yet, Hansen managed to win some recognition for Kierkegaard. When asked about his opinion of Ibsen, Tolstoy, in harmony with his disposition at that time—"the chief thing in art is that it is non-existent"[23]—answered that such

---

[18] Tolstoy's words spoken to Hansen's wife are quoted in *Scando-Slavica*, vol. 24 (Copenhagen) 1968, p. 61.
[19] Quoted from Hansen's letter to Tolstoy (1885), published in *Литературное наследство*, vol. 75, Moscow: Nauka 1965, p. 316.
[20] *Переписка Льва Толстого с Николаем Страховым* [Correspondence between Tolstoy and Strakhov], St. Petersburg: Society of Tolstoy's Museum Publishers 1914, p. 310.
[21] Ганзен [Hansen], "Пять дней в Ясной Поляне" [Five Days in Yasnaya Polyana], *Исторический вестник*, no. 1, 1917, p. 143.
[22] See the unpublished Tolstoy letter to Hansen from April 25, 1890, which is kept in the Russian State Archive of Literature and Art (RGALI), fund 84, record 1, storage unit 32, page 1.
[23] Лев Толстой [Leo Tolstoy], *Письмо Н. Ге* [Letter to N. [ikolay] Ga [y]], in *Собрание сочинений* [Collected Works], vols. 1–22, Moscow: Khudozestvennaja literatura, vols. 19–20 (1984), p. 264.

literature is too artificial. *Brand* bears too little relation to life; it is fantastical and false, and the character is not true and consistent. "How much better are Kierkegaard and Bjørnson. Both of them, being different in the genre, have the main quality of the writer—sincerity, ardor and seriousness. They both think seriously and express what they think,"[24] wrote Tolstoy to Hansen.

II. The Era of Modernist Style

The twentieth century made a new attempt to get acquainted with Kierkegaard. The essays of Georg Brandes on Danish literature in his collected works,[25] and the books of Harald Høffding, *Den nyere Filosofis Historie*[26] and *Psychologi i Omrids paa Grundlag af Erfaring*,[27] where some space was dedicated to Kierkegaard, had been published in Russian by that time. But the epoch of modernity, which first and foremost appreciated the individual vision of cultural phenomena and which had legitimatized the author's right to one's own subjective evaluation, could neither offer any comprehensive image of Kierkegaard nor develop an objective approach to his creative work.

In 1908, the printing house "Shipovnik" ["Dog-rose"], the herald of the Modern Style in Russia, commissioned a famous symbolist poet Jurgis Baltrušaitis (1903–88)[28] to translate something from *Either/Or*; he chose "The Unhappiest One" and "Diapsalmata."[29] To please the fashion at the time, this publication depicted the creative work of Kierkegaard in dull, decadent tones and did not mention a word about *Either/Or*. Nevertheless, the translation, despite all its literalness, which is due to Baltrušaitis' uncertainty as a translator, was livelier and more convincing than Hansen's heavy renditions. Hansen, who criticized Baltrušaitis' translations from the Norwegian (the latter had translated several dramas by Ibsen), ignored this publication.

Due to the same reason, the first attempt at an academic approach to Kierkegaard in Russia among the philologists also failed. Karl Friedrich Tiander (b. 1873), professor at Helsingfors (Helsinki) University, who contributed to the work *The*

---

[24] Толстой [Tolstoy], *Письмо П. Ганзену* [Letter to P. Hansen], in *Собрание сочинений* [Collected Works], vols. 19–20 (1984), p. 224.

[25] Георг Брандес [Georg Brandes], *Собрание сочинений* [Collected Works], trans. and ed. by М.В. Лучицкая [M.V. Luchitskaya], vols. 1–12, Kijev: B.K. Fuks 1902–3, vol. 2.

[26] Гаральд Гефдинг [Harald Høffding], *История новейшей философии* [The History of Modern Philosophy], trans. n.n., St. Petersburg: izdaniye zhurnala "Obrazovaniye" 1900.

[27] Гефдинг [Høffding], *Очерки психологии, основанной на опыте* [Psychology in Outline based on Experience], trans. n.n., ed. by Jakov Kolubovsky, St. Petersburg: M.A. Aleksandrov 1908.

[28] Jurgis Baltrušaitis, author of several collections of poetry. After the October Revolution, he became an ambassador, a diplomat, and a plenipotentiary representative of Lithuania in the USSR. After 1939, he lived in Paris.

[29] "Несчастнейший" ["Diapsalmata"], *Шиповник*, no. 4, 1908, pp. 24–45. Later "The Unhappiest One" was republished in *Альманах мировой литературы*, vols. 1–4, Moscow: Svobodniy zhurnal 1914, vol. 4, pp. 59–88.

History of Western Literature (1800–1910),[30] dedicated to Kierkegaard a chapter entitled "Echoes of Romanticism in Denmark and Sweden."

Despite Tiander's desire to introduce Kierkegaard into the history of Western literature, the Danish thinker remained a mystery for him. Kierkegaard was for Tiander a character from his own books, more a literary hero than a writer. The researcher tried to guess this riddle by resorting to Dostoyevsky. He realized that the "aesthetic," "ethical," and "religious" writings of Kierkegaard had the same author, who in the long run wrote about one thing. But it was more comfortable for Tiander to bring this "one thing" to the state of Kierkegaard's soul, to a related mystery kept by Kierkegaard's Russian equal, prince Myshkin—the protagonist in the novel *The Idiot*. The "paradox" of the prince[31] and the "paradox" of Kierkegaard were for Tiander one and the same. But if he presumably assumed a difference between Dostoyevsky and prince Myshkin, between the author and the character, then Kierkegaard (who was also subject to fits of epilepsy and showed "signs of mental abnormality"[32]) was, for Tiander, fully identical with his pseudonyms and literary characters. The prince, according to Dostoyevsky, is a "positively beautiful" creature, and his openness and understanding of everything reveal the mystery of "the beautiful," Kierkegaard is the same; he is the writer for whom there opened "the mystery of private life, which…always remains the book with seven seals for another person, thanks to which he becomes an individual, who is indivisible and eternally alone."[33] His mystery is revealed when he begins to write, and, as Tiander thinks, in these moments he goes through the greatest sufferings because he does not recognize himself and cannot unravel his mystery. He flees from himself, not recognizing himself; he is haunted by "the fear of publishing his works under his name."[34] The choice of strange pseudonyms shows a "psychopathologic element" in him.[35]

But his pathology should find an explanation for itself: Kierkegaard wants his ideas to reach human hearts, and that is why he shifts the responsibility onto his readers, demanding in a cruel way from them the "idealness" "to bring an ideal into reality in order to create a new element in nature, which is as alien to nature as the absolute, which requires the entire force, and which is alien to the relative, which requires only a part of the force. The absolute is cruel to this extent because

---

[30] Карл Фридрих Тиандер [Karl Friedrich Tiander], "Отклики романтизма в Дании и Швеции" [Echoes of Romanticism in Denmark and Sweden], in *История западной литературы* [The History of Western Literature], ed. by Ф. Д. Батюшков [F.D. Batyushkov], vols. 1–3, St. Petersburg: Izdaniye obshchestva "Mir" 1910–4, vol. 3 (1914), pp. 430–40.

[31] Федор Достоевский [Fyodor Dostoyevsky], *Идиот* [*The Idiot*], in *Собрание сочинений* [Collected Works], vols. 1–15, Leningrad: Nauka 1989, vol. 6, p. 227. In Dostoyevsky's words, "the problems of the highest self-consciousness and self-awareness, and, accordingly, of the highest being, are nothing else but an illness, a distortion of the normal condition, and if so, then this is not the highest being, but it must be equal to the lowest one."

[32] Тиандер [Tiander], "Отклики романтизма в Дании и Швеции" [Echoes of Romanticism in Denmark and Sweden], p. 433.

[33] Ibid., p. 432.

[34] Ibid., p. 433.

[35] Ibid.

it requires everything."[36] Kierkegaard wants from man himself an immediate demonstration of his own belonging to "the highest being," while man at the same time remains in reality as before. But without the ideals, Tiander explains, we cannot live "by our nature...we are all choked on the mystery."[37] That is why one can forgive Kierkegaard for his demand "that everyone personally suffers the tragedy of crime and punishment, which leads to knowledge of God,"[38] the highest ideal. In Tiander's opinion, Kierkegaard's tragedy is the tragedy of every contemporary person, the tragedy of "religious double faith of our time, its permanent wavering between the absolute ideal and temporary well-being, between God and Tempter. Which one of us is not ill with this 'either/or'?"[39] The author finishes the chapter in this hopeful mood.

Tiander's later notes on Kierkegaard did not have the same justificatory tone as his earlier publications. When the mystery of Kierkegaard's soul eventually turned into the subject of his study, then, loyal to his passion, he did not rely on the facts, even when he wrote an article on Kierkegaard for the encyclopedical dictionary: "All 14 volumes of his works have a fragmentary character and in their way are a great dialectician's diary, constantly interrupted by the erotic visions of a madman."[40] The later interpretations of his creative work became in a way too simple: Kierkegaard "failed to give an account of the demands of flesh," and ultimately "we are witnessing the religious-erotic conflict as suffered by a person of a fiery-passionate nature and a mercilessly courageous mind."[41]

An anonymous author of an article "Kierkegaard" in the *Large Encyclopedia* edited by Sergey Nikolaevitch Yuzhakov (1849–1910) was less sharp and more diffuse in his judgments:

> All of Kierkegaard's works have subtle, witty dialectics and share passionate inspiration in defence of Christianity....His language is always noble, full of poetic loftiness and breath-taking eloquence, although in places it is difficult to understand. His works had a great influence on his contemporaries and on the development of Danish literature.[42]

But this author did not feel comfortable with Kierkegaard either, and in order to understand him, he, like Tiander, resorted to a comparison with another thinker—Ludwig Feuerbach. The author of the article pointed out that Feuerbach's and Kierkegaard's strong interest in Christianity drives them in different ideological directions. From the

---

[36]   Ibid., p. 437.
[37]   Ibid., p. 432.
[38]   Ibid., p. 440.
[39]   Ibid.
[40]   Тиандер [Tiander], "Кьеркегор" [Kierkegaard], in *Новый энциклопедический словарь Брокгауза-Ефрона* [Brockhaus-Efron New Encyclopedical Dictionary], vols. 1–29, St. Petersburg: izdatel I.A. Efron 1911–16, vol. 23 (ca. 1915), p. 805.
[41]   Тиандер [Tiander], "Кьеркегор" [Kierkegaard], in *Энциклопедический словарь Гранат* [Granat's Encyclopedical Dictionary], vols. 1–58, Moscow: Granat 1910–48, vol. 26, p. 298.
[42]   Анонимно [Anonymous], "Киркегор" [Kierkegaard], in *Большая энциклопедия* [Large Encyclopedia], ed. by Сергей Николаевич Южаков [Sergey Nikolayevich Yuzhakov], vols. 1–22, St. Petersburg: Prosveshcheniye 1903–4, vol. 10 (1903), p. 754.

point of view of the author of the dictionary article, the aim of Feuerbach's search is to understand the essence of the Christian teaching in order to reject it later on.

Later, in 1909, *The Orthodox Encyclopedia of Theology* made another attempt at a detached assessment of Kierkegaard's teaching. To do this, the publishers turned to the psalm-singer of the Alexander-Nevsky Church at the Emperor's Mission in Denmark, Magister of Theology Nikolay Aleksandrovich Yegorov. Yegorov's sources were presumably local publications, which he corrected and completed for the Orthodox edition. Realizing the importance of Kierkegaard for theology and understanding all the seriousness of his teaching, Yegorov wrote: "to comprehend Kierkegaard…one would have to sacrifice one's life."[43] But nevertheless he comfortably dissociated himself from him and presented him as a thoroughly Protestant thinker.[44] In this way it was easier for Yegorov to formulate what in Kierkegaard's teaching the Orthodox readers should "have with them," namely, "the deep rich sermon on the Christian ideal and Christian asceticism" and what should be "abandoned," namely, "his literature from the 'period of conflict with the Church' as the expression and sign of his known morbid development, which brought him to an untimely death and which does not follow from the author's huge preceding creative work."[45] "To abandon" for Yegorov meant not to take seriously the pages of *The Moment*, since "no one knows what Kierkegaard was talking about with his passionate attacks on the Church" and because of which he "overstrained his feeble organism."[46] Yegorov pointed out that Kierkegaard's sermon would have been justified if he had suffered persecution only from the journal, the *Corsair* ("a true Christian is a certain martyr among the crowd,"[47] Yegorov reminds us), but in no way from the official Church. But as far as Kierkegaard's teaching about how "man should…live in a Christian way…and personify Christianity in his life," this was directed exclusively against the Protestant Church for which "asceticism was something obsolete, imposing bounds, suppressing everything 'natural and human.'"[48] This interpretation allowed the Orthodox Church to judge his activity positively.

Mikhail Vladimirovich Odintsov (1879–ca. 1965) was the only Russian pre-revolutionary author who wrote about Kierkegaard and did not try to apply the latter's idea to the momentary necessities of Russian social life and did not try to fit his teaching into the ready schemes in accordance with the profile of his own works, but who was ready to patiently and attentively treat him entirely as a thinker in his own right. But little is known about Odintsov, who read Kierkegaard extensively and seriously in the original.[49] He did not even turn up before his auditors in person;

---

[43]   Николай Егоров [Nikolay Yegorov, "Киркегор" [Kierkegaard], in *Православная Богословская энциклопедия* [The Orthodox Encyclopedia of Theology], vols. 1–12, St. Petersburg: A.P. Lopukhin 1900–11, vol. 10 (1909), p. 439.
[44]   Ibid., p. 451.
[45]   Ibid.
[46]   Ibid., p. 450.
[47]   Ibid., p. 446.
[48]   Ibid., p. 451.
[49]   I only know that he was born in Irkutsk region in 1879 and died in about 1965. He learnt Danish himself and visited Denmark in 1909. After the Revolution, in the beginning of the 1920s, he taught history of ethics on Law Department of Irkutsk University.

his lecture "The Philosophy of Religious Action. Søren Kierkegaard" was read by Piotr Berngardovich Struve (1870–1944) at a session of the Petersburg Religious-Philosophical Society held on October 18, 1912.[50]

At this meeting (which included the cultural elite of that time—Dmitry Merezhkovsky (1866–1941), Zinaida Hippius (1869–1945), Dmitry Filosofov (1872–1940), Aleksandr Blok (1880–1921), Mikhail Prishvin (1873–1954), and others) Odintsov presented Kierkegaard's philosophy as an attempt, consonant with the Russian philosophy of that time, to cross an abyss separating "speculation" and "action." But Odintsov's premises and the results of his constructions turned out to be closer to the pragmatism of William James, as well as to so-called *life philosophy*. That is why the word "experience," which Odintsov often and willingly resorted to—the word from an old, positivist lexicon—acquired in his usage a new meaning, close to the notion "life," i.e., the experience which is always understood, comprehended. He named this kind of experience "religious action," the meaning of which he formulated thus:

> If the consciousness of our time begins to listen to the imperative voice of the living inner experience more attentively and apprehends its religious discovery more perceptibly, if we aspire to find a mediocre [sc. indirect] connection between philosophical contemplation and religious experience, then the traces of life preserved in Kierkegaard's philosophy may…save us from digressing to the fruitless desert of the pure logic of intellectualism and the lifeless mechanicalness of naturalism.[51]

The role of a connecting link between contemplation and action is performed by the "will." This is another key word which Odintsov uses to explain Kierkegaard's philosophy. Under Nietzsche's influence, he found in Kierkegaard's works an understanding of the will as a "condition of a personality's being or non-being."[52] In the tradition of voluntarism, he interprets Judge William's considerations about the meaning of the choice in *Either/Or*, the entire content of *Fear and Trembling* and *Practice in Christianity*, and in particular the following passage from *The Sickness unto Death*: "The more consciousness, the more self; the more consciousness, the more will, the more self. A person who has no will at all is not a self; but the more will he has, the more self-consciousness he has also."[53] Odintsov presents the becoming of one's own self—the religious action proper—as the willing activity of an individual; God in this scheme occupies the place of an absolute beginning, which makes it possible for man to become the absolute self. In this way Kierkegaard's theology, the teaching about the Absolute, turns out to be the basis of a metaphysics of the human will. So Odintsov annuls Kierkegaard's paradox, according to which "the single

---

[50] Piotr Struve published it in the same month in the journal which he edited—*Russkaya Mysl*.

[51] Михаил Одинцов [Mikhail Odintsov], "Философия религиозного действия. Серен Керкегор" [Philosophy of the Religious Action. Søren Kierkegaard], *Русская мысль*, no. 10, 1912, p. 30.

[52] Ibid., p. 8.

[53] *SKS* 11, 145 / *SUD*, 29.

individual as the single individual stands in an absolute relation to the absolute."[54] Instead, he is interpreted as offering man the possibility of becoming God-man that is an eternal and absolute being in the form of an individual man, living in time and according to conventions and subject to suffering and death. Odintsov fails to hear Kierkegaard's warning that "the doctrine of the God-man has made Christendom brazen."[55] According to Odintsov, Kierkegaard's task is to overcome the "physical nature of the individual" by dissolving it in the Absolute, and in the course of this movement to an ideal of "absolute spirituality" denying everything "exclusively human"—culture, education, even natural human love, marriage and friendship.[56] Odintsov expresses a reservation that, of course, Kierkegaard perfectly understood that his demands were impossible to fulfill completely: "that is why he stated that the heart of the matter is not only in outward forms, but in inner doing."[57]

This awkward reservation prejudiced the perplexed members of the Religious-Philosophical Society against the lecture. An expression "inner doing" (evidently, Odintsov rendered Kierkegaard's notion *Inderlighed* in this way) in the context of a practical program for spiritual renewal, which the speaker promised to extract from Kierkegaard's teaching, ultimately nonplussed them. The people present claimed that they did not understand how they personally could fulfill the demands of "fighting with the world and the asceticism of voluntary sufferings," which accompany man's liberation from the "exclusively human." The lecture sounded to them like an abstract and unrealizable call for action. Aleksandr Blok noted the ambiguity of the situation in his diary: "Today Struve, the most 'positive' of the smart people sitting around the table, was speaking so habitually and simply about 'the greatest suffering' as if it were something one owed. The rest did not even talk about it—it was written on their faces."[58]

III. Russian Emigration: Lev Shestov

After the October Revolution of 1917, interest in Kierkegaard shifted, as almost all the main representatives of Russian non-Marxist philosophy left the country. Lev Zander (1893–1964), a future prominent representative of the Ecumenical movement,

---

[54] *SKS* 4, 207 / *FT*, 120.
[55] *SKS* 11, 230 / *SUD*, 118.
[56] Одинцов [Odintsov], "Философия религиозного действия. Серен Керкегор" [Philosophy of the Religious Action. Søren Kierkegaard], p. 27.
[57] Ibid., p. 29.
[58] Александр Блок [Aleksandr Blok], *Дневник* [Diaries], Moscow: Sovetskaya Rossiya 1989, p. 142.

traveled a long and difficult path, studying Kierkegaard in Siberia (University in Perm[59]), the Far East[60] and, eventually, France.[61]

In 1933 in Paris Ivan Tkhorzhevsky (1878–1951),[62] who had become famous in Russia as a translator, wrote an article under the title "The *Symposium*"[63] in which he laid down the essence of Kierkegaard's "In vino veritas" in connection with the first edition of this work in French. And in 1936 in *Quart*, a Czech journal, there appeared an article "Dostoyevsky and Kierkegaard" written by Sergey Levitsky (1909–83), who later became a well-known sociologist and the author of the concept of "solidarism."[64]

Once a famous historian of Russian theology, Georgy Florovsky (1893–1979), turned to Kierkegaard for the purpose of creating a contrast to Schelling's philosophy: "one should read Kierkegaard, his *Philosophische Brocken* in order to immediately see, what Schelling did not feel. The God enters the world, says Kierkegaard, in Christ's Advent. Something new happens. And this new thing is the beginning of eternity!"[65]

Lev Shestov (1866–1938) also became acquainted with Kierkegaard's works after settling down in Paris; the history of this acquaintance is common knowledge. Shestov learned about Kierkegaard for the first time in April 1928 from conversations with Edmund Husserl and Martin Buber. Shestov's road to Kierkegaard was arduous. He could not decide for a long time to which camp to assign Kierkegaard, the camp of "Speculation" or "Revelation." The translator Bengamin Fondane wrote, "when I noticed that Shestov became meager and looked tired, he…said: 'It's nothing, it's the results of fighting with Kierkegaard.'"[66] By December 1932 Shestov was already giving a course entitled "Dostoyevsky and Kierkegaard" at the Department of Russian Studies at the Sorbonne. From then on Shestov included Kierkegaard in the line of his lifelong companions together with Plato, Plotinus, Luther, Pascal, and Nietzsche.

In November 1932, Shestov wrote to his friend Boris de Schloezer (1881–1969):

---

[59] The report of this appeared eight years later in Сборник общества истории, философии и социальных наук при Пермском университете [Collection of the Society of History, Philosophy and Social Studies at Perm University], vol. 2 (Perm), 1927.

[60] Лев Зандер [Lev Zander], "Жизнь и философия Киркегора" [Kierkegaard's Life and Philosophy], *Русское обозрение* (Vladivostok), 1922.

[61] Lev Zander, "Aux sources de l'existentialisme," in *Vues sur Kierkegaard*, Cairo: La Part du sable 1955.

[62] Ivan Ivanovich Tkhorzhevsky, translator of Verlaine, Valéry, Omar Hayam, editor of the journal *Vozrozhdeniye*.

[63] Ivan Tkhorzhevsky, "The *Symposium*," *Возрождение*, no. 3033 (Paris), 1933, pp. 5–6.

[64] Сергей Левицкий [Sergey Levitsky], "Достоевский и Киркегор" [Dostoyevsky and Kierkegaard], *Quart* (Prague) 1936.

[65] Георгий Флоровский [Georgy Florovsky], "Спор о немецком идеализме" [Debate on German Idealism], *Путь*, no. 25 (Paris), 1930, pp. 51–81.

[66] Bengamin Fondane, "Heraclite le pauvre," *Cahier du Sud*, no. 177, 1935, p. 579.

> I still have my mind set on Kierkegaard. I even want to write a short article about him and him alone, once again about "Abraham and Socrates." Especially after I received two new books by Martin Buber, which convinced me again that even Kierkegaard's most ardent enthusiasts…construe him as Socrates' follower….A German philosophical journal invited me, through Buber himself, to write a review of his last book. But it is very strenuous for me, since in a review, i.e., in a short article, it will be impossible to clarify all the barely noticeable nuances, which result in the incommensurability between Abraham, who went he knew not where, and Socrates, who demanded that a person should know where he is going. I do not know your impression of Kierkegaard's book, but I always have the feeling that, according to Kierkegaard, even God is powerless against the atrocities of existence and that horror cannot argue with the immediate data of conscience. And still Kierkegaard (and it is to his everlasting credit) did not stop discussing these atrocities, which cannot argue with the immediate data of conscience. And it seems to me, this is the most remarkable point of his writings.[67]

It appears that at that time Shestov finally discovered the key line in Kierkegaard's philosophy, that new "revelation," which allowed him to make a decisive break in his own thinking. While Shestov gets the reader to be absorbed with Tolstoy in the discoveries of the dying Ivan Ilyitch, to think about the paradoxes of Dostoyevsky's "underground man," to listen to the fierce Plotinus' speeches and Job's wailing, he tried again and again to present hard labor, tragedy, catastrophe, and despair as revelations of death. These things should highlight some fundamental existential error of man, a certain initial "fault." Kierkegaard helped him to capture the initial sense of this fault and to find its source and ever-present essence in the event of the Fall. In interpreting *The Concept of Anxiety*, Shestov follows Kierkegaard, but modifies the trend of his thoughts and begins to understand the Fall as a result of a certain dread, a dread of nothingness. But Shestov construed it such that reason itself whispers into man's ear this dread and lack of confidence in his divine freedom. Reason compels man to prefer the rational necessity and guaranteed distinction between good and evil to the arcane, uncertain and paradoxical freedom of faith. So, in the end, reason is the biblical serpent.

This conclusion guides Shestov's further reading of Kierkegaard. When he was writing a review of the then published books by Buber and was in correspondence with him, the subject of his future book was, in general outline, clear to him. Shestov represented the life and work of Kierkegaard as an ever-lasting dramatic antagonism between two kinds of existential "pathos"—the absurdity of Abraham's faith and the autarchy of Socrates' reason, which with serpent-like wickedness enslaves both the thought and the very life of Kierkegaard. Kierkegaard negated the idealistic metaphysics of Hegel, "who turned the whole of creation into a trinket," but could not overcome Socrates' offence. He did not trust the experience of Abraham and Job, which he himself described so eloquently. He felt ashamed of his human, alas, all too human, disaster, which made him part with Regine Olsen. He interpreted his loss as

---

[67] Наталья Баранова-Шестова [Natalya Baranova-Shestova], *Жизнь Льва Шестова. По переписке и воспоминаниям современников* [The Life of Lev Shestov. Through Correspondence and Memoirs of his Contemporaries], vols. 1–2, Paris: La Presse Libre 1983, vol. 2, pp. 104–5.

a sacrificial refusal of the "finite" for the "infinite." He did not have the heart for the "movement of faith," for the valor of faith, believing in the divine blessing of life here and now, in the nonsensical possibility of obtaining that which was once lost, despite the laws of impersonal necessity. He preferred Socrates' valor in death, the valor of the wise, i.e., the cloistered, stoic, and indifferent calm in "Phalaris' bull," to the valor of faith. That is why, wrote Shestov in 1931, "Kierkegaard drew his Christian edification not from the Absurd, that he glorified, and not from the Holy Scripture, which he considered the revelation of truth, but from that 'knowledge,' which the wisest of men brought us, when he dared to taste the fruit of the forbidden tree."[68]

At the beginning of 1933 Shestov started working on the book *Kierkegaard and the Existential Philosophy. Vox Clamantis in Deserto*. He finished the draft by March–April 1934. Initially, the book was to be published in French with the NRF (Nouvelle Revue Française) publishers. However, this plan never succeeded because the chief editor, the writer André Malraux (1901–76), who was collaborating with the Communists at that time, vetoed Shestov's book upon his return from the USSR. Grasset publishers also refused to produce it. On May 5, 1935 Shestov gave a public lecture entitled "Kierkegaard and Dostoyevsky" (which became a preface to the book) at the meeting of Religious and Philosophical Academy. The transcript of the report was published in the magazine *The Road*[69] and in *Cahier du Sud*[70] in French. In autumn 1937 Shestov delivered the lectures "Kierkegaard as a Religious Philosopher" on the radio. The transcript of these lectures was published in *Cahiers de Radio-Paris*, and a translation of it in *Russian Notes*.[71]

At the beginning of 1936, on the occasion of Shestov's seventieth birthday, the Committee of Shestov's Friends was established, which took upon itself the task of publishing his book about Kierkegaard in French by organizing a subscription to the work. Lucien Lévy-Bruhl (1857–1939), Nikolay Berdyaev (1874–1948), and Albert Camus (1913–60) actively helped Shestov. The book was published in 1,000 copies in July 1936 among the philosophical works of Vrin publishing house. In 1937 Robert Paine translated the book into English but could not find a publisher. After the War the book appeared in Danish (1947), Spanish (1947) and German (1949).

The book *Kierkegaard and the Existential Philosophy* appeared on July 8, 1939 in Paris with a small print-run of 400 copies. It was reprinted in Moscow at the Progress"-Gnosis publishing house in 1992.[72] The thoughts expressed by Shestov in previous works are now clearly chiseled, formulated, and widely generalized.

---

[68] Лев Шестов [Lev Shestov], "В фаларийском быке" [In Phalaris' Bull], in his *Афины и Иерусалим* [Athens and Jerusalem], Paris: YMCA-Press 1951, p. 146.

[69] Шестов [Shestov], "Киргегард и Достоевский" [Kierkegaard and Dostoyevsky], *Путь*, no. 48, 1935, pp. 20–37.

[70] Léon Chestov, "Kierkegaard et Dostoyevski," *Cahier du Sud*, no. 18, 1936, pp. 170–200.

[71] Шестов [Shestov], "Киргегард—религиозный философ" [Kierkegaard as Religious Philosopher], *Русские записки*, no. 3 (Paris), 1938, pp. 196–221.

[72] Шестов [Shestov], *Киргегард и экзистенциальная философия (Глас вопиющего в пустыне)* [Kierkegaard and the Existential Philosophy (Vox clamantis in deserto)], Paris: Sovremenniye zapiski i Dom Knigi 1939 (republished, Moscow: Progress-Gnosis 1992) (in

He created a finished and accomplished view in which he places different accents. Rationalism still appears to be a curse on human thought since Socrates. It perverts both a human attitude toward necessity and the notion of freedom. "Freedom" for the rationalists is neither the elimination of necessity nor its banishment from existence, nor a victory over it, but only the cognition of it, passive comprehension, recognition of its sovereign, inalienable, and inviolable rights.

Facing the humanly comprehended reality, the human will becomes not freedom but the tool of necessity. Spinoza formulated this concept by saying that necessity governs everything, and even "*Deus non operari ex libertate voluntatis*"[73]—even God "does not act of free will." That is why the task of philosophy, according to Shestov, amounts not merely to recognizing the power and actual authority of one or another order of things. In the sovereignty of necessity, the philosophy of rationalism strives to see the truth as something universal and essential. This knowledge assures a person that he is insignificant in the face of the unconquerable and monstrous force of necessity, and that his maximal possible freedom may only amount to fully submitting to the power of necessity, being bent by its force, hostile and fatal to man, ruthless and indifferent to him and his fate. Shestov finally fixed this conception of rationalism under the title "theoretical philosophy," and turned against it with the entire force of his mind and soul.

In the book *Kierkegaard and the Existential Philosophy* Kierkegaard is presented as a character of biblical proportions. He is not a mere writer, but an individualist genius, who invokes doom and fate. Job, Abraham, Luther stand beside him. Shestov carefully words the main point of Kierkegaard's philosophy:

> It is either the thinking of Abraham, Job, the Prophets and the Apostles or the thinking of Socrates. It is either theoretical philosophy, which takes wonder as its starting point and seeks "understanding," or existential philosophy, which proceeds from despair (I repeat once more: from the Biblical *de profundis ad te, Domine, clamavi*) and leads to the revelation of Holy Scripture.[74]

According to Shestov, Kierkegaard is aware of the fact that the contraposition of Job to Hegel or Abraham to Socrates is utter madness to the common mind. But his task is namely to "to tear himself free from the power of the commonplace; it is for a good reason that he has told us that the starting point of philosophy is not wonder, but despair, which reveals a new source of truth to man."[75]

It is Shestov's belief that what we call "understanding" ("*intellegere*" in Spinoza), crushed and flattened our knowledge, beat it into a two-dimensional plane of a nearly illusive existence, and debilitated thinking. Now

---

English as *Kierkegaard and the Existential Philosophy*, trans. by Elinor Hewitt, Athens: Ohio University Press 1969).

[73] Spinoza, *Ethica*, Pars I prop. 32, cor.
[74] Шестов [Shestov], *Киргегард и экзистенциальная философия (Глас вопиющего в пустыне)* [Kierkegaard and the Existential Philosophy (Vox clamantis in deserto)], 1992, p. 71.
[75] Ibid.

> We can only "accept"—we are not yet able to challenge, we are convinced that "challenging" only spoils and corrupts human thought; Job, Abraham, and the Psalmist, in our opinion, think badly. But, for existential philosophy, the greatest defect in our thinking is its loss of the ability to "challenge," because it has thus forfeited the one dimension that alone is able to guide it to the truth.[76]

To find faith in salvation, according to Shestov, one must lose one's mind. This faith is painful, and it is impossible to leave reason light-heartedly. It is martyrdom to believe against reason. But, for Kierkegaard, existential philosophy was built on martyrdom and despair. Job's wailing, alleges Shestov, opens a new dimension of *thinking:* he feels real power in wailing, which can knock down walls. The knight of faith cannot be distracted like a speculative philosopher from the finite for the sake of the infinite, but he possesses the whole of finitude. Kierkegaard's faith, like the faith of Shestov, is not only a way to the truth, unavailable to reason. This faith is a way to beatitude. It is not the joy of speculation but a genuine bliss.

Nonetheless, the conclusions in this book are more pessimistic in comparison to Shestov's earlier reflections. According to Shestov, Kierkegaard not only contemplates Abraham's gesture but actually compares himself to him, as his situation also demanded faith from him, a kind of faith like that of Abraham, who believed God would return Isaac to him. But he did not find Abraham's powers within himself. When he found the solution to the contradiction in the movement in faith, he, according to his own confession, was unable to perform it, unlike Abraham, unable to embrace the absurdity. But Shestov believes this pessimism to be a distinctive feature of Kierkegaard's philosophy, which meets and yields to evil, which is incorporated in the very structure of human existence.

It is a rigid claim: "everything *is* namely what it *is*." Shestov sees that existence is obliged to conform to it, but ethics, the moral law, is a mediator of such an answer. By looking deeply into man, Shestov more and more sees in his existence the features which make final victory over reason more than questionable. Athens not only won over Jerusalem in antiquity. Its triumph is steadfast; it is rooted in the depth of existence, the essence of which lies in a fundamental acceptance of the world as it is. Existence is more interested in being than in the miraculous or the impossible. When Kierkegaard turns from his heroes, he "turns his attention from the miraculous,"[77] as he touches what is common without noticing it. This commonness is a force much more powerful than his personal faith, a force, which has only one adequate movement aimed at the cognition of *how* it is and namely *what* it is. And then, according to Shestov, he submits to it, feeling that he "cannot make the movement of faith," and so cognition infatuates him, tempting him, like nothingness. Philosophy, in its turn, loses all access to the cognition of creative freedom, and even God is submitted to necessity, i.e., the autonomy of the moral law and the necessity of salvation:

> Every time we try to give an answer to the question, *cur Deus homo*, we inevitably come up against the moment of necessity, which is evidence of the existence of some primordial principles of existence over which even God has no power; in order to save man, God is

---

[76] Ibid., p. 72.
[77] Ibid., p. 156.

obliged to become man, to suffer, to accept death...to accept the conditions set for Him by necessity, for the sake of the salvation of mankind. The situation is altogether the same as in human affairs: reason shows God the limits of possibility; ethics praises God for scrupulously fulfilling all the "you must's" stipulated by impossibilities.[78]

Shestov concludes that genuine freedom was lost when man tasted the fruit from the tree of knowledge. And it will return only when cognition loses its power over man, when man sees the irresistible lust in reason's striving for the truths which transmitted sin to the world, and sin is a synonym of "cognition," since man, according to Shestov, has an immeasurably greater and alternate variety of freedom: not to choose between evil and good, but to become like the God of Old Covenant and save the world from evil.[79]

Feedback from Shestov's nearest Russian acquaintances was scarce.[80] The simplest explanation for this is provided by Nikolay Berdyaev: "as regards the book of L. Shestov it is impossible to learn about Kierkegaard himself, and one learns only of the author of the book."[81] Emmanuel Levinas (1906–95) reproached him of the same thing in his review of the book: "The author is more present therein than his subject."[82] Shestov made it into the history of thought as an author of striking, original ideas. With Kierkegaard acting as an impulse and a splendid illustration, his ideas exerted for a long time only an indirect influence on the fate of European thought.

IV. Stalin's Epoch and Khrushchov's Thaw

Being in an isolated position, Shestov's book found itself on historic grounds as well. Its publication in the USSR was initially impossible. Shestov hated Bolshevism. His philosophical interests were in the sphere of existentialism, and he took absolutely no interest in the social sciences that could bring him closer to those emigrants' circles which sympathized with the Soviet authorities. Since the end of the 1920s, the contacts with Berlin, Prague, and Paris—permissible though not often practiced in the Soviet cultural life of the time of the New Economic Policy—were eventually controlled by the State Security bodies. In the 1930s the Party leadership fully dominated philosophy—the whole culture became, according to Lenin's formula "part of the common party cause," the means for the mobilization of the Soviet population to accomplish the party's programs for reconstructing the country. In the Communist Party's view, only materialistic Marxist philosophy could express the world outlook of a new ruling class and a new culture, and all other philosophies

---

[78] Ibid., p. 111.
[79] Ibid., p. 197.
[80] See Леонид Чертков [Leonid Tchertkov], "Серен Киркегор в русской литературе" [Søren Kierkegaard in Russian Literature], *Вестник религиозного христианского движения*, no. 148 (Paris), 1986, pp. 44–6.
[81] Николай Бердяев [Nikolay Berdyaev], *Собрание сочинений* [Collected Works], vols. 1–4, Paris: YMCA-Press 1985–90, vol. 3 (1989), p. 399.
[82] Emmanuel Levinas, "Léon Chestov, *Kierkegaard et la philosophie existentielle*," *Revue des études juives*, vol. 2, nos. 1–2, 1937, p. 141.

should be annihilated. Existentialist problems were eventually moved to the rank of the "religious" and consequently forbidden themes.

At the beginning of the 1930s Kierkegaard's name was still mentioned in the Soviet Union in a neutral tone—one could read a short review of his criticisms of Christianity and a feature article about his influence on Henrik Ibsen (1828–1906) and Bjørnstjerne Bjørnson (1832–1919) in the *Literature Encyclopedia*.[83] The following comments on Kierkegaard firmly tied him to existentialist philosophy and were made exclusively in exegetical tones. I happened to have to hand the commentaries of a leading political journalist of a central Soviet newspaper *Pravda* David Zaslavsky (1880–1965)[84]: they show the painful effort with which he read Kierkegaard, trying to understand him and becoming angry when he found himself unable to do so. His notes are full of odd remarks "idiot," "schizophrenic"—Zaslavsky's commentary strikes one first of all with its sincerity and simplicity, as was the case ten years later, when he took command of a witch-hunt campaign against Boris Pasternak (1890–1960). But publicly censored statements from that time were no less outrageous. The editors of the fourth edition of the *Short Philosophical Dictionary*, Mark Rosenthal (1906–75) and Pavel Yudin (1899–1968), presented existentialism to Soviet readers as a "decadent subjective-idealistic philosophical trend of an imperialistic epoch." Its principal aim, it claimed, was the "demoralizing of society's consciousness, the struggle against the revolutionary organizations of the proletariat."[85] An author of a section in the six-volume *History of Philosophy*, A.G. Myslivchenko concluded that Kierkegaard's conservatism stemmed from his "hatred of the masses, democratic ideas and especially—socialism."[86] In addition, Kierkegaard rejected the existing material world and put in its place the "subjective religious-ethical world of the sensations of the individual"[87]—the author of the section even managed to quote a "bourgeois philosopher," György Lukács (1885–1971), about the definition "religious atheist," which, in Myslivchenko's opinion, was devoid of meaning.

The 1960s required from Soviet historians of philosophy more than presentations and labels. Society was no longer satisfied with harsh epithets—the time demanded proofs. Gradually it became a norm to quote philosophers instead of simply dividing them into "progressive" and "reactionary." The USSR was emerging out of its international isolation, its foreign contacts broadened, and a good knowledge of the sources (as a rule, in German translations from the beginning of a century) and of the critical literature became imperative. But it was an unstable time: on the one hand, conditions were created for intelligent, sympathetic or at least adequate,

---

[83] Л. Г. Б[люмфельд] [L.G. B[lumfeld]], "Киркегор" [Kierkegaard], in *Литературная энциклопедия* [Literature Encyclopedia], vols. 1–11, Moscow and Leningrad: Izdatelstvo Kommunisticheskoy Akademii 1929–39, vol. 5 (1931), p. 26.

[84] Zaslavsky's archive is kept in RGALI, fund 2846, record 1, storage unit 52.

[85] Марк Моисеевич Розенталь [Mark Moyseyevich Rosenthal] and Павел Федорович Юдин [Pavel Fyodorovich Yudin] (eds.) "Киркегор" [Kierkegaard], in *Краткий философский словарь* [Short Philosophical Dictionary], Moscow: Izdatelstvo politicheskoy literatury 1954, p. 677.

[86] *История философии* [History of Philosophy], vols. 1–6, Moscow: Izdatelstvo Akademii Nauk 1957–65, vol. 3 (1959), p. 583.

[87] Ibid., p. 584.

by academic standards, comments on Kierkegaard for young scholars—in Sergey Averintsev's (1937–2004) and Yuri Davydov's (b. 1929) articles in the *Philosophical Encyclopedia*,[88] in the works of Vladimir Karpushin (1920–90),[89] Tatyana Gaidukova (b. 1944),[90] and, especially, those of Piama Gaidenko (b. 1934),[91] the fellow worker of the Institute of Philosophy, on whom we will dwell later. On the other hand, the printing house Mysl, that published the propaganda series "Thinkers of the Past," published a monograph by Bernard Emmanuilovitch Bykhovsky (1898–1980).[92] It appeared in 1972 and was an alarming reminder of those times when thinking could cost one one's freedom and even one's life.

Bykhovsky, a renowned Soviet philosopher, a graduate of the "Red Professors' Institute" and laureate of the Stalin prize, represented our country abroad as a Corresponding Fellow of the editorial board of the journal *Philosophy and Phenomenological Research* and a member of the editorial board of the magazine *Revolutionary World: An International Journal of Philosophy*. He proceeded from the point of view that "the entire history of philosophy has been the history of a struggle of materialism against idealism, dialectics against metaphysics, and progressive trends against reactionary ones"[93] and could not countenance any deviations from this view. He judged Siger de Brabant, Berkeley, Kierkegaard and other "thinkers of the past," whom he happened to write about, according to this set of criteria. Though a very elderly man, he adhered to the views of the 1930–1940s, when philosophy was an expression of state policy and was explained in a language which the broad masses could easily understand. That language was not a mere continuation of Marxist philosophy; it was worked out in Russia at the end of the nineteenth century in social-democratic workers' groups, when Russian Marxists had as their task to put a very difficult world into a package for very simple minds. It could be done only

---

[88] Сергей Аверинцев [Sergey Averintsev,] and Юрий Давыдов [Jury Davydov], "Кьеркегор" [Kierkegaard], in *Философская энциклопедия* [Philosophical Encyclopedia], vols. 1–5, Moscow: Sovetskaya Entsiklopediya 1960–5, vol. 3 (1964), pp. 128–30.

[89] Владимир Карпушин [Vladimir Karpushin], "Серен Киркегор—предшественник экзистенциальной антропологии" [Søren Kierkegaard as a Forerunner of Existentialist Humanism], *Вопросы философии*, no. 12, 1967, pp. 103–13.

[90] Татьяна Гайдукова [Tatyana Gaidukova], "Проблема выбора в философии Кьеркегора" [The Problem of Choice in Kierkegaard's Philosophy], *Вестник МГУ*, no. 6, series 8, 1969, pp. 32–44; Татьяна Гайдукова [Tatyana Gaidukova], "Принцип иронии в философии Киркегора" [The Principle of Irony in Kierkegaard's Philosophy], *Вопросы философии*, no. 9, 1970, pp. 109–20.

[91] Пиама Павловна Гайденко [Piama Pavlovna Gaidenko], "Киркегор и философско-эстетические истоки экзистенциализма" [Kierkegaard and the Philosophic-Aesthetical Sources of Existentialism], in *Вопросы литературы*, no. 7, 1967, pp. 133–157; Пиама Павловна Гайденко [Piama Pavlovna Gaidenko] and Юрий Бородай [Jury Boroday], "Серен Киркегор и критика Гегеля с позиций экзистенциализма" [Søren Kierkegaard and his Criticism of Hegel from the Existentialistic Point of View], *Вестник МГУ. Серия экономики и философии*, no. 2, 1961, pp. 45–54.

[92] Бернард Быховский [Bernard Bykhovsky], *Кьеркегор* [Kierkegaard], Moscow: Mysl 1972.

[93] Быховский [Bykhovsky], *Сигер Брабантский* [Siger Brabantsky], Moscow: Mysl 1980, p. 51.

by simplifying things because people's minds had been ruined by the practice that nobody demanded from them that they make any effort to enhance and develop their intellect; on the contrary, one assumed that, the proletarians possessed everything they needed by right. And even if someone with the peasant-workers' background became a professor of philosophy, no education and no international contacts could break the person's relation with these schemes. That is why the question of to what rank the "Danish blasphemer of Hegel" could be classified was solved for Bykhovsky ahead of time:

> History knows…a lot of such mistakes, illusions, figments, which for many years, sometimes for many centuries after their origination remained a hindrance to social progress, and a spiritual weapon of reactionary forces….One such example is the spiritual heritage of Søren Kierkegaard. His morbid psyche, wounded consciousness, and defective thinking brought about in Copenhagen—a God-forsaken place—ideas, feelings, inducements that greatly appealed to people of another century, and which corresponded to the mood and aspirations of people living not only in other countries, but under different social conditions—under conditions of a general crisis of the capitalist system.[94]

Bykhovsky's approach is striking by his complete inability to read between the lines, as if Kierkegaard's works were a political document that were in no need of sophisticated interpretation and contained nothing ambiguous. His limitation leads to some quite curious things like a reminder that, despite the fact that Kierkegaard and Marx were born on the same day, the latter was a "thinker of entirely different type and level,"[95] or comparing Kierkegaard's comments on Schelling's lectures with those of Engels, who did not hear the lectures themselves. The book had a new feature in comparison with those of Stalin's times, namely, it was free from the barbaric mistakes in names and titles that were characteristic of earlier sources, and it contained references to authoritative Western experts on Kierkegaard—in line with contemporary trends. All this was only done to show that one could never come close to the truth without a Marxist method.

That is why it is no use trying to understand Bykhovsky's "point of view" on Kierkegaard's philosophy—he solely concentrates on what Kierkegaard "could not understand" or "did not share": on Hegel's objective idealism, on the revolutionary pathos of German right-wing Hegel followers, on the class-struggle basis of morals invented by Marx, on Feuerbach's anthropological atheism or on rationalism that differs among progressive philosophers of all times and peoples. This book is a grotesque example of an official Marxist approach rather than an example of Kierkegaard studies proper. It could only spur interest in Kierkegaard among a differently thinking part of the Soviet intelligentsia that determined interesting thinkers by a label "reactionary" and "decadent" and that discovered for itself Vassiliy Rozanov (1856–1919), Konstantin Leontyev (1831–91), Nietzsche, and Heidegger in this way.

---

[94] Быховский [Bykhovsky], *Кьеркегор* [Kierkegaard], p. 215.
[95] Ibid., p. 37.

A book by Piama Pavlovna Gaidenko, *The Tragedy of Aestheticism. On the Weltanschauung of Søren Kierkegaard* (1970),[96] though its author did not pursue notoriety of this kind, was sold on the black market, which was rare for books published by a Soviet state publishing house and not brought from abroad or printed in a blind, scarcely legible copy from the pre-revolutionary edition. As a disciple of Aleksey Fyodorovitch Losev (1893–1988), the only surviving representative of Russian religious philosophy in the USSR, the follower of the tradition of Vladimir Solovyov (1853–1900), Pavel Alexandrovich Florensky (1882–1937), and Sergey Bulgakov (1871–1944), Gaidenko combined the high spirituality of a closed country's inhabitants, by which one still recognizes our intelligentsia, with an impartiality rare for this group, and with a desire to learn and a readiness to think independently. There were few historical-philosophical works of such a high level in the USSR. She was so much interested in Kierkegaard that the book was not ruined by the uncertainty, inevitable for a Russian thinker, about a circle of the ideas of the West.

Gaidenko came to Kierkegaard after she had received inspiration from Heidegger's existentialism and published some works on that topic. But her understanding of existentialism differed from that of Shestov, for whom existential thinking was a sensation of the entire world's diseased being and a strained effort to discover its origin. The starting point for Gaidenko, a child of the 1960s, was essentially different. An individual life is a one-time experience. It cannot be repeated, and this constitutes its strength. Gaidenko's existentialism was expressed in the fact that, without taking into account academic approaches, which she was no doubt familiar with, she was not afraid to show her strongest personal interest in the idea and in the desire to "work on" this idea first of all individually, for herself. Kierkegaard was comfortable for her to dwell on as he also "considered philosophy a private matter, something very personal."[97] A tradition of Russian philosophy to create everything that was best with the efforts of single thinkers and not of representatives of trends or schools contributed to the success of her book.

The main and the most painful question for Gaidenko, which served as a starting point for her, is the inexpressibility of Abraham's situation, that is, of a man "getting into the hands of the living God." But she does not see in this situation the fatalism of a man of the Old Testament. In her opinion, this situation expresses for Kierkegaard a new European "aestheticism," which sharpens the Christian problem of freedom of choice in an unsolvable contradiction, in the impossibility of keeping one's word or bearing the responsibility for one's action. Like Lev Shestov, Gaidenko thinks that Abraham's silence, his suspension of the ethical is a willing act, a voluntarily made decision, which distinguishes him from the tragic hero only by the fact that a responsibility of this kind cannot be expressed before the world and remains

---

[96] Пиама Гайденко [Piama Gaidenko], *Трагедия эстетизма. О миросозерцании Серена Киркегора* [The Tragedy of Aestheticism. On the *Weltanschauung* of Søren Kierkegaard], Moscow: Iskusstvo 1970. Republished as Пиама Гайденко [Piama Gaidenko], *Прорыв в трансцендентному* [Breakthrough towards the Transcendental], Moscow: Respublica 1997.
[97] Ibid., p. 19.

itself without an answer. He himself suspends the space of the ethical, leaving it open for any sort of evaluation. Neglecting Johannes de silentio's words about the incomprehensibility of Abraham's act, Gaidenko characterizes his silence as "demonical," as equally good and evil, a saint and a criminal. This fundamental suspension of judgment makes her, in its turn, suppose that the source of Abraham's "demonism" is generally not the Hebrew Jehovah, but some new god which appeared in the middle of the nineteenth century, an ironic god, who relates Abraham to Johannes the seducer, Don Juan, and Faust:

> Demonical aestheticism is ironic due to its ambiguity as long as everything in it turns out to be determined through its opposite; demonic religiousness—belief in the absurd, as the only form of overcoming the will that "loved evil"—turns out to be unusually overturned irony. Here the subject of irony is not an individual himself but God....Just as a romantic remains in relation to his works, and something transcendental keeps a distance to them and does not let him understand himself in them and through them because he always turns out to be higher than his creation, so also the God of an absurd faith is on the other side from His creations, not letting Himself understand Himself and at the same time being merciless to them—they are both ironic.[98]

It should be pointed out that Gaidenko understands irony not simply as a speech act, but as an act that refers to a certain person. In this interpretation she follows her teacher Aleksey Losev, who wrote: "Irony appears when I, wishing to say 'no,' say 'yes,' and at the same time I say this 'yes' exclusively to express and find out my sincere 'no.' My 'no' does not remain an independent fact, but it depends on the expressed 'yes,' needs it, establishes itself in it and has no meaning without it."[99] This subconscious denial of the autonomy of speech and the desire to tie it firmly to human personality is rooted in the old Russian tradition of mistrust of anything having to do with logic. The desire not to let the author out of view is explained by the prejudice, inherent to Russian religious thought, that everything kind is straightforward and simple, and that is why it is clearly positioned and directly expressed; whereas indirect, complexly built or ironic speech is always a language of evil, the language of an aggressor, the language of authority which does not lead to direct discovery or is simply incomprehensible. This prejudice, that in the nineteenth century there arose a conflict between aesthetics and morality, art and reality, explains Gaidenko's other constructions as well. For her, the opposite of "irony" is "seriousness," and the criterion for seriousness is the author's readiness to take responsibility for his characters' stances. And when the Romantics' irony remains play, the aesthetical moment of their creative work, then Kierkegaard's existentialism was what makes one carry out this artistic "experiment on oneself."[100] It is noteworthy that the first attempt in Russia to conceptually approach the problem

---

[98]   Ibid., p. 204.
[99]   Алексей Федорович Лосев [Aleksey Fyodorovitch Losev] and В.Н. Шестаков [V.N. Shestakov], *История эстетических категорий* [History of the Aesthetical Categories], Moscow: Iskusstvo 1965, pp. 326–7.
[100]   Гайденко [Gaidenko], *Прорыв к трансцендентному* [Breakthrough towards the Transcendental], p. 79.

of the pseudonyms in Kierkegaard's works resolved it as the problem of an "indirect way of writing, indirect way of thinking, indirect way of being,"[101] i.e., it was drawn from the identity of an utterance and existence that coincide in "seriousness," in other words, an "existential position." More generally, for Gaidenko, "to exist" means "to express one's position in speaking." This shaky foundation is, in particular, a reason why Kierkegaard's religious "left-hand" writings are not among the texts which she considers. Any indirect communication, including ironic speech, turns out to be completely brought to the "aesthetical" way of existence. But if Romantic irony—here Gaidenko supports a view given by Kierkegaard in *The Concept of Irony*—is a voluntarily taken position of an eternal "I," for which no actuality is adequate, then Kierkegaard's irony testifies to the fact that he already did not have the possibility of a choice:

> Kierkegaard's position, despite his passionate desire to overcome the ironic point of view, despite his struggle for "finding one's own self in faith," remains ironic to the end. Irony is not an outer mask with which Kierkegaard clothed his works…irony turned out to be his own existential position….That is why Kierkegaard is a writer-pseudonym, that is why paradox is the final word in his teaching.[102]

After almost ten years Gaidenko returned to Kierkegaard again in her book on J.G. Fichte,[103] but her interest in him was probably exhausted by that time. A small paragraph in this book included a short synopsis of *The Concept of Anxiety* in comparison with Fichte's and Schelling's ideas on freedom and—somewhat unexpectedly in the given context—Franz Kafka's *The Trial*. An explanation of this context was that Kierkegaard tried to take the problem of freedom from the sphere of a speculative construction and carry it over to the field of psychology, while preserving the possibility of its ethical solution. That is why Gaidenko was interested in the question to what extent the limits of consciousness coincide with the limits of guilt, and in particular, as in Kafka's works, guilt without the act, that is without guilt. But Kierkegaard's decision was interpreted in a way typical for her:

> As far as the sphere of freedom does not coincide with the sphere of conscious but concerns also the unconscious, man should then be responsible not only for what he did with a clear mind and sober memory. He is responsible for the latter before the human court, but before the court of his own conscience, he, according to Kierkegaard, should be responsible for his secret thoughts as well, and even for what he did not think about. This is because not everything with which a human soul lives reaches consciousness. Man, according to Kierkegaard, bears the responsibility also for his unconscious, and that is why he cannot mark the limits of his guilt.[104]

---

[101]   Ibid., p. 49.
[102]   Ibid., pp. 206–7.
[103]   Гайденко [Gaidenko], *Философия Фихте и современность* [The Philosophy of Fichte and the Present], Moscow: Mysl 1979.
[104]   Ibid., p. 271.

V. The Late Soviet and Post-Soviet Epoch

A book such as *The Tragedy of Aestheticism* could only appear in the rebellious 1960s. Frankly speaking, they brought for our country not the revolutionary methods of "deconstruction" but only the possibility of a relatively independent thinking that did not depend on momentary Party directives. The last years of the Soviet epoch were their exact antithesis. It was too lifeless and aesthetic a time to create similarly fundamental books. Moreover, the decline of any ideology, be it Marxism or its opponent, Russian religious philosophy, was also felt in the USSR. The customary systematic study of philosophic teachings and the attempt to "apply" them to life began to look like something outdated and artificial. But the ideological barriers had not yet fallen. The Soviet historians of philosophy, not having the opportunity to choose any of the modern or post-modern methods openly, sought for themselves other strategies and mostly concentrated on particular problems, which were narrowly formulated. But such material was often accompanied by a translated extract from Kierkegaard's works. This is how excerpts from *From the Papers of One Still Living* and some materials related to "the *Corsair* affair" were published. Thanks to these new articles, the Soviet readers learnt about the new, unknown aspects of Kierkegaard's works,[105] and also about his art of indirect communication.

The first to pay attention to this as a separate theme was Sergey Aleksandrovich Isayev (1951–2000)—the second person (after Hansen) whom one may call Kierkegaard's translator. But his translations were done later, when he became the Rector of the State Institute of Theatre Art. At the beginning of the 1980s, reading Kierkegaard in German, he wrote a thesis on him that was dedicated to existential dialectics. At that same time, he wrote his conclusions in an article "Kierkegaard as a Founder of Existential Dialectics" that deserves some attention.[106]

Unlike Piama Gaidenko, who thought that Kierkegaard's pseudonyms were his many I's, which he tried in vain to gather together, and who explained this phenomenon by his "torn consciousness" as an ironic man, Isayev reminded his readers that Kierkegaard was a religious thinker who "had already overcome the

---

[105] See Валентин Асмус [Valentin Asmus], "Лев Шестов и Кьеркегор (Об отношении Л. Шестова к зачинателю западноевропейского экзистенциализма)" [Lev Shestov and Kierkegaard (On L. Shestov's Attitude towards the Pioneer of European Existentialism)], *Научные доклады высшей школы. Философские науки*, no. 4, 1972, pp. 70–80; Алексей Богомолов [Aleksey Bogomolov] and Наталья Эфендиева [Natalya Efendiyeva], "Проблема диалектики в учении С. Кьеркегора о 'Стадиях на жизненном пути" [The Problem of Dialectics in S. Kierkegaard's Teaching on Stages on Life's Way], *Научные доклады высшей школы. Философские науки*, no. 5, 1976, pp. 101–10; Наталья Мудрагей [Natalya Mudragey], "Проблема человека в иррационалистическом учении С. Кьеркегора" [The Problem of Man in S. Kierkegaard's irrationalistic Teaching], *Вопросы философии*, no. 6, 1979, pp. 76–86; Наталья Эфендиева [Natalya Efendiyeva], "Проблема времени в философии С. Кьеркегора" [The Problem of Time in S. Kierkegaard's Philosophy], *Вопросы философии*, no. 5, 1980, pp. 152–64.

[106] Сергей Исаев [Sergey Isayev], "Кьеркегор как создатель экзистенциальной диалектики" [Kierkegaard as a Founder of Existential Dialectics], *Вестник МГУ*, no. 5, series 7, 1980, pp. 23–34.

'ironical' stage of existence."[107] But this argument of definitions—in the absence of contemporary translations and proper historical-philosophical reviews—seemed to lack proof, though Isayev, unlike Gaidenko, did not build any constructions, but tried to rely strictly on the text of the *Concluding Unscientific Postscript*, which Gaidenko almost completely neglected. But the ambiguity of the situation was deepened by the fact that Johannes Climacus was quoted directly as if it were not Isayev who raised the problem of Kierkegaard's pseudonyms. But the students of Moscow University, in whose bulletin the article was published, received a short ten-page synopsis, from which one could learn, first, how, according to Johannes Climacus, a scientific objective statement differs from an indirect artistic one, second, why the notion of an indirect method of communication is broader than the notion of "pseudonymity," and third, what role irony and humor play in existential communication. Unfortunately, this article repeated the common Soviet practice of "knowledge-expansion" by stating a philosopher's main ideas, supported by freely chosen quotations in sufficient volume such that the point of view of the author of the article was never clearly expressed.

But Isayev was among the first thanks to whom this practice was done away with during *perestroika*. His translation of *The Sickness unto Death* from Danish was published in 1990.[108] Three years later this work, together with *Fear and Trembling* and *The Concept of Anxiety*, was published again in a separate book.[109] In the Foreword, Isayev continued his old argument with Gaidenko, and this time he openly expressed his position. Here, as earlier in the book *Theology of Death. Writings on Protestant Modernism* (1991), where a separate chapter was dedicated to Kierkegaard, Isayev labeled him a Protestant theologian, to whom Orthodox problems of the Russian religious philosophy could hardly be applied.[110] To Gaidenko, who excluded Abraham from human society because of his "demonism," Isayev opposed the idea that "spirituality generally only begins when one does not seek the law of one's action in another man, and the motives of one's action—outside of himself. The universal (i.e., the state, the society, the social group) does not dominate an individual, but an individual dominates the universal."[111] To make such a statement seemed, for Isayev, to be very brave and timely in the country that was only recently freed from political oppression, and, in addition, it added a "pivotal feature" to Kierkegaard and enabled him to justify the publication of the book.

But by the middle of the 1980s there emerged in the Soviet Union a generation of non-engaged philosophers, who, rather phenomenologically, were interested

---

[107] Ibid., p. 24.

[108] Болезнь к смерти [*The Sickness unto Death*], trans. by Sergey Isayev, Moscow: Izdatelstvo politicheskoy literaturi 1990 (Series Этическая мысль. Научно-публицистические чтения).

[109] Страх и трепет [*Fear and Trembling*], Moscow: Republica 1993.

[110] Исаев [Isayev], "Теология страха и трепета Серена Кьеркегора" [The Theology of Fear and Trembling in Kierkegaard], in his *Теология смерти. Очерки протестантского модернизма* [The Theology of Death. Sketches of Protestant Modernism], Moscow: Izdatelstvo politicheskoy literaturi 1991, pp. 75–118.

[111] Исаев [Isayev], "Диалектическая лирика РР. Кьеркегора" [Kierkegaard's Dialectical Lyric], in *Страх и трепет* [*Fear and Trembling*], 1993, p. 8.

exclusively in the subject and, accordingly, in reflection and its techniques. Valery Aleksandrovich Podoroga (b. 1946), a scholar at the Institute of Philosophy, belonged to this new generation. His book, *The Metaphysics of the Landscape. Communicative Strategies in the Philosophical Culture in the 19th–20th Centuries*, stood far apart from the overwhelming ideological discussions of that time but was not aloof to the philosophical ideas accumulated in the twentieth century.[112] This book is the work of a very knowledgeable person, who managed both to incorporate the main trends of modern and post-modern thought (mainly, structural analysis and deconstruction) into his area of interests and to take his own stand in relation to these ideas.

The main principle of his approach may be described as follows: a book is like a sound, which exists only when it is played, though we still have musical notation of this musical sound. A book is read and exists only when it is read; it has no other existence apart from this one. Thought exists only as expressed, and so it is more appropriate to consider Kierkegaard's maieutic philosophizing not as an artificial technique, foreign to thought, but, on the contrary, thought is a thought expressed only when it envisages an after-effect produced on the reader.

It is Podoroga's opinion that the works of Kierkegaard, Nietzsche, and Heidegger, the three main persons in *Metaphysics of the Landscape*, stand out by the common standards for historical-philosophical analysis, namely because they possess individual communicative dimensions and values, which are not considered in classic and academic patterns of philosophical reflection. According to Podoroga, such works are exterritorial: "when reading, we leave the boundaries of category, genre, discipline, as if we were drifting from one content of meaning to another without any hindrance."[113] Podoroga contrasts his new approach with the traditional historical-philosophical analysis that strives to appropriate even the most daring, most "deviant" text by means of an interpretation which establishes the priority of one possible way of reading over all the others. Podoroga's goal is to free the text from the supremacy of one sole interpretation so that reading becomes not a linear uninterrupted reader-ridden process, but on the contrary reveals its gaps and pauses which manipulate the reader and make him forget himself. In this situation, the reader finds himself under the power of various textual currents, or "communicative strategies" in Podoroga's terminology, that determine both the inner textual structure and the methods of its influence on the reader. Kierkegaard's indirect communication represents one variety of this kind of strategy.

This distinguishes Podoroga's approach to Kierkegaard from that of the others. He claims that Kierkegaard is primarily interested in the formation-of-faith which in itself has little in common with the question "what is faith?" A "what is...?" question cannot approach the essence of faith. Hence there follows a criticism of Shestov, who, it is claimed, searches for "direct" answers in Kierkegaard's works

---

[112] Валерий Подорога [Valery Podoroga], *Метафизика ландшафта* [Metaphysics of the Landscape], Moscow: Наука 1993.
[113] Подорога [Podoroga], "Авраам в земле Мориа. Серен Киркегор" [Abraham in the Land of Moriah. Søren Kierkegaard], in his *Выражение и смысл* [Expression and Sense], Moscow: Ad Marginem 1995 [1993], p. 18.

and constantly confuses the formation-of-faith with its ultimate image: Shestov's book is

> absorbing reading, a kind of philosophical novel on a private thinker, who surrendered to despair due to the impossibility of accepting faith....But Kierkegaard did not give any helpful advice and did not answer questions with a strong accentuation on "what" and, probably would be surprised by such questions, which deny that his philosophical writings include the main answer: the answer to how faith can be performed, not understood.[114]

Paradoxically, such "understanding" is fraught with misunderstanding. On the whole, any interpretation (here and later Podoroga refers to the experience of the "Exordium" of *Fear and Trembling*) creates a fallacious experience of textual depth. This is precisely what Johannes de silentio strives to avoid.

"Any interpretation-oriented extracting of the 'inner sense' from the biblical text creates innumerable possibilities to develop church ideologies, while religious faith itself is no more considered a religious event,"[115] writes Podoroga. Johannes de silentio's task is to stop the transformation of a sacred text into a neutral element in historical narration, and Kierkegaard finds a way to perform it: like a skillful stage director, he edits four intertwined shots, four versions of an event. His purpose is to slow as much as possible the speed of the epic reading and show that it is supported by the neutrality of an absolute distance, which separates the Elohist narrator from the event itself. The reader, who does not see ruptures in the narration, may regard Abraham's ordeal as a simple informative event or a historical myth devoid of any religious content. But due to Kierkegaard's technique of "freezing the picture" aimed at slowing the reading, the reader receives the impression that this Old Testament event, which has no place and no time in history, is performed in a specific existential reality which connects the reader to Abraham. As regards other parts of *Fear and Trembling*, there and in some other works, i.e., the journals and notebooks, scattered passages from *Either/Or*, *The Concept of Anxiety* and, especially, the *Concluding Unscientific Postscript*, Podoroga finds and interprets in his own way those statements by Kierkegaard that refer to his poetics and cohere with communicative principles stated in *Metaphysics of the Landscape*.

This book is an absolutely creative and original work. It is senseless to try to decide while reading it whether the author in his understanding of Kierkegaard approaches the "authentic" Kierkegaard, which reflects a certain reference pattern of the research tradition. While not a moot work, *Metaphysics of the Landscape* shows that Kierkegaard's discourse with the reader may exist apart from the strict framework created by an academic interpretation of philosophical texts.

---

[114] Ibid., pp. 138–9.
[115] Ibid., p. 59.

VI. Summing Up

By the end of the 1980s, when the barriers of ideological censorship collapsed in the Soviet Union, there arose a free space, which, in the context of the persisting information vacuum, was quickly and without hindrance filled by various ideas of the historical-philosophical process and the most liberal versions of cultural phenomena. It became clear that in the changed political situation Kierkegaard, who was previously nearly outlawed, should be introduced to the public once again. Therefore, in December 1990 it was decided to hold a conference entitled "The Cultural Heritage of Søren Kierkegaard" at Moscow University, which was organized by Alex Fryszman under the auspices of the Danish Embassy in the USSR. In addition to other specialists, such as Finn Hauberg Mortensen and Jørgen Dehs, leading Soviet historians of philosophy took part in the conference; the high level of their speculative contemplation and comparisons was certainly indisputable.

However, the conference proved that for the ponderate Russian mind Kierkegaard is still too sophisticated a figure, and it would be more convenient to approach his works through other philosophers and artists, who were more often studied in Russia than Kierkegaard. There Hegel and his critic Trendelenburg helped, as did Gogol, who was an embodied conflict of an artist and a preacher, and even Mozart, as an author of music and aesthetic interpretation of Don Juan's character.[116] Incidentally, Peer Hultberg and Wladimir Herman staged in the "U Nikitskih Vorot" theater-studio "The Seducer's Diary" in the genre of *commedia dell'arte*. The success of such introductory events, as has often happened in Russian intellectual culture, was not the result of a patient and careful immersion in the works of a thinker, but of the advantages of a responsive acquired taste, deep insight, and even some ignorance of a writer, which allowed for a fresher opinion.

To tell the truth, this fresh opinion was very often justified by references to Kierkegaard's variety of faces and his inexhaustible philosophical appearances. An odd result of such multiplicity is the variable polyphony of his last name, which went on and on here ever since Hansen's transcription of "Kirkegor"; Tiander and Odintsov offered respective alternatives: "Kjerkegor" and "Kerkegor"; Shestov, who learned about Kierkegaard from the Germans, wrote his surname in a way close to its spelling, "Kirgegard," and Berdyaev, in episodic references, inflected it far and wide, "Kirhegardt," "Kirkegard(t)," and sometimes "Kirkegor."

But if we try to sum up the reception of Kierkegaard in Russia in a nutshell, then we should assume that even the most talented and successful interpretations of his philosophy would rather ignore its sources and purposes, while invariably seeing in "the complex of problems called Kierkegaard" something of their own, that they had snatched during the first still unintelligent acquaintance. This first impression—that Kierkegaard talks about "man," and, therefore, "about all of us," and preaches ideas of moral (evaluative) content and even public concern, all prevented the respective

---

[116] See *Мир Кьеркегора: Русские и датские интерпретации творчества Кьеркегора* [The World of Kierkegaard: Russian and Danish Readings of Kierkegaard's Works], ed. by Александр Иванов [Aleksandr Ivanov], Moscow: Ad Marginem 1994.

authors from, so to speak, "tuning in to his frequency." Too early and insensibly even for themselves, they started to seek a solution for the "privacy" and irony of Kierkegaard, who comprehended the essence of man through peering into a single individual (*Den Enkelte*)—in the humanity-oriented religious problematic of Russian thought.

One cannot say that in the last fifteen years the situation has changed drastically, although maybe there was an increase in the volume and quantity of sources. Something was added to the list of translations, when in 1997 there was published an amended version of *Repetition* (which I retrieved from the Hansen's archive in St. Petersburg), *Philosophical Fragments* and my articles and translations of extracts from the *Concluding Unscientific Postscript*. Pre-revolutionary publications by Hansen and Baltrušaitis are often reprinted nowadays, and Kierkegaard's Day in Moscow organized by Moscow University together with Moscow St. Andrews' Biblical Theological Institute was timed to coincide with one such reprint in October 2002. My translation of *Philosophical Fragments* and two volumes of *Concluding Unscientific Postscript*, translated by Sergey Isayev shortly before his death, are having a long wait to be published.

Bibliography

I. Russian Translations of Kierkegaard's Works

"Гармоническое развитие в человеческой личности эстетических и этических начал" ["The Balance between the Esthetic and the Ethical in the Development of the Personality"], trans. by Peter Hansen, *Северный вестник*, nos. 1, 3, 4, 1885, pp. 102–52.

"Афоризмы эстетика" [Aesthetical Aphorisms] (an extract from "Diapsalmata"), trans. by Peter Hansen, *Вестник Европы*, no. 3, 1886, pp. 108–15.

Наслаждение и долг [Pleasure and Debt] (extracts from "The Balance between the Esthetic and the Ethical in the Development of the Personality," "Diapsalmata," and "The Seducer's Diary"), trans. by Peter Hansen, St. Petersburg: Izdaniye M.M. Lederle and Co. 1894. (Republished and supplemented with the articles of Lev Shestov, "Kierkegaard as Religious Philosopher" and V. Yakovlev, "Søren Kierkegaard and Lev Shestov," in С. Кьеркегор [S. Kierkegaard], *Наслаждение и долг* [Pleasure and Debt], Rostov na Donu: Phoenix 1998, pp. 201–378 and in *Несчастнейший* [The Unhappiest One], ed. by A. Sukhovey, Moscow: Bibleycko-Bogoslovskiy Institut cv. Apostola Andreya 2002.)

"Несчастнейший" [The Unhappiest One] (extracts from "Diapsalmata" and "The Unhappiest One"), trans. by Jurgis Baltrušaitis, introduced by Harald Høffding, *Шиповник*, no. 4, 1908, pp. 24–45. (Republished in *Альманах мировой литературы*, vols. 1–4, 1914, vol. 4, pp. 59–88 and in *Несчастнейший* [The Unhappiest One], St. Petersburg: Intellekt 1991.)

"Непосредственные воплощения любовного начала или музыкальное любовное начало. Древний трагический мотив, отраженный в современном" [The Immediate Erotic Stages or The Musical-Erotic. The Tragic in Ancient Drama Reflected in the Tragic in Modern Drama] (extracts from "The Immediate Erotic Stages or The Musical-Erotic" and "The Tragic in Ancient Drama Reflected in The Tragic in Modern Drama"), trans. by Vyacheslav Vs. Ivanov, in *История эстетики. Памятники мировой эстетической мысли*, vols. 1–5, Moscow: Iskusstvo 1961–70, vol. 3 (1967), pp. 485–96.

"Из записок еще живущего" [From the Papers of One Still Living] (extracts from *From the Papers of One Still Living*], trans. by A. Sergeyev and A. Chekansky, in С. Киркегор [S. Kierkegaard], *Писатели Скандинавии о литературе* [Scandinavian Writers on Literature], ed. by K. Muradyan and I. Kupriyanova, Moscow: Raduga 1982, pp. 14–7.

Страх и трепет [Fear and Trembling] (translation of parts of *Fear and Trembling*), trans. by Peter Hansen, New York: Chalidze Publications 1982. (Republished in С. Киркегор [S. Kierkegaard], *Страх и трепет* [*Fear and Trembling*], St. Petersburg: Sovetskiy fond kultury. Otdeleniye "Stupeni" 1991.)

"Отрывки из *Дневника* 1847 г (с 'оценками' и пометками Льва Толстого)" [Extracts from the Journals of 1847 (With "Marks" and Marginal Notes by Leo Tolstoy)], trans. by Peter Hansen, *Вестник религиозного христианского движения*, no. 148 (Paris), 1986, pp. 55–81.

Болезнь к смерти [*The Sickness unto Death*], trans. by Sergey Isayev, Moscow: Izdatelstvo politicheskoy literatury 1990 (Series *Этическая мысль. Научно-публицистические чтения*).

"Дневник обольстителя" ["The Seducer's Diary"], trans. by Peter Hansen, in *Скандинавия: литературная панорама* [Scandinavia: Literary Panorama]. (2nd ed., Moscow: Khudozhestvennaya literatura 1991, pp. 11–160; republished in Серен Кьеркегор [Søren Kierkegaard], *Дневник обольстителя* ["The Seducer's Diary"], Kaluga: Zolotaya alleya 1993; Серен Киркегор [Søren Kierkegaard], *Дневник обольстителя*, ["The Seducer's Diary"], Moscow: EKSMO-Press 1999 and in Серен Кьеркегор [Søren Kierkegaard], *Дневник обольстителя* ["The Seducer's Diary"], St. Petersburg: Limbus-Press 2000.)

Несчастнейший [The Unhappiest One] (extracts from "Diapsalmata," "The Unhappiest One," and *Repetition*), St. Petersburg: Intellekt 1991.

Или-или [*Either/Or*], trans. by S.A. Sklyarenko, Moscow: Arktogeya 1993.

Болезнь к смерти [*The Sickness unto Death*], trans. by Sergey Isayev, Moscow: Respublica 1993. (Republished in С. Кьеркегор [S. Kierkegaard], *Страх и трепет* [Fear and Trembling], Moscow: Respublica 1998, pp. 251–350.)

"...*И это было светом его очей*..." ["...It was his eyes' joy..."] (extracts from the *Journals* of 1834–42 and 1849), trans. by Valeriya Mazepa, *Новая юность*, no. 2, 1993, pp. 133–45.

"Мгновение Серена Киркегора" [The Moment of Søren Kierkegaard] (extracts from *The Moment*), trans. by Alex Fryszman, *Независимая газета*, April 1, 1993.

"О понятии иронии" [On the Concept of Irony] (translation of parts of *The Concept of Irony*), trans. by A. Koskova and S. Koskov, *Логос*, no. 4, 1993, pp. 176–98.

Страх и трепет [*Fear and Trembling*], trans. by Sergey Isayev and Natalya Isayeva, Moscow: Respublica 1993 (2nd ed., Moscow: Terra 1998).

Повторение [*Repetition*], trans. by Peter Hansen, completed and ed. by Darya Loungina, Moscow: Labyrinth 1997. (Republished in *Несчастнейший* [The Unhappiest One], ed. by A. Sukhovey, Moscow: Bibleycko-Bogoslovskiy Institut cv. Apostola Andreya 2002.)

Заключительное ненаучное послесловие к 'Философским крохам' [Concluding Unscientific Postscript to "Philosophical Fragments"] (translation of Part Two, Section II, chapter III, §§ 1, 2 from *Concluding Unscientific Postscript*), trans. by Darya Loungina, *Логос*, no. 10, 1997, pp. 139–47. (Republished, *Культурология. XX век*, vol. 2, no. 6, 1998, pp. 232–44.)

Несчастнейший [The Unhappiest One] (extracts from "The Balance between the Esthetic and the Ethical in the Development of the Personality," "Diapsalmata," and "The Seducer's Diary"), ed. by A. Sukhovey, Moscow: Bibleysko-Bogoslovskiy Institut cv. Apostola Andreya 2002.

"Философские крохи" [Philosophical Fragments] (translation of chapter III from the *Philosophical Fragments*), trans. by Darya Loungina, *Вопросы философии*, no. 1, 2004, pp. 161–74.

Заключительное ненаучное послесловие к "Философским крохам" [*Concluding Unscientific Postscript to Philosophical Fragments*], trans. by Tatyana Valeryevna Shchittsova, Minsk: Logvinov 2005.

Заключительное ненаучное послесловие к "Философским крохам" [*Concluding Unscientific Postscript to Philosophical Fragments*], trans. by Sergey Isayev and Natalya Isayeva, St. Petersburg: S.-PGU 2005.

"Философские крохи" [Philosophical Fragments] (translation of Chapter I from the *Philosophical Fragments*), trans. by Darya Loungina, *Вопросы философии*, no. 12, 2005, pp. 138–52.

Философские крохи [*Philosophical Fragments*], trans. by Darya Loungina, forthcoming.

II. Secondary Literature on Kierkegaard in Russia

Аверинцев, Сергей [Averincev, Sergey] and Юрий Давыдов [Jury Davidov], "Кьеркегор" [Kierkegaard], in *Философская энциклопедия* [Philosophical Encyclopedia], vols. 1–5, Moscow: Sovetskaya Entsiklopediya 1960–5, vol. 3 (1964), pp. 128–30.

Адмони, Владимир [Admoni, Vladimir], "Кьеркегор" [Kierkegaard], in *Краткая литературная энциклопедия* [Little Literary Encyclopedia], vols. 1–9, Moscow: Sovetskaya Entsiklopediya 1962–78, vol. 3 (1966), p. 940.

Анонимно [Anonymous], Рецензия на *Наслаждение и долг* [Review of "Pleasure and Debt"], *Русское богатство*, no. 6, 1894, pp. 80–1.

Анонимно [Anonymous], "Предшественник Ибсена" [Ibsen's Forerunner], *Русский вестник*, no. 8, 1901, pp. 567–73.

Анонимно [Anonymous], "Киркегор" [Kierkegaard], in *Большая энциклопедия* [Large Encyclopedia], ed. by Сергей Николаевич Южаков [Sergey Nikolaevitch Yuzhakov], vols. 1–22, St. Petersburg: Prosveshcheniye 1903–4, vol. 10 (1903), p. 754.

Асмус, Валентин [Asmus, Valentin], "Лев Шестов и Кьеркегор (Об отношении Л. Шестова к зачинателю западноевропейского экзистенциализма)" [Lev Shestov and Kierkegaard (On L. Shestov's Attitude towards the Pioneer of European Existentialism)], *Научные доклады высшей школы. Философские науки*, no. 4, 1972, pp. 70–80.

Б[люмфельд], Л. Г. [Blumfeld, L.G.], "Киркегор" [Kierkegaard], in *Литературная энциклопедия* [Literary Encyclopedia], vols. 1–11, Moscow and Leningrad: Izdatelstvo Kommunisticheskoy Akademii 1929–39, vol. 5 (1931), p. 26.

Богомолов, Алексей [Bogomolov, Aleksey] and Наталья Эфендиева [Natalya Efendiyeva], "Проблема диалектики в учении С. Кьеркегора о 'Стадиях на жизненном пути" [The Problem of Dialectics in S. Kierkegaard's Teaching on Stages on Life's Way], *Научные доклады высшей школы. Философские науки*, no. 5, 1976, pp. 101–10.

Буткевич, Тимофей [Butkevitch, Timophey], "Датский философ Серен Киркегор как проповедник ифических начал в развитии личности" [The Danish Philosopher Søren Kierkegaard as a Preacher of the Ethical Principles in the Composition of a Personality], *Вера и разум*, no. 16, 1886, pp. 185–225.

Быховский, Бернард [Bykhovsky, Bernard], "Датский анти-Гегель" [The Danish Anti-Hegel], *Вопросы философии*, no. 11, 1971, pp. 80–90.

— *Кьеркегор* [Kierkegaard], Moscow: Mysl 1972.

Ганзен, Петр [Hansen, Peter], "Киркегор" [Kierkegaard], in *Энциклопедический словарь Брокгауза-Ефрона*, vols. 1–43, St. Petersburg: izdatel' I.A. Efron, 1890–1907, vol. 15 (1895), pp. 124–7.

Гайденко, Пиама Павловна [Gaidenko, Piama Pavlovna], "Киркегор и философско-эстетические истоки экзистенциализма" [Kierkegaard and the Philosophic-Aesthetical Sources of Existentialism], *Вопросы литературы*, no. 7, 1967, pp. 133–57.

— *Трагедия эстетизма. О миросозерцании Серена Киркегора* [The Tragedy of Aestheticism. On the *Weltanschauung* of Søren Kierkegaard], Moscow: Iskystvo 1970 (republished as Пиама Гайденко [Piama Gaidenko], *Прорыв в трансцендентному* [Breakthrough towards the Transcendental], Moscow: Respublica 1997).

— "Свобода как метафизический страх" [Freedom Expressed as Anxiety], in her *Философия Фихте и современность* [The Philosophy of Fichte and the Present], Moscow: Mysl 1979, pp. 261–73.

Гайденко, Пиама Павловна [Gaidenko, Piama Pavlovna] and Юрий Бородай [Jury Boroday], "Серен Киркегор и критика Гегеля с позиций экзистенциализма" [Søren Kierkegaard and his Criticism of Hegel from the Existential Point of View], *Вестник МГУ. Серия экономики и философии*, no. 2, 1961, pp. 45–54.

Gaidenko, P.P. [Piama Pavlovna], "Kierkegaard and the Philosophical-Esthetic Sources of Existentialism," *Russian Studies in Philosophy. A Journal of Translations*, vol. 43, no. 4, 2005, pp. 5–34.

Гайдукова, Татьяна [Gaidukova, Tatyana], *Эстетическое существование в философии Кьеркегора* [The Aesthetic Mode of Existence in Kierkegaard's Philosophy] in *Из истории зарубежной философии XIX–XX веков* [From the History of Foreign Philosophy of the Nineteenth and Twentieth Century], Moscow: Izdatelstvo MGU 1967.

— "Проблема выбора в философии Кьеркегора" [The Problem of Choice in Kierkegaard's Philosophy], *Вестник МГУ*, no. 6, series 8, 1969, pp. 32–44.

— "Принцип иронии в философии Киркегора" [The Principle of Irony in Kierkegaard's Philosophy], *Вопросы философии*, no. 9, 1970, pp. 109–20.

— "Кьеркегор об иронии" [Kierkegaard on Irony], in her *У истоков* [At the Origins], St. Petersburg: Alethea 1995, pp. 1–98.

Дионео, [Исаак Шкловский], [Dioneo, [Isaak Shklovsky]], "Датский моралист" [The Danish Moralist], *Одесские новости*, November 25, 1894.

Доброхотов, Александр [Dobrokhotov, Aleksandr], "Апология Когито или Проклятие Валаама. Критика Декарта в *Ненаучном послесловии* Керкегора" [Apology for the Cogito or Bileam's Curse. Kierkegaard's Criticism of Descartes in his *Unscientific Postscript*], *Логос*, no. 10, 1997, pp. 129–38.

Долгов, Константин [Dolgov, Konstantin], "Серен Киркегор—предтеча современного экзистенциализма" [Søren Kierkegaard as a Forerunner of Contemporary Existentialism], in his *От Киркегора до Камю* [From Kierkegaard to Camus], Moscow: Iskustvo 1990, pp. 7–42.

Егоров, Николай [Yegorov, Nikolay], "Киркегор" [Kierkegaard], in *Православная Богословская энциклопедия* [The Orthodox Encyclopedia of Theology], vols. 1–12, St. Petersburg: A.P. Lopukhin, 1900–11, vol. 10 (1909), pp. 440–53.

Зандер, Лев [Zander, Lev], "Жизнь и философия Киркегора" [Kierkegaard's Life and Philosophy], *Русское обозрение* (Vladivostok), 1922.

Заславский, Давид [Zaslavskiy, David], "Юродство и юродивые в современной буржуазной философии" [Idiocy and Idiots in Contemporary Bourgeois Philosophy], *Вопросы философии*, no. 5, 1954, pp. 138–51.

Зотов, Анатолий [Zotov, Anatoliy] and Юрий Мельвиль [Jury Melvil], "Христианский предэкзистенциализм С. Кьеркегора" [The Christian Pre-Existentialism of S. Kierkegaard], in their *Буржуазная философия середины 19—начала 20 в.* [Bourgeois Philosophy from the Middle of the 19th to the Beginning of the 20th Century], Moscow: Izdatelsvo MGU 1988, pp. 221–43.

Иванов, Александр [Ivanov, Aleksandr] (ed.), *Мир Кьеркегора: Русские и датские интерпретации творчества Кьеркегора* [The World of Kierkegaard: Russian and Danish Readings of Kierkegaard's Work], Moscow: Ad Marginem 1994.

Исаев, Сергей [Isayev, Sergey], "К вопросу о 'косвенной' форме изложения в произведениях Серена Кьеркегора" [About "Indirect Communication" in Søren Kierkegaard's Works], in his *Человек, сознание, мировоззрение* [The Human Being, the Consciousness, the Life-View], Moscow: Izdatelsvo MGU 1979, pp. 24–34.

— "Кьеркегор как создатель экзистенциальной диалектики" [Kierkegaard as a Founder of Existential Dialectics], *Вестник МГУ*, no. 5, series 7, 1980, pp. 23–34.

— "Теология страха и трепета Серена Кьеркегора" [The Theology of Fear and Trembling in Kierkegaard], in his *Теология смерти. Очерки протестантского модернизма* [Theology of Death. Sketches of Protestant Modernism], Moscow: Izdatelsvo politicheskoy literaturi 1991, pp. 75–118.

— "Кьеркегор" [Kierkegaard], in *Новая философская энциклопедия* [New Philosophical Encyclopedia], vols. 1–4, Moscow: Mysl 2000–01, vol. 2, pp. 358–9.

Карпушин, Владимир [Karpusin, Vladimir], "Серен Киркегор—предшественник экзистенциальной антропологии" [Søren Kierkegaard as a Forerunner of Existential Humanism], *Вопросы философии*, no. 12, 1967, pp. 103–13.

Левицкий, Сергей [Levitsky, Sergey], "Достоевский и Киркегор" [Dostoyevsky and Kierkegaard], *Quart* (Prague), 1936.

Лунгина, Дарья [Loungina, Darya], "Об экзистенции в *Понятии страха*" [On Existence in *The Concept of Anxiety*], in *Кьеркегор и современность* [Kierkegaard and the Present], ed. by Т.В. Щитцова [T.V. Shchittsova], Minsk: Ribs i Go 1996, pp. 66–72.

— "Керкегор" [Kierkegaard], in *Энциклопедический словарь Кирилл и Мефодий* [The Cyril and Methodical Encyclopedical Dictionary], Moscow: KM 2000 (published as CD-Rom).

— "Керкегор и проблема науки" [Kierkegaard and the Problem of Science], *Вопросы философии*, no. 1, 2000, pp. 161–7.

Mareeva, E.V., "Unity of Soul through the Power of Choice," *Russian Studies in Philosophy. A Journal of Translations*, vol. 43, no. 4, 2005, pp. 34–50.

Мудрагей, Наталья [Mudragey, Natalya], "Проблема человека в иррационалистическом учении С. Кьеркегора" [The Problem of Man in S. Kierkegaard's Irrationalistic Teaching], *Вопросы философии*, no. 6, 1979, pp. 76–86.

— "Иррациональное и иррационализм на материале философии Кьеркегора" [The Irrational and Irrationalism on the Material of Kierkegaard's Philosophy], in her *Рациональное и иррациональное*, Moscow: Наука 1985, pp. 68–99.

Одинцов, Михаил [Odintsov, Mikhail], "Философия религиозного действия. Серен Керкегор" [Philosophy of the Religious Action. Søren Kierkegaard], *Русская мысль*, vol. 10, no. 7, 1912, pp. 1–31.

Подорога, Валерий [Podoroga, Valery], "Авраам в земле Мориа. Серен Киркегор" [Abraham in the Land of Moriah. Søren Kierkegaard], in his *Метафизика ландшафта* [Metaphysics of the Landscape], Moscow: Наука 1993, pp. 1–167.

Розенталь, Марк Моисеевич [Rozental, Mark Moyseyevich] and Павел Федорович Юдин [Pavel Fyodorovich Yudin] (eds.), "Киркегор" [Kierkegaard], in *Краткий философский словарь* [Short Philosophical Dictionary], Moscow: Izdatelstvo politicheskoy literaturi 1954, p. 77.

Стрельцова, Галина [Streltsova, Galina], "Парадокс философии Серена Кьеркегора" [The Paradox of Søren Kierkegaard's Philosophy], *Вестник МГУ*, no. 4, series 7, 2000, pp. 106–20.

Тиандер, Карл Фридрих [Tiander, Karl Friedrich], "Отклики романтизма в Дании и Швеции" [Echoes of Romanticism in Denmark and Sweden], in *История западной литературы* [The History of Western Literatures], ed. by Ф.Д. Батюшков [F.D. Batyuskov], vols. 1–3, St. Petersburg: Izdaniye obshchestva "Mir," 1910–14, vol. 3 (1914), pp. 430–40.

— "Кьеркегор" [Kierkegaard], in *Энциклопедический словарь Гранат* [Granat's Encyclopedical Dictionary], vols. 1–58, Moscow: Granat 1910–48, vol. 26, p. 298.

— "Кьеркегор" [Kierkegaard], in *Новый энциклопедический словарь Брокгауза-Ефрона* [Brockhaus-Efron New Encyclopedical Dictionary], vols. 1–29, St. Petersburg: izdatel I.A. Efron 1911–16, vol. 23 (ca. 1915), p. 805.

Tsypina, L.V., "Introduction to the Philosophical Poetics of Soren Kierkegaard," *Russian Studies in Philosophy. A Journal of Translations*, vol. 43, no. 4, 2005, pp. 71–87.

Тхоржевский, Иван [Tkhorzhevsky, Ivan], "Пир" [The Symposium], *Возрождение*, no. 3033, 1933 (Paris), pp. 5–6.

Фришман, Алекс [Fryszman, Alex], *Достоевский и Киркегор* [Dostoyevsky and Kierkegaard], *Достоевский и мировая культура*, no. 1, 1993, pp. 575–91.

Чичнева, Елена [Tchitchnyova, Yelena], "Философия как проповедь (С. Киркегор)" [Philosophy as Preaching (S. Kierkegaard)], *Вестник МГУ*, no. 5, series 7, 2000, pp. 62–74.

Шестов, Лев, [Shestov, Lev], "В фаларийском быке" [In Phalaris' Bull], *Revue philosophique*, nos. 1–4 (Paris) 1932. (Republished in Лев Шестов [Lev Shestov], *Афины и Иерусалим* [Athens and Jerusalem], Paris: YMCA-Press 1951, pp. 79–154.)

— "Киргегард и Достоевский" [Kierkegaard and Dostoyevsky], *Путь*, no. 48 (Paris) 1935, pp. 20–37. (Republished as a preface in Лев Шестов [Lev Shestov], *Киргегард и экзистенциальная философия* (Глас вопиющего в пустыне) [Kierkegaard and the Existential Philosophy (Vox clamantis in deserto)], Paris: Sovremenniye zapiski i Dom Knigi 1939.)

— *Киргегард и экзистенциальная философия* (Глас вопиющего в пустыне) [Kierkegaard and the Existential Philosophy (Vox clamantis in deserto)], Paris: Sovremenniye zapiski i Dom Knigi 1939 (reprinted, Moscow: Progress-Gnosis 1992).

— "Киргегард—религиозный философ" [Kierkegaard as Religious Philosopher], *Русские записки*, no. 3 (Paris), 1938, pp. 196–221. (Republished in Лев Шестов [Lev Shestov], *Умозрение и откровение* [Speculation and Revelation], Paris: YMCA-Press 1964, pp. 231–60.)

Эфендиева, Наталья [Efendiyeva, Natalya], "Проблема времени в философии С. Кьеркегора" [The Problem of Time in S. Kierkegaard's Philosophy], *Вопросы философии*, no. 5, 1980, pp. 152–64.

Э [фруси], [Б. О.] [E[ffrusi], B.[oris] O.[sipovitch]], "Датский философ Серен Киркегаард" [The Danish Philosopher Søren Kierkegaard], *Мир Божий*, no. 7, 1894, pp. 211–12.

III. Secondary Literature on Kierkegaard's Reception in Russia

Djakowska, Alina and Alex Fryszman, "Drei Stadien in der polnischen Rezeption von *Furcht und Zittern* und *Die Wiederholung*," *Kierkegaard Studies. Yearbook*, 2002, pp. 310–29.

Grimsley, Ronald, "Chestov," in *The Legacy and Interpretation of Kierkegaard*, ed. by Niels Thulstrup and Marie Mikulová Thulstrup, Copenhagen: C.A. Reitzel 1981 (*Bibliotheca Kierkegaardiana*, vol. 8), pp. 276–77.

Nagy, András, "Kierkegaard in Russia. The Ultimate Paradox: Existentialism at the Crossroads of Religious Philosophy and Bolshevism," in *Kierkegaard Revisited. Proceedings from the Conference "Kierkegaard and the Meaning of Meaning It" Copenhagen, May 5–9, 1996*, ed. by Niels Jørgen Cappelørn and Jon Stewart, Berlin and New York: Walter de Gruyter 1997 (*Kierkegaard Studies. Monograph Series*, vol. 10), pp. 107–38.

Лунгина, Дарья [Loungina, Darya], "Узнавание Керкегора в России" [Recognition of Kierkegaard in Russia], *Логос*, no. 7, 1996, pp. 168–83.

— "On the Original Reception of Kierkegaard in Russia, 1880–90s," *Søren Kierkegaard Newsletter*, no. 48, 2004, pp. 20–4.

Lungina, D.A [Loungina, Darya], "Russia's Acquaintance with Kierkegaard," *Russian Studies in Philosophy. A Journal of Translations*, vol. 43, no. 4, 2005, pp. 50–70.

Passy, Isaac, "Søren Kierkegaard and the Russian Religious Renaissance," in *Søren Kierkegaard. Philosoph, Schriftsteller, Theologe. Vorträge des bulgarisch-dänischen Seminars Sofia 31. März–2. April 1992*, Sofia: Internationale Kyrill und Method-Stiftung 1992, pp. 22–7.

Чертков, Леонид [Tchertkov, Leonid], "Søren Kierkegaard in Russian Literature," *Kierkegaardiana*, vol. 13, 1984, pp. 128–48.

— "Серен Киркегор в русской литературе" [Søren Kierkegaard in Russian Literature], *Вестник религиозного христианского движения*, no. 148 (Paris) 1986, pp. 27–55.

Bulgaria:
The Long Way from Indirect Acquaintance to Original Translation

Desislava Töpfer-Stoyanova

It could be considered a peculiarity of the Bulgarian cultural milieu that Søren Kierkegaard has been one of the most translated philosophical authors in the last fifteen years. The removal of ideological barriers after the political changes in 1989 created conditions promoting a flourishing activity of translation in the country. The Danish philosopher with his eight translated works certainly occupies a special place in the process of opening of Bulgarian culture to European thought. In 1991 *Either/Or*,[1] *Fear and Trembling*,[2] *Repetition*,[3] and *The Sickness unto Death*[4] were published in Bulgarian; *The Concept of Anxiety* appeared in 1992,[5] followed by *The Concept of Irony* (1993),[6] *Practice in Christianity* (1994),[7] and *Philosophical Fragments* (2002).[8] This increased interest of translators, publishers, and the reading audience could be explained by the need to overcome a clear lack that was present at that time: no complete work of the Danish philosopher had been translated into Bulgarian until 1991. Another positive tendency in the translation of Søren Kierkegaard into Bulgarian is worth mentioning. In contrast to the old translation, all the translations in the last fifteen years (with the single exception of *Philosophical Fragments*) were

[1]   *Или—или, част 1* [*Either/Or*, vol. 1], trans. by Stefan Nachev, Sofia: Narodna kultura 1991; *Или—или, част 2* [*Either/Or*, vol. 2], trans. by Stefan Nachev, Sofia: Narodna kultura 1991.
[2]   *Страх и трепет* [*Fear and Trembling*], trans. by Stefan Nachev, Sofia: Narodna kultura 1991.
[3]   *Повторението* [*Repetition*], trans. by Stefan Nachev, Sofia: Narodna kultura 1991.
[4]   *Болка за умиране* [*The Sickness unto Death*], trans. by Radosveta Teoharova, Varna: Steno 1991.
[5]   *Понятието страх* [*The Concept of Anxiety*], trans. by Radosveta Teoharova, Varna: Steno 1992.
[6]   *Понятието ирония* [*The Concept of Irony*], trans. by Stefan Nachev, Sofia: Universitetsko izdatelstvo Sv. Kliment Ohridski 1993.
[7]   *Въдворение в християнството* [*Practice in Christianity*], trans. by Radosveta Teoharova, Varna: Steno 1994.
[8]   *Философски фрагменти* [*Philosophical Fragments*], trans. by Krasimir Abdelhalil, Sofia: Kota 2002.

made from Danish. This was possible thanks to the pioneering work of the translator Stefan Nachev and the translating activity of Radosveta Teoharova.

Only short parts of Kierkegaard's works were translated before 1991; despite this, he was not completely unknown to the Bulgarian reading public. Already at the beginning of the twentieth century Bulgarian literary circles were acquainted with the name and some of the ideas of Søren Kierkegaard. Their sources were mainly translations and secondary literature in German and Russian, seldom in French or English. The interest in Kierkegaard's work was provoked by the popularity of another Danish author, who had decidedly influenced Bulgarian literary criticism—Georg Brandes (1842–1927). At the end of the nineteenth and the beginning of the twentieth century, parts of his essays on modern European literature were translated in different Bulgarian magazines and newspapers. In accordance with Brandes' understanding, Kierkegaard was popular as a forerunner of Henrik Ibsen (1828–1906). Thus, the interest in the Danish philosopher was related to Ibsen's popularity.

The first Bulgarian translation of a Kierkegaard text appeared in 1914 in the magazine *Rodno izkustvo*. A part of "Diapsalmata" was translated by Dimiter Stoichev.[9] He belonged to a group of Bulgarian modernist poets and writers. It is not clear from what language the translation was made—most probably Russian or German. A short note about the personality of Kierkegaard accompanied the text. According to it, he was an author of many poetic, religious, and philosophical works and a representative of the reaction against Romanticism.

In 1920 a translation of "The Unhappiest One" was printed in the modernist magazine *Vezni*.[10] It is noteworthy that this magazine played a very important role on the Bulgarian literary scene at that time and was considered a great authority on literature. The translator was the prominent Bulgarian poet Ljudmil Stoyanov (1888–1973). In this case again it is not clear from what language the translation was made. It seems rather probable that it was made from Russian since the same excerpt had been published in Russian twelve years before the Bulgarian translation. Kierkegaard's text was accompanied by a short translator's commentary about the life and the ideas of the Danish thinker. Stoyanov refers to Harald Høffding (1843–1931) as the best authority on Kierkegaard's work. In agreement with Høffding, he sees the Danish philosopher as a representative of the reaction against Romanticism. As the central point in Kierkegaard's philosophy he singles out his teaching about personality and subjective passion. He emphasizes Kierkegaard's idea of the inadequacy of scientific knowledge. The Bulgarian poet agrees with the Danish philosopher that human existence, as temporal, requires much more hope and faith than science could provide. According to the translator, with this idea Kierkegaard is very close to contemporary philosophy and is a forerunner of William James (1842–1910) and Henri Bergson (1859–1941). Stoyanov states that neither Høffding nor Brandes were able to estimate the true importance of the work of the Danish thinker for contemporary metaphysics.

---

[9]   "Diapsalmata," trans. by Димитър Стойчев [Dimiter Stoichev], *Родно изкуство*, no. 6, 1914.
[10]   "Най-нещастният" ["The Unhappiest One"], trans. by Людмил Стоянов [Ljudmil Stoyanov], *Везни*, nos. 4–5, 1920.

The short commentary contains also some biographical notes, concerning the conflict between the official Danish church and Kierkegaard, and his complicated inner life, torn between reality and dream. Stoyanov claims that the inner struggle of the Danish thinker with himself led him to a psychological crisis and caused his death. It seems that in the next decades interest in Kierkegaard among literary circles in Bulgaria declined somewhat. The Danish philosopher was likewise of almost no interest to Bulgarian philosophers. The intellectual climate in the years after the Second World War did not promote any serious research on Kierkegaard's work. In the period before the political changes in the country, only very few articles on Kierkegaard appeared in Bulgarian philosophical magazines.

In the 1970s Dobrin Spasov, one of the leading figures of Marxist philosophy in Bulgaria and a professor at the University in Sofia, presented a short survey of the ideas of the Danish thinker in an article about Danish philosophy. The article was also published in English in the *Yearbook of the University of Sofia*. Spasov assigns to himself the modest task not of adding to "the rich literature on the great Danish philosopher,"[11] but only of helping the Bulgarian reader to supplement his too simplified evaluation of Kierkegaard as "religious thinker and political reactionary."[12] As we learn from Spasov, the main source of information about Kierkegaard for the Bulgarian reader had for a long time been Harald Høffding's *History of Modern Philosophy* in its Russian translation.

Spasov emphasizes the close connection between Kierkegaard's philosophy and Kierkegaard's own existence. The Marxist professor devotes particular attention to the question about the motivation of Kierkegaard's productivity. Not surprisingly, he sees as decisive Kierkegaard's supposed illness. A proof of its existence he finds in the complaint, frequently repeated through the most sincere pages of Kierkegaard's journals, that he has "a thorn in the flesh." The philosophy of Kierkegaard is defined as a philosophy of individual existence. Spasov sees a "bright individualistic mentality" in Kierkegaard's critique of Hegel and classical German idealism. Still, the Bulgarian professor considers it important to stress that "it would be exaggeration to think that German systematic philosophy did not leave any stamp"[13] on Kierkegaard's thinking. His argument is that the Danish thinker himself systematized his existential philosophy. What is meant here are the three stages of life—the aesthetic, the ethical, and the religious as well as the intermediate phases—the ironical and the humorous.

One of Spasov's important generalizations is that in spite of being a predominantly religious thinker, Kierkegaard interprets religion "morally and not too much theologically."[14] The Bulgarian Marxist argues that Kierkegaard emphasizes those moments in the Christian doctrine which are harmonious with his individualism.

The conclusion of the part of the article devoted to the Danish philosopher is that Kierkegaard's work is one of the main sources of the most prominent philosophical

---

[11] Добрин Спасов [Dobrin Spasov], "Contemporary Danish Philosophy," *Yearbook of the University of Sofia*, no. 1, 1971, p. 71.
[12] Ibid.
[13] Ibid., p. 73.
[14] Ibid., p. 74.

tradition in Denmark. Spasov sees his influence on modern Danish philosophy in the skeptical and individualistic character of this philosophy, in its intimacy with psychology, and in the merits of its literary style.

In 1981 an article "With and Without Kierkegaard—a Dilemma of the Young Lukács," by Dimiter Zashev was published in the magazine *Filosofska misul.*[15] The article investigates the influence of Kierkegaard's philosophical heritage on the work of the Hungarian philosopher György Lukács (1885–1971). Zashev finds traces of Kierkegaardian thought already in Lukács' early work, *History of the Development of the Modern Drama* (1911). He states that Kierkegaard's concept of "modern tragedy" influenced Lukács' understanding of drama. The common point between the two authors is the idea that the changes of dramatic style in the modern epoch could not be explained from a merely aesthetic point of view, but rather result from more general changes in society. Outlining Lukács' dialogue with Kierkegaard in the later works of the Hungarian philosopher, Zashev stresses the critical distance at which Lukács formulates his own ideas. The center of Zashev's investigation is Lukács' so-called essayistic period and primarily his essay on Kierkegaard entitled "Søren Kierkegaard and Regine Olsen" published in the volume *Chaos and Forms.*[16] In the essay the breaking off of the engagement with Regine is interpreted as Kierkegaard's "gesture." According to Lukács, with this gesture Kierkegaard aims to shape his life and to express it in a symbolic form. Zashev shows how the existential dialectic of Kierkegaard is interpreted by Lukács in the perspective of the aesthetic problem of form.

The great number of recently translated works of the Danish philosopher in the last fifteen year might give the impression that Kierkegaard research is presently flourishing in Bulgaria. But this is only partly true. The interest in the Danish thinker, though constant, has nevertheless been limited. Yet several books and articles have indeed been published in this period. It is characteristic for Bulgarian reception that only the pseudonymous writings and very often only those, which are translated into Bulgarian, are object of investigation. It is remarkable that the most frequently quoted authorities on Kierkegaard are still Georg Brandes and Miguel de Unamuno (1864–1936). This is due to the fact that their works dealing with the philosophy of Kierkegaard have been translated into Bulgarian.[17] It is also noteworthy that the Russian reception of Kierkegaard has undoubtedly influenced Kierkegaard research in Bulgaria, which is due to the close relationship between the languages. The most popular Russian authors are Lev Shestov (1866–1938) with his book *Kierkegaard*

---

[15] Димитър Зашев [Dimiter Zashev], "Със и без Киркегор—една дилема на младия Лукач" [With and Without Kierkegaard—a Dilemma of the Young Lukács], *Философска мисъл*, no. 11, 1981, pp. 76–87.

[16] See Georg Lukács, *Хаос и форми* [Chaos and Forms], trans. by Димитър Зашев (Dimiter Zashev), Sofia: Universitetsko izdatelstvo Sv. Kliment Ohridski 1987 (Lukács' essay on Kierkegaard and Regine Olsen is in English published as "The Foundering of Form against Life. Sören Kierkegaard and Regina Olsen," in *Soul and Form*, Cambridge, Mass.: MIT Press 1974, pp. 28–41).

[17] See Georg Brandes, *Литературата на 19 век* [The Literature of the Nineteenth Century], Sofia: Nauka i izkustwo 1980; Miguel de Unamuno, *Есета* [*Essays*], Sofia: Universitetsko izdatelstvo Sv. Kliment Ohridski 1995.

and Existential Philosophy, and Piama Gaidenko with *The Tragedy of Aestheticism*.[18] Of course, these remarks about Kierkegaard research in Bulgaria sketch only a general tendency and do not exhaust the diversity of references to other Kierkegaard scholars.

In 1998, Sofia University professor Isaac Passi published his book *Søren Kierkegaard*.[19] A shorter version of the same text appeared in 1994 in the book *On the Philosophy of Life. Eight Philosophical Portraits*,[20] and again in year 2001 in the book *Schopenhauer, Kierkegaard, Nietzsche*. *Søren Kierkegaard* offers short biographical notes and an overview of some of the main ideas of the Danish philosopher on the basis of the pseudonymous writings with the emphasis on *Either/Or*, *Fear and Trembling*, and *Stages on Life's Way*.[21] In the perspective of the history of philosophy Kierkegaard is described as a representative of the philosophy of life and as a forefather of existentialism. Passi agrees with Shestov, who draws a comparison between the ideas of Kierkegaard and those of Fyodor Dostoevsky and sees both the Russian writer and the Danish thinker as rebels against the hypertrophied claims of reason.

The book devotes particular attention to the controversy with Hegel. This conflict results, according to Passi, from Kierkegaard's interest in individual existence, which Hegel's philosophy completely neglects. According to the Bulgarian author, in spite of the controversy, the German philosophical tradition and particularly Hegel have had a strong influence on Kierkegaard's thinking. This influence is evident in the method of dialectics. Nonetheless, Passi claims that the similarity between the subjective dialectics of Kierkegaard and Hegel's dialectical method is only formal. Subjective dialectics deals with stage of individual existence, whereas Hegelian dialectics is concerned with stages of the development of the Absolute. The transition from one stage of existence to another depends on the will of the individual and does not result from an objective law of development. This difference is closely connected with the method of describing the stages. Kierkegaard does not give an account of them from an objective point of view. He rather describes the stages with many individual voices, speaking from their subjective point of view. That is why, according to Passi, the different pseudonyms are essential to his work, which is constructed on the principle of drama.

Considerable space in the book is devoted to the description of the three stages of life—the aesthetic, the ethical, and the religious. Passi draws a parallel between the moods described by Kierkegaard as "aesthetic" and the Romantic moods. He

---

[18] Лев Шестов [Lev Shestov], *Киркегард и екзистенциалная философия* [Kierkegaard and Existential Philosophy], Paris: Dom knig i sowrem. zapiski 1939; Пиама Гайденко [Piama Gaidenko], *Трагедия эстетизма* [The Tragedy of Aestheticism], Moscow: Iskustvo 1970.

[19] Исак Паси [Isaac Passi], *Сьорен Киркегор* [*Søren Kierkegaard*], Sofia: Universitetsko izdatelstvo Sv. Kliment Ohridski 1998.

[20] Исак Паси [Isaac Passi], *Към философият на живота. Осем философски портрета* [On the Philosophy of Life. Eight Philosophical Portraits], Sofia: Universitetsko izdatelstvo Sv. Kliment Ohridski 1994.

[21] Исак Паси [Isaac Passi], *Шопенхауер, Киркегор, Ницше* [Schopenhauer, Kierkegaard, Nietzsche], Sofia: Kiril i Metodii 2001.

claims that Romanticism, though in a transformed form, lives in the work of the Danish thinker. Irony is discussed on the basis of *The Concept of Irony*. In agreement with Georg Brandes, Passi argues that Kierkegaard's dissertation is the real starting point of his work. Themes and features of the later writings of Kierkegaard can be recognized already in this work. In his exposition of the ethical stage, Passi emphasizes the importance of the category of "choice." Not unlike Kant, the Danish thinker connects morality with will, but his understanding of ethics is contradictory to that of Kant. The choice as category in Kierkegaard's philosophy does not have any foundation in what is universal and valid for everyone; rather, it depends only on the individual subject. In this way, Passi argues, Kierkegaard's ethics cannot escape the danger of moral relativism. According to Passi's interpretation, the aesthetic and the ethical existence are only stages leading to the superior way of life—the religious. Nevertheless, he claims that in the religious way of life the ethical is not completely neglected, but rather gains a new dimension. Kierkegaard is criticized with the argument that, with his description of the religious stage as a complete devotion to God, he leaves no room for individual freedom and the possibility of real choice. The Bulgarian author emphasizes the opposition between paradox as the main characteristic of Christian faith, on one hand, and knowledge and reason, on the other.

Kierkegaard is appreciated as sociologist and social critic on the basis of his review of Thomasine Gyllembourg's *Two Ages*. In this work, according to Passi, he "makes a virtuous analysis of his epoch and the possibility of choice, which it leaves."[22] The ideas of Kierkegaard are interpreted as very close to those of Schopenhauer and Nietzsche. The similarity is seen in the description of the contemporary epoch as hostile to individuality. The social criticism of the Danish thinker, according to the Bulgarian author, outlines themes that would become central for the most prominent social critics of the nineteenth and twentieth centuries.

In conclusion Passi states that "the starting point, the center and the aim of Kierkegaard's philosophy is man."[23] Kierkegaard, like the philosophy of the eighteenth century, seeks the cause of every individual and historical phenomenon in human nature. Passi points out that the central idea of Kierkegaard's thought is subjective freedom and criticizes Kierkegaard's understanding of history as a product of freedom. Opposing Kierkegaard to Hegel, he agrees with the German philosopher, who sees the work of necessity in history.

Passi interprets the individualism of Kierkegaard's philosophy in such a manner that the Danish thinker becomes a "prophet" of pragmatism. According to Passi, for Kierkegaard, "truth...is truth, only because it is helpful and useful, because it makes life and makes existence easier."[24]

Opposing existential philosophy to rational philosophy, Passi comes to the surprising conclusion that "the philosophy of Kierkegaard is irrelevant to what is

---

[22] Паси [Passi], *Шопенхауер, Киркегор, Ницше* [Schopenhauer, Kierkegaard, Nietzsche], p. 143.
[23] Ibid., p. 146.
[24] Ibid., p. 149.

intellectual and rational."[25] Being an existentialist, Kierkegaard is also automatically designated an irrationalist. Such an interpretation of Kierkegaard's philosophy as irrationalism is often met in contemporary Bulgarian reception. To this interpretative trend belongs the article "The Christian Preexistentialism of Søren Kierkegaard" published in 1998 and written by Alexander Dimitrov and Vladimir Ivanov. According to the authors, the Danish philosopher claims that man and human existence are objects of a new, "irrational type of knowledge."[26] Kierkegaard is seen as a forerunner of a new tradition of philosophizing, the tradition of existentialism. It is in his writings that the human personality and faith for the first time in the history of philosophy become the sole topics. The authors emphasize the close connection between the work and the personal life of the Danish thinker and claim that the reader must deal with the tormented personality of Kierkegaard in all of his works.

To the same interpretative trend, which stresses the irrationalism of Kierkegaard's philosophy, belongs the book *The Tree Of Life. Faith in the Works of Dostoevsky, Kierkegaard and Hesse* written by Maria Krusteva and published in 1999.[27] This book does not have the character of a philosophical investigation; it aims rather to make a religious suggestion on the basis of some cultural considerations. In the writings of Dostoevsky, Kierkegaard, and Hermann Hesse (1877–1962) the author sees the vestiges of a transition from one "paradigm of consciousness" to a new one. The transition is from the consciousness determined by reason to that of faith or, as Krusteva expresses it metaphorically, from the "Tree of Knowledge" to the "Tree of Life" (the same metaphor is used by Shestov). Krusteva interprets reason as the source of man's unhappy, split consciousness and his alienation from God. Reason and faith are seen as irreconcilable; the transition to faith should mean a new form of life and attitude towards the world, a form of life, in which reason is negated. The author interprets Kierkegaard's concepts of repetition, contemporaneity, and sin as illustrations of her thesis, emphasizing the freedom of will on the way to faith and the individual in this way.

Also close to this interpretative trend is Ralica Sapundjieva in her article "The Personal Choice in the works of Kierkegaard and Schopenhauer" published in 2001 in the magazine *Filosofia*.[28] The author sees both philosophers as rebels against the philosophical myth of omnipotent reason. She describes how choice is executed or not executed in the aesthetical, ethical, and religious existence and on this basis discerns a similarity between the stages in Kierkegaard's writings and Schopenhauer's ages of life. Yet Sapundjieva herself does not want to carry her thesis too far and modestly

---

[25] Ibid., p. 147.
[26] Александър Димитров [Alexander Dimitrov] and Владимир Иванов [Vladimir Ivanov], "Християнският предекзистенциализъм на Сьорен Киркегор" [The Christian Preexistentialism of Søren Kierkegaard], *Научни трудове: ВВОУ "В. Левски,"* no. 62, 1998, p. 386.
[27] Мария Кръстева [Maria Krusteva], *Дървото на живота. Вярата в творчеството на Достоевски, Киркегор и Хесе* [The Tree of Life. Faith in the Works of Dostoyevsky, Kierkegaard and Hesse], Sofia: Prozorec 1999.
[28] Ралица Сапунджиева [Ralica Sapundjieva], "Личният избор при Киркегор и Шопенхауер" [The Personal Choice in the Works of Kierkegaard and Schopenhauer], *Философия*, nos. 5–6, 2001, pp. 87–92.

maintains that the similarity is only limited and that a parallel to the religious stage of life could not be found in the work of Schopenhauer.

Ralica Sapundjieva is also the author of the article "Hesse and Wilde—a Reflection on the 'Philosophy of Pleasure,' Based on the Aesthetic Stage of Life in the Philosophy of Søren Kierkegaard" published in the magazine *Filosofski alternativi* in 2002. The author illustrates the aesthetic stage of life on the basis of *Either/Or* and emphasizes that the aesthete lives in the "now" of the moment and of the concrete situation. She describes how life in immediacy leads to a crisis in the aesthetic way of life. In the philosophical novel *Steppenwolf* by the aforementioned German writer, Herman Hesse, Sapundjieva finds another description of an aesthete in crisis. She claims that, in a manner similar to Kierkegaard, Hesse interprets the aesthetic existence as reflection, which leads only towards despair. The dangers of the aesthetic way of life are, according to Sapundjieva, the topic in the novel *The Picture of Dorian Gray* by the English writer Oscar Wilde. She argues that all the characters in the novel are aesthetes, and all of them become victims of their view of life. As a conclusion, Sapundjieva states that "the only opportunity of choice in the aesthetic life is the choice of self-destruction."[29] This fact, however, "shows the only direction for the survival of the human being—the choice of life which is equivalent to the choice of the ethical way of life."[30]

A different interpretation is offered by Valentin Kanavrov in his book *The Restlessness of Reason*.[31] The aim of the author is to investigate how reason is at work in the philosophy of Kierkegaard. The writings of the Danish thinker are interpreted in the context of the development of philosophical ideas in the nineteenth century. Kierkegaard, together with Nietzsche, Dostoevsky, and Marx, is seen as a representative of the stage of development of the philosophical reason called "the illness of reason." Typical for this stage is that reason is no longer understood as an infinite and eternal Self. According to Kanavrov, "The falling of absolute reason to the individual man, the identification of reason not with the infinite and eternal God, but with the mortal man, pushes the problem of existence to the fore."[32] Thus, reason is at work in the philosophy of Kierkegaard as the self-investigation of the individual, mortal, suffering human life. Whereas classical rationalism penetrates reality and interprets it as rational (and that is, as constituted by reason), the "ill reason" penetrates reality only to display its paradoxical character.

The chapter devoted to Kierkegaard is entitled "The Illness." The author emphasizes the peculiarity of Kierkegaard's philosophy, which is situated between Hegelian philosophy and the Christian theology, but is neither rational theology nor Christian dogmatics. Being "schismatic to everyone and everything," the philosophy

---

[29] Ралица Сапунджиева [Ralica Sapundjieva], "Хесе и Уайлд—едно разсъждение върху 'Философията на мига' основано на естетическия стадий на живот на Киркегор" [Hesse and Wilde—a Reflection on the "Philosophy of Pleasure," Based on the Aesthetic Stage of Life in the Philosophy of Søren Kierkegaard], *Философски алтернативи*, nos. 1–2, 2002, p. 40.

[30] Ibid.

[31] Валентин Канавров [Valentin Kanavrov], *Размирието на разума* [The Restlessness of Reason], Sofia: Universitetsko izdatelstvo Sv. Kliment Ohridski 1994.

[32] Ibid., p. 120.

of Kierkegaard does not belong to any philosophical tradition of its time. On the basis of *Either/Or, Repetition, Fear and Trembling, The Concept of Anxiety, Philosophical Fragments*, and *The Sickness unto Death*, the author shows how the rationalist means and notions of philosophizing (dialectics, abstract and concrete, triad, form and content, reflection, understanding), which are "literarily borrowed from Hegel,"[33] function in Kierkegaard's writings. According to Kanavrov, this rationalist manner is often in contradiction with the articulated intentions of the author. Kierkegaard is criticized for not articulating clearly enough the rational basis of his work. Thus, for example, the Bulgarian author sees in *Either/Or* a presupposed rationalist identity of a rational construction and the real development of personality, an identity, which stands in contradiction with Kierkegaard's claimed individualism. The pseudonymity of Kierkegaard's writings is interpreted as a form of the cunning of reason in the Hegelian sense. The position of the Danish thinker is the position of the observing manipulator, who penetrates every different opinion and always manages to impose his own intention. According to Kanavrov, the main difficulty in Kierkegaard's work arises from the fact that he defines existence as differentiation between being and thinking and then tries somehow to connect them. In Kanavrov's understanding, "the ill reason" which is at work in Kierkegaard's writings, knows and aims at the identity of thinking and being, but is not able to carry it out. That is why it turns to faith. But the faith, to which "the ill reason" turns, could only have a paradoxical character. It is not the faith of Christian dogma, because "the ill reason" searches for a rationalist access to faith through doubt, reflection, and contemplation. The foundation of Kierkegaard's philosophy should be faith and dogma, yet he makes use of the rationalist method. Kanavrov interprets this as a "contradiction in the premises." As a result of this contradiction, the concepts in Kierkegaard's writings are "ill and powerless, illogical and paradoxical."[34]

Another interpretation, which does not define Kierkegaard's philosophy as irrationalism, is offered by Radosveta Teoharova in her article "The Architectonic in the System of Ideas of Immanuel Kant and Søren Kierkegaard" published in 1990 in the magazine *Filosofska misul*.[35] She considers Kierkegaard's philosophy to be very close to the transcendental position of Kant. The starting point of the investigation in the article is the problem of subjective causality: how does subjectivity, as autonomous cause, relate to reality? Unfortunately, the author does not discuss the difference in the concept of reality in the works of Kant and Kierkegaard. She argues that both philosophers define in the same way the *a priori* character of subjectivity as autonomous essence. The common point is the understanding that while relating to itself as a person, the subject (namely, its thinking capacity), creates the concept of a noumenal essence in man—the concept of God. Teoharova asserts that, with regard to the problem of the divine, Kierkegaard takes the methodological position of transcendentalism. The author draws the parallel between the two philosophers even

---

[33] Ibid., p. 106.
[34] Ibid., p. 129.
[35] Радосвета Теохарова [Radosveta Teoharova], "Архитектониката в системата на идеите на И. Кант и С. Киркегор" [The Architectonic in the System of Ideas of Immanuel Kant and Søren Kierkegaard], *Философска мисъл*, no. 12, 1990, pp. 11–9.

further. According to her, both Kant and Kierkegaard define the self as immanently antinomic. Thus, "the main problem, which human existence faces is to achieve the unity of God and world in man, who himself determines his existence."[36] God and world are interpreted as regulative principles in the Kantian sense, principles which are of practical use for the synthetic self-determination of man. Teoharova formulates the question about the system in Kierkegaard's work as the question of how the Danish philosopher conceives the unity of the two contradictory principles (God and world). She claims that the solution to this problem is presented when "the whole is articulated and shows an inner order of the relation of the parts to each other."[37]

The article "Absurdity—The Existential Dimension of Faith" by Elena Lavrencova published in 1999 in the magazine *Filosofia* is also worth mentioning.[38] On the basis of *Fear and Trembling* and with reference to *Repetition*, the author explores the problem of absurdity as the form of the relation to God in Christian faith. The faith of Abraham is absurd because he intends to kill his son in contradiction with the universal ethical norms, which have their source in the divine, and at the same time, he believes against human reason that he will not lose his son. Considerable attention is paid to the transformation of the ethical in Christian faith. The author ascertains that the theological suspension of the ethical does not mean its negation, but rather only its temporary abolition. Referring to the work of Gregor Malantschuk and in accordance with his thesis, she points out that the sacrifice of Isaac is only an exception in the life of Abraham, who lives his everyday life within the ethical norms. Absurdity as the existential dimension of faith is not identical with irrationality according to Lavrencova. She inquires into the problem of faith as second immediacy and stresses the role of resignation as a preliminary stage on the way to faith. She comes to the important conclusion that, according to Kierkegaard's interpretation, Christian faith is "a complex phenomenon, which has resignation as its preliminary stage and absurdity as its main existential dimension."[39] In the end Lavrencova points out that the story of Abraham cannot display the whole nature of Christian faith. Since the important Christian concept of sin is missing in this story, it can show only one side of the absurdity of Christian faith.

A very important event for Kierkegaard research in Bulgaria was the Bulgarian–Danish conference *Danish Literature in Bulgaria—One Century of Enchantment* which took place in Sofia in 2000. The conference was organized and held by the Department of German and Scandinavian Studies at the University of Sofia during the official state visit of Margrethe II, Queen of Denmark. One of the conference days was devoted to the work of Søren Kierkegaard and its Bulgarian reception. The papers held during the three days were printed in a volume bearing the same title as the conference. The second part of this volume is devoted to Kierkegaard

---

[36] Ibid., p. 16.
[37] Ibid., p. 19.
[38] Елена Лавренцова [Elena Lavrencova], "Абсурдът—екзистенциалното измерение на вярата" [Absurdity—Existential Dimension of Faith], *Философска мисъл*, no. 5, 1999, pp. 38–45.
[39] Ibid., p. 44.

and contains six contributions. Joakim Garff's paper "A Man of Letters: a New Biographical Reading" is published only in English without a Bulgarian translation. The other five contributions are from Bulgarian authors.

The paper of Dimka Gocheva, "Notes on Kierkegaard's Notion of Irony in *The Concept of Irony*,"[40] is divided into three parts. The first part is entitled "The Antithesis of Irony and the Synthesis proposed by Kierkegaard." Here the main claims of the German Romantics on one hand, and those of Hegel on the other, are sketched. Kierkegaard's own understanding of irony is interpreted as a synthesis of antithetical positions. Gocheva considers the main feature of Kierkegaard's achievement to be that he interprets irony from the perspective of the old and ever topical philosophical question: how do words designate thoughts? In the second part of the article, Kierkegaard is treated as a thinker who manages to propose a solution to ardent debates on the question: on whom can we best rely when we seek the image of the real Socrates? Kierkegaard defends the novel position that neither Plato nor Xenophon reveal the authentic personality of Socrates. It is only the writer of comedies Aristophanes who adequately approached Socrates and his method. In the third part, "Kierkegaard as Philosopher and Writer of an Artistic Prose," Kierkegaard is praised as one of the very few thinkers who are able to express profound philosophical content in an intriguing and exquisite verbal form.

In "The Existential Philosophy in 'The Diary of the Seducer'" Petar Hadzinakov offers a piece of literary criticism in an essayistic form.[41] Søren Kierkegaard is seen as a representative of modernity in European philosophy and literature and as the first existentialist. At the center of the paper is "The Diary of the Seducer" interpreted as a fragmentary, yet organic unity of numerous emotional and semantic layers. The author emphasizes the role of the "woman" depicted as the bearer of the category of otherness. The character of the seducer is interpreted as a man, having the soul and sensitivity of an artist, turning his philosophy into poetry and love of arts, and his eroticism into philosophy.

The paper of Atanas Igov is entitled "On Kierkegaard or the Tragedy of Being" and is also written in essayistic form. The author draws attention to the close connection between poetry, drama, and metaphysics in the writings of Kierkegaard. The work of the Danish thinker is defined as a "poetical reflection on the drama of his own life"[42] and discussed from this point of view.

The contribution of Katia Kuzmanova-Zografova entitled "Søren Kierkegaard and Bulgarian Literature" argues against the widespread thesis about the "late

---

[40] Димка Гочева [Dimka Gocheva], "Бележки за Киркегоровото разбиране за иронията във *Върху понятието ирония*" [Notes on Kierkegaard's Notion of Irony in *The Concept of Irony*], in *Датската литература в България—един век очарование* [Danish Literature in Bulgaria—One Century of Enchantment], ed. by the Department of German and Scandinavian Studies at the University of Sofia, Sofia: Simolini 2000, pp. 124–34.

[41] Петър Хаджинаков [Petar Hadzinakov], "Екзистенциалната философия в Дневник на прелъстителя" [The Existential Philosophy in "The Seducer's Diary"], in *Датската литература в България* [Danish Literature in Bulgaria], pp. 135–41.

[42] Атанас Игов [Atanas Igov], "За Киркегор или трагедията на битието" [On Kierkegaard or the Tragedy of Being], in *Датската литература в България* [Danish Literature in Bulgaria], p. 141.

reception" of Kierkegaard's works in Bulgaria.[43] The author points out that already at the beginning of the twentieth century Kierkegaard's ideas had influenced Bulgarian modernist literature. Kuzmanova-Zografova refers to the above-mentioned publication in the magazine *Vezni*, which includes a translation of "The Unhappiest Man" and a philosophical portrait of the Danish thinker by the Bulgarian poet Ljudmil Stoyanov.[44] She draws a parallel between the ideas of Kierkegaard and those of the Bulgarian modernist poets and finds in their works and in his writings the characters of Don Juan and Ahasverus.

The contribution of the author of the present article is entitled "The Peculiarity of the Christian Time Experience in *Philosophical Fragments* by Søren Kierkegaard and the *Phenomenology of Religious Life* by Martin Heidegger." This piece draws a parallel between Kierkegaard's interpretation of the Christian time experience and Heidegger's interpretation of the same on the basis of the authors' common understanding that the attitude towards time constitutes the way of existence. In contrast to Heidegger, Kierkegaard defines time in opposition to eternity. Yet this metaphysically defined time is not the time of human existence. The temporality of human existence is constituted only by the "breaking-in" of eternity in time. Only in this way do the three modi of time come into being and does time gain meaning for human existence. In *Phenomenology of Religious Life* the constitutive function of the relation to time for the Christian way of living is understood in another way. Heidegger interprets the relation to time as the relation to the future, which constitutes the present of Christian existence.

During the course of ninety years Kierkegaard's philosophy has been an object of fickle interest in Bulgarian philosophical and literary circles. Most of this time his ideas were not completely unknown, and the acquaintance with them was usually indirect, mediated by other authors. This was due to the fact that he did not write in one of the major European languages. The last fifteen years have been a period in which interest in his philosophy has grown and led to a better acquaintance with his thinking. It is characteristic for the Bulgarian reception of Kierkegaard's philosophy that his ideas are often explored in the more general context of the philosophical problematic of reason. In this perspective the theme of faith also becomes a topic of investigation. Still, relatively little attention has been devoted to the religio-philosophical and theological problematic. This fact can be explained by the absence of a prominent theological tradition in Bulgaria. Kierkegaard's doctrine of the three stages of existence evokes great interest among Bulgarian philosophers. The description of the stages and the investigation of their peculiarity are popular topics in the Bulgarian reception of Kierkegaard.

---

[43] Катия Кузманова–Зографова [Kuzmanova–Zografova, Katia], "Сьорен Киркегор и модерната българска литература" [Søren Kierkegaard and Modern Bulgarian Literature], in *Датската литература в България* [Danish Literature in Bulgaria], pp. 146–51.

[44] Людмил Стоянов [Ljudmil Stojanov], "Сьорен Киркегор" [Søren Kierkegaard], *Везни*, nos. 4–5, 1920, pp. 199–201.

Bibliography

I. Bulgarian Translations of Kierkegaard's Works

"Diapsalmata," trans. by Dimiter Stoichev, *Родно изкуство*, no. 6, 1914.

"Най-нещастният" ["The Unhappiest One"], trans. by Ljudmil Stoyanov, *Везни*, nos. 4–5, 1920.

Или—или, част 1 [*Either/Or*, Part 1], trans. by Stefan Nachev, Sofia: Narodna kultura 1991.

Или—или, част 2 [*Either/Or*, Part 2], trans. by Stefan Nachev, Sofia: Narodna kultura 1991.

Страх и трепет [*Fear and Trembling*], trans. by Stefan Nachev, Sofia: Narodna kultura 1991.

Повторението [*Repetition*], trans. by Stefan Nachev, Sofia: Narodna kultura 1991.

Болка за умиране [*The Sickness unto Death*], trans. by Radosveta Teoharova, Varna: Steno 1991.

Понятието страх [*The Concept of Anxiety*], trans. by Radosveta Teoharova, Varna: Steno 1992.

Понятието ирония [*The Concept of Irony*], trans. by Stefan Nachev, Sofia: Universitetsko izdatelstvo Sv. Kliment Ohridski 1993.

Въдворение в християнството [*Practice in Christianity*], trans. by Radosveta Teoharova, Varna: Steno 1994.

Философски фрагменти [*Philosophical Fragments*], trans. by Krasimir Abdelhalil, Sofia: Kota 2002.

II. Secondary Literature on Kierkegaard in Bulgaria

Гочева, Димка [Gocheva, Dimka], "Бележки за Киркегоровото разбиране за иронията във *Върху понятието ирония*" [Notes on Kierkegaard's Notion of Irony in *The Concept of Irony*] in *Датската литература в България—един век очарование* [Danish Literature in Bulgaria—One Century of Enchantment], ed. by the Department of German and Scandinavian Studies at the University of Sofia, Sofia: Simolini 2000, pp. 124–34.

Димитров, Александър [Dimitrov, Alexander] and Иванов, Владимир [Ivanov, Vladimir], "Християнският предекзистенциализъм на Сьорен Киркегор" [The Christian Preexistentialism of Søren Kierkegaard], *Научни трудове: ВВОУ "В. Левски,"* no. 62, 1998, pp. 383–391.

Зашев, Димитър [Zashev, Dimiter], "Със и без Киркегор—една дилема на младия Лукач" [With and Without Kierkegaard—a Dilemma of the Young Lukács], *Философска мисъл*, no. 11, 1981, pp. 76–87.

Игов, Атанас [Igov, Atanas], "За Киркегор или трагедията на битието" [On Kierkegaard or the Tragedy of Being] in *Датската литература в България—един век очарование* [Danish Literature in Bulgaria—One Century of Enchantment], ed. by the Department of German and Scandinavian Studies at the University of Sofia, Sofia: Simolini 2000, pp. 141–5.

Канавров, Валентин [Kanavrov, Valentin], *Размирието на разума* [The Restlessness of Reason], Sofia: Universitetsko izdatelstvo Sv. Kliment Ohridski 1994.

Кръстева, Мария [Krusteva, Maria], *Дървото на живота. Вярата в творчеството на Достоевски, Киркегор и Хесе* [The Tree of Life. Faith in the Works of Dostoyevsky, Kierkegaard and Hesse], Sofia: Prozorec 1999.

Лавренцова, Елена [Lavrencova, Elena], "Абсурдът—екзистенциалното измерение на вярата" [Absurdity—Existential Dimension of Faith], *Философска мисъл*, no. 5, 1999, pp. 38–45.

Mineva, Emilia, "Kierkegaard und Marx. Thesen," in *Søren Kierkegaard. Philosoph, Schriftsteller, Theologe. Vorträge des bulgarisch-dänischen Seminars Sofia 31. März–2. April 1992*, Sofia: Internationale Kyrill und Method-Stiftung 1992, pp. 118–25.

Паси, Исак [Passi, Isaac], "Søren Kierkegaard and the Russian Religious Renaissance," in *Søren Kierkegaard. Philosoph, Schriftsteller, Theologe. Vorträge des bulgarisch-dänischen Seminars Sofia 31. März–2. April 1992*, Sofia: Internationale Kyrill und Method-Stiftung 1992, pp. 22–7.

— *Към философият на живота. Осем философски портрета* [On the Philosophy of Life. Eight Philosophical Portraits], Sofia: Universitetsko izdatelstvo Sv. Kliment Ohridski 1994.

— *Сьорен Киркегор* [*Søren Kierkegaard*], Sofia: Universitetsko izdatelstvo Sv. Kliment Ohridski 1998.

— *Шопенхауер, Киркегор, Ницше* [Schopenhauer, Kierkegaard, Nietzsche], Sofia: Kiril i Metodii 2001.

Passy, Isaac, Сапунджиева, Ралица [Sapundjieva, Ralica], "Личният избор при Киркегор и Шопенхауер" [The Personal Choice in the Works of Kierkegaard and Schopenhauer], *Философия*, nos. 5–6, 2001, pp. 87–92.

— "Хесе и Уайлд—едно разсъждение върху 'Философията на мига' основано на естетическия стадий на живот на Киркегор" [Hesse and Wilde—a Reflection on the "Philosophy of Pleasure," Based on the Aesthetic Stage of Life in the Philosophy of Søren Kierkegaard], in *Философски алтернативи*, nos. 1–2, 2002, pp. 40–51.

Спасов, Добрин [Spasov, Dobrin], "Впечатления от философския живот в Дания" [Impressions from the Philosophical Life in Denmark], *Теоретичен орган на Института по философия при БАН*, no. 12, 1971, pp. 48–61.

—"Contemporary Danish Philosophy," *Yearbook of the University of Sofia*, no. 1, 1971, pp. 68–81.

Стоянов, Людмил [Stojanov, Ljudmil], "Сьорен Киркегор" [Søren Kierkegaard], *Везни*, nos. 4–5, 1920, pp. 199–201.

Теохарова, Радосвета [Teoharova, Radosveta], "Архитектониката в системата на идеите на И. Кант и С. Киркегор" [The Architectonic in the System of Ideas of Immanuel Kant and Søren Kierkegaard], in *Философска мисъл*, no. 12, 1990, pp. 11–19.

— "Stadien auf des Lebens Weg und Weltalter. Mensch- und Kulturkonzepte bei Schelling und Kierkegaard," in *Søren Kierkegaard. Philosoph, Schriftsteller, Theologe. Vorträge des bulgarisch-dänischen Seminars Sofia 31. März–2. April 1992*, Sofia: Internationale Kyrill und Method-Stiftung 1992, pp. 28–36.

Theoharov, Vladimir, "Die Symbolik des Spiegels bei Kierkegaard und Nietzsche," in *Søren Kierkegaard. Philosoph, Schriftsteller, Theologe. Vorträge des bulgarisch-dänischen Seminars Sofia 31. März–2. April 1992*, Sofia: Internationale Kyrill und Method-Stiftung 1992, pp. 98–105.

Todorov, Christo, "Das Thema des Todes als Verbindungslinie zwischen Kierkegaard und Jaspers," in *Søren Kierkegaard. Philosoph, Schriftsteller, Theologe. Vorträge des bulgarisch-dänischen Seminars Sofia 31. März–2. April 1992*, Sofia: Internationale Kyrill und Method-Stiftung 1992, pp. 41–9.

Хаджинаков, Петър [Hadzinakov, Petar], "Екзистенциалната философия в Дневник на прелъстителя" [The Existential Philosophy in "The Seducer's Diary"], in *Датската литература в България—един век очарование* [Danish Literature in Bulgaria—One Century of Enchantment], ed. by the Department of German and Scandinavian Studies at the University of Sofia, Sofia: Simolini 2000, pp. 135–41.

Янева, Десислава [Ianeva, Desislava], "Своеобразието на християнския опит за време във *Философски трохи* на Сьорен Киркегор и *Феноменология на религиозния живот* на Мартин Хайдегер" [The Peculiarity of the Christian Time Experience in *Philosophical Fragments* by Søren Kierkegaard and in *Phenomenology of Religious Life* by Martin Heidegger], in *Датската литература в България—един век очарование* [Danish Literature in Bulgaria—One Century of Enchantment], ed. by the Department of German and Scandinavian Studies at the University of Sofia, Sofia: Simolini 2000, pp. 152–8.

III. Secondary Literature on Kierkegaard's Reception in Bulgaria

Кузманова-Зографова, Катия [Kuzmanova-Zografova, Katia], " Сьорен Киркегор и модерната българска литература" [Søren Kierkegaard and Modern Bulgarian Literature], in *Датската литература в България—един век очарование* [Danish Literature in Bulgaria—One Century of Enchantment], ed. by the Department of German and Scandinavian Studies at the University of Sofia, Sofia: Simolini 2000, pp. 146–51.

Romania:
A Survey of Kierkegaard's Reception, Translation, and Research

Nicolae Irina

One of the major events in the more recent history of Kierkegaardian research in Romania was the First International Symposium "Kierkegaard Today" (Bucharest, April 23–24, 1999). The conference was jointly organized by the Faculty of Philosophy (University of Bucharest) and the Søren Kierkegaard Research Centre (University of Copenhagen). It was the fruit of a cooperation agreement and mutual exchange between the two parties, which was signed in 1998. A couple of the conference papers from this event, which gathered more than a dozen scholars from both sides, were published in the *Revue Roumanie de Philosophie* in 2001.[1] Among them, Madalina Diaconu's article titled "Die Kierkegaard-Rezeption in Rumänien," offers a comprehensive historical overview of Romanian Kierkegaard scholarship.[2]

My aim in this article is to explore in a little more detail certain areas treated there (for example, Mircea Eliade, Gabriel Liiceanu, etc.). I will then briefly address the subsequent developments in Romanian Kierkegaard research, analyzing its progress and tendencies. I will basically follow the time frame indicated by Diaconu, who argues that the development of Kierkegaard's reception in Romania has gone through various stages, which she divides into four temporal periods: (I) 1928–46, (II) 1947–66 (III), 1967–89, (IV) 1990–present. She maintains that with this division, structured according to the way in which Romanian philosophy developed in the twentieth century, the second period could be easily disregarded since it could be characterized as "an absolute silence, a vacuum between the very productive philosophical activity in the 1930s and 1940s and the rediscovery of Kierkegaard as an existentialist figure in the late 1960s."[3]

---

[1]   *Revue Roumaine de Philosophie*, vol. 45, nos. 1–2, 2001, pp. 133–75.
[2]   For a thoroughly detailed exposition of the topic, I suggest that the reader also refer to Diaconu's article, although I will here try to indicate many of its central claims.
[3]   Madalina Diaconu, "Die Kierkegaard-Rezeption in Rumänien," *Revue Roumaine de Philosophie*, vol. 45, nos. 1–2, 2001, p. 149 (my translation).

I. Before the Second World War

Romanian scholarly reactions to Kierkegaard's writings can be traced back to the late 1920s. In his autobiography, the internationally well-known historian of religions Mircea Eliade (1907–86) notes that his article published in 1928, "Søren Kierkegaard—Fiancé, Pamphleteer, and Hermit,"[4] was "probably the first article on Kierkegaard to appear in the Romanian language."[5] Eliade's interest in Kierkegaard is noted by one of his biographers, Mac Linscott Ricketts, who claims that, with regard to Eliade's philosophy, "it is clear that in the early years he was strongly impressed by Kierkegaard."[6]

At the time when Eliade wrote this article, he was in his early twenties. He wrote it as a means of indirect communication, as he later explains in his *Autobiography*, where, in the section entitled, "The Lesson of Søren Kierkegaard," Eliade writes, "Such [a 'coded dialogue'] was the article dedicated to Søren Kierkegaard...in which, speaking of his love for Regine Olsen, I did not fail to quote the famous fragment that says a fiancée can help the man she loves to become a genius, while a wife can only make him [a general]."[7] In this context, Ricketts argues that "the unhappy Dane could only be a hero for [Eliade]—all the more so in that, like him, Kierkegaard chose to refuse the commonplace of marriage in order to ensure the well-being of his spirit."[8] The "famous fragment" invoked by Eliade is chosen from *Stages on Life's Way*, more precisely from "In vino veritas," where Kierkegaard writes:

> Many a man became a genius because of a girl; many a man became a hero because of a girl, many a man became a poet because of a girl, many a man became a saint because of a girl—but he did not become a genius because of the girl he got, for with her he became only a cabinet official; he did not become a hero because of the girl he got, for because of her he became only a general.[9]

The passage in Eliade's article in which he indirectly communicates his message is also worth mentioning here. Let us remark its persuasive powers and, not least, its literary value:

---

[4] Mircea Eliade, "Sören Kierkegaard—Logodnic, pamfletar si eremit," *Cuvantul*, vol. 4, no. 1035, 1928, p. 1.

[5] Mircea Eliade, *Autobiography*, vols. 1–2, trans. by Mac Linscott Ricketts, San Francisco: Harper & Row 1981, vol. 1 (*1907–1937. Journey East, Journey West*), p. 129.

[6] Mac Linscott Ricketts, *Mircea Eliade. The Romanian Roots, 1907–1945*, vols. 1–2, New York: Columbia University Press 1988 (*Boulder East European Monographs*, no. 248), vol. 2, p. 1212.

[7] Eliade, *Autobiography*, vol. 1, p. 129. Eliade makes here a parallel between his relation with Rica and Kierkegaard's relation with Regine Olsen. (Ricketts recognizes that he has initially translated "general" in the Romanian original version as "commonplace." Cf. Note 37, in Ricketts, *Mircea Eliade*, vol. 2, p. 1260.)

[8] Ricketts, *Mircea Eliade*, vol. 1, p. 214.

[9] *SKS* 6, 60 / *SLW*, 59. Compare with Ricketts' translation of Eliade's article version, in *Mircea Eliade*, vol. 1, p. 215. See also *Pap.* V B 178:8, p. 309: "No man has ever become a poet because of a woman."

Søren's heart was dark and tormented; love for his fiancée illumined and cheered it. After a year, he broke off the engagement. His fiancée—fascinated by his powerful and enigmatic personality—was humiliated. She followed him around, wept, wrote to him, called to him. Søren loved his fiancée, and her appeals tore his poor soul to shreds. And yet their lives were not to be united. Søren was a melancholic man, with an incandescent interior life, with impulses which would have perished in the comfortable and mediocre happiness of marriage. That year of happiness had terrified him.[10]

Eliade's article, says Diaconu, presents "nothing but a romanticized biography and a psychological portrait"[11] of the Danish thinker, offering the first, but rather brief and approximate, outline of Kierkegaard's theory of stages in the Romanian philosophical milieu. Beyond the autobiographical context, it is also worth noting that in a journal entry from April 13, 1962, after reading Kierkegaard's *The Point of View for My Work as an Author*, Eliade spells out the meaning of Kierkegaard's "duplicity." He claims that, in appearance, Kierkegaard was an "author of aesthetic and moral works...but in reality an exclusively religious author, camouflaged, a 'double agent,' for it was the only way to make contact with 'the individual' [and] the man in the street."[12]

It is Ricketts' contention that, from the perspective of the historian of religions, Eliade considers Kierkegaard "a direct precursor of Brand (since Ibsen was influenced by Kierkegaard)."[13] Eliade claims that Kierkegaard's attempt to show that the Denmark of his time was not "Christian," although "christianized," illuminates an issue that in theology today has become a *locus communis*. But Eliade argues that "the important point lies elsewhere: modern man, radically secularized, believes himself or styles himself an atheist, areligious, or, at least, indifferent, [but] he is wrong, [for] he has not yet succeeded in abolishing the *homo religiosus* that is in him: he has only done away with (if he ever was) the *christianus*."[14] Eliade concludes that modern man is left with "being 'pagan,' without knowing it."

A more argumentative account of Kierkegaard's perspective on Christian dogmas is Lucian Blaga's (1895–1961) "The Dogmatic Eon."[15] In this article, as Diaconu puts it, the Romanian philosopher criticizes the type of dualism characteristic of Tertullian, Pascal, and Kierkegaard, whose spirit is "split between intellect and faith." Blaga claims that Kierkegaard confuses "the dogmatic" and "the dialectical," for he allows that "many of the [Christian] paradoxes dissolve dialectically."[16] Later,

---

[10] Ricketts' translation, see *Mircea Eliade*, vol. 1, p. 214.
[11] Diaconu, "Die Kierkegaard-Rezeption in Rumänien," p. 150.
[12] Mircea Eliade, *Journal II: 1957–1969*, trans. from the French by Fred H. Johnson, Jr., Chicago and London: University of Chicago Press 1989, p. 164.
[13] Ricketts, *Mircea Eliade*, vol. 1, p. 214.
[14] Eliade, *Journal II*, pp. 164–5.
[15] Lucian Blaga, "Eonul Dogmatic," first published in *Gandirea. Literara, artisitca, sociala*, vol. 11, no. 2, February, Cluj 1931, pp. 70–8.
[16] Diaconu, "Die Kierkegaard-Rezeption in Rumänien," p. 150.

in 1942, Blaga published an article titled "Sören and His Great Trembling,"[17] this time to offer a "psychological portrait of the Dane."[18]

The *inter bellum* years were very productive for the Romanian philosophical endeavor in general, but also with particular regard to the interpretation of the Danish philosopher. Diaconu mentions a couple of other brief references to Kierkegaard in articles written by Mircea Florian, Nicodim Ion Matei, and Benjamin Fundoianu, but she indicates that the most significant Romanian scholarly interpretations in the first stage of Romanian Kierkegaard research are attributable to Nicolae Balca (1903–83) and Grigore Popa (1910–94). Balca wrote the chapter dedicated to Kierkegaard in the standard Romanian work, *History of Modern Philosophy*.[19] He also reviewed Erich Przywara's *Das Geheimnis Kierkegaards*[20] and Alois Dempf's *Kierkegaards Folgen*.[21]

Balca divides Kierkegaard's philosophy into two parts. In the first part, he includes "Kierkegaard's opposition to the Hegelian System, the impossibility of a system of existence, the concept of paradox, and the close relation between Kierkegaard and Lessing's thinking."[22] The second part encompasses Kierkegaard's theory of stages and the categories of "individual" (*der Einzelne*) and "repetition" (*Wiederholung*). Balca read Kierkegaard in German translations, like Eliade (who also used Italian), but other Romanian philosophers became interested in Kierkegaard's thinking through the intermediary of French versions of the Danish original. This was also the case with Grigore Popa.

During his doctoral studies, Grigore Popa obtained a scholarship at the Ecole Roumaine en France in Paris, between 1936 and 1938. As a result of his French readings in Kierkegaard's writings and the secondary literature related to it, Popa produced his Ph.D. thesis in 1939. Popa published *Existence and Truth in Søren Kierkegaard* in 1940,[23] and it thus became the first Romanian monograph on Kierkegaard. Its publication was reviewed in many journals and generated a strong interest within both philosophical and theological circles in Romania.

The thesis has a tripartite structure. A preliminary analysis aims at deciphering the "ontological meaning of life" and offers a conceptual framework in which "interiority" and "existential authenticity" play a central role. In this first part, Popa develops his personal views under the influence, as Diaconu shows, of Blaga, Rosca (Popa's thesis supervisor), Eliade, and Kierkegaard. Popa then sketches the Kierkegaardian theory of stages, relying on an analysis of the concepts of existence,

---

[17] Lucian Blaga, "Sören si marele sau cutremur," *Luceafarul*, vol. 2, no. 1, 1942, pp. 2–6.
[18] Diaconu, "Die Kierkegaard-Rezeption in Rumänien," p. 156.
[19] In *Istoria filosofiei moderne, vol. 2: De la Kant pana la evolutionismul englez* [History of Modern Philosophy, vol. 2: From Kant to English Evolutionism], Bucharest: Tiparul Universitar 1938, pp. 531–62.
[20] Erich Przywara, *Das Geheimnis Kierkegaards*, Munich and Berlin: Oldenbourg 1929.
[21] Alois Dempf, *Kierkegaards Folgen*, Leipzig: Hegner 1935.
[22] Diaconu, "Die Kierkegaard-Rezeption in Rumänien," p. 153.
[23] Grigore Popa, *Existenta si adevar la Soeren Kierkegaard*, Sibiu: Tip. Arhidiecezana 1940. A new edition was published a few years ago (Cluj: Ed. Dacia 1998).

the existential categories, the method of existential communication, the leap, etc. In the end, Popa claims that the subjective truth has an "edifying" and a "revelatory" function.

II. After the Second World War

In the aftermath of the Second World War, Romanian philosophy had to readjust its aims within the confines of the new political climate. Thus, only the relaxing of constraints in the late 1960s allowed a resurgence of the interest in Kierkegaard's thought. The first contributions, in 1967, belong to Nicolae Bagdasar (1896–1971) and George Călinescu (1899–1965). But, as Diaconu claims, the only one who, in the 1960s, rose to the level of the previous Kierkegaard interpretation in Romania was Alexandru Posescu.[24]

In the 1970s and the beginning of the 1980s, a strong *historical* interest in Kierkegaard developed. Many historical accounts aimed at introducing and integrating Kierkegaard's thought in the overall picture of the history of philosophy and the contemporary philosophical debates. In this context, Diaconu mentions the contributions of Dumitru Ghise, Alexandru Boboc, Constantin Ionescu Gulian, Florica Neagoe, Ernest Stere, Lucia Dumitrescu-Codreanu, and Ludwig Grünberg.[25]

In the different context of literary criticism, Aurel Dragos Munteanu offered a theoretical analysis of Kierkegaard's concept of the "interesting." Also, in 1979, the literary periodical *Secolul 20* dedicated a special issue to Denmark, in which Gabriel Liiceanu published "Kierkegaard—Landmarks for a Biography."[26] In the first ten pages of the article, a comprehensive examination of the most important moments in Kierkegaard's spiritual development provides the reader with a grasp of an evolution that left Kierkegaard with no other option than "to live in the world of spirit."[27] Liiceanu supports his remarks with frequent quotations from Kierkegaard's journals.

With regard to Kierkegaard's relation to Regine Olsen, Liiceanu points out that, "giving up the finite that confines every conjugality," Kierkegaard chose "the infinite." This is, according to Liiceanu, the movement that defines Kierkegaard's authorship: "the striving to obtain a technique [that would enable him] to extract the infinite camouflaged in finite existence."[28] Moreover, Liiceanu indicates the role of "the incognito" in Kierkegaard's existential communication, claiming that the essence of Kierkegaard's maieutic method relies on the attempt to reach the other. Thus "the whole 'aesthetic' work of Kierkegaard becomes...*a metaphysics of the incognito.*"[29]

---

[24] Cf. Diaconu, "Die Kierkegaard-Rezeption in Rumänien," p. 158.
[25] Ibid., p. 159.
[26] Gabriel Liiceanu, "Kierkegaard—Repere pentru o biografie," *Secolul 20*, nos. 222–4, 1979, pp. 54–118.
[27] Ibid., p. 57.
[28] Ibid., p. 59.
[29] Ibid., p. 63.

Reviewing the significance of the life and work of the Danish thinker, Liiceanu contends that "Kierkegaard's 'existentialism'—unlike that of the twentieth century, especially in its ostentatious and noisy (*tapageuse*) form as French existentialism—is the projection *par excellence* of a *passio*; it is a philosophy produced by vocation and not by atmosphere."[30] Contrary to the later developments of "existentialism" in its French versions, Kierkegaard's emphasis on loyalty and seriousness could have been richer and more fruitful, according to Liiceanu, for an "existentialist" philosophy and would have allowed the movement to be characterized as the pursuit of "the concordance between the moral practice and its ideology."

Among others, Liiceanu was one of the disciples of the Romanian philosopher Constantin Noica. During his time spent at Paltinis (near Sibiu), he kept a rigorous record of his discussions that every now and then turned to issues related to Kierkegaard's thinking. In *The Paltinis Diary. A Paideic Model in Humanist Culture*,[31] Liiceanu notes on February 17, 1979: "I came…with a massive amount of readings in Kierkegaard, from which I had to put together an article and a micro-anthology for the issue of *Secolul 20*, which focused on Denmark."[32] A couple of days later, on February 21, he mentions that he gave a presentation of his reading of Kierkegaard's *The Point of View for My Work as an Author.* Liiceanu's remarks were entirely integrated in the article published in *Secolul 20* later that year.[33] After the publication of that article, on November 22, 1980, Liiceanu added in a different context yet another brief comment on Kierkegaard, who reportedly "attacked the practice of the institutionalized *faith,* which has lost the vigor of its New Testament origin."[34]

III. After 1990

The interest in Kierkegaard's thought regained its pre-war vigor soon after the radical change of the political climate in the post-1989 Romania.

In 1996, Madalina Diaconu offered the second Kierkegaard monograph in Romanian research: *On the Edge of the Precipice. Søren Kierkegaard and the Nihilism of the Nineteenth Century.* It was first designed as a thesis for the Department of Philosophy at the University of Bucharest, under the supervision of Ion Ianosi. (The thesis was initially entitled *Søren Kierkegaard's Nihilism and the Literature of the Nineteenth Century.*) Ianosi later wrote the foreword to the published version.

Ianosi describes the first four chapters of Diaconu's work as being critical and analytical *par excellence*. The overall picture of Diaconu's book is characterized by

---

[30] Ibid., pp. 66–7.
[31] Gabriel Liiceanu, *Jurnalul de la Paltinis: un model paideic in cultura umanista*, Bucharest: Ed. Cartea Romaneasca 1983 (2nd and 3rd editions, Bucharest: Ed. Humanitas 1991 and 1996).
[32] Ibid., p. 83.
[33] Ibid., p. 95. In *Secolul 20*, see Liiceanu "Kierkegaard—Repere pentru o biografie," pp. 62–3.
[34] Liiceanu, *Jurnalul de la Paltinis*, 2nd ed., p. 176.

Ianosi as a "rigorous, challenging and knowledgeable endeavor."[35] Diaconu outlines her project in the "Summary" section of the published version, offering a brief account in English, French, and German.

Diaconu distinguishes between the "nihilism of the exception" and the "nihilism of *das Man*," thus indicating the shift from the dissolution of reality through "the imagination by means of the ironical, arbitrary and sovereign ego of the early Romantic" to the collapse into "lack of spirituality and into anonymity, indifference and conformism."[36] As outlined in the "Summary," Diaconu tries to prove that one can identify all forms of nihilism in Kierkegaard's work, "the nihilism of the exception in his pseudonymous writings and in *The Concept of Irony*...and the mass-nihilism especially in Kierkegaard's late writings, during and after the polemics with the *Corsair.*"[37]

Diaconu examines the relation of nihilism to the individual's inwardness and finds that a causal explanation for the birth of nihilism in a person is uncertain. Yet, she says, "according to Kierkegaard's writings, one can judge nihilism to be the consequence either of *vita ante acta*...or of the failure in a limit situation, in a religious ordeal."[38] The first path leads to faith, the second requires the intervention of the alterity (divine or human).

Diaconu deals more specifically with Kierkegaard's nihilism (a word never used by Kierkegaard, as Diaconu mentions) in the third chapter, "Hypostases of Nihilism in Kierkegaard's Pseudonymous Writings and in *The Concept of Irony.*" She first identifies it as melancholy, in *Either/Or* and *Repetition*; secondly as a typical aspect of the historical moment, in *The Concept of Irony*; and thirdly as a "phenomenology of the negative feelings (irony, dread, despair)." In conclusion, it is Diaconu's contention that one can talk about the problem of Kierkegaard's "underground nihilism," which is characteristic of "[his] life and philosophy, his equivocal attitude, [i.e.,] on the one hand, his negative 'temptations' and on the other, both the rejection of nihilism by the believer and the form of the religious existence, described by him, as itself a sort of nihilism."[39]

The aforementioned First International Symposium "Kierkegaard Today" (Bucharest, April 23–4, 1999) benefited from the presence of the many internationally renowned Kierkegaard scholars: Jon Stewart ("Kierkegaard's Criticism of Martensen in the *Philosophical Fragments*"[40]), Darío González ("L'esprit et la lettre"), Pia Søltoft ("Before God and Before Man"), Christian Tolstrup ("Kierkegaard's Socrates and Christ—Irony and Incarnation"), and Begonya Sàez Tajafuerce (" 'Without Authority': On Kierkegaard's Ethical Assignment").

---

[35]   See Ion Ianosi's "Foreword," in Madalina Diaconu, *Pe marginea abisului. Søren Kierkegaard si nihilismul secolului al XIX-lea*, Bucharest: Ed. Stiintifica 1996, p. 12.
[36]   Diaconu, *Pe marginea abisului*, p. 230.
[37]   Ibid.
[38]   Ibid., p. 231.
[39]   Ibid.
[40]   Published in the *Revue Roumaine de Philosophie*, vol. 45, nos. 1–2, 2001, pp. 133–48.

The Romanian contribution at the Bucharest Symposium included Adrian Arsinevici's "Philosophizing about the Philosophy of Translating a Philosophical Text," Madalina Diaconu's aforementioned "Kierkegaard-Rezeption in Rumänien," Vasile Macoviciuc's "Le concept 'desespoir' chez Kierkegaard," Mihaela Pop's "Le Concept Kierkegaardien de *Moment*," Nicolae Irina's "Le Concept de Choix dans *Ou bien...ou bien...*," Alexandru Boboc's "Welt und Zeit bei Kierkegaard und Nietzsche," and Florin Leonard Stan's "Kierkegaard's Concept of 'Repetition.'"

Only three of all the conference papers were published in *Revue Roumaine de Philosophie* (2001). One of the published papers from the Romanian Symposium (in addition to the contribution of Jon Stewart and Diaconu), is Mihaela Pop's article "L'Influence Platonicienne sur le Concept Kierkegaardien de *Moment*."[41] According to Pop, "the moment" is a central category in Kierkegaard's thinking. She claims that Kierkegaard transfers this ontological category into the ethical realm, offering to it "a completely new signification in the realm *of subjectivity*."[42] Pop aims to show, as the title of her paper directly suggests, that Plato's ontological view of time had a major influence on Kierkegaard's understanding of the moment.

Pop begins her investigation with *The Concept of Anxiety*.[43] In her analysis, Kierkegaard holds that the moment is, on the one hand, the temporal instrument that enables eternity to penetrate the temporal existence and that, on the other hand, it enables the individual to turn towards eternity. Thus, Pop indicates that "the fundamental category [of] this double movement, [of] this transition or passage is *repetition*."[44]

One other aspect that Pop investigates in her article is the way in which Plato's doctrine of recollection determines Kierkegaard's views on the nature of sin, which, according to the Christian religion, prevents the individual from reaching the truth. Again, "the moment" enables the individual to arrive at a "new epistemological condition," which, as Pop puts it, presupposes "the awareness of the sin and thus of the difference that separates him from the divine."[45]

A couple of the unpublished Romanian Conference papers (Bucharest, April 1999) have been gathered in the reprint collection of the Hong Kierkegaard Library,[46] i.e., Leo Stan's "Søren Kierkegaard Repetition and Freedom: Two Conditions of Becoming *den Enkelte* (the Individual)," and Nicolae Irina's "The Concept of Choice in *Either/Or*."

Stan's purpose is to emphasize the contrast between Kierkegaard's "repetition" and Plato's theory of recollection. His thesis is that the "genuine sense" of repetition, as it appears in *Practice in Christianity*, is already anticipated in *Repetition*, *Fear and*

---

[41] Mihaela Pop, "L'Influence Platonicienne sur le Concept Kierkegaardien de *Moment*," *Revue Roumaine de Philosophie*, vol. 45, nos. 1–2, 2001, pp. 165–75.

[42] Pop, "L'Influence Platonicienne sur le Concept Kierkegaardien de *Moment*," p. 165 (my translation).

[43] Pop quotes from the French version of Knud Ferlov and Jean-Jacques Gateau (Paris: Gallimard 1990).

[44] Pop, "L'Influence Platonicienne sur le Concept Kierkegaardien de *Moment*," p. 170.

[45] Ibid., p. 172.

[46] St. Olaf College, Northfield, Minnesota, USA.

Trembling, and *The Concept of Anxiety*. Stan also argues that Kierkegaard's approach to "repetition" in *Practice in Christianity* is "*avant la lettre* phenomenological."

Stan has previously published an article in the Romanian *Psychoanalysis. Review of Cultural Psychoanalysis,* "Kierkegaard on the Couch. Outline for a Psychoanalytical Approach of His Life,"[47] and more recently has co-authored a review titled "On Zhuangzi and Kierkegaard."[48] Stan has also translated and written a comprehensive introduction to *Fear and Trembling*.[49]

Irina's main concern is to offer the conceptual framework for a discussion of the ethical implications of the concept of choice in Kierkegaard's work, mainly focusing the analysis, as stated in the title, on *Either/Or*. The conference paper later developed into a graduation thesis (Faculty of Philosophy, University of Bucharest, 2001, under Alexandru Boboc's supervision). The work was presented in the Dissertation Panel of the Fourth International Kierkegaard Conference (St. Olaf College, June 5–13, 2001).

Irina has also published "In Between Actuality and Ideality. The Structure and the Characteristics of the Kierkegaardian Ethical Discourse,"[50] where he first investigates the characteristics of the Kierkegaardian "art of communication" (*Meddelelses Kunst*), and then evaluates the way in which its requirements were developed in the ethical existential communication of Judge William. He concludes by noting the insufficiency of the ethical discourse in the broader context of Kierkegaard's thought. Part of the material in this article was developed into an M.A. thesis (Faculty of Philosophy, University of Bucharest, 2002) and later published as "On the Modal Categories in S. Kierkegaard."[51]

Apart from the participants that gave papers at the Bucharest conference in 1999, other Romanian scholars also dedicated part of their research to Kierkegaard's work. Catalina Elena Dobre from the University "Dunarea de Jos" (Galati) has recently published a good number of materials related to Kierkegaard. For example, in "On the Footsteps of Kierkegaard,"[52] Dobre traces the main biographical details in

---

[47] Leonard Stan, "Kierkegaard pe canapea. Schita pentru o posibila abordare psihanalitica a vietii sale," *Psihanaliza. Revista de cultura psihanalitica*, vol. 6, no. 4, 1999, pp. 7–11.

[48] Leonard Stan and Hans-Georg Moeller, "On Zhuangzi and Kierkegaard, a Review of *The Sense of Antirationalism: The Religious Thought of Zhuangzi and Kierkegaard*, by Karen L. Carr and Philip J. Ivanhoe," *Philosophy East & West. A Quarterly of Comparative Philosophy*, vol. 53, no. 1, 2003, pp. 130–5.

[49] Graduation work from the Faculty of Philosophy (University of Bucharest, 2001, supervisor: Remus Rus). Stan also wrote *The Moment as Presence in Kierkegaard's View of Temporality*. Major essay (M.A.), St. Catharines, Brock University 2002.

[50] Nicolae Irina, "Intre actualitate si idealitate. Structura si caracteristicile discursului etic kierkegaardian," *Analele Universitatii Bucuresti. Filosofie*, vol. 49, Bucharest: University of Bucharest 2000 (printed in 2002), pp. 69–79.

[51] Nicolae Irina, "Despre categoriile modale la S. Kierkegaard," *Analele Universitatii "Dunarea de Jos." Filosofie*, no. 2, 2003, pp. 13–22. Irina also wrote *Will, Belief and Faith: Kierkegaard's Volitionalism in the Context of Contemporary Debates*. Thesis (M.A.), St. John's: Memorial University of Newfoundland 2004.

[52] Catalina Elena Dobre, "Pe urmele lui Kierkegaard," *Eidos. Revista de Filosofie*, vol. 1, no. 1, 2002, pp. 59–82.

Kierkegaard's life confined "between two crises: an exterior one—the impossibility of his union with his beloved Regine Olsen; and an interior one—the impossibility of the union with God."[53] Dobre also reviewed the translation of Kierkegaard's "'Guilty?'/'Not Guilty?'"

IV. Romanian Translations and Resource Centers

In the 1990s, after the political change in Romania, a great deal of interest was shown in the translation of Kierkegaard's work. Various new publishing houses finally started to release in Romanian full versions of Kierkegaard's texts, for until then only small fragments were occasionally published.

In 1992, "The Seducer's Diary"[54] was the first to see the light of day in the bookstores, followed, in 1995, by *Practice in Christianity*.[55] Then, again from *Either/Or*, "Diapsalmata" and "The Balance Between the Esthetic and the Ethical,"[56] and from *Stages on Life's Way* "In vino veritas" in 1997.[57] *The Concept of Anxiety* was published in 1998[58] and so was a first version of *The Sickness unto Death*.[59] Also from *Either/Or*, "The Esthetic Validity of Marriage" was issued in 1998.[60] In 1999, *Philosophical Fragments*[61] and yet another version of *The Sickness unto Death* were added to the growing number of Romanian translations in the 1990s.[62]

The process continues ceaselessly in recent years with the publication of *Repetition*[63] and " 'Guilty?'/'Not Guilty?' " from *Stages on Life's Way* in 2000.[64]

---

[53] Ibid., p. 77.
[54] Translated from Danish (*SV2*), by Kjeld Jensen and Elena Dan.
[55] Translated from German (*Einübung in Christentum*, Jena: E. Diederichs 1912), by Mircea Ivanescu; Romanian version title: *The School of Christianity*.
[56] Translated from Danish (*SV2*), by Kjeld Jensen and Elena Dan; Romanian version title: "Letter to a Friend."
[57] Translated from Danish (*SV2*), by Kjeld Jensen and Elena Dan; Romanian version title: "The Banquet."
[58] Translated from Danish (*SV3*), by Adrian Arsinevici.
[59] Translated from Italian (*La malattia mortale*, Florence: Lacerba Edizioni 1926), by George Popescu.
[60] Translated from Danish (*SV2*), by Kjeld Jensen and Elena Dan.
[61] Translated from Danish (*Philosophiske Smuler*, Copenhagen: Gyldendal 1983), by Adrian Arsinevici. Arsinevici's project is outlined in "Translation of *Philosophical Fragments*" ["Oversættelse af *Philosophiske Smuler* til rumænsk"], in *Kierkegaard 1993—Digtning, filosofi, teologi* [Kierkegaard 1993—Poetry, Philosophy, Theology], ed. by Finn Hauberg Mortensen, Odense: Odense University, Institute for Literature, Culture and Media 1993, p. 137.
[62] Translated from German (*Die Krankheit zum Tode*, Hamburg: Felix Meiner 1995), by Madalina Diaconu.
[63] Translated from Danish (*SV3*), by Adrian Arsinevici.
[64] Translated from Danish (*SV2*), by Alexandra Jensen and Elena Dan.

Fear and Trembling was published in two versions, one in 2001[65] and the other in 2002.[66]

In addition to the absolutely necessary translations into Romanian, of great help for Kierkegaard research in Romania is the recent increase in the amount of Kierkegaard's writings in English, German, and French translations. The Library of the Faculty of Philosophy (University of Bucharest) is the recipient of a generous donation of the complete edition of *Kierkegaard's Writings*, from the Hong Kierkegaard Library (St. Olaf College, Northfield, Minnesota, USA). Also, the New Europe College (NEC, Bucharest) has added to its valuable collections the most recent German and French editions.

It is easy to see that it is mainly the so-called "philosophical writings" from Kierkegaard's authorship that preponderantly retain the overall interest of Romanian researchers. Apart from the politically determined syncope, Romanian research has been continuously interested in Kierkegaard's thought, but the most fruitful phases have been: (a) the interval between the 1930s and the 1940s, and (b) the time elapsed since the Romanian political change in 1989. Thus, on the one hand, during the first phase of Kierkegaardian research, Romanian scholars read Kierkegaard with a strong interest in the discovery of the work of the Danish philosopher, in an attempt to integrate his thought into the Romanian philosophical vocabulary. The second phase shows a very significant tendency towards translating and making Kierkegaard's work more accessible to a larger Romanian audience, accompanied by a more focused study of the conceptual analyses in Kierkegaard's writings.

---

[65] Translated from German (*Furcht und Zittern*, Munich: Deutscher Taschenbuch 1976), by Dragos Popescu.
[66] Translated from Danish (*SV3*), by Leonard Stan.

Bibliography

I. Romanian Translations of Kierkegaard's Works

Jurnalul seducatorului ["The Seducer's Diary"], trans. by Kjeld Jensen and Elena Dan, Bucharest: Scripta 1992.
Scoala crestinismului [*Practice in Christianity*], trans. by Mircea Ivanescu, Bucharest: Adonai 1995.
"Banchetul" ["In Vino Veritas" A Recollection Related by William Afham], trans. by Kjeld Jensen and Elena Dan, Bucharest: Universal Dalsi 1997.
Diapsalmata. Jurnalul seducatorului ["Diapsalmata," "The Seducer's Diary"], Bucharest: Masina de Scris-Universal Dalsi 1997.
Scrisoare catre un prieten ["The Balance between the Esthetic and the Ethical in the Development of the Personality"], trans. by Kjeld Jensen and Elena Dan, Bucharest: Masina de Scris 1997.
Conceptul de anxietate [*The Concept of Anxiety*], trans. by Adrian Arsinevici, Timisoara: Ed. Amarcord 1998 (*Scrieri*, vol. 1).
Farame Filosofice [*Philosophical Fragments*], trans. by Adrian Arsinevici, Timisoara: Ed. Amarcord 1998 (*Scrieri*, vol. 2).
Legitimitatea estetica a casatoriei ["The Esthetic Validity of Marriage"], trans. by Kjeld Jensen and Elena Dan, Bucharest: Masina de Scris 1998.
Maladia mortala: eseu de psihologie crestina întru edificare si desteptare de Anti-Climacus [*The Sickness unto Death. A Christian Psychological Exposition for Upbuilding and Awakening*], trans. by George Popescu, Craiova: Ed. Omniscop 1998.
Boala de moarte: un expozeu de psihologie crestina în vederea edificarii si a desteptarii [*The Sickness unto Death. A Christian Psychological Exposition for Upbuilding and Awakening*], trans. by Madalina Diaconu, Bucharest: Ed. Humanitas 1999.
Repetarea [*Repetition*], trans. by Adrian Arsinevici, Timisoara: Ed. Amarcord 2000 (*Scrieri*, vol. 3).
" 'Vinovat?'/'Nevinovat?' " [" 'Guilty?'/'Not Guilty?' "], trans. by Alexandra Jensen and Elena Dan, Bucharest: Ed. Masina de Scris 2000.
Frica si cutremurare/Sören Kierkegaard. Spiritul iudaismului/G.W.F. Hegel [*Fear and Trembling. A Dialectical Lyric*], trans. by Dragos Popescu, Oradea: Antaios 2001.
Frica si cutremur [*Fear and Trembling*], trans. by Leo Stan, Bucharest: Ed. Humanitas 2002.

Din hârtiile unuia încă viu [*From the Papers of One Still Living*]; *Despre conceptul de ironie, cu permanentă referire la Socrate* [*On the Concept of Irony with Continual Reference to Socrates*], trans. and ed. by Ana-Stanca Tabarasi, Bucharest: Humanitas 2006.

II. Secondary Literature on Kierkegaard in Romania

Arsinevici, Adrian, "Oversættelse af Philosophiske Smuler" [Translation of the *Philosophical Fragments*], in *Kierkegaard 1993: digtning, filosofi, teologi* [Kierkegaard 1993—Poetry, Philosophy, Theology], ed. by Finn Hauberg Mortensen, Odense: Odense University, Institute for Literature, Culture and Media 1993, p. 137.

Bagdasar, Nicolae, "Sören Kierkegaard. Omul" [Søren Kierkegaard. The Man], *Ramuri*, vol. 4, no. 11, November 15, 1967, p. 16.

Balca, Nicolae, "E. Przywara's *Das Geheimnis Kierkegaards*" [Kierkegaard's Secret of E. Przywara], *Revista de filosofie*, vol. 21, no. 3, 1936, pp. 315–7.

— "Kierkegaard," in *Istoria filosofiei moderne, vol. 2: De la Kant pana la evolutionismul englez* [History of Modern Philosophy, vol. 2: From Kant to English Evolutionism], Bucharest: Tiparul Universitar 1938, pp. 531–62.

— "A. Dempf's *Kierkegaard Folgen*" [*To Follow Kierkegaard* by A. Dempf], *Revista de filosofie*, vol. 26, nos. 3–4, 1941, pp. 393–6.

Blaga, Lucian, "Eonul Dogmatic" [The Dogmatic Eon], *Gandirea. Literara, artistica, sociala*, vol. 11, no. 2, 1931, pp. 70–8.

— "Sören si marele sau cutremur" [Sören and His Great Trembling], *Luceafarul*, vol. 2, no. 1, 1942, pp. 2–6.

Bleicher, M[ax], "Conceptul repetitiei la Kirkegaard (sic)" [The Concept of Repetition in Kierkegaard], *Vremea*, vol. 9, no. 431, March 29, 1936, p. 11.

Boboc, Alexandru, "Sören Kierkegaard (1813–1855)," in *Istoria filosofiei Universale*, fascicles 1, 2 and 5, ed. by Florica Neagoe, Bucharest: University of Bucharest 1975, fascicle 2, pp. 125–9.

Diaconu, Madalina, *Pe marginea abisului. Søren Kierkegaard si nihilismul secolului al XIX-lea* [On the Edge of the Precipice. Søren Kierkegaard and the Nihilism of the Nineteenth Century], Bucharest: Ed. Stiintifica 1996.

— "Kierkegaard-Rezeption in Rumänien" [Kierkegaard's Reception in Romania], *Revue Roumaine de Philosophie*, vol. 45, nos. 1–2, Bucharest: Ed. Academiei Romane 2001, pp. 149–64.

Dobre, Elena Catalina, *Angoasa ca fenomen existential* [Anxiety as an Existential Phenomenon], Galati: Galateea 2000.

— "Despre iubire. Reflectii 'estetice' si 'inestetice' (Perspective kierkegaardiene)" [On Love. "Aesthetic" and "Unaesthetic" Remarks (Kierkegaardian Perspectives)], *Akademia*, no. 3, 2000, pp. 8–10.

— "Eternitatea clipei" [The Eternity of the Moment], *Porto Franco*, nos. 9–11 (68), 2001, pp. 51–2.

— "Pe urmele lui Kierkegaard" [In the Footsteps of Kierkegaard], *Eidos. Revista de Filosofie*, vol. 1, no. 1, 2002, pp. 59–82.

— "Conceptul de sine cu specifica referire la Søren Kierkegaard" [The Concept of Self with Special Reference to Søren Kierkegaard], *Analele Universitatii "Dunarea de Jos." Filosofie*, no. 2, 2003, pp. 65–71.

Eliade, Mircea, "Sören Kierkegaard—Logodnic, pamfletar si eremit" [Søren Kierkegaard—Fiancé, Pamphleteer, and Hermit], *Cuvantul*, vol. 4, no. 1035, 1928, p. 1.

Irina, Nicolae, "Intre actualitate si posibilitate. Structura si caracteristicile discursului etic Kierkegaardian" [In Between Actuality and Ideality. The Structure and the Characteristics of the Kierkegaardian Ethical Discourse], *Analele Universitatii din Bucuresti. Filosofie*, vol. 49, Bucharest: University of Bucharest 2000 (2002), pp. 69–79.

— "Despre categoriile modale la Kierkegaard" [On Modal Categories in Kierkegaard], *Analele Universitatii "Dunarea de Jos." Filosofie*, no. 2, 2003, pp. 13–22.

Liiceanu, Gabriel, "Kierkegaard—Repere pentru o biografie" [Kierkegaard—Landmarks for a Biography"], *Secolul 20*, nos. 222-4, 1979, pp. 54–118.

Pop, Mihaela, "L'Influence Platonicienne sur le Concept Kierkegaardien de *Moment*" [Plato's Influence on Kierkegaard's Concept of the *Moment*], *Revue Roumaine de Philosophie*, vol. 45, nos. 1–2, 2001, pp. 165–75.

Popa, Grigore, "Actualitatea lui Soeren Kierkegaard" [The Actuality of Søren Kierkegaard], *Gandirea*, vol. 16, no. 8, 1937, pp. 395–404.

— *Existenta si adevar la Sören Kierkegaard* [Existence and Truth in Søren Kierkegaard], Sibiu: Tip. Arhidiecezana 1940 (2nd ed., Cluj: Ed. Dacia 1998).

Posescu, Alexandru, "Sören Kierkegaard despre pluralitatea stadiilor existentei" [Søren Kierkegaard on the Plurality of the Stages of Existence], *Revista de filozofie*, vol. 15, no. 8, August, 1968, pp. 921–5.

Stan, Leonard, "Kierkegaard pe canapea. Schita pentru o posibila abordare psihanalitica a vietii sale" [Kierkegaard on the Couch. Outline of a Possible Psychoanalytical Approach to His Life], *Psihanaliza. Revista de cultura psihanalitica*, vol. 6, no. 4, 1999, pp. 7–11.

— "The Lofty Struggle for Salvation: Søren Kierkegaard on the Heroic Resistance of Religion" (review of Sylvia Walsh, *Living Poetically. Kierkegaard's Existential Aesthetics*; George Pattison, *Kierkegaard's Upbuilding Discourses: Philosophy, Theology, Literature* and Jon Stewart, *Kierkegaard's Relations to Hegel Reconsidered*), *Archaeus. Studii de istorie a religiilor*, vol. 8, nos. 1-4, 2004, pp. 235–62.

Stan, Leonard and Hans-Georg Moeller, "On Zhuangzi and Kierkegaard" (review of *Sense of Antirationalism: The Religious Thought of Zhuangzi and Kierkegaard* by Karen L. Carr and Philip J. Ivanhoe), *Philosophy East & West. A Quarterly of Comparative Philosophy*, vol. 53, no. 1, 2003, pp. 130–5.

Tabarasi, Ana-Stanca, "Dialog intre marii ginditori danezi" [Dialogue Between the Great Danish Thinkers], *Romania literara*, no. 24, 2002, p. 27.

— "Jurnalul iubitei lui Kierkegaard: Seducatoarea seducatorului" [Regine Olsen's Diary: The Seducer of the Seducer], *Romania literara*, no. 1, 2002, pp. 20–1.

— "Pseudonimele lui S. Kierkegaard" [S. Kierkegaard's Pseudonyms], *Secolul 21. Publicatie periodica de sinteza: Alteritate*, vols. 1–7, nos. 442-8, 2002, pp. 260–7.

III. Secondary Literature on Kierkegaard's Reception in Romania

Diaconu, Madalina, "Die Kierkegaard-Rezeption in Rumänien" [Kierkegaard's Reception in Romania], *Revue Roumaine de Philosophie*, vol. 45, nos. 1–2, 2001, pp. 149–64.

Macedonia:
The Sunny Side of Kierkegaard

Ferid Muhic

Søren Kierkegaard arrived in Macedonia relatively very recently, hardly thirty years ago. A fifteen-page article of condensed comparative analysis by Ferid Muhic, entitled "Reason and Faith in Kierkegaard's Philosophy" represents the welcoming speech on the occasion of Kierkegaard's first official visit to this country.[1]

Why then "relatively recently?" Given that this event happened not only in the previous century, but also in the previous millennium! Since this milestone, there has appeared not more than one text every two years specifically treating the great philosopher. Today the total number of texts dealing with Kierkegaard in Macedonian publishing history does not exceed fifteen. This is far from sufficient, measured by any standard. What may be offered as a plausible explanation for this lack of systematic and creative exchange of thought with "the melancholic Danish philosopher"? It was not the language barrier since English, French, German, and even Russian translations of Kierkegaard's philosophy circulated in Macedonia long before the above-mentioned first textual reaction. Ideological pressure or political opportunism may have been a part of the problem. Despite the exaggerated stories of the "socialist censure and control" in Yugoslavia (of which The Socialist Republic of Macedonia was an integral part, with more or less the same level of party control), neither existentialism nor Kierkegaard was ever on the list of *Index librorum prohibitorum*, either in Yugoslavia or in Macedonia.

The general conditions of social life and the more urgent issues connected with daily aspects of political themes, together with the very distant and abstract speculations concerning the *conditio humana*, may arguably be among the important reasons. In other words, the attention of the vast majority of Macedonian philosophers and writers of that time was attracted by very different topics, which were considered to be more immediate, more urgent, or more lucrative.

And now, when the words of Kierkegaard are becoming more and more relevant everywhere, including Macedonia, the average capacity of human beings to raise fundamental questions concerning their individual existence and personal identity has dropped dramatically in the world, as well as in Macedonia. Who is

---

[1] Ферид Мухиќ [Ferid Muhic], "Ставот на Киркегор кон верата и разумот6 некои дилеми" [Reason and Faith in Kierkegaard's Philosophy], *Зборник на Филозофски факулūеū*, 1978, pp. 365–79.

really capable of devoting his or her life to the basic dilemmas, which Kierkegaard promoted during his entire life? Is there a single person today whom Kierkegaard would accept without hesitation as an equal partner in a dialogue on his philosophy, without risking overestimating the partner and underestimating himself? Who could follow the intensity and passion of his personal search for certainty, not to mention the complexity of his thought and the subtleness of his writing and style?

Still, there is one point which differentiates the reception of Kierkegaard in Macedonia from that in most other countries. It is the lack of predominantly dark colors in the existing paintings of his philosophy, the absence of gloomy and depressive sounds in the presentation of the inner melody of Kierkegaard's song. This fundamental distinction is definitely the common denominator of all texts dealing with Kierkegaard in Macedonia so far.

This is why the title of this short sketch points to "the sunny side of Kierkegaard," since not only is it a *differentia* specific to the Macedonian reception, but also it is accentuated as the immanent feature of his spirit, which was traditionally overshadowed by its strong melancholic tones. In this respect, "concluding this unscientific introduction," I would say that Macedonian philosophers presented another Kierkegaard, and recognized in him different qualities from those commonly shared, less foggy, less windy, with all his longings preserved and all his dramatic dilemmas intact, but far brighter!

In what follows I present the Macedonian texts which deal with Kierkegaard with a brief explanation of their content.

The sole Macedonian translation of Kierkegaard is *The Seducer's Diary. Either/Or, Fragment from Life*, which was made from English by Aleksandar Temkov (B.A. in Philosophy from the Faculty of Philosophy in Skopje) and published in 1996.[2] This is the first integral translation of any text of Kierkegaard in the Macedonian language, which reserves a special place for both the translator and the edition. This work contains a preface entitled, "Søren Kierkegaard—the Socrates of Denmark."[3] The translator introduces the history and genesis of this book, with elements of critical evaluation.

The article "Reason and Faith in Kierkegaard's Philosophy" was a pioneering work, appearing in 1978.[4] In this text the interest of the author, Ferid Muhic (Ph.D., Professor of Contemporary Western Thought at the Faculty of Philosophy in Skopje), is to explore and compare critically the relationship of the two seemingly mutually contradicting philosophical fascinations of Kierkegaard: reason and faith. His conclusion is that the dialectical coherence of Kierkegaard's philosophy preserved a conceptual unity, not in spite of, but exactly because of the contradictions, proving

---

[2] *Дневникот на заводникот. Или-Или, Еден фрагмент од животот* [The Seducer's Diary. Either/Or, Fragment from Life], trans. by Aleksandar Temkov, Skopje: Epoha 1996.

[3] Александар Темков [Aleksandar Temkov], "Сорен Киркегор—Данскиот Сократг" [Søren Kierkegaard—the Socrates of Denmark], *Дневникот на заводникот*, pp. 5–13 (Preface to the translation of "The Seducer's Diary").

[4] Ферид Мухиќ [Ferid Muhic], "Ставот на Киркегор кон верата и разумот—некои дилеми" [Reason and Faith in Kierkegaard's Philosophy].

that they are derived not from the postulates of formal logic but from the authenticity of the deepest strivings, basic needs, and highest goals of the human soul and spirit.

The article "The Concept of Solitude in Philosophy and Literature," also the work of the present author, appeared in 1979.[5] This work is probably the most extensive analysis of Kierkegaard's philosophy published in Macedonian periodicals so far. The essay presents an account of Kierkegaard's attitude concerning the situation and the feeling of solitude as one the key situations of human existence.

The present author also makes use of Kierkegaard in a book of poetry from 1986.[6] To make the list complete, as well as to justify once again the title of this modest contribution, it should be mentioned that "the sunny side of Kierkegaard" is to be found in the poetry of Macedonian authors. The poem "Kierkegaard's Pass" devoted to Kierkegaard, describes a narrow pass high in the mountain, through which only one person at a time could pass and only in this way reach the top.

The book *The Magic of Existentialism* represents the M.A. thesis from 1994 by Ivancho Atanasovski, who is now an assistant on the subject of ethics at the Faculty of Philosophy in Skopje.[7] This work discusses Kierkegaard's philosophy in all key aspects throughout the text. The main value of this analysis is a comparison of Kierkegaard with other philosophers traditionally included in the existentialist tradition.

The book *Ideology and Subjectivity* by Professor Branislav Sarkanjac (Ph.D. in Philosophy from the Faculty of Philosophy in Skopje) presents a philosophical discussion concerning the social and the conceptual dynamics of ideology and subjectivity.[8] The position of Kierkegaard is focused primarily on the issue of subjectivity, and, as such, it is an original and exciting contribution to the reception of Kierkegaard as a politically relevant thinker, important for the understanding of many dilemmas of the contemporary world.

Sense and Virtue from 1997 is a textbook for university students.[9] The philosophy of Kierkegaard is presented as the most important attempt to preserve the perennial character of human values, and to regenerate the feeling of dignity for human personal individuality.

---

[5] Ферид Мухиќ [Ferid Muhic], "Поимот на осаменоста во филозофијата и во уметноста" [The Concept of Solitude in Philosophy and Literature], *Razgledi*, vol. 21, no. 3, 1979, pp. 311–43.

[6] Ферид Мухиќ [Ferid Muhic], "Kirkegorov Prolaz" [Kierkegaard's Pass], in *Falco Peregrinus*, Plav: Zavichajni biseri 1986, p. 27.

[7] Иванчо Атанасовски [Ivancho Atanasovski], *Магијата на егзистенцијализмот* [The Magic of Existentialism], Skopje: Metaforum 1994.

[8] Бранислав Саркањац [Branislav Sarkanjac], *Идеологијата и Субјективитетот* [Ideology and Subjectivity], Skopje: Metaforum 1994, see pp. 58–9; p. 74; p. 80; pp. 92–5; p. 100; p. 111; p. 118; p. 126; p. 134; p. 139; pp. 141–3; pp. 156–7; p. 178; p. 187; pp. 199–202; p. 211; pp. 213–4; pp. 216–8; p. 233; p. 257.

[9] Ферид Мухиќ [Ferid Muhic], *Смислата и Доблеста* [Sense and Virtue], Bitola: Sv. Kliment Ohridski 1997, pp. 192–5; pp. 197–8.

The article "The Transcendence of Eros and the Melancholy of the Aesthetic" was published in 1998.[10] Although presented on only six pages of the magazine, this text covers about twenty pages in A4 format. The author, Ms. Kitsa Kolbe (Ph.D. in Philosophy from the Faculty of Philosophy in Skopje), follows the main subject of her doctoral thesis devoted to the philosophical problems of the "principle of hope," and the "principle of longing." This is why the English translation, given by the magazine, of the notion of Eros, would be closer to the originally intended concept of longing. The key point is that, for Kierkegaard, longing and melancholy are not the causal functions of social factors, but transcendent, or trans-social and trans-historical postulates of human contemplation.

The chapter "On Irony—with Constant Reference to Kierkegaard" appeared in a book published in 2000.[11] The author, Ivan Dzheparoski, is Professor of Aesthetics at The Faculty of Philosophy. He presents the aesthetic views of Kierkegaard in his book *Beyond the System*. Allusion to the Kierkegaard's masters' thesis, in combination with an inspired approach, adds specific quality to Kierkegaard as a philosopher as well as a writer.

The article "My Choice: Kierkegaard, Nietzsche, Dostoyevsky" compares and interconnects the three thinkers, explaining the reasons of each author's personal preference.[12] The author, Trajche Stojanov, is a B.A. from the Philosophy Faculty of Philosophy in Skopje.

The work *Philosophy*,[13] which appeared in 2002, is from the hand of Professor emeritus Jonche Josiffovski. This text offers a readable and didactically appropriate presentation of Kierkegaard's philosophy for secondary school students.

The work by Risto Soluntchev (B.A. in Philosophy from the Faculty of Philosophy in Skopje) entitled *The Spheres of Existence in Søren Kierkegaard* introduces systematically to the Macedonian reader the main features of these spheres, together with some comments designed to help in the understanding of Kierkegaard's view.[14]

---

[10] Кица Колбе [Kitsa Kolbe], "Трансценденцијата на копнежот и меланхолијата на естетското" [The Transcendence of Eros and Melancholy of Aesthetical], *Културен Живот*, vol. 4, no. 90, 1998, pp. 54–60.

[11] Иван Џепароски [Ivan Dzheparoski], "За иронијата—со постојано навраќање на Кјеркегор" [On Irony—with Constant Reference to Kierkegaard], in *Оттаде системот* [Beyond the System], Skopje: Kultura 2000, pp. 21–39.

[12] Трајче Стојанов [Trajche Stojanov], "Мојот избор: Кјеркегор, Ниче, Достоевскиг" [My Choice: Kierkegaard, Nietzsche, Dostoyevsky], *Сум-списание за уметност*, vol. 8, no. 31, 2001, pp. 112–24.

[13] Јонче Јосифовски [Jonche Josiffovski], *Филозофија* [Philosophy], Skopje: Prosvetno delo-Skopje 2002, pp. 125–7.

[14] Ристо Солунчев [Risto Soluntchev], "Сферите на егзистенција кај Сорен Киркегор" [The Spheres of Existence in Søren Kierkegaard], *Филозофија*, vol. 3, no. 12, 2004, pp. 51–72.

Bibliography

I. Macedonian Translations of Kierkegaard's Works

Дневникот на заводникот. Или-Или, Еден фрагмент од животот [The Seducer's Diary. Either/Or, Fragment from Life], trans. from English by Aleksandar Temkov, Skopje: Epoha 1996.

II. Secondary Literature on Kierkegaard in Macedonia

Атанасовски, Иванчо [Atanasovski, Ivancho], *Магијата на егзистенцијализмот* [The Magic of Existentialism], Skopje: Metaforum 1994, p. 18; pp. 22–4; p. 26; p. 29; p. 32; p. 37; p. 41; pp. 45–9; pp. 64–5; p. 70; p. 76; p. 78; pp. 80–1; p. 86; p. 88; p. 90; pp. 92–7; p. 99; p. 121; p. 124; p. 133; pp. 152–3; p. 157; pp. 160–1; pp. 167–8; pp. 170–1; p. 173; p. 176; p. 178; p. 183; pp. 200–201; p. 203; p. 207.

Јосифовски, Јонче [Josifovski, Jonche], *Филозофија* [Philosophy], Skopje: Prosvetno delo-Skopje 2002, pp. 125–7.

Колбе, Кица [Kolbe, Kitsa], "Трансценденцијата на копнежот и меланхолијата на естетското" [The Transcendence of Eros and Melancholy of Aesthetic], *Културен Живот*, vol. 4, no. 90, 1998, pp. 54–60.

Мухиќ, Ферид [Muhic, Ferid], "Ставот на Киркегор кон верата и разумот - некои дилеми" [Reason and Faith in Kierkegaard's Philosophy], *Зборник на Филозофски факултет*, ед. бs Филозофски факултет на универзитетот, Skopje 1978, pp. 365–79.

— "Поимот на осаменоста во филозофијата и во уметноста" [The Concept of Solitude in Philosophy and Literature], *Razgledi*, vol. 21, no. 3, 1979, pp. 311–43.

— "Kirkegorov Prolaz" [Kierkegaard's Pass], in *Falco Peregrinus*, Plav: Zavichajni biseri 1986, p. 27.

— *Смислата и Доблеста* [Sense and Virtue], Bitola: Sv. Kliment Ohridski 1997, pp. 192–5; pp. 197–8.

Саркањац, Бранислав [Sarkanjac, Branislav], *Идеологијата и Субјективитетот* [Ideology and Subjectivity], Skopje: Metaforum 1994, pp. 58–9; p. 74; p. 80; pp. 92–5; p. 100; p. 111; p. 118; p. 126; p. 134; p. 139; pp. 141–3; pp. 156–7; p. 178; p. 187; pp. 199–202; p. 211; pp. 213–4; pp. 216–8; p. 233; p. 257.

Солунчев, Ристо [Solunchev, Risto], "Сферите на егзистенција кај Сорен Киркегор" [The Spheres of Existence in Søren Kierkegaard], *Философија*, vol. 3, no. 12, 2004, pp. 51–72.

Стојанов, Трајче [Stojanov, Trajche], "Мојот избор: Кјеркегор, Ниче, Достоевскиг " [My Choice: Kierkegaard, Nietzsche, Dostoyevsky], *Сумсписание за уметност*, vol. 8, no. 31, 2001, pp. 112–24.

Темков, Александар [Temkov, Aleksandar], "Сорен Киркегор—Данскиот Сократг " [Søren Kierkegaard—the Socrates of Denmark], in *Дневникот на заводникот* [The Seducer's Diary], pp. 5–13 (Preface to the translation of "The Seducer's Diary").

Џепароски, Иван [Dzheparoski, Ivan], "За иронијата—со постојано навраќање на Кјеркегор" [On Irony—with Constant Reference to Kierkegaard], in *Оттаде системот* [Beyond the System], Skopje: Kultura 2000.

III. Secondary Literature on Kierkegaard's Reception in Macedonia

None.

Serbia and Montenegro:
Kierkegaard as a Post-Metaphysical Philosopher

Safet Bektovic

Søren Kierkegaard became known in Serbia and Montenegro only after the Second World War. In the beginning, he was only discussed in narrow circles of specialists, where he was regarded respectively as a modern philosopher and a literary author and most often in connection with existentialism, i.e., as a forerunner of Jean Paul Sartre, Albert Camus, and other authors whose works were already known in the region.

A growing interest in Kierkegaard's philosophical ideas in the 1970s and 1980s resulted in the first Kierkegaard translations. These translations were, however, not made directly from the Danish original but rather from German translations. Nevertheless, this represented the beginning of a Kierkegaard research where individual authors, primarily philosophers, began to write about Kierkegaard. The most zealous translator—not only in Serbia but also in the entire area of the former Yugoslavia—was Milan Tabaković from Belgrade. He translated the greater part of Kierkegaard's authorship into Serbo-Croatian.[1] It is also worth noting that Gligorije Ernjaković was the only one to translate directly from the Danish original (*The Concept of Anxiety*).[2] The print run of the first editions of these Kierkegaard

---

[1] *Ponavljanje: pokušaj u eksperimentalnoj psihologiji Konstantina Konstantinusa* [*Repetition. A Venture in Experimental Psychology by Constantin Constantinus*], trans. by Milan Tabaković, Belgrade: Grafos 1975 (republished, 1980, 1982, Belgrade: Moderna 1989 and Belgrade: Dereta 2005); *Ili-ili* [*Either/Or*], trans. by Milan Tabaković, Sarajevo: Veselin Masleša 1979 (republished, 1990 and Belgrade: Grafos 1989); *Filozofske mrvice* [*Philosophical Fragments*], trans. by Milan Tabaković, Belgrade: Grafos 1980 (republished, 1982 and 1990); *Dve kratke etičko-religiozne rasprave* [*Two Ethical-Religious Essays*], trans. by Milan Tabaković, Belgrade: Grafos 1982 (republished, Belgrade: Moderna 1989 and Belgrade: Grafos 1990); *Knjiga o Adleru* [*The Book on Adler*], trans. by Milan Tabaković, Belgrade: Grafos 1982; *Dnevnik zavodnika* ["The Seducer's Diary"], trans. by Milan Tabaković, Novi Sad: Svetovi 2000.

[2] *Pojam strepnje: obično, psihološki usmerenorazmatranje u pravcu dogmatičkog problema o naslednom grehu* [*The Concept of Anxiety. A Simple Psychologically Orienting Deliberation on the Dogmatic Issue of Hereditary Sin*], trans. by Gligorije Ernjaković, Belgrade: Grafos 1970 (republished, Belgrade: Plato 2002).

translations was not particularly large (around 2000-3000 copies), but when interest in Kierkegaard continued to grow, most of them were quickly reprinted.

In the 1980s, when the present author himself studied philosophy in Serbia, Kierkegaard's works, *Philosophical Fragments, Fear and Trembling,* and *Either/Or,* were a part of the obligatory reading for students of philosophy in the field of modern philosophy. At that time Kierkegaard became regarded as one of the most important post-metaphysical philosophers, alongside Marx, Nietzsche and Heidegger, and there were people with an interest in Kierkegaard at several of the university centers in the former Yugoslavia including Zagreb, Sarajevo, Belgrade, and Priština.

With what concerns the scholarly study of Kierkegaard in Serbia and Montenegro, I will draw attention to two books, which in my view are the most relevant for a presentation of the reception of Kierkegaard in the region. These are *Søren Kierkegaard's Philosophy* and *Thought and Passion*.[3]

Søren Kierkegaard's Philosophy is written by a philosophy and university professor from Montenegaro, Vujadin Jokić (1928–86), who taught modern philosophy and aesthetics at several universities in Serbia and Montenegro. This book is in actuality a reworked edition of Jokić's lectures on Kierkegaard, which he gave at the Department of Philosophy in Podgorica during the academic year 1985–86 and which were only published after the death of the author. One of Jokić's students was responsible for the edition, the present professor of philosophy in Novi Pazar—Šefket Krcić.

Jokić regards Kierkegaard's authorship as a complete unity and tries to discover the guiding idea or, as he himself says, the "synthetic thought" in Kierkegaard's philosophy. According to Jokić, this thought consists in "a reflexive understanding of the concept of the individual" situated in a Christian religious perspective. The understanding of this thought, i.e., the individual's Christian existence, is connected, according to Jokić, with the understanding of the time and the environment in which Kierkegaard lived and wrote, and not least of all with Kierkegaard's relation to the official Christianity and Christian theology.[4]

In the first part of the book, Jokić systematically presents Kierkegaard's main works by following their chronological and thematic course. Here he underscores, among other things, Kierkegaard's philosophical originality in relation to the understanding of the existence of human beings. At the same time, he draws attention to Kierkegaard's *Lebensphilosophie* and existential analysis which transcends the limits of Christianity and has a universal philosophical character, which makes Kierkegaard one of the most important European thinkers of the nineteenth century.

In the second part of the book, Jokić treats Kierkegaard's key concepts such as existence, individual, paradox, sin, despair, anxiety, faith, and repetition. Here one can see Jokić's aesthetic approach and his sense for the aeesthetic-philosophical dimension in Kierkegaard. He points out a connection between Kierkegaard's life and his works. It was, according to Jokić, "a melancholy and passionate life," and

---

[3] Vujadin Jokić, *Filozofija Serena Kjerkegora*, Podgorica: Unireks 1999; Milos Todorović, *Misao i strast: filozofija Serena Kjerkegora*, Belgrade: Prosveta 2001.
[4] Jokić, *Filozofija Serena Kjerkegora*, p. 19.

the contemplation on this life is clearly reflected in Kierkegaard's "passionate philosophical production."[5]

The book *Thought and Passion* written by the professor of philosophy at the University of Novi Sad, Milos Todorović, is without doubt the most comprehensive work on Kierkegaard written by an author from Serbia and Montenegro. It testifies, among other things, to a many-faceted research on Kierkegaard's philosophy and a broad use of the relevant secondary literature on Kierkegaard written in European languages. Todorović's book takes the main philosophical themes in Kierkegaard to be the self, freedom, truth, and actuality, and gives the issue of the relation between thinking and passion, philosophy and existence, a central position.

The first part of *Thought and Passion* aims, among other things, to give an account of the main features of idealist philosophy from Descartes via Fichte, Kant, and Hegel with respect to the idea of the "subject–object relation." Kierkegaard is regarded as a key person in the post-metaphysical philosophical tradition whose criticism of speculative reason and emphasis on reflexivity and the inward nature of human existence opens up an entirely new way of doing philosophy. Instead of a "speculative subjectivity" and "methodological doubt," Kierkegaard places "the existence of the individual" at the center in which "the ways of the formation of existence," as Todorović calls it, are the determinations for the character of truth and actuality. These ways can, according to Todorović, also be regarded as the main aspects of existence which constitute "the mood of existence," and they are expressed in special pairs of concepts: "sins and doubt," "spirit and anxiety," "the self and despair," "the paradox and offence."[6]

In the second part of his book—which has the subtitle "Being and Existence"—Todorović treats Kierkegaard's key concepts in light of an "existential ontology." These include the concepts of becoming, repetition, existential truth, and faith. Their forms and mutual connections have, according to Todorović, a dialectical character and cannot be regarded as independent or static terms. Becoming, which contains a contemporaneity in relation to the past and the future is thus dialectically related to repetition. In the same way truth and faith stand in a reciprocal relation and together with the preceding pair (becoming and repetition) contribute to making possible an understanding of existence.[7]

One can say by way of conclusion that Todorović's book, written primarily for specialists and philosophy students, represents required reading and a very useful tool for anyone in Serbia and Montenegro who seeks to gain an insight into the whole of Kierkegaard's authorship and his main philosophical thoughts.

Translated by Jon Stewart

---

[5] Ibid., p. 47.
[6] Todorović, *Misao i strast*, pp. 49–87.
[7] Ibid., p. 251.

Bibliography

I. Serbo-Croatian Translations of Kierkegaard's Works

Osvrt na moje delo [*The Point of View for My Work as an Author*], trans. by Lela Matić, Belgrade: Grafos 1965.

Pojam strepnje: obično, psihološki usmerenorazmatranje u pravcu dogmatičkog problema o naslednom grehu [*The Concept of Anxiety. A Simple Psychologically Orienting Deliberation on the Dogmatic Issue of Hereditary Sin*], trans. by Gligorije Ernjaković, Belgrade: Grafos 1970 (republished, Belgrade: Plato 2002).

Bolest na smrt [*The Sickness unto Death*], trans. by Milan Tabaković, Belgrade: Grafos 1974 (republished, Belgrade: Plato 2000).

Ponavljanje: pokušaj u eksperimentalnoj psihologiji Konstantina Konstantinusa [*Repetition. A Venture in Experimental Psychology by Constantin Constantinus*], trans. by Milan Tabaković, Belgrade: Grafos 1975 (republished, 1980, 1982, Belgrade: Moderna 1989 and Belgrade: Dereta 2005).

Strah i drhtanje [*Fear and Trembling*], trans. by Slobodan Žunjić, Belgrade: Grafos 1975.

Brevijar [Letter-Holder. Religious Fragments from Different Works of Kierkegaard], trans. by Dimitrije Najdenović, Belgrade: Grafos 1979 (republished 1981, 1986, Belgrade: Moderna 1990 and Nova Pazova: Bonart 2001).

Ili-ili [*Either/Or*], trans. by Milan Tabaković, Sarajevo: Veselin Masleša 1979 (republished 1990 and Belgrade: Grafos 1989).

Filozofske mrvice [*Philosophical Fragments*], trans. by Milan Tabaković, Belgrade: Grafos 1980 (republished 1982 and 1990).

Osvrt na moje delo [*The Point of View for My Work as an Author*], trans. by Lela Matić, Belgrade: Grafos 1981.

Osvrt na moje delo [*The Point of View for My Work as an Author*], trans. by Lela Matić, Belgrade: Grafos 1981 (republished 1985).

Dve kratke etičko-religiozne rasprave [Two Ethical-Religious Essays], trans. by Milan Tabaković, Belgrade: Grafos 1982 (republished, Belgrade: Moderna 1989 and Belgrade: Grafos 1990).

Knjiga o Adleru [*The Book on Adler*], trans. by Milan Tabaković, Belgrade: Grafos 1982.

Selingova pozna filozofija [Schelling's Later Philosophy] (translation of *Schellings Seinslehre und Kierkegaard*, ed. by Anton Mirko Koktanek, München: Oldenbourg 1962 (this work contains a German translation of Kierkegaard's notes to Schelling's Philosophy of Revelation)) trans. by Milutin Stanisavać, Belgrade: Grafos 1984.

Bolezen za smrt: krščanska psihološkarazprava za spodbudo in prebujo [*The Sickness unto Death. A Christian Psychological Exposition for Upbuilding and Awakening*], trans. by Janez Zupet, Celje: Mohorjeva družba 1987.

In vino veritas, trans. by Života Filipović, Čačak: Dom Kulture 1994.

Dnevnik zavodnika ["The Seducer's Diary"], trans. by Milan Tabaković, Novi Sad: Svetovi 2000.

Strah i drhtanje [*Fear and Trembling*], trans. by Slobodan Žunjić, Belgrade: Plato 2002.

Dnevnici i zapisi 1834–1855 [Journals and Papers 1834–1855], trans. by Predrag Šaponja and Smiljka Jovetić-Veber, Novi Sad: Svetovi 2003.

II. Secondary Literature on Kierkegaard in Serbia and Montenegro

Bektovic, Safet, *Paradoksalnost vere u filozofiji S. Kjerkegora* [The Paradox of Faith in S. Kierkegaard's Philosophy], Priština: Filozofski fakultet 1989.

Jokić, Vujadin, *Filozofija Serena Kjerkegora* [Søren Kierkegaard's Philosophy], Podgorica: Unireks 1999.

Kuzmanović, Nebojsa, *Kjerkegorove sfere egzistencije* [*The Existential Spheres in Kierkegaard*], Sremski Karlovci: Krovovi 1997.

Marković, Vito, "*Esteticko, eticko i religiozno*" [The Aesthetical, the Ethical and the Religious], Preface to *Brevijar*, pp. 7–9.

Mojsić, Sofija, "*Dijalektika 'estetske egzistencije' Serena Kjerkegora*" [The Dialectic of the Aesthetical Existence in Søren Kierkegaard's Writings], *Filozofija i drustvo*, nos. 9–10, 1996, pp. 377–96.

— "Kierkegaard—nas savremenik Problemi formiranja identiteta modernog coveka" [Kierkegaard—The Contemporary Problems of the Identity Formation of Modern Man], *Filozofija i drustvo*, nos. 9–10, 1996, pp. 311–6.

Prošić, Luka, "*Kjerkegor u romanu*" [Kierkegaard in the Novel], *Književnost*, nos. 10–2, 2002, pp. 976–83.

Sarcević, Abdulah, "Dijalektika trazenja apsolutnog" [The Dialectic of Seeking the Absolute], Preface to *Pojam strepnje*, pp. 7–56.

Tabaković, Milan, "Intencija, struktura i terminologija Filozofskih mrvica" [Intention, Disposition and Terminology of the *Philosophical Fragments*], Epilogue to *Filozofske mrvice*, pp. 119–24.

Todorović, Milos, "*Susret poietickog i praktickog*" [The Meeting-Place of the Poetical and the Practical], in *Sreca i stvaranje. Kulturni centar i Odsek za filozofiju Filozofskog fakulteta u Novom Sadu*, 1997, pp. 79–95.

— *Misao i strast—filozofija Serena Kjerkegora* [Thought and Passion—Søren Kierkegaard's Philosophy], Belgrade: Prosveta 2001.

Životić, Miladin, *Egzistencija, realnost i sloboda* [Existence, Reality and Freedom], Belgrade: Ideje 1973.

Žunjić, Slobodan, "*Dijalekticka lirika Straha i drhtanja*" [The Dialectical Lyric in *Fear and Trembling*], Preface to *Strah i drhtanje*, pp. 5–24.

Žurović, Mirko, "*Dijalektika egzistencije u filozofiji Serena Kjerkegora*" [The Dialectic of Existence in Søren Kierkegaard's Philosophy], Preface to *Bolest na smrt*, 1974.

III. Secondary Literature on Kierkegaard's Reception in Serbia and Montenegro

None.

Index of Persons

Abbagnano, Nicola (1901–90), Italian philosopher, 82–9 passim.
Adinolfi, Isabella, 96.
Adorno, Theodor W. (1903–69), German philosopher, 36, 161.
Ady, Endre (1877–1919), Hungarian poet, 164.
Agacinski, Sylviane, 175.
Aizpún de Bobadilla, Teresa, 43, 49, 50.
Alcorta y Echeverría, José Ignacio, Spanish philosopher, 31.
Alemquer, Mário, 1.
Alves, João Lopes, 3.
Alvira, Rafael, 43, 50.
Amorós, Cèlia, 43, 49.
Andersen, Hans Christian (1805–75), Danish poet, novelist and writer of fairy tales, 156.
Antunes, Manuel, S.J. (1918–85), 7.
Aquinas, Thomas (ca. 1225–74), Scholastic philosopher and theologian, 46.
Aristophanes, 295.
Arsinevici, Adrian, 308.
Artigas, José, 30.
Atanasovski, Ivancho, 319.
Augustine of Hippo, Saint (354–430), philosopher and theologian, 38, 215.
Averintsev, Sergey, 265.

Babits, Mihály (1883–1941), Hungarian poet, 164.
Bachtin, Michaił, 220.
Bacsó Béla, 175.
Bagdasar, Nicolae (1896–1971), Romania philosopher, 305.
Balassa, Péter, 172.
Balázs, Béla (1884–1949), Hungarian film aesthete and script writer, 160.
Balca, Nicolae (1903–83), Romanian philosopher, 304.
Baltrušaitis, Jurgis (1903–88), Russian poet, 252, 275.
Banfi, Antonio (1886–1957), Italian philosopher, 85, 86, 88.
Bonhoeffer, Dietrich (1906–45), German Lutheran pastor and theologian, 170.
Baroja, Pío (1872–1956), 25, 26.
Barth, Karl (1886–1968), Swiss theologian, 85, 162, 170, 190.
Belletti, Bruno, 94.
Berdyaev, Nikolay (1874–1948), Russian philosopher, 260, 263, 274.
Bergson, Henri (1859–1941), French philosopher, 167, 286.
Berkeley, George (1685–1753), Irish philosopher, 265.
Bessa-Luís, Agustina, Portuguese novelist, 9, 10.
Bienenstock, Maks (1881–1918), Polish scholar, 213.
Bignone, Ettore (1879–1953), 83.
Billeskov-Jansen, Frederik (1907–2002), Danish literary scholar, 39.
Bjørnstjerne, Bjørnson (1832–1910), Norwegian dramatist, 252, 264.
Blackham, Harold John, 37.
Blaga, Lucian (1895–1961), Romania poet, dramatist and philosopher, 303, 304.
Bloch, Ernst (1885–1977), German philosopher, 160.
Blok, Aleksandr (1880–1921), Russian cultural figure, 256, 257.
Boboc, Alexandru, 305, 308, 309.
Boesen, Emil (1812–81), Danish theologian, 40.
Borgese, Giuseppe Antonio (1882–1952), Sicilian writer, 83.
Borso, Dario, 95.
Bosco, Maria Angélica, 33.
Brabant, Siger de (ca. 1240–80), philosopher, 265.
Brandenstein, Béla (1901–89), Hungarian philosopher, 162.
Brandes, Georg (1842–1927), Danish literary critic, 23, 84, 86, 87, 157, 208, 286, 288, 290.
Buber, Martin (1878–1965), Jewish philosopher, 160, 258, 259.
Bulgakov, Sergey (1871–1944), Russian Orthodox theologian, 267.

Butkevitch, Timophey Ivanovich (1854–1925), Russian theologian, 249.
Bykhovsky, Bernard Emmanuilovitch (1898–1980), 265, 266.

Călinescu, George (1899–1965), Romanian philosopher, 305.
Calò, Giovanni (1882–1970), Italian scholar, 82.
Camus, Albert (1913–60), French author, 167, 169, 260, 323.
Canals Vidal, Francisco, 38.
Cañas, José Luis, 44.
Canclini, Arnoldo, 52.
Cândido Pimentel, Manuel, 10.
Cantoni, Remo (1914–78), Italian philosopher, 89, 92.
Cappelørn, Niels Jørgen, 53, 175.
Careaga Guzmán, Virginia, 41, 50, 51.
Casais Monteiro, Adolfo (1908–72), Portuguese-Brazilian philosopher, writer, 2, 3.
Castagnino, Franca, 83, 89.
Castilla del Pino, Carlos, 32.
Černý, Václav (1905–87), Czech literary critic, 207.
Chacel, Rosa (1898–1994), Spanish writer, 38.
Clair, André, 50.
Coimbra, Leonardo (1883–1935), Portuguese philosopher, 2, 5.
Colao, Alberto, 33.
Collado, Jesús Antonio, 35, 36.
Collins, James Daniel (1917–85), American philosopher, 31.
Corssen, Meta, 88.
Cortese, Alessandro, 84, 87, 93, 94.
Czakó, István, 175.

Davini, Simonella, 96.
Davydov, Yuri, 265.
Dehs, Jørgen, 274.
Dempf, Alois, 304.
Démuth, Andrej, 192.
Derrida, Jacques (1930–2004), French philosopher, 175.
Descartes, René (1596–1650), French philosopher, 228, 325.
Diaconu, Madalina, 301–8 passim.
Díaz, Carlos, 50.
Dimitrov, Alexander, 291.
Djakowska, Alina, 219.
Dobre, Catalina Elena, 309, 310.
Donadoni, Dino, 92.
Dostoevsky, Fyodor Mikhailovich (1821–81), Russian author, 159, 160, 169, 253, 258–60, 289, 291, 292, 320.
Dru, Alexander, 90.
Dumitrescu-Codreanu, Lucia, 305.
Dzheparoski, Ivan, 320.

Effrusi, Boris Osipovich, 250.
Eliade, Mircea (1907–86), Romanian historian, 301–4.
Engels, Friedrich (1820–95), German philosopher, 266.
Ernjaković, Gligorije, 323.
Estelrich i Artigues, Joan (1896–1958), Spanish author, 17, 23–7 passim.
Evans, C. Stephen, 195.

Fabro, Cornelio (1911–95), Italian Kierkegaard scholar, 7, 31, 33, 51, 52, 55, 87–95 passim.
Farré, Luis, 35.
Fazekaš, Ľudovít, 191, 192.
Fehér M., István, 175.
Ferlov, Knud (1881–1977), translator of Kierkegaard's works, 2, 3, 81, 83.
Fernández, Clemente, 38.
Ferreira, Alberto (1920–2000), Portuguese author, 4.
Ferreira, Vergílio (1916–96), Portuguese novelist, 9.
Ferrer Bonifaci, Consuelo, 36.
Ferro, Nuno, 9, 10.
Feuerbach, Ludwig (1804–72), German philosopher, 87, 223, 254, 255, 266.
Fichte, Johann Gottlieb (1762–1814), German philosopher, 269, 325.
Filosofov, Dmitry (1872–1940), Russian cultural figure, 256.
Florensky, Pavel Alexandrovich (1882–1937), Russian Orthodox theologian and philosopher, 267.
Florian, Mircea, 304.
Florovsky, Georgy (1893–1979), Russian theologian, 258.
Fodor Géza, 175.
Fondane, Bengamin, 258.
Fontán Jubero, Pedro, 38.

Fragata, Júlio S.J. (1920–85), Portuguese philosopher, 7, 8.
Franco Barrio, Jaime, 41.
Fryszman, Alex, 220, 221, 274.
Fundoianu, Benjamin, 303.

Gabriel, Leo (1902–87), 39.
Gama, João, 4.
Gangale, Giuseppe (1898–1978), 85.
Gaidenko, Piama Pavlovna, 169, 265–71 passim, 289.
Gaidukova, Tatyana, 265.
Gaos, José, 29.
García, José, 51.
García Amilburu, María, 43, 49–51.
Garin, Eugenio (1909–2004), Italian philosopher, 81, 85.
Gateau, Jean-Jacques (1887–1967), French translator of Kierkegaard's works, 2, 3.
Gelabert, Martín, 40.
Gentile, Giovanni (1875–1944), Italian philosopher, 85, 86.
Gigante, Mario, 95.
Glicksman Grene, Marjorie, 30.
Gocheva, Dimka, 295.
Gogol, Nikolai (1809–52), Russian author, 274.
Goldmann, Lucien (1913–70), French philosopher, 157.
Gombrowicz, Witold (1904–69), Polish author, 227.
Gómez de Liaño, Ignacio, 38.
Goncharov, Ivan (1812–91), Russian author, 248.
Goñi Zubieta, Carlos, 47.
González, Darío D., 53, 307.
González Álvarez, Ángel (1916–91) Spanish Thomist philosopher, 31.
Gorbunov-Posadov, Ivan, 251.
Gottsched, Hermann, (1848–1916), German protestant theologian, 23.
Granat, Wincenty (1900–79), Polish Catholic scholar, 216, 217.
Grifo, Carlos, 3.
Gromczyński, Wiesław, 224, 225.
Grøn, Arne, 49, 50.
Grünberg, Ludwig, 305.
Guardini, Romano (1885–1965), German Catholic priest, author and academic, 30.

Guerrero Martínez, Luis Ignacio, 41.
Guldbrandsen, Kirsten Montanari, 91.
Gulian, Constantin Ionescu, 305.
Gutiérrez Rivero, Demetrio, 34, 40.
Gyenge, Zoltán, 172, 175.
Gyllembourg-Ehrensvärd, Thomasine Christine (1773–1856), Danish author, 290.

Hadzinakov, Petar, 295.
Haecker, Theodor (1879–1945), German writer, 30, 89, 90.
Hamvas Béla (1897–1968), Hungarian thinker and writer, 164, 169.
Hansen, Peter Emmanuel (1846–1930), Russian translator of Kierkegaard's works, 247–52 passim, 270, 274, 275.
Hartmann, Nikolai (1882–1950), German philosopher, 6.
Hegel, Georg Wilhelm Friedrich (1770–1831), German philosopher, 5, 26, 37, 39, 40, 86–8, 156, 160, 166, 169, 170, 206, 215, 216, 222–4, 228, 259, 261, 266, 274, 287, 289–95 passim, 304, 325.
Heiberg, Johanne Luise (1812–90), Danish actress, 10.
Heidegger, Martin (1889–1976), German philosopher, 6, 26, 85, 87, 95, 157, 162, 164, 167, 169, 172, 213, 217, 266, 267, 272, 296, 324.
Heim, Josef, 206.
Hejdánek, Ladislav, 208.
Heller, Ágnes, Hungarian philosopher, 39, 171, 175.
Herman, Wladimir, 274.
Herman, Włodzimierz, 229.
Hesse, Hermann (1877–1962), German-Swiss author, 291, 292.
Hippius, Zinaida (1869–1945), Russian cultural figure, 256.
Høffding, Harald (1843–1931), Danish philosopher, 23, 27, 29, 81–3, 87, 252, 286, 287.
Hong, Edna H. (1913–2007), American translator, 4, 90.
Hong, Howard W. (b. 1912), American translator, 4, 90.
Hromádka, Josef Lukl (1889–1969), Czech theologian, 190.

Hulka-Laskowski, Paweł (1881–1946), Polish writer and translator, 214.
Hultberg, Per, 274.
Humpál, Martin, 206.
Husserl, Edmund (1859–1938), German philosopher, 7, 88, 228, 258.

Ianosi, Ion, 306, 307.
Ibsen, Henrik (1828–1906), Norwegian dramatist, 19, 82, 83, 86, 156, 157, 158, 164, 169, 250–2, 264, 286, 303.
Igov, Atanas, 295.
Iiritano, Massimo, 96.
Irina, Nicolae, 308, 309.
Isayev, Sergey Aleksandrovich (1951–2000), Russian translator of Kierkegaard's works, 270, 271, 275.
Ivanov, Vladimir, 291.
Iwaszkiewicz, Jarosław (1894–1980), Polish poet, 217, 223.

Jacobsen, Jens Peter (1847–85), Danish author, 158.
Jakubowska, Janina, 226.
James, William (1842–1910), American psychologist and philosopher, 35, 256, 286.
Jarauta Marión, Francisco, 37, 41.
Jaspers, Karl (1883–1969), German philosopher, 30, 39, 85, 87, 160, 162, 167, 169, 172, 213.
Jesi, Furio, 93.
Jokić, Vujadin (1928–86), Montenegrin philosopher, 324.
Jolivet, Régis (1891–1966) French Catholic thinker, 29, 30, 31.
Josiffovski, Jonche, 320.
József, Attila (1905–37), Hungarian poet, 164.

Kafka, Franz (1883–1924), Austrian writer, 164, 169, 269.
Kampmann, Theoderich (1899–1983), German theologian and literary scholar, 30.
Kanavrov, Valentin, 292, 293.
Kant, Immanuel (1724–1804), German philosopher, 87, 194, 222, 226, 290, 293, 294, 325.
Karpushin, Vladimir (1920–90), 265.
Kasperski, Edward, 221–3, 226.

Kassner, Rudolf (1873–1959), Austrian philosopher and writer, 158.
Kavelin, Konstantin Dmitrievich (1818–85), Russian thinker, 250, 251.
Kesselring, Rudolf (ca. 1880–ca. 1945), Polish Protestant clergyman and professor, 214, 215.
Kierkegaard, Søren Aabye (1813–1855),
The Battle between the Old and the New Soap-Cellars (in *Journals BB*) (1838), 93, 173.
From the Papers of One Still Living (1838), 53, 270.
The Concept of Irony (1841), 3, 53, 95, 170, 173, 218, 269, 285, 295, 307.
Either/Or (1843), 1–3, 9, 19, 25, 28, 34, 35, 38, 40, 43, 49, 51, 54, 81, 83, 87, 162, 170, 285, 289, 292, 295, 307–10, 171, 193, 205, 206, 208, 213–8 passim, 228, 229, 248, 249, 251, 252, 256, 273, 318, 324.
Repetition (1843), 54, 170, 172, 218, 248, 275, 285, 293, 294, 308, 310.
Fear and Trembling (1843), 3, 4, 40, 43, 49, 54, 165, 171, 193, 213, 217, 248, 256, 271, 273, 285, 294, 308–10, 324.
Prefaces (1844), 95, 218.
Upbuilding Discourses (1843–1844), 9, 91, 95, 162.
Philosophical Fragments (1844), 31, 33, 37, 52, 88, 92, 218, 275, 285, 293, 296, 307, 310, 324.
The Concept of Anxiety (1844), 2–5, 29, 34, 50, 54, 87–9, 92, 170, 172, 218, 222, 259, 269, 271, 273, 285, 290, 293, 308–10, 323.
Stages on Life's Way (1845), 2–5, 32, 34, 35, 51, 83, 87, 206, 248, 251, 258, 289, 302, 310.
Concluding Unscientific Postscript (1846), 19, 20, 37, 54, 92, 170, 218, 271, 273, 275.
A Literary Review of Two Ages (1846), 54, 95, 205, 208.
Upbuilding Discourses in Various Spirit (1847), 49.
Works of Love (1847), 34.
Christian Discourses (1848), 46, 51, 92.
The Point of View for My Work as an Author (ca. 1848), 2, 4, 33, 45–7, 162, 303, 306.

The Lily in the Field and the Bird of the Air: Three Devotional Discourses (1849),
The Sickness unto Death (1849), 2–6 passim, 34, 87, 92, 96, 172, 217, 228, 256, 271, 285, 293, 310.
Two Ethical-Religious Essays (1849), 2, 4.
Practice in Christianity (1850), 34, 91, 172, 218, 256, 285, 309, 310.
For Self-Examination (1851), 248, 251.
The Moment (1855), 8, 85, 193, 206, 213, 218, 255.
Søren Kierkegaards Papirer, 19, 53, 55, 90.
Søren Kierkegaards Skrifter (1997–), 4, 53, 172, 173, 218.
Journals, Notebooks, *Nachlaß*, 45.
Keil, Ana, 4.
Khan, Abraham H., 189, 195.
Kirmmse, Bruce, 175.
Klein, Alessandro, 94.
Koch, Carl, 5, 84.
Kołaczkowski, Stefan, 214.
Kołakowski, Leszek, 217.
Kolbe, Kitsa, 320.
Koncz, Sándor (1913–83), Hungarian theologian, 162.
Kosterka, Hugo, 205.
Koštiaľ, Rudolf (1913–91), Slovak thinker, 191.
Kosztolányi, Dezső (1885–1936), Hungarian poet, author and translator, 164.
Kowalczyk, Stanisław, 225, 226.
Králik, Roman, 192, 194.
Kraus, Arnošt, 206, 208.
Krcić, Šefket, 324.
Krusteva, Maria, 291.
Kuzmanova-Zografova, Katia, 295, 296.

Larrañeta Olleta, Rafael (1945–2002), Spanish philosopher, 37, 38, 40, 41, 50–4 passim.
Lavrencova, Elena, 294.
Lázaro Ros, Amando, 30.
Leibniz, Baron Gottfried Wilhelm von (1646–1716), German philosopher and mathematician, 82.
Lenin, Vladimir Ilyich (1870–1924), Russian statesman, 165, 263.
Le Senne, Rene (1882–1954), French philosopher, 87.

Lesná-Krausová, Milada, 206.
Lévinas, Emmanuel (1906–95), French philosopher, 175, 263.
Levitsky, Sergey (1909–83), Russian sociologist, 258.
Lévy-Bruhl, Lucien (1857–1939), French philosopher, 260.
Liiceanu, Gabriel, 301, 305, 306.
Lochman, Jan Milič, 195.
Locke, John (1632–1704), English philosopher, 228.
Lombardi, Franco (1906–89), Italian Feuerbach scholar, 86, 87, 93.
López Aranguren, José Luis (1909–96), Spanish thinker, 31, 33.
López Ibor, Juan José, 32.
López Quintás, Alfonso, 38.
Losev, Aleksey Fyodorovitch (1893–1988), Russian philosopher, 267, 268.
Lourenço, Eduardo (b. 1923), Portuguese philosopher, 4, 8.
Löwith, Karl (1897–1973), German-Jewish philosopher, 36, 86.
Lowrie, Walter (1868–1959), American translator, 86, 90.
Loyola, Íñigo de (Ignatius of) (1491–1556), founder of the Society of Jesus, 22, 25.
Lubańska, Stefania, 226.
Lukács, György (or Georg) (1885–1971), Hungarian philosopher, 36, 39, 84, 157–71 passim, 176, 264, 288.
Lund, Cynthia, 175, 195.
Luther, Martin (1483–1546), German religious reformer, 94, 215, 258, 261.

Maceiras Fafián, Manuel, 38.
Macoviciuc, Vasile, 308.
Madách, Imre (1823–64), Hungarian poet, 156.
Malantschuk, Gregor (1902–78), 294.
Malewska, Hanna (1911–83), Polish Catholic scholar, 216.
Malraux, André (1901–76), French author, 260.
Marcel, Gabriel (1889–1973), French existentialist philosopher, 87, 213.
Marinho, José (1904–75), Portuguese philosopher, 4, 6.
Marini, Sergio, 95.

Markuš, Jozef Ondrej, 191.
Marx, Karl (1813–83), German political philosopher, 86, 160, 161, 166, 170, 171, 206, 215, 227, 266, 292, 324.
Masci, Filippo, 82.
Matei, Nicodim Ion, 304.
Mátrai László (1909–83), Hungarian philosopher, 167.
Matuštík, Martin, 189.
McKinnon, Alastair, 43, 49.
Melchiorre, Virgilio, 95, 96.
Melendo, Tomás, 51
Merezhkovsky, Dmitry (1866–1941), Russian cultural figure, 256.
Mikołajczyk, Hubert, 222, 223.
Mikszáth, Kálmán (1847–1910), Hungarian author, 157.
Miranda Justo, José, 4, 5.
Modica, Giuseppe, 95, 96.
Møller, Poul Martin (1794–1838), Danish poet and philosopher, 10.
Mollo, Gaetano, 95.
Montaigne, Michel de (1533–92), French philosopher, 159.
Monteiro, Casais, 5, 6.
Mortensen, Finn Hauberg, 274.
Mounier, Emmanuel (1905–50), French philosopher, 29.
Mozart, Wolfgang Amadeus (1756–91), Austrian composer, 274.
Muhic, Ferid, 318.
Munk, Kaj (1898–1944), Danish pastor and author, 191.
Munteanu, Aurel Dragos, 305.
Mynster, Jakob Peter (1775–1854), Danish theologian and bishop, 26.
Myslivchenko, A.G., 264.

Nachev, Stefan, 286.
Nagy, Imre (1896–1958), Hungarian politician, 168.
Nandrásky, Karol, 191, 192.
Navarria, Salvatore, 93.
Neagoe, Florica, 305.
Negre, Montserrat, 50, 51.
Nicoletti, Michele, 95.
Niecikowski, Jerzy, 224.
Nietzsche, Friedrich (1844–1900), German philosopher, 85, 95, 162, 216, 229, 256, 266, 272, 289, 290, 292, 308, 320, 324.

Noica, Constantin, 306.

Odintsov, Mikhail Vladimirovich (1879–ca. 1965), Russian author, 255–7, 274.
Oliveira e Silva, Luís de (b. 1945), 9.
Olsen, Regine (1822–1904), 10, 36, 40, 84, 162, 259, 288, 302, 305, 310.
Ondrejovič, Dušan, 191, 192.
Ordass, Lajos (1901–78), Hungarian Evangelical bishop, 168.
d'Ors, Eugeni (1881–1954), Catalan essayist, 27.
Ortega y Gasset, José (1883–1955), Spanish philosopher and author, 26, 27.

Paci, Enzo (1911–76), Italian philosopher, 82, 88, 89.
Paine, Robert, 260.
Papini, Giovanni (1881–1956), Italian author, 81.
Pareyson, Luigi (1918–91), Italian philosopher, 82, 88, 92.
Pascal, Blaise (1623–62), French scientist and philosopher, 22, 229, 258, 303.
Pascoaes, Teixeria de (1877–1945), Portuguese poet, 9.
Pascual, Anna, 51.
Passi, Isaac, 289, 290.
Pasternak, Boris (1890–1960), Russian poet, 264.
Pastuszka, Józef (1897–1989), Polish Catholic priest and professor, 214, 216, 217.
Pattison, George, 175.
Paul, 22.
Pedro, Valentin de, 1, 28.
Pelagius (ca. 354–ca. 420), ascetic monk and reformer, 88.
Pelikán, Jaroslav, 189, 195.
Peñalver Gómez, Patricio, 44.
Penzo, Giorgio (1925–2006), 95, 96.
Pessanha, Camilo (1867–1925), Portuguese poet, 9.
Pessoa, Fernando (1888–1935), Portuguese poet and author, 4, 8, 9.
Petit, Paul (1893–1944), French Catholic thinker, 31.
Petkanič, Milan, 192.
Petrucci, Gualtiero, 83.
Pilinszky, János (1921–81), Hungarian poet, 169.

Index of Persons 335

Pizzuti, Giuseppe Mario, 91, 94.
Plato, 3, 159, 258, 295, 308.
Plazaola, Juan, 38.
Plotinus (ca. 204–70), founder of Neoplatonism, 258, 259.
Płużański, Tadeusz, 223.
Podoroga, Valery Aleksandrovich, 272, 273.
Polo, Leonardo, 40, 49.
Pontopiddan, Henrik (1857–1943), Danish author, 158.
Pop, Mihaela, 308.
Popa, Grigore (1910–94), Romanian philosopher, 304.
Pope Pius XI (1857–1939), 85.
Pope Pius XII (1876–1958), 90, 224.
Posescu, Alexandru, 305.
Prezzolini, Giuseppe (1882–1982), Italian author, 82.
Prini, Pietro, 89.
Prishvin, Mikhail (1873–1954), Russian cultural figure, 256.
Procházka, Arnošt, 206.
Przywara, Erich (1889–1972), German Catholic theologian, 90, 304.

Quinzio, Anna Giannatiempo, 95, 96.

Rácz, Péter, 171, 172.
Radnóti Sándor, 175.
Ravasz, László (1882–1975), Hungarian Protestant bishop, 161.
Redaelli, Luigi, 1, 83.
Regina, Umberto, 95, 96.
Remete, László (1910–45), Hungarian speaking Slovak Lutheran pastor.
Ribeiro, Álvaro (1905–81), 3, 5, 6.
Rickert, Heinrich (1863–1936), German philosopher, 162.
Ricketts, Mac Linscott, 302, 303.
Ricoeur, Paul (1913–2005), French philosopher, 175.
Rieger, František Ladislav, 190.
Rilke, Rainer Maria (1875–1926), German poet, 164, 169.
Rizzacasa, Aurelio, 96.
Rocca, Ettore, 93, 96.
Rodríguez Rosado, Juan José (1933–93), Spanish thinker, 36.
Rof Carballo, Xoan (1905–94), 32.
Rohde, Peter P. (1902–78), 30, 37.

Roos, Heinrich (1904–77) Danish Jesuit, 31.
Rosado, Rodríguez, 39.
Rosenthal, Mark (1906–1975), Soviet philosopher, 264.
Rozanov, Vassiliy (1856–1919), Russian thinker, 266.
Rozsnyai, Ervin, 170, 171.
Rousseau, Jean Jacques (1712–78), French philosopher, 38.
Roubiczek, Paul, 37.
Rudas, László (1885–1950), Hungarian philosopher, 167.
Rugási Gyula, 175.

Sáez Tajafuerce, Begonya, 48–53 passim, 307.
Šajda, Peter, 192, 196.
Sánchez Barbudo, Antonio (1910–95), Spanish literary critic and writer, 35.
San Miguel Conde or José Ramón, Spanish philosopher, 31.
Santos, Delfim (1907–66), 6.
Sapundjieva, Ralica, 291, 292.
Saraiva, Maria Manuela, 7.
Sarkanjac, Branislav, 319.
Sartre, Jean-Paul (1905–80), French philosopher, 9, 87, 172, 213, 217, 224, 323.
Sawicki, Franciszek (1877–1952), Polish Catholic scholar, 216.
Sciacca, Michele Federico (1918–75), 88.
Schelling, Friedrich Wilhelm Joseph von (1775–1854), German philosopher, 37, 156, 258, 266, 269.
Schiappa, Margarida, 3.
Schlegel, Johan Frederik (1817–96), Danish jurist, Regine Olsen's husband, 10.
Schleiermacher, Friedrich (1768–1834), German theologian, 37, 163.
Schloezer, Boris de (1881–1969), friend of Lev Shestov, 258.
Schopenhauer, Arthur (1788–1860), German philosopher, 39, 49, 289, 290, 291, 292.
Schrempf, Christoph, (1860–1944), German Protestant theologian, 23, 82, 85, 87, 213.
Schulzová, Anežka, 209.
Seidler, Irma (1883–1911), Hungarian painter, 158, 159.
Serra de Sala, Mariona, 35.

Shestov, Lev (1866–1938), Ukrainian-French philosopher, 29, 161, 169, 257–63 passim, 267, 272, 273, 288, 289, 291.
Shklovsky, Isaak Vladimirovich (1865–1935), Russian journalist, 250.
Simmel, Georg (1858–1918), German philosopher and sociologist, 167.
Simón Merchán, Vicente, 40.
Sinkó Ervin (1898–1967), Hungarian author, 165.
Sirovič, František, 192.
Smolík, Josef, 190.
Socrates, 8, 25, 259–61, 295, 318.
Solovyov, Vladimir (1853–1900), Russian philosopher, 159, 267.
Søltoft, Pia, 307.
Soluntchev, Risto, 320.
Sousa, Elisabete M. de, 9.
Spasov, Dobrin, 287, 288.
Spera, Salvatore, 93–5.
Spinoza, Baruch (1632–77), Dutch philosopher, 261.
Stack, George J., 39.
Stalin, Iosif Vissarionovich (1878–1953), 166, 167.
Stan, Florin Leonard, 308.
Stere, Ernest, 305.
Stewart, Jon, 175, 307, 308.
Stoichev, Dimiter, 286.
Stojanov, Trajche, 320.
Stoyanov, Ljudmil (1888–1973), Bulgarian poet, 286, 287, 296.
Strakhov, Nikolay Nikolayevich (1828–96), Russian thinker, 250, 251.
Strindberg, August (1849–1912), Swedish dramatist, 158, 169.
Struve, Piotr Berngardovich (1870–1944), Russian philosopher, 256.
Suances Marcos, Manuel, 44, 45, 54.
Świderski, Bronisław, 218, 221.
Szeberényi, Lajos Zsigmond (1890–1941), Hungarian Protestant pastor, 163.
Széles, László, 162.
Szendrey, Júlia (1828–68), wife of the Hungarian poet Sándor Petőfi (1823–49), 156.
Szigeti József (1892–1973), Hungarian philosopher, 167.
Szilasi, Vilmos (1889–1966), Hungarian philosopher, 164.

Szwed, Antoni, 218, 220, 223, 226.

Tabaković, Milan, 323.
Tatár, György, 175.
Tavaszi Sándor (1888–1951), Hungarian philosopher, 163.
Temkov, Aleksandar, 318.
Teoharova, Radosveta, 286, 293, 294.
Tertullian (ca. 160–235), church father, 225, 303.
Thomas, see "Aquinas."
Thulstrup, Marie Mikulová, 190–6 passim, 208.
Thulstrup, Niels (1924–88), Danish theologian, 93.
Tiander, Karl Friedrich, Russian philologist, 252–4, 274.
Tillich, Paul Johannes, (1886–1965), German-American theologian and philosopher, 170, 190.
Tischner, Joseph (1931–2000), Polish Catholic priest, 228.
Tisseau, Paul-Henri (1894–1964), French translator of Kierkegaard's works, 4, 52, 90.
Tkhorzhevsky, Ivan (1878–1951), Russian translator, 258.
Todorović, Milos, 325.
Toeplitz, Karol, 217, 218, 222–5.
Tolstoy, Leo (1828–1910), Russian writer and philosopher, 159, 247, 248, 250, 251, 259.
Tolstrup, Christian, 307.
Torralba, Francesc, 45, 46, 47, 52.
Trendelenburg, Friedrich Adolph (1802–72), German philosopher and philologist, 274.
Troeltsch, Ernst (1865–1923), German Protestant theologian, 94, 160.
Trotsky, Leon (1897–1940), Russian Bolshevik revolutionary and Marxist theorist, 164.
Trtík, Zdeněk (1914–83), Czech theologian, 190.

Unamuno, Miguel de (1864–1936), Spanish philosopher, novelist and essayist, 17–28, 35, 40, 54, 288.
Urbina, Pedro Antonio, 38.
Urdanibia, Javier, 49.
Urdanoz, Teófilo, 38.

Urmeneta, Fermín de, 38.
Urs von Balthasar, Hans (1905–88), Swiss theologian, 46.
Uscatescu, Jorge, 40.

Valádez, Leticia, 50.
Valverde, José María (1926–96), Spanish thinker, 44.
Vasseur, Álvaro Armando (1878–1969), Uruguayan poet, 28.
Veverka, Lukáč Ján, 192, 193.
Vidari, Giovanni (1871–1934), Italian scholar, 82.
Viallaneix, Nelly, French philosopher, 39.
Vidiella, Jorge, 36.
Vörösmarty Mihály (1800–55), Hungarian poet, 156.

Wahl, Jean (1888–1974), French philosopher, 2, 4, 29, 30, 39, 88.
Warkocz, Antoni (1908–92), Polish Catholic scholar and priest, 216.
Wat, Alexander (1900–67), Polish futurist and critic of communism, 229.

Watkin, Julia, 43, 49, 50, 195.
Weber, Max (1864–1920), German sociologist, 160.
Weiss, János, 175.
Wilde, Oscar (1854–1900), Irish playwright and poet, 292.

Xenophon, 295.

Yegorov, Nikolay Aleksandrovich, 255.
Yudin, Pavel (1899–1968), Soviet philosopher, 264.
Yuzhakov, Sergey Nikolaevitch (1849–1910), editor, 254.

Zander, Lev (1893–1964), Russian philosopher, 257.
Zashev, Dimiter, 288.
Zaslavsky, David (1880–1965), Soviet journalist, 264.
Žilina, Miloslav, 208.
Žitný, Milan, 193.

Index of Subjects

Abraham, 4, 43, 259, 261, 262, 267, 268, 271, 273, 294.
absurd, the, 92, 225, 226, 260, 294.
Ahasverus, see "Wandering Jew."
alienation, 171.
anxiety, 5, 6, 25, 32, 88, 169, 227, 324, 325.
atheism, 166, 170.

beauty, 228, 229.
being, 46.
boredom, 227.

Catholicism, 7, 17, 29, 31, 32.
choice, 290, 308.
Christology, 225.
communication, 46, 221–7 passim, 305, 309.
    indirect, 45, 92, 219–27 passim, 249, 269, 270, 272, 302.
contemporaneity, 291.
Corsair, the, 255, 307.

daimonic, the, 268.
despair, 6, 25, 166, 169, 216, 223, 226, 229, 262, 292, 307, 324, 325.
Don Juan, 24, 43, 296.
doubt, 4.
drama, Greek, 156.

eternity, 48, 296, 308.
existence, 43, 157, 220, 223, 225, 296, 304, 324, 325.
existentialism, 3, 6, 7, 10, 17, 29–31, 39, 44, 85–95 passim, 164, 168–73 passim, 205, 207, 213, 215–7, 223–9 passim, 262–4, 267, 268, 289–91, 295, 306, 318, 319, 324.

faith, 8, 21, 87, 90–2, 165, 216–8, 222, 223, 226, 259, 260, 262, 272, 273, 290, 291–6 passim, 318, 324, 325.
Faust, 268.
freedom, 43, 46, 87, 91, 220, 223, 226, 227, 259, 261, 263, 269, 290, 325.

Hong Kierkegaard Library at St. Olaf College, 48, 49, 53, 195, 310.
humor, 5, 222, 271.

idealism, 90.
imagination, 38.
immanence, 227.
immortality, 21.
Incarnation, the, 92, 225.
individual, the, 8, 20, 27, 33, 46, 207, 256, 275, 303, 304, 308, 324.
individualism, 293.
interesting, the, 305.
irony, 6, 221, 222, 268, 269, 271, 275, 290, 295, 307.
irrationalism, 19, 36, 87, 166, 169, 207, 225, 291, 293.
irrationality, 294.

Job, 4, 259, 261, 262.

leap, 2, 4, 19, 158, 223, 225, 227, 305.
literature, 156.

maieutics, 216, 272, 305.
marriage, 3.
martyrdom, 262.
mediation, 223.
melancholy, 5, 32, 307, 320.
memory, 38.
moment, the, 38, 308.
movement, 223.
mysticism, 215.

nihilism, 166, 306, 307.

offence, 325.

paradox, the, 4, 8, 92, 158, 223, 225, 226, 253, 256, 290, 304, 324, 325.
phenomenology, 7, 88, 95, 215, 228, 307.
positivism, 5.
possibility, 87, 88.
pseudonymity, 5, 8, 41, 44, 45, 48, 218, 220, 249, 271, 293.

recollection, 5, 308.
relativism, 290.
repetition, 2, 27, 38, 51, 227, 291, 304, 308, 324, 325.
revelation, 215.
Romanticism, 156, 286, 290.

sin, 21, 217, 227, 263, 291, 294, 308, 324, 325.
Søren Kierkegaard Library at the University of Copenhagen, 41, 45.
Søren Kierkegaard Research Centre at the University of Copenhagen, 48, 96, 97, 173, 174, 218.

stages, 2, 6, 38, 50, 157, 217, 220, 223, 287, 289, 296, 303, 304.
subjectivism, 169, 207, 214, 216.
subjectivity, 6, 8, 37.

theory, 50.
time, 38, 48, 296, 308.
transcendence, 227.

Wandering Jew, 296.